140 - 248
370 - 471

Marriage & Family in the Modern World

A BOOK OF READINGS

THIRD EDITION

EDITED BY

Ruth Shonle Cavan

Marriage and Family in the Modern World
A BOOK OF READINGS

Marriage and Family in the Modern World

A BOOK OF READINGS

Third Edition

Edited by Ruth Shonle Cavan

Professor Emeritus of Sociology and Social Work, Rockford College

THOMAS Y. CROWELL COMPANY
New York   Established 1834

Preface

This third edition of *Marriage and Family in the Modern World: A Book of Readings* continues the purpose of the first two editions: to place in the hands of college students and other readers a carefully selected collection of articles and excerpts from books that contribute to the understanding of marriage and family living. Certain articles used in previous editions have been omitted, chiefly those of a non-sociological nature, and have been replaced by articles that emphasize newer sociological interests. The volume is planned for courses in preparation for marriage, family living, and the sociology of the family. Some articles report specific research findings; others are descriptive or interpretative; and still others apply to education in family living, counseling, or case work. The student bent on guidance in marriage and family living or an understanding of the sociology of the family, the teacher of the appropriate courses, and the general reader should find the book understandable and useful. Although deeper meaning may be given to some of the articles by background preparation in sociology, psychology, or biology, genuine appreciation of the articles is not dependent upon such preparation.

The sixty-four articles are organized into twenty chapters. The first four chapters give the setting for the study of marriage and family life in the United States; a brief historical perspective from the colonial family to the family of the future; a discussion of subcultural family types in the United States; and a contrast with marriage in three contemporary non-American cultures. Chapters 5 through 11 introduce the concept of the family life cycle and traverse the subjects of dating, engagement, love, intimacies, unmarried parenthood, and legal regulations. Chapters 12 through 14 deal with husband and wife in the experience of marriage, the nuclear family and the kinship web, and the middle and later years. Chapters 15 and 16 are concerned with stresses, conflict, divorce, and readjustment. Chapters 17 through 19 focus on parents and children, both in normal situations and under stress. Chapter 20 presents several approaches to treatment when the family cannot handle its problems.

Marriage and Family in the Modern World covers the subjects included in most textbooks on marriage and the family. The difficult problems of marriage that come to a minority of couples (alcoholism, prolonged unemployment, divorce) or that may come only once in a lifetime (bereavement) have not been bypassed, although it is often easier to overlook them in a field of study that is generally optimistic.

One difficulty of readings books is that the great number of authors included prevents the reader from coming into rapport with them, as he may do with the single author of a book. To overcome this difficulty, a brief biographical note gives salient facts about each author so that the reader may feel that he is being addressed by a person and not merely by a name.

Finally, to increase the usefulness of the book a chart has been placed in the appendix listing recent texts in marriage preparation and the family by chapter and citing appropriate articles in the readings by number. With this system the instructor may easily refer students to the articles that may clarify or amplify any specific chapter in the text being used.

The editor wishes to thank the many colleagues who gave helpful written or verbal suggestions or who gave permission to reprint articles and consented to revisions of articles. The book has been made possible also by the generous willingness of many publishers to have articles or parts of books reprinted.

RUTH SHONLE CAVAN
DeKalb, Illinois
April, 1969

Contents

Marriage and Family in the Modern World
A BOOK OF READINGS

Chapter 1: Significance of Marriage and the Family Today

1. THE FAMILY AS AN ELEMENT IN THE SOCIAL STRUCTURE

William J. Goode

§ In this selection, the author views the family as the link between the individual and society, whose strategic function is to mediate between the two. He supports this position with a review of the emphasis on the importance of the family in historical writings and in Utopian social experiments. It is through the family, the author states, that "society is able to elicit from the individual his necessary contribution. The family, in turn, can continue to exist only if it is supported by the larger society." He points out the fallacy of many preconceived notions about the family, the universal existence of families, and the interlinkage of family functions.

In all known societies, almost everyone lives his life enmeshed in a network of family rights and obligations called role relations. A person is made aware of his role relations through a long period of socialization during his childhood, a process in which he learns how others in his family expect him to behave, and in which he himself comes to feel this is both the right and the desirable way to act. Some, however, find their obligations a burden, or do not care to take advantage of their rights. This wide range of behavior leads to one of the commonest themes of conversation found in all societies—just what the duties of a given child or parent, husband or wife, cousin or uncle ought to be, and then, whether he *has done* his duty. This type of discussion is

SOURCE: William J. Goode, *The Family* (Englewood Cliffs, N.J.: Prentice-Hall, 1964), pp. 1–6. Copyright © 1964 by Prentice-Hall and reprinted by permission.

The author received his doctorate from Pennsylvania State University and is professor of sociology at Columbia University. He is the author of *After Divorce* and *World Revolution and Family Patterns* as well as numerous articles concerning the family.

1

especially common in societies undergoing industrialization, where arguments are frequent concerning the duties of women.

Various Views of the Family

The intense emotional meaning of family relations for almost all members of a society has been observable throughout man's history. Philosophers and social analysts have noted that society is a structure made up of *families*, and that the peculiarities of a given society can be described by outlining its family relations. The earliest moral and ethical writings suggest that a society loses its strength if people fail in their family obligations. Confucius thought, for example, that happiness and prosperity would prevail in the society if only everyone would behave "correctly" as a family member—which primarily meant that no one should fail in his filial obligations. The relationship between a ruler and his subjects, then, was parallel to that of a father and his children. Similarly, much of the early Hebrew writing, in Exodus, Deuteronomy, Ecclesiastes, Psalms, and Proverbs, is devoted to the importance of obeying family rules. In India, too, the earliest codified literature (the *Rig-Veda*, about the last half of the 2nd millennium B.C., and the Law of Manu, about the beginning of the Christian Era) devote great attention to the family.

From time to time, imaginative social analysts or philosophers have sketched out plans for societies that *might* be created—utopias—in which new definitions of family roles are presented as solutions to traditional social problems. Plato's *Republic* is illustrative of this approach. He was probably the first to urge the creation of a society in which all people, men and women alike, would have an equal opportunity to develop their talents to the utmost, and to achieve a position in society solely through merit. Since family relations in all known societies prevent a selection based solely on individual worth, in Plato's utopia the tie between parents and children would play no part, because no one would know who was his own child or parent. Conception would take place at the same times each year at certain hymeneal festivities. Children born out of season would be eliminated (along with those born defective); all children would be taken from their parents at birth, and reared under challenging conditions by specially designated people. Similarly, experimental or utopian communities, like Oneida, the Shakers, and the Mormons in this country, insisted that changes in family relations were necessary to achieve their goals.

Included among the aims of many revolutions since the French Revolution of 1789 has been a profound alteration in family relations. Since World War II, the leaders of all countries undergoing industrialization have introduced new laws, well ahead of public opinion, intended to create family patterns that would be more in conformity with the demands of urban and industrial life.

All these facts, by demonstrating that philosophers, reformers, and religions, as well as secular leaders, have throughout history been at least implicitly aware of the importance of family patterns as a central element in the social structure, also suggest that the social analyst must understand family behavior in order to understand social processes generally.

The strategic significance of the family is to be found in its *mediating* function in the larger society. It links the *individual* to the larger social structure. A society will not survive unless its many needs are met, such as the production and distribution of food, protection of the young and old, the sick and the pregnant, conformity to the law, the socialization of the young, and so on. Only if *individuals* are motived to serve the needs of the society will it be able to survive. The formal agencies of social control (such as the police) are not enough to do more than force the extreme deviant to conform. Socialization makes most of us wish to conform, but throughout each day we are often tempted to deviate. Thus both the internal controls and the formal authorities are insufficient. What is needed is a set of social forces that responds to the individual whenever he does well or poorly, supporting his internal controls as well as the controls of the formal agencies. The family, by surrounding the individual through much of his social life, can furnish that set of forces.

The family, then, is made up of individuals, but it is also part of the larger social network. Thus we are all under the constant supervision of our kin, who feel free to criticize, suggest, order, cajole, praise, or threaten, so that we will carry out our role obligations. Even in the most industrialized and urban of societies, where it is sometimes supposed that people lead rootless and anonymous lives, most people are in frequent interaction with other family members. Men who have achieved high position usually find that even as adults they still respond to their parents' criticisms, are still angered or hurt by a brother's scorn.

Thus it is *through the family* that the society is able to elicit from the *individual* his necessary contribution. The family, in turn, can continue to exist only if it is supported by the larger society. If the society as a larger social system furnishes the family, as a smaller social system, the conditions necessary for its survival, these two types of systems must be interrelated in many important ways. The two main foci in this volume will be the relations among family members and the relations between the family and the society.

Preconceived Notions about the Family

Such a task presents many difficulties. One of the greatest lies in ourselves. We know too much about the family to be able to study it both objectively and easily. Our emotions are aroused quickly by the behavior of families, and we are likely to feel that family patterns other than our own are queer or improper. We are too prone to argue about what is *right*, rather than coolly to demonstrate what *is*. In addition, we have had an opportunity to observe many people engaged in family behavior, so that when we consider almost any generalization (such as "the lower social strata have a higher divorce rate than the upper") we can often find a specific experience that seems to refute the generalization. Thus our personal experience is really a narrow sample of the wide range of family behavior, but it is so vivid to us, that we are likely to see no reason to look for broader data with which to test it.

Our emotional involvement and reliance on individual experience often convince people that the findings of family sociology must be "obvious," since they deal with what we already know. Many "well known" beliefs about the family, however, are not well-grounded in fact. Others are only partly true, and require precise study in order to be understood better. One such belief is that "children hold the family together." In fact, most divorcing couples do not have children. But the most valid data now suggest, rather, that the causal nexus is this: People who have not become well adjusted, who for many reasons may be prone to divorce, are also less likely to have children.

Perhaps the need for testing apparently self-evident ideas about the family may be seen in another way. Suppose that a researcher in the field of the family had demonstrated the following set of facts. Would it have been worth doing? Or were the facts already known?

1. The present divorce rate in the U.S. is much higher than the rates in primitive societies, and higher than any other nation has ever experienced.

2. Because of the importance of the extended family in China and India, the average size of the household has always been very high, with many generations living under one roof.

3. In Western nations, the age at marriage among peasants was always low, since early marriage meant that children would soon be produced, and these were useful in farming. By contrast, the average age at marriage among the nobility was generally higher.

Although these statements sound plausible to many people, and impressive arguments could be adduced to support them, in fact they are all false. A majority of primitive societies have higher rates of marital dissolution than our own, and several nations in the past have at various times equaled or exceeded our present rate—notably Japan in the 1880's, when even her official rate (certainly an underestimate) was over 300 divorces per 1,000 marriages. Every survey of Chinese and Indian households has shown that they are relatively small (about 3.3 to 5.5, from one region to another). Peasant marriages were later, on the average, than the nobility, requiring as they did that the couple have land of their own.

Thus we see that in the instances just cited, common beliefs *did* require testing. Of course, many popular beliefs about how families work *are* correct, but we cannot simply assume their correctness. We must examine many of our individual observations to see how well they fit other societies or perhaps the different family types in our own society.

To understand family behavior we must be self-conscious in our method. We must adopt an approach that will yield reliable results. Vast tables of figures, such as the ages of all the married couples in the world, taken from national censuses, would contain many facts, but might add very little to our grasp of family behavior. What we seek is *organized* facts, or a structure of propositions, that will illuminate one another. That is, we seek theory as well as facts. Theory without facts is blind speculation; facts without theory are random and often insignificant observations.

The Family as a Unique Institution

A brief consideration of certain peculiarities of the family as an element of the social structure will suggest how better theory and a fruitful general approach are needed in this area.

The family is the only social institution other than religion which is *formally* developed in all societies. Indeed, the term "social structure" in anthropology is often used to mean the family and kinship structure. By contrast, some have argued that in certain societies legal systems do not exist because there is no formally organized legislative body or judiciary. Of course, it is possible to abstract from concrete behavior the legal *aspects* of action, or the economic aspects, or the political dynamics, even when there are no explicitly labeled agencies formally in control of these areas in the society. However, the kinship statuses and their responsibilities are the object of both formal and informal attention in societies at a high or a low technological level.

Family duties are the *direct* role responsibility of everyone in the society, with rare exceptions. Almost everyone is both born into a family and founds one of his own. Each person is kinsman to many. Many people, on the other hand, may escape the religious duties which others take for granted, or the political burdens of the society. Almost no family role responsibilities can be delegated to others, as more specialized obligations can be in a work situation.

Participation in family activities has a further interesting quality, that though it is not backed by the formal punishments supporting many other kinds of obligations, almost everyone takes part nonetheless. We must, for example, engage in economic or productive acts, or face the alternative of starving. We must enter the army, pay taxes, and appear before courts, or face physical penalties and force. However, no such penalties face the individual who does not wish to marry, or refuses to talk with his father or brother. Nevertheless, so pervasive and recurrent are the social pressures, and so intertwined with indirect or direct rewards and punishments, that almost everyone either conforms, or claims to conform, to family demands.

Next, as suggested earlier, the family is the fundamental *instrumental* foundation of the larger social structure, in that all other institutions depend on its contributions. The role behavior that is learned within the family becomes the model or prototype for role behavior required in other segments of the society. The content of the socialization process is the cultural traditions of the society; by passing them on to the next generation the family acts as a conduit or transmission belt by which the culture is kept alive.

Next, each individual's total range of behavior, how he budgets his time and energies, is more easily visible to the family than to outsiders. Family members can evaluate how the individual is allocating his time and money in various of his role activities. Consequently, the family acts as a source of pressure on him to adjust—to work harder and play less, or go to church less and study his school lessons more. In all these ways, the family is an instrument or agent of the larger society; its failure to perform adequately means that the goals of the larger society may not be attained effectively.

A further striking characteristic of the family is that its major functions are separable from one another, but in fact are not separated in any known family system. These functions will be discussed in various contexts in this book, and need no great elaboration at this point. The family contributes these services to the society: reproduction of the young, physical maintenance of family members, social placement of the child, socialization, and social control. Clearly, all these activities could be separated. The mother could send her child to be fed in a neighborhood mess hall, and of course some harassed mothers do send their children to buy lunch in a local snack bar. Those who give birth to a child need not socialize the child. They might send the child to specialists, and indeed specialists do take more responsibility for this task as the child grows older. Parents might, as some eugenicists have suggested, be selected for their breeding qualities, but these might not include any great talent for training the young. Status-placement might be accomplished by random drawing of lots, by IQ tests or periodic examinations in physical and intellectual skills, or by polls of popularity, without regard to an individual's parents, those who socialized or fed him, or others who controlled his daily behavior.

Separations of this kind have been suggested from time to time, and a few hesitant attempts have been made here and there in the world to put them into operation. However, three conclusions relevant to this kind of division can be made. (1) In all known societies, the *ideal* (with certain qualifications to be noted) is that the family be entrusted with all these functions. (2) When one or more family tasks are entrusted to another agency by a revolutionary or utopian society, the change can be made only with the support of much ideological fervor, and sometimes political pressure as well. (3) These instances are also characterized by a gradual return to the more traditional type of family. In both the Israeli *kibbutzim* and the Russian experiments in relieving parents of child care, the ideal of completely communal living was urged, in which husband and wife were to have only a personal and emotional tie and not be bound to each other by constraint. The children were to see their parents at regular intervals but look to their nursery attendants and mother-surrogates for affection and direction during work hours. Each individual was to contribute his best skills to the cooperative unit without regard to family ties or sex status (i.e., there would be few or no "female" or "male" tasks). That ideal was maintained for a while, but behavior has gradually dropped away from the ideal. The only other country in which the pattern has been attempted on a large scale is China. Whether the Chinese commune will retreat from its high ambitions remains to be seen, but chances are good that it will follow the path of the *kibbutz* and the Russian *kolkhoz*.

Various factors contribute to such a deviation from the ideal, but the two most important sets of pressures cannot easily be separated from each other. First is the problem, also noted by Plato, that individuals who develop their own attitudes and behaviors in the usual Western (i.e., European and European-based) family system do not adjust to the problems of the communal "family." The second is the likelihood that when the family is radically changed, the various relations between it and the larger society are changed, so that new strains are created, demanding new kinds of adjustments on the part of the individuals in the society. Perhaps the planners must develop somewhat different agencies, or a different blueprint, to transform the family.

Concretely, some of the factors reported as "causing" a deviation from the ideal of family living are the following. Some successful or ambitious men and women wish to break away from group control, and leave to establish their lives elsewhere. There, of course, they do not attempt to develop a communal pattern of family living. Parents do try to help their own children secure advantages over other children, where this is possible. Parents not only feel unhappy at not being with their children often enough (notice that youngsters need not "be home for meals"!), but perhaps some feel the husband-wife relationship itself is somewhat empty because children do not occupy in it their usually central place. Husband and wife usually desire more intimacy than is granted under communal arrangements. Finally, the financial costs of taking care of children outside the family are rather high.

These comments have nothing to do with "capitalism" in its current political and economic argument with "communism." It merely describes the historical fact that though various experiments in separating the major functions of the family from one another have been conducted, none simply evolved slowly from a previously existing family system; and the two modern important instances represent a retreat from the ideals of a previous generation. It is possible that some functions can be more easily separated than others; or that some family systems (for example matrilineal systems, to be discussed later) might lend themselves to a separation of functions more easily than others. Nevertheless, we have to begin with the data available now. Even cautiously interpreted, they suggest that the family is a rather stable institution.

A Sociological Approach to Family Research

The unusual features the family exhibits as a type of social subsystem require that some attention be paid to the approach to be used in studying it. First, neither ideal nor reality can be excluded from focus. It would, for example, be naive to suppose that because onefourth to one-third of all couples marrying will eventually divorce, they do not cherish the ideal of monogamy. Kinsey estimated that about half of all married men engage in extra-marital intercourse, but perhaps nearly all these men believed in the ideal of faithfulness. On a more personal level, every reader of these lines has lied, but nevertheless most believe in the ideal of telling the truth.

A sociologist ascertains the ideals of family systems partly because they are a guide to behavior. Knowing that people believe in telling the truth, we can expect them to do so unless there are advantages in telling a lie, and we can even (as a manipulative measure) create the conditions under which people are more likely to tell the truth. We know also that when an individual violates the ideal, he is likely to conceal the violation, to find some internal excuse for the violation, and to be embarrassed if others find him out.

A sociologist may also be interested in ideals as values, as sets of norms which are passed on from one generation to another as a major constituent of culture. The organization of values, how norms in different areas change or are translated into a different form, how they are qualified by still other norms—all these are legitimate questions for a sociologist.

2. THE AMERICAN FAMILY

M. F. Nimkoff

§ Nimkoff points to freedom in family relationships as the distinguishing mark of the American family. Although this freedom makes possible a diversity of family forms, a general American family type nevertheless exists: it is characteristically nuclear in structure, independent of kin, and tends toward equalitarian status of husband and wife. Socialization of children is shared with outside agencies, and personal happiness is regarded as the key to success. The family is fragile and the divorce rate high; however, a second marriage re-establishes the family in most instances.

The United States, including Alaska and Hawaii, embraces a geographic region that ranges in climatic conditions from subpolar to tropical. Its 179 million inhabitants (1960) [1] occupy an area of 3.6 million square miles, with an average density of 50.5 persons per square mile. One state, Texas, covers 267,339 square miles, with 36.5 persons per square mile, and Rhode Island has 1214 square miles, with 812.4 persons per square mile. English is the common language but there are large groups that speak German in Pennsylvania, Italian and Yiddish in New York, the Scandinavian languages in the Middle West, Chinese and Japanese in California, French in Louisiana and Spanish in the Southwest, to mention only the largest linguistic groups. Protestants constitute approximately 66 per cent of the population, Roman Catholics 26 per cent, Jews 3 per cent, with smaller representations of other religious groups and of persons with no religious affiliation. About one-tenth of the population is Negro. The economy is mainly industrial, with only 8.1 per cent of the civilian labor force employed in agriculture. The average

SOURCE: M. F. Nimkoff, ed., *Comparative Family Systems* (New York: Houghton Mifflin Company, 1965), 329–39. Reprinted by permission of the publisher.

The author, who was chairman of the Sociology Department of Florida State University at the time of his death in 1966, had been editor of the journal *Marriage and Family Living*. He is the author of *Marriage and the Family* and *Comparative Family Systems*, and the co-author of *Technology and Social Change*.

[1] All of the data of this chapter are for 1960, unless otherwise indicated.

(median) income per family is $5600 per year, roughly double that of the richest European country, but 13 per cent of the families have incomes under $2000 a year. Politically, the United States is a federal republic of 50 states, with the right of legislation pertaining directly to marriage and the family reserved to the states, not the federal government. In Nevada and Idaho, a divorce may be had on the ground of mental cruelty after a legal residence period of only six weeks, whereas Massachusetts has a five-year residency requirement if the marriage was not contracted in the state, and in New York, a divorce action can be brought only on the ground of adultery.[2]

The foregoing paragraph is presented to dramatize the fact that while there is basic unity in the culture of the United States, there is also diversity according to region, rural-urban residence, ethnic and religious affiliation, race and socio-economic position. These variations are reflected in differences in family structure and behavior. For example, Catholics generally have higher birth rates than Protestants, and Protestants, than Jews, but the Southern Baptists have more children than the Catholics, and Presbyterians have fewer children than Jews.[3] The family organization of the upper classes is more patriarchal, that of the middle classes more equalitarian and that of the lower classes more matricentric than that of the other classes. In the discussion that follows, we shall focus, unless otherwise indicated, on the family organization of the dominant group in the American scene, the white Protestant, urban, middle class. It is this group which sets the tone and direction for the whole society.

If we ask what it is that gives distinction or uniqueness to the American family, a significant part of the answer can be given in terms of one of the dominant cultural values of American society, namely, freedom.[4] Freedom acts as an organizing principle in American culture to give coherence to the society. It is possible to say that in few other modern societies has the principle of freedom been so fully applied. We shall consider how the norm of freedom infuses the structure and functions of the American family.

In addition to freedom, a highly important explanatory factor in accounting for the unique characteristics of the American family is the relatively high economic standard of living. Freedom and affluence are

---

[2] There are however a number of grounds for annulment, which may be used as a substitute for divorce. Annulments constitute some 40 per cent of all marital dissolutions in New York, compared to 3.5 per cent for the United States at large. [In 1966, New York increased its grounds for divorce from one to five.—Ed.]

[3] Paul Glick. *American Families.* New York: John Wiley, 1957, Table 25.

[4] The American creed of equality and freedom is set forth in the Declaration of Independence, the Preamble to the Constitution, and the Bill of Rights. Promoting these values were the settlement patterns of an expanding frontier, which existed over a long period of years and which helped to develop a tradition of individualism.

not altogether independent variables; on the contrary, they are mutually reinforcing factors, with freedom a significant influence in the growth of the American economy, and prosperity, in turn, a source of freedom. Nor, of course, are freedom and affluence the only determinants of the unique aspects of the American family scene. Sociologists have long recognized that the causes of complex social phenomena are multiple. While it is not possible to explain everything distinctive about the American family in terms of freedom and affluence, these two factors in combination—the one ideological and the other economic—have great explanatory value.

Structure

The pattern of kinship structure of the American family includes bilateral descent, a strongly emphasized nuclear family and a distinct but subordinate kindred. The family of procreation is neolocal (residentially independent) and, more important, fiscally independent. In terms of freedom, we may say the nuclear family is relatively free from economic obligation to kin. Crucial evidence of the economic independence of the small conjugal unit is the complete testamentary freedom the law accords the head of the household, except for the dower rights vested in the widow. There is an ideological independence also. If you ask a middle-class white American: "Who are the members of your family?" he will probably (if married) mention first his wife and children. If he mentions his father, mother, sisters and brothers, he regards them as a separate unit, to say nothing of relatives further removed such as aunts, uncles and cousins. This is unlike the situation in the Hindu joint family, a form of extended family comprising a single corporate unit.

Freedom implies privacy, and where the means exist, as they generally do in the United States with its high per capita income, privacy is translated concretely into separate residences. The percentage of parents living with their married children is only 4.2. Where co-residence exists, it is generally regarded as undesirable and perhaps a temporary expedient, occurring most often when the parent is aged, widowed or chronically ill. Impartiality is the ideal as between the families of orientation of husband and wife, even though more aged parents live with married daughters than with sons. It is said that the American model of the nuclear family, with bilateral kinship, was established in the United States even before the Industrial Revolution and derives from the Anglo-Saxon heritage.[5]

[5] Conrad M. Arensberg. "The American Family in the Perspective of Other Cultures," in Eli Ginzberg (Ed.), *The Nation's Children. Vol. I: The Family and Social Change.* New York: Columbia University Press, ˙960.

The key relationship in the nuclear family, that between husband and wife, is similarly based on freedom. There is first the freedom to marry or not to marry. One woman in 12, one man in 13, 75 years of age and over, has never married. This ratio seems high, when compared with primitive societies, or with Eastern societies such as India, where the unmarried woman is a great rarity, but not when the comparison is with other Western societies.

Fewer women remain spinsters in the United States than in any other Western country,[6] and the marriage rate is higher than in most other nations.[7] The marriage rate is high because the age at marriage is low—in the early twenties—on the average.[8] In turn, early marriage is probably encouraged by the moral dilemma occasioned by the conflict between the strict sanctions against premarital sex on the one hand and the intense sexual stimulation by mass media on the other. Early marriage is possible because in an affluent society young wives as well as young husbands are able to find employment, and where some additional financial aid is necessary, parents are able to provide it informally and inconspicuously, without loss of freedom on the part of the recipients.

There is next the freedom to choose one's mate. The limitations on freedom as defined by law are relatively minor. Generally a male may not marry under 18 years of age, with parental approval, nor under 21 without such approval; for females, the corresponding ages are 16 and 18. Some states limit choice to members of the same race. Most persons do marry within the same religious and socio-economic classes, but there is no legal obligation to do so. Marriage is non-preferential and no material consideration is involved in obtaining a mate. In most states first cousins may not marry; in about half the states the marriage of affinal relatives such as stepparents and stepchildren is prohibited. Marriage is typically based on personal rather than utilitarian considerations.

Authority Pattern

In the modern middle-class American family, the ideal type is the equalitarian relationship between husband and wife. This follows logically from the postulate of freedom, for if the wife is to be free, she must be the equal of her husband in power. Technically and legally, the husband is the head of the household, and his work determines the

[6] John Hajnal. "The Marriage Boom," *Population Index*, Vol. 18 (April 1953), Tables 2 and 4.
[7] Paul H. Jacobson. *American Marriage and Divorce*. New York: Rinehart and Winston, 1959, p. 121.
[8] Paul C. Glick, *op. cit.*, Table 16.

legal place of residence. An equalitarian relationship poses special problems when there are differences of opinion to be resolved, inasmuch as it is not possible to resolve such differences in a dyad by the simple democratic rule of taking a vote and abiding by the will of the majority. Adjustments must be made by a meeting of minds, or by compromise and conciliation. Under the circumstances, a high divorce rate is scarcely surprising.

Freedom, although a hoary tradition in American culture, has been an expanding factor, not static or constant. A force which has given great impetus to freedom for women is the increased opportunity for employment, to which further reference will be made later. The employment of wives is important for many reasons, not the least of which is the effect on the power structure of the family. A study [9] comparing families in which the wife was employed and others in which she was not, failed to find that her employment significantly altered the power structure of the family. This is interesting but beside the point, which is that the status of women generally is higher today than in earlier times when jobs were less plentiful. Many non-working wives used to work and assume they can find jobs if they want to. The possibility of an independent income for the wife increases her freedom, lessens her dependence on her husband and diminishes his authority.[10]

In the domestic sector, women have rights equal to those of men. They are co-guardians of their children, have equal rights to acquire and dispose of property, have equal rights to legal actions for divorce.

The equalitarian ideal applies also to the children, whose rights are supposed to be respected and whose points of view are to be considered. Their potentialities for development ideally take precedence over the ambitions their parents have for them, if these two sets of forces conflict.

Sex and Reproduction

A deep-seated viewpoint that stems from the Judaeo-Christian tradition, and more recently from Puritanism, sees sex apart from marriage as sinful, and, in marriage, as a necessary evil. This negative evaluation stimulates sexual interest, although in a devious and uneasy manner.

Ideally, there is a single standard regarding premarital coitus which taboos it for both sexes. In practice, there is a double standard which condemns premarital coitus more severely for women than for men. Since 1900 the proportion of women engaging in premarital coitus has

[9] Robert O. Blood, Jr., and Robert L. Hamblin. "The Effects of the Wife's Employment on the Family Power Structure," *Social Forces*, Vol. 26 (May 1958), pp. 347–352.
[10] W. F. Ogburn and M. F. Nimkoff. *Technology and the Changing Family*. Boston: Houghton Mifflin, 1955.

increased, but evidence suggests that this proportion has tended to stabilize in recent years.[11]

The rule in marriage is that children are desirable but not essential. If the couple is childless, adoption is not imperative, although common. There are more couples wanting to adopt a child than there are children available for adoption, but this may in part be due to the fact that some children are kept in institutions and are not available for adoption. Women in 1957 who had completed childbearing had borne, on the average, 2.80 children. Over the last half-century the trend has been toward more moderate-sized families. American women now have generally completed their families by their late twenties. The long-term reduction in the maternal role, together with the earlier age at marriage and the increase in longevity, has occasioned an increase in other roles for married women, namely, the wifely and the non-domestic roles. Both are strengthened by the fact that on the average the last child has married and left home by the time the father is 50 and the mother 47, and by the further fact that this leaves the median couple with 14 years of life together before the death of one spouse.

Economic Maintenance

As in almost all societies, American husbands are invariably breadwinners unless they are handicapped persons. About one-third of the wives are also in the labor force. The proportion has increased to this number from about 5 per cent in 1900, and the indications are that the percentage will further increase in the future. The pattern in the United States is for girls to work before marriage, and after marriage until a child is born. With the birth of the child, the mother usually leaves the labor force, but she may return to it after her children are in school. Thus the largest segment of working wives is in the age group from 35 to 54. Part of the explanation for the withdrawal of mothers of young children from the labor force is the lag in services for working mothers, such as public day-care centers and nursery schools. These exist but not in such relative numbers as in, say, Russia. Another part of the explanation is the official policy of the government, as represented by its Children's Bureau, which discourages employment of mothers of preschool children. Even so, 2,884,000 working mothers in 1962 had children under six, or about one-fifth (21.3 per cent) of the women with children under six in the total population.[12]

Husbands and wives seldom compete vocationally. The wife's work is usually more episodic, more poorly paid. But the income of wives

[11] William Kephart. *The Family, Society and the Individual.* Boston: Houghton Mifflin, 1961, p. 352.
[12] U.S. Department of Labor. *Monthly Labor Review.* Reprint 409. (Special Labor Force Report no. 26). January, 1963. Table 7, p. 31.

is an important factor in the total income of American families, and helps to account for the relatively high standard of living.

Children are generally required to attend school until the age of 16 and are prevented by law from full-time employment. They do not contribute significantly to economic maintenance and are seldom economic assets. The desire of married couples for children is therefore more often based on sentimental rather than material considerations. The non-economic value of children is a force for planned parenthood.

When we consider how the money income is managed, we note that the male head is usually the chief fiscal agent in the American family. If there are investments, he makes them, as well as such larger expenditures as those for insurance, car, rent and fuel. Yet we are told that more than half of all investments in the United States are owned by women. The explanation is that men generally predecease their wives and leave their property to them. Widows who own stocks and bonds often turn the management of the property over to men, who manage it for a fee.

If in the middle class the husband is the chief manager of family income, the wife is the chief purchasing agent. She does the everyday buying of food and clothing. She does most of the housework. Essentially the division of labor in the middle-class American family is quite traditional, like that in most cultures. Its distinguishing feature, resulting from changes associated with increased industrialization and urbanization, is the sharing of functions by husbands and wives. The division of labor is progressively less sharp, as wives become breadwinners and as husbands reciprocate by helping with marketing, housekeeping and child care. But the exchange is not equal. The changes in the masculine role, while perhaps more extensive than those in the wifely role, are nevertheless more symbolic, whereas the changes in the wifely role are more intensive. A husband who works all day may help his wife with the supper dishes, whether she has a job or not; the working wife still does most of the housework as a rule, including meal preparation. Many women who do not work have a relatively easy time of it, what with smaller families, smaller houses, labor-saving devices and the help of husbands; the women who work are often heavily burdened.

The high real income of American families together with the appreciable leisure of wives who do not work free them for a wide variety of community, church and social welfare activities on a volunteer basis. An important phenomenon in American society is the great number of women engaged in such volunteer services.

Status

The new-born child in nearly every society takes the status of his family of orientation. In many societies he keeps this status throughout his lifetime. Because the United States is an open society with relatively high rates of social mobility, the American child may in due course achieve a higher status than that of his parents or siblings. Indeed, it is one of the norms of the middle class to encourage the child to rise in the economic and social scale. If there is a discrepancy in the social status of family members, the relationship between them may be marked by strain. This is more likely to occur, however, when the child is an achiever and the parents are lower class and retain the habits of that class.

Socialization

During the pre-school period, the socialization of the middle-class child is typically managed mainly by the parents, with only occasional assistance from grandparents and other kin. With the father at work away from home, responsibility for the education of the children, sons as well as daughters, is largely in the hands of the mother. It has been said [13] that the dependence of sons on their mothers leads to reaction-formation in the latency period, because the sons realize they must become emancipated if they are to fill the expected masculine role in adulthood. The reaction formation may take the form of "getting tough." The mother may overtly deplore such behavior while covertly encouraging it if her love for her son is conditional, as it often is, on his success in manly pursuits. Daughters have an easier task of role fulfillment, because mothers can serve more appropriately and effectively as models for daughters than for sons. The over-protectiveness of boys in American society is said to be further continued and accentuated during the school years by virtue of the fact that there are many more women teachers, especially in the elementary schools.

Foreign observers,[14] in particular, often comment on American child-rearing practices as being more permissive than European or Asian. The focus is more on the needs and desires of the child, less on the claims of the tradition. Foreign observers note the greater independence of American children, an independence which they think often borders on impudence and disrespect for elders. They are not so often impressed by a display of good manners on the part of American children. On the other hand, the observers report more spontaneity in American children, more initiative and ambition.

The orientation of middle-class American children is to the family and to peers, not to other adults. This leads to a segregated children's world,

[13] Talcott Parsons and Robert F. Bales. *Family, Socialization and Interaction Process*. New York: The Free Press of Glencoe, 1955, Ch. 2.
[14] Francis L. K. Hsu. *Americans and Chinese: Two Ways of Life*. New York: Henry Schuman, 1953.

in which maturation is relatively slow, responsibilities are few and time is ample in which to develop one's abilities. This situation contrasts with that of many other societies in which the child's incorporation into the world of adults comes relatively early.

Middle-class parents stress the discipline and inhibition of the emotions, especially those of sex and rage. Physical aggression is discouraged. Adherence to a time schedule is somewhat compulsive. The result of this discipline is said to be an uncommon amount of anxiety.

As to life goals, for sons a college training is a must; for daughters, it is deemed desirable but more optional. Business or a profession is the usual vocational goal for sons; for daughters, marriage. The parental ambition for sons must be in general terms, since particular jobs are not amenable to control by parents. Middle-class parents want their sons to be responsible, show initiative, be competitive and aggressive, perform adequately in school, show athletic prowess and manifest emotional stability and heterosexual interests. Daughters should be nice, sweet and popular.

One element of socialization that merits special mention is the religious education of the American child which has certain paradoxical aspects. On the one hand, at a superficial level American society stresses religious values in relation to the home. Two states require a religious marriage service and in the rest (where the type of service is optional), the great majority of weddings are celebrated by ministers, priests or rabbis. Most American families are church members and the percentage of families belonging to a church has increased fairly steadily since 1900. It is not clear that church attendance has increased, and it is quite likely that religious knowledge has declined. Studies conducted a decade or so ago show that only 35 per cent of Americans questioned could name the four gospels of the Bible.[15] It appears that many American families join churches for social rather than religious reasons. Bible reading, grace at meals and family prayers are less common in urban than in rural families.[16] The decline in Biblical knowledge appears to be associated with the increase in urbanization and with the lack of religious education in the schools.

Recreation

The high per capita income and the short workweek encourage sociability and recreation as prominent activities of the American family. In many societies, husbands and wives play little, if at all, together. The

---

[15] In Great Britain, the response was higher, 61 per cent, whereas only 22 per cent were church members compared to 57 per cent in the United States. Michael Argyle, *Religious Behaviour*. London: Routledge and Kegan Paul, 1958. Table 8, p. 35.
[16] M. F. Nimkoff. *Marriage and the Family*. Boston: Houghton Mifflin, 1947, p. 150.

struggle for existence may be too severe to afford much leisure, or the prevailing norms may discourage public displays of companionship between mates. Even in traditional Western rural society, where the struggle may have been less than in many primitive hunting societies, husbands and wives had little time for sheer play. Much recreation was of a practical nature, tied to economic pursuits such as corn-husking or quilting bees. Now, with more ample leisure for both, and more real income, American husbands and wives have more opportunity for joint recreation. Congeniality in play becomes an important test of compatibility, and the success or failure of the marriage turns more often than ever before on whether the mates are congenial playmates.

The newly evolving concept of marriage as recreation is diffused throughout the marital experience. Coitus is more for mutual pleasure than for procreation. Children, too, are for pleasure, not for profit. With increasing income, marketing becomes a growing and ever more significant function. Marketing can be fun, and a visit by the whole family to the shopping center is for the American family a kind of modern equivalent of the old-fashioned family picnic. Eating, which is for survival, is replaced more and more by dining, which is for pleasure. The home, originally a shelter, becomes more of an art museum and a theatre. The criterion of a successful marriage, which traditionally in other times and places was children or economic cooperation or religious salvation is, in the United States, personal happiness. This is an emotion like the joy in play. It is volatile compared to the enduring values of duty or necessity. Happiness differs from the other values in that it cannot be taken for granted but must be repeatedly validated.

Disorganization

The United States has one of the highest divorce rates in the world, exceeded in 1950 only by that of Egypt.[17] In interpreting this rate, the reader should remember what was said earlier about freedom as a dominant value in American life. If a marriage is not successful, the couple is generally free to terminate it. The divorce rate increase in the United States from 4 per 1000 married females 15 years of age and over in 1900 to a high of 17.9 in 1946, then declined to 9.2 in 1960.[18] While the rate showed signs of stabilizing from 1950 to 1960, high rates are likely to continue in a society which does not sanction premarital sexual experimentation and which is most unlikely to forbid divorce or even to

[17] Paul H. Jacobson, *op. cit.*, pp. 30 and 98.
[18] *Trends in Divorce and Family Disruption.* (Preprint from August 1963 Health, Education, and Welfare Indicators.) National Vital Statistics Division, Public Health Service, U.S. Department of Health, Education, and Welfare. Washington, D.C.: U.S. Government Printing Office.

make it much more difficult, since this would not be consistent with the accent on freedom.

Even more disturbing to many than the incidence of divorce is the number of desertions. No national data are available but figures for some cities show that the number of desertions exceeds the number of divorces. Of special concern to social workers and government officials is the heavy financial and moral burden occasioned by deserting fathers. Some idea of the magnitude of the problem can be had from the report that the cost of the Aid to Dependent Children program in 1960 amounted to nearly a billion dollars, and has been rapidly rising in recent years. Not clear, however, is the possible impact of the ADC program itself on the incidence of desertion. Critics of the program point to the fact that desertion may be encouraged by the provision of the law which extends aid only to economically dependent children in broken homes or to those without a legal father.[19]

Marriages are more fragile in the United States than in most countries because the ties that bind are fewer or weaker. This is especially true for the basic economic bonds between spouses. In discussing the bases of marital stability in primitive societies, Linton[20] observes that economic interdependence of husband and wife probably outweighs all other factors combined. The male is essentially the producer of raw materials and the female is the processor. By contrast in modern American urban industrial society, this economic interdependence of spouses is greatly reduced, since—as we have seen—about one-third of all married women have paying jobs and many of those who do not work are confident they could support themselves if they wished to. The married men need depend less than in the past on their wives for "all the comforts of a home," thanks to restaurants, hotels, tailors, dry-cleaning establishments, laundries, doctors, hospitals, drugstores and other service establishments.

The dependence of members of the family upon one another is further reduced by modern mass production and the increasing real income. For instance, when the usual arrangement was for an American family to have only one car, it was commonly referred to as "the family car" because all members of the family had to accomodate to it. If one member used it excessively, the others would be deprived. If this was to be avoided, careful planning by all and synchronization of schedules was required. It meant outings for the family as a whole. With the advent of the second car, the wife is freed from dependence on her

[19] Under the Social Security Act, federal grants are made to the states for the support of children in their own homes, where economic need is occasioned by the death, incapacity or absence of a parent.
[20] Ralph Linton. "The Natural History of the Family" in Ruth Nanda Anshen (Ed.), *The Family: Its Function and Destiny,* rev. ed. New York: Harper & Row, 1959, p. 35.

husband for her transportation needs, and vice versa. The second car increases freedom; it also increases individualism. Husband and wife need each other less than before. The second car is of course only one of an increasing number of individualizing instruments in American life. Nor is the automobile industry content to stop with the sale of the second car. Geared as the industry is, like the economy as a whole, to continued expansion, it is seeking to increase the market for its product by promoting an additional car for each adolescent in the family.

With ties of economic interdependence weakened, there is greater reliance on ties of psychological interdependence. These sentimental ties are, however, more volatile and less enduring than those of economic and religious interdependence. Research shows [21] that in the United States there is a decrease in marital happiness with duration of marriage.

The accent on happiness in marriage is an expression of the emphasis on individualism in American society. Individualism is an expression of the American creed of freedom, freedom of the individual to develop his own tastes, and to live according to his own plan. The happiness of the individual, more than the welfare of the group, is the controlling consideration. The family is said to exist for the individual, not the individual for the family. What matters most is the development of the individual, sometimes at the expense of group and general interest.

The American family is therefore in a precarious balance. When marriage and parenthood are successful, the satisfaction in interpersonal relations may be deeper and more evident than in societies in which the more traditional, institutional values are emphasized. On the other hand, the family more readily falls apart, since hostility and aggression when they occur are more disruptive than in societies in which marital roles are more impersonal and are taken for granted as a matter of destiny.

In the United States, perhaps the most extreme of modern individualistic societies, the precarious balance of the family has been maintained by a high rate of remarriage after divorce. Over 98 per cent of those divorced before age 30 remarry, usually within two to three years. In many cases, the new love begins before the old love formally ends. The distinction made [22] between transitional and terminal divorce is important from the standpoint of the stability of the family as a social institution. In the case of terminal divorce, no new domestic unit is established and the divorced person continues to live in domestic isolation, a potentially disorganizing situation, whereas in transitional divorce, the divorce is followed by remarriage and the prospect

---

[21] Peter C. Pineo. "Disenchantment in the Later Years of Marriage," *Marriage and Family Living*, Vol. 23 (February 1961), pp. 3–11.
[22] Cited by Jessie Bernard, *Remarriage*. New York: Dryden Press, 1956, p. 334.

of social stability. For the most part, in the United States, divorce disorganizes particular families but remarriage reorganizes them.

Thus it can be seen that within the framework of the tradition of freedom and the environment of economic affluence, the characteristics of the family in the United States that make for both stability and instability become socially intelligible.

Chapter 2: From Colonial Family to the Family of the Future

3. THE CHANGING AMERICAN FAMILY

Ernest W. Burgess

§ The family is subject not only to changes of the family life cycle but also to pressures from the technological advances of our society. A series of changes that has almost run its course is from farm to city to suburb.

The following descriptions should be read not merely for their interest but in the light of their relationship to their rural or urban environment. The colonial family was necessarily well organized, and the form of organization it took was the traditional patriarchal form. The rural colonial family was not only a social group but a work group as well. As does a small business, the farm had a manager (the father), a foreman (the mother), and workers of various degrees of skill (relatives and children). In semi-isolation, it had to depend upon itself for most of its needs; it had to be resourceful, loyal, helpful to all it members. The farm family of the early 1900's was still family-centered, but it depended to some extent upon community facilities and therefore did not need to be so rigidly organized. In the 1920's the city family was often the rural or small-town family transplanted to the city, breathless in its effort to swing into the rapid and uneven pace of the many streams of city life. By the 1960's there were more special services to help city families and a pattern of city living had begun to develop.

The most evident and perhaps the most fundamental change that has taken place in American family life is the emergence of what may be called the urban family. It is different in many striking ways from the traditional American family which is characteristically rural. The

SOURCE: *Religious Education*, 23 (May, 1928), 408–11. Reprinted by permission of the publisher, The Religious Education Association, New York, New York.

The author, now deceased, had a long and notable career as an innovator and leader in research on marriage and the family. He received his doctorate from the University of Chicago, where he taught for many years. He co-authored *Predicting Success or Failure in Marriage, Engagement and Marriage,* and *The Family from Institution to Companionship*; edited several books; and published dozens of articles.

changes in the American family caused by the transition from the rural to the urban environment may be seen in a comparison of three families (1) a colonial American family; (2) a rural family before the [first] World War; and (3) an ultra-modern urban family.

The colonial American family was of the patriarchal type. The following case of the Lay family stands for what might be termed a survival of or a reversion to this large patriarchal type of family like that of the Hebrew patriarchs or that still found in China, Japan and India. Almost every American rural community has a large family group more or less resembling the Lay family:

Mr. and Mrs. Lay were pioneer farmers in an area of virgin forest. The draining of the water made the swamp district available for agriculture. The deep black soil once drained of the excess water proved to possess almost inexhaustible fertility. The land now became valuable. And Mr. Lay gradually acquired the status of a well-to-do, prosperous farmer.

The family increased in numbers. Five sons and two daughters were born to Mr. and Mrs. Lay. As soon as the boys and girls were able, they were called upon to do their share of the farm work. With the increase of labor resources a large acreage became possible. The draining of the land provided this increased acreage. With the increase and growth of the children the additional labor was provided. They made that farm blossom like a garden. It is true the schooling facilities were meagre, and the school attendance was sadly curtailed because of the necessary work on the farm, but the cultivation of the farm was deemed of greater importance than the cultivation of the mind.

From the very beginning Mr. Lay considered himself as the ruling spirit of the family group. The farm was his, and the income was his to control. All moneys received, even that from the sale of poultry and dairy products, passed into the family treasury, that was absolutely controlled by the father. Nothing was bought without his consent and approval. He ruled absolutely from barn to kitchen. He was not tyrannical nor harsh in the execution of his authority. His despotism was of a benevolent kind, but he demanded recognition of his authority as something self-evident, and the family submitted to it in the like spirit.

There was some kind of social life in which the family participated. Every Sunday morning the entire family attended church. The drive to town was an event in their life. After church the afternoon was spent visiting their relatives. Or possibly the relatives would accompany them to their home. In later years, after the children had established their own homes, the entire family would meet either at the homes of the parents or at one of the children's homes for a Sunday afternoon reunion. As the family constituted a large group, this resulted in limiting the circle of their social intercourse to the family circle. The group thus became an inner group of prime importance.

As the boys married, it became evident that additional farm lands must be secured to provide the family with their means of livelihood. It is needless to state that the prospective bride was always thoroughly inspected and her virtues, particularly her capacity for work and willingness to save money, discussed before permission to marry was given by the father. No son married without the father's consent. But once the permission to marry was granted, the father set out to acquire a farm for the young couple, where they might reside. But the farm remained the father's property and the young people were considered his tenants. They were permitted to enjoy larger liberties, but in matters pertaining to the cultivation of the farm, the purchase of farm equipment, and of livestock, the father always had control. No calf was ever purchased or sold without his consent. Every little detail, such as planning the cultivation of the land, the sowing of a particular kind of wheat or other grain, was left to the father. He was the head of the group, and his will ruled supreme. The fact that the father possessed good judgment and business ability, and that his advice was always good, and the other fact that his authority was not wielded in a tyrannical manner, brought about a willingness on the part of the sons to continue their submission to this head of the family government.

This case brings out vividly the dominating control of the husband and father as the head of the family, a power that recalls that of the *pater familias* in the large Roman household or resembles that of the house manager or the head of the large patriarchal Chinese family. This case may be regarded as extreme because the title to all the property is held by the father and because he exercises the deciding voice in the marriage of his children. The entire social life of its members is concentrated in the family and in the wider kinship circle. In fact, the will of each individual is definitely subordinate to the family interests as embodied in the will of its dominating head.

The A. family is a more typical representative of the rural family of [about 1900], in the generation before the automobile and the [first] World War.

The A. family had five children, James, 19, Albert, 16, Carrie, 14, Aileen, 12, and Edmund, 2. They lived on a farm of four hundred acres four miles from Chermont. They attended a country school two miles from home.

The boys always worked for their father and the girls helped their mother. Once in a while Carrie worked for Mrs. B., who lived about two miles away. This was when her mother did not need her. Carrie was allowed to keep her money but was expected to get her clothes with it.

Mr. A. gave the boys their spending money each week.

The friends of the family were the C., B., P., M., L. and K. families. These families often had dances at their respective homes and all the family attended and danced.

Albert, Carrie, and Aileen always asked their parents if they might go to a skating party, box social or to the large town to the corn palace. Mr. and Mrs. A. let them go but not very often for they thought it was best for them to stay at home and not start running around too young. You always found all the family at home or else all away to visit some neighbor.

When Albert, Carrie, and Aileen started to go with girls and boys they first went with school mates whom they had known many years. Carrie was married to a neighbor boy and they went to live on a near-by farm. Albert married a Chermont girl and went to live on a farm about ten miles from home. Aileen was married to a neighbor boy whom she had known since childhood.

While the old type of patriarchal domination is absent from the A. family, the central place of the family in the life of its members is most evident. The family is both an economic and a social unity.

A day in the life of a city family [in the 1920's] presents a thought provoking contrast to the two types of rural families.

Mr. Jay is awakened at 7 o'clock, and dresses quietly in the bathroom in order not to awaken his sleeping wife. He eats breakfast alone, with his newspaper, and leaves the house at 8 o'clock without a member of his family. Mrs. Jay never awakens before 8:30 or 9, and then has her coffee in bed. The two children, James, aged 17, and Julia, aged 12, eat breakfast at 8:10, and leave for school at 8:30. If it is a rainy morning the limousine takes them after it returns from taking their father to his office. They seldom say good-bye to their mother as she is usually asleep.

Mrs. Jay, in negligée, commences with the cook, and does the ordering for the day, over the telephone. She never goes to market. After giving the two servants their directions for the day's work, she looks after her bills or writes letters at her desk.

If she has not a luncheon engagement, or some shopping downtown, she has an engagement for the afternoon—cards, or calling, or a concert or matinee. She is usually dressing for dinner when her husband returns from work. She languidly asks him about his business and receives monosyllabic replies. He is vice-president of a large bond house and is very busy in his office all day.

Dinner is at seven, and the children do most of the talking. In the evening, Mr. Jay either goes to the club to play cards or goes to the theatre or to a party with his wife. They have many wealthy friends who entertain a great deal. During the ride home and while they are going to bed they are too tired to talk much.

James goes to high school. After he has deposited his books in his locker, he runs to his class room, bluffs through the morning classes, chats with the girls and "fellows" between classes, and eats lunch with the "gang." His lunch usually consists of three sandwiches and a cream puff, which are eaten on the street. After his afternoon classes, he either goes to the movies or plays baseball in the yard of one of his friends. He returns in time for supper, after which he pretends to study until his parents have gone out. Then he, too, goes out.

Julia, aged 12, goes to a private school for girls. The work is not strenuous and she has plenty of time to scribble notes to the girl on her left and whisper. She takes English, arithmetic, French, reading, geography, and sewing. At 10:30, hot chocolate is served; at 12:30, a hot luncheon is given to the pupils. School is out at 2, and Julia hurries home for her music lesson or to practice piano. Twice a week she is tutored in arithmetic, because she is backward. If several of her girl friends interrupt her practicing, they make fudge and giggle. Julia seldom goes outdoors except for her walk from school.

After she has washed and dressed for dinner, and eaten with her parents, she studies or reads "The Little Colonel Books," and telephones to all her little friends whom she has seen during the day. She retires at 9:30, and usually keeps her light burning in order to read in bed. She seldom receives a good-night kiss from her parents. Her companionship with her brother is very slight, as they quarrel continually. He delights in teasing her.

Altogether, the home life of this family is very neglected. The four members only meet together once during the day, at dinner. They all tell what they have done during the day, but they scarcely know each other. If Julia enters her mother's room, she usually is told, "Go away, dear, I'm dressing now." James does not approach his father much except to ask for some new article or funds with which to buy it. Mr. Jay is usually too busy reading or dressing to do anything but grant his son's request.

The children have practically no home life, nor connection with their parents. They are quite independent. Mrs. Jay takes little interest in her husband's work, and he cares not at all for her social interests during the day. His cards and his business occupy him completely.

This not altogether sympathetic account of the external behavior of the different members of the Jay family introduces us to many, if not all, of the changes which urban life has wrought in the rural pattern of the traditional American family. First of all, the urban family no longer possesses the economic unity of its agricultural prototype. In the rural family even today all its members are united by the roles which they play in a common economic enterprise of which the husband and the father is the manager. In the city the husband's business tends to be remote not only spacially, but also as in this case, spiritually from the others in the family. The wife has become a woman of leisure and the two children are unencumbered by the necessity of performing any household tasks.

Added to this lack of economic unity is the absence of social unity in this family. The dinner at night is the only meal that brings together all the members of the family. The independence of each individual is so well nigh complete that the question may well be raised, "what is keeping the family together."

The objection may be raised that this is an extreme case of family life in the urban environment. That charge is no doubt quite true. But the point is that this extreme case, just because it is unusual, causes us to realize the nature and intensity of certain forces that are changing family life under city conditions.

4. THE FUTURE OF THE FAMILY REVISITED

John N. Edwards

§ A long list of causes and results of social change—for example, loss of functions, increased mobility, declining status ascription, and the ascendency of materialistic values—is often attributed to family change. A re-examination of these factors suggests, however, that they give only limited explanations of family change. Edwards contends that the current value predicament in American society does not point to a revolution in family values, as some writers have suggested. He does find, however, strong evidence of increased interpenetration and interdependence between the family and the economic sphere.

Familial change and institutional interpenetration are subjects which have attracted the continued but sporadic attention of sociologists and social scientists.[1] For the most part observers of the family, in essence, have considered the interchange between various institutional sectors and the family a one-sided affair. Familial change is perceived, in other words, as resulting from social changes in other institutional spheres with few, if any, reciprocal effects. A considerable amount of

SOURCE: *Journal of Marriage and the Family,* 29 (August, 1967), 505–11. Reprinted with permission of the publisher and the author.

John N. Edwards received his doctorate from the University of Nebraska and is presently associate professor of sociology at the University of Kentucky. He is the author of *The Family and Change* as well as a number of articles relating to family sociology.

[1] See, for example, William F. Ogburn, *Social Change,* New York: Viking Press, 1922; William F. Ogburn and Meyer F. Nimkoff, *Technology and the Changing Family,* New York: Houghton-Mifflin, 1955; Pitirim A. Sorokin, *The Crisis of Our Age,* New York: E. P. Dutton, 1941; Carle C. Zimmerman, *Family and Civilization,* New York: Harper and Brother, 1947; Margaret P. Redfield, "The American Family: Consensus and Freedom," *American Journal of Sociology,* 52 (November, 1946), pp. 175–183; Ernest Burgess, "The Family in a Changing Society," *American Journal of Sociology,* 53 (May, 1948), pp. 417–422; Lawrence K. Frank, "Social Change and the Family," *Annals of the American Academy of Political and Social Science,* 160 (March, 1932), pp. 94–102; Joseph K. Folsom, *The Family and Democratic Society,* New York: John Wiley and Sons, Inc., 1934; Ruth N. Anshen, "The Family in Transition," in *The Family: Its Function and Destiny,* ed. by Ruth N. Anshen, New York: Harper, 1959, pp. 3–19; Sidney M. Greenfield, "Industrialization and the Family in Sociological Theory," *American Journal of Sociology,* 67 (November, 1961), pp. 312–322; Meyer F. Nimkoff, "Biological Discoveries and the Future of the Family. A Reappraisal," *Social Forces,* 41 (December, 1962), pp. 121–127; and Reuben Hill, "The American Family of the Future," *Journal of Marriage and the Family,* 26 (February, 1964), pp. 20–28.

evidence has been and can be marshalled to substantiate this interpretation. Yet, one of the consequences of adopting this prevailing view is that it has frequently resulted in the formulation of a unifactorial "theory" or in the development of a theory of such a general nature that it has little heuristic and predictive utility. Ogburn and Nimkoff's [2] citation of technological innovations as the determinants of functional losses typifies the unifactorial approach, while Burgess' [3] suggestion that familial changes are the consequences of alterations in economic conditions and societal ideology is indicative of the level of abstraction with which change has been treated.

In addition to their predilection for unifactorial and highly general formulations, it has been noted that our earlier analysts of the family and social change were far from dispassionate observers. Either by implication or explicitly, the majority of writers during the 1940's took a stance on our perennial, theoretical antistrophe between persistence and change.[4] With few exceptions, social and family change was treated as a unique and disturbing occurrence. The views of these sociologists were not only tainted with traditional nostalgia in the midst of generalized and rapid change but reflected an over-rigid model of society which was then current.

Despite an increased awareness of the limitations of prior discussions of changes in the American family, many of the issues recently have been raised anew. Hobart, in contending that the family serves as a humanizing influence in modern society, suggests four significant changes being undergone: functional losses, increased personal mobility, declining status ascription, and the continued ascendency of materialistic values.[5] Although there is a certain amount of confusion at times as to whether these are consequences or causes of change, all of these factors have been isolated as important explanatory variables by previous theorists of familial change. In combining these four factors, Hobart argues that they have led to a profound value predicament in which the primary commitment and meaning of the family are being lost. Material abundance and our present commitment to its expenditure, he maintains, threaten the centrality of "human" values and our prospects of "self-realization." Consequently, if the current trends persist, it is possible "that something more or less than man might emerge to carry on something more or less than human society." [6]

Within the limited compass of this paper, this interpretation of the

---

[2] Ogburn and Nimkoff, *op. cit.*   [3] Burgess, *op. cit.*
[4] Sorokin and Zimmerman during this period were two outstanding proponents of the theme of family decay and deterioration.
[5] Charles W. Hobart, "Commitment, Value Conflict and the Future of The American Family," *Marriage and Family Living*, 25 (November, 1963), pp. 405–412.
[6] *Ibid.*, p. 409.

variables will be examined and an attempt will be made to indicate, whenever appropriate, their limitations as explanations of change. In doing so, the efficacy of these variables as explanations of change, whether employed singly or in concert, will be evaluated. Secondly, an alternative interpretation of marriage and the family will be suggested as a base line for the development of future theories of change.

Variables of Familial Change

1. Loss of Functions

Hobart, in discussing the American family's loss of functions, points to the provision of companionship and emotional security as the basic function and reason for family formation today. Without question, many of the former functions such as economic production, education, protection, and recreation have been shifted to other institutional spheres or, at the very least, their content and form as they are carried out by the American family have been altered. Juxtaposed against this is evidence which suggests that the attractiveness of family formation has increased over the decades, However, Hobart's assertion that Americans seek divorce when they fail to attain a sufficient level of companionship and emotional security lacks empirical support. The precipitating influences in the initiation of divorce proceedings are, in fact, a matter of some debate. In making such as assertion, Hobart appears to be in accord with Ogburn that "the dilemma of the modern family is due to its loss of function"[7] and that family instability and disintegration are a consequence.

In the words of Barrington Moore, the American family today may have "obsolete and barbaric features,"[8] but family units have persisted and the vast majority continue to persist despite the ongoing loss of functions. Durkheim's classic proposition concerning social differentiation is most suggestive in this connection. Increasing specialization and differentiation, concomitants of societal complexity, Durkheim contended, lead to an increment in interdependence.[9] This is no less true of familial functions than it is of the division of labor. Our present family system, organized around whatever tasks, is more highly interdependent with other institutional sectors than previously. Even the

[7] William F. Ogburn, "The Changing Functions of the Family," in *Selected Studies in Marriage and the Family*, ed. by Robert F. Winch, Robert McGinnis, and Herbert R. Barringer, New York: Holt, Rinehart, and Winston, 1962, pp. 159–163.
[8] Barrington Moore, "Thoughts on the Future of the Family," in *Identity and Anxiety*, ed. by Maurice R. Stein, Arthur J. Vidich, and David M. White, New York: The Free Press, a division of the Macmillan Co., 1960, p. 394.
[9] Emile Durkheim, *The Division of Labor in Society*, New York: The Free Press, a division of the Macmillan Co., 1947.

various totalitarian experiments with the eradication of family functions, including those of childrearing and socialization, tentatively suggest the ultimate functionality of the family in societal maintenance, regardless of its specific structure and functions.[10] It thus would appear that the issue of functional losses as a source or indication of instability is a misleading one. It is indeed questionable if family instability (divorce and separation) can be eliminated or reduced however many or few functions the family performs. The issue for any theory of family change seems to be, rather, the identification of the specific direction of interdependence and the concomitants which accompany and lead to increased interdependence.

2. *Increased Personal Mobility*

The relatively high rate of spatial mobility within industrialized society, according to Hobart, affects the family in at least three ways: (1) it precipitates a larger amount of crises and adjustments, (2) it breaks the family from its external supports such as friendship and kinship groups, and (3) it weakens the proscriptions against divorce as a means of resolving family difficulties.[11] Increased personal or spatial mobility undoubtedly occasions the need for more adjustments. Generally such mobility is related to changes in work and, at times, to shifts in family status. The transitions attendant to these alterations are not to be underestimated. Yet, as the Rapoports indicate, conflicts and stresses are not necessarily multiplied by these transitions.[12] They may, in actuality, have desirable consequences. As a result of mobility, the functions of the family are by no means residual but become an inextricable background in the free choice of work and career. The prescriptions of work may allow, in turn, considerable latitude in the organization of family structure that was not formerly possible. The pursuit of higher education by women has enabled them to share occupational positions with their spouses and, in so doing, their involvement in the structuring of the family as well as in economic activities has been intensified.

The contention that the American family lacks external support during crisis periods is a corollary of the notion tht the nuclear family is

[10] Nicholas S. Timasheff, "The Attempt to Abolish the Family in Russia," in *The Family*, ed. by Norman W. Bell and Ezra F. Vogel, New York: The Free Press, a division of the Macmillan Co., 1960, pp. 55–63. Reiss has argued that Timasheff's interpretation of the Russian failure to eradicate the family may be based on a logical fallacy. See Ira L. Reiss, "The Universality of the Family: A Conceptual Analysis," *Journal of Marriage and the Family*, 27 (November, 1965), pp. 443–453.
[11] Hobart, *op. cit.*, p. 406.
[12] Robert Rapoport and Rhona Rapoport, "Work and Family in Contemporary Society," *American Sociological Review*, 30 (June, 1965), pp. 381–394.

isolated in an urban's situation. There are now a number of empirical indications which contradict or at least modify this view. Data from a Cleveland study, presented by Sussman, suggest that, in spite of extensive spatial mobility, nuclear families operate within a matrix of mutual kin assistance.[13] It is, in fact, during periods of crises that the aid of kin is most likely to be offered and accepted. Axelrod's research in Detroit indicates that relatives rather than non-relatives are the most important type of informal group association.[14] Babchuk and Bates, in a study of primary relations, also suggest that a large number of close friendships are maintained on a nonlocal and non-face-to-face basis.[15] On the whole, the evidence indicates that the high rate of annual movement by families has a relatively negligible effect on their external supports and does not, as often contended, weaken the informal controls of primary groups. It is patent that family transitions of one sort or another have always existed. The possibility that mobility as a crisis point in family life has merely superseded others is not to be discounted; but, if this is true, the impact of mobility on the family still remains to be demonstrated.

3. Declining Ascribed Relationships

In identifying the decline of traditionally defined or ascribed relationships as another element in the weakening of family bonds, Hobart concedes that the emphasis on achieved relationships fosters greater choice in establishing social relations. He argues, though, that the cross-sex contact, particularly in voluntary associations, subjects the marriage bond to greater stress.[16] To view voluntary organizations as potential agents for family dissolution is to oversimplify and distort the complexity of these organizations. Expressive voluntary groups (a dance club, for example) and those whose memberships are comprised of both sexes may serve to reinforce family relations. By their very nature, expressive associations are organized to supply immediate and personal gratification to their respective members. Their focus is, in other words, integrative at an individual level, while instrumental groups (such as the Chamber of Commerce) provide integration at a communal level.

[13] Marvin B. Sussman, "The Isolated Nuclear Family: Fact or Fiction?" *Social Problems*, 6 (Spring, 1959), pp. 333–340. Similar findings based on New Haven, Connecticut, data are contained in Marvin B. Sussman, "The Help Pattern in the Middle-Class Family," *American Sociological Review*, 18 (February, 1953), pp. 22–28.

[14] Morris Axelrod, "Urban Structure and Social Participation," *American Sociological Review*, 21 (February, 1956), pp. 13–18.

[15] Nicholas Babchuk and Alan P. Bates, "The Primary Relations of Middle-Class Couples: A Study in Male Dominance," *American Sociological Review*, 28 (June, 1963), pp. 377–385.

[16] Hobart, *op. cit.*, pp. 406–407.

Particularly where expressive organizations are bisexual in composition, solidarity may be enhanced.[17]

It is, on the other hand, among those organizations which attract their constituencies from only one sex or the other that the probability of affiliation disturbing familial equilibrium is increased. In the one-sex groups, family members become geographically dispersed and may expend considerable amounts of time apart from one another. Even still, a number of relevant studies suggest that these are exceptional cases.[18] A sizeable proportion of the population are not affiliated with any type of voluntary association. Moreover, among those who do belong, their participation is neither extensive nor intensive. Americans, all folklore to the contrary, are not a nation of joiners, and it is thus difficult to perceive achieved relationships as a threat to family and marital solidarity.

In conceiving the proliferation of associations and achieved relationships as causes of dissolution and change, there is also an implicit assumption made about the nature of man. Basically, in positing cross-sex contact as a disruptive force, man is viewed as primarily a sexual being. Presumably, social control of the sexual drive is tenuous and exposure to the opposite sex is sufficient to deteriorate this control altogether. Since every society is interested in controlling sexual outlets to some extent, it is particularly imperative for an industrialized society which severely limits such outlets to segregate the sexes. This conception of man is not only incompatible with most sociological theories, but it is ultimately an untenable position. Even if we grant that adultery is a widespread experience, there remains the intricate, and as yet unaccomplished, task of sorting out extramarital involvement from other causes of instability.

4. Ascendency of Materialistic Values

Materialistic values are seen as fundamentally incongruous with the more important values of the family; therefore, value confusion and instability result. The resolution of the present value confusion, Hobart notes, is doubly important for the family in that it is one of the basic

[17] The integrative impact of voluntary organizations is discussed at length in Nicholas Babchuk and John N. Edwards, "Voluntary Associations and the Integration Hypothesis," *Sociological Inquiry*, 35 (Spring, 1965), pp. 149–162.
[18] For instance, see Charles Wright and Herbert Hyman, "Voluntary Association Memberships of American Adults: Evidence from National Sample Surveys," *American Sociological Review*, 23 (June, 1958), pp. 284–294; John Foskett, "Social Structure and Social Participation," *American Sociological Review*, 20 (August, 1955), pp. 431–438; Wendell Bell and Maryanne Force, "Urban Neighborhood Types and Participation in Formal Associations," *American Sociological Review*, 21 (February, 1956), pp. 25–34; and John Scott, Jr., "Membership and Participation in Voluntary Associations," *American Sociological Review*, 22 (June, 1957), pp. 315–326.

socializing agents and it symbolizes many of the more fundamental humane values. Either human values must become preeminent in American society or the values of success, efficiency, and prosperity will continue to alter the family institution and eventually erode it. Hobart suggests, in this regard, that a value revolution is essential for continued societal survival. Such a revolution, he argues, cannot be a mere emergence of a consistent value hierarchy but must be a total displacement of our now-prevailing economic values. Although current trends appear to make such a revolution remote, the position set forth by Hobart is in essence optimistic. As a key to renewed commitment to marriage, he suggests that, increasingly, individuals in our affluent society are becoming more important for what they are, rather than for what they are capable of doing. Individuals are perceived and cared for in terms of their intrinsic value, rather than their extrinsic and utilitarian worth. Thus, despite the current prominence of utilitarian values, it is felt that the family is evolving in a new direction.[19]

The Family Today and Tomorrow

To this juncture, I have attempted to point out several limitations in invoking functional loss, spatial mobility, and the emphasis on achieved relationships as explanations for familial change. I should like, at this point, to offer an alternative interpretation of contemporary marriage and family living as a base line for further analysis, since it is quite apparent with the data now at hand that there is some measure of disagreement. Specific alternative explanatory variables of change will not be indicated; it is equally important in the formulation of any future theories of change, however, that we avoid stereotyping our present situation as we have done with the rural family of the past. In offering this admittedly tentative and sketchy analysis, Hobart's excellent example is followed by focusing on value orientations.

A basic underlying theme of American culture, Jules Henry has noted, is a preoccupation with pecuniary worth or value that is a consequence of what he terms "technological driveness." [20] Though our institutional structure is highly interdependent, the point is that our economic system and its values have become so pervasive that American life can be characterized as being driven by the constant creation of new wants and desires. Each new want—with considerable impetus from advertising— aids in the destruction of self-denial and impulse control, both virtues of a previous era. Where an economic system has no ceiling or production limits, all hesitation to indulgence must be overcome. And overcome it is, as witnessed by the tremendous growth of the advertising industry.

[19] Hobart, *op. cit.*, pp. 407–412.
[20] Jules Henry, *Culture Against Man*, New York: Random House, Inc., 1963.

The preoccupation with pecuniary worth appears to be a necessary complement to a social system dominated by its economic institutional sphere. The nature of an economy of such a social system is that rewards must be transferable and negotiable; hence, the institutionalization of a monetary system. Whether one is selling the products of his labors or his personality and training, tangible rewards are mandatory. No doubt the efficacy of religious thought has suffered for this reason. Eternal damnation is not sufficiently definite, nor the prospect of heaven sufficiently imminent, to normatively persuade many who exist in a society where most rewards are quantified. Quantified rewards and our nearly obsessive concern with them are not identical with status achievement which other writers have cited as a crucial factor in the dissolution of the family. Status achievement may take many forms, of which the accumulation of monetary rewards is only one manifestation. The point is, rather, that the prospect of quantified rewards has become so pervasive in our society that it permeates virtually all social relationships including that between husband and wife and the progeny. The non-rewarding character of unlimited procreation has partially contributed to the diminution of that function and family size. To speak of "human obsolescence" and to consider the treatment accorded the elderly in our society are also evidence of the importance attached to tangibly rewarded behavior. In many instances it is not too much of an overstatement to consider as objects those that have not yet developed exchangeable resources (the young) and those who have exhausted theirs (the elderly). Even those occupying the middle ground, however, are not necessarily in an enviable position, for their relationships often lack all but a vestige of emotional interchange.

Insofar as marriage and the family are concerned, the first difficulties arising from this emphasis on pecuniary rewards are encountered in the dating process. The emergence of the rating and dating complex, Waller suggested, has fostered exploitative relationships in dating.[21] In such a relationship each partner attempts to maximize his or her returns with the least amount of concessions. Control and therefore the maximization of rewards are vested in that individual who has the least investment in the situation. Were it not a serious matter, it would be ironical that low commitment should be so highly rewarded. Indeed it is significant and symptomatic of contemporary society that rewards from this type of relationship should be consciously and avidly pursued. The exploitative nature of dating, were it merely confined to dating, would be less problematic. Due to the lengthy dating period, ranging from the preteen years to the early twenties, this orientation becomes

[21] Willard Waller and Reuben Hill, *The Family: A Dynamic Interpretation*, New York: Holt, Rinehart and Winston, 1951, pp. 131–157.

reinforced through repetition. It cannot fail, therefore, to have an impact on marital relationships, particularly in the first years of marriage, the period when couples are most vulnerable to divorce.

Marital relationships, ideally at least, are defined in our society as relationships involving mutual sacrifice, sharing, and giving. Magoun states in this regard: "Anyone going into marriage with the expectation of being thanked for bringing home the bacon—even against dismaying odds—or for shining the ancestral silver tea service till it glistens from the buffet in little pinwheels of light, is headed for heartache." [22] And heartache is precisely what a large proportion of marriages, not only those that terminate in divorce but also the so-called normal marriages, garner. With monotonous repetition we are conditioned, primarily as a result of the pervasiveness of our economic institutions, to react to situations in a manner designed to elicit rewards. When the potential of tangible rewards is absent, interaction tends to be halting and random. Through the conditioning of the economic system and the lengthy continuation of this basic orientation during the dating process, the newly married are grossly unprepared for the prescriptions of marriage.

Recent findings amply illustrate this trend. The marriages of what Cuber refers to as the "significant Americans" are predominantly utilitarian in nature. The partners of these marriages are primarily interested in what each derives from the relationship. There is little concern with mutual sacrifice and sharing other than that which is essential to the maintenance of the marital bond. Moreover, the types of rewards sought in these marriages are not psychic or emotional but those which enhance material security. In fact, these marriages are, as Cuber points out, characterized by continual conflict, passivity, and a lack of vitality. Only a minority of the marriages approximate the cultural ideal of an intimate, emotional attachment between partners that results in mutual concern and sharing; and it is these marriages which are most vulnerable to divorce.[23] Thus, it would appear that, like the devil, the family in contemporary, industrialized society must take the hindmost. As an institution it is unorganized and, therefore, lacks the influence that may be exercised by those institutions which are. Through necessity it must be flexible and adaptable; those that are not fail.[24]

A central proposition of functional analysis is that a change in one element of an integrated system leads to changes in other elements. The major impetus for social change in our society has been and continues to be our dynamic economic institutions, which seek to create

[22] F. Alexander Magoun, *Love and Marriage,* New York: Harper and Brothers, 1956, p. 44.
[23] John F. Cuber and Peggy B. Harroff, *The Significant Americans: A Study of Sexual Behavior Among the Affluent,* New York: Appleton-Century, 1965.
[24] Clark E. Vincent, "Familia Spongia: The Adaptive Function," *Journal of Marriage and the Family,* 28 (February, 1966), pp. 29–36.

ever new wants and markets for their products and services. Due to its decreasing size, the family's adaptability for change has kept pace. From many perspectives the various social alterations, such as the employment of women, have resulted in greater independence and increased potentialities for individual family members. In other respects, of course, the changes have been dysfunctional. As we have tried to indicate, the disparity that now exists between the ideal marriage and the real is considerable—just as considerable as it probably was in the past. Future alterations are of a high order of probability, particularly adjustments pertaining to the normative emphasis on material rewards and the affective character of marriage. Still, the desinence of the family appears to be a phantasm born of the anxiety accompanying rapid social change.

If, indeed, contemporary marriages are based more on what the marital partners *are* rather than what they *do* as Hobart suggests, the major disjunctive feature of current family life is that what individuals *are* is primarily reward-seeking organisms. This commitment to economic values is logically incompatible with the values of family life, but it is not a source of major dislocation or dissolution of the family group.

Given this condition, what future has our present family system? Earlier industrialization has relieved a major proportion of our female population from the more onerous activities associated with household management. In spite of the unprecedented opportunity for experimentation, women in general have found it to be a frustrating era. Either they have found a combination of childrearing and outside activities unrewarding or they have felt that the channels for careers remain severely limited. Ongoing social change with respect to career expansion has been marked, nonetheless, and it is highly probable that the tempo will be increased.

This may have major significance for future marital relationships. The tremendous expansiveness of the insurance industry signifies, to some at least, the import attached to the economic aspects of marriage. This is again highlighted by the frequency with which insurance enters into divorce suits. More importantly, it is clear that marriage for men is more desirable, if not perhaps more necessary, than it is for women. Bernard's study of remarriage adequately illustrates the greater dependence which men have on the marital relationship; women, especially those that are economically secure, are less likely to remarry.[25] With increased avenues for more satisfying gainful employment, women will be afforded an enhanced alternative to wedlock. The generalized societal expectations regarding the desirability of marriage for everyone

[25] Jessie Bernard, *Remarriage*, New York: The Dryden Press, 1956, pp. 55, 62–63.

is quite pervasive, to be sure. But marriage, to put it simply, has become a habit—a habit which many young women with attractive career alternatives are beginning to question, however.

Economic overabundance, it is submitted, in the long run will have a repressive effect on the rate of marriage. The recognition of alternatives to wedlock, as that concerning alternatives to premarital chastity, will not occasion sudden behavioral consequences. But change is overdue. When women, already imbued with the economic ethos, fully realize their equality in this sphere, much of the *raison d'etre* of marriage will no longer be present. This is not to say, it should be emphasized, that family formation will precipitously decline; it is merely contended that the consequences of our reward-seeking orientation will become more evident, and this will be reflected in the marriage rate. In other words, one of the present structural supports which buttresses the attractiveness of the marital relationship will cease to exist. Women will no longer find economic dependence a virtue and worthy byproduct of marriage, for, given the opportunity, they will succeed for themselves as ably as any male might.

Numerous other current trends support this contention. The availability of reliable contraceptive devices, the expectations regarding small family size, and the declining influence and authority of men all suggest that the supports for the marital bond are weakening. Educational opportunities for women and the impetus these provide for the pursuance of careers are another consideration. Universities and colleges will probably attract even larger numbers of women in the future, as they have done for each of the last seven decades. Although most of these women may anticipate marriage eventually, more equitable hiring practices and salaries guaranteed by the Civil Rights Act of 1964 will alter this to some extent. The current popularized literature on the single state also dramatizes the interest in alternatives to marriage.

As stated earlier, the family is not and is not likely to be a nonfunctional entity. The prominence of affective behavior in familial relationships as an ideal appears to be a central support for the continuance of these relationships. Still, just how important affective behavior will remain for individuals and how well these needs will be met in the family stand as primary issues in family research. It is illuminating that study after study to date has found that interaction among couples tends to be halting.[26] It is difficult to conceive of warm, intimate, and emotional relationships being maintained over time when vital interaction is almost non-existent. Perhaps even sporadic episodes of sponta-

---

[26] Robert S. Ort, "A Study of Role-Conflicts as Related to Happiness in Marriage," *Journal of Abnormal and Social Psychology*, 45 (October, 1950), pp. 691–699; Peter C. Pineo, "Disenchantment in the Later Years of Marriage," *Marriage and Family Living*, 23 (February, 1961), pp. 2–11; and Cuber and Harroff, *op. cit.*

neous communication are sufficient to sustain these relationships, but the accessibility of legal outlets suggests that, without these and other structural supports, many marriages will terminate in divorce.

Despite the many elements of organizational life that are incompatible with our more humane values, bureaucratic structures in many respects recognize the desirability of maintaining intimate familial relationships. W. H. Whyte has noted, in his inimitable analysis of bureaucracies, the attempt to integrate the wife into the organizational structure.[27] In many ways and in many corporations, of course, this is a defensive act. Even as a mechanism of defense, though, this maneuver implicitly recognizes the wife's role as a supportive agent. Regardless of corporate motivation, the attempted integration of wives into the system can have beneficial consequences for the family. Where such an attempt is not made, the abyss between the economic and family group is only widened. Naturally, from the viewpoint of many individuals, this is not an ideal solution. It is, nonetheless, an alternative— an alternative upon which improvement may be made and, in view of increasing societal bureaucratization, one which demands attention.

A man and woman marrying today can contemplate, in the majority of cases, over 40 years' duration of the relationship, encompassing over one-half of their lives. In a society in which group membership is extremely transitory, this represents a significant departure. Because of its duration and its small size, the individual has no greater opportunity in influencing the character and quality of a group.

[What we are presently witnessing, moreover, is not a revolution of societal values or the demise and increased instability of the American family. Rather, given the current preeminence of economic orientations in our value system, the marital union and family are becoming more highly interdependent with the economic sphere. Cross-culturally and historically, the family, irrespective of its particular structure and functions, has been and is primarily an instrumental group from a societal perspective.] It is not accidental, therefore, that marriage in most societies is based on considerations other than an affective and human orientation. That this is less true in the United States is not an indication of incipient instability but intimates that we are engaged in a radical experiment of familism. It is an experiment in which [we are seeking to integrate a new individualism with the other more highly organized institutions. Insofar as our value orientations are dominated by economic values, marriages and family formation in the future are more likely to be based on reason rather than the impulse of habit.]

[27] William H. Whyte, Jr., *The Organization Man*, Garden City, New York: Doubleday and Company, Inc., 1957.

Chapter 3: Family Subcultures in the United States

5. THE ITALIAN-AMERICAN FAMILY

Herbert J. Gans

§ Prior to World War I, great numbers of immigrants from Europe flooded certain American cities, among them Boston. In time the European-based culture gave way to a modification, strongly interlaced with American values and customs. Such a blending constitutes a subculture —a step on the way to complete assimilation into American culture. At the point in time when the Italians in the West End of Boston were in the ethnic stage, the author of this article lived among them, making careful observations of their way of life. The second-generation Italian family was a strong conservator of the old values and customs, but receptive to changes that would move the third generation into American culture.

Family Types

Sociologists and anthropologists generally distinguish between the *nuclear* family, made up of husband, wife, and children but separated from other relatives; and the *extended* family, in which a group of nuclear families and related individuals from several generations act together as a virtual unit. The extended family is found most often in agricultural or hunting societies, where such groups are functioning economic units. The nuclear family is associated with the urban-industrial society in which family members cannot be employed together, and in which, because of rapid social change, cultural differences between the generations and the resulting conflict between young and old make life together difficult.

SOURCE: Herbert J. Gans, *The Urban Villagers: Group and Class in the Life of Italian-Americans* (New York: Free Press, 1962), pp. 45–61. Reprinted with the permission of the publisher.

The author received his doctorate from the University of Pennsylvania and is presently at the Center for Urban Education, New York. He is the author of *The Levittowners: Ways of Life and Politics in a New Suburban Community.*

West Enders fall squarely between the two ideal types. The nature
of the family, however, can best be understood if one can distinguish
between households and families. West End households are nuclear,
with two qualifications. Married daughters often retain close ties with
their mothers and try to settle near them. They do not share the same
apartment, because however close the ties, there are differences
between the generations—or at least between husband and mother-in-
law—that are likely to create conflict. Some households take in close
relatives who would otherwise be alone, especially unmarried brothers,
sisters, or even cousins, because of feelings of obligation, love, and
the desire to reduce the loneliness of the single person. Pitkin, observing a similar pattern in his study of a Southern Italian village, described
this family as *expanded*.[1] Since rents were low in the West End, unmarried siblings often had their own apartments. Much of their spare time,
however, was spent with married brothers or sisters, and they often
participated in child-rearing as quasi-parental aunts and uncles.

But although households are nuclear or expanded, the family itself
is still closer to the extended type. It is not an economic unit, however,
for there are few opportunities for people to work together in commercial or manufacturing activities. The extended family actually
functions best as a social circle, in which relatives who share the same
interests, and who are otherwise compatible, enjoy each other's company. Members of the family circle also offer advice and other help on
everyday problems. There are some limits to this aid, however, especially
if the individual who is being helped does not reciprocate. For example,
one family I met in the West End had a member who suffered from
spells of deep depression. The family circle visited him frequently to
cheer him up, to give advice, and to urge him to join in family activity,
but when he failed to accept their ministrations, his relatives became
impatient. They continued to visit him, but did so grudgingly. As one
of his relatives put it: "He has no interests, why should anyone care
about him?"

The extended family system is limited generationally, for relationships between adults and their parents—the immigrant generation—
are fewer and less intimate than those between adults of the same
generation.[2] Visits with parents are exchanged, but parents are gen-

[1] Donald Pitkin, "Land Tenure and Farm Organization in an Italian Village,"
Unpublished Ph.D. Dissertation, Harvard University, 1954, p. 114.
[2] Others have reported the lack of contact between the generations and the frequency of contact within them among second-generation Italians. See Philip Garigue
and Raymond Firth, "Kinship Organization of Italianates in London," in Raymond
Firth, ed., *Two Studies of Kinship in London*, London: Athlone Press, 1956, especially pp. 74, 82. Comparative studies of Italian and Irish populations have also
reported this pattern, noting the difference in the Irish family, where old people
are venerated and powerful. See M. K. Opler and J. L. Singer, "Ethnic Differences

erally not part of the continuing social life of the family circle. Widowed parents do not live with their children if other alternatives are available. While old people are allowed to function as grandparents, they are freely criticized for spoiling their grandchildren, or for insisting on outmoded ideas. Compared with the middle class, in fact, the older generation receives little respect or care. Social workers in the West End told of families who sent old people to welfare agencies even when they could afford to support them, although this is not typical. The lack of respect toward the older generation is especially noticeable among children, who tease and insult old people behind their backs, including their own grandparents.

The only exception to this pattern is the previously mentioned tie between mother and married daughter, and a more infrequent one between mother and unmarried son. Even so, mothers tend to assist rather than guide their married daughters. They help out in the household and in the rearing of children, but they have neither the power nor authority of the "Mum," the ruling matriarch of the English working-class family.[3]

The expanded family that I have described is common to both the routine-seekers and the action-seekers. The analysis of family life in the following pages will deal principally with male-female and parent-child relationships among the routine-seekers. As already indicated, most West Enders are routine-seekers—or become so when they marry—and families in which the husband is an action-seeker are relatively few in number.

Male-Female Relationships

I pointed out in Chapter 2 that West Enders socialize primarily with people of their own age and sex, are much less adept than middle-class people at heterosexual relationships. In many working-class cultures, the man is away from the house even after work, taking his leisure in the corner taverns that function as men's clubs. But, since the Italian culture is not a drinking one, this is less frequent among West Enders. Consequently, much of their segregation of leisure takes place within the home: the women sit together in one room, the men in another. Even when everyone gathers around the kitchen table, the men group together at one end, the women at the other, and few words are

in Behavior and Psychopathology," *International Journal of Social Psychiatry*, vol. 2 (1956), pp. 11–22; and Ezra F. Vogel, "The Marital Relationships of Parents of Emotionally Disturbed Children," Unpublished Ph.D. Dissertation, Harvard University, 1958, Chap. 6.

[3] The role of the "Mum" has been described in many studies of English working-class life. See, for example, Michael Young and Peter Willmott, *Family and Kinship in East London*, London: Routledge and Kegan Paul, 1957. See also Chapter 11.

exchanged between them. Men are distinctly uncomfortable in the company of women, and vice versa, but the men find it harder to interact with the women than the women with the men. At social gatherings I attended, whenever women initiated conversations with men, the men would escape as quickly as possible and return to their own group. They explained that they could not keep up with the women, that the women talked faster and more readily, turning the conversation to their own feminine interests and that they tried to dominate the men. The men defended themselves either by becoming hostile or by retreating. Usually, they retreated.

The men's inability to compete conversationally with women is traditional. Second-generation Italians grew up in a patriarchal authority system with a strictly enforced double standard of behavior for boys and girls. The boys were freer to indulge their gratifications than the girls. In order to be able to do what they wanted, the girls thus had to learn early how to subvert the male authority by verbal means —"how to get around the men"—and what they did not learn elsewhere, they learned from the mother's wile in getting her way with her husband. As will be noted subsequently, the father enforces discipline and administers punishment; he does not need to talk. The mother can influence her husband only by talking to him, reinterpreting the child's deeds so that he will not punish the child any more than she feels desirable. Talk is the woman's weapon for reducing inequities in power between male and female.

With unrelated women, the male reaction sometimes resembles fear. The men are afraid that the women will overpower them through their greater verbal skill, and thus overturn the nominal dominance of the man over the woman. In a culture that puts great stress on what David Riesman has called "male vanity," placing a man in an inferior position is thought to impugn his masculinity. In other situations, his fear is based on an opposite motive, that undue contact with a woman may produce sexual desire that cannot be satisfied. Among West End men, the unrelated woman is conceived mainly as a sexual object. At the same time, the strict double standard makes her sexually inaccessible. Consequently, while men are freely aggressive, both sexually and verbally, with a "bad" girl, they must control themselves with an inaccessible "good" girl. Among unmarried people, for example, when a "good" girl enters an all-male group, profanity and sexual talk are immediately halted, and the men seem momentarily paralyzed before they can shift conversational gears.

What the men fear is their own ability at self-control. This attitude, strongest among young, unmarried people, often carries over into adulthood. The traditional Italian belief—that sexual intercourse is unavoidable when a man and a woman are by themselves—is maintained intact among second-generation West Enders, and continues even when sexual interest itself is on the wane. For example, I was told of an older woman whose apartment was adjacent to that of an unmarried male relative. Although they had lived in the same building for almost twenty years and saw each other almost every day, she had never once been in his apartment because of this belief.

As a result, the barriers between the sexes are high, and they are crossed mainly by deviant types. The only men who carry on a consistent social relationship with women are "ladies' men," who are in varying degrees effeminate. Likewise, the only women who carry on such a relationship with men are likely to be those with strong masculine tendencies. Some of my neighbors used to anger their wives by sharing sexually connotative jokes and indulging in sexual banter with a young woman who appeared to be masculine in some of her ways. They were able to do this because the girl did not represent a potential sexual object. Although she still saw herself as a potential bride, and expressed great, though false, embarrassment at the men's behavior, she was a safe target for the expression of the sexual hostility of the males toward the women. At the same time, she never discouraged these attacks because they were the only kinds of advances she was likely to get from men, and perhaps because she was masculine enough to be able to enjoy the joking. West End women indulged in sexual banter, too, but only among themselves.

The male fear of "good" girls was vividly portrayed one evening when a group of men in their twenties were pursuing another man who had slashed one of the group in a tavern brawl. The man ran into his apartment building, leaving the entrance blocked by his mother and his sister. Armed with sticks, the men pushed the mother—a women in her sixties—out of the way. The girl, however, was able to stop them from coming into the building. While they did attack her verbally, they did not touch her, and then, promising to carry out justice at some other time, they eventually withdrew.

Husband-Wife Relationships

The general pattern of male-female interaction carries over into the relationship between husbands and wives. The barriers between male and female are translated into a marital relationship that can be best described as *segregated*, as distinguished from the *joint* relationship that characterizes the middle-class family.[4] Bott's description of his phenomenon among English families applies to the West Enders as well:

---

[4] These terms are taken from Elizabeth Bott, *Family and Social Network*, London: Tavistock Publications, 1957, pp. 53–54.

Husband and wife have a clear differentiation of tasks and a considerable number of separate interests and activities. They have a clearly defined division of labor into male tasks and female tasks. They expect to have different leisure pursuits, and the husband has his friends . . . the wife hers.[5]

While the husband's main role is breadwinning, the wife is responsible for all functions concerning home and child, even the finding of an apartment. Women speak of the family apartment as "my rooms"; husbands speak to wives about "your son." Responsible for overseeing the rearing of the child, the mother may even administer discipline, although this is usually left to the father when he comes home from work.

On the surface, this pattern differs little from the middle-class one. In middle-class society, as in most societies, most of the tasks connected with home and child are also the mother's duty. In the West End, however, the boundary between tasks is quite rigid. As one West End housewife put it, "when my husband comes home with the pay, I can't ask him to help in the house." Whereas the middle-class husband expects to help out in the household, and to share the responsibilities of child-rearing, the West End husband does not expect to do so, and will help out only in unusual situations. It is not that he rejects the possibility of joint action; it is simply something outside of his experience.

The segregation of functions is more clearly visible in the emotional aspects of the husband-wife relationship. Although young West Enders are as much concerned with romantic love as other Americans, and although couples do marry on the basis of love, the marital relationship is quanitatively different from that of the middle class. Not only is there less communication and conversation between husband and wife, but there is also much less gratification of the needs of one spouse by the other. Husbands and wives come together for procreation and sexual gratification, but less so for the mutual satisfaction of emotional needs or problem solving. Among my neighbors was a bachelor. When I asked one of his relatives whether he would every marry, it was explained that he would probably not, since his work brought him into contact with women who satisfied his sexual needs. In addition, his frequent visits to his married sister's household provided the opportunity for the little relationship with children expected of the man.

Thus the marriage partners are much less "close" than those in the middle class. They take their troubles less to each other than to brothers, sisters, other relatives, or friends. Men talk things over with brothers, women with sisters and mothers; each thus remains on his side of the sexual barrier.

[5] Bott, *op. cit.*, p. 53.

I can best illustrate the nature of the marital relationship anecdotally. Most of the small stores in the West End were family enterprises. Two of the Italian stores that I frequented were each run by a man and a woman who I knew to be related, and who I thought were either brother and sister, or cousins. In both cases, my assumption was based on the man's lack of interest in the woman's children when they were in the store, as well as her total lack of interest in his business. One day, when I raised the question of relocation plans in one of the stores, the woman replied curtly, "I don't care about the store, it's his; it's his business to make a living, not mine." This was said matter of factly, without a trace of anger or malice. If the woman did interfere in the man's activities, especially in one of the many extracurricular ones that commonly took place in small stores,[6] she was rebuked and told to mind her own business. In both stores, the lack of communication convinced me that the relationship was that of two individuals who were brought together by economic necessity and by kinship ties, but who otherwise were not close. My assumption that they were siblings or cousins had been based on my middle-class expectations, and I was much surprised to discover that, in both places, they were husband and wife.

The segregated conjugal pattern is closely associated with the extended family, for the functions that are not performed by husband and wife for each other are handled primarily by other members of the extended family. In a society where male and female roles are sharply distinguished, the man quickly learns that, on many occasions, his brother is a better source of advice and counsel than his wife. The recruitment of the family circle on the basis of compatibility enhances this pattern, for those relatives who provide helpful advice are also likely to be compatible in other ways, and thus to be part of the circle.

Although the middle-class observer may find it hard to imagine the absence of the marital closeness that exists in his own culture, this pattern has been functional for people like the West Enders. Until recently, they have lived under conditions in which one of the spouses could easily be removed from the household by mental or physical breakdown, or premature death. In years past more than today, job insecurity, occupational hazards, and poor living conditions meant that every wife might have to reckon with the incapacitation or removal of the breadwinner—even though male desertion was and is rare. Likewise, illness or death in childbirth might remove the woman before her time. The lack of closeness, however, makes it easier for the remaining parent to maintain the household, raise the children—usually with the help of members of the extended family—and to overcome the emotional loss of the spouse. For example, a West Ender I met had

[6] See [Gans] Chapter 5.

lost her husband, with whom she was said to have been exceptionally close, a few months earlier. With her children married, however, she began to think of herself as a single woman again, and participated in social activities with a number of unmarried women of whom she said —only half in jest—she would join in "man-catching" endeavors. At the same time, however, she was able to talk about events which she had shared with her husband as if he were still alive. She did not have to shut him out of her mind in order to overcome the pain of her loss.

Although the segregated conjugal pattern is clearly dominant among the West Enders, signs of its eventual disappearance are making themselves felt.[7] Between the first and second generation, the major change has been that of bringing the men into the house for their evening activities. While Italians have never been frequenters of neighborhood taverns, the immigrant generation did set up club houses for card playing and male sociability that kept some men away from the house after work. These have disappeared, however, and, as already noted, second-generation men now segregate themselves from the women inside the home, and spend only one or two evenings a week in activities "with the boys." The women also have begun to conceive of their husbands as helping them in the home, although they are not yet ready to insist or even to ask for their aid. The move to the suburbs is probably one indication of the ascendancy of the wife to greater equality, for in these areas, where the joint conjugal pattern is dominant, it is somewhat harder for the man to maintain the old pattern. West Enders occasionally mentioned couples in which the wife, shortly after marriage, had persuaded the husband to move out of the West End in order to "get him away from the boys." But this does not always work; some men, even after twenty years of living elsewhere, return to the West End for evening visits to male friends. One man I knew, who used to come back for male companionship, was kidded about being dominated by his wife, and this has driven him further away from his old peers.

Child-Rearing

In the West End, children come because marriage and God bring them. This does not mean that West Enders believe children to be caused by God, but that the Catholic church opposes birth control, and that this is God's wish. There is some planning of conception, either through the use of the church-approved rhythm method, or, more rarely, through contraception. But while the sale of contraceptives is illegal in Massachusetts, this does not prevent their acquisition. West Enders,

---

[7] These changes are discussed further in [Gans] Chapter 10.

however, do reject their use—or at least talking about their use—on religious grounds. The major method of family planning seems to be ex post facto. Should the wife become pregnant after a couple has had what they deem to be enough children, she may attempt to abort herself, using traditional methods that she has learned from other women. If the attempt fails, as it probably does in many cases, the new child is accepted fatalistically—and usually happily—as yet another manifestation of the will of God. Even so, families are smaller among second-generation Italians than among their parents. The couple with six to eight children, which seems to have been prevalent among the first generation, now has become a rarity. A large family is still respected, however, because children themselves are still highly valued.

The fact that children are not planned affects the way in which parents relate to them, and the methods by which they bring them up. Indeed, American society today is characterized by three types of families: the *adult-centered*—prevalent in working-class groups—run by adults for adults, where the role of the children is to behave as much as possible like miniature adults; the *child-centered*—found among families who plan their children, notably in the lower middle class—in which parents subordinate adult pleasures to give the child what they think he needs or demands; and the *adult-directed*—and upper-middle-class pattern—in which parents also place lower priorities on their own needs, in order to guide the children toward a way of life the parents consider desirable.[8]

In the lower middle class of the present generation, husband and wife are likely to have finished high school, perhaps even the same one. This shared background helps them to communicate with each other, and creates some common interests, although much spare time still is spent with peers of the same sex. The most easily shared interest is the children, and the parents communicate best with each other through joint child-rearing. As a result, this family is child-centered. Parents play with their children—which is rare in the working class—rear them with some degree of self-consciousness, and give up some of their adult pleasures for them. Family size is strongly influenced by educational aspirations. If the parents are satisfied with their own occupational and social status, and feel no great urgency to send their children to college, they may have as many children as possible. For each child adds to their shared enjoyment and to family unity—at least while

---

[8] S. M. Miller and Frank Riessman have used similar terms—parent-centered and child-centered—to distinguish working-class families from middleclass ones in "The Working-Class Subculture: A New View," *Social Problems*, vol. 9 (1961), p. 92. For a different typology of family organization, using somewhat the same terms, see Bernard Farber, "Types of Family Organization: Child-Oriented, Home-Oriented, and Parent-Oriented," in Arnold Rose, ed., *Human Behavior and Social Process*, Boston: Houghton Mifflin, 1962, pp. 285–306.

the children are young. Sometimes, the child will dominate his parents unmercifully, although child-centered parents are not necessarily permissive in their child-rearing. Rather, they want the child to have a happier childhood than they experienced, and will give him what they believe is necessary for making it so. One of their child-centered acts is the move to the suburb, made not only for the child's benefit, but also to make their child-rearing easier for themselves, and to reduce some of the burdens of child-centeredness. They give the child freely over to the care of the school, and to organizations like the Scouts or Little League, because these are all child-centered institutions.

Among college-educated parents, education and educational aspirations shape family life. College education adds immeasurably to the number of common interests between husband and wife, including activities other than child-rearing. Consequently, these parents know what they want for their children much more clearly than does the child-centered family, and their relationship to the children is adult-directed. Child-rearing is based on a model of an upper-middle-class adulthood characterized by individual achievement and social service for which parents want the child to aim. As a result, the child's wants are of less importance. Such parents devote much time and effort to assuring that the child receives the education which will help him to become a proper adult. For this purpose, they may limit the size of their families; they will choose their place of residence by the quality of the school system; they will ride herd on the school authorities to meet their standards; and, of course, they will exert considerable pressure on the children to do well in school.[9]

The West End family is an adult-centered one. Since children are not planned, but come naturally and regularly, they are not at the center of family life. Rather, they are raised in a household that is run to satisfy adult wishes first. As soon as they are weaned and toilet-trained, they are expected to behave themselves in ways pleasing to adults. When they are with adults, they must act as the adults want them to act: to play quietly in a corner, or to show themselves off to other adults to demonstrate the physical and psychological virtues of their parents. Parents talk to them in an adult tone as soon as possible, and, once they have passed the stage of babyhood, will cease to play with them. When girls reach the age of seven or eight, they start assisting the mother, and become miniature mothers. Boys are given more freedom to roam, and, in that sense, are treated just like their fathers.

But while children are expected to behave like adults at home, they are able to act their age when they are with their peers. Thus, once

[9] For an example of what I call adult-directed child-rearing, see J. Seeley, R. Sim, and E. Loosley, *Crestwood Heights*, New York: Basic Books, 1956, especially Chaps. 7–9.

children have moved into their own peer group, they have considerable freedom to act as they wish, as long as they do not get into trouble. The children's world is their own, and only within it can they really behave like children. Parents are not expected to supervise, guide, or take part in it. In fact, parent-child relationships are segregated almost as much as male-female ones. The child will report on his peer group activities at home, but they are of relatively little interest to parents in an adult-centered family. If the child performs well at school or at play, parents will praise him for it. But they are unlikely to attend his performance in a school program or a baseball game in person. This is his life, not theirs.[10]

Schoolteachers and social workers who dealt with West End children often interpreted the family segregation patterns from a more child-centered perspective, and assumed that the parents had lost interest in their children or were ignoring them. But this is not the case. At home, they are still part of the family circle, and continue to play their assigned roles. In fact, West End children continue to attend family gatherings at ages at which middle-class children are usually excused from them. They also sit in on social gatherings from which middle-class children might be excluded altogether. But then West Enders do not make the same distinction between family and social gatherings, since they usually involve the same people.

There are parents among the West Enders who do ignore their children, and take no interest in them. Usually, these are people who for one reason or another are incapable of playing a parental role, and most West Enders consider them to be immoral, or pathological.

The departure of the children from home to peer group functions to support the adult-centered family. When the adults have complete authority over what goes on in the home, the children's need to behave like children must take place outside the view of adults. In the case of an acculturating ethnic group, the segregation of children and adults also reduces some of the conflict that would otherwise result from culture clashes between the children and the parents. At the same time, the children are able to bring home some of the dominant American culture patterns, and thus to act as an acculturating influence on the parents.

The children's movement into the peer group proceeds gradually, with the latter taking up more and more of their time as the children

---

[10] Covello reports that immigrant Italians criticized their children for participating in such childish activities as school sports, and tried to prevent their playing. They were expected to behave like grown adults by the time they reached the age of eight, and to have outgrown the need for play. Leonard Covello, "The Social Background of the Italo-American School Child," Unpublished Ph.D. Dissertation, New York University, 1944, p. 467. Changes in the conception of the child's role are discussed further in Chapter 10.

become older. As already noted, boys are allowed more freedom than girls, but when girls reach their teens, they also move into peer groups outside the home, performing their household functions grudgingly. Although parents would like to keep the girls closer to home, they find it difficult to fight the peer group attractions that draw their daughters out of the household. By adolescence, then, children spend little time in the parental home.

Mothers do attempt to teach their departing children rules of proper behavior, namely, the rules of the adult-centered and routine-seeking home, and urge them to adopt these in peer group activities. During this time, however, the child is also learning what are called the rules of the street, that is, those of the peer group. Thus, for some years, parents fight the ascendancy of street rules over home rules, especially if the former appear in his behavior at home. When a boy reaches the age of ten to twelve, however, parents feel that he is now responsible for his own actions. If he gets into "trouble," through behavior bringing him to the attention of the police or the priest, the blame must be attached to the influence of bad companions. Having done their best by urging him to follow home-rules, parents hope that he will do so. Should he fail to do so, however, the consequences are ascribed fatalistically to his peer group and his own moral failings. But whereas parents are concerned about the results, they neither feel the same responsibility for the child that is found in the middle-class family, nor develop the same guilt feelings should he get into trouble.

Interestingly enough, the home-rules that are preached to the child differ little from those held by the middle class. Mothers are more likely to be routine-seeking than action-seeking, and their desire for stability creates values which are also found in the middle class. The extent to which these rules are enforced, however, varies between action-seeking and routine-seeking or mobile families. The former, for instance, seem to surrender earlier, with less resistance to the child's inevitable adoption of the rules of the street. Moreover, the child himself reacts differently to the enforcement of these ideals. The child of a routine-seeking family, discovering that there are home rules and street rules, soon learns therefore to act accordingly in both places. In an action-seeking family, however, the child learns that the rules which the parents preach and those which they themselves practice diverge sharply. Thus he is more likely to reject the preached rules, and behave according to the street rules both at home and on the street.

The predominant method of child-rearing is punishment and reward. Children are punished when they misbehave, and rewarded—though not always—when they are obedient. Punishment is both physical and verbal: mothers slap and beat their children, tell them not to do this or do that, and threaten to tell the fathers when they come home. Indeed, to a middle-class observer, the parents' treatment often seems extremely strict and sometimes brutal. There is a continuous barrage of prohibitions and threats, intertwined with words and deeds of reward and affection. But the torrents of threat and cajolery neither impinge on the feelings of parental affection, nor are meant as signs of rejection. As one mother explained to her child, "We hit you because we love you." People believe that discipline is needed constantly to keep the child in line with and respectful of adult rules, and that without it he would run amok.

West Enders raise their children impulsively, with relatively little of the self-conscious, purposive child-rearing that is found in the middle class. Parents tell their child how they want him to act without much concern about how he receives their message. They do not weigh their words or methods in order to decide whether these are consistent with earlier ones, or with the way they want to raise the child. Since the child is viewed as a little adult, parents do not think much about how he reacts qua child. Nor do they worry whether too strict a punishment or too permissive rewarding will have subsequent detrimental consequences. Even while they are conscious of the possibility of children being "spoiled," especially by relatives, they mean by this only that the child may get more attention than is compatible with an adult-centered family system.

Impulsive child-rearing is possible because West Enders are not concerned with *developing* their children, that is, with raising them in accordance with a predetermined goal or target which they are expected to achieve. Unlike adult-directed or even child-centered families, West Enders have no clear image of the future social status, occupational level, or life-style that they want their children to reach. And even when they do, they do not know how to build it into the child-rearing process.

West Enders want for their children what they want for themselves —a secure existence as persons who are both accepted and somewhat envied members of their family circle and peer group. They hope that their children will seek a better education and obtain a better job than they, but the children are not pushed hard toward this goal. If a child does not achieve the parental wishes, he is pressed no further. Indeed, the parents' greatest fear is that the child will become a "bum." The worry about downward mobility is stronger than any desire for upward mobility. Consequently, the major hope is that in education, occupation, and general status, the child will not fall below that of his peers.

The impact of these child-rearing patterns on the child himself is less confusing than one might imagine. As the child learns largely by imitation, parents often try to behave as models—in censoring their own profanity, for example. But as they cannot long keep up such behavior, the child soon learns what is considered normal. He accepts the unending mixture of physical or verbal reward and punishment in the same way. Public reactions, of course, are no index to possible deeper impact, but judging by what is visible to the observer, the child is guided by the torrent of words to avoid behavior that results in punishment. He pays less attention to the rest of what is said. He reacts similarly to the verbally stated norms which he is asked to follow, but which he sees are being violated by his parents and the world around him. The child, thus becoming aware of the inconsistencies between word and deed, soon learns that what people say is less significant than what they do. Although he neither rejects the words, nor the norms they state, he quickly learns to dichotomize between what is and what ought to be.

These conclusions not only color his later life, but many of them stand him in good stead. The child learns the morality imbedded in the stated rules, but seems to internalize little of it. Instead, he accepts it as an ideal guide by which to judge the reality he faces, and to measure the deviation between the two. This allows him to justify his own failure to act in terms of the ideal, and to develop a protective cynicism, especially toward the stated norms of the outside world. In turn, this skepticism protects him from the deprivations and disappointments he encounters as a member of a low-income population. But it also blinds him to people's good intentions. When such intentions might result in desirable innovations, his failure to respond to them other than cynically often deprives him of the benefits offered by the outside world.[11]

The child's pragmatic outlook impresses him with the need to obey authority that can implement power and to ignore that which cannot. The dichotomy between word and deed allows him to develop a posture of respect for authority and the cunning to subvert it for his own aims. At first, he uses this to negotiate between the conflicting rules of street and home. Later, it will allow him to develop strategy to maneuver through the intricate mixture of words and deeds in the peer group. Words, he learns, are meant to impress people, but deeds and only deeds count.[12]

[11] This creates problems in community participation and in relationships with the outside world generally. See [Gans] Chapters 5 and 7.
[12] Thus, words are used as means to an end, rather than as conceptual tools. This may explain why the Italian-American community has produced so few analytically inclined intellectuals, but a larger number of critical and moralizing polemicists. For they also have come out of working-class parental backgrounds similar to those in the West End.

6. THE AMISH FAMILY

John A. Hostetler

§ The great amount of religious and political freedom permitted in the United States drew organized groups from other parts of the world who found their original environment inhospitable. Many such groups sought isolation from conventional communities, asking only to be left in peace to develop their own social system and search for fulfillment of their values. One such group, with a religious base, was the Amish. The Amish have been able to maintain partial isolation to the extent that they can be distinguished not only as a religious organization but as a subculture.

The family is a strong unit in Amish society. The author was reared in a strict Amish community, which he left as an adult. He writes of the Amish family sympathetically but objectively as a professional sociologist.

No social group is more intimate, informal, and primary than the family. Infants are born into a family; they do not join a family. The family is a closed system in many respects, for in it the basic wishes and needs of its members are expressed. The home is the place where individual interests first collide with group interests. Here members of a family vacillate between their own will and those of others, a process which has been called antagonistic co-operation.[1] Procreation, protection, and training are accomplished in most societies in the family. Much could be related about the Amish family, but we shall examine only selected aspects dealing with function and form.

Married-Pair Living

Family organization among the Amish has always been strictly monogamous and patriarchal rather than matriarchal. Over-all authority tends to belong to the father, with varying degrees of modification and application in specific families. Patriarchal authority is illustrated in many daily functions. A family of ten was seated about the table. When the husband took the pie, he cut one large piece for himself, one

SOURCE: John A. Hostetler, *Amish Society* (Baltimore, Md.: The Johns Hopkins Press, 1963), pp. 148–64. Reprinted by permission of the publisher and the author.

The author received his doctorate from Pennsylvania State University and teaches in the State University system.

[1] William G. Sumner, *Folkways* (Ginn and Co., 1906), 345.

of a smaller size for his wife, and then divided the balance among the eight children. The illustration is not necesarily typical.

Co-operation between husband and wife prevails in differing degrees, depending somewhat on the make-up of the personalities and their adjustment. The line of authority is not rigid, however, as another example will indicate. A man and his wife called at the home of a neighbor to see a bed which was for sale. He remained seated in the buggy while she entered the house and inspected the bed. Undecided, and not willing to commit herself without the encouragement of her husband, she called him. After both looked at the bed and pondered over the price, she said, "What do you think?" He replied, "You are the boss of the house." After a few gestures which indicated that she approved of the purchase, he wrote out a check for the amount.

The wife is often consulted when family problems arise, and she exercises her powers in rearing children, but her husband's word is regarded as final in domestic matters. This conforms to the biblical standard; "The head of the woman is the man." [2] God created woman as a helper for man; she is her husband's helper but not his equal. An Amish woman knows what is expected of her in the home, and her attitude is normally one of willing submission. This is not suggesting that there are no exceptions, for the writer has known families where the wife exerts influence out of proportion to the usual pattern. In real practice, the farm is the Amishman's kingdom, and his wife is his general manager of household affairs.

Property, whether household goods or farm equipment, is spoken of as "ours" within the family. In actuality, however, any transaction involving the sale or purchase of property is made through the husband, or has his approval. Farms are usually owned jointly by husband and wife to insure legal ownership in case of the death of the husband. In public affairs men are regarded as more fit for leadership than women. Banking, writing checks, and depositing money are the business of the husband. Women as well as men bid for household items at public sales. The experienced housewife generally has the authority to make decisions pertaining to the house, but husband and wife usually confer with each other before making any large purchases, and the considerate husband will consult his wife before purchasing any household item. The wife generally has a purse of her own which is replenished periodically by her husband for the purchase of household supplies, groceries, and clothing. When her supply of money is exhausted, she asks for more.

Major household expenses or anticipated medical expenditures are usually discussed mutually, and if the wife decides she would like to

[2] I Corinthians 11:3.

patronize a certain doctor, her husband is likely to consent. The husband, on the other hand, may purchase farm equipment or livestock without seeking the advice of his wife. The wife sometimes may keep the income from eggs sold.

The extent to which the farmer aids his wife in household tasks is nominal. Of course, he helps on special occasions such as butchering and cooking apple butter, but does not help in the routine preparation of food or washing dishes. At weddings, the men serve as cooks and table waiters with their wives. Guests at an Amish table are often addressed by the husband: "Now just reach and help yourselves."

The wife's duties include care of the children, cooking and cleaning, preparation of produce for market, making clothes for the family, preserving food, and gardening. Women and adolescent girls frequently help with the harvest of crops, especially cornhusking. In one family each of the older girls manages a team of horses during the summer months. They plow the fields, cultivate the soil, and do the work of adult males. This is exceptional, however, since women are not generally called upon to help with the heavier jobs in farming. It is the woman who sees that the fences, posts, grape arbors, and frequently the trees about the farm buildings are whitewashed in the spring. The appearance of the lawn and the area surrounding the house is largely the responsibility of the wife, and she feels obligated to keep the inside as well as the outside clean and neat in appearance.

The wife aids the husband in work not usually considered household tasks more than the husband helps his wife in household work. While the men and carpenters were remodeling the barn, in anticipation of the oldest son's marriage, the mother of one home arranged to have neighbor women and relatives come for a day to paint the barn's window sashes.

Gardening, except perhaps for the initial spading in the spring, is the sole responsibility of the wife. The Amish housewife usually has a large variety of edibles, with as many as twenty-two kinds of vegetables. She makes sure that there are plenty of cucumbers and red beets, because they are part of the standard lunch at Sunday services. Typical Amish gardens abound with flowers. One garden had twenty-four varieties. Order and cleanliness tend to be distinctive features of Amish gardening. Orchards are a part of the typical Amish landscape, and spraying, if done at all, is the man's job. More often than not fruits are purchased from commercial sources, because expensive equipment for spraying is considered too costly for a small orchard.

Food processing consumes a large part of the wife's time. In summer she preserves fruits and vegetables and in winter, various kinds of meats. One housewife estimated that she had a thousand quarts of canned goods in the cellar at the end of the summer. The frozen-food locker establishment in a nearby village is also used for preserving meats, fruits, and vegetables. Meat curing is done by the husband, often at the suggestion and according to the plans of the wife.

With regard to the woman's role in religious services the teaching of the Apostle Paul is literally obeyed: "Let the woman learn in silence with all subjection." In leadership activities, the woman is not "to usurp authority over the man." At baptismal services, boys are baptized before girls. Women never serve as church officials, but women as well as men participate in the *Rat* (counsel) of the church.

Voting in state and national elections, which was more widespread among the Amish in the past than at present, is done by men but rarely by the women.

The Amish woman's role is well defined, circumscribed by duties involving home and family. The man, as husband and father, is expected to assume the leadership role.

Personal Relationships

Personal relationships between husband and wife are quiet and sober, with no apparent demonstration of affection. The relationship is strikingly different from the way sentiments are indicated and affection expressed in American society. Patterns of conversation vary among Amish mates, but terms of endearment, or gestures which would indicate any overt expression of affection, are conspicuously absent.

The husband may address his wife by her given name, or by no name at all. He may merely begin talking to her if he wants her attention. In speaking about his wife to others he may use "she," or "my wife," but rarely her given name. The mother of the family in like manner may refer to him simply as "my husband" or "he."

Irritation between mates is expressed in a variety of ways, but is conditioned by informally approved means of expressing dissatisfaction. As a rule institutional patterns outweigh personal considerations. Little irritation is observable among the Amish. Displeasure or disapproval is expressed by the tone of voice, by gesture, or by direct statement. The husband many express disapproval by complete silence at the dinner table and the wife is left to guess what is wrong. The usual conversation may lag for several days before it is completely restored to a normal level. Harsh and boisterous talk between mates occurs infrequently and then is known to be manifest only by more or less maladjusted partners.

The bond between husband and wife tends to be one of respect rather than personal attraction based on romantic love. The role of the parents is defined in terms of traditional familial patterns, and this relationship is to some degree controlled by kinship ties. The husband

and wife are not individuals connected only by personal sentiments, but they are members of a group who must maintain the standards and dignity of that group. This tendency toward the consanguineal system compares favorably to the findings of Thomas and Znaniecki in their discussion of the Polish peasant family in which they say, ". . . the marriage norm is not love, but 'respect.' . . ." They explain further the meaning of this respect: "The norm of respect from wife to husband includes obedience, fidelity, care for the husband's comfort and health; from husband to wife, good treatment, fidelity, not letting the wife do hired work if it is not indispensable. In general, neither husband nor wife ought to do anything which could lower the social standing of the other, since this would lead to a lowering of the social standing of the other's family. Affection is not explicitly included in the norm of respect, but is desirable. As to sexual love, it is a purely personal matter, is not and ought not to be socialized in any form; the family purposely ignores it, and the slightest indecency or indiscreetness with regard to sexual relations in marriage is viewed with disgust and is morally condemned." [3]

The Polish pattern of marital relationships compares very favorably with the Amish. The Amish are in addition very conscious of the biblical pattern: "Wives, submit yourselves unto your own husband, as unto the Lord . . . So ought men to love their wives as their own bodies . . . and the wife see that she reverence her husband." [4]

Children and Growing Up

Amish children appear innocent and unspoiled by the things of this world. The birth of a child brings joy to the family and community, for there will be another dishwasher or wood chopper, and another church member. Thus children are wanted. At no time in the Amish system are they unwelcome, for they are regarded as "An heritage of the Lord."

The first two years of life are undoubtedly the happiest. Baby obtains what he wants. He is given permissive care with great amounts of love from mother, father, brothers, sisters, aunts, uncles, grandfathers, grandmothers, and cousins.

After about the second year, restrictions and exacting disciplines are continuously imposed upon the child until well into adolescence. He must be taught to respect the authority of his parents and to respond properly to their exactness. The child is considered sinless since he does not know the difference between right and wrong. It is the duty of

[3] William I. Thomas and Florian Znaniecki, *The Polish Peasant in Europe and America* (Knopf, 1927), Vol. I, 90.
[4] Ephesians 5:22, 28, 33.

parents to teach him this difference, so that he will realize his moral inadequacy and choose the "right way" of the Amish religion.

The Amish home is an effective socializing agent, directed at making the child a mature person in the Amish way of life. Early in life the child learns that Amish are "different" from other people. Thus, he must learn to understand not only how to play the role at home and in the Amish system, but also how to conduct himself in relation to the norms of his "English" neighbors.

He cannot have clothes and toys just like the "English" people have. He soon learns to imitate his parents, to take pride in the "difference," and appears no longer to ask "why" until adolescence.

The Amish boy or girl is raised so carefully within the Amish family and community that he never feels secure outside it. The faces of many Amish boys and girls reflect pure intent, a sincere, honest, cordial, and well-bred disposition. The extraordinary love and discipline they get prepares them well for Amish womanhood and manhood.

Each family is expected to transmit to the child a reading knowledge of German. This is done traditionally on Sunday, alternating with the preaching service. The family members gather about the sitting-room table, and each having a German Testament, take their turn spelling, enunciating the alphabet, and reading. In some families, this program is carried on daily in connection with the family worship. Even preschool children, ages four and five, take their turn by repeating words or syllables as they are pronounced by the family head.

Amish children do not receive regular allowances from their parents. A young person who works a day or half day for a neighbor is often permitted to keep the earnings, but is expected not to spend them. When parents take their children to town they may be given a small sum for buying candy. Early in life parents may provide a bank in which to save pennies. The necessity of taking good care of one's clothing and other personal items is strongly emphasized to the child.

Teaching the child to work and to accept responsibility is considered of utmost importance. The child begins to assist his parents at the age of four and is given limited responsibility at the age of six. The boy learns to feed the chickens, gather eggs, feed the calf, and drive the horses. The girl is trained to perform small jobs for her mother and to learn early the art of cooking and housekeeping. Some parents give a pig, sheep, or calf to the child with the stipulation that he tend the animal and take care of it. In this way the child is motivated to take an interest in the farm.

The role of the child and the work performed by each is well illustrated in a family of six children, five boys and one girl. Five are old enough to perform certain tasks. Their ages are: 22, 17, 15, (girl) 12, 8, and 3. The two oldest boys, ages 22 and 17, and the father, carry on the farming operations and field work. The 15-year-old boy, who is still in puberty, and though regarded capable of doing a full day's work, performs the lighter tasks about the barn. The girl, age 12, and a boy 8 attend public school, and the youngest, a three-year-old, is in the age of curiosity.

The girl enjoys helping her mother with the household duties, especially setting the table and preparing meals. She and her younger brother help their mother with the garden. When the time comes to do the chores, each has his specific assignment, but their duties also overlap. The four oldest children and the father milk 15 cows regularly. The oldest son feeds and beds the horses, hogs, and calves. The second feeds the laying hens, and the third tends the pullets on range and carries wood for his mother. The girl milks three cows, feeds the rabbits, and gathers the eggs. The eight-year-old boy has no regular work assignment but assists his mother or one of the older members of the family. The two older sons frequently help on washday with the heavier tasks such as carrying water. The third son has a decided dislike for house work.

In the Amish family, sons who reach the age of 21 are paid monthly wages if they are unmarried and continue to work at home. A young man may hire out for the summer, but this practice has almost completely disappeared among the Amish who farm with tractors. Farmers who need assistance frequently request help from a neighbor or a relative for a few days. Single girls, occasionally work as maids in local villages but more frequently assist in another Amish home. A *Maut* (maid) among the Amish enjoys the same privileges as other members of the family.

The solidarity of the family and its ability to act as a unit in an emergency is illustrated by the co-operation at occasions when the livestock breaks out. Charles P. Loomis, who worked at an Amish place as a farm hand, describes such an incident. As they were seated at the supper table: "Mattie got up to get some milk and saw that the cows were getting through the gate. She screamed and the whole family dashed to the door. Mother hurriedly put the baby into the carriage. We ran after the 22 cows. The big family encircled them, one girl having run over a mile on plowed ground. We got them back in. They had not been out this spring and were wild. Mother said she has read in books about stampedes in the west. Chris and I put them back in their stanchions after supper. He fed them grain first, but still we had a job. He said, 'They're out of practice. When they get to going to the meadow each day they will do better.'" [5]

From the discussion this far, it will be seen that the relations among

[5] Charles P. Loomis, "Farm Hand's Diary" (unpublished, 1949).

family members have many economic functions concerned with production. In this respect the Amish family is like the rural-farm type in America, but unlike the urban family.

Masculine dominance is evident in brother-sister relationships. The father and boys sit down first at the table while the mother and girls bring on the food. At a family ice-cream supper the boys went to the cellar to refill the big dish with ice cream, and, upon returning, they helped themselves first before passing the dish.

Strict obedience to parents is a profound teaching stressed over and over by Amish parents and by the preachers, a principle based upon several passages in the Bible. An Amish lad who runs away from home, or even an adult who leaves the Amish church, is held guilty of disobedience to his parents.

Amish children manifest resentments as do all children, by pouting, or by negative responses. But when these manifestations are overt, "smackings" are sure to follow either with the palm of the hand, a switch, a razor strop, or a buggy whip. Temper tantrums, making faces, name calling, and sauciness among youngsters are extremely rare, as the child learns early that his reward for such rebellion is a sound thrashing.

Disputes between boys are perhaps as frequent in Amish as in non-Amish families. The manner of expressing dissatisfaction is mostly verbal, especially among youngsters, but broken noses do occur. Profanity is not permitted, and if discovered by the parents, is usually promptly treated with punishment. Resentment toward a brother or sister is expressed rather mildly in the presence of older persons. In the presence of parents, a quarrel may be expressed to a chum by silence, hesitancy, or by completely ignoring the situation.

The subject of sex in Amish life is regarded as a purely personal matter. Adults purposely ignore any mention of the subject, especially in the presence of children. Very little sex instruction is given to the ordinary Amish child. In spite of this suppression the child acquires gradually, piece by piece, an elementary knowledge of the process of biological reproduction. Perhaps not until he arrives at the age of marriage does he have a fair knowledge of the subject.

The Amish child most certainly does ask questions about the sexual behavior of animals on the farm. To satisfy his curiosity, the child more often than not talks such matters over with associates of his own age. The jokes of young men show that sexual interests are developed before marriage and long before courtship. Any remark about sex in private conversation between a boy and girl of courting age is inopportune, but an indecent joke is not uncommon among a group of men.

Mate-Finding

The young Amishman's choice of a wife has several limitations conditioned by his value system. He must obtain a partner from his own Amish faith, but not necessarily from his own community. Because of minimum contact with Amish young people of other communities and states, marriage in the large settlements has been limited largely to the immediate community. The choice of a mate is also governed by core values. First-cousin marriages are taboo while second-cousin marriages are discouraged but infrequently do occur.

The rule that marriage must be endogenous with respect to the religious clan has certain exceptions. It is always permissible to marry into a more orthodox Amish group if the nonmember joins the more conservative group. Young people intermarry freely among Amish districts and settlements which maintain fellowship with one another. It is impossible without serious consequences to leave a church and join a more progressive one through marriage. This act would bring *Meidung* upon oneself in a strict group.

The occasion which provides best contact for young people is the Sunday-evening singing. The singing is usually held at the same house where the preaching was held. The youth from several districts usually combine for the singing. This occasion provides interaction among young people on a much broader base than in the single district.

On Sunday evening after the chores are done, the young folks make preparations for the singing. The young man puts on his very best attire, brushes his hat and suit, and makes sure that his horse and buggy are clean and neat in appearance. He may take his sister or his sister's friend to the singing, but seldom his own girl friend. If he does take his own girl, he will arrange to pick her up about dusk at the end of a lane or at a crossroad. In Lancaster County, Pennsylvania, the young people meet in villages to pair off, but this is not customary in other settlements.

A singing is not regarded as a devotional meeting. Young people gather around a long table, boys on one side and girls on the other. The singing is conducted entirely by the unmarried. Only the fast tunes are used. Girls as well as boys announce hymns and lead the singing. Between selections there is time for conversation. After the singing, which usually dismisses formally about ten o'clock, an hour or more is spent in joking and visiting. Those boys who do not have a date usually arrange for a *Mädel* (girl) at this time.

Although there are other occasions when young folks get together, such as husking bees, weddings, and frolics, the singing is the regular medium for boy-girl association. Both the boy and the girl look upon each other as possible mates. Social activity is naturally arranged with marriage in view. A boy or girl may "quit" whenever they please, but limited selection also limits variation. The usual age for courtship, called *rumspringa* (running around), begins for the boy at sixteen, and for the girl at fourteen to sixteen. Secrecy pervades the entire period of courtship and is seldom relaxed regardless of its length. If a boy is charged with having a girl friend he will certainly be very slow to admit it. Courting that cannot be successfully disguised becomes a subject for teasing by all members of the family.

In one home a girl's handbag was found by the children in the farm hand's buggy. It had been forgotten and left there by the boy's girl friend, and it became the subject of much laughter and joking. The maid in this home said, "That's as bad as I. Once, I left a tablecloth in his [meaning her escort's] buggy."

Among themselves, young people seldom refer to their boy or girl friends by first name. The pronoun "he" or "she" is used instead. The terms "beau" and "*Kal*" (fellow) are used in general conversation. The term "dating" is used, but has no dialect equivalent.

Besides taking his girl home after the singing on Sunday evening, the young man who has a "steady" girl will see her fortnightly on Saturday evening. When Saturday evening comes, he dresses in his best; he makes little ado about his departure and attempts to leave the impression that he is going to town on business.

Before entering the home of his girl he makes sure that the "old folks" are in bed. Standard equipment for every young Amishman of courting age is a good flashlight. With his light focused on her window, the girl has the signal that her boy friend has arrived; she quietly goes downstairs to let him in. The couple may be together until the early morning hours in the home on such occasions.

Courting normally takes place in the kitchen or sitting room. The Amish feel that it is none of the "outsider's" business how their courting is conducted. The clatter of horses' hoofs on hard-surface roads is evidence of lovers returning home in the early hours of the morning.

The old way of spending the time together was for a boy and girl to lie on the bed without undressing. The Amish have no uniform word in their speech for this practice, which to them, in earlier times was very ordinary. *Bei-schlof* (or with sleep) is a usage in one area. In English this behavior pattern is known as bundling, but the modern American society does not approve of this practice. It is little wonder that Amish persons in the most "nativistic" settlements, who are sometimes asked whether they bundle, do not know the meaning of "bundling." There seems to be a tendency for this form of courting to disappear among the Amish as their communities change, but it still prevails in some districts. Unfortunately the subject has been exploited by pamphleteers and story writers. The practice has been sharply condemned by some Amish ordained men and defended by others as something almost sacred.[6] Already in the nineteenth century new settlements had been started by those families who wanted to get away from the practice. Those communities that have assimilated most to the American society have felt the depreciating attitude of outsiders and tend thus to oppose the practice of bundling. Those which have retained their traditional culture most consistently have been least opposed. The practice has disappeared without argument in other areas with the influx of modern home conveniences (living-room suites, etc.), and with a wider range of social contact with the outside world.

Premarital relations are disapproved of and condemned by the church. Transgressors are expelled from the church and shunned for a period of several weeks or until reinstatement, which requires a statement of confession before the church assembly. Violation of the rule of chastity is hardly regarded worse than other faults—at least the moral stigma does not remain with the individual as it often does in the great society. Finding a mate takes place in the confines of the little community, rather than outside it. Conflict and casualties resulting from mismating are absorbed by the culture. Conflicts appear less obvious than in the great society. The wedding is a climactic experience for family and community and the families of both bride and bridegroom take an active part in helping the newlyweds to establish a home.

It is an important task of the family to provide a dowry. Homemade objects and crafts play an important part in the family. Furthermore, it is understood that each person invited to a wedding brings a gift for the new couple. These tokens of friendship, which are usually displayed on the bed in an upstairs bedroom, consist of dishes, kerosene lamps, bedspreads, blankets, tablecloths, towels, clocks, handkerchiefs, and small farm tools.

The parents of the bride and bridegroom also provide furniture, livestock, and sometimes basic equipment when the couple moves into their home. For instance, one bridegroom, an only son, had the farm deeded over to him together with the farm machinery and livestock. The bride received from her parents a cow, tables, chairs, a new stove, dishes, bedding, and many other items. The dowry of the bride was in this case not unusual. All mothers by tradition make a few quilts and comforters

---

[6] Reported in *Eine schädliche Ubung* (n.p., 1929). Other tracts are: D. J. Stutzman, *A Call to Repentance* (Millersburg, Ohio, n.d.), and *Our Youths, A Collection of Letters Pertaining to the Conditions Among our Youths, The Amish Mennonites* (Lynnhaven, Va., n.d.).

for each child. These are usually made years in advance so they will be ready when needed. One housewife made three quilts and two comforters for each child; she had seven boys and three girls.

The Mature Years

Respect for the aged, already obvious among youth, is even more pronounced with regard to mature Amish people. The individual never outgrows the command to obey his parents. The command is binding not until parents die, but even after they are gone. All age groups in both sexes revere parents, grandparents, and great-grandparents. The duty to obey one's parents is one of the main themes in Amish preaching. Perhaps the verse most often repeated on this point is one of the Ten Commandments: "Honor thy father and thy mother, that thy days may be long upon the land which the Lord thy God giveth thee." [7]

Not only is there respect for the aged, but authority is vested in the old people. This arrangement naturally lends itself to increased control of life by the aged. Preservation of the religious ideals and more is thereby insured, and the younger people who are inclined to introduce change can be held in check.

A strong consciousness of kinship is peculiarly favorable to gerontocracy, or social control by the older members of society. As in the ideal type of the little community, this control is informal rather than formal or obvious, but nevertheless, "closer to us than breathing, nearer than hands or feet." [8] The part which old people have "in drawing forth and molding the character and life-policy of every younger person in the kinship group makes the necessity for direct control much less frequent in isolated culture than in more accessible communities." [9] The relatively integrated community is associated with effective rules imposed by the aged, be they parents or church leaders. Thus deference to age pervades not only familial relationships, but also the religious leadership of the group. Furthermore, the counsel of the older bishop or minister carries more authority than that of younger ones.

The Amish farm typically contains two dwellings, one of which is the *Grossdaadi Haus* that houses the grandparents. At retirement the older couple moves into this house and a married son or daughter falls heir to the farm responsibility. The grandparents may retain some type of control of the farm until the couple demonstrates its ability to manage the farm. The grandparents have not only a separate

[7] Exodus 20:12; also Ephesians 6:1 and Colossians 3:20.
[8] Howard Becker and Harry Elmer Barnes, *Social Thought from Lore to Science* (Dover, 1961), 11.
[9] *Ibid.*

household unit, but a horse and buggy of their own. Instead of dual houses, many farm dwellings are large enough to accommodate two separate household operations. When there are no grandparents to occupy these quarters, they are sometimes rented to other Amish people, or occupied by the hired man and his wife.

Some of the Amish who retire in or near a small village will erect a small barn beside their dwelling so that they can feed and maintain a horse. Those families living in town do not take their turn for the preaching service, as facilities are not adequate to accommodate 80 to 120 people and from 25 to 30 horses. Instead, they may ask another family to take the service while supplying food and costs.

By the time they are 60, most Amish have accumulated enough wealth for a satisfactory retirement. Traditionally, no Amish accepts old age assistance or public assistance of any kind. Neither do Amish take any life insurance. Needy older persons are aided by relatives. Should close relatives be incompetent or unwilling, the church will come to their assistance.

The retirement of father and mother from active life on the farm stabilizes the social organization of the entire Amish community. While the young man is free to make his own decisions, the very presence of the parents on the farm influences the life of the younger generation. The young couple is not obligated to carry out the wishes of the parents, yet an advisory relationship stimulates not only economic stability but also religious integrity. The Labrador Eskimos, for example, regarded the words of their aged as final, believing that the old contain the wisdom of the ancestors. The Iroquois Indians reverenced the aged, in spite of the fact that the old were often helpless. The Kwakiutl made their old men masters of ceremonies at public gatherings. The Dahomeans respected both aged men and women because of their close affinity to the ancestral dead.[10]

The Amish consider their practice as merely a continuation of the old Hebrew attitude. For them, the Hebrew system provides a rational explanation. "The hoary head is a crown of glory . . . the beauty of the old men is the hoary head. A wise son heareth his father's instruction. Hearken unto thy father that begat thee, and despise not thy mother when she is old. Thou shalt rise up before the hoary head, and honor the face of the old man. . . . Honor thy father and thy mother, . . . and he that smiteth his father, or his mother, shall be surely put to death. I said days shall speak and a multitude of years shall teach wisdom." [11]

[10] Leo W. Simmons, *The Role of the Aged in Primitive Society* (Yale University Press, 1945), 51–61.
[11] The quotations are from Proverbs 16:3; 20:39; 13:1; 23:22; Leviticus 19:32; Exodus 20:12; 21:15; and Job 32:7.

One cross-cultural study of the aged in seventy-one widely different societies concludes that: ". . . when conditions called for respect to the aged they got it; when these conditions changed, they might lose it." [12] The respect for the aged in Amish life seems to be connected with the permanence of residence, and a conservative attitude stemming from a religious concept. Respect for the aged is thus consistent with the social and cultural behavior patterns in the little Amish community.

7. THE CULTURE OF POVERTY

Oscar Lewis

§ When Lewis developed the idea of a culture of poverty in his study of slums in Mexico City, he not only provided insight into these slums but added a new concept adaptable to the study of deep-rooted poverty everywhere. In the United States the culture of poverty underlies the deep concern of the 1960's for this lowest subcultural stratum in an otherwise affluent society.

Because the research design of this study was concerned with testing the concept of a culture of poverty in different national contexts and because this concept is helpful in understanding the Ríos family, I shall briefly summarize some of its dimensions here.

Although a great deal has been written about poverty and the poor, the concept of a culture of poverty is relatively new. I first suggested it in 1959 in my book *Five Families: Mexican Case Studies in the Culture of Poverty.* The phrase is a catchy one and has become widely used and misused.[1] Michael Harrington used it extensively in his book *The Other America* (1961), which played an important role

---

[12] Simmons, *op. cit.,* 50.

SOURCE: Oscar Lewis, *La Vida* (New York: Random House, 1965), pp. xlii–lii. Reprinted by permission of the publisher.

The author, an anthropologist who received his doctorate from Columbia University, is noted for his carefully compiled and interpretative books on village life in India and Mexico and the slums of Mexico City and Puerto Rico. In his *Five Families: Mexican Case Studies in the Culture of Poverty,* the concept of culture of poverty was first developed.

[1] There has been relatively little discussion of the culture of poverty concept in the professional journals, however. Two articles deal with the problem in some detail: Elizabeth Herzog, "Some Assumptions About the Poor," in *The Social Service Review,* December 1963, pp. 389–402; Lloyd Ohlin, "Inherited Poverty," Organization for Economic Cooperation and Development (no date), Paris.

in sparking the national anti-poverty program in the United States. However, he used it in a somewhat broader and less technical sense than I had intended. I shall try to define it more precisely as a conceptual model, with special emphasis upon the distinction between poverty and the culture of poverty. The absence of intensive anthropological studies of poor families from a wide variety of national and cultural contexts and especially from the socialist countries, is a serious handicap in formulating valid cross-cultural regularities. The model presented here is therefore provisional and subject to modification as new studies become available.

Throughout recorded history, in literature, in proverbs and in popular sayings, we find two opposite evaluations of the nature of the poor. Some characterize the poor as blessed, virtuous, upright, serene, independent, honest, kind and happy. Others characterize them as evil, mean, violent, sordid and criminal. These contradictory and confusing evaluations are also reflected in the in-fighting that is going on in the current war against poverty. Some stress the great potential of the poor for self-help, leadership and community organization, while others point to the sometimes irreversible, destructive effect of poverty upon individual character, and therefore emphasize the need for guidance and control to remain in the hands of the middle class, which presumably has better mental health.

These opposing views reflect a political power struggle between competing groups. However, some of the confusion results from the failure to distinguish between poverty *per se* and the culture of poverty and the tendency to focus upon the individual personality rather than upon the group—that is, the family and the slum community.

As an anthropologist I have tried to understand poverty and its associated traits as a culture or, more accurately, as a subculture [2] with its own structure and rationale, as a way of life which is passed down from generation to generation along family lines. This view directs attention to the fact that the culture of poverty in modern nations is not only a matter of economic deprivation, of disorganization or of the absence of something. It is also something positive and provides some rewards without which the poor could hardly carry on.

Elsewhere I have suggested that the culture of poverty transcends regional, rural-urban and national differences and shows remarkable similarities in family structure, interpersonal relations, time orientation, value systems and spending patterns. These cross-national similarities are examples of independent invention and convergence. They are common adaptations to common problems.

The culture of poverty can come into being in a variety of historical

[2] While the term "subculture of poverty" is technically more accurate, I have used "culture of poverty" as a shorter form.

contexts. However, it tends to grow and flourish in societies with the following set of conditions: (1) a cash economy, wage labor and production for profit; (2) a persistently high rate of unemployment and underemployment for unskilled labor; (3) low wages; (4) the failure to provide social, political and economic organization, either on a voluntary basis or by government imposition, for the low-income population; (5) the existence of a bilateral kinship system rather than a unilateral one; [3] and finally, (6) the existence of a set of values in the dominant class which stresses the accumulation of wealth and property, the possibility of upward mobility and thrift, and explains low economic status as the result of personal inadequacy or inferiority.

The way of life which develops among some of the poor under these conditions is the culture of poverty. It can best be studied in urban or rural slums and can be described in terms of some seventy interrelated social, economic and psychological traits.[4] However, the number of traits and the relationships between them may vary from society to society and from family to family. For example, in a highly literate society, illiteracy may be more diagnostic of the culture of poverty than in a society where illiteracy is widespread and where even the well-to-do may be illiterate, as in some Mexican peasant villages before the revolution.

The culture of poverty is both an adaptation and a reaction of the poor to their marginal position in a class-stratified, highly individuated, capitalistic society. It represents an effort to cope with feelings of

[3] In a unilineal kinship system, descent is reckoned either through males or through females. When traced exclusively through males it is called patrilineal or agnatic descent; when reckoned exclusively through females it is called matrilineal or uterine descent. In a bilateral or cognatic system, descent is traced through males and females without emphasis on either line.

In a unilineal system, the lineage consists of all the descendants of one ancestor. In a patrilineal system, the lineage is composed of all the descendants through males of one male ancestor. A matrilineage consists of all the descendants through females of one female ancestor. The lineage may thus contain a very large number of generations. If bilateral descent is reckoned, however, the number of generations that can be included in a social unit is limited, since the number of ancestors doubles every generation.

Unilineal descent groups ("lineages" or "clans") are corporate groups in the sense that the lineage or clan may act as a collectivity: it can take blood vengeance against another descent group, it can hold property, etc. However, the bilateral kin group (the "kindred") can rarely act as a collectivity because it is not a "group" except from the point of view of a particular individual, and, furthermore, has no continuity over time.

In a unilineal system, an individual is assigned to a group by virtue of his birth. In contrast, a person born into a bilateral system usually has a choice of relatives whom he chooses to recognize as "kin" and with whom he wants to associate. This generally leads to a greater diffuseness and fragmentation of ties with relatives over time.

[4] "The Culture of Poverty," in John J. TePaske and S. N. Fischer, eds., *Explosive Forces in Latin America*. Columbus, Ohio State University Press, 1964, pp. 149–173.

hopelessness and despair which develop from the realization of the improbability of achieving success in terms of the values and goals of the larger society. Indeed, many of the traits of the culture of poverty can be viewed as attempts at local solutions for problems not met by existing institutions and agencies because the people are not eligible for them, cannot afford them, or are ignorant or suspicious of them. For example, unable to obtain credit from banks, they are thrown upon their own resources and organize informal credit devices without interest.

The culture of poverty, however, is not only an adaptation to a set of objective conditions of the larger society. Once it comes into existence it tends to perpetuate itself from generation to generation because of its effect on the children. By the time slum children are age six or seven they have usually absorbed the basic values and attitudes of their sub-culture and are not psychologically geared to take full advantage of changing conditions or increased opportunities which may occur in their lifetime.

Most frequently the culture of poverty develops when a stratified social and economic system is breaking down or is being replaced by another, as in the case of the transition from feudalism to capitalism or during periods of rapid technological change. Often it results from imperial conquest in which the native social and economic structure is smashed and the natives are maintained in a servile colonial status, sometimes for many generations. It can also occur in the process of detribalization, such as that now going on in Africa.

The most likely candidates for the culture of poverty are the people who come from the lower strata of a rapidly changing society and are already partially alienated from it. Thus landless rural workers who migrate to the cities can be expected to develop a culture of poverty much more readily than migrants from stable peasant villages with a well-organized traditional culture. In this connection there is a striking contrast between Latin America, where the rural population long ago made the transition from a tribal to a peasant society, and Africa, which is still close to its tribal heritage. The more corporate nature of many of the African tribal societies, in contrast to Latin American rural communities, and the persistence of village ties tend to inhibit or delay the formation of a full-blown culture of poverty in many of the African towns and cities. The special conditions of apartheid in South Africa, where the migrants are segregated into separate "loca-tions" and do not enjoy freedom of movement, create special problems. Here the institutionalization of repression and discrimination tend to develop a greater sense of identity and group consciousness.

The culture of poverty can be studied from various points of view: the relationship between the subculture and the larger society; the nature of the slum community; the nature of the family; and the attitudes, values and character structure of the individual.

1. The lack of effective participation and integration of the poor in the major institutions of the larger society is one of the crucial characteristics of the culture of poverty. This is a complex matter and results from a variety of factors which may include lack of economic resources, segregation and discrimination, fear, suspicion or apathy, and the development of local solutions for problems. However, "participation" in some of the institutions of the larger society—for example, in the jails, the army and the public relief system—does not *per se* eliminate the traits of the culture of poverty. In the case of a relief system which barely keeps people alive, both the basic poverty and the sense of hopelessness are perpetuated rather than eliminated.

Low wages, chronic unemployment and underemployment lead to low income, lack of property ownership, absence of savings, absence of food reserves in the home, and a chronic shortage of cash. These conditions reduce the possibility of effective participation in the larger economic system. And as a response to these conditions we find in the culture of poverty a high incidence of pawning of personal goods, borrowing from local moneylenders at usurious rates of interest, spontaneous informal credit devices organized by neighbors, the use of second-hand clothing and furniture, and the pattern of frequent buying of small quantities of food many times a day as the need arises.

People with a culture of poverty produce very little wealth and receive very little in return. They have a low level of literacy and education, usually do not belong to labor unions, are not members of political parties, generally do not participate in the national welfare agencies, and make very little use of banks, hospitals, department stores, museums or art galleries. They have a critical attitude toward some of the basic institutions of the dominant classes, hatred of the police, mistrust of government and those in high position, and a cynicism which extends even to the church. This gives the culture of poverty a high potential for protest and for being used in political movements aimed against the existing social order.

People with a culture of poverty are aware of middle-class values, talk about them and even claim some of them as their own, but on the whole they do not live by them. Thus it is important to distinguish between what they say and what they do. For example, many will tell you that marriage by law, by the church, or by both, is the ideal form of marriage, but few will marry. To men who have no steady jobs or other sources of income, who do not own property and have no wealth to pass on to their children, who are present-time oriented and who want to avoid the expense and legal difficulties involved in formal marriage and divorce, free unions or consensual marriage makes a lot of sense. Women will often turn down offers of marriage because they feel it ties them down to men who are immature, punishing and generally unreliable. Women feel that consensual union gives them a better break; it gives them some of the freedom and flexibility that men have. By not giving the fathers of their children legal status as husbands, the women have a stronger claim on their children if they decide to leave their men. It also gives women exclusive rights to a house or any other property they may own.

2. When we look at the culture of poverty on the local community level, we find poor housing conditions, crowding, gregariousness, but above all a minimum of organization beyond the level of the nuclear and extended family. Occasionally there are informal, temporary groupings or voluntary associations within slums. The existence of neighborhood gangs which cut across slum settlements represents a considerable advance beyond the zero point of the continuum that I have in mind. Indeed, it is the low level of organization which gives the culture of poverty its marginal and anachronistic quality in our highly complex, specialized, organized society. Most primitive peoples have achieved a higher level of socio-cultural organization than our modern urban slum dwellers.

In spite of the generally low level of organization, there may be a sense of community and *esprit de corps* in urban slums and in slum neighborhoods. This can vary within a single city, or from region to region or country to country. The major factors influencing this variation are the size of the slum, its location and physical characteristics, length of residence, incidence of home and landownership (versus squatter rights), rentals, ethnicity, kinship ties, and freedom or lack of freedom of movement. When slums are separated from the surrounding area by enclosing walls or other physical barriers, when rents are low and fixed and stability of residence is great (twenty or thirty years), when the population constitutes a distinct ethnic, racial or language group, is bound by ties of kinship or *compadrazgo*, and when there are some internal voluntary associations, then the sense of local community approaches that of a village community. In many cases this combination of favorable conditions does not exist. However, even where internal organization and *esprit de corps* is at a bare minimum and people move around a great deal, a sense of territoriality develops which sets off the slum neighborhoods from the rest of the city. In Mexico City and San Juan this sense of territoriality results from the unavailability of low-income housing outside the slum areas. In South Africa the sense of territoriality grows out of the segregation enforced by the government, which confines the rural migrants to specific locations.

3. On the family level the major traits of the culture of poverty are the absence of childhood as a specially prolonged and protected stage

in the life cycle, early initiation into sex, free unions of consensual marriages, a relatively high incidence of the abandonment of wives and children, a trend toward female- or mother-centered families and consequently a much greater knowledge of maternal relatives, a strong predisposition to authoritarianism, lack of privacy, verbal emphasis upon family solidarity which is only rarely achieved because of sibling rivalry, and competition for limited goods and maternal affection.

4. On the level of the individual the major characteristics are a strong feeling of marginality, of helplessness, of dependence and of inferiority. I found this to be true of slum dwellers in Mexico City and San Juan among families who do not constitute a distinct ethnic or racial group and who do not suffer from racial discrimination. In the United States, of course, the culture of poverty of the Negroes has the additional disadvantage of racial discrimination, but as I have already suggested, this additional disadvantage contains a great potential for revolutionary protest and organization which seems to be absent in the slums of Mexico City or among the poor whites in the South.

Other traits include a high incidence of maternal deprivation, of orality, of weak ego structure, confusion of sexual identification, a lack of impulse control, a strong present-time orientation with relatively little ability to defer gratification and to plan for the future, a sense of resignation and fatalism, a widespread belief in male superiority, and a high tolerance for psychological pathology of all sorts.

People with a culture of poverty are provincial and locally oriented and have very little sense of history: They know only their own troubles, their own local conditions, their own neighborhood, their own way of life. Usually they do not have the knowledge, the vision or the ideology to see the similarities between their problems and those of their counterparts elsewhere in the world. They are not class-conscious, although they are very sensitive indeed to status distinctions.

When the poor become class-conscious or active members of trade-union organizations, or when they adopt an internationalist outlook on the world, they are no longer part of the culture of poverty, although they may still be desperately poor. Any movement, be it religious, pacifist or revolutionary, which organizes and gives hope to the poor and effectively promotes solidarity and a sense of identification with larger groups, destroys the psychological and social core of the culture of poverty. In this connection, I suspect that the civil rights movement among the Negroes in the United States has done more to improve their self-image and self-respect than have their economic advances, although, without doubt, the two are mutually reinforcing.

The distinction between poverty and the culture of poverty is basic to the model described here. There are degrees of poverty and many kinds of poor people. The culture of poverty refers to one way of life shared by poor people in given historical and social contexts. The economic traits which I have listed for the culture of poverty are necessary but not sufficient to define the phenomena I have in mind. There are a number of historical examples of very poor segments of the population which do not have a way of life that I would describe as a subculture of poverty. Here I should like to give four examples:

1. Many of the primitive or preliterate peoples studied by anthropologists suffer from dire poverty which is the result of poor technology and/or poor natural resources, or of both, but they do not have the traits of the subculture of poverty. Indeed, they do not constitute a subculture because their societies are not highly stratified. In spite of their poverty they have a relatively integrated, satisfying and self-sufficient culture. Even the simplest food-gathering and hunting tribes have a considerable amount of organization, bands and band chiefs, tribal councils and local self-government—traits which are not found in the culture of poverty.

2. In India the lower castes (the Chamars, the leather workers, and the Bhangis, the sweepers) may be desperately poor, both in the villages and in the cities, but most of them are integrated into the larger society and have their own *panchayat* [5] organizations which cut across village lines and give them a considerable amount of power. [6] In addition to the caste system, which gives individuals a sense of identity and belonging, there is still another factor, the clan system. Wherever there are unilateral kinship systems or clans one would not expect to find the culture of poverty, because a clan system gives people a sense of belonging to a corporate body with a history and a life of its own, thereby providing a sense of continuity, a sense of a past and of a future.

The Jews of eastern Europe were very poor, but they did not have many of the traits of the culture of poverty because of their tradition of literacy, the great value placed upon learning, the organization of the community around the rabbi, the proliferation of local voluntary associations, and their religion which taught that they were the chosen people.

4. My fourth example is speculative and relates to socialism. On the basis of my limited experience in one socialist country—Cuba—and on the basis of my reading, I am inclined to believe that the culture of poverty does not exist in the socialist countries. I first went to Cuba in 1947 as a visiting professor for the State Department. At that time I began a study of a sugar plantation in Melena del Sur and of a slum

---

[5] A formal organization designed to provide caste leadership.
[6] It may be that in the slums of Calcutta and Bombay an incipient culture of poverty is developing. It would be highly desirable to do family studies there as a crucial test of the culture-of-poverty hypothesis.

in Havana. After the Castro Revolution I made my second trip to Cuba as a correspondent for a major magazine, and I revisited the same slum and some of the same families. The physical aspect of the slum had changed very little, except for a beautiful new nursery school. It was clear that the people were still desperately poor, but I found much less of the despair, apathy and hopelessness which are so diagnostic of urban slums in the culture of poverty. They expressed great confidence in their leaders and hope for a better life in the future. The slum itself was now highly organized, with block committees, educational committees, party committees. The people had a new sense of power and importance. They were armed and were given a doctrine which glorified the lower class as the hope of humanity. (I was told by one Cuban official that they had practically eliminated delinquency by giving arms to the delinquents!)

It is my impression that the Castro regime—unlike Marx and Engels —did not write off the so-called lumpen proletariat as an inherently reactionary and anti-revolutionry force, but rather saw its revolutionary potential and tried to utilize it. In this connection, Frantz Fanon makes a similar evaluation of the role of the lumpen proletariat based upon his experience in the Algerian struggle for independence. In his recently published book [7] he wrote:

> It is within this mass of humanity, this people of the shanty towns, at the core of the lumpen proletariat, that the rebellion will find its urban spearhead. For the lumpen proletariat, that horde of starving men, uprooted from their tribe and from their clan, constitutes one of the most spontaneous and most radically revolutionary forces of a colonized people.

My own studies of the urban poor in the slums of San Juan do not support the generalizations of Fanon. I have found very little revolutionary spirit or radical ideology among low-income Puerto Ricans. On the contrary, most of the families I studied were quite conservative politically and about half of them were in favor of the Republican Statehood Party. It seems to me that the revolutionary potential of people with a culture of poverty will vary considerably according to the national context and the particular historical circumstances. In a country like Algeria which was fighting for its independence, the lumpen proletariat was drawn into the struggle and became a vital force. However, in countries like Puerto Rico, in which the movement for independence has very little mass support, and in countries like Mexico which achieved their independence a long time ago and are now in their postrevolutionary period, the lumpen proletariat is not a leading source of rebellion or of revolutionary spirit.

In effect, we find that in primitive societies and in caste societies,

[7] Frantz Fanon, *The Wretched of the Earth.* New York, Grove Press, 1965, p. 103.

the culture of poverty does not develop. In socialist, fascist and in highly developed capitalist societies with a welfare state, the culture of poverty tends to decline. I suspect that the culture of poverty flourishes in, and is generic to, the early free-enterprise stage of capitalism and that it is also endemic in colonialism.

It is important to distinguish between different profiles in the subculture of poverty depending upon the national context in which these subcultures are found. If we think of the culture of poverty primarily in terms of the factor of integration in the larger society and a sense of identification with the great tradition of that society, or with a new emerging revolutionary tradition, then we will not be surprised that some slum dwellers with a lower per capita income may have moved farther away from the core characteristics of the culture of poverty than others with a higher per capita income. For example, Puerto Rico has a much higher per capita income than Mexico, yet Mexicans have a deeper sense of identity.

I have listed fatalism and a low level of aspiration as one of the key traits for the subculture of poverty. Here too, however, the national context makes a big difference. Certainly the level of aspiration of even the poorest sector of the population in a country like the United States with its traditional ideology of upward mobility and democracy is much higher than in more backward countries like Ecuador and Peru, where both the ideology and the actual possibilities of upward mobility are extremely limited and where authoritarian values still persist in both the urban and rural milieus.

Because of the advanced technology, high level of literacy, the development of mass media and the relatively high aspiration level of all sectors of the population, especially when compared with underdeveloped nations, I believe that although there is still a great deal of poverty in the United States (estimates range from thirty to fifty million people), there is relatively little of what I would call the culture of poverty. My rough guess would be that only about 20 percent of the population below the poverty line (between six and ten million people) in the United States have characteristics which would justify classifying their way of life as that of a culture of poverty. Probably the largest sector within this group would consist of very low-income Negroes, Mexicans, Puerto Ricans, American Indians and Southern poor whites. The relatively small number of people in the United States with a culture of poverty is a positive factor because it is much more difficult to eliminate the culture of poverty than to eliminate poverty *per se.*

Middle-class people, and this would certainly include most social scientists, tend to concentrate on the negative aspects of the culture of poverty. They tend to associate negative valences to such traits as present-time orientation and concrete versus abstract orientation. I do not intend to idealize or romanticize the culture of poverty. As someone has said, "It is easier to praise poverty than to live in it"; yet some of the positive aspects which may flow from these traits must not be overlooked. Living in the present may develop a capacity for spontaneity and adventure, for the enjoyment of the sensual, the indulgence of impulse, which is often blunted in the middle-class, future-oriented man. Perhaps it is this reality of the moment which the existentialist writers are so desperately trying to recapture but which the culture of poverty experiences as natural, everyday phenomena. The frequent use of violence certainly provides a ready outlet for hostility so that people in the culture of poverty suffer less from repression than does the middle class.

In the traditional view, anthropologists have said that culture provides human beings with a design for living, with a ready-made set of solutions for human problems so that individuals don't have to begin all over again each generation. That is, the core of culture is its positive adaptive function. I, too, have called attention to some of the adaptive mechanisms in the culture of poverty—for example, the low aspiration level helps to reduce frustration, the legitimization of short-range hedonism makes possible spontaneity and enjoyment. However, on the whole it seems to me that it is a relatively thin culture. There is a great deal of pathos, suffering and emptiness among those who live in the culture of poverty. It does not provide much support or long-range satisfaction and its encouragement of mistrust tends to magnify helplessness and isolation. Indeed, the poverty of culture is one of the crucial aspects of the culture of poverty.

The concept of the culture of poverty provides a high level of generalization which, hopefully, will unify and explain a number of phenomena viewed as distinctive characteristics of racial, national or regional groups. For example, matrifocality, a high incidence of consensual unions and a high percentage of households headed by women, which have been thought to be distinctive of Caribbean family organization or of Negro family life in the U.S.A., turn out to be traits of the culture of poverty and are found among diverse peoples in many parts of the world and among peoples who have had no history of slavery.

The concept of a cross-societal subculture of poverty enables us to see that many of the problems we think of as distinctively our own or distinctively Negro problems (or that of any other special racial or ethnic group), also exist in countries where there are no distinct ethnic minority groups. This suggests that the elimination of physical poverty *per se* may not be enough to eliminate the culture of poverty which is a whole way of life.

What is the future of the culture of poverty? In considering this question, one must distinguish between those countries in which it represents a relatively small segment of the population and those in which it constitutes a very large one. Obviously the solutions will differ in these two situations. In the United States, the major solution proposed by planners and social workers in dealing with multiple-problem families and the so-called hard core of poverty has been to attempt slowly to raise their level of living and to incorporate them into the middle class. Wherever possible, there has been some reliance upon psychiatric treatment.

In the underdeveloped countries, however, where great masses of people live in the culture of poverty, a social-work solution does not seem feasible. Because of the magnitude of the problem, psychiatrists can hardly begin to cope with it. They have all they can do to care for their own growing middle class. In these countries the people with a culture of poverty may seek a more revolutionary solution. By creating basic structural changes in society, by redistributing wealth, by organizing the poor and giving them a sense of belonging, of power and of leadership, revolutions frequently succeed in abolishing some of the basic characteristics of the culture of poverty even when they do not succeed in abolishing poverty itself.

Chapter 4: Courtship, Marriage, and the Family in Other Cultures

8. THE FRENCH FAMILY: A PRIVATE SOCIAL WORLD

Rhoda Metraux and Margaret Mead

§ Each society—each culture—produces its own peculiar form of family life. The American family has had to make rapid adaptations from rural to urban to suburban living, and from hand labor to technological devices. Looseness of relationships, adaptability, and sometimes disorganization mark the American family. In France, the family clings more closely to traditions. It is distinguished by permanence, loyalty, and privacy of family life. This highly perceptive discussion by two anthropologists interprets the French family of today to American readers, who, when they travel in Europe, often complain of the difficulty of learning what family life means to the French.

The Frenchman at home is *chez-soi,* in his own place. For the French, *le foyer* is *un petit bien complet, un petit bien indépendant*—a small possession, complete and independent. But *bien* means not only possession or, more specifically, a piece of property; it also conveys, among other meanings, those of comfort, excellence, and well-being, all of which—together with the idea of its privacy and autonomy—combine in the feeling about *le foyer.*

SOURCE: Rhoda Metraux and Margaret Mead, *Themes in French Culture: A Preface to a Study of French Community* (Stanford, Calif.: Stanford University Press, 1954), pp. 1, 2, 3, 5. Copyright © 1954 by Rhoda Metraux and Margaret Mead. Reprinted by permission of the authors.

Rhoda Metraux received her doctorate (anthropology) from Columbia University. She has had extensive research experience in different parts of the world.

Margaret Mead, anthropologist, also received her doctorate from Columbia University, and is a member of the professional staff of the American Museum of Natural History. Although her interests and professional connections are extensive, her anthropological field work has centered on the peoples of the Pacific Islands. Among her books that are of special interest to students of marriage and family living are *Coming of Age in Samoa, Growing Up in New Guinea,* and *Male and Female.* Other books and articles cover a wider range.

The term is an untranslatable one; to render it inadequately as *house* or *home* or *family*, with the connotations these words have for Americans, is to distort the total meaning which *le foyer* has for those who belong to it. It is a truism that this is a little used word in French daily conversation and, from one point of view, a discussion of French family life is itself an anomaly. For, generally speaking, this is a subject which in its intimate details is reserved to those close to the family and, as an entity, to formal, even solemn public occasions.

. . . . .

The arrangement of French dwellings conveys something of the distance between the world without and the world within the *foyer*. One need only recall houses in provincial France where a high wall, enclosing the garden or the court behind or the plot of land around the house, shuts out too-curious neighbors and passers-by; where a bell on garden gate or door rings, perhaps automatically, to announce each person—stranger or member of the family—who approaches; where every footfall around the house sounds on gravel. Or one may visualize the urban apartment building where the incomer must first pass the sharp scrutiny of the concierge [attendant or house superintendent] next to the entrance before proceeding, up briefly lighted stairs, to the door of his destination. Designs of nineteenth-century luxury apartments in Paris provide another, although somewhat different, image of the privacy of the *foyer*. Here each apartment occupies an entire floor of a building which also, on the first two floors, houses a business establishment and, in the attics, has rooms for servants and poor tenants. The close proximity of these unrelated worlds implies the detachment of each from the other. The specific image alters from one type of house, from one region of France to another. Common to them is the sense of the boundary set, the protection against possible intrusion. Not everyone, by any means, owns a house, a garden, or a plot of land; on the contrary, housing is a major problem in France today (including both the provision of housing in crowded cities and the utilization of antiquated housing in provincial towns). But ownership—and the maintenance of privacy and independent security—is something which the adult desires and expects: a home is inherited, bought or worked towards for eventual retirement, ideally, though it may not be attained in fact.

The household, established at marriage, is intended to have permanence. The furniture and appliances that are then installed are meant to last not until a change in fashion but throughout a lifetime. For the home, however agreeable, is arranged neither for extensive display nor as a meeting place with outsiders, but chiefly to please the taste and to suit the convenience of those who live in it. However, the house (or the apartment) is not in itself the *foyer*. In its figurative sense—and this is the way in which it is most commonly used—*le foyer* refers to a group of people—a married couple and their children—who live in a fixed place and form a closed circle.

. . . . .

Of these circles [all types of social groups], the family—especially the *foyer*—is the most self-contained and enduring in that family relationships are regarded as all but indestructible and the individual's obligations to and benefits from the immediate family continue throughout life. For the child (especially the girl) who has grown up and become independent, the door to the parental home remains "always open"; reciprocally, parents feel that they have a continuing right to participate in major decisions made by their grown children that may affect the larger family. Parents and children have a mutual responsibility for each other's well-being that is reflected in legal arrangements about inheritance and the care of the indigent; parents cannot disinherit children nor can children disclaim responsibility for the care of elderly or ailing parents. Yet, ideally, reciprocity consists not in making return gifts for what has been received, but in protecting what one has and passing on to the next generation what one has received and cared for. Thus, the past is continually made part of the present and the *foyer*, like other social circles, is not isolated but is one of an interlocking series.

The larger family (*la famille, les parents*)—including grandparents, parents' siblings, cousins, and so on, as well as those who have married in—is regarded as having unity as it also has extension in time. But in fact, when "the family" is referred to, it is usually the members of the *foyer* and the closest, most congenial relatives and those from whom one expects to inherit (or to whom one expects to bequeath) who are meant. The household itself reflects something of this larger family with its extension over time. Describing what she misses in the American family, a young war-bride writes:

> One doesn't find that good French family tradition; the habits, the reminders (*souvenirs*), the family pictures, the family house and furniture. The family in the United States is in the present. In France, it is in the present, but in the past and future also.

The traditional symbol of the unity of the larger family and its exclusiveness is the *conseil de famille* (family council), which links together the several related *foyers*. Meeting formally or informally, this group may act for its members and in certain situations can be a legally responsible intermediary between the family and the rest of the world. Here the individual may ask advice from or may be called upon to give account to members of his family acting in concert.

. . . . .

The *foyer* that is established at marriage is, ideally, autonomous. The fact that actual independence may be postponed or renounced until the death of the parents (as when a peasant son continues to live with his own family in his parental *foyer*) does not detract from this conception, as it concerns the intimate relationships of husband and wife and children to one another.

. . . . .

Parents welcome children warmly and responsibly. With their birth, the human plan of the *foyer* is realized. Yet, though desired and loved, the child is regarded as a heavy charge upon its parents, for its upbringing requires foresight and long years of patient effort. Men and women alike stress the vital importance of bringing up the child properly (*élever l'enfant proprement*); they point out, besides, that all parents, according to their means, want to do well (*faire quelque chose de bien*) for each child. Consequently, people feel one should be able to decide upon the number of children one wishes to have and—though informants are quick to point one that they themselves know of large families—the general expectation is that the family will remain small.

9. SOCIAL LIFE AND COURTSHIP IN A FRENCH VILLAGE

Laurence Wylie

§ In contrast to the generalized account of the French family given in the preceding selection, this selection gives a first-hand intimate view of adolescence, courtship, and marriage roles as found in a typical village in Southern France. Dr. Wylie, his wife, and two sons, then aged three and five, spent the year of 1950–1951 living on neighborly terms in a commune of about two thousand people, called Peyrane. Dr. Wylie mingled with the villagers in their public life, and his children played with the French children and attended the village school; in time he was invited into the homes. The commune is an old one. In the village are predominantly artisans, industrial miners, and tradesmen; small farmers nearby are also part of the commune.

SOURCE: Laurence Wylie, *Village in the Vaucluse* (Cambridge, Mass.: Harvard University Press, 1957), pp. 99, 102, 103, 110, 111, 124–27. Copyright 1957 by The President and Fellows of Harvard College. Reprinted by permission of the publisher.

The author, who received his doctorate from Brown University, is C. Douglas Dillon Professor of the Civilization of France, Harvard University. He is especially interested in French community studies and in French literature as a vehicle of French culture.

Points to notice in contrast to our culture are the expectation that each boy or girl will begin to support himself upon leaving school, the close financial and personal control by the parents, and the relative freedom allowed the adolescent boys before marriage. The roles of married life are in contrast to this freedom; responsibilities of husband and wife are firmly fixed and enforced by public opinion.

For the children who are not sufficiently intelligent or ambitious to go away to school, life suddenly becomes enjoyable and simple after they have reached the age of fourteen. They are no longer children. They are young people, and only two things are expected of the young people of Peyrane: to support themselves and to have a good time. They will have no other obligations until they become sufficiently *sérieux* [mature] to settle down and establish a household of their own. The five or ten years between school and marriage are relatively free, free of the harsh discipline of school which the young people have left behind them, free of the family responsibilities they will eventually have thrust upon them. This is the period of life which the people of Peyrane call "the happiest years of one's existence."

·   ·   ·   ·   ·

[The boys work with their fathers—on the family farm, in the father's store, or in the nearby ocher mines if the father is a miner.]

It is usual for adolescent girls in Peyrane to have a job although often it is only a temporary arrangement to support themselves until they are married. Of course, they do not all seek a paying job. Their first duty is to their mother. If she needs help at home, the daughter will stay with her and share the household tasks and the woman's work on the farm. This work is considered especially appropriate, since by helping run the household, a girl is preparing for her future adult role. [The daughters of wealthy fathers may take lessons, for example, sewing or hairdressing, instead of working.]

·   ·   ·   ·   ·

Of course, the children who take lessons earn no money. Neither do the boys who work on the farms with their father or the girls who work at home with their mother. But their financial situation is no different from that of the children who work for wages, since wages for adolescents are not given to the children but to their parents. Although adolescents are considered mature enough to earn money, they are not sufficiently *sérieux* to be entrusted with the money they earn.

No matter whether they work for the parents or work for wages, all adolescents are faced with the same situation: they have no money of their own. If their earnings are more than enough for their support, the excess goes not to them but to the household.

On the other hand, a father is duty bound to give his adolescent children enough money so that they may have a good time. Not only do adolescents expect spending money, but society demands that a father be generous with them. The niggardly father is criticized. . . . [The people of Peyrane] believe it to be the right of a young person to have a good time. More than that, they believe it is the *duty* of a young person to have a good time. And it is the duty of their parents not only to tolerate, but to abet their adolescent children in the quest for pleasure. An adult who has in some way been deprived of pleasure during his adolescent years is considered to a degree an incomplete person. He is looked upon with pity, or even with suspicion.

. . . . .

[With release from school, young people enter into adult recreational activities. Girls join the women in their groups where work and talk are combined and boys begin to go to the café where the men congregate and to play cards with the men. Boys and girls participate in dances held in Peyrane and in neighboring villages. As a rule they do not attend the dances in pairs: the boys come together and the girls are brought in small groups by a father or older brother. They return home in the same way. The parents of one girl in Peyrane were criticized for permitting their daughter to ride to a neighboring village on the back of her fiancé's motorcycle; even though engaged, the couple should have been chaperoned. At the dance, boys congregate on one side of the room, girls on the other; but after a while they begin to dance. At intervals they visit the café to sit around the tables, talking and laughing, and drinking in moderation.]

The amusement the young people are most enthusiastic about, after dancing is taking a *promenade*. A *promenade* is so vague and formless that it can be defined only as "an occasion on which people go somewhere for recreational purposes only." It may be a short walk through the village, a picnic in the woods, or a long anticipated trip to the top of Mont Ventoux. It may be made by a family group to celebrate a first communion, by a group of girls to see the annual parade at Apt, or by a boy and girl in love. Even a single person walking in what seems to be an aimless manner may be said to be taking a *promenade*.

. . . . .

The dances, the *promenades*, and the usual forms of adult recreational activity are supposed to offer adolescent girls adequate opportunities to have a good time. A well-behaved girl will not seek others, and most of the girls seem content. . . . As they get older they can expect suitors to call in the evening.

Boys are expected to seek wilder forms of amusement.

. . . . .

By the time young people are ready to marry they are acquainted with other young people from the whole area of the Apt Basin and even from more distant parts of the département. Family connections, visits, *prom-enades*, and above all the dances which they have attended have en-larged their circle of acquaintances beyond the limits of Peyrane.

. . . . .

When a young man decides he would like to marry a certain girl, his behavior makes his intentions obvious. At dances she is his only partner and he tries to keep other men from dancing with her. He tries to be with the girl on *promenades*. He drops into her home frequently, some-times bringing a bottle of his sparkling wine. After a while the visits become so much a part of the family routine that he is almost accepted as a member of the family. In most families he is allowed to take the girl to a dance without a chaperone. He may take her on his motorcycle to visit relatives in a neighborhood hamlet. The girl's family makes a point of retiring a little earlier than usual so that the young people may be alone.

After a few months the young man surprises no one when he asks the girl to marry him. If she consents, it is traditional for him to ask her father officially for his consent. This is legally necessary if the young people are minors. Family approval is not hard to obtain if it is evident that two conditions are fulfilled.

The first condition is that the couple should be in love. . . . The other important condition is that both the young man and the young woman should be *sérieux*. *Sérieux* means several things in his context. A serious husband or a serious wife is first of all faithful. A man who might "run after other women" or a woman who might be capable of "making horns grow on her husband's brow" is not serious. The most disgraceful thing that can happen to a person is for one's spouse to be so flagrantly un-faithful that the infidelity becomes generally known in the village.

Seriousness implies more than fidelity, however. A serious husband will try to earn as much money as the family needs to live "decently." He will not drink immoderately or spend too much time playing cards or boules. He will supplement his income by cultivating a garden. He will live so that he will be loved and respected by his wife and children.

A serious wife will be a hardworking, reasonable, and moderate woman. She will keep her house neat. She will feed and clothe the fam-ily economically and well. She will be on good terms with her neighbors but will not spend too much time gossiping. She will know how to stretch a hundred-franc note without having the reputation for being stingy. She will supplement her husband's income by making clothes, raising chickens and rabbits. If the need for money is desperate she will even take over the arduous task of raising silkworms or working in the grape harvest, without neglecting her regular household duties. She will not object if her husband goes to the café so long as he does not spend too much money or drink too much or come home too late for meals.

She will not even object if he is moderately immoderate—that is, if now and then he goes on a bit of a binge. She will keep the children from running the streets when they are young and she will keep them clean. She will teach them good manners and will encourage them to love and fear their father. She may expect her husband to coöperate in disciplining the children, but except on rare occasions she may not ask him to spend his free time taking care of the children.

There are other qualities besides "seriousness" that one welcomes in a prospective son- or daughter-in-law. Since marriage brings the families of both spouses into close contact it would be preferable that the two families be compatible with each other, so that neither will be ashamed of the other or awed by it. Then there is the matter of money. Everyone says that it is stupid to marry for money, but when conversation falls on a particular ménage it becomes obvious that people do associate the question of money with the question of marriage.

10. THE CHANGING MOSLEM FAMILY OF THE MIDDLE EAST

Dorothy Fahs Beck

§ Moslemism is more than a religion; it is an entire cultural pattern, very different in values and customs from the Christian or Hebraic cultures. Although contact with the West has begun to crack the hard shell of the Moslem culture, much of the old remains. Spotted unevenly throughout the Arab nations of the Middle East, one finds remnants of the older ways: the families of great wealth, with numerous wives and servants catering to the prestige and comfort of the male head of the household; the patriarchal family organization; the low social status of women; and, paralleling these households of wealth, the abject poverty of large segments of the population. Where the older culture remains, contacts with the West have sometimes simply added expensive cars and private planes to the possessions of the wealthy. But in many Middle Eastern countries, more fundamental changes have occurred and continue

SOURCE: *Marriage and Family Living*, 19 (November, 1957), 340–44. Reprinted by permission of the publisher and the author.

The author, who received her doctorate in sociology from Columbia University, has carried out numerous research projects in the medical field. She is Director of Research, Family Service Association of America. A year spent in the Middle East as assistant professor of biostatistics at the American University of Beirut and in travel plus library research contributed to a long article on the Moslem family, from which the present selection has been taken.

to occur: women are no longer forced by their families or public opinion to wear the veil; the harem is declining or has disappeared; women may hold jobs and vote. The changes have come unevenly to different countries or within the same country, where the cities tend to follow western ways but the villages still follow traditional Moslem ways. Turkey is the most completely westernized; Saudi Arabia the least. The Moslem religion is still the prevalent religion throughout.

In her article, based on first-hand experience and on reading, Dr. Beck does not confine herself to one country but gives a panoramic view of the Moslem family of the present in the midst of change. It is well to remember that the old patterns existed for many centuries and that men and women accepted and adapted to them without protest until the social and economic conditions of the countries began to change as a result of increased contacts with the western world. Note also in Dr. Beck's article that the change creates strains in family relationships. The change-over to the western style of marriage is not complete; the framework of the older Moslem marriage is often poorly concealed beneath new western customs.

The remarkable changes of Moslem family living patterns which has been accomplished in recent decades is perhaps best symbolized by the lifting of the veil that for more than a thousand years has held the Middle Eastern women in seclusion. While the veils used in different countries have varied in detail, they have all accomplished the same purpose, namely the hiding of the hair and usually also the face, and the prevention of any feminine appeal in public. Until the last three decades, the veil was worn almost universally by middle and upper class women throughout the area and has been an essential badge of social status and morality. To have said that a woman was without a veil was to have said she was "without shame."

.   .   .   .   .

A second major technic for the seclusion of women is also passing, namely the harem, or "hareem" as it is called in the Near East. While I had always associated this term with polygyny, it is primarily used to mean either the separate quarters for women within the household or the women and children themselves thus held in seclusion. Every device was used to keep these family members hidden. Windows were covered with fancy but concealing carved wood latticework. Shades were drawn. Gardens were protected from the view of neighbors by high outer walls or the house structure itself. Only women, children, the husband, close relatives, blind men, and eunuchs were permitted to enter. Since even men servants were excluded, small boys provided the major link with the outside world.

. . . . .

Today the harem is fast passing with the veil. The modern Moslem man of means builds himself a western-style house without separate quarters for the women. He shares his open balcony with his wife on a summer evening and when he goes out, she sometimes accompanies him. When he entertains at home, she joins the circle. The new homes have no carved wooden latticework in the windows and only in Iran, Iraq, and Afghanistan do they still build an outer wall for each compound to hide the family from view.

. . . . .

This increased freedom for interpersonal contact, together with the impact of mass communication from the West, has placed a heavy strain on the old mores prohibiting premarital courtship. According to Moslem tradition, it was the parents' responsibility to arrange before they died a suitable match for each child. To avoid any moral slips, the Islamic norms provided for child betrothals and early marriage, especially for the girl. A suitable partner for a girl was defined as a man of Moslem faith who could maintain or enhance her social and economic status. Age and compatibility were ignored. Kinship marriages were common, cousins being especially preferred. The choice was entirely in the parents' hands and the well-bred girl was expected neither to offer objections to their choice nor to see her future mate prior to the final ceremony.

With the impact of higher education for women and contact with the Western pattern, this ethic is also changing. Both the age of betrothal and the age of women at marriage are rising, especially among the well-to-do where educational demands interfere with early marriage. The modern family now consults the children about the choice of spouse and the more daring children may themselves suggest the partner and ask their parents to arrange a contract.

. . . . .

If she does marry, the modern woman may find it very difficult to play her role in the patriarchal family where the husband or his father has unlimited authority. From the first, she will be expected to join the groom's extended and often quite large family household where she will share a communal living and a common purse. Her status will become that of junior assistant to her mother-in-law who will continue to direct the household chores. The young brides of an earlier era accepted this status as a matter of course, but with the trend toward the education of women and a later age at marriage, the older girls with modern notions from school sometimes have a difficult time adjusting to the ways and direction of their mothers-in-law. In time the more modern educated couples often break away from these larger family units and establish independent homes. When this happens, it is likely to be considered a reflection on the family. Separate units within the same compound are sometimes tried as a compromise. Few escape a period of dominance by a generation conditioned to the old family pattern.

In addition to adjusting to a new husband and a strange house full of new relatives, the young wife must worry about how to stay married. Moslem law permits the man to divorce his wife at will merely by pronouncing the words, "I divorce you," three times, preferably on separate occasions. The woman, except in Turkey where Swiss law has replaced Moslem law, cannot divorce her husband unless this right has been specified in the original marriage contract.

. . . . .

The third major threat to the security of the Moslem wife is the chance that her husband may tire of her and take a second, permanent or temporary wife. The Qur'an [Koran] says: ". . . marry of the women who seem good to you two or three or four, and if ye fear that ye cannot do justice then one . . ." (IV, 3). This requirement that justice be done to all wives has usually been interpreted as requiring that the husband provide each wife with a separate household of equal comfort to that of the other wives and clothes and food of comparable quality. In the agricultural village the extra wife paid her way with her extra pair of hands, but in the city an extra wife was never a luxury a poor man could afford. Even among the rich, polygyny was not typical. Now it is declining in repute also among the urban wealthy and is only a small factor in the total picture. It is forbidden in Turkey and characterizes only about 2 per cent of the marriages in Egypt at any one time. The figure for Iraq is 9 per cent, while in Saudi Arabia it is much higher.

11. PERSIAN COURTSHIP AND WEDDING

Najmeh Najafi, as told to Helen Hinckley

§ The description of a typical Persian courtship and a Persian wedding shows that although the rituals are different from our own and the roles of husband and wife in contrast to those of Americans, nevertheless the girl enters marriage with all the eagerness and anticipation of an American bride. Marriage gives the girl prestige and carries both bride and groom into the adult world.

SOURCE: Najmeh Najafi, *Persia Is My Heart* (New York: Harper and Row, 1953), pp. 87–90, 92–93, and 120–24. Copyright 1953 by Najmeh Najafi and Helen Hinckley Jones. Reprinted by permission of the publisher.

The author, who is a native of Persia (now Iran), studied at Pasadena City College, California. She is also the author of *Reveille for a Persian Village*, written with Helen Hinckley.

The author, Najmeh Najafi, grew up during a period of great change, when Persia became Iran, the veil for women was abolished legally by the reformer Reza Shah, and women gained the privilege of meeting in such public places as tearooms and westernized stores. She notes, however, that the old, conservative families clung to the old ways and tended to seclude their women. Her own family life began under the old ways. Her mother, at the age of twelve, married a man of forty, and bore him eight children, of whom the author was the youngest. An older sister married when thirteen and had her first child the following year. At this time, women still wore the veil when they went out, and the only places for women to go were the church and the community bathhouse, which served as a kind of social club where women met to discuss, gossip, and predict who the next bride would be.

In the city bathhouse and in the bathhouse of the village, the conversation is the same. Always in the minds of the women there is a lively interest in the young girls. For the women are the suitors of Persia. When a young girl leaves her tray to go into the hot pool or to dip screaming into the adjacent cold pool, many eyes will follow her. The girl does not mind. She knows that the place that a woman must occupy in her country is at best beloved doll to her husband and respected mother to her children.

. . . . .

It is the custom for the mother, with as many female relatives as care to make the call, to send a servant ahead to announce that she is making a call, object matrimony for her son. She goes into the house. The call is a polite one, but all eyes are open. The girl knows the eyes are upon her and she feels her knees knocking together, her smile made of cardboard on her face, her hands trembling. For this call she has prepared herself without make-up. Make-up might hide a blemish which the mother must see if she is not to be deceived.

. . . . .

If the suitors are pleased with the girl, with her accomplishments, with the wealth and position of her family, next time, very soon, the prospective groom will visit, too. The man will be older than the girl, maybe five years or so. Or maybe he will be a middle-aged or even an old man, looking for a wife to take the place of one lost by death or to add to his harem.

. . . . .

Reza Shah made a law forbidding child marriages. The girl, according to law, must be sixteen. But still many girls marry at eleven, twelve, thirteen.

. . . . .

Wives are not purchased in Persia as some people believe. Nevertheless, a wife from the highest class is worth at least five thousand dollars in gifts.

After the call by the female relatives, after the boy (or man) has visited the home and has said that he is satisfied, then the parents of both the boy and the girl get together to talk about the dowry of the girl, the gifts of the boy, the wedding, the ceremony, other matters.

The first gift of the groom's parents to the bride will be, most likely, a diamond ring. If the parents can afford it, the stone will be enormous. It reflects the position of the family. After this will come the handwritten, beautifully illuminated copy of the Koran. This too is a very expensive gift. Later there will be such gifts as silver candlesticks done with the care and creative precision of the Persian artisan, silver mirror, lacquered chests—the gifts are reflections of the artistic culture of Persia.

For two or three months, maybe even for a year the bride will remain in the home of her mother getting her dowry arranged. In my country this is a happy time in the girl's life and in the mother's too, when the two work together for the life-long happiness of the girl.

.   .   .   .   .

[The author visits a girl friend, Shikuh, who is soon to be married.]

Shikuh's girl friends in Kasvin came very early and we began to sew. We cut and made the white wedding dress, the slips, the brassieres, all of the dainty things the bride would need.

.   .   .   .   .

Four days seemed like one day. The next day we went to the public bath, fifteen laughing, merry girls. All day we spent in the bath. There was a special expert to pluck our eyebrows, treat our lashes, there was the shampoo, the soothing rub with the bath mitten, the steaming that makes one clean clear to the inside, the plunge in the hot water and the sharp chill of the cold water as we went shrieking into it for only a moment.

During the last part of the bath there had been a band of musicians playing outside the bathhouse. Our instruments are different from yours, but there are strings and drums and cymbals. As we came out the village people and the people of Kasvin threw flowers and little white candies on the street in front of Shikuh's feet.

The next night two mullahs [interpreters of the Islamic faith] came for the marriage ceremony. In my country there are mullahs of different prices. If you are wealthy you may buy the best mullah for the occasion. If you are not, poor mullahs will marry you as tightly.

.   .   .   .   .

In Moslem weddings the bride, dressed in white and with a veil over her face, sits alone in a room close to the court, and close to the room for the women. She sits on the floor on a special piece of finest Persian pure silk with maybe threads of real metal worked into the design. Behind her is a mirror and tall candelabra. At each side there is a long piece of bread almost like a rug. You don't have anything in America like these very long pieces of flat bread, square at one end, the other end pointed. Into the bread, in beautiful Persian design, is placed colored incense for future burning.

Outside the door of the bridechamber the two mullahs stand one on each side, reading from the Koran. Two times the bride must not answer the questions of the mullah. At this time it is the custom of the boy's mother to bring a gift of gold to show that she is willing. Hoseh's [the groom] mother is dead so a kinswoman brings the golden bracelets. Now Shikuh answers "Yes," and there is a squeal from all the women at the celebration and a great clapping of hands from everyone. Two women of the family—women who have been especially happy in their lives— come and stand before the incense-covered bread. One has two cubes of sugar between her palms. As she rolls her palms together a thin stream of sugar falls upon the floor. The bride will be sweet to her husband. It is the best quality in women in my country. The other woman has needle and thread. She sews while she says she is closing the mouth of the new relatives.

In Persia the boy takes the bride to the home of his mother. Shikuh would go to the home of Hoseh. There are many who whisper that Shikuh is fortunate to be at once mistress of her house. It is hard, sometimes, for the young girl to go to the home of the mother-in-law, especially if there are other sons and their wives already in the home.

Then the groom is led into the bride's room and the two are left behind a drawn curtain while the mullahs make the marriage papers. One is for the parents of the girl, one for the parents of the boy.

[However, the bride does not immediately go to the home of her new husband. For several months she continues to live with her parents; she prepares her dowry and is instructed by her mother on the duties and responsibilities of a Moslem wife. Finally the day comes for her to leave her parents' home. Porters carry the dowry to the home of the groom, which will become her new home. Then the groom and his kinsmen come to accompany the bride to the new home; her parents may not go with her, as they cannot enter into her new life.]

12. MARRIAGE AND THE FAMILY IN KOREA

Un Sun Song

§ In Korea, as in France, the Moslem countries, and the United States, marriage is important to the bride and groom, their families, and the society. As is marriage in each of the other countries, Korean marriage is colored by religious concepts—in this case, by Confucianism. Korean society is also undergoing change, which touches courtship and marriage. Dr. Song, a sociologist from Korea, points out the old customs, some of the changes, and the values of marriage.

It has been said that in order to understand a people you must first understand their family system. Especially in the case of Korea is this true, since every facet of life revolves around the family and the relations between its members. In the Western world, and especially the United States, love is the motivating force which leads to marriage. In Korea this ideal of romantic love is less evident; the most important reason for marriage in Korea is to continue the family line. To have a son who will continue the family name and reverence the family ancestors is the goal of every Korean, a fact which helps to explain the importance of the male in our culture.

Mate Selection and Courtship

Although the Western influence has brought about some variations in the old patterns of culture, it is the traditional customs which are still observed by the greater part of the people. Most Americans are usually surprised to learn that in Korea we have no "dating" custom such as there is in their country. Of course, this stems from the fact that romantic love does not determine marriages. In fact, there is an old proverb which says that, "Love does not always lead to marriage, but marriage often leads to love." The statement that we have no dating custom invariably elicits the question: "Well, how do boys and girls get to know each other well enough to get married?" The answer is that they don't—at least not

SOURCE: *Korean Survey*, 7 (April, 1958), 4–6, 12. Reprinted by permission of the publisher and the author.

The author, who was born in Seoul, Korea, completed her college education in Tokyo and her graduate training in the United States, where she received her doctorate in sociology from the University of Maryland in 1958.

as well as the American girls and boys do. Although there are increasing numbers of so-called "love matches" to be found in Korea (since 1945), these are often frowned upon by the more tradition-minded elders. But this is getting somewhat ahead of the story. Let us take a look at the customs of an earlier day.

From the time that a child was born in Korea the parents were concerned about finding a mate for him or her. Although sometimes a child was "engaged" at a very young age this custom has passed away. Today, by the time the daughter is about eighteen and the son is twenty-two, the parents probably have already picked out some mate for them. It is interesting to note that the future spouse's family background and name is much more important than whether or not he is wealthy. Naturally, every family is anxious to get the best possible match for their children, but if it is a question of whether to marry a person with excellent family background and little money or poor family background and much money, they will choose the good family background.

Aside from family background, there are traditionally several other things which will determine whether or not a couple should be married. To begin with, there is a taboo which prohibits two families with the same surname and genealogy from marrying among themselves. In addition, the signs of the zodiac were consulted and the year, month, day, and hour of the couple's birth dates were compared and if they were found to be harmonious it was a good omen that the marriage should take place.

After the parents have chosen some likely candidates they show their son or daughter several pictures of them. The children are usually given an opportunity to pass judgment on whether or not they like the looks of the spouse-to-be, and choose the one they would like to marry. Then the parents make arrangements for their children to meet. Usually it is the girl's parents who send an "invitation" to the boy's family. Although in some cases this is the first time that the boy and girl have ever met, it often happens that they have gone to school together or were neighbors. At this formal meeting the two young people have a chance for a brief conversation and can learn something about each other. If the boy and girl want to know each other better, they may, with the approval of both families, see each other more often. In general, however, the couple will become engaged after the first meeting and will marry as soon as possible, usually as soon as the girl's trousseau is ready. The interval between the first meeting and the wedding ceremony may be anywhere from several weeks to six months or more.

It often happens that if the parents are unsuccessful in finding a suitable mate for their child, they consult a *chung-mai*, or professional match-maker. This marriage broker is usually a widow who is well acquainted with a number of families; or it may be an old and respected member of the community, one's employer, or a person of influence or position. They all fulfill the same function, however, in that they seek to find the most eligible mate for their client or friend. If the *chung-mai* is professional, then it is customary to give her some kind of reward for her services. She receives commissions of money or gifts from both the families, which are given according to their financial situation. It is said that if a *chung-mai* succeeded in finding a good wife for a rich man's son, she would have no worries for the rest of her life.

Going back somewhat to the engagement period, one might ask just what the young couple may do while they are waiting for their marriage day. Well, here again there is much variation from place to place and from time to time. Generally speaking, the husband-to-be may visit his fiance at her home, where they may talk to each other, have dinner together, or play cards with each other under the strict eye of some third party. This is a custom which is not unfamiliar in Spain, where the *duenna* acts as chaperone for the young people. If the couple would like to go out for a walk there is usually someone following them not far behind; or if they want to go to a movie they are chaperoned by some member of the family.

During this brief engagement period the girl's family is busily preparing her trousseau, and she is brushing up on her housekeeping. She is taught to take over such duties as cooking, sewing, and home management. Usually this is not too difficult for her, since she has been helping her mother keep house since she was very young. The mother, female relatives and friends, meanwhile, are preparing the things that she will need in order to set up housekeeping—kitchen utensils, furniture, and clothes or fabrics. This is a very expensive undertaking for the bride's family, especially if there is more than one daughter. In fact, Koreans have a proverb: "No thief attempts to rob the house of a man who has three daughters."

But when the time for the wedding finally arrives it is a time of great rejoicing. In fact, the marriage is probably the most important celebration in Korea. The traditional wedding ceremony is filled with color and symbolism and ritual, but the Western influence has been introducing many Christian aspects to the marriage until today many people have a Christian religious marriage. In any case, whether the ceremony itself is traditional or modern, it is always followed by a sumptuous feast to which many guests are invited. Everyone enjoys going to a wedding feast because there is such a variety of tasty delicacies—several meat dishes including beef, pork, and chicken; fish, both smoked and dried; fruits, pastries, and candies; vegetables and rice; and, of course, plenty of wine. The number and variety of dishes varies with the financial status of each family, but it is said that some rich families often have between sixty and seventy-five dishes at one feast.

If their families are well-to-do, the bride and groom may decide to go on a honeymoon to the famous hot springs at Onyang or Paikchon. If they decide not to go on a honeymoon then the couple will settle down to live with the parents of the husband, for according to tradition it is the responsibility of the son to live with his parents and take care of them in their old age. Although this custom is not practiced extensively among modern families, it is still prevalent among the majority and will probably reflect the ancient concept of filial piety for years to come, in spite of the passing of many folkways in the face of growing modernization and secularization.

The Korean Family

The traditional Korean family, as it exists in the rural areas of Korea, is patriarchal and monogamous. The key figure in the household is the patriarch, the oldest male member, in most cases. It is he who manages the family affairs. Insofar as ritual is concerned, the patriarch is the priest in the family worship, the breadwinner of the family, and, consequently, it is he who regulates the income of the family. The word of the patriarch is law. His decisions must be accepted by the other members of the family.

As a result of the patriarch's supervision of family members, he represents the family as a group to the outside world. The family's social status can be no higher than that of the father. The entire life of the family is subordinated to the wishes and desires of the patriarch; however, the attitude and behavior of the patriarch is seldom determined by self interest or concern. Rather he is controlled by the institutional demands of the family.

The key element in the relationship between the patriarch and his wife is just as Confucius decreed it should be thousands of years ago: respect. Their relationship must be harmonious; the husband is active and the wife is passive—he is like a needle and she like the thread. He is heaven; she is earth. All these analogies point out that each of them has a specific role to fulfill and that the one cannot fulfill the role of the other. Nor do the husband and wife show their affection toward each other in the presence of their children or friends. There is no kissing custom in Korea—this is strictly a Western innovation—therefore husbands don't kiss their wives. Or if they do, they don't do it where other people might see them and make fun of them. Public opinion is a very strong means of social control in Korea!

Although there are modern exceptions to the rule, women are supposed to walk behind their husbands, not beside them, when they are out in public. Formerly, whenever the men went out to some party or special dinner they would not take their wives, for in Korea there was a special class of female entertainer, the *kisaeng,* who would dance and sing for the guests. Even inside the home the traditional attitude of the husband is that a man should not work in the kitchen because it is beneath his dignity. But here again there are many husbands, who, when there are no outsiders around, will help their wives with the cooking and washing the dishes. Some men will not admit it, but they actually *enjoy* cooking.

The relationship of the husband and wife is expressed also in the language. When they speak to each other they may use the somewhat affectionate term, *yobo.* Most important, however, they may not call each other by their first name! This would be a most serious and insulting thing to do. Instead, they use many different terms such as *pakkanyangpan* (husband), *uri chuin* (my master), *chip-e saram* (person of the house), *anhai* (wife). More common in the husband-wife interaction is the use of the term *aigi aboji* (father of the child) or *aigi omoni* (mother of the child) to refer to the husband or the wife. Also the name of the child may be used, for example, *Poktong-ui-aboji* meaning Poktong's father. Another interesting fact about the Korean husband-wife relationship is that when they marry, the wife keeps her maiden surname. Thus, if Kim Soon Hi marries a man named Lee, she is still referred to as Kim Soon Hi. If you wanted to call her "Mrs. Lee," you would have to say the equivalent of "Mr. Lee's Wife."

Sociologically speaking, the Korean family is parent-child centered rather than husband-wife centered, as most Western families are today. It is this parent-child relationship, more specifically the father-son relationship, which is the key to the understanding of the Korean family system. The importance of a son in the family can be readily understood in view of the Korean attitude toward ancestor reverence and ancestral tablets in continuing the family line, and "face," an attitude which is strengthened through the teachings of Confucianism. Only through a son can there be a continuation of the family line. Girls will marry into some other families and will no longer be considered members of their true family. In this social context lies the strong preference for male children rather than female. Nevertheless, Koreans would prefer to have daughters than to have no children at all. Another practical reason for the preference of a son is, of course, that sons are better able to work on the farms and can provide for the sustenance of the aged parents.

The father's attitude toward his children is an interesting one. He must always try to be very dignified, so that the children will show him the proper respect; therefore he is not too affectionate toward them, even though he loves them very much. There is no concept in Korea that the father is the "boy's best friend." It is the father's job to discipline the children. Sometimes he spanks them if he thinks it is necessary or makes them go to bed without eating their supper. When they speak to their father, they must use a respectful form of language. (Korean language is based upon a system of polite forms, some very polite and others less polite, being used between very close friends.) If a child ever used other than the honorific level to his father, he would expect to be punished very quickly. Korean children respect and fear their fathers and it is rare to find children who are hard to handle.

If we compare the parents to the human body, the father is the head and the mother is the heart. It is she who takes care of the food and clothing for the family. As all of the father's activity is carried on outside the home, the mother works inside the home. She works from dawn to dusk just managing the home. She can not go to bed until the father has gone, and she must get up before him in the morning. You will never find a Korean wife making her husband prepare his own breakfast before going to work.

Mother must do the thousand and one little things which often go unnoticed—things like remembering all the relatives' birthdays—so she doesn't go out very often. Therefore, she often asks her husband on some family occasion to invite their friends to the house and she prepares a big meal and spends the whole day chatting and gossiping with her friends.

Until quite recently the Korean wife did not work outside the home to earn money even if she was able to do so. It was considered a disgrace for such a thing to happen and the father would lose "face" among his friends and neighbors. Girls were trained to be good wives and mothers —not to be office girls. Boys are brought up so that they might become responsible husbands and fathers in the future. Today, as far as the girls are concerned, however, this old attitude is losing ground and many young girls and wives have found it necessary to seek work in offices and factories of the large cities in order to meet the demands of a war-shattered economy.

In most other ways, though, Korea retains the old customs. This helps to explain why there is very little divorce in Korea. In our culture divorce carries a stigma which is greater than in most Western countries, so couples are less inclined to seek a divorce as a solution to their problems. But, on the other hand, there is less reason to need a divorce because of the very nature of the roles of the husband and wife. The husband knows what is expected of him and he knows that no one will try to take over his duties unless he gives his permission. The wife is brought up to respect her husband and love her children. There is no conflict as to whether a woman should turn to a career or to housekeeping. The culture solves that problem. In the Western world there are many role conflicts between husband and wife, and the value of individualism deemphasizes the importance of the family group. In Korea the men are supposed to be authoritarian and active while women are taught to be submissive and passive. Men and women cooperate in order to bring up their children and continue the family name.

The importance of a son to continue the family name helps to explain one of the ancient institutions which has recently been abolished, that is, concubinage. In the old days when a wife was barren the husband had the right to take a concubine in order to have a son. If the concubine had a son he would become the legal heir and she would receive much prestige. Even so, the wife's position would not be endangered, for she was still the wife and no one could take over her position.

I mentioned earlier that the patriarch was the authority in the family. This is quite true, but as he gets older he becomes more of a figurehead and it is the wife who has the greatest influence. Usually the patriarch knows that his wife is assuming more and more responsibility, but he lets her gradually take over more of his duties. If the wife has several sons it is easier for her to gain more power in the household because she already has a great deal of prestige. It often happens that the wife is able to make herself the real authority in the family without the husband's knowing or realizing it. In other words, the husband *thinks* he is the authority, but the wife *knows* that she is. This is one of the most important secrets for a happy marriage in Korea.

And when the couple is old they may expect that their children (the eldest son in particular) will take care of them for the rest of their lives. So old age, in Korea, becomes a time, not of worry and anxiety, but of peace and happiness, the aged parents secure in the knowledge that they have done their part in continuing the family line and contributing respectable citizens to their society.

Chapter 5: The Family Life Cycle

13. STAGES OF THE FAMILY LIFE CYCLE

Ruth Shonle Cavan

§ When life is full of many interests and activities, it is all but impossible not to become absorbed in the present. These are the best years, we think; the past fades into insignificance; the future has not yet arrived. Of the past we say, "it's all water under the bridge," and of the years to come, "let the future take care of itself." But of course the present never stands alone; no one period of life is detached from what has gone before or what will come after. Life is all of a piece—a long river of experience that begins at birth, already loaded with heredity from the past of the family, that flows on until the end of life, passing along in its turn hereditary factors and learned values to younger lives in the earlier stages of the process of living.

It is often possible and practical to select one or two phases or stages of life and study them intensively. That is really what this book does. Most of the articles deal with the years shortly before or soon after marriage. So that perspective will not be lost, it seems wise to emphasize the on-flowing quality of life, whether of the individual or of the family. Dating, courtship, marriage, and early family building are part of the life span that appeal as being dramatically important to individuals and society. They are but one segment of the whole of life.

The idea of the unbroken flow of a person's life from birth through childhood, adolescence, adulthood, and old age is a fairly familiar one. Any one of us can look backward at the stages we have passed through,

SOURCE: This article is based on Robert J. Havighurst, *Human Development and Education* (New York: Longmans, Green & Company, Inc., 1953), Evelyn Millis Duvall's book *Family Development* (Philadelphia: J. B. Lippincott Company, revised 1967) and her article "Implications for Education through the Family Life Cycle," *Marriage and Family Living*, 20 (1958), 334–42, and the author's own book, *The American Family*, 4th ed. (New York: Thomas Y. Crowell Company, 1969).

The author is editor of this book of readings and author of numerous books and articles dealing with various aspects of the family, including two texts, *The American*

assess our present stage, and from our observation of those around us anticipate the stages to come. All in all, eight or nine stages can readily be distinguished during one person's life. These stages can be thought of in terms of his individual development, as Robert J. Havighurst has presented them, or in terms of his family relationships, as Evelyn Millis Duvall has emphasized. Each person has his own life, but for most people personal development is closely linked to family life. The discussion that follows merges the Havighurst and Duvall approaches.

Family and Individual Developmental Stages

Prior to marriage, husband and wife have passed through the developmental stages of infancy, early and middle childhood, and adolescence, living with the family into which they were born, sometimes referred to as the family of orientation. Since these stages are discussed under family stages 2, 3, 4, 5, and 6 in terms of the children of our hypothetical couple, they are omitted here.

1. The Beginning Family

With marriage, a man (average age, twenty-three) and a woman (average age, twenty) change their family relationships. If they have been living with their parents, or in close relationship to them, they have usually thought of themselves and been considered by others as members of their fathers' families. With marriage, the two individuals, previously members of two separate family units, loosen these early bonds and join together to begin the task of building a unique family life, according to their own ideals and to fit their needs. Dr. Duvall refers to this newly married couple as a beginning family.

Husband and wife draw on earlier family experiences and on the general cultural expectations and values for family life, but the particular combination of factors and the special points of emphasis are their own. If this beginning of family life is strongly structured, the couple will be ready for the next stage.

In this developmental stage the young husband is often confronted

---

Family and *American Marriage*. Her doctorate is from the University of Chicago, and she is professor emeritus of sociology at Rockford College.

Robert J. Havighurst received his doctorate from Ohio State University. He is professor of education at the University of Chicago. He is author or coauthor of numerous books and articles on educational subjects and on adjustment to old age.

Evelyn Millis Duvall, who received her doctorate from the University of Chicago, has held professional positions with the Association for Family Living, Chicago, and the National Council on Family Relations. She is now a family life consultant who devotes much of her time to conducting workshops, lecturing, and writing. Among her many publications are *Family Living, Facts of Life and Love for Teenagers, When You Marry* (coauthor), *In-Laws Pro and Con,* and *Family Development.*

with a number of tasks, overlapping in time or closely following one another: training for and establishing himself in an occupation, fulfilling his military service requirements, and learning to fit into his domestic roles. The wife also has her tasks in learning to manage a household and gaining experience as a hostess. Often she aids in financing a home; 60 per cent of new wives are employed. Together, husband and wife adjust conflicting roles and interests and develop compatible intimate relationships.

2. The Childbearing Family

The beginning family typically shifts into the childbearing family (sometimes called the family of procreation) during the second year of marriage. In many ways the change is not abrupt, for the roles of new parents gradually develop during the months of pregnancy. Nevertheless the actual physical arrival in the family of a live baby with its own demands changes the marriage relationship. The new roles of mother and father are added to the earlier roles of wife and husband. The wife may also exchange a previous role as employed woman for the combined role of homemaker, mother, and soon nursery school teacher, all in her own home. Only 13 per cent of mothers of preschool children are employed.

The husband, as father, may think first in terms of added financial burdens, especially if his wife previously was employed. He must develop a new sense of responsibility. He also must allow time in his schedule to spend with his wife, who may be more dependent upon him than before for companionship. Typically he also wants free time to spend with his child.

Together husband and wife need to reach common goals for their children and to agree on methods of child rearing. They need to build up their social life and their intimate personal life, both of which may have been subordinated to the needs of the wife and new baby.

Usually, other children are soon added to the first-born, with the last child being born when the mother is about twenty-six and the father about twenty-nine years old.

Not only has the family passed into a new developmental stage, but each baby in turn has its own developmental tasks to accomplish. Although the baby is unaware of "tasks," he is most happy when able to try out and put to use his developing abilities. During the first two years of life the baby typically learns the rudiments of handling various physiological processes, such as when and where to sleep, how to eat in a way suitable to his age, the routine of elimination, coordination of muscles, walking, and talking. He begins to learn how to adjust to other people and how to maintain some simple forms of self control; he begins, also, to recognize himself as a distinct personality.

3. *The Family with Preschool Children*

As husband and wife learn to accept each new pregnancy and birth with confidence, their attention is focused on the development of the older children. The family with preschool children refers to the family whose oldest child is approaching the age of six. Typically, younger children have been born—in fact the family may be complete. Although at first glance it may seem that each child simply brings a repetition of the parents' first-child adjustment, actually with each child the situation changes for everyone. Parents repeat their care of the infant with each child—but each child has his own individual characteristics. At the same time, they must also keep advancing with the oldest child into his new stages of growth. Responsibilities increase, more money and a larger house are needed, more household tasks must be done. The father and mother are now threatened with the possibility of losing their marriage in family life. The mother, especially, may become almost completely absorbed in keeping her home running and personally caring for her children.

The older children, aged four to six, are no longer infants; they have passed into the recognizable stage of early childhood. They are able to manage their bodies and their conversation with a fair degree of adequacy. They can accept limited responsibilities not only for themselves but for tasks around the house. They know what they want and are able to express themselves in demanding fulfillment; at the same time they can delay fulfillment a moderate length of time. They are able to learn a moderate degree of self control and how to manage limited independence. Conscience, or a sense of right and wrong, begins to develop as they internalize their parents' values.

4. *The Family with School Children*

Soon the family has developed into the family with children in school, between the ages of six and thirteen. Littler ones may still be preschoolers. The parents are in their thirties. This is the stage at which parents must begin to let go of their children. They are aided by the school, which takes the children many hours each day. Soon Scouts and other organizations claim them for outings and camping trips. Nevertheless the parents are usually pretty well submerged in family life and in trying to meet the needs of rapidly growing children. They have little privacy or time for themselves. Family life has become a complex set of interrelationships as each child strives for physical and mental space in which to develop.

The child is now in middle childhood, which carries him through the elementary school years. Most of his associates are of his own age and sex, and it is important that he learn how to adjust well to them. His abilities from earlier years continue to develop; he also has new tasks in development. As he becomes more aware of himself, he formulates attitudes toward himself as a boy or girl. The acceptance of a masculine or feminine self conception and role is important as a forerunner to later adolescent development. He is also becoming accustomed to organized groups and to cooperation with adults other than his parents.

5. The Family with Teen-agers

By the time the parents are in the middle or late thirties, their family life changes sharply. The elementary school child has given way to the high-school teen-ager, whose interests change almost overnight as he enters into an entirely new world and feels the impact of new cultural expectations. For approximately seven years parents go through a period fraught with anxiety for their children and insecurity for themselves, as the children more and more turn toward their peers for life satisfactions. The mother often begins to change her pattern of life, seeking part- or full-time employment; 40 per cent of mothers between ages thirty and forty are employed. Expenses increase rapidly and her earnings help to ease the burden on the father and to provide children and adults with additional opportunities or luxuries that they crave. The center of family life is still primarily in the children.

Although teen-agers still have some of their closest ties with their own age-sex group, they are becoming aware of the opposite sex. One of the developmental tasks of the teen years is to learn to adapt to the opposite sex; mixed groups increase in number. Girls learn to look upon themselves and other girls as potential women; and boys see themselves and other boys as fast developing into men. Sexual attraction between boys and girls must be admitted and managed within the scope of social conventions. With mixed-group activities comes a new type of social life, with the need to learn social skills—how to dance, carry on a conversation, and play social games. Other group skills are also learned through committees and the planning and carrying out of school, church, or club projects. Independence from parents increases. Toward the end of the teen period comes a definite interest in marriage as a foreseeable part of future life.

6. The Family as a Launching Center

This is the name given by Dr. Duvall to the family whose children are leaving home to attend college, find employment in some other community, or marry. The parents themselves are entering middle age; the marriage of the last child typically finds the mother in the late forties, the father entering the fifties. The father is probably nearing the peak of his earning power and of his influence in the community. The specter of retirement and old age has not yet appeared. As the mother loses status in the family with the departure of children, she seeks and gains status in the community or through employment. Nevertheless, she sometimes feels lost, unwanted, as though the most significant part of her life had ended. The impersonal success on the job or some board or committee does not seem to compensate for the warm, personal relationship she once had with her children. She also often is experiencing the menopause, which may be a symbol of loss of youthfulness that she finds hard to accept. The father also has adjustments to make, not only to the removal of his children but also to his wife's new role as an independent employed woman. He may have to accept less catering to his individual wishes and may feel he should assume new obligations at home to prevent overburdening of his wife. An important task for both husband and wife is to rethink their philosophy of life and search for new values to carry them into middle age.

Children have completed the transition from adolescence into young adulthood. For a time the young person becomes more or less detached from his family group. He is able to act with a high degree of independence as an individual. Unless he is in college, he loses contact with his age group, a contact that has carried him along all through school, and he becomes an adult among adults of all ages. He no longer gains status from his family connections in the same degree as earlier in his life. This is the period when he must prove himself on his own merits. For the young man, settling into an occupation is all important; finding a mate and marrying is highly significant. The girl looks upon work as temporary and actively though modestly works on the problem of finding a husband. Both young men and women sometimes doubt their ability to select the proper mates for themselves and seek books, lectures, and courses on preparation for marriage. Young men also must adjust to military service and adjust this service to their other major interests of vocation and marriage.

It may be said that this period from approximately eighteen to twenty-five is probably the most significant in the lives of most people. Childhood is definitely and conclusively left behind and adulthood is embraced in all phases of life. The development that began with conception has now found fruition in adult life; the pattern set at this time tends to color the remainder of life, although the person does not stand still in his development.

7. *The Family in the Middle Years*

Husband and wife are in their fifties and early sixties. Their children have left home. They are again a couple, again primarily husband and wife and secondarily father and mother. This is the period for mending fences of communication and joint living, which may have become ragged or even damaged in the busy years of child rearing. In one sense this phase is a renewal of the early married years, as the couple again seek a new personal adjustment. It differs, however, as it is based on years of experience together and the memories of their joint enterprise in rearing a family. They must put these experiences away as memories and turn to their future as a couple, a future of some twelve to fifteen years before death begins to create a significant number of widows or widowers.

Husband and wife must adjust to declining sexual interests and some loss of physical vigor and youthful appearance on both sides. The way is open, however, for growth of personal companionship.

During middle age, the couple usually become grandparents. They step into new roles, different from the roles of parents. The roles must be learned and must not be allowed to intrude on the parental roles of the parents of their grandchildren, for in our society each parent-child combination must be allowed its own freedom to develop. The middle-aged couple are now in the position that their parents were when they were in stages 2 and 3 of family development.

The married children now have their own homes, their own family life. They are becoming parents and entering upon stages 2, 3, and 4, through which their parents passed some twenty-five to thirty years earlier; these stages have already been described above.

8. *The Aging Family*

This stage is usually thought of as beginning with retirement and lasting until the death of both husband and wife. The couple have already adjusted to the independence of their married children and are well versed in the arts of grandparenthood. The early part of the aging period is dominated by adjustment to retirement, which typically brings both lowered income and decline in social status.

The later part of the period is marked by physical and sometimes mental decline and eventually by the death of either husband or wife; typically the husband dies first and an elderly widow must adjust to a single life after forty or more years as one of a married couple. If the wife dies first, the widower has the adjustment to make. The remaining one has the difficult task of becoming accepted into other groups at a time of life when adaptation is difficult.

The married children are now themselves middle-aged; their children are adolescent or marrying and having children, and another swing of the life cycle has begun. Their attention now comes back to their aging parents with concern for their welfare. Sometimes the aging parents, especially a widowed mother, joins them in their home, but often the bond is the one of maintaining a helpful friendship with a parent in his or her own home.

In time, the married children themselves pass into the old-age stage of the cycle and in their turn look to their children for security and love. Thus the never-ending cycle of family life moves through the generations.

Overlapping Stages

The preceding discussion is highly simplified. Families with three or four children, especially if they are widely spaced, typically are in several phases of family development at one time. From the point of view of the oldest child the family may be one with teen-agers; but the youngest child may demand that the family still adjust to the preschooler.

This dual process may place additional strains on the family and between the members since the needs of the teen-ager may conflict with those of the young child. The parents are caught between the needs of the two and somehow must help each child to satisfy his needs. From another point of view, however, the slow movement from stage to stage may help the family. Perhaps the tensions would be even greater if the family had to move abruptly from one stage to another, a situation which could happen only if a family consisted simply of twins or triplets, or in lesser degree in the case of one child. As it is, the family "learns" on the oldest child and then more confidently and with more composure accepts the developing needs of each succeeding child and the changes in their own family and personal relationships. As Dr. Duvall phrases the situation in *Family Development* (pages 9–10):

> We see a family being pushed out into new unknowns in its experience as its oldest child becomes a preschooler, goes to school, gets into the teens, and finally leaves for a life of his own. As younger children come along, they arrive in a family already somewhat familiar with these normal events and stages of children's growth through the induction given by the eldest.

Developmental Tasks

In the passage of person or family from one stage to another certain general trends may be noticed. At each stage, individual or family, young person or old, is faced with certain developmental tasks. A developmental task, according to Havighurst, who is referring to the individual, "is a task which arises at or about a certain period in the life of the individual, successful achievement of which leads to his happiness and to success with later tasks, while failure leads to unhappiness in the individual, disapproval by society, and difficulty with later tasks." Dr. Duvall adopts this definition and applies it to family life.

Thus a developmental task, well done, produces a well-adjusted individual or family for the present and creates the competence for moving on to the next stage and achieving success there also. Each stage of development rests on the stage that has preceded. Successful childhood rests on successful development in infancy, adolescence on childhood, early adulthood on adolescence, and so on. If the person fails to accomplish adequately the tasks of any one stage, he is hampered in achieving success in the next stage, and the next. In either individual or family, it is not possible to ignore some stages as unimportant and to feel that only certain stages are significant. Each stage, its tasks well achieved, brings immediate reward and also lays the foundation for success in the next stage. Conversely, failure at any one stage brings immediate unhappiness or dissatisfaction and makes success at later stages difficult.

The developmental tasks of any one stage rest on three factors, according to Havighurst and Duvall. The basic factor is the person's physical readiness for a particular function. A baby cannot learn to talk, walk, or control elimination until mind and body have matured to the place where these things are possible for him. The older boy or girl cannot become a parent until sex organs mature. At the other end of life, when physical and mental powers are declining, the developmental tasks are to adjust to lessened capacities. The time comes when the athlete can no longer play successfully with or against younger people; there comes a time when the scholar cannot read without glasses, grasp difficult concepts readily, nor originate new concepts. Thus for the first part of life the person's powers are expanding and his tasks are concerned with learning to use these expanding powers successfully. During the latter part of life, powers are contracting and the person's task is to conserve and learn to live successfully with his lessening powers.

A second, strong factor in development is the expectations of the society in which the person lives as to what form development should take, and what the specific tasks should be. Children become able to learn to talk between the ages of one and two. They are expected to learn at this time; parents become greatly concerned if their children do not begin to talk at this age; they encourage, coax, and praise. The child of five or six is able to take care of his bodily needs and to endure separation from his mother. Therefore social expectation is that he will enter school and be successful in school life. Older children and parents help to prepare the child for school, and if he does not enter school as expected, parents are called to account. Sometimes the expectations of society are that the child will not immediately make use of his growing powers but will control and restrain them, fitting them into a larger pattern of life. The adolescent is not expected to use his sexual powers but quite conversely to refrain from using them until other cultural expectations have been met—education, personal maturity, and economic competence.

Third is the factor of personal aspirations and values. These are closely related to the first two factors, but in time become a motivating force in their own right. The youth makes his own choice of occupation and young men and women choose whom they will marry. Each person develops his own scale of values and philosophy of life.

Recurrent Tasks

Another important point developed by Havighurst is that certain tasks are learned once and for all, but other tasks recur at different levels of maturity or development. Getting along with other people is an important task that recurs in different forms at different stages. The child of six to ten years is expected to get along with age mates of his own sex. In adolescence, boys and girls are expected to learn how to get along with each other, without however abandoning their previous ability to get along with their own sex. In adulthood, both sexes are expected to learn to cooperate for impersonal purposes and projects. And in old age people are expected to learn to associate with other old people. Thus each stage of development adds a new type of association to those learned before, but at no point is the early learning lost or unneeded.

Other tasks are accomplished only once in a lifetime. Talking and walking are illustrations. The person may increase his capacity for talking and walking and apply the skills in various ways, but the actual physical skills do not need to be learned more than once.

The Continuity of Family Life

An individual is born and dies; but if we think in terms of family, there is no beginning and no end, unless, in some given generation, there are no descendants. Even though one given couple have no children, the family in a larger sense does not die, since married brothers or sisters of the couple may have children who carry on the family inheritance and culture. People who have pride in the idea of family continuity sometimes take great pains to maintain a record of the family tree which traces the generations back for hundreds of years, without a break in continuity. The family continuity is most clear in societies in which the different generations continue to live in the same community, perhaps even in the same households. In old China, such a living arrangement was the accepted thing: each son brought his wife into his father's household and reared his children there as part of a large family group. In time, when the father died, the eldest son became head of the family, or perhaps the brothers separated, each brother to become head of a branch family that continued on down through the generations.

In the United States we often lose this sense of continuity, since at marriage each couple tends to splinter off from the parental families and to set up an independent and autonomous household, sometimes many miles distant from either set of parents.

Nevertheless, family continuity continues in a biological sense. If families of different generations maintain close contact, the continuity also usually incorporates family traditions, values, and customs. In spite of the high degree of mobility in this country, members of many families do remain in close contact with each other. Dr. Duvall reports the following figures, credited to Robert O. Blood, Jr., sociologist, based on a study of Detroit, Michigan, an industrial city where one would expect to find a high degree of mobility. Among 731 Detroit families, 89 per cent had relatives living in the metropolitan area of Detroit. Among these Detroit families, intrafamily visiting was frequent: 29 per cent visited daily, 37 per cent weekly, 20 per cent monthly, and 13 per cent yearly.

Whenever we talk about the developmental stages of an individual family, we are simply dipping into the continuous stream of family life and lifting out a small segment of the total, the experiences of one couple. Stretching out behind them is the family of their parents and grandparents, and reaching into the future is the family of their children and grandchildren. Since couples now tend to marry in the late teens and early twenties and have children before they are thirty, there is a lag of about twenty-five years between equivalent stages of two generations. When one couple are in the twenties, their parents are middle-aged, and the members of the next generation are being born. When the couple are passing into old age, the second generation is middle-aged and the third generation is already leaving home to start yet another generation. Thus there is no end to the continuous flow of family life.

14. LIFE CYCLE PATTERNS IN JAPAN, CHINA, AND THE UNITED STATES

Kiyomi Morioka

§ The life-cycle concept as developed in the United States is only partially applicable to other cultures. Morioka approaches his analysis of the Japanese family life cycle by studying the process of role changes

SOURCE: *Journal of Marriage and the Family*, 29 (August, 1967), 595–606. Reprinted by permission of the publisher and the author. Revised version of a paper originally presented at the Sixth World Congress of Sociology, Evian, France, September, 1966. The author wishes to express his sincere thanks to Professor Akira Ohta of Tokyo Kyoiku University and Mr. and Mrs. Richard J. Smethurst of the University of Michigan for their kind assistance in translation. However, all responsibilities for possible errors remain with the author.

Kiyomi Morioka is associate professor of sociology, Tokyo Kyoiku University, Bunkyoku, Tokyo, Japan.

through the generational cycle. He emphasizes the stem family with its continuity through several generations, but with role changes depending upon whether at a given time the household contains one, two, or three generations. The traditional Chinese family is also linked to intergenerational changes, but in a different way. In contrast, studies of American families are concerned only with role changes in the one-generation nuclear family.

The present paper aims at clarifying characteristics of the life cycle pattern of the Japanese stem family in comparison with that of the Chinese joint family and of the American conjugal family and, by doing so, at widening the scope of the study of family development which has almost totally been confined to the conjugal family so far. The developmental framework should not remain provincial, but be applicable to any family patterns. This paper attempts to demonstrate an extensive cross-cultural applicability of the emerging conceptual framework of family development.

From among a little more than a dozen existing life cycle studies of the Japanese family, three distinctive approaches to the subject can be identified. The three approaches are:

(1) The family composition approach, which emphasizes the changes in household composition and focuses on establishing a series of stages with the aid of a predetermined household typology, as best represented by Takashi Koyama's work.[1]

(2) The approach whereby the life cycle is regarded as a demographic, independent variable. This approach, which is best exemplified

[1] Takashi Koyama, "Cyclical Changes of the Family Composition," in *Ie: Its Structural Analyses*, ed. by Y. Okada and S. Kitano, Tokyo: Sobunsha, 1959, pp. 67–83. This is the first longitudinal study ever attempted by a Japanese sociologist, making use of official documents of an agricultural neighborhood from 1802 to 1861 under the Tokugawa Shogunate which registered people by household for the purpose of religious inspection. Koyama classified a total of 1,556 households appearing in the 60 books (one for each year) into seven types of households, and in each instance he carefully traced the transition of household types from one to another. Moreover, he delineated the main course of the transitions by highlighting the directions of change which occurred most often. The four stages thus made discernible are as follows:

1. The household with collateral relatives. This is a stage in which two couples in the family line cohabitate, the parents being retired and family headship lying with the younger generation. The unmarried sons and daughters are supported by their eldest brother, the family head, and leave the natal home as they marry or establish new branch families under his aid and protection. This stage lasts for 3.4 years on the average.
2. The household with lineal ascendants and descendants. This is also a stage of cohabitation of two couples with the headship in the hands of the younger genera-

by Eitaro Suzuki's pioneer study,[2] accentuates fluctuation in economic activities over a period of several decades in the family life history and elucidates the fact that the Japanese stem family undergoes a definite cycle of prosperity and decline caused by regular changes in the household composition, even though economic conditions outside the family remain the same.

(3) The approach which regards the life cycle as process, focusing attention on the role complex characteristic of each stage and tracing changes in it from the early stage to the later one mainly through a comparison of synchronic cross-sectional data on families in different stages.

The present writer has employed the third approach, for he finds it

---

tion. However, all siblings of the family head have now left home, and only lineal relatives remain. This lasts for 8.5 years.

3. The household with unmarried children. This is the stage in which the parents are dead and the family head and his wife live alone with their unmarried children. The family takes the form of a nuclear family household. This lasts for 8.7 years.

4. The household with married children. This is the stage in which two lineal couples live together, and the family headship is kept by the father rather than by his married heir. When the heir takes over headship, the household shifts back to the first stage and a new cycle starts. This lasts for 2.7 years.

[2] Eitaro Suzuki, *Principles of Japanese Rural Sociology*, Tokyo: Nippon-Hyoron-sha, 1940, pp. 258–262. Also, Suzuki, "On Cyclical Regularity in Generational Development of the Japanese Family," in *Family and Rural Village*, Vol. 2, ed. by T. Toda and E. Suzuki, Tokyo: Nikko-shoin, 1942, pp. 1–50. Suzuki's inspiration came from Russian and American contributions to the subject, in particular from writings by P. A. Sorokin and C. E. Lively. He held that one would be able to identify a recurring cycle in the course of changes in the composition of the stem family if basic demographic information were available. He further maintained that it would be possible to calculate a coefficient of consumption and productivity for each year of family development which would indicate the family's level of living and its changes. His ideas were embodied in a "scheme of cyclical development of the stem family" based on national averages of life expectancy, ages at the first marriage, the number of children, and infant mortality. Regularities he found through this procedure are as follows:

(1) The length of each cycle is 59 years, including two family heads in successive generations.

(2) The family when largest is made up of seven members, and when smallest only three. The average family size during the whole cycle is 4.712 persons, which is close to the 1920 national average.

(3) The family is made up of two generations of parents and children during a period of 40 years (68 percent of one cycle) and of three generations of grandparents, parents, and children for 19 years (32 percent of the cycle). Contrary to popular belief, the Japanese family exists in the form of a two-generation household for a longer period of time than it does in the form of a three-generation household.

(4) The Japanese proverbs which read that "the family reaches its greatest poverty when the eldest son is fifteen" and "the family passes its height of prosperity when the youngest son is fifteen" are confirmed by the findings regarding the fluctuation of the coefficient of consumption and productivity during a cycle.

(5) From the pattern of family development, three types of the Japanese family, namely, joint, stem, and conjugal, are identifiable.

inadequate either to put emphasis on discovering a successive order of stages on the basis of a certain household typology or to try to find the existence of a cyclic regularity in family development without identifying stages; he regards it more important to clarify characteristics of the role complex associated with each stage of the cycle.[3]

A life cycle study of the Japanese family ought to include demarcation of cycle stages as tools for further investigation. In this regard, there arises the problem of how to establish a set of stages which does not merely reflect transformations of a household, but represents major changes in a role complex. Dependence on a ready-made household typology as seen in Koyama's case does not offer a fully satisfactory delineation. One should remember that household typology and stages of a life cycle are of different natures, although they have some important elements in common and hence are interchangeable to a certain extent.

For the task of delineating cycle stages of the Japanese stem family, which is a supragenerational entity, it is necessary, first of all, to set aside the traditional notion of an endless continuation of the family line from generation to generation and instead to direct attention to its discontinuing aspect which has often been hidden from institution-oriented students; such a supragenerational continuance is possible only because couples from two or three generations live together under the same roof with the same family name. Here, with the aid of G. P. Murdock's useful concept of a composite form of the family,[4] the Japanese stem family is viewed as a vertically composite form of nuclear families one from each generation. This position enables us to apply theories of the life cycle developed in the United States to the study of the life cycle of the stem family in Japan and to solve the problem of stage delineation as well.

This idea was substantiated in the writer's first article treating the family life cycle,[5] with numerical data of 1950, according to which the average age at the first marriage was 25.9 for a man and 23.0 for a woman and the average life expectancy of a man was 67.2 and of a woman, 69.8. On the assumption that the first child or the second is an heir, one gets Figure 1. Since time is read from the left of the figure to the right, a horizontal line represents the duration of marriage, and generations come down from the top to the bottom.

[3] A fuller discussion of the three approaches is presented in Kiyomi Morioka, "A Critical Review of Studies in the Family Life Cycle" (2), *International Christian University Journal of Social Sciences*, 5 (September, 1964), pp. 1–26.
[4] George Peter Murdock, *Social Structure*, New York: Macmillan, 1949, p. 2.
[5] Kiyomi Morioka, "A New Approach to the Family Study: Theory and Method of Family Life Cycle," *Monthly Bulletin of Family Courts*, 5:2 (February, 1953), pp. 66–73.

In Figure 1, one can identify with little trouble the following two stages which appear alternately:

1. The period of two nuclear families of parents and the heir.
2. The period of a single nuclear family when parents are dead and the heir in the next generation remains unmarried.

This finding is consonant with Suzuki's view which referred to a cyclical regularity in the recurrence of the two stages.[6] But this preliminary demarcation of stages is inadequate, for the Japanese family is not a mere federation of nuclear families of different generations, but a single social entity that exists for generations. One should proceed further to take into consideration the succession of family headship which symbolizes the lineal continuity of the stem family. With the locus of the family headship as a criterion, life stages can be delineated as follows:

Stage I: Two couples of successive generations cohabitate, but headship lies with the father (from A to Y in Figure 1).

Stage II: The father has either retired or died, and the headship has been transferred to the son (from Y to Z).

Stage III: The mother is dead also, and the nuclear family of the younger generation is left alone. Upon marriage of the heir, the stage is shifted to Stage I (from Z to A).

In this scheme, the period when two nuclear families of the parents

TABLE 1   *Length of Stages in 1930, 1950, and 1960*

STAGE	1930 (in years)	1950 (in years)	1960 (in years)
I	5.5	14.4	15.7
II	4.0	5.5	6.5
III	20.0	7.0	6.8
Total	29.5	26.9	29.0

and the heir overlap is divided into two stages and, thus, the period of a complete stem family household is separated largely from that of an incomplete stem family household. The above three stages can be said to reoccur in the life cycle of the stem family in Japan. Table 1 shows the length of each stage based on Suzuki's data for 1930[7] and

---

[6] See (3) in footnote 3.
[7] The relative lengths of the stages are debatable, because the time of the heir's birth seems to have been much earlier in actuality than Suzuki had supposed in his calculation of lengths of the periods.

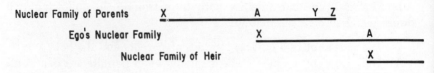

X   Marriage
Y   Death of husband
Z   Death of wife
A   Marriage of heir

FIGURE 1

census data for 1950 and 1960. It is due at least partly to prolonged life expectancy that Stage I has become longer, occupying a little more than half a cycle in 1960, and that Stage III has become correspondingly shorter.

The level of living of the family, as well as the household composition, changes with an advancement in the stages, but more important are the differences in the human relationships characteristic of each stage. In Stage III, human relationships resemble those of the conjugal family, although special treatment toward and expectations of the heir can be fully explained in the context of the stem family. On the other hand, Stages I and II typically manifest the nature of the stem family. Characteristics of human relationships in these stages are focused upon in-law relations.

Stage I is an especially difficult period for a daughter-in-law and also an uncomfortable one for her husband and parents-in-law. Figure 2 illustrates the family composition at the time of receipt of a daughter-in-law. If adjustment between her and other members of her new family is not made, the dotted circle around the nuclear family of the parents-in-law or that of hers tends to become a solid circle. If the adjustment is made, the solid circle around the two nuclear families is completed at the bottom. Adjustment is mainly required of the daughter-in-law, because it is she who is to be adapted to the existing life patterns of the husband's family. But, since others are also required to readjust somewhat, there exists a special source of tension in the family at this stage. Moreover, this is also the stage in which daughters are to be married and sons to be matched and made independent of their parental family. This dual task may be expressed, as Figure 2 shows, in the task of linking generational discontinuity of component nuclear families to lineal continuity of the stem family. It is not an exaggeration to say that the key to understanding the essence of the Japanese stem family (*ie*) lies here.

Next, Stage II is the one in which the young take up leadership and support their aging parents. The position of the young wife is already firmly established, and she assumes the responsibility of taking care of the consumption aspect of the household's life after the retirement of her mother-in-law. Naturally the relationship between mother-in-law and daughter-in-law also changes, and the mother-in-law, especially after the death of her husband, is placed in a weaker position.[8]

In Stage I and the early part of Stage II, the family tends to become

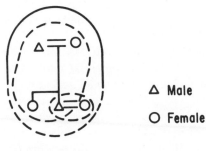

△ Male

O Female

FIGURE 2

prosperous economically and influential politically through the cooperation of father and son. On the other hand, in-law tensions often develop, sometimes leading to family discord or even separation or divorce, and thus economic deterioration ensues. Here the question arises as to why such a composite form of family can persist without disintegrating into component nuclear families in the regular fashion of the Chinese family. The reason is the institutional and ethical requirements placed on the traditional Japanese family, namely, the succession of the family line and the support of aged parents.

Family life cycle studies in the United States elucidate the following circumstance in answer to the present question. American farm families in the latter period of the second stage, in the early period of the third stage, and in the fourth stage—based on the classic four-stage theory —are especially vulnerable to economic stresses.[9] This would be true with Japanese farm families, too, if they retained the form of a nuclear family household without becoming a stem family household. In fact, economic stress would be felt much more strongly in general by Japanese

[8] Paragraphs describing in-law relations over-represent the prewar situation where a young wife was subjugated to her mother-in-law, accordingly more or less distorting the postwar picture. Nowadays the lengthened period of Stage I is balanced with the lessened control of a housewife over her daughter-in-law.

[9] G. W. Blackwell, "Correlates of Stages of Family Development among Farm Families on Relief," *Rural Sociology*, 7:2 (June, 1942), pp. 161–174.

farm families than by their American counterparts. (This is understandable, if one remembers that the ratio per capita in production of calories between Japanese and American farmers was 100 to 1,060 for the period of 1926–1940.) In those days when the oldest child is about 15 years of age, a family is confronted with the heavy economic burden of bringing up children (the first period of financial pinch), and after the children have become married, the aged parents are not strong enough physically or financially to support themselves (the second period of pinch). In order to surmount these two financial squeezes, a family often needs social relief, but in Japan the popular way of living during these periods is to have the two nuclear families of parents and the heir cohabitate, sharing a single livelihood. The family overcomes these economic crises effectively, because the parents in the second pinch help their son in the first pinch by taking care of the grandchildren or providing extra hands for chores and family enterprises, while the son helps the aged parents by supporting them. In other words, the stem family performs the function of *concomitant mutual insurance*, in addition to that of mutual insurance between the parents and the son with an interval of about 30 years. This interpretation is applicable not only to farmers but perhaps to those engaging in other industries of low productivity, and provides a partial answer to why the stem family system continues.

The Life Cycle Pattern of the Conjugal Family and of the Joint Family

A considerable number of life cycle studies of the conjugal family have been made in the United States since the early 1930's. In this section, the present writer will begin by summarizing American achievements insofar as they are relevant to his comparative review and then proceed to a discussion of life cycle patterns of the joint family as exemplified by the traditional Chinese family, making use of reports of firsthand studies conducted by Japanese scholars during the military invasion of the mainland of China.

The American Family

When the conjugal family does not take any composite form during its life span, it has a predictable natural history—from its formation at marriage, through the usual process of expansion and contraction in the number of positions and interpersonal relations, to total disappearance at the death of the original couple. One reason that scholars began life cycle studies of the conjugal family fairly early is the predictability of the history of this type of family which recurs with each newly married couple. On the other hand, life cycle studies in Japan developed later because of the difficulty of defining the life cycle of the stem family, which appears to have no predictable course of development and finality other than constant loss and addition of members.

Although there were some American scholars who observed variables in terms of the duration of marriage,[10] many divided the family cycle into stages of growth and development. The number of stages and criteria by which they delineated stages varied according to the various intentions of research. But generally speaking, studies in the 1930's and 1940's undertaken mostly by rural sociologists divided the cycle into four stages: the prechild family, the growing family, the contracting family, and the aging family. An appellation of stages was not, however, always the same.[11] Since about 1950, scholars have tended to identify six or more stages, probably in reflection of a shift of interest from household composition and the accompanying level of prosperity to more microscopic aspects of family life such as buying patterns, saving patterns, mobility patterns, role complex, and social participation including contact with relatives. This shift was concomitant with the spread of the use of this approach from rural sociology, where it had developed originally, to the study of urban families also.

The essential features of existing studies in this field are well-known to us elsewhere.[12] It would be enough, therefore, to pay passing attention to one of the latest investigations, that of Reuben Hill, which deserves special note. He developed an elaborate set of nine stages of the life cycle employing three criteria: numbers of positions in the family, the age composition as represented by the developmental stages of the oldest child, and the retirement of the husband-father from active employment. The stages thus differentiated are: I. Establishment (newly married, childless); II. New Parents (infant to three years); III. Preschool Family (child three to six years and possibly younger siblings); IV. School-Age Family (oldest child six to 12 years, possibly younger siblings); V. Family with Adolescent (oldest 13-19, possibly younger siblings); VI. Family with Young Adult (oldest 20, until first child leaves home); VII. Family as Launching Center (from departure of first to last child); VIII. Postparental Family, The Middle Years

[10] C. E. Lively, *The Growth Cycle of the Farm Family*, Mimeographed Bulletin No. 51, Wooster: Ohio Agricultural Experiment Station, 1932, pp. 1–22. Allen Beegle and Charles P. Loomis, "Life Cycles of Farm, Rural-Nonfarm, and Urban Families in the United States as Derived from Census Materials," *Rural Sociology*, 13:1 (March, 1948), pp. 70–74.
[11] Pitirim A. Sorokin, Carle C. Zimmerman, and C. J. Galpin, *A Systematic Source Book in Rural Sociology*, Vol. 2, Minneapolis: University of Minnesota Press, 1931, pp. 30–32. Lively, *op. cit.*; C. P. Loomis, "The Study of the Life Cycle of Families," *Rural Sociology*, 1:2 (June, 1936), pp. 180–199; and Blackwell, *op. cit.*
[12] Reuben Hill and Roy H. Rodgers, "The Developmental Approach," in *Handbook of Marriage and the Family*, ed. by Harold T. Christensen, Chicago: Rand McNally, 1964, pp. 171–211.

(after the children have left home until father retires); IX. Aging Family (after retirement of father). Hill views these stages of the family life cycle as distinctive in role complexes, anticipating peculiar types of family interaction for each of them.[13] What he has found from a comparative study of three generations of the same family lines would be changes in the decision-making pattern among the three groups—grandparents, parents, and married children—rather than over the life cycle. Nevertheless, the framework of the family cycle opens up the way for insights into changes taking place over the life span of the family.

Of the three sets of data as criteria, the first serves mainly to delineate the first and last stages in which the couple studied is childless, the second to demarcate the middle stages, and the third to divide the last stage into two parts, before and after retirement. While the third criterion represents a new approach to the study of the expanding post-parental stage, the first two criteria have been applied before. The first, the most basic criterion, is quite simple to apply; but the second one, the age composition of the family, includes judgments as to which series of developmental stages of which child are best applied. The variety of stage delineations stems mainly from differences in these judgments.[14] Many, including Hill, used the oldest child; but some used all children,[15] and still others, the youngest child as the key child.[16]

In the demarcation of stages of the Japanese family, the first criterion has been employed in combination with the third, the retirement of the father from the position of family head, which is closely linked to his giving up active participation in the family enterprise. However, the content of the first criterion is not the same in Japanese and American families. In American conjugal families, expansion and contraction in the number of positions occur exclusively in the younger generation and not in the parents, because broken families are eliminated from the study of the life cycle.[17] On the contrary, changes in the number of positions take place in every generation in the Japanese family, and the changes in the number of positions which are relevant to stage delineation are confined to those in the family line—to the marriage of the heir and the addition of his wife to an existing household, to

---

[13] Hill, *op. cit.*, pp. 116–117.

[14] E. L. Kirkpatrick, R. Tough, and M. L. Cowles, *The Life Cycle of the Farm Family in Relation to its Standards of Living and Ability to Provide*, Research Bulletin 121, Madison: University of Wisconsin Agricultural Experiment Station, 1934, pp. 1–38. Blood and Wolfe, *op. cit.*

[15] Anderson, *op. cit.*, Part I, pp. 7–8.

[16] John B. Lansing and Leslie Kish, "Family Life Cycle as an Independent Variable," *American Sociological Review*, 22:5 (October, 1957), pp. 512–519.

[17] An exception is the conceptualization by R. H. Rodgers in his paper, *Improvements in the Construction and Analysis of Family Life Cycle Categories*, Kalamazoo: Western Michigan University, 1962.

the death of the father, and later to that of the mother. The minor importance of noting changes in the number of the younger family members reduces the importance of the second criterion. This is not because the second criterion is regarded as unessential, but simply because its application would make the resultant set of stages too complicated. A similar consideration has prevented us from including changes in the number of the younger family members in the first criterion. The recent and rapid changes in the Japanese family, however, demand a reformulation of the stages by an application of the second criterion. This will be discussed later in more detail.

The Traditional Chinese Family

The Chinese family to be discussed here is not the present-day family under the Communist regime, but the past one under Japanese military occupation. Thus, what is meant by the word "traditional" differs from the meaning intended by an American authority on the Chinese family.[18]

The Chinese family is a patrilineal, patrilocal family which can include all male descendants from common ancestors and their wives and children. However, this kind of very large household cannot endure for a long period of time, and family dissolution is inevitable. Since the Chinese family underwent steady growth as well as disintegration in almost every generation, it is obvious that the period from one disintegration to the next can be designated as the life span of a cycle. One cycle beginning with a nuclear family household may be divided into the following four stages:

I. The stage of a nuclear family household from the time it is formed to the marriage of its oldest son.
II. The stage of a stem family household from the time of the marriage of the oldest son to that of the second.
III. The stage of a joint family household from the time of the marriage of the second son to the death of his parents.
IV. The stage of a joint family household without common ancestors who are still alive.

In Stage I there is no in-law relation living in the family. This comes into being in Stage II and becomes more and more complicated in Stage III with the addition of the son's wife who comes from a different clan, usually from a remote place. In spite of the existence of possibilities for internal discord, a family in Stage III is relatively stable because of the effective control exercised by the family head, the

[18] Marion J. Levy, Jr., *The Family Revolution in Modern China*, Cambridge: Harvard University Press, 1949, pp. 41–42.

father. Stage IV, on the other hand, reveals a marked decline in the power of the family head over his younger brothers and sisters-in-law, and consequently, various forms of inner tension are manifested which finally lead to the splitting-up. The fact that most constituent family units have passed the first period of financial squeeze during this period and now are not so vulnerable may facilitate dissolution. It has been reported, however, that some families break down in Stage III before the death of the parents, and that many disintegrate in the latter part of the same stage, namely, after the death of the father while the mother is still alive. It is not a fixed rule, therefore, that an expanded family reaches its eventual dissolution in Stage IV. But, in view of the institutional requirement not to divide family property before the death of the parents, it is reasonable to set up the fourth stage. After this last stage, some constituent families begin a new cycle with Stage I and others with Stages II or III, depending on the degree of maturity of each family unit at that time.

Since averages of the age at the first marriage, of the number of sons born to a wife, and of life expectancy are not available for Chinese, the average length of each stage cannot be calculated. Instead, the writer presents one example of family development, which appears in the reports prepared by Megumi Hayashi [19] and which is the only relevant example the present writer has ever seen. It is the life history of the Wongs, a wealthy peasant family in an agricultural village in central China. In 1915 when the Wongs broke up into component family units, the whole family was in Stage IV, and the four independent families produced upon dissolution were all in Stage I, only one being childless. Hayashi traced the development of the family of the oldest brother, who had been the head of the family before it broke up, from 1915. In 1930, i.e., 15 years after the dissolution, his family was in Stage III and consisted of four nuclear families, one of his own and the others of his three sons. In the ten years following, he and his wife died and three independent nuclear households, those of his sons, appeared. Although the reports do not tell us whether the family disintegration occurred after the death of the parents or before, one can identify the stages of development through which the Wongs passed during the period of a quarter of a century. Those are Stages IV, I, II, III, IV, and I or IV, I, II, III, and I.

Why do all married sons of the Chinese family remain in the parental household with their wives and children? Answers to this question can

[19] Megumi Hayashi, "A Study of the Equal Division Inheritance in Chinese Peasant Families," in *Main Issues of Contemporary Sociology*, ed. by M. Hayashi *et al.*, Tokyo: Kobundo, 1949, pp. 65–119. Also, Hayashi, "A Study of Large and Small Families Viewed from Population Census of Chinese Peasants," in *Main Issues of Sociology*, ed. by K. Komatsu *et al.*, Tokyo: Yuhikaku, 1954, pp. 37–73.

be readily found in the Chinese custom of emphasizing dutiful service to one's parents and faithful performance of ancestor worship. But these ethical or religious motivations have economic and political foundations. The joint family household is preferred, because it can maintain the wealth of a family and its social status, which is dependent on the size of the family fortune, by preventing the partition of family property among the male descendants. It is also preferred for the accumulation of property which is facilitated by its efficient system of division of labor in production and by its economization of living expenses. It can furnish help with relative ease for the aged, the ill, the crippled, and the infirm. Further, in the days when political and military unrest prevailed, a large family far excelled a small family with only a single male adult in performing the role of protection and defense. These economic and political benefits in combination with the institutional requirements seem to have fostered the joint family system in China.

We have another question: Why does the Chinese family usually fail to maintain a joint family household over the generations, in spite of the negative sanction given to dissolution and the actual benefits derived from living together? The answers are both social-psychological and legal. Firstly, the failure is due partly to the tendency on the part of each component family unit to cohere within itself. (Naturally, there are institutional safeguards to defend the joint family against this tendency and to discourage cohesion of component units.) Secondly, the failure is due also to the legal right of male offspring to inherit an equally divided portion of family fortune. The fortune of a joint family is the accrued property, part of which each son assumes he will obtain sooner or later. The institution of equal division coupled with the coherence of constituent family units forms the basic impetus for family dissolution.

An explanation of cyclical dissolution of the Chinese family cannot be complete without a mention of the conditions that promote the aforesaid impetus. Those come from various types of internal discord. Japanese scholars in field interviews with Chinese peasants obtained the following as the conditions that led to dissolution.[20] Obviously, the first listed is the most important.

1. Quarrels among sisters-in-law, often over children or the unequal contributions of their husbands to the household.
2. Discord between mother-in-law and daughter-in-law.
3. Disharmony among brothers because of discrepancies in a variety of areas such as the degree of financial success, idleness versus diligence, frugality versus extravagance, and personal opinions.

[20] Noboru Niida, *Chinese Peasant Families*, Tokyo: University of Tokyo Press, 1952. Tomoo Uchida, *Family Dissolution in Rural China*, Tokyo: Iwanami-shoten, 1956.

Sometimes, brothers' quarrels reflected those existing between their wives.

4. Tension between father and son, often closely linked to discord between mother-in-law and daughter-in-law.
5. Poverty. In cases where it was difficult to make a living, frustration on the part of sons or brothers tended to become so intense that the family was ready to find an outlet in quarrels.
6. Numerous family members, especially brothers. The existence of many brothers resulted in the inclusion of many sisters-in-law and complicated in-law relationships in the household. This was fertile soil for all manner of domestic discord.

Well-to-do families preferred to maintain themselves over generations without dissolution for reasons given in a foregoing paragraph. However, the larger the family size became and the more complicated the household composition, the greater the possibility for disharmony to occur and to lead to eventual disintegration. It was just for the purpose of avoiding such tensions that wealthy families had rules of avoidance or reserve and applied them as rigidly as possible.

The developmental cycle of the Chinese family suggests that the Japanese family would often fail to endure beyond a generation if all sons with their wives and children stayed in the natal household. A married son other than the heir may remain in the parental home, but only until the establishment of a new branch family.[21] It is the son's destiny to leave home before, at, or shortly after marriage and to find his own fortune, usually with financial aid from parents or the eldest brother, who lives with the parents and inherits almost all the property left by the former head. The institution to discourage all married sons except the heir from staying in the parental home for a long period of time minimizes possible in-law conflicts which are harmful for the continuation of the *ie*, the supragenerational entity. In this sense, the institution of primogeniture is a functional part of the stem family of Japan; and, similarly, that of equal division of property among coparceners is functionally linked to the cyclical growth and dissolution of the joint family of China.

Comparative Remarks

Some comparative remarks have been made in the previous section. Here, the life cycle pattern of each of the major family types will be reviewed in terms of household types, and then the changes in the life

---

[21] It is reported that joint family households existed very often in Japan's remote underdeveloped districts in the early part of the Edo Period (1603–1867). They were, however, not joint-family-oriented but represented a variety of the stem family with a prolonged stay of married cadets in their parental households.

cycle pattern of the contemporary Japanese families will be discussed from the cross-cultural standpoint.

Family Types, Household Types, and Life Cycle Patterns

Employing composition as the criterion, the present writer classifies households into three types: the nuclear family household with no married offspring, the stem family household with a single married son or daughter, and the joint family household with two or more married offspring in one generation. Household is an actual manifestation, regulated by conditions of time and place, of the family as an institution. Household and family are not identical, but separate and yet interrelated orders. For example, the emergence of more nuclear family households does not necessarily indicate expanding support for the value of the conjugal family system.

With institutional orientation concerning household composition as the criterion, one can set up three family types, i.e., the conjugal family, the stem family, and the joint family, which have been employed in the present paper from the outset. As already suggested, a particular family type does not always take the form of a particular, seemingly corresponding household type. But, there is an undeniable link, of course, making exact correspondence likely. This correspondence can be explained by reference to the stages of the life cycle.

1. The conjugal family manifests itself mainly in the nuclear family household, seldom in the stem family household except in its incomplete form, and virtually never in the joint family household. The forms which a family takes over its life span are within the range of the nuclear family household.
2. The stem family demonstrates itself best in the stem family household, but often takes the form of a nuclear family household during its life cycle. It also occasionally appears as a joint family household but only when the married second or third son stays home temporarily. In Japan the intervention of a joint family household in a stem family household stage was more common formerly than today when the custom of married cadets remaining in the home has come to extinction.
3. The joint family demonstrates itself typically in the joint family household, but also takes the form of a stem family household when the family has only one married son. It also appears as a nuclear family household for some years immediately following the dissolution of the joint family household.[22]

[22] Kiyomi Morioka, "Structure and Functioning of the Family," in *Family, Rural Village and City*, ed. by T. Fukutake *et al.*, Tokyo: University of Tokyo Press, 1957, p. 27.

Figure 3 summarizes the foregoing discussion. Since this figure is a device to describe the transformation of the stem family, it does not fit the conjugal family or the joint family as satisfactorily. However, it is useful in showing the relationship of family types, household types, and life cycle patterns.

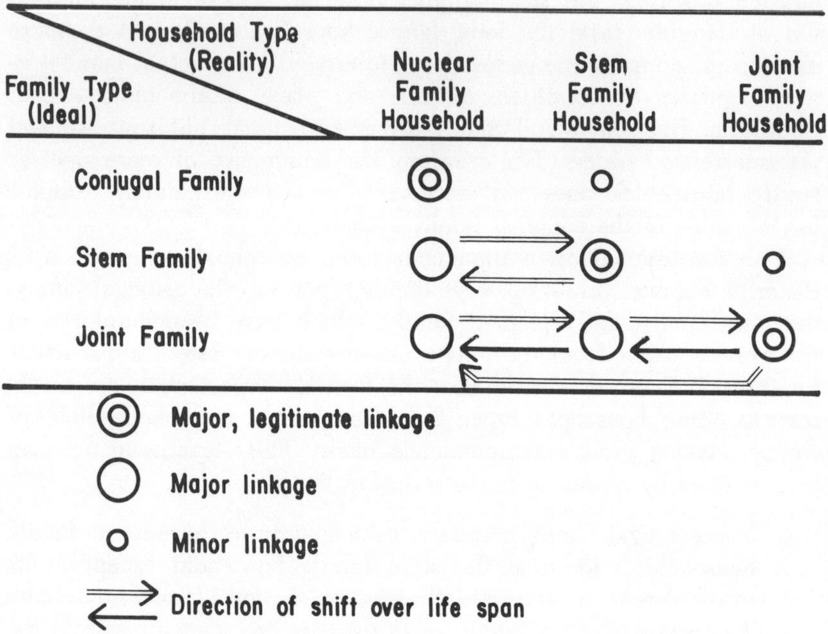

FIGURE 3

The Changing Japanese Family and Its Life Cycle Pattern

In the previous subsection the present writer discussed tendencies of shifts in household types during the life span of a family, keeping the family type as a constant. With respect to changes in the family type, Conrad M. Arenberg has pointed out the irreversible trend of a shift from joint families to stem families and again from stem families to small (conjugal) families.[23] We can add the Japanese family to the list of examples in which a shift from the stem to the conjugal family has occurred or is occurring.

The conjugal family made inroads into Japan with official support

[23] Conrad M. Arenberg, "The American Family in the Perspective of Other Cultures," in *Selected Studies in Marriage and the Family*, ed. by Robert F. Winch *et al.*, New York: Holt, Rinehart and Winston, 1962, pp. 40–49.

in the wake of the last world war and has received widespread support. But it is hazardous to conclude that the traditional concept of the stem family has been displaced by this new pattern. There are rural-urban and generational variations in the attitudes toward this new concept of the family as illustrated in Takashi Koyama's comparative study of three districts in Tokyo.[24] The conjugal family is popular in cities, and the younger generation is particularly enthusiastic about it. On the other hand, farmers and others with family enterprises handed down from forebears tend to adhere to the stem family. Naturally, the aged are suspicious of or even hostile toward this new invader. Even middle-aged urban white-collar workers who are converts to the new doctrine still retain some of the behavior patterns characteristic of the stem family. On the whole, we may say that the Japanese family is in a period of transition from the stem to the conjugal family.[25]

The changing status of the Japanese family permits us to compare it and the American family with regard to ages of wives at important events in the family's life. Table 2 is compiled from a combination

TABLE 2 *Ages of Wives at Important Events*

IMPORTANT EVENTS	UNITED STATES		JAPAN	
	1940	1950	1950	1960
First marriage	21.6	20.1	23.0	24.4
(Husband)	(24.3)	(22.8)	(25.9)	(27.2)
Birth of first child	22.6			26.3
Birth of last child	27.2	26.1		28.7
Marriage of first child	45.6			52.1
Marriage of last child	50.1	47.6		54.5
Death of husband	60.9	61.4	64.3	69.1
Death of wife	73.5	77.2	69.8	75.6

of the numerical data prepared by Paul C. Glick on the American family [26] and my own materials on the Japanese family.

Although this table does not provide us with information which is completely comparable, nobody will miss some parallel trends in both

[24] Takashi Koyama, (ed.), *A Study of Contemporary Families in Japan*, Tokyo: Kobundo, 1960, pp. 67–72.
[25] This view is not shared by some Japanese family sociologists including Kizaemon Ariga, who claims that the stem family of Japan is substantially maintained despite the impacts of the reformed postwar Civil Code and rapid industrialization since 1950. See K. Ariga, *The Japanese Family*, Tokyo: Shibundo. 1965, pp. 1–57.
[26] Paul C. Glick, "The Family Cycle," *American Sociological Review*, 12:2 (April, 1947), pp. 164–174. Also, Glick, "The Life Cycle of the Family," *Marriage and Family Living*, 17:1 (February, 1955), pp. 3–9.

countries. One is the decrease in the length of the childbearing period, which is astonishing if the 1890 data for the U.S.A. are presented for comparison and which is undeniable with regard to Japan also, even though data for 1950 on this point are lacking. Another is the remarkable expansion of the postparental period resulting from lengthened life expectancy and the shortened period of time for having children. In the United States the age at the time of marriage is another contributing factor to this trend, while in Japan it is a negative factor. Except for age at marriage, the American and the Japanese family reveal a similar trend so far as numerical data in Table 2 are concerned.

Another study which the present state of the Japanese family urges us to attempt is a reformulation of the set of life cycle stages. The one the present writer developed more than a dozen years ago is apt for the stem family, but not useful for the conjugal family. A new set should be applicable to both types; otherwise it cannot be useful for a study of the contemporary Japanese family which is changing from the stem to the conjugal family.

The procedure followed in the setting up of a new set of stages was, first of all, to divide a concrete family into component nuclear units and to record the number of units on the family line with the Roman numerals I, II, and II. ("I" means that the family is a nuclear family household, for example.) Then, eight stages of development were distinguished for each component nuclear unit and represented with the letters O, A, B, C, D, E, F, and G as follows: Stage O (a newly married couple, prechild period); Stage A (the oldest child being an infant to six years old, preschool period); Stage B (the oldest child being seven to 12 years old, grade-school period); Stage C (the oldest child being 13 to 18 years old, middle-school period); Stage D (the oldest child being 19 years old or over until the last child leaves home, launching period); Stage E (after the last child has left home and until the father retires, postparental period); Stage F (after the father has retired and until his death, aging period); Stage G (after the father has died and until the mother's death). This new set of cycle stages is obtained on the basis of Reuben Hill's three criteria and, therefore, it is, in substance, a Japanese translation of his nine stages.[27]

Then Roman numerals and letters were combined to designate household composition and stages of development of each component nuclear unit, as exemplified in the following lines:

IB: A nuclear family household in the grade-school period.
IIF-C: A stem family household with parents in the aging period and the son's nuclear unit in the middle-school period.

[27] Hill, *op. cit.*

IIG-D-A: A stem family household with a widowed grandmother, parents in the launching period, and the son's nuclear unit in the preschool period.

This new categorization is useful in describing the developmental status of particular families and in tracing in what generational combination of stages the shift from the stem to the conjugal family tends to occur. In a longitudinal panel study of about 50 stem family households in an agricultural neighborhood, in which this set of stages was applied, the present writer found that the departure of married heirs from parental households, which undermines the stem family, took place fairly often, however, only in the earlier stages of development, in O, A, or at latest B, and when the parents were in D, E, or F. In other words, pressures that bind a married heir to the natal household weaken during the period when his oldest child is about ten years old or under and his parents are still active enough to live without their son's help.[28] If the heir has taken advantage of this period and left for a job in a large urban center, which pays far more than farming, nobody can exactly predict, under present conditions of Japanese industrial growth and ideological climate, whether he will eventually return to his old home. He may come home to take care of his aged parents on the farm, or he may stay in town and have his parents join him if he is successful in business. When a farm family is uprooted, the concept of the stem family will gradually decline and fade away. This is because the primary props of the stem family of Japan are assumed to be family property and/or family enterprise handed down from the forefathers and the mutual aid network of the neighborhood in which families are interlocked by an endless number of payments and repayments over the generations.

Conclusion

The developmental framework is applicable not only to the conjugal family, but also to the Japanese stem family and the Chinese joint family. It serves to uncover the role complex unique to each of them as well as characteristic of each stage of their life cycle, and it brings to light the interrelatedness and differences between a family typology and a household typology. One should remember here that the applicability and usefulness of this framework has been achieved by the view that the stem family and the joint family (household) are composite forms of the nuclear family.

[28] Kiyomi Morioka, "Family Change and Reformulation of Cycle Stages," *International Christian University Journal of Social Sciences*, 6 (October, 1965), pp. 317–349.

This framework is useful also for capturing changes of the family pattern as occurring in present-day Japan. This is one of the most promising tools in our hands for conducting a cross-cultural study of changing family structure under the impact of modernization, if some longitudinal techniques, preferably segmented longitudinal panels with controls,[29] are used instead of cross-sectional data gathering.

[29] Hill and Rodgers, *op. cit.*, pp. 205–206.

Chapter 6: Differences between Men and Women

15. WHY WOMEN LIVE LONGER THAN MEN

Selig Greenberg

§ One of the mysteries of the normal life expectancy is that the average length of life of women is at least six years longer than that of men. One result of this difference is that many more women than men lose their marriage partners by death. Under present conditions, middle and old age bring widowhood to many women, who then must adjust to a single and often lonely existence after the partnership of marriage. The period of widowhood is prolonged because of the custom of women marrying men who are several years older than themselves.

Mr. Greenberg examines first physical and then social reasons that contribute to the shorter lives of men. At the end of his article he suggests two unconventional solutions to the prevalence of widowhood.

For some time now American women have been gaining on the men —at least in numbers. Back in 1930, the men in this country outnumbered the women by about a million and a half. Today the women hold a lead of about the same size, and the Census Bureau is predicting that by 1975 they will be ahead of the men by perhaps as many as 3,600,000.

One explanation is the decline in immigration, which at one time brought millions of single men into the country. Another—and more significant—is that American females have developed a habit of outliving the men; and recent figures indicate that the gap between life span of the sexes is widening steadily.

For example, at the turn of the century, the average American woman

SOURCE: *Harper's Magazine*, 215 (October, 1957), 70–73. Copyright © 1957 by Harper's Magazine, Inc. Reprinted by permission of the author.

The author has been on the staff of the Providence, Rhode Island, *Journal-Bulletin* since he graduated from Brown University. He specializes in articles on medical science.

lived two years and ten months longer than the average man. Today she is outliving him by more than six years. If she is typical, she will not die until she is a little over seventy-three years and six months old—which gives her the longest life expectancy of any women in the world.

The men in her family, however, can expect to last only a few months past sixty-seven. The men of seven other countries do better than that —Dutchmen, Israelis, Norwegians, Swedes, New Zealanders, Danes, and Britons, in that order. At birth a boy in Holland can look forward to outliving the average American boy by more than three years. Furthermore, the older the American grows, the worse his prospects look. By the time he is forty, his life expectancy is poorer than that of the men of fifteen other nations; and at fifty his chances of living another ten years are 24 per cent less than they would be if he were an Italian and 55 per cent less than if he were a Swede.

These facts foreshadow some interesting changes in American society —in our courting and marriage habits, family life, the job market, and even politics. But before we try to figure out what is likely to happen as a result of the growing surplus of women, it might be well to look at two other questions:

(1) Why do women—traditionally regarded as the weaker sex—live so much longer than men?
(2) Why has their life expectancy increased so much more than that of American males during the past few decades?

The answer to the first is easy, if not flattering to the male ego. Except for their greater muscular strength—which is no longer the asset it was in the Good Old Days of sweaty physical toil and hand-to-hand combat—men actually are the *weaker* sex. In most species, the female outlives the male. Among humans, nature compensates for this by arranging to have 105 boys born for every 100 girls. The proportion of male babies conceived is even larger than this, but their greater vulnerability makes its appearance even before birth. More boy babies fail to come to full term and are lost through miscarriages. The ratio of boys born with congenital malformations is also larger.

Even the normal boy baby has a physiological disadvantage, compared to the normal girl baby, from the very start. A girl is born with two complete X-chromosomes—the minute hereditary particles that substantially influence the fate of the organism—while boys have only one. As she grows older, she has a higher count of white blood cells which help to combat infections. And a woman's glandular system is superior to a man's. Her thyroid is larger, and her pituitary—the master gland which controls the body's over-all hormone productions—enlarges during pregnancy and remains somewhat larger from then on. This bolsters the performance of her adrenal glands, enabling her to resist stress more effectively; it keeps her blood pressure at a lower level and gives her greater tolerance for fatigue and illness. The female sex hormones apparently protect their owner against arterial disorders by helping to keep down the fat content of the blood. This may account for the fact that hardening of the arteries and subsequent heart disease are comparatively rare among women until after the menopause when the output of ovarian hormones drops off sharply.

The death rate is higher for males in every age group; but particularly in early adulthood and middle age. The initial male superiority in numbers lasts through the age of twenty-four. From that point on, the females in any given generation pull ahead, and their plurality gets progressively larger with the years. Last year there were 103.9 boys for every 100 girls in the age group under eighteen in the United States. In the eighteen to twenty-four category, males still predominated slightly. But in the twenty-five to forty-four group there were only 96.6 men for every 100 women, and in the sixty-five plus category, 85.7.

The Built-in Medicine Chest

Biologists reason that women's physiological advantages are nature's way of ensuring that the race will be carried on. A pregnant woman needs special reserves of strength. Her heart, for example, must be strong enough to meet both the ordinary needs of her own body and those of the developing fetus. Her lungs must supply her blood with extra oxygen. Every organ in her body must be able to work at a higher pitch. Because of this, one authority claims, women are provided with "better internal medicine chests" than men.

In any case, almost every disease kills more men than women. The only exceptions are diabetes and what the professional calls sex-specific conditions—like childbirth and cancer of the breast and genital organs. But diabetes, while it cannot be cured, is now relatively easy to control; in the last two decades alone deaths of mothers during childbirth have been slashed from eighty-five to five for every 10,000 live births; and encouraging progress has been made in the cancer field.

Here, too, women are doing better than men. Not only is the mortality rate from all forms of cancer about 5 per cent higher for men; the female cancer rate has been gradually declining while the male rate has remained static in some forms of the disease and risen in others. The overall cancer mortality rate among women has dropped 10 per cent in the past fifteen years. In the same period, male fatalities from cancer of the lung and respiratory system have nearly tripled. One explanation may be that female cancers are usually easier to detect,

more accessible, and more amenable to treatment; another possibility is
that women are more apt to seek prompt medical advice when they
discover any suspicious symptoms.

Nevertheless, the cancer picture is only one part of a larger picture
which follows the same pattern. Although there are now about 1,500,000
more women than men in the United States, 200,000 more men than
women have died annually in recent years. Diseases of the heart, blood
vessels, and kidneys are about two and a half times more prevalent
among men than women in the middle-aged group and account for well
over 100,000 more male than female deaths each year. The male death
rate from arteriosclerotic heart diseases is some 75 per cent higher than
the female.

So we come to our second question: Why is the difference between
the life spans of the sexes becoming wider in this country? The answer
to this is hard to document, for it involves many intangibles. But I
believe that, in addition to their biological superiority, women are
psychologically better able to adapt themselves to the strains of our
highly competitive society—that it is, in effect, easier to be a woman
than a man in mid-twentieth century America.

The Pace That Kills

It is fashionable these days to say that American men are dying
prematurely because they drive themselves beyond endurance to get
things for their women. This broad and pat generalization can be neither
proved nor disproved. What can be proved is that the modern American
man is subject to a multitude of special pressures and frustrations, and
that there has been a fundamental change in his position in society. Yet
society still expects him to be the strong, silent male of tradition, above
the temper tantrums and tears with which women help to dissipate and
relieve their tensions. Since he has been trained to believe that it is
unmanly to be too vocal about his feelings, the man tends to bury them
as much as he can.

Medical authorities suspect that the damaging effect of such inhibition
may be one reason why five times as many men as women die of
stomach and duodenal ulcers which are attributable, at least in part, to
excessive tension. And three times as many men as women commit
suicide every year. (It must be said that more women *try* to kill themselves, but a large proportion of them bungle the job—either because
they are less efficient than men, or because they never really meant to
go through with it.)

In the decades which have marked women's increasing life expectancy,
there has been a significant shift in the pattern of the American family
—a shift which includes new concepts of the husband-wife relation-

ship, the raising of children, and the management of the home. All these things, combined with the competitiveness of American life, have undermined the American man's sense of security. No longer king of the roost, the undisputed authority in his own house, he is ridden with anxieties, and some of the strongest are fears of sexual inadequacy.

It has become generally accepted in our society that the wife is expected to receive as well as give pleasure in sexual intercourse. While this frequently makes for a more deeply satisfying relationship, it is also apt to put a strain on the man, for whom sexual performance has always been something of a testing and a challenge. As he grows older, the inevitable decline in his potency can become a source of deep-seated insecurity. In other societies, where age increased rather than decreased social prestige and where the man's position in the community as well as the home was stable, the falling off of sexual powers did not represent so grave a threat to self-esteem. But since America has never developed these comforting traditions, too many of our men feel compelled to prove themselves as they age by increased activity in other spheres, often to the detriment of their physical and emotional health.

Compare this with the situation facing modern American women. They have been liberated both from the Victorian taboos regarding sex and from most of the perils of childbirth. The vast majority of them have also come to accept the planning of families so that there are very few women today, as there were in the past, who are exhausted by childbearing before thirty.

It would be fatuous to deny that women, too, are confronted with difficult problems of adjustment, especially in regard to their still shifting position in our society. But on the whole they have things a whole lot easier than their mates. Ironically, man-made mores, stemming from the days when women were still in short supply in this country, are at least partially responsible. An American woman still expects—and generally receives—from the men around her certain considerations which, while they flatter the man's vanity, also put an added strain on him.

Far more than men, women are able to set their own pace. It is acceptable for them either to remain at home—where mechanical appliances and the easy availability of processed foods have vastly lightened the burden of housekeeping—or to take a job. And even when they work they are usually spared the grinding pressure to get to the top of the ladder which bears upon most men. Moreover, a woman who is taking care of a house is pretty sure to get a full daily quota of regular exercise, while her husband leads an essentially sedentary life and sometimes kills himself by sporadic bouts of strenuous physical activity. Then, too, as she grows older, a woman can taper off her work gradually; but her husband, in whom the whole aging process starts later, is apt to be brought suddenly face to face with the devastating jolt of retirement.

Women to Burn?

Whatever the causes, there are at present no signs that the trend in the life expectancy of the sexes will change—and the repercussions of a growing majority of women upon our society are certain to be formidable. Inevitably, the influence of women on social and political action will grow; they will control more and more of the nation's wealth (a sizable proportion of it is already in their hands); and they will invade the job market in greater and greater numbers, out of both economic and psychological necessity.

At present there are 7,600,000 widows in the United States, a good proportion of them in their early fifties and many in a precarious economic position. Even those who are financially comfortable face years of loneliness and frustration, and their chances of remarriage—never very strong—are growing steadily slimmer as the male deficit increases. For many of these women, a job may provide at least a partial solution. But we will still be faced with the rising number of women over sixty-five. The Census Bureau predicts that this group of women over the retirement age will climb at the rate of about two million per decade.

We may also expect that the surplus of women of marriageable age, not yet too serious, will begin to soar, and that it will become harder and harder for a girl to marry if she has not done so by a fairly early age. What the effect of more spinsterhood will be upon our morals and how great a threat it will present to the monogamous marriage system is hard to say, but we will undoubtedly be hearing more about it. Already a Tennessee state senator has introduced a bill to legalize polygamy as a means of alleviating the surplus of women, and Dr. Marion Langer, a sociologist specializing in marriage counseling, recently advised girls not to worry about cradle-snatching.

The best way to avoid being widowed, she suggested, is to "marry a man five, six, or seven years your junior." She conceded, however, that under existing conditions a girl might have a hard time snaring a younger man and concluded by saying that our society has only two possible solutions to the mounting man shortage—polygamy or finding some way to lengthen man's life expectancy.

It is unlikely that we will ever adopt her first alternative. But her second involves almost as radical a modification in our mores and way of life. The male would have to jettison his cult of manliness and abandon his illusion of biological superiority. And the female would have to give up her demand for special consideration and accept the responsibilities of her greater stamina. The shock to both egos might be severe. All the same it is a possibility worth trying—for the sake of both men and women.

16. THE PRIVATE WORLDS OF MEN AND WOMEN

American Institute of Family Relations

§ Men and women differ not only physically and in the social stresses to which they are subjected but also in their modes of thought, interests, and customary activities. Understanding of these worlds and tolerance of them are essential to successful marriage adjustment.

In large and important areas of life, men and women have entirely different standards of value—or else they are not good specimens of their own sex. They do not speak the same language. Note, for instance, how often women use the adjective "little" as compared with its use by men. Sociologist James H. S. Bossard remarks, "This sex distinction is evident at every turn—in the words used, habits of exclamation, intensity of expression, and stock phrases, as well as the subjects discussed. The child learns early and is constantly reminded that there is prestige in learning the sex-appropriate forms of expression."

In short, boys and girls spend the first 10 or 15 years of their lives in relatively distinct social worlds. In marriage these two worlds have to be fused, in part, and much of the difficulty of marital adjustment grows out of the difficulty of this fusion, and frequent failure in it. This point is developed in sociologist E. E. LeMasters' new college textbook, *Modern Courtship and Marriage*,[1] more fully than in any other recent treatise.

Not only are there almost entirely different sexual worlds for males and females in our culture, Dr. LeMasters insists, but there are many male worlds into which a female can hardly enter. What he calls tavern society is basically a male world—the world of the Elks, Moose, Masons, American Legion and other veterans' organizations, of the luncheon clubs, athletic clubs, hunting clubs, and the like. "It is unwise for women approaching marriage to conclude that male society is now completely open to them, or to condemn their husbands for wanting to participate

SOURCE: *Family Life*, 18 (October, 1957), 1–3. Reprinted by permission of the publisher, The American Institute of Family Relations.

This article is based in large part on a discussion by E. E. LeMasters in his book, *Modern Courtship and Marriage*. Dr. LeMasters, who received his doctorate from Ohio State University, is at the University of Wisconsin. He is the author of a number of professional articles on marriage and the family.

[1] New York: The Macmillan Co., 1957.

in the man's world, as he has been accustomed to doing since he can remember."

Hardly any women have a realistic understanding of what it means to participate for several years in the armed forces, as most men have done. The world of sports participation is foreign to women, and so on. The world of business, into which so many millions of women have now entered, is still essentially a man's world, and such an expression as "Business is business" is as foreign to women's basic way of thinking as the expression, "I haven't a thing to wear" is foreign to men's.

Now, how can a wife adjust herself to these facts? First, says Dr. Le-Masters, by respecting the man's world and realizing that she can never be fully admitted to it; then by a determination to understand it as far as she can; and finally by accepting the way of life of *her own* sex instead of trying to repudiate it and make an imitation man out of herself (Alfred Adler's *masculine protest*), an ambition in which she can never succeed.

On the other hand, men will have to try to understand (or accept resignedly if they can not understand) the separate world of women. This centers largely in clothes, and growing partly out of this is a difference in ideas about the value of money. It involves the matter of diet, which becomes an obsession with so many women. But there are many more deeply-rooted differences, associated with the constitutional differences between the sexes. "The average wife seems to need a good cry every so often," Dr. LeMasters observes; and the husband need not necessarily feel like a guilty brute to think that he has precipitated these tears.

Religion means more to women than to men. So do children: "married couples sometimes develop basic conflicts related to this intense preoccupation of the mother with her children. The husband with his outside work and interests may feel that his wife is becoming a slave to the children, which to some extent she usually is. The wife, on the other hand, may decide that her husband isn't interested in the children." It is useless for a woman to ask a potential husband whether he likes children, the author insists; of course he does—if he doesn't have to take care of them. There is, he admits, a "marginal man" who has been domesticated. He is not a full-fledged member of the Male Society, but prefers to enjoy his leisure with his wife. He will spend his spare time tinkering around the house. If he goes hunting or fishing, he may take his wife with him. Such men, the author asserts, "may not scale the heights of economic success as well as their more masculine brothers, but for many women they make ideal husbands."

Excessive use of alcohol is more a masculine than a feminine pattern in our society, and men should remember that habits which "the gang" may tolerate, will be offensive to their wives. But some other supposed differences do not appeal to Dr. LeMasters as being well-founded. He doubts if wives have any more tendency to worry than do their husbands nowadays, nor that they have as much greater craving for security as is commonly imputed to them. But he thinks there is an important difference in their attitudes toward their own background families, which may be the cause of much conflict in marriage. Men are largely emancipated from their fathers and mothers, while women are always daughters who remain closer to their parents. There is certainly some truth in this; on the other hand several recent studies have pointed to the boy, overprotected by "Mom," as a serious source of difficulty in marriage.

Summarizing, Dr. LeMasters argues that it is important for each sex to accept the other as a distinct social group, and to recognize its right to be different.

17. DIFFERENCE IN ATTITUDE TOWARD LOVE AND SEX

Percival M. Symonds

§ Dr. Symonds, an educational psychologist, points out that either love or sex may be overvalued, but that it is men who typically overvalue sex and women who overvalue love. Here again is a difference in attitudes between men and women which, misunderstood, may easily lead to tensions in courtship or marriage.

Overvaluation of Love and Sex

By Men

While love tends in our present civilization to be overvalued and sex to be undervalued, in certain individuals this is not true. Some men, for instance, tend to place too strong a value on sex. To them sex is

SOURCE: Percival M. Symonds, *The Dynamics of Human Adjustment* (New York: D. Appleton-Century Company, 1946), pp. 559–60. Copyright 1946 by D. Appleton-Century Company, Inc. Reprinted by permission of Appleton-Century-Crofts, Division of Meredith Corporation.

The author, now deceased, received his doctorate from Columbia University, where he was long a professor in Teachers College. His special fields of interest included dynamic psychology, psychology of personality and character, and parent-child relationships. Among the books he wrote in these fields are *Diagnosing Personality and Conduct, Psychology of Parent-Child Relationships, The Ego and the Self,* and *Dynamics of Psychotherapy.*

the most exciting and important thing in the world; everything is measured in terms of its contribution to sex needs. A man may overvalue sex as a way of meeting certain anxieties and of contributing in a neurotic way to the satisfaction of other needs. First of all there is the fear many men have of not being normal, particularly of not being sexually virile. This probably is a final repository of earlier anxieties which have settled on a concern over sexual adequacy. One may suspect that the man who overvalues sex is struggling with more pervasive doubts as to his adequacy as a person. The man who overvalues sex has strong needs to surpass his male rivals. Perhaps he has had these exaggerated rivalries as a boy, and they may go back to his original rivalry with his father. The sexually ardent man is attempting to restore his wounded self-esteem. He wants to prove that he can attract women and to dispel doubts as to any weakness that he may have in this direction.

In a more specific sense, sex may be overvalued because of specific early experiences. The boy who has been sexually stimulated or seduced as an infant may be made by such experiences to have an increased need for such pleasures, particularly when he feels they are to be denied.

By Women

Women in particular are inclined to set a high premium on love experiences, and while they may also overvalue sex, the sexual aspects typically play a lesser role. The woman for whom love experiences have an exaggerated significance perhaps doubts her own love qualities. Frequently she is attempting to surpass female rivals and to prove to herself that she is more attractive and more to be desired than others in her circle. This, too, goes back to a rivalry with sisters or, in the first instance, with the mother.

Women seek love experiences for the restoration of wounded self-esteem. Love serves as a compensation for the inferior sex role they are forced to play. Since a woman does not play the aggressive sex role, she has to prove that she can attract men. Horney [1] emphasizes the need of some women to be constantly surrounded by men and build themselves an entourage as protection against the anxieties their own feelings of inferiority arouse. Another explanation sometimes adduced for the overvaluation of love by women is the fact that they have been commonly denied other pleasures and satisfactions granted to men. In the Victorian era the compartmentalization of life allotted few other interests to women than love, whereas men had the whole range of life's interests from which to draw.

Women as well as men may have been overstimulated in early child-

[1] Horney, Karen, "The Overevaluation of Love," *Psychoanalytic Quarterly*, 3 (1934), 605–638.

hood, and these early experiences may have forced love and sex relations to assume a place of large importance.

A little girl, for instance, who was forced by her parents to sing and dance in a tavern and was fondled by the rough visitors may have developed a taste for sensuous experiences which afterward when repressed contributed to the development of a chronic depression arising from persistent guilt.

Chapter 7: Dating, Mate Selection, and Engagement

18. DATING BEHAVIOR: A FRAMEWORK FOR ANALYSIS AND AN ILLUSTRATION

James K. Skipper, Jr., and Gilbert Nass

§ The authors suggest that dating serves at least four main functions: recreation; socialization into techniques of interaction between men and women; status-grading achievement; and courtship. They also hypothesize a continuum of motivation from dating as an end in itself to dating as a means to a larger goal, and another continuum of degree of emotional involvement. In a study of middle-class nursing students, the authors came to the conclusion that the girls were dating as a means to marriage and tended to become deeply involved, whereas the men they dated had a recreational motivation and were not emotionally involved. The framework of the study is applicable to many types of dating situations.

Dating is a form of behavior which most people in the United States experience during adolescence and early adulthood.[1] Usually dating is stereotyped as a romantic, exciting, interesting, and valuable experience in and of itself. Moreover, it is felt that it makes a salient contribution to the individual's socialization into the adult roles of the society, eventual marriage, and establishment of home and family. Although it is recog-

SOURCE: *Journal of Marriage and the Family*, 28 (1966), 412–20. Reprinted by permission of the publisher and the authors.

James K. Skipper, Jr., is associate professor of sociology at Case Western Reserve University. He is the author of sixteen published articles, and is co-editor of *Social Interaction and Patient Care* and co-author of *Sociology in Hospital Care*. Gilbert Nass is associate professor in the Department of Child Development and Family Relations at the University of Connecticut.

[1] When one thinks of dating, he usually refers to the time span of the teens and early twenties. However, the limitations of this approach should be recognized. For example, see the organization of mating data according to Farber's "permanent availability model." Bernard Farber, *Family: Organization and Interaction*, San Francisco: Chandler Publishing Company, 1964, pp. 103–184.

nized that dating may sometimes be problematic and filled with frustrations, the eventual rewards are thought to greatly outweigh momentary uncertainty.

Because the general American view of dating is positive and optimistic, one often fails to appreciate some of the important problems inherent in different types of dating situations. This sometimes prevents a systematic examination of dating and an analysis of how it affects and is affected by other social structures and processes.

This paper presents a framework for studying dating situations which was derived from the analysis of a particular type of dating encounter, that involving the young Caucasian female, age 18 to 21, from working-class or middle-class background, away from home, pursuing a specialized education in a large, urban, hospital school of nursing.[2] This analysis is used to illustrate the usefulness of the framework, but in no way does it *test* the hypotheses which the authors suggest. The data and general impressions presented here were gathered informally and do not constitute a systematic nor complete study of the topic. They are based on the authors' observations and interviews with 120 student nurses, 25 male medical students, interns, and residents, and on questionnaire material collected from 50 college males.

Framework for Analysis

A number of writers have discussed the various functions of dating.[3] In summary, their work indicates that dating probably serves at least four main functions for the individual:

1. Dating may be a form of recreation. It provides entertainment for the individuals involved and is a source of immediate enjoyment.
2. Dating may be a form of socialization. It provides an opportunity for individuals of opposite sex to get to know each other, learn to adjust to each other, and to develop appropriate techniques of interaction.

[2] The analysis was made at the School of Nursing, Presbyterian St. Luke's Hospital, Chicago, Illinois. It should be recognized that this type of dating situation is not unique or uncommon. Corwin and Taves report that "nationally, about 1 out of every 16 girls who graduate from high school enters nursing." A large proportion of these attend urban nursing schools. Ronald Corwin and Martin Taves, "Nursing and other Health Professions," in *Handbook of Medical Sociology*, ed. by Howard Freeman, Sol Levine, and Leo Reeder, Englewood Cliffs, New Jersey: Prentice-Hall, 1963, p. 193.

[3] See especially: Willard Waller, "The Rating and Dating Complex," *American Sociological Review*, 2 (1937), pp. 727–734; Robert Winch, "The Functions of Dating in Middle-class America," in *Selected Studies in Marriage and The Family*, ed. by Robert F. Winch, Robert McGinnis, and Herbert R. Barringer, New York: Holt, Rinehart & Winston, 1962, pp. 506–509; Robert Blood, "Uniformities and Diversities in Campus Dating Preferences," *Marriage and Family Living*, 18 (1956), pp. 37–45.

3. Dating may be a means of status grading and status achievement. By dating and being seen with persons who are rated "highly desirable" by one's peer group, an individual may raise his status and prestige within his group.

4. Dating may be a form of courtship. It provides an opportunity for unmarried individuals to associate with each other for the purpose of selecting a mate whom they may eventually marry.

We suggest that in most cases the functions of dating are manifest, not latent. In other words, individuals' most common motivations in dating correspond roughly to the most common functions of dating, even though all possible motivations would not so correspond.[4] Although individuals may have several motivations for dating each other, we suggest that each has one motivation which is probably more important (primary) than the others. However, individuals' primary motivations in dating each other may or may not be the same. For example, a girl may date a wealthy boy who drives an expensive sports car just in order to be seen with him (status seeking). The boy on the other hand may be dating the girl in order to learn something about women (socialization). In another case a boy may date an attractive girl because he desires a sexual experience with her (recreation). The girl may be dating the boy because she views him as a potential husband (courtship).

For purposes of analysis, in any dating relationship the individuals' primary motivations in dating may be placed on a continuum ranging from completely expressive (dating as an end in itself) to completely instrumental (dating as a means to some larger goal). The individuals' emotional involvement in the dating relationship may also be placed on a continuum ranging from no emotional involvement to complete emotional involvement. Although it may be possible empirically for individuals to fall anywhere on the two continua, theoretically it seems logical that there would be a positive correlation between the degree of instrumentality implicit in an individual's motivation for dating and his degree of emotional involvement. The authors suggest that:

1. An individual whose primary motivation in dating is mate selection is likely to have a strong instrumental orientation and a strong emotional involvement.

2. An individual whose primary motivation in dating is either socialization or status seeking is likely to have a low instrumental orientation and a low emotional involvement.

[4] There may be a number of other motives for dating which are not directly related to the functions listed. For instance, a girl may date a boy simply to make another boy jealous or to take the boy away from another girl. If spy novels and films are any criteria, individuals sometimes date with the sole motivation of gaining information. However, the authors assume (subject to empirical check) that these are relatively uncommon motivations for dating.

3. An individual whose primary motivation in dating is recreation is likely to have a strong expressive orientation (low instrumental) and a low emotional involvement.

Whenever an individual (A) has much to gain from maintaining a social relationship with another individual (B), (A) is likely to become distressed if it appears the relationship is going to discontinue before he has a chance to derive his full satisfaction from it. If (B) has less to gain from maintaining the relationship with (A), than (A) does with (B), then (B) is in a better position to control the relationship than (A). (B) has the better bargaining position. He can attempt to win concessions from (A) by threatening to discontinue the relationship. To the extent to which (A) is willing to meet (B's) demands, (B) controls the relationship.[5]

In reference to dating relationships it is suggested:

1. The greater the emotional involvement of individuals dating each other, the greater will be their desire to continue their relationship.
2. The greater the instrumental orientation of individuals dating each other, the greater will be their desire to continue their dating relationship.
3. The greater the disparity between the emotional involvement and/or the instrumental orientation between individuals dating each other, the greater the likelihood that conflict and distress will occur in their dating relationship.
4. In the disparate dating situation, the individual with the greater emotional involvement and/or instrumental orientation will suffer the greater distress.
5. In the disparate dating situation, the individual with the greater emotional involvement and/or instrumental orientation will have the least control over the relationship.

With this framework in mind, in the remainder of this paper the authors will be concerned with analyzing a dating situation where the males' primary motivation is recreation and the females' primary motivation is courtship. Particular attention will be paid to the question of why the parties have the motivations they do in dating each other, the consequences of these motivations for their dating, and how their interaction is affected by other social structures and processes.

An Illustrative Dating Situation

Considerable evidence suggests that many post-high school females attending institutions of higher learning are vitally concerned with their

[5] These thoughts are based in part on Homans' discussion of "The Origination of Interaction." George Homans, *Social Behavior: Its Elementary Forms*, New York: Harcourt, Brace & World, 1961, pp. 201–203.

dating experience and their marital prospects. A great deal of their expressed concern centers around what they regard as "the limited quantity and quality" of available and eligible prospective mates. Often their distress leads them to compulsive and blind involvement with "anyone who shows the slightest interest." These involvements are usually disappointing from the female point of view. They seldom lead to either rewarding or lasting relationships, let alone permanent ones.[6]

For the young girl attending nursing school, this problem appears to be escalated. Both Davis and Mauksch, among other expert observers, have noted the great number of nursing students who have expressed concern about their difficulties in establishing meaningful relationships with young men. These were difficulties they evidently did not have before entering nursing school.[7] We also observed such behavior at an urban nursing school. This type of problem was encountered frequently. Typically, it was expressed as follows:

> I never had these kinds of problems before I came here. I was never what you call shy and I always thought I was kind of attractive and had a good personality. I never had any difficulty in getting dates with the right type of boys in high school. But then it was not so important. Now it is, and all I do is keep getting mixed up with the wrong kinds of guys and I don't even know it. It is making me miserable and I can hardly think of anything else. I used to think I knew what was right to do and what was wrong. Now I am not sure. I just don't know. Maybe that's my problem. Anyway, I have got to latch on to someone pretty soon. After all, I am almost twenty-one years old. Most of my friends are married already, or at least engaged.
>
> Well of course I have been looking for a man, for about two years now. I have met some nice ones. But it is gosh darn hard to get them to think about marriage. They are just happy fooling around with you.

An intriguing question is, why should this problem exist at all? Why should these young girls be so anxious about dating, their relationships with men, and their prospects for marriage? Objectively, it would seem reasonable to assume that the pursuit of higher education and a career in nursing would provide them with a feeling of security for the future, increase their confidence and ability to establish relationships with men,

---

[6] Coombs and Kenkel have speculated that women are more likely than men to be serious minded about dating and view dating partners in a marriage context since their future socioeconomic status and life chances are going to be largely determined by their future husband. Robert Coombs and William Kenkel, "Sex Differences in Dating Aspirations and Satisfaction with Computer Selected Partners," *Journal of Marriage and the Family*, 28 (1966), pp. 62–66.

[7] Fred Davis and Virginia Olsen, "Initiation into a Woman's Profession: Identity Problems in the Status Transition of Coed to Student Nurse," *Sociometry*, 26 (1963), pp. 89–101; Hans Mauksch, "Becoming a Nurse: A Selective View," *Annals of the American Academy of Political and Social Science*, 346 (March, 1963), pp. 88–98.

and generally enhance their marketability and potential for marriage.[8] But in many cases this did not seem to happen. The authors' investigation uncovered a number of potential hypotheses which may aid in understanding and explaining this phenomenon.

Examination of social class behavior suggests that the working class adheres strongly to defining the adult role of women in terms of homemaker-mother. The range of vocational alternatives is often limited by such factors as opportunity, motivation, and money. Given this focus of commitment to the homemaker-mother role, role behaviors avoiding appropriate socialization are discouraged. An excellent example of this is the oft-stated idea that college is not necessary for girls who desire to get married and raise a family. Rather, working class girls are directly trained to seek as their paramount societal position that of homemaker-mother. The security of this position is seldom questioned. High school and immediate post-high school dating are directed toward landing a "good young fellow," establishing a home, and having children.[9]

The middle-class female in late high school and immediately after high school is also trained for the homemaker-mother position.[10] However, the parameters of her training are far more extensive. She can consider higher education as a legitimate right resulting from her socioeconomic status. She can consider a career-oriented rather than job-oriented occupational position. She can consider learning skills which qualify her for assuming a companionship position in her marriage and/or becoming an active community member. Nevertheless, these other activities are not evaluated so much as alternatives to the homemaker-mother role as they are activities likely to enrich it and be supportive and complementary to it. In other words, they are viewed more as means toward the goal of establishing a more successful homemaker-mother position than as alternatives to it. Thus, in spite of a number of differences in social background and socialization, the main goal in life of many working-class and middle-class girls is exactly the same: marriage, home, and family.[11]

Since most student nurses come from working-class or middle-class homes, it is understandable and predictable, although perhaps contrary

[8] J. Richard Udry, *The Social Context of Marriage*, Philadelphia: J. B. Lippincott Company, 1966, pp. 212–213.
[9] Ruth Cavan, *The American Family*, New York: Crowell, 1963, pp. 149–152; Lee Burchinal, "Trends and Prospects for Young Marriages in the United States," *Journal of Marriage and the Family*, 27 (1965), p. 249; William Goode, *World Revolution and Family Patterns*, New York: Free Press of Glencoe, 1963, pp. 10–18, 65–66, 371, 373.
[10] Cavan, *op. cit.*, pp. 121–124.
[11] Udry, *op. cit.*, p. 57; Lamar Empey, "Role Expectations of Young Women Regarding Marriage and a Career," *Marriage and Family Living*, 20 (1958), pp. 152–156.

to some popular beliefs, that these young women are not primarily interested in a career in nursing. A commitment to a professional career had little to do with their recruitment to the field.[12] The overriding goal of nursing students is marriage, home, and family and the roles of wife, homemaker, and mother. So strong is this orientation to the traditional female role that in one study it was discovered that even in a school placing strong emphasis on the development of career and leadership orientation in its students, over 87 percent at both admission and graduation ranked "home and family" as *the* adult female role which they stressed the most.[13] Corwin and Taves summarized the crucial importance of the marriage goals to the prospective nurse when they wrote:

> The prospect of marriage and children permeates every aspect of nursing; no aspect of the profession can be completely understood apart from the influence of marriage plans and their frustration.[14]

Given this focus of commitment, it is understandable why nursing students may place such great emphasis on the courtship function of dating. However, this only partially explains their unusual anxiety over their dating and their subjectively perceived failure to make adequate progress toward the marriage goal. Several other variables must be considered if one is to understand the true nature of the nursing student's difficulties.

The dating dilemma begins with the ecological setting. Most nursing schools are set in urban environments. This fact has far-reaching consequences. The school which is the primary basis of this report was located in a metropolitan complex of several million inhabitants. It was situated approximately two miles from the central business district in an area of light industry populated by lower income classes of various ethnic groups. It was part of a large medical center consisting of several hospitals, medical school, and a number of auxiliary institutions. Due to the type of schooling, the extent of on-the-job training, and the restrictive curfews on leaving the dormitory during free night hours, the nursing students were virtually imprisoned within the confines of the medical center for the greater part of each week. The physical boundaries directed and dictated the types of dating contacts available for them. These contacts may be classified into four main categories:

    I. High school acquaintances from the home town area.

    II. Local lower-class working boys.

[12] Fred Katz and Harry Martin, "Career Choice Processes," *Social Forces*, 41 (1962), pp. 149–154.

[13] Fred Davis and Virginia Olsen, "The Career Outlook of Professionally Educated Women," *Psychiatry*, 28 (1965), pp. 334–345.

[14] Corwin and Taves, *op. cit.*, pp. 200–201.

III. College boys from schools located some distance from the medical center but within the greater metropolitan area.

IV. Medical men; students, interns, residents, and occasionally attending physicians working in the medical center.

For each of these categories of male contacts there were built-in deterrents to sequential courtship for the nursing student. Although objectively these obstacles were not necessarily inherent in the situation and without solution, from the student's point of view they often seemed to be and were a constant source of worry, strain, and anxiety. Various major problems were involved with each category of male contacts.

Time and space were the major difficulties involved in continuing relationships with former high school acquaintances. The vast majority of the girls' homes were not situated in the local metropolitan area but in the surrounding hinterland. Thus, the simple fact of physical distance was a barrier. Combined with limited free time during the work week and vacations which were few and far between, dating of "home town" boys with any regularity was possible only in rare cases. Although relationships firmly established before the girl left for school were often maintained by mail, those which were not so established very often ended in frustration. Many of the girls perceived this time-distance problem at an early stage in their student career and consequently directed their energies and attentions to other, more accessible categories of males.[15] Nevertheless, those girls who did manage to maintain successful dating interactions "back home," culminating in formal engagement with the symbolic ring, received high esteem and were much admired and envied.[16]

On occasion the students would come in casual contact with boys living in the area contiguous to the medical center. These young men were of low social class origin and either unemployed or holding unskilled or semiskilled jobs. Few had been graduated from high school. The girls maintained a high degree of social distance between themselves and this category of boys and rarely dated them. In fact, they were usually shunned and avoided at all costs. To put it very bluntly, the girls did not consider these boys to be "good enough" for them.

In contrast to the boys back home and those in the immediate area, college boys from various metropolitan schools afforded a dating oppor-

---

[15] Cotton and Smircich have emphasized time and energy as crucial factors in establishing norms regarding dating-mating behavior. William R. Cotton Jr. and R. S. Smircich, "A Comparison of Mathematical Models for the Effect of Residential Propinquity on Mate Selection," *American Sociological Review*, 29 (1964), pp. 522–529.

[16] The "engagement success" of these girls was a source of anxiety to the other students who were having dating problems. It served as a constant reminder of their own difficulties and perceived failure.

tunity which continually appealed to the girls. They were quite optimistic about college boys as dates. In a few instances, from the girls' definition of the situation, a highly romantic, rewarding, and successful (engagement) dating experience evolved from these contacts. From these few successful courtships a myth developed among the "less fortunate" girls that college boys offered unlimited opportunities for normal dating. This was far from the reality of the situation. There existed a barrier to successful dating interaction with college boys that almost none of the girls perceived immediately, and which the vast majority of the girls persisted in refusing to recognize. The barrier concerned the college boys' definition of what "kind of girl" a nurse or nursing student is. By training and practice, the nurse becomes a manipulator of human bodies. This manipulation involves intimate knowledge, contact, and actual handling of all parts of the human body including the "private parts" of both males and females. This knowledgeability marks the student nurse. The content of her work role overlaps into her social relationships, especially dating situations. She is defined by college boys as "someone who knows the score," "an easy mark," "a good-time girl," "a chick who likes it," etc. This common, stereotyped image is frequently portrayed in widely circulated magazines.

For example, the following passage concerning the off-duty nurse appeared in an article titled "The Private World of Nurses":

> Under this prophylactic white uniform beats a black lace heart. Ripe and shining peach-slice legs where the ghostly Supp-hose was. Fat pink moons of flesh backing out of sling back pumps, gone the Hi-Treads of day. Perfume. Ruby cashmere. Color, color, color, then back to the hospital floor, on any old pretense.
>
> Only a skirt and sweater, but it is the metamorphosis that hits them. Real hair, naked heels and ruby cashmere shoulders contrast sharply with the great white vestal virgin pyre of the nurses' station. Miss Rachik and the wilder of her uniformed sisters learn that fast. Any excuse, but drop back to your floor dressed like real people. Maybe one night Dr. Brown will. . . .[17]

A quotation from another article, "Is it True What They Say About Nurses?" is even more to the point.

> The girl who chooses a career in nursing almost automatically acquires a "reputation"—in the old-fashioned sense of the word—whether or not she wants or deserves it. For somehow the out-of-the-sickroom connotation of the word "nurse" implies a promiscuity that's unmatched by any other female profession except the oldest.
>
> This libidinous public image stems in part from popular writers, who seem to delight in ascribing chameleon-like charms to the nurse; she's cool, starched, and impersonal by day, unstarched to the point of nym-

[17] Gail Sheely, "The Private World of Nurses," *Cosmopolitan*, May (1966), p. 54.

phomania by night. Indeed, if one is to accept as believable the sexual goings-on in doctors-and-nurses novels, movies, and TV shows, one can only conclude that nurses swing *on* the job as much as off.[18]

At one of the universities in the area, a sample of 50 college boys (sophomores, juniors, and seniors) were asked to rate their expectations of college girls, working girls, and student nurses regarding permissiveness in sexual intimacies during casual dating.[19] The results of this survey are presented in Table 1. The data indicate that, in the college boys' expectations, student nurses were "faster" in sexual permissiveness than either working girls or college girls.

This stereotype of the basic nature of the kind of girl who would become a nurse plays an important part in defining the dating situation. Many college boys define the student nurse in terms of her "glamour-girl-fun value" and only later, if at all, her potential as a wife and homemaker. As one of the young men put it:

> When one of the guys starts dating one of those student nurses, you know damn well he is just out "to get a little." Oh, he may try to "con" her a bit. But that's the story, Dad.

TABLE 1 *Comparison of College Boys' Expectations of the Sexual Permissiveness of College Girls, Working Girls, and Student Nurses during Casual Dating*

	VERY PERMISSIVE		AVERAGE PERMISSIVENESS		NOT VERY PERMISSIVE		TOTAL
	N	%	N	%	N	%	N
I. College girls	4	8	20	40	26	52	50
II. Working girls	5	10	23	46	22	44	50
III. Student nurses	19	38	22	44	9	18	50
Comparison I–III	$X^2=$		9.07		$<.02$		
Comparison II–III	$X^2=$		6.82		$<.05$		
Comparison I–II	$X^2=$		.326		$<.90$		

This stereotype is the basis for college boys' defining the dating of student nurses in terms of recreation (sex) and not courtship. Not only is the student nurse defined as "knowing the score," particularly about sexual matters, but in addition the "knowing" is transformed into "she

[18] Colette Hoppmann, "Is It True What They Say About Nurses?" *Pageant*, 21:9 (March, 1966), pp. 33–34.
[19] All the respondents were Caucasians between the ages of 18 and 22, and almost all were from middle-class background. Sexual permissiveness was defined as petting and beyond, and casual dating as anything less than "going steady."

likes it!" From the typical college boy's definition of the situation, these are girls to have fun with but not the type one takes home to mother. In this respect the student nurse and the divorcee may have comparable problems which tend to obstruct the attainment of a courtship relation.

The student nurse is placed in a precarious position. If she is not cooperative and does not meet the college boys' expectations of sexual permissiveness, she is likely to be dropped immediately and have no further dates. If she is cooperative, she easily builds a reputation and becomes fair game for her current dating partner and later his friends and fraternity brothers. The authors suspect that more girls than not choose to solve the dilemma by being more permissive than they normally would, just in order to keep dating. As one young lady commented:

> Whether you like it or not, you have to go along with them, at least some of the time. Otherwise, you get left out and sitting in the dorm all the time.

This type of behavior, of course, is evidence that there is an element of truth in the stereotype. Further evidence is provided by 12 of the college boys included in the survey presented in Table 1, who claimed to have dated all three classes of girls; student nurses, working girls, and college girls. Table 2 indicates that the reported experiences of these boys roughly substantiates the stereotype. Only one of the 12 boys placed either college girls or working girls in the very permissive category, compared to five who placed student nurses in that category.

TABLE 2   *Comparison of College Boys' Reported Experience of the Sexual Permissiveness of College Girls, Working Girls, and Student Nurses during Casual Dating*

	VERY PERMISSIVE		AVERAGE PERMISSIVENESS		NOT VERY PERMISSIVE		TOTAL
	N	%	N	%	N	%	N
I. College girls	1	8.3	5	41.7	6	50.0	12
II. Working girls	1	8.3	7	58.3	4	33.3	12
III. Student nurses	5	41.7	5	41.7	2	16.7	12

Strangely enough, few of the nursing students were able to forecast the difficulties involved in these dating encounters in advance or to recognize them realistically when they did occur.

> I always think things are going along fine. We seem to be getting along fine and then "bam" it's all over. I guess it must be me.

It is hard for me to believe what you are suggesting. I am not like that at all. Where do the boys get that idea about nurses? They are wrong about us. I am sure of that.

The girls seemed incapable of taking the college boys' definition of the situation, even after they had been hurt several times. Characteristically, they failed to see any patterns evolving in these situations. Usually they tended to place the blame entirely on themselves and/or the boy or the unique circumstances of the particular dating encounter. Perhaps one of the major factors involved in partially explaining why the girls did not become more aware of these patterns in their dating was that the great majority of them attempted to deal with the problem alone. Very seldom did they share these confidences with each other.

I would like to talk about my problems in dating some of these guys, but I don't want to be the only one. You know what I mean? You look pretty foolish when you tell all and nobody else does.

Although the problems of boys and dating were popular topics of group sessions, the discussions were almost always on the superficial level. Very rarely did the girls come to grips with the real issues that were bothering them. If they had, they might have discovered that their own individual problems were far from unique, being commonly shared with many other girls.[20] This might have allowed them to take a more rational approach to their own individual difficulties and saved them a great deal of mental anguish.

Ecological restrictions tended to expose student nurses to males involved in the medical profession more frequently than to any other of the three categories. Medical students, interns, and residents formed the bulk of the men with whom the girls came in constant contact. Almost all the difficulties in dating which the girls experienced with college boys were equally true of their encounters with males attached to the medical profession. However, the magnitude of the problem was exaggerated by several additional variables.

First, most of the nursing students' potential dating partners in the cultural milieu of the medical center were "occupational transients." They were spending only a few short interim years in the community before leaving to establish roots and practice elsewhere. Many of these men were not ready to get serious and establish a sequential courtship pattern with any girl. Similar to the patterns of other types of transients, it was often difficult for them to develop a sense of commitment within the community setting and especially in their interactions with student

[20] Udry has observed: "Overt sexual conversation is taboo among most girl groups. If it is discussed at all in a group, it will be a far cry from the sexual conversation of male groups." Udry, *op. cit.*, p. 91.

nurses.[21] Also, these men were subject to long hours of work and study, usually under great pressure. They had limited free time for fun and amusement. When they did, they often wanted to take advantage of every minute. One intern commented in an informal interview:

> When I get a chance, I want to cut loose and really live a little. I need an immediate and complete release from all the stress and pressure.

Another explained:

> We don't have much time to fool around. So when we do, we want to date a girl who is pretty lively and ready to go; I mean a real swinger. Do you understand?

Similar to the college boys, the medical men had an entirely expressive orientation in dating student nurses. Their motivation was strictly recreation with as little emotional involvement as possible. However, this orientation was not always clear to the girls they were dating. In fact the medical men sometimes went out of their way to convince the girls that their motivation and emotional involvement were much stronger than they actually were.

In their interaction with college boys, the student nurses were approximately of equal age and experience as their potential dating partners. This was not the case with medical functionaries, where a definite age differential existed favoring the male. Expose the female to males four to ten years her senior, and in this type of situation the weight of differential experience becomes a crucial factor. The opportunity for controlling the relationship rides overwhelmingly with the male. It is he who possesses the superior power, experience, and interactional skills in the dating relationship.

Another variable impinging upon the dating relationship was the occupational prestige structure. The medical doctor possesses great status, prestige, respect, and authority in his formal work relationships with patients, nurses, and other hospital personnel. He is perfectly aware of his dominant position as are all other parties with whom he interacts. The assumption of one's own charisma[22] can be a powerful, positive psychological mechanism for any male medical student, intern, resident, etc. Not unlike the student nurse, the medical man's work role also overlaps into the dating situation, not so much in terms of the actual content of the role, but more in terms of rank and authority in the occu-

[21] Farber presents an excellent discussion of mutual personal commitment as the emerging basis for courtship-marriage behavior. Our data are directed to the point that these eligibles, as transients, in the dating situation are unable to provide a personal commitment which allows minimal "mutual" dimensions. These male eligibles consider consequences for the other person largely in terms of their own immediate dating goals. Farber, *op. cit.*, pp. 153–4, 333–387.

[22] Harvey Smith, "The Hospital's Dual Status System," in *Social Organization and Behavior*, ed. by R. L. Simpson and I. H. Simpson, New York: Wiley, 1964, pp. 303–308.

pational prestige structure. In the dating sequence, the medical man does not set aside lightly the legitimate authority claims of his professional work role. The medical trainee—be he student, intern, or resident—is an heir apparent to the highest authority position in the hospital, and he quickly and easily incorporates a self-conception compatible with his evolving elite status. This attitude pervades the medical trainee's social contacts with subordinate nurses. He tends to expect them to follow and obey his wishes as they are required to do in the work relationship. Moreover, he often uses his power and authority to gain his way. When the student nurse believes the physician is to be admired and venerated and also to be trusted and obeyed, then in a dating relationship she is placed in a vulnerable and compromising situation.

The possibility of exploitation is very high. For example, one nursing student reported she became acquainted with an intern, started seeing him in a group dating situation, became sexually intimate and eventually very serious about him, only to discover he was already married; the whole charade was carried out with the knowledgeable aid of the intern's friends and cohorts.[23]

The student nurse's dilemma in dating medical men appeared to be even more distressful than in her dating college boys. If the girl was not sexually permissive in dating, she faced not only the threat of never being asked for future dates but also the possibility of some petty reprisal in the work relationship. If she was permissive, she had to live with the feeling (very often warranted) that many of the males with whom she came in contact during working hours in the hospital would be well-informed about her off-duty activities, and, if her degree of sexual permissiveness went against her own norms, she was also likely to suffer severe distress and guilt.

Summary and Conclusions

The preceding paragraphs have presented an illustration of a dating situation in which the males' primary motivation in dating is recreation and the females' primary motivation is courtship. The authors have attempted to analyze some of the reasons behind the motivations, the consequences of the motivations for interaction, and some of the social factors affecting both the motivations and the interaction. However, it must be understood that this illustration was not presented as an example of *all* dating situations involving student nurses, for it is not.

[23] Kirkpatrick and Kanin have observed that a female's tolerance limit for erotic intimacy seems to rise as she becomes more emotionally involved and the relationship becomes more meaningful to her. Clifford Kirkpatrick and Eugene Kanin, "Male Sex Aggression on a University Campus," *American Sociological Review*, 22 (1957), pp. 52–58.

Based on the authors' experience at one urban nursing school, they estimate that the type of dating problems described in this paper resulted in severe distress for only about one out of every four girls. Whether this is a representative pattern for student nurses or not is a problem for further, more extensive, and much more systematic research.

The real concern of this paper is not with this particular dating situation per se, but with the dating problems it illustrates, some important sociological variables which affect dating interaction, and the usefulness of the theoretical framework presented earlier for analyzing dating situations. Individuals' motivations in dating are affected by social variables, as are their choices of actual dating partners and the course of their dating relationship. In the authors' example the girls' primary motivation in dating was courtship, which was directly related to their desire to get married and their definition of the ideal adult role of women as homemaker-mother. Ecological restrictions forced the girls into contact with two types of dating partners, college boys and medical men, both of which tended to date student nurses for recreation, not courtship. In the case of college boys, this was directly related to their belief in the stereotype of a nurse as a sexually permissive woman. In addition to the stereotype, the medical men were influenced by their occupational transiency, their need but little time for recreation, and the ecological availability of the student nurses.

The authors suggest that if one is able to learn individuals' primary motivations in dating, their degree of instrumental orientation and their degree of emotional involvement, one will be able to predict something about the conflict which is likely to take place in the relationship, which partner is likely to control the relationship, and which partner is likely to experience the most distress.

The student nurses' courtship motivation involved a higher degree of instrumental orientation and emotional involvement than the males' recreation motivation. These differences produced conflict in the dating encounters. The male controlled the relationship in large part because he had less to lose if it was discontinued. He was not emotionally involved with *the* student nurse and could easily find another for purposes of recreation. The student nurse on the other hand had to keep the relationship "going" if she was to achieve the goal of eventual marriage. Under the circumstances her emotional involvement with a particular boy was bound to be greater than his to her. Therefore, the student nurse was in a poor bargaining position and forced to make concessions (in this case being more sexually permissive than she would normally) in order to maintain the relationship. This situation caused the girls much distress.

The variables which the authors isolated in the dating of student nurses may be of equal importance in other settings. For example, what part do ecological barriers play in determining dating partners in rural as opposed to urban areas, small schools vs. large schools, all-male or female institutions compared to those which are coed? Is courtship the main motivation in dating of most college and working girls? Are there other groups besides nurses who have acquired social stereotypes which may influence the motivation of their dating partners? Are athletes and beauty queens dated primarily by those seeking status?

The type of framework presented here may be used to analyze any dating situation. To test the authors' hypotheses, procedures must first be instituted to ascertain dating partners' motivations in dating each other, their degree of instrumental orientation, and their emotional involvement. From an analysis of these data, one should be able to test whether the degree of instrumental orientation and the degree of emotional involvement are in fact associated with individuals' motivations in dating. One would also be able to discover from these data the relative frequencies of the motivations between the sexes, whether individuals have other motivations than those cited, and if individuals have more than one primary motivation in dating. A wide range of dating situations must be examined varying the individuals' primary motivations. Assuming just four primary motivations, there are ten separate combinations to be analyzed: courtship-courtship, courtship-recreation, courtship-status seeking, courtship-socialization, recreation-recreation, recreation-status seeking, recreation-socialization, status seeking-status seeking, status seeking-socialization, and socialization-socialization. Finally, the degree to which motivations may vary in importance or perhaps even change completely during the course of dating should be considered.

19. ATTITUDES OF COLLEGE STUDENTS TOWARD INTER-FAITH MARRIAGE

Alfred J. Prince

§ People tend to marry others with backgrounds like their own, of the same religious faith, race, and socioeconomic status. A minority of people, however, cross cultural and racial lines. When they do they may face special problems of adjustment of beliefs, customs, values, and attitudes in order to bring harmony into the marriage. The most frequent type of

SOURCE: *Coordinator*, 5 (September, 1956), 11–23. This article is based on the author's unpublished master's thesis of the same title, completed at the University

intermarriage in the United States occurs between people of markedly different religious faiths. This article gives the attitudes of more than a thousand students in one state university to dating and marrying persons of other religious faiths than their own, some of their experiences with interreligious dating, and their opinions as to how their parents would react if they married outside their faith. Research of the 1960's, some of it unpublished, indicates little change in attitudes since this article was written.

The purpose of this study was to find out how young people of marriageable age—students attending the state university in Idaho, in particular—feel about inter-faith marriages. More specifically, the study was designed to seek answers to the following questions: (1) Are young people willing to marry outside their religious faith? (2) Will they do so only under certain conditions? If so, what are some of these conditions? (3) Are they willing to adopt the religion of their chosen mate, if by so doing, it will make marriage possible? (4) What are some of the reasons young people give why they do not want to marry outside their faith? (5) Is there any relationship between a person's expressed attitudes toward an inter-faith marriage and the attitudes he thinks his parents hold toward such a marriage? These are a few of the questions this paper hopes to throw light upon.

The data were obtained by pretested questionnaires from students living on the University of Idaho campus in January, 1955. Questionnaires were distributed to the students in their living groups following the evening meal. Questionnaires were completed by approximately two-thirds of the students, some 810 males and 483 females.

As shown in Table 1, 97 per cent of the students reported a willingness to date outside their faith. Ninety-five per cent would also date a person who had no church affiliation.

Approximately one student in four would not "go steady" with someone of a religious faith different from his own. One student in eight would not "go steady" with a person who had no church affiliation. Girls were less willing to "go steady" outside their faith than were boys.

When it came to the question of marriage, 59 per cent of the students stated that they would cross religious lines and marry and 41 per cent would not. One student in four was opposed to marrying a person who had no church affiliation. Girls were also less willing to marry outside their faith than were boys.

---

of Idaho in 1955. Reprinted by permission of the author and the publisher, E. C. Brown Trust Foundation, Portland, Oregon.

The author is on the staff at Eastern Washington State College, where he teaches sociology and social work. His special interests are counseling, interfaith marriages (on which he continues research), courtship behavior, and social work.

TABLE 1 *Attitudes of College Students toward Dating, Going Steady, and Marrying outside Their Religious Faith**

	MALE (N = 779)		FEMALE (N = 475)		TOTAL (N = 1254)	
Attitude	Yes Per Cent	No Per Cent	Yes Per Cent	No Per Cent	Yes Per Cent	No Per Cent
Would Date outside Religious Faith	97	3	97	3	97	3
Would "Go Steady" outside Religious Faith	80	20	72	28	77	23
Would Marry outside Religious Faith	62	37	52	48	59	41

* The 41 students in the study who stated that they had "no church affiliation" are not included in this table. With one exception, these 41 students would "date," "go steady with," and "marry" a Catholic, Protestant, or Jewish person, or a person with "no church affiliation." One student would date and go steady with a person in any of the aforesaid categories, but he would marry only a person with "no church affiliation."

One girl wrote:

My main objection to inter-faith marriages does not reflect any prejudice against either faith. It, to me, represents the possibility of an unstable family—not necessarily separation and divorce possibilities, but lack of an important spiritual bond. I feel that children are given an unfair chance even if I could bring my child up in my own faith. It could raise doubt and wonder when my husband and I went to separate churches. If the child wanted to go with one parent, then the other, he may end up indifferent to and/or confused by his own religion.

Another commented:

We have had two mixed marriages in our closely knit family circle—one, Jewish-Protestant, and the other, Protestant-Catholic—both have proven unsuccessful. Therefore, I could not enter such a relationship with much confidence, since both marriages failed because of religious differences. I am engaged to a Protestant; and if by chance he turned Catholic, our engagement would be broken. I have no confidence in the possible success of inter-faith marriages.

Another wrote:

I know that it is possible to have a happy and successful inter-faith marriage, but I think it depends on how strongly a person believes in his faith. Myself, I could never be happy with a man of a different faith from my own.

Another commented:

I can get along with people of faiths different from mine, but I could not build a successful marriage. Religion enters the picture too much.

When the data in Table 1 were related to the religious affiliation of the students, it was found that almost all Protestant and Catholic students would date someone of a religious faith different from their own. Only three per cent of the Protestant students and only one Catholic student would not date a person of a different faith.[1]

One Protestant student explained to the writer why she would date a Catholic but not a Jew as follows:

It is a result of the social pressures caused in my community. All Jewish friends of mine are banned from the clubs, etc. to which my parents and I belong. Therefore, it would cause embarrassment to both parties if it were not possible for us to attend dinner, etc. together.

More Catholic students than Protestants were willing to "go steady" with someone of a different faith. The percentages were 90 per cent and 75 per cent, respectively.

Catholic students were also more willing to marry across religious lines than were Protestant students. Only 29 per cent of the Catholic students reported that they would not marry outside their faith but more than 40 per cent of the Protestant students reported that they would not be a partner in an inter-faith marriage. It was also interesting to note that 70 per cent of the Catholic students were willing to marry a Protestant but only 54 per cent of the Protestant students were willing to marry a Catholic.

Thus, Catholic students were not only more willing to marry outside their faith than Protestant students were, but they were also more willing to marry a Protestant than Protestant students were willing to marry a Catholic. At the same time, however, more Catholic students wanted their mate to adopt their religion and/or to agree to have the children brought up in their faith than did Protestant students. A large percentage of Protestant and Catholic students—33 per cent of each group —stated that they would marry a Jewish person. Would similar results be obtained if this study is repeated at an eastern university having a larger percentage of Jewish students?

Students who attended church infrequently tended to be more willing

[1] The two Jewish students in the study would date, go steady with, and marry someone outside their faith. The eight students whose religious faith was classified as "other" (i.e., Greek Orthodox, etc.) were all willing to marry outside their faith.

to cross religious lines and marry than were students who attended church regularly. Of the 453 students who did not attend church or attended less than once a month, more than 75 per cent reported that they would marry outside their faith. On the other hand, of the 794 students who attended church once a month or more less than 50 per cent would marry a person of a different faith.

Table 2 summarizes the attitudes of the students toward inter-faith marriages. It will be seen that a slightly larger percentage of girls than the boys checked statements one and two. Both of these statements require a condition to marriage. On the other hand, but 17 per cent of the

TABLE 2   *Present Feelings of College Students toward Inter-Faith Marriage*

Statement	MALE Per Cent	FEMALE Per Cent	TOTAL STUDENTS CHECKING STATEMENTS Per Cent
1. I would marry outside of my religious faith if my mate were willing to change his (or her) faith to mine.	22	23	22
2. I would marry outside of my religious faith without requiring that my mate change his (or her) faith to mine, but he (or she) would have to be willing to bring up our children according to my faith.	25	28	26
3. I would marry outside of my religious faith without requireing that my mate change his (or her) faith to mine, and I would not object to our children being brought up in his (or her) faith.	30	17	26
4. In order to make marriage possible with my chosen mate, I would be willing to adopt his (or her) faith.	6	9	7
5. I would not marry outside of my religious faith.	17	23	19
Total	100	100	100

girls checked statement three which does not require a condition to marriage while 30 per cent of the boys checked the same statement. It appears, therefore, that girls were less willing to marry outside their faith unless the mate adopted their religion and/or agreed to have the children brought up in their faith than were boys.

In view of the foregoing statement, it is interesting to note in Table 2 that a somewhat higher percentage of girls were willing to adopt the religious faith of their mate than were boys. Baber [2] and Hoover [3] also found that girls are more opposed to inter-faith marriages than boys. Baber found that more boys were willing to adopt the spouse's faith than were girls.[4] Nine per cent of the men in his study were willing to adopt the mate's faith; but only five per cent of the women were willing to do so. In the present study, the percentages obtained were almost the reverse, with six per cent of the boys and nine per cent of the girls stating that they were willing to adopt their mate's religious faith.

No significant differences were found in the responses of the lower and upper classmen to the statements in Table 2. However, students who attended church regularly tended to check statements one or two more often than did students who attended church infrequently.

As noted earlier, more Catholic than Protestant students reported a willingness to marry outside their faith. The question now arises: Are Catholic students also more likely to require the mate to adopt their faith than are Protestant students? Analysis of the data showed the answer to be yes. Seven out of ten Catholic students checked statements one or two. (See statements in Table 2.) Only four out of ten Protestant students checked these same statements. Furthermore, over 50 per cent of the Catholic students checked statement two, i.e., they would marry outside their faith if the mate agreed to have the children brought up in their religion but slightly less than 25 per cent of the Protestant students checked this same statement.

Although Catholic students appeared more willing to cross religious lines and marry than Protestant students did, Catholic students also expressed a desire for their spouses to adopt Catholicism and/or by insisting that the children be brought up in the Catholic faith. For example:

> Regarding whether I would marry outside my Catholic faith, my husband-to-be would have to consent to let the children be brought up in my faith and not interfere with my religious practices and beliefs. How-

[2] Ray Baber, *Marriage and the Family* (New York: McGraw-Hill Book Company, Inc., 1939), p. 149.
[3] Harry F. Hoover, *Attitudes of High School Students toward Mixed Marriage* (Washington, D.C.: Catholic University of America Press, 1950), p. 52.
[4] This tendency also appeared to be true for the remaining 51 students in the study who were not included in Tables 3 and 4.

ever, I would never insist that he alter his own ideas on religion should he be willing to agree to the above.

Another commented:

I approve of inter-faith marriages; but in my case, I would want the party to be a Catholic or become a convert. However, I would still marry a non-Catholic providing the children were brought up in the Catholic religion.

Another wrote:

I would marry a person of another faith if that person would change his faith to mine. I am going steady with a Protestant boy and we have discussed this problem and he has agreed to adopt my religion before we get married.

A Catholic male student wrote:

A mixed marriage has two strikes against it from the start. Difference in religion is a spawning place for much friction. However, my marriage would depend on the girl, not her religion, provided the children are brought up in my faith.

One male student who was seriously considering marrying a Catholic stated that he would not marry her unless he could first accept the teachings of the Catholic Church. He wrote:

At present I, a Protestant, intend to marry a Catholic. I am studying the Catholic beliefs, but if I find that I can't accept them, I don't believe I'll marry her. She is a strong Catholic; and if I were to marry her without being able to believe in her religion, there would almost surely be undesirable results later in our marriage.

Another student commented:

I was pinned to a boy who is Catholic and I am Protestant. For over a year, I went to church with him and tried to understand and accept the Catholic religion. I seemed to be unable to do so; thus, our relationship was broken.

To summarize briefly the data in Table 2, (1) slightly more than one-fourth of the students would cross religious lines and marry (apparently, without requiring any of the conditions specified in the statements in Table 2), (2) more than one student in five would consider an inter-faith marriage if the prospective mate would adopt the student's religion, (3) slightly more than one-fourth of the students would consider an inter-faith marriage if the children are brought up in their faith, (4) approximately one student in five would not marry outside his faith (even if the prospective mate were willing to adopt the student's faith or to allow the children to be brought up in the student's religion), and (5) seven per cent of the students were willing to adopt the religious faith of their mate, if by so doing, it would make marriage possible.

At this point, brief mention should be made of some of the reasons given by students as to why they do not want to marry outside their faith. Students were asked to check one or more of the following reasons: (1) Because of my religious convictions; (2) Because of parental objection; (3) Because I believe there is a probability that such a marriage would be unsuccesful; and (4) Other reasons (explain).

Briefly, it was found that 50 per cent of the students who were opposed to inter-faith marriages checked reason number three, i.e., "because I believe there is a probability that such a marriage would be unsuccessful." The other reasons, in order of frequency checked, were: one, two, and four. The majority of the students who checked category four wrote that they did not want to marry outside their faith because they foresaw difficulty arising over the religious training of the children. One student wrote:

> The biggest objection to inter-faith marriage to me is the problem of raising the children in a religious faith. The parents often can agree which church each wishes to attend, but rarely can they agree on which church the children should attend.

Another commented:

> I would not marry into the Catholic church because there would be the question of having to raise the children in the Catholic religion. Once they were Catholic, it would be almost impossible for them to choose freely any other religion.

One student whose parents are of different faiths wrote:

> I, myself, don't believe in an inter-faith marriage particularly because of the case in my own family. I feel very strongly on this subject. It seems that when young people marry they only see themselves, and being in love, they don't seem to realize at the time how much religion may or can mean to their marriage in later years, and the trouble it may cause, especially when children arrive.

Another commented:

> I am the result of a mixed marriage. It has worked out fairly well as my father belongs to no church and my mother had complete control of our education. Unless I change my view, I would not marry a person who is not a Catholic because I might be at a disadvantage in educating my children and because a major item like religion can cause undue friction.

This study examined the relationship between a person's expressed attitudes toward an inter-faith marriage and the attitudes he *thinks* his parents hold toward such a marriage. Students who would marry outside their faith felt also that their parents would approve an inter-faith marriage. On the other hand, students who were opposed to an inter-faith marriage also felt that their parents would disapprove if they married outside their faith. As seen in Table 3, 68 per cent of the Protestant students who would marry a Catholic felt that both parents would approve the marriage, and 16 per cent felt that both their parents would disapprove. Similarly, 76 per cent of the Catholic students who would marry a Protestant felt that both their parents would approve the marriage, but only four per cent felt that both parents would disapprove.

TABLE 3 *Students Who Would Marry outside Their Faith and How They Think Parents Would Feel if They Attempted Such a Marriage*

Students Who Would Marry outside Faith	BOTH PARENTS WOULD APPROVE Per Cent	ONLY ONE PARENT WOULD APPROVE Per Cent	BOTH PARENTS WOULD DIS-APPROVE Per Cent	NO RESPONSE Per Cent	TOTAL Per Cent
Protestant Students (N–1053)					
Would marry a Catholic person (N–565)	68	11	16	5	100
Would marry a Jewish person (N–359)	60	9	20	11	100
Would marry a person with no church affiliation (N–846)	82	6	5	7	100
Catholic Students (N–189)					
Would marry a Protestant person (N–133)	76	16	4	4	100
Would marry a Jewish person (N–57)	69	12	7	12	100
Would marry a person with no church affiliation (N–114)	70	9	11	10	100

In contrast, Table 4 shows that students who would not marry outside their faith also felt that their parents would *disapprove* an inter-faith marriage. Only a small percentage of them felt that their parents would approve such a marriage. It will be seen in Table 4 that 34 per cent of the Catholic students who would not marry a Protestant felt that both their parents would disapprove the marriage; but 43 per cent of them felt that both parents would approve. Perhaps Catholic students are more apt to feel that as long as their mate is willing to adopt the Catholic faith and/or is willing to agree to have the children brought up in the

Catholic religion, their parents will not disapprove if they marry outside their faith.

One should keep in mind, however, that the data in Tables 3 and 4 show only what the students *think* their parents' feelings are toward inter-faith marriages. Some students who answered the question, of course, knew their parents' attitudes toward inter-faith marriages. On the other hand, some, perhaps, had never heard their parents express any attitudes for or against inter-faith marriages but they assumed that their parents would disapprove of an inter-faith marriage for some reason or another. The point, however, is that there appears to be a relationship between a student's expressed attitudes toward an inter-faith

TABLE 4   *Students Who Would Not Marry outside Their Faith and How They Think Their Parents Would Feel if They Attempted Such a Marriage*

Students Who Would Marry outside Faith	BOTH PARENTS WOULD APPROVE Per Cent	ONLY ONE PARENT WOULD APPROVE Per Cent	BOTH PARENTS WOULD DIS-APPROVE Per Cent	NO RESPONSE Per Cent	TOTAL Per Cent
Protestant Students (N–1053)					
Would not marry a Catholic person (N–482)	26	10	59	5	100
Would not marry a Jewish person (N–690)	17	7	69	7	100
Would not marry a person with no church affiliation (N–205)	28	11	55	6	100
Catholic Students (N–189)					
Would not marry a Protestant person (N–56)	43	16	34	7	100
Would not marry a Jewish person (N–131)	17	5	70	8	100
Would not marry a person with no church affiliation (N–75)	23	8	60	9	100

marriage and the attitudes he *thinks* his parents hold toward such a marriage. And, in the final analysis, it is perhaps the attitude a person *thinks* his parents have toward a particular subject that more than likely will influence his own attitudes toward the same subject. Many students commented on their parents' attitudes toward inter-faith marriages. One student wrote:

I put that my parents would disapprove of my marrying outside my faith, but they would not forbid it. They would, however, discourage it.

Another commented:

Both of my parents would disapprove of my marrying a Jewish person, not because of prejudice but because of little knowledge of the faith. My father would disapprove of a Catholic because he cannot agree with their philosophy of faith.

Another wrote:

My parents would permit my marrying almost anyone with whom I was deeply in love, providing I retain my faith and the children are brought up in the Catholic faith.

A Catholic male student wrote:

I have no doubt that my parents would have preferences, probably Catholic. But they would not disapprove of any other religion, as long as the children were brought up Catholic.

The final excerpt, written by a student in her junior year, shows the pressure some parents will exert on their children to prevent them from marrying someone of a different religious faith. She wrote:

The past few years, I went with a Catholic boy. When I informed my parents that we were pinned, they refused to let me announce it, and insisted that I return the pin immediately. Because of my parents' strong objections, we cancelled the announcement of the pinning, but because we were both very much in love, I secretly kept his pin. I kept on going out with the boy and for this reason my parents almost had me transferred to a private Protestant college in the East.

The fellow was willing to give up his religion and join my church. My own religious convictions would not allow for any other decision, but my parents still objected—saying that he would eventually return to the Catholic faith.

This problem caused much unhappiness for everyone concerned. In time, I developed an ulcer from worrying about it. I transferred schools, thinking that it would help me in thinking out matters more clearly— hoping I would forget the boy in time. I don't know whether this has helped or not, but I do know that I will never go through this same religious problem again. . . .

In conclusion, the findings in the present study show clearly that young people of marriageable age are well-aware of some of the problems that accompany inter-faith marriages. Although these students expressed a liberal view toward such marriages, they themselves would marry outside their faith only under certain conditions.

20. SOCIAL CLASS AND CAMPUS DATING

Ira L. Reiss

§ After a brief review of earlier studies of campus dating, Reiss presents the results of research that bring together the factors of parental social class and the student's campus rating in tracing the lines of campus selection of dating partners. New interpretation is given to earlier studies. One of the conclusions Reiss reaches is that the supposedly free dating system is limited by sociocultural factors.

General Background of the Research Area

About 30 years ago, there began to appear in the sociological literature accounts of dating practices on college campuses. Although earlier writers had mentioned the same phenomenon, it was a 1937 journal article by Willard Waller that has come to epitomize this early literature on campus dating customs.[1] Waller reported that the older accepted code of a courtship system that led to formal engagement and marriage in a predictable fashion had decayed and was being replaced by a thrill seeking and exploitive type of relationship which was not integrated with marriage. This new type of relationship was a dalliance relationship, needed to fill in the time it took to get a college education and establish oneself financially. Connected with this type of dating was the "rating-dating complex" which was a set of customs that established one's prestige on campus and which in turn determined one's dating desirability. The key prestige variables were things like popularity, access to cars and money, and belonging to the best Greek organizations. Serious, marriage oriented dating did not involve these prestige ratings. Thus, such prestige rating-and-dating was not viewed as "true" courtship. This campus dating system was discerned by Waller

SOURCE: *Social Problems*, 13 (Fall, 1965), 193–205. Reprinted by permission of the author and the publisher, The Society for the Study of Social Problems.

The author, whose doctorate is from Pennsylvania State University, is professor of sociology at the University of Iowa. He is the author of *Premarital Sexual Standards in America* and the *Social Context of Premarital Sexual Permissiveness*.

[1] Willard Waller, "The Rating and Dating Complex," *American Sociological Review*, 2 (October, 1937), pp. 727–734. Joseph K. Folsom was one of the sociologists who presented similar ideas before Waller's article.

at the Pennsylvania State University in the early 1930's and was documented by discussion and interviews with students.

In order to clarify the place of my research, it may be well to recount very briefly a few of the relevant studies that followed the Waller article. In the 1940's Hollingshead brought forth considerable evidence indicating the social behavior of adolescents was functionally related to the social class of their parents.[2] Particularly relevant here was Hollingshead's finding that dating among high school students was heavily controlled by social class background. Then shortly after the war Harold Christensen, Robert Blood, and William Smith, in separate research work, tested college students to see if the sort of rating factors (cars, money, dancing ability, etc.) which Waller found to hold at Penn State would also hold true in their samples.[3] They each found that the students in their sample largely rejected the "competitive materialistic" items that Waller reported and instead favored "personality" factors such as "sense of humor, cheerful, good sport, natural and considerate."[4] Blood found that the type of value system Waller was speaking of was most likely to be found among the Greeks on campus but that even there it was not supported unanimously by any means. These findings brought into question Waller's own views.[5] Nevertheless, it must be borne in mind that Waller's observations may have been correct for the time and place they were made.

In 1960 Everett Rogers and Eugene Havens published a study done on Iowa State College students.[6] They had 11 judges rank the Greek organizations and the major residence on campus and then, by interviews with a random sample of 725 students and by checking the student newspapers, they gathered evidence regarding the relation of prestige to dating of various types. They found a high probability for

2 August B. Hollingshead, *Elmtown's Youth*, New York: John Wiley and Son, 1949.
3 Harold T. Christensen, *Marriage Analysis*, New York: Ronald Press, 1958, 2nd edition, esp. pp. 235–243, 261–264; Robert O. Blood, Jr., "A Retest of Waller's Rating Complex," *Marriage and Family Living*, 17 (February, 1955), pp. 41–47; William M. Smith, Jr., "Rating and Dating: A Restudy," *Marriage and Family Living*, 14 (November, 1952), pp. 312–317.
4 See in particular Robert O. Blood, Jr., "Uniformities and Diversities in Campus Dating Preferences," *Marriage and Family Living*, 18 (February, 1956), pp. 37–45. An interesting report of a similar research project on a Negro campus can be found in Charles S. Anderson and Joseph S. Himes, "Dating Values and Norms on a Negro College Campus," *Marriage and Family Living*, 21 (August, 1959), pp. 227–229.
5 At about this same time an article by Samuel H. Lowrie had questioned Waller's characterization of campus dating. See "Dating Theories and Student Responses," *American Sociological Review*, 16 (June, 1951), pp. 334–340. A more recent discussion of this point can be found in Jack Delora, "Social Systems of Dating on a College Campus," *Marriage and Family Living*, 25 (February, 1963), pp. 81–84.
6 Everett M. Rogers and A. Eugene Havens, "Prestige Rating and Mate Selection on a College Campus," *Marriage and Family Living*, 22 (February, 1960), pp. 55–59.

people to date those who are ranked similar to themselves. They concluded from this:

> Therefore, Waller's hypothesis that prestige ranking governs casual campus dating but not more serious mate selection is not substantiated to any great degree by the present findings. Instead, these findings indicate that students follow prestige lines at all stages of the mate selection process.[7]

A study of fraternity pledging at an Eastern college by Gene Levine and Leila Sussmann lent support to the Rogers and Havens findings on prestige factors in dating.[8] Levine and Sussmann found that it was the wealthier students who more often pledged and who more often were accepted into fraternities and who in addition had the "proper" attitudes toward fraternities. Thus, there seemed to be a class factor not only in campus ratings but in parental background that distinguished the Greek and non-Greek student.

In effect, these findings on campus dating radically revamped much of Waller's position. The "competitive-materialistic" system of values that Waller described seems to be present on college campuses today mainly as a sub-cultural element, most likely to be found among the Greek organizations. But the more recent findings on class prestige factors in dating are even more important theoretically. Waller's view of the prestige system at Penn State was not a view of people of different parental social classes dating along those class lines. Rather, Waller explicitly stated that he did not believe there were any basic social class background differences among the students:

> The students of this college are predominantly taken from the lower half of the middle classes, and constitute a remarkable homogeneous group. Numerous censuses of the occupation of fathers and of living expenses seem to establish this fact definitely.[9]

The prestige that Waller spoke of was obtained by success in dating the highest ranked girls and boys. The rating-dating system was a popularity system in which having a good line, knowing how to dance, dressing nicely, all had a part. It was, to Waller, based predominantly on dating desirability, and social class in any fundamental sense was not the basis of it. The system produced a sort of superficial rating-dating class of its own rather than depending on any more basic class system. Thus, one important question now is, is there a more fundamental class system both on and off campus with which the campus dating system is integrated and which Waller has overlooked? The

---

[7] Rogers and Havens, *ibid.*, p. 59.

[8] Gene N. Levine and Leila A. Sussmann, "Social Change and Sociability in Fraternity Pledging," *The American Journal of Sociology*, 65 (January, 1960), pp. 391–399.

[9] Waller, *op. cit.*, p. 729.

Levine and Sussmann study of fraternities lends support to a positive answer to this question as does the Rogers and Havens study. Research on social class homogamy in marriage and engagement also strongly supports the view of the importance of social class in mating.[10] Careful research of this sort has not often been done on the college campus. In fact, some writers stress the democratization effects of college life and the homogeneity of social class on campuses.[11] Nevertheless, I am suggesting that the social classes on campus are not simple "popularity" classes but that they are stable class structures based on many campus values and that they reflect parental social class and affect serious as well as casual dating.

Theory and Hypotheses

In its broadest sense the orientation of my research embodies the well tested theory that *the dating patterns of a group will follow the social class lines of that group and thereby encourage class endogamous dating and mating.*[12] The implications of this theory have only rarely

[10] The classic study establishing homogamy in mating is Ernest W. Burgess and Paul Wallin, *Engagement and Marriage*, New York: Lippincott, 1953. There is an excellent account of the relation of parental class and student dating in Winston W. Ehrmann, *Premarital Dating Behavior*, New York: Henry Holt, 1959, pp. 144–169. For interesting evidence that sorority and fraternity people marry each other, see A. Philip Sundal and Thomas C. McCormic, "Age at Marriage and Mate Selection: Madison, Wisconsin, 1937–1943," *American Sociological Review*, 16 (February, 1951), pp. 37–48, esp. p. 47. Sixty-one per cent of the sorority girls married fraternity boys. A recent study reporting class homogamy in campus marriages and showing parental influence is Robert H. Coombs, "Reinforcement of Values in the Parental Home as a Factor in Mate Selection," *Marriage and Family Living*, 24 (May, 1962), pp. 155–157. For a much older statement along these lines see Alan Bates, "Parental Roles in Courtship," *Social Forces*, 20 (May, 1942), pp. 483–486. For evidence on the continued importance of social class in mate selection in general see Simon Dinitz, Franklin Banks, and Benjamin Pasamanick, "Mate Selection and Social Class: Changes During the Past Quarter Century," *Marriage and Family Living*, 22 (November, 1960), pp. 348–351; J. Daniel Ray, "Dating Behavior as Related to Organizational Prestige," (M.A. Thesis), Indiana University, 1942; Ernest A. Smith, "Dating and Courtship at Pioneer College," *Sociology and Social Research*, 40, 1955, pp. 92–98. Marvin Sussman has shown the ways parents control marriage in a New Haven study: "Parental Participation in Mate Selection and Its Effect Upon Family Continuity," *Social Forces*, 32 (October, 1953), pp. 76–81.

[11] Listed below is one such study that tested for class homogamy in campus marriages and found little evidence of it. These authors believe that the campus is a democratizing influence which *reduces* class endogamy. Clark R. Leslie and Arthur H. Richardson, "Family Versus Campus Influences in Relation to Mate Selection," *Social Problems*, 4 (October, 1956), pp. 117–121. The literature on intermarriage also mentions that the campus breaks through traditional barriers. See Albert I. Gordon, *Intermarriage*, Boston: Beacon Press, 1964. However, there could be a democratization concerning interfaith marriage, without affecting class endogamy.

[12] The references in footnote 10 are relevant here. Also, the role of stratification in love relations has been dealt with in William J. Goode, "The Theoretical Importance of Love," *American Sociological Review*, 24 (February, 1959), pp. 38–47.

been tested on college campuses although it is often spoken about.[13] It follows from this theory that one should expect to find a stratified dating system on any campus, except those campuses where, due to extremely small size and homogeneity, there is no class distinction among the students. It also follows from our knowledge that student behavior reflects parental class, that the social class differences among students should reflect class differences among the parental adult population.[14] It is of theoretical value to know not only whether or not the campus is stratified but to know whether the class system tends to reflect in some ways the parental class lines. If it does, then one latent consequence of such a system may be to maintain some remnant of adult control over mating via the promotion of class endogamous marriages which parents generally seem to favor.

The Waller approach to campus dating focused on specific date-rating factors and took them to be the essence of the dating system. It is my contention that the rating factors are merely symptoms of basic campus and parental class distinctions and that the entire system can best be understood from this social class perspective. The rating-dating system of any sort, competitive or personality based, is believed to be a direct reflection of the campus and parental class system and a way of clarifying and identifying class differences. Such clarification is viewed as part of a serious mate-selection system. Thus, Waller's view that rating-dating is a dalliance system and not integrated with serious dating or mating is questioned.

In summary, I am proposing to test two hypotheses related to the basic "class-dating" theory: (1) serious dating on campus will be in line with an existing campus stratification system, and (2) campus dating will reflect the parental class system.

Methodology

The data on campus dating were gathered at a coeducational liberal arts college in Virginia. The 19 Greek organizations (ten fraternities and nine sororities) had 840 members and 151 pledges out of a total student body of 1800 single students. There were 809 single independent

---

[13] For a relatively early statement in this area and an interesting test of courtship among college men see Robert F. Winch, "Interrelations Between Certain Social Backgrounds and Parent-Son Factors in A Study of Courtship Among College Men," *American Sociological Review*, 11 (June, 1946), pp. 333–341, esp. p. 338. For a study showing similarities and changes in basic values see Robert McGinnis, "Campus Views in Mate Selection: A Repeat Study," *Social Forces*, 36 (May, 1958), pp. 368–373.
[14] Hollingshead had found considerable evidence that the social class of one's parent was a good predictor of adolescent behavior. Hollingshead, *op. cit.*

students. There was a relatively even sex ratio in both Greek and independent groupings. It was decided that full information on Greek serious dating practices would be obtained as one test of the stratification-dating theory. If in 19 highly organized fraternities and sororities there was no indication of the relation of social class and serious dating, then the theory and its derivative hypotheses would be brought into question. In addition to the sample of all seriously dating Greeks, I drew a random sample which I could use to rank all campus groups, to obtain information on parental social class, and to further test on a representative sample the relation of campus class to dating patterns in both independent and Greek student groups. The random sample was an important group since it represented the entire campus. The all Greek sample was used to give a fuller and more detailed picture of the serious dating patterns of the Greeks.

The Greek organizations all met on Monday nights and usually had over 90% attendance at meetings. I sent one student assistant to each Greek organization to obtain information regarding all "serious" dating relationships.[15] A serious dating relation was defined as a relatively exclusive dating relation such as going steady, being pinned or engaged. All such relations were reported to my informants together with information on the Greek, independent, or off-campus status of the dating partner. If class-dating were found in these serious relations it would be evidenced that serious dating relationships were not *just* based on "personality factors" but that these very personality factors could possibly be viewed as influenced by stratification factors.[16] Finally, if one wanted to check on the relation of mating to stratification then serious dating and not just casual dating must be checked.

The check of all 19 Greek organizations yielded 133 serious dating relations for sorority girls and 112 such relations for fraternity boys. About 30% of the Greek members were involved in serious relations. Sixty-two of these relations were between a sorority girl and a fraternity boy. (These figures are for members only, not pledges. Pledges were also investigated and they will be reported on later.) The 62 couples consisting entirely of Greeks on campus afforded a check on the reliability of our information. If our data were accurate the sororities and fraternities should each report 62 matched serious relations. This was the case.[17]

In addition to this all-Greek sample, a random sample of all single

---

[15] The student assistants went back two more times to verify and check all information they had received the first time.
[16] Blood, *op. cit.*, Smith, *op. cit.*; both stress personality factors as crucial in dating.
[17] One additional couple broke up due to differences in the definition of their relationship that came to the foreground during the research.

students on the campus was drawn and given a questionnaire. One hundred forty-four questionnaires were obtained.[18] There were 25 non-responses who were mostly students who were not located by my research assistants. Questionnaires were given out and picked up within a few hours by my 19 assistants. The questionnaires asked the respondent to rank each of the 10 fraternities as high, medium, or low, and to do the same for the 9 sororities, and to give reasons for the rankings assigned. In addition, questions were asked concerning the students' background including income and occupation of father, their own dating behavior, and the relative rank they would give to male and female independents and Greeks.

The all-Greek sample containing all 245 seriously dating Greeks was used as one test of Hypothesis One concerning the congruence of the dating system with the campus class system. The random sample of the campus was used to further check this hypothesis for both Greeks and independents, to rank all campus groups, and also to check the second hypothesis concerning the relation of campus class to parental social class.

The Campus Stratification System

If the first hypothesis is correct there should be a significant association between the rank of the various campus segments and the serious dating patterns of these groups. Table 1 presents information on all the Greek students who were involved in serious dating. The fraternities and sororities were listed according to the ranking assigned by the random sample of campus students. The majority of students agreed on all rankings, although the rankings on sororities were more unanimous than the rankings on fraternities. The fraternities were divided into five high and five low ranked groups and the sororities into five high and four low ranked groups. It should be noted that many other cuts were tried on these data and the results were the same, i.e., there is a significant and strong relation between one's organizational rank and that of one's serious date. This is particularly true for the high ranked Greeks.

Table 1 also shows that although all Greek organizations have roughly the same per cent involved in serious dating, the high ranked Greek organizations (particularly the fraternities) have a significantly higher per cent involved in serious dating with members of Greek organizations rather than with off-campus or independents. Serious dating within the Greek system is dominated by the high ranked organizations. The low

[18] There were 16 pledges and 5 No Answers on organizational membership which were not included in the general analysis of Greeks and independents in this paper. This left 123 respondents to be used in the general analysis. The pledges were analyzed separately.

ranked Greeks, for the most part, obtain their serious dates outside the Greek system. It should be noted here that the Greek dating reported by our random sample was very similar and this is evidence of the representativeness of our random sample.

When we look in Table 1 at the relation of sorority ranking to the choice of dating an off-campus or an independent male, the results are rather striking. Of the high ranked sorority girls who are not dating within the Greek system, all of them are dating off-campus and not one is seriously dating an independent male on campus. Whereas, of the low ranked sorority girls, 19% seriously date independent males. Since there are an equal supply of Greeks and independents on campus and an equal sex ratio, this pattern seems to imply an avoidance of independents, perhaps due to a low ranking on campus. This avoidance is particularly pronounced for the high ranked sororities.

If we look at fraternity members in Table 1 to see their choice of off-campus or independent dates, we find a pattern somewhat similar to that of the sororities. Table 1 shows that the high ranked fraternity men prefer off-campus dates significantly more than the low ranked fraternity men. In fact, the low ranked fraternity men date independent females more than they date off-campus girls. Here too, then, is evidence that

TABLE 1   *Percentage Distribution of Types of Serious Dating Partners Among Greeks in the all Greek Sample**

	PERCENTAGE OF EACH TYPE OF PARTNER				Number of Serious Dating Relations†
	High Ranked Greeks	Low Ranked Greeks	Off-Campus	Inde-pendent	
High Ranked Fraternities	63	12	17	8	(60)
Low Ranked Fraternities	14	19	23	44	(52)
High Ranked Sororities	44	8	48	0	(86)
Low Ranked Sororities	15	21	45	19	(47)

* Significant differences exist between high and low ranked Greeks in their choice of a Greek dating partner and in the per cent dating Greeks and in the per cent dating independents. Also, a significant difference exists between fraternities and sororities in per cent dating off-campus.

† The percent of total members involved in serious relations is not significantly different for these four groups. Going from top to bottom of the table the per cent is: 31, 27, 32, 25.

the independents are ranked low particularly by high ranked Greeks, but it would seem that the independent females are not avoided to the extent that the independent males are. Our double standard culture dictates that in a dating relation, if one person is to be higher in status than the other, it should be the male; and perhaps this is why independent females are not avoided as much as independent males.[19]

There is direct evidence of the relative ranking of campus groups from our random sample which can be compared with the above evidence from the Greek sample. We asked the random sample respondents to state their relative ranking of independent males and fraternity males and of independent females and sorority girls. Rankings were asked for in terms of one's personal views and not in terms of what one thought others would generally say. The results indicated that most individuals, except independent males, feel that independent males rank below fraternity males. The independent females were evenly divided regarding their own superiority, and the independent males closely agreed with them. However, most all the Greeks were convinced that sorority girls outranked the independent girls.[20]

It should be noted that this view of the independents is generally shared by both high and low ranked Greeks.[21] Thus, it would seem that when low ranked Greeks date independents, they believe they are dating "down" but are willing to do so for other compensatory reasons or, in the case of males, simply because they don't feel the distance is so great and that it is accepted for males to date down. Perhaps some of the low ranked fraternity males date independent females with sexual goals uppermost in mind. However, in serious dating relationships this is less likely to happen.[22]

Additional evidence on this relative campus ranking comes from a further look at serious dating patterns of the independents in our random sample.[23] If independent males are ranked lower than the independent females, then it follows that the independent females in our random sample should report more serious relations with the upper classes, namely, the Greeks. This was the case—of 19 independent

---

[19] For evidence and elaboration on the double standard see Ira L. Reiss, *Premarital Sexual Standards in America,* Glencoe, Ill.: The Free Press, 1960, esp. ch. 4.
[20] Eighty per cent of the independent males thought they ranked higher than fraternity men but all other groups had over 80% who said the opposite. Fifty per cent of the independent females felt they ranked higher than sorority girls. Although the independent males agreed, over 80% of the Greeks disagreed.
[21] Low fraternity as compared to high fraternity men are somewhat kinder in their ratings of independents whereas low sorority girls are almost unanimous in giving low rank to independents. These differences were not quite significant.
[22] For data on this see Winston W. Ehrmann, *op. cit.,* chs. 4 and 5.
[23] The independent females reported the largest group of friends from the other three campus groups, thereby further showing their pivotal positions and their tendencies to date both independent and Greek boys.

females with serious dates, 7 were with fraternity men. It should be noted that 5 of the 7 fraternity men dating independent females were from low ranking fraternities. This, too, would be expected. There were 11 independent males with serious dates, and only one was with a sorority girl and this was with a girl from the lowest ranking sorority on campus. Further, the independent females are more likely to have their serious dates on campus than are the independent males. Only one third of the serious dates were off campus for independent females, whereas two thirds of the serious dates of independent males were off campus. Finally, the independent females are involved with fraternity men about as much as the low ranked sorority girls, while the independent males are involved with sorority girls much less than low ranked fraternity males. The evidence on independents here is based on a small number of cases. However, since the results are consistent with several other checks, the confidence in the findings is increased.

In sum then, the stratification system which emerges at this point is one in which the Greeks are clearly at the top, but the low ranked Greeks are more likely to date seriously outside the Greek part of the system. In addition, the independents seem stratified by sex, with females ranked higher than males; and here too it is noted that the females have their serious dates more within the total campus system and the independent males have their serious dates predominantly outside the entire campus system.

Casual dating was also checked in the random sample and proved to follow stratification lines quite similar to serious dating. Many independents, especially males, do not date at all in Greek organizations. Table 2 shows the distribution of those students who do date Greeks. The same relations among high and low Greeks and male and female independents prevail in casual dating as prevailed in serious dating.[24] It may be argued that if casual dating and serious dating both show a similar relation to the campus rating system, then the rating system is integrated with serious dating and mating and is "true" courtship and not just a dalliance system as Waller contended.

An additional search was made via the questionnaire and campus records to see whether the above noted differences in campus prestige are related to differences in some key characteristics of the students in the four major campus groups. A comparison of age at which dating

---

[24] Table 2 is composed of answers from those who do date in Greek organizations to the question, "In which Greek organizations have you dated the most?" Some respondents will include serious dating as well as casual. However, the bulk of the dating reported is casual. Further, when known serious dating is eliminated, the relationship still holds up the same as reported although a little weaker. Actually, the relation is understated since about 35% of the independent females and almost 60% of the independent males do not date Greeks at all. This fact supports the relation of social class and dating but is not presented in the table.

TABLE 2 *Percentage of Those Who Date Greeks, Who Are Dating in High Ranked Greek Organizations, in the Random Sample*

Group	Per cent Dating High Ranked Greeks
High Ranked Greeks	$78_{(41)}$ *
Low Ranked Greeks	$54_{(24)}$
Independent Females	$50_{(20)}$
Independent Males	$20_{(10)}$

$$X^2 = 8.95$$
$$P < .05$$
$$G = .53\dagger$$

* The number to the right and below the percentage is the base for the percentage.
† G = Gamma or Index of Order Association devised by Goodman and Kruskal.

began among sorority and independent females revealed no significant differences. However, the same comparison of independent males and fraternity males revealed a moderately strong and almost significant difference.[25]

A stronger and a significant difference appeared between the fraternity and independent males when compared on whether they had been in love before. There was no significant difference among females.[26] Thus, it seems the fraternity males started dating earlier and had more love experiences. This "sociability" factor is one that was found to characterize fraternity men in the Levine and Sussmann study referred to above.[27] Such "sociability" background may well represent a social class difference in this sample as it did in the Levine and Sussmann sample.

A check of attitudes toward premarital intercourse was also undertaken. The independent males were the most conservative male group. This somewhat fits with their lack of dating and love experience. The low fraternity males were the most liberal group with high fraternity males falling in the middle. All females were about equally conservative.

The reasons for the relative ranking of the fraternities and sororities given by the total random sample were also examined to see if inde-

[25] Sorority girls had 74% who started dating by age 16 to the independent girls 66%. The percentages for fraternity and independent males were 65 and 41 respectively.
[26] Sorority girls had 84% who had been in love to the independent girls 94%. The percentages for fraternity and independent males were 96 and 60 respectively.
[27] Levine and Sussmann, *op. cit.*

pendents and Greeks differed here. All groups agreed that high ranking was given to a Greek organization for things such as sociability, intelligence and maturity, and campus activities. These were the most frequently mentioned ranking factors. There is evidence that these reasons are accurate perceptions of differences among the Greek organizations. A search of school records revealed that the high ranked Greeks control the student assembly and its officers. All but 7 of the 125 student assembly members during a three year period preceding the study were Greeks, and of the 118 Greeks, 87 were from high ranked Greek organizations. Of 63 Greek class officers, 53 were high ranked Greeks. This relation held up for sororities as well as fraternities.

Good looks and good grades were evaluated differently by Greek and independent males. The Greeks stressed good looks and the independents stressed good grades. Available evidence generally fits these rankings. In the three years preceding this study, 30 beauty queens were chosen. Five of them were low ranked Greeks; 25 were high ranked Greeks; none of the beauty queens were independents. In terms of academic grades, the high ranked sororities outdo the low ranked sororities. However, among males the situation is different and the high ranked fraternities do not outdo the low ranked fraternities in grades. The independent males are better than the fraternity males in grades; but the independent females are poorer than the sorority females. The academic grade records for a ten year period were checked and verified that this was a stable patterning of grades.

Finally, independent males valued dancing, sports, and parties less than fraternity males. The differences among sorority and independent females in rankings were fewer than those between fraternity and independent males. The sorority females gave more importance to such items as good manners, dress, and dancing ability, but otherwise there was general agreement. So here, too, the independent females are closer to the Greek females than the independent males are to the Greek males.

Some of the reasons for ranking Greek organizations are similar to the sort of factors about which Willard Waller wrote. In particular, this is true of such factors as "good dancer," "good dresser," "good looking." These factors were not the most frequently mentioned; nevertheless, here is evidence of the sort of rating-dating that Waller had in mind. However, and this is my major point here, to focus on these factors as the heart of the dating system and to conclude that the system is superficial and unintegrated with marriage is to miss the crux of the matter. I am suggesting that these factors are merely part of the complex of factors which defines what sort of organization the high ranked students on campus achieve. These prestige factors are some of the variables that go with belonging to a certain campus social class and serve to identify that class. They are merely symbols of campus class status, and it is that class status that is crucial, not the symbols.[28]

I should add here that an examination of the dating behavior of the 151 pledges in the Greek organizations revealed a very similar pattern to that of Greek members. This examination involved all pledges from all Greek organizations. Also, a study checking Greek rating and dating was done on this same campus in 1954 with quite similar results.[29] Thus, the stratification we are describing has roots in the past and our examination of pledges indicates that it is being extended into the future.

Campus Social Class and Parental Social Class

Although other studies have shown that parental social class affects dating and mating, there is very little data on the relation of campus social class to parental social class. Evidence from our own sample is relevant here, although our testing of this hypothesis is nowhere near as thorough as was our testing of Hypothesis One. We have shown above that the fraternity men are more socialized in terms of dating and love experience. There is also evidence showing that Greeks value elements such as dress, parties, dancing, sports, and drinking activities more than independents. Such values are again part of a "socialized" image of man which the Greeks promote and which Levine and Sussmann have identified as part of the middle classes.[30]

In the random sample, I also have information on fathers' income and occupation. Here too some differences appear among the campus strata. As can be seen in Table 3 the overall occupations of Greeks are significantly higher than those of the independents. High status occupation here is defined as executive or professional. There is also a difference in occupation of father between high and low fraternities and high and low sororities. However, these differences are not quite significant. The differences in Table 3 reflect the general rank of each campus group as discussed in this paper.[31]

The females in sororities are somewhat higher in class background than the independent females and are also somewhat above the fra-

[28] For a discussion of how fashion in dress symbolizes status, see Bernard Barber and Lyle S. Lobel, "Fashion in Women's Clothes and the American Social System," *Social Forces*, 31 (December, 1952), pp. 124–131.
[29] This unpublished study was done by two students: Withers Davis and Penny Hutchinson.
[30] Levine and Sussmann, *op. cit.* Religious differences were also checked and the only religious difference discovered was that low fraternity men were highest on Catholic and Baptist members.
[31] An unpublished study by two of my students (Rusty Dietrich and Barbara Clarke) at this same college did show that, among Freshmen, independent females as compared to sorority girls had lower income, less church attendance, and fewer parents who had been in sororities. No test of males was done in this study.

ternity men. Females in college often come from higher class back-grounds than males. Possibly this is due to females' college attendance being considered of secondary importance to males' college attendance and so those females that do go to college come from wealthier homes.[32] This higher background may further explain the reluctance of sorority girls (particularly high ranked ones) to date independent males.

A check on income revealed one interesting relationship. Although the differences between high and low ranked Greeks and male and female independents were present, the difference between all inde-pendents and all Greeks disappeared.[33] Independent females in par-ticular came out quite high on income. One might interpret these occupational and income results as indicating that although Greeks come

TABLE 3 *Percentage of Fathers with High Status Occupations for Various Campus Groups in the Random Sample**

Groups	Per cent of Fathers in High Status Occupations
High Fraternity	$69_{(13)}$†
Low Fraternity	$54_{(13)}$
High Sorority	$80_{(25)}$
Low Sorority	$60_{(10)}$
Independent Female	$42_{(31)}$
Independent Male	$41_{(22)}$

* Differences within the three pairs in this table are not significant but the difference between all Greeks and all Independents is significant.

† The number to the right and below the percentage is the base for the percentage.

from higher social classes as indicated by occupation, they do not come from wealthier homes. Thus, the overall campus class differences be-tween Greeks and independents reflect the style of life of each group as related to occupational background more than income background. It may be argued that the occupation of a father affects male values more than female values. Thus, despite their wealth the independents, particularly the males, lack the values that go with the high occupational groupings and thus are ranked lower on campus. Although this *post*

[32] Recent evidence of females' higher status on other specific campuses can be found in Leslie Richardson, *op. cit.*, p. 120, and Robert P. Bell and Leonard Blum-berg, "Courtship Intimacy and Religious Background," *Marriage and Family Living*, 21 (November, 1959), pp. 356–360, esp. p. 357.

[33] The mean income based on questionnaire response of the random sample is esti-mated to be: High Fraternity, $12,400; Low Fraternity, $9,400; High Sorority, $12,600; Low Sorority, $11,100; Independent Females, $13,000; and Independent Males, $12,400.

factum explanation does make sense of these findings, it must, of course, be tested in new research.

The question raised in Hypothesis Two asks how parental social class affects the relationship, found in Hypothesis One, between one's own campus class rating and the campus class rating of one's date. Unfortunately, the more crucial tests of Hypothesis Two cannot be made with the existing data I have available. Such tests would involve checking the various possible relations between parental social class and campus social class dating more directly. For example it is possible that, even though high campus class individuals are more likely to come from high parental classes (see Table 3), parental social class does not affect the campus class dating system. For example, even though the higher parental class boys join the higher ranking fraternities, the reasons why these boys most often date equally high campus ranked girls may well be fully independent of their parental social class. This possibility does *not* fit with Hypothesis Two. On the other hand, it is possible that parental class would fully explain the tendency of high campus ranked boys to date high campus ranked girls. If so, when one held parental social class constant and looked at only one parental social class at a time, the relation showing high campus ranked boys dating high campus ranked girls would disappear. If this happened, then one could conclude that parental class fully explained why boys and girls dated as they did within the campus class system. This would fit with Hypothesis Two.

Finally, there is another possible way that the parental social class system could influence the campus class dating system. It could be that one's campus social class acts as an intervening variable between one's parental social class and one's choice of a dating partner. Possibly it is because one has high parental social class that one gets involved in high campus class groups and these high campus class groups might develop a style of life which in turn would make one more likely to date others from similar high campus groups. This eventuality would also fit with Hypothesis Two for it would show the influence of parental class on the campus social class dating system. It is hoped that future research will test these several possibilities and thereby afford us a more precise test of Hypothesis Two.[34]

In sum, then, this check of Hypothesis Two shows that there is some

---

[34] I did ask each person in the random student sample to give me information on his or her parental social class. However, in order to make the checks suggested it would be necessary to have parental social class information on *both* the boy and the girl involved in a dating relationship. My random sample consisted mostly of students who were seriously dating someone else *not* included in the sample and this left us with a lack of knowledge about the parental class of their dates. Because of this we could only perform the partial testing of Hypothesis Two which appears in the text and in Table 3.

evidence to support the hypothesis that the stratification system on the college campus reflects the stratification system of the students' parents. However, the evidence is surely more suggestive than conclusive and is not nearly as complete as that supporting Hypothesis One.

Conclusions

The importance of this theoretical approach is its relevance for much of the past work on campus dating. In part, it tests ideas often verbalized but seldom tested, and tries to organize the many *ad hoc* findings in this area into one theory. The theory bears on Waller's position in that it defines his "materialistic-competitive" system as but one set of rating factors that can be used to symbolize the class differences among students. The rating-dating system (whether "competitive" or "personality" based) doesn't block mating; it is more an indication of the presence of an underlying campus stratification system than it is an indication of a thrill-centered, exploitative dating system unintegrated with marriage or social class. As a matter of fact, the rating system operates not only on casual dating but in serious dating also and therefore seems well integrated with marriage. The manifest consequences of this dating system may well be involved with the establishment of one's rating, as Waller suggested, but the latent consequences are the support of campus and parental class endogamy. It may further be hypothesized that since parents usually favor matings within the same social class, then another latent consequence is to aid in achieving such parental goals. Awareness of such latent consequences is crucial to the understanding of the campus dating system. Without this awareness the system may appear to be merely an "irrational" system of dalliance.

There is need for several types of additional research. First it would be important to examine a more representative sample of American college students to see how this theory and its derivative hypotheses fare on different types of campuses. Stratification on campuses without Greek organizations needs investigation. My data indicate that independents do indeed have hierarchical divisions just as Greeks do, but more investigation is needed. Testing this theory on various size campuses with differing proportions of Greeks would also be valuable. In addition, how individual choice operates within the limits of a stratification system should be conceptualized more clearly. There is the important problem of how such factors as propinquity, ideal mate image, parental images, basic values, and other variables operate in relation to social class and in relation to mate selection in general. Finally, the relation of other institutions such as the political, economic, and religious to campus dating and campus class should be explored.

It is particularly important in the analysis of a "free dating system," such as we possess, to keep in mind the ways in which the system is structured and the controls of a socio-cultural nature that are operative. It is all too easy to believe the cultural ideology that we have a "free" system. The theory put forth in this paper keeps the socio-cultural limitations of our dating system in the foreground. It is by focusing on such socio-cultural factors that we may obtain insight into the functional relations of mate-selection to the overall institutional structure of our society.

21. THE AMERICAN COLLEGE SORORITY: ITS ROLE IN CLASS AND ETHNIC ENDOGAMY

John Finley Scott

§ The college sorority has a special function in channeling members' dating to achieve endogamy within whatever ethnic, religious, or social-class stratum the sorority represents. The sorority tends to offset the great variety of contacts and wealth of new ideas prevalent on the campus, and maintains the ascribed status of the student. Scott's keen analysis of the functions of the sorority also throws light on dating in other groups.

All who study higher education in America sooner or later encounter college sororities. They are visible centers of the rites of feminine adolescence—rites so amusing and so seemingly trivial that academicians tend not to give them serious attention. But "sorority membership" as an antecedent variable has earned the more serious respect of many research workers who study the behavior of college students. Sororities are

SOURCE: *American Sociological Review*, 30 (August, 1965), 514–27. Reprinted by permission of the publisher and the author.

Revision of a paper read at the 1964 annual meeting of the American Sociological Association, in Montreal. Several persons read earlier versions and offered useful criticisms; especially helpful were Warren Hagstrom and Christopher Jencks. Sandra Saunders provided valuable liaison with informants. But my fundamental obligation is to the informants themselves, including several necessarily anonymous sorority members who respected my sociological mission more than the National Panhellenic Conference rule of silence to outside inquiry. The research was supported in part by grants from the National Science Foundation and from the Committee on Research, University of California, Davis.

The author is at the University of Washington, Seattle.

most common at the large campuses of public land-grant schools; formally, they are private associations providing (where college administrations permit) separate dormitory facilities for female students, sharply distinguished from other such facilities by "Greek-letter" names, a strict and invidious policy of recommendatory and invitational membership, and substantial control by organized adult "alumnae" rather than the college.

The basic research problem here is that sororities are known only by their effects. There is little public record of their internal structure and little more on their relation to the environing society. Then too sororities, when academicians do take note of them, are usually seen as alien to the values of liberal education. Thus they have been mainly studied as an exercise in academic morality, and only so that they might thereby be better deplored. Especially is this the case regarding their membership criteria in such categories of ascribed status as religion and "race." Sociological explanation of these criteria is thereby neglected. *Tout comprendre, c'est tout pardonner;* thus the moralist cannot venture to explain what he only wants to condemn.

Sororities claim to be secret societies and in many respects they are: their mystery is designed, their structure hidden, their liaisons discreet. What is this peculiar institution? Why is it what it is? In answering these questions my proximate concern is to explain a parochial and now embattled institution; ultimately I want to show more generally how control of material choice by ascriptive group, a topic most thoroughly studied and most clearly understood in simple and agrarian societies, can be adapted to the conditions imposed by such modern institutions as mass higher education. The sorority may expire, but the motives behind it will persist: thus it provides an interesting introduction to some of the variables involved in the relation between the ancient institutions of kinship and novel forms of industrial social organization.

Even with this abstract and generalizing concern, however, the analysis rests on concrete details. Here then is a brief note of what sororities are *not*, because so many common beliefs about them, influenced by their mystery and circumlocution, are in fact largely wrong, and if believed render implausible the explanation that follows. Sororities are much more than a simple feminine counterpart to the more widespread college fraternity; less variable in their form, they differ from fraternities mainly because marriage is a profoundly more important determinant of social position for women than for men and because the norms associated with marriage correspondingly bear stronger sanctions for women than for men. Though what is called "youth culture" shapes much sorority activity, recruitment, membership, and activities are only narrowly governed by college-age members; effective control rests with parent-age "alumnae." Though many college women wish to join sororities and many more affect sorority manners, conduct, and dress, recruitment and the maintenance of membership are chronic organizational problems. The prototypical sorority is not so much the servant of youthful interests as it is an organized agency for controlling them; dominated by ascriptive groups and concerned to maintain their norms, it operates at a physical remove from these groups and in a larger and frequently hostile institutional setting.

In this paper I do not outline the structure of sororities completely, but instead consider on a more abstract or theoretical level some of the variables that relate kinship to other social processes, especially as regards the choice of marital partners. From the combination of these variables that obtains in higher education in industrial society, it is possible to derive the idea or "model" of an organization designed to maintain the norms of ascriptive groups in the face of opposition from other parts of the society. This hypothetical organization corresponds remarkably well to sororities as they exist in fact.

The factors or variables that account for the evolution of the sorority are:

1. The relation between kinship institutions and those of higher education;
2. Rules of mate selection that inhere in the persistence of strata and ethnic groups;
3. Hypergamy and its derivative "Brahmin problem;"
4. Love;
5. The social heterogeneity of tax-supported colleges; and
6. The bargaining advantage for women of timely marriage and the institutionalization of feminine youth.

These variables do not account for all that goes on in concrete sororities, but they do account for much that is otherwise difficult to explain.

Kinship and Higher Education

Structural differentiation in industrial societies has evolved a system of education wherein the more technical and cognitive aspects of socialization are removed from the control of family and ascriptive groups and assigned to special agents. Nowhere has this differentiation gone further than in the United States, and nowhere are the societal "substructures" relating kinship institutions and education more specialized.

Familial and extra-familial agents of socialization are inherently disposed to conflict. Even when their teaching is complementary they still compete for the child's limited attention. The potential for conflict increases as the content of what is taught diverges, being realized most fully in "higher education." No prior stage in formal education is so sharply set off from familial socialization; this is signalled by the frequent separation of the student's residence from that of his family of orientation. And while higher education may complement socialization by ascriptive groups, simply passing on the same culture in a more specialized way (and indeed many regional and religio-ethnic colleges do little more than this) higher education is both theoretically and factually important not where it complements the values of ascriptive groups but where it challenges them. University education is literally universal in the variety of ways in which it celebrates excellence in achievement; necessarily it thereby threatens the persistence of ascription. Where kinship, based on nuclear families, tends to suppress competition, higher education must select and place persons who are already approximate ascribed equals. It therefore encourages competition explicitly in its curricular matters and implicitly in its extra-curricular ones as well (including courtship on the campus).

But higher education can serve ascriptive interests as well as threaten them. All families ascribe their social and economic status to their children; this process fundamentally connects the family to the system of stratification. But the many technical positions in industrial societies require that pure ascription be reinforced by learned (and therefore achieved) skills. Education and especially higher education are perhaps the most efficient general way to impart these skills. When a family desires upward mobility of the children, achievement has to be the principal basis for the increment in status, and the importance of education is thereby increased. Finally, higher education is not only a means of mobility, but becomes a symbol of what it facilitates, so that the degrees conferred by colleges and universities, as well as other visible indicators of college attendance, come to be valuable in themselves, and higher education is thus respected as a symbol of status even by persons who may strongly depreciate its instrumental value. Effective familial ascription to higher strata comes therefore to mean "sending the children to college," despite the risks it also entails.

Now, from the point of view of ascriptive groups the "ideal" college would reinforce ascription where it needed to be reinforced, without threatening it otherwise. To such an "ideal" college kinship groups could, for example, delegate control over the technical details of education, but they would retain control over the less technical processes more likely to be undone by educational "universalism" and vital to their own interests, such as mate selection, religious or ethnic ritual, and symbolic representation of class position. In practice, ascriptive groups have countered the general threat at the colleges they cannot control as primary institutions, by inaugurating or coöpting (where possible) ancillary secondary institutions. A dormitory, for example, because of the time students spend in it, can often influence behavior more than the formal curriculum of the primary institution itself. So long as children live at home, the family of orientation exercises control over them simply because they spend so much time there; and thus the collegiate break in familial residence is a salient threat to familial control. This is why ascriptive groups have invested so much in the operation and defense of residence halls catering to their own members, and of which the college sorority is the most extreme example.

Endogamy

Familial ascription in industrial societies, just as in nonindustrial ones, involves a principle of endogamy, a norm of marriage within some particular group. A status can be taught to children more thoroughly when both parents occupy it to begin with. Two forms of endogamy bear on sororities: ethnic endogamy and stratum or class endogamy. As for the first, sororities are differentiated along ethnic lines; the stronger the desire for endogamy by the ethnic group, the more complete the differentiation. The best examples are the Jewish sororities, because among all normatively endogamous American ethnic groups only the Jews so far have made much use of higher education. Stratum or class endogamy, however, is more pervasive; and it is additionally important because it is also respected by those committed to norms of ethnic endogamy. Norms of endogamy generally apply more strongly to women than to men because a man derives his status from an occupational position (whether gained by ascription or achievement) and confers that status on his wife, whereas a woman leaves her antenuptial status to assume that conferred by her husband. In industrial societies women can gain a tolerable status by their own occupational achievements, but such a status, as every college girl knows, is still stigmatized as secondary and inferior to that conferred by a husband. This stigma motivates marriage, preserves the equivalence of stratum level between parents that status ascription to progeny requires, and facilitates employment of women in positions less prestigeful than their husbands'.

A variety of organizations and activities can reinforce behavior appropriate to a particular stratum or ethnic group, but only a few can maintain control over mate selection. Especially in their routine activities, sororities too reinforce much that is class-specific but not very important to the control of courtship. But without the latter they could not count on the long-run support from interested ascriptive groups that they now command. The specifically feminine skills appropriate to middle- or higher-class women still largely require marriage to a man of similarly high status for their exercise: if spinsterhood or unfitting marriage is the price of learning them their achievement is empty and meaningless.

Hypergamy and the "Brahmin Problem"

Stratum mobility through marriage occurs widely, being effectively prohibited only in racial caste systems. The movement of a woman through marriage to a stratum higher than that to which she was born is named *hypergamy*, and to a lower one, *hypogamy*. Especially in industrial societies, norms of stratum endogamy (as distinct from the practice) seldom exist as such except where they reinforce stronger norms of ethnic endogamy; instead they reflect the emphasis on mobility that prevails in these societies. A social class is not the same kind of ascriptive group as a caste: though both rely mainly or wholly on ascription for recruitment, a caste ascribes the *same* status, whereas members of a mobility-oriented class desire to ascribe a *higher* status. This means that hypergamy rather than class endogamy is to be sought, and hypogamy avoided. The reasons for this are clear. First, mobility from low status to high is widely desired. Second, industrial societies encourage and facilitate mobility. Primarily they do so for men, stressing the possibility of achieving highly ranked positions in the labor force. But in these societies the typical family is small, and given its function of instilling strong generalized motives for achievement, it has neither the inclination nor the resources (compared with large families in simple societies) for much differential socialization by sex. Emphasis on the rewards given to the higher strata, and on the use of efficient means for entering those strata, though addressed mainly to sons, will hardly be lost on daughters. Third, stratum mobility through marriage is simply easier than stratum mobility through work. And it is made easier still by such differential socialization as persists in industrial societies, whereby women are relatively well trained in the strategems of attracting men and relatively poorly motivated (as compared with men) to compete for and maintain a well-rewarded position. So efficient is hypergamy as a means of improving one's status that it comes to be institutionalized as an aspiration of both parents and daughters (though more unequivocally for parents than for daughters). Available data suggest that sororities facilitate hypergamy rather than stratum endogamy as such.

Marriage always involves an element of exchange and hypergamy figures in the exchange. It gives men of higher status a marketing advantage, since they have a more valuable status to confer; but it also disadvantages women of high antenuptial status. I call this the *Brahmin problem.* It occurs in courtship bargaining with respect to any valuable status or attribute that cannot be reciprocally conferred between marital partners. Generally the most valuable of these statuses and attributes are related to stratum level, but not all of them are: handsomeness and beauty, wit, kindness, intelligence, if not equally distributed among different strata, are at least in no society the monopoly of any one, and this provides motives for marriage across stratum boundaries. Yet a man's status, if high, is valuable enough in exchange to offset greatly his personal defects, because he can confer it; whereas the high status to which a woman may be born is not so valuable in exchange, because she is relatively unable to confer it. Because her status is valuable to her and to her parents, she prefers to marry a man whose status is at least equally high, but for these men she must compete to some extent against women from all strata. Further, except in societies where the status of women is low generally, women born to high strata are disadvantaged by a peculiar pattern of what may be called "class-specific vanity;" for they expect to receive in courtship the same extravagant favors and attention that their well-situated parents have made available to them. But men who court them are seldom wholly insensitive to vanity, and where inter-stratum contact is frequent they often discover that the favors, including the prospect of marriage, of lower-status women can be had for a smaller investment of their own scarce time, money, and emotion. Higher-strata women are therefore often indisposed for the potentially sanguinary competition they must face anyway. The Brahmin problem is inherent in hypergamy, and it is important because of the structures that have grown up to contend with it.

Some possible solutions—each of which has been used by the higher strata of some society—are female infanticide, spinsterhood, polygyny, and dowries and groom-service fees. Except for spinsterhood, all of these are structurally incompatible with industrial organization, and even spinsterhood, though apparently more common in industrial societies than in simple ones, is disesteemed. Further, since family institutions in industrial societies have many functions besides solving the Brahmin problem, the solution must be economical, and applicable where it will be most effective—namely, where the most suitable men are likely to be met, and at an age where they are disposed to marry. Both of these criteria imply concentration on the institutions of higher education, for here are found both men born to higher strata and men moving into them. The campus presents an excellent marriage market, though (because it also facilitates hypogamy) a risky one; and consequently in societies where substantial proportions of the population go to college, courtship and marriage are as much a part of what happens there as is the formal curriculum.

Within the college population, one way to relieve the Brahmin problem to some degree is to maximize encounters with men who are themselves mobile, who aspire to a group to which they do not yet belong. More than others, these men will value the symbolic reassurance provided by social contact with girls whose skills are those of the class to which they aspire; they will be tempted less than others, then, by charms that women of all strata possess. Since college fraternities are filled with men who aspire to stratum mobility, their members, indisposed to hypergamy, are the sorority girls' most convenient suitors.

Love[1]

The emotions called "love" characteristically fail to guarantee respect for any prior classification of the persons involved, including classification into strata or ethnic groups. Lovable traits vary among societies but in none are they distributed solely according to any principle of ascribed status. The theoretical importance of love derives from its capacity to motivate exogamy in the face of some norm of endogamy; if the norm is to prevail, then love must be controlled. No organization can prevent its members from falling in love; indeed sororities use love to motivate timely marriage. Their distinctive office is to see that their nubile participants fall in love only with men who qualify as desirable mates under the principle of endogamy involved.

Love is also important to the educational setting and to sororities because it appeals most strongly to adolescents. It tempts the young into exogamy and hypogamy; the burden of normative control is thus left to the old.

Heterogeneity of Public Education

The general factors mentioned so far do not by themselves account for sororities. Imagine a system of higher education in which admission policies were such that free mate selection within each college would be in complete accord with the appropriate principles of endogamy. Thus young members of endogamy-seeking ethnic groups would all attend ethnically segregated schools, while women aspiring to hypergamy would choose schools where they might meet men above their own stratum, but never below it. This system would be ideal so far as endogamy is the object, and many actual schools approach it. In that system the maintenance of endogamy would not require special independent secondary organizations, and class- and religion-specific schools are in fact relatively devoid of them.

A large and growing proportion of American college enrollment, however, is in tax-supported colleges and universities, where the cost of attendance is relatively low and admission and matriculation are com-

[1] This section summarizes William Goode's concise and excellent discussion in "The Theoretical Importance of Love," *American Sociological Review*, 24 (1959) pp. 38–47.

petitively based on ability.[2] These schools draw students from many strata and ethnic groups: from the relatively poor, because they can afford nothing else; and to a considerable extent from more affluent groups (especially in the American west and midwest) because their academic reputations often compete with those of private schools. But the variety of students exacerbates the Brahmin problem. Those parents who are afflicted with it and choose to enroll their daughters in public schools are motivated to devise some way to restrict interstratum and interethnic contact in college, generally in residential proximity to other women and crucially in courtship encounters with men.

The total costs of rather expensive sorority residence, together with the nominal tuition at a public school, are usually much less than dormitory residence would be at a class-specific private school with its high tuition. Then, too, many girls, whose parents hope they will marry "the right kind of man," lack the intellectual fortitude (because they learn the techniques for hypergamy instead)[3] to meet the increasingly severe performance standards of high-status private colleges, even if their parents could afford the tuition. Co-educational schools of high repute, whether public or private, are characterized by a high sex ratio (a preponderance of men); those of low repute by a low sex ratio; and the social strata represented by the students are consistent with the academic reputation. Thus the disposition of nubile girls to feminine charm, which brings them profound rewards, and their indisposition to abstract thought, excludes many of them from one fine source of high-status men, private schools of high prestige; they must instead rely on what can be found at the less selective public schools.

Sorority girls attend tax-supported schools and benefit from their capacity to reinforce a familially ascribed status with marketable technical skills (e.g., educated conversation and taste, as well as occupational training, should employment be contemplated after marriage), while the organizations in which they reside vastly reduce the potential for interstratum and interethnic contact and the corollary risk of exogamous love. It is at the great state universities, free, open, and competitive, that the sorority system is most fully developed.

But the relative scarcity of high status men at the public schools, and the relative surplus of low-status women, are still to be contended with. Although sororities can do little about the first problem, they can do quite a bit about the second by establishing and maintaining the belief that, at least at particular colleges, dating opportunities are severely

[2] In 1949, 49.3 per cent of 2.45 million college students were enrolled in public schools; in 1961 both figures had risen, to 60.5 per cent of 3.89 million students. U.S. Office of Education, *Digest of Educational Statistics*, Washington: Government Printing Office, 1962, p. 86.
[3] See Ralph H. Turner, "Some Aspects of Women's Ambition," *American Journal of Sociology*, 70 (1964), pp. 271–285.

curtailed for girls who are not sorority members. Thus many high school girls, fearing that they will not be invited into sorority membership at a particular college, enroll at other colleges where sororities are absent or are thought to be less dominant.[4] Since these girls will generally be unsophisticated, unattractive, or of lower-class or subordinated ethnic descent, less afflicted with general or class-specific vanity and thus easier to court, the Brahmin problem is relieved at the school with the strong sorority system to the extent that they are frightened away from it.

Importance of Timely Marriage

Even given all the preceding conditions, however, an exogamy-deterring alternative to the sorority can still be imagined: postponement of the time of marriage until the risk of college-inspired exogamous love is past. This might be called an "Irish Solution to the Brahmin Problem," in view of Eire's late age at marriage since the potato famine. Yet women are constrained, if they contemplate marriage at all, to be timely about it. Whether endogamous or exogamous, arranged or romantic, marriage is an exchange in which (among other things) the sexual attractiveness of women is offered in return for status and support from men. Men can confer status and extend support for relatively many years; women are sexually attractive for relatively few. Since youth and nubile beauty are such important aspects of women's exchange in marriage, the problem of avoiding an undesirable marriage cannot be solved by postponing marriage indefinitely. Demographically, late marriage is associated with a high proportion of spinsters; this is the price the Irish have paid for late marriage.

Among all the age-graded statuses through which a woman passes, the period of nubility is the most rewarded; indeed, the rewards are so great relative to other periods that "feminine youth" is not simply an abstract age-graded status but a veritable institution, consciously recognized, celebrated in folklore and literature, the object of anticipatory socialization of female children and a time to which later memories return. This situation favors the sororities, for they are explicitly designed to maximize the rewards of nubility, to enhance with symbol and ceremony a highly valued yet ephemeral status, quite apart from the services they offer to endogamy. As the youthful condition is cherished, so stands to be also its organizational expression.

[4] Thus in questionnaires I distributed in 1963 and 1964 among undergraduate women at the University of California at Davis, the modal response (about 30 per cent) to the open-ended question "Why did you choose to come to Davis?" was "no sororities," and their absence was mentioned together with other factors in another 20 per cent of the responses. More intensive interviewing suggested that the belief that sororities dominate social life at certain other campuses is widely and strongly held among high school girls.

Sororities: A Brief Description

Given the conditions just reviewed, an organization can be imagined whose purpose it would be to encourage the timely marriage of women in conformity with norms of endogamy or hypergamy in the face of exceptional risks of exogamous or hypogamous love, by restricting heterosexual encounters to the appropriate groups. This set of conditions seems too complex as a "latent function" ever to be made manifest. Yet in fact it is the *consciously* designed (if largely unacknowledged) purpose of sororities; the difference between sociological and lay conceptions is not so much a matter of latency *v.* manifestation as one of terminology. The threat to endogamy and the conditions of its maintenance are more or less understood by those who control sororities—their middle-aged "alumnae." These women know perfectly well that a young girl probably will not meet the right kind of man unless she goes to college, but that if left to herself at a large school she may fall in love with the wrong kind, that the best way to assure marriage to one of the right kind of men is to arrange for meaningful encounters with lots of them, and that marriage must not be put off too long. The problem in more technical and general terms is that of maintaining the norms of the ascriptive group at the critical point when the person moves by marriage from his family of orientation to his family of procreation. Although the homiletical tone appropriate to her era avoids the problems of courtship control, a founder of one of the great national sororities posed the general issue well enough:

> . . . In taking a girl out of the crowd and making her a permanent member of a small group, the sorority is rendering her an inestimable service. It is providing her during her college course with family affiliations and with the essential elements of a home—sympathetic interest, wise supervision, disinterested advice. Incidentally society itself is benefited. The corner stone of the social structure is the family, and it is not altogether wise that college girls, or college boys for that matter, should cut loose from youth's anchorage and drift far from home moorings during four long years. There is a danger, and a very grave danger, that four years' residence in a dormitory will tend to destroy right ideals of home life and substitute in their stead a belief in the freedom that comes from community living. . . . Culture, broad, liberalizing, humanizing culture, we cannot get too much of, unless while acquiring it we are weaned from home and friends, from ties of blood and kindred.[5]

Because endogamy and other familial interests seem less important to girls than to their parents, an organization dedicated to maintaining

[5] Sarah Ida Shaw Martin (Mrs. William Holmes Martin), *The Sorority Handbook* (11th ed.), Boston: privately published, 1931, pp. 41–42.

them at the expense of other activities will have problems of recruitment, especially if it is at least partly voluntary. Sororities indeed have such a problem. The folklore of student life stresses that many who wish to live in sororities are not invited into them. This is true enough, but it obscures the equally true point that many whom the sororities want as members do not wish to join. Recruitment thus depends on a number of special techniques.

First, parents often pressure daughters to join sororities; many girls join only because parents insist. Second, sororities do their most effective recruiting not among college students, but at high schools, where a picture of college life can be drawn for prospective recruits who cannot readily test it by direct experience. Sororities are claimed to have a monopoly on all that is pleasant; especially are they claimed to have cornered all masculine attention. Although the extent to which these claims are true varies among colleges—depending in part on the heterogeneity of student culture—their effect depends on the extent to which they are believed, and (as noted above) apparently they are believed even where they are largely false. Third, in all respects save those that increase the risk of exogamy sorority life is not only represented but is in fact made as attractive as possible to prospective recruits. This is why the "subculture" of the sorority, especially in its public manifestations, often seems so studiously adolescent and, by adult standards, trivial. Its prospective members are mainly pre-college girls, who seldom understand, and often fear, much of their future collegiate role, and as a result the sorority must be oriented more to the world of the high school where it solicits than to that of the college where it resides. Just as girls tend to flock to the "party schools" of low academic repute, avoiding those that emphasize scholarship, and to seek less competitive courses and departments within the school, so historically the most effective way to recruit pre-college girls has been to maintain sorority life as one of fun and frolic with an abundance of masculine attention. For that life to prevail the rigors of scholarship must necessarily be reduced to the minimum required for continued attendance at the school.

Institutionalized hedonism, as a solution to problems of recruitment, poses other problems of membership retention. The sorority does not serve the interests of youth, but those of an earlier generation; and it maintains a number of rules that are issues of conflict between sorority alumnae and active members just as, in the home, they are issues between parents and children. Not surprisingly, therefore, sorority life is regularly reported even by its partisans among undergraduate women to involve a great deal of constraint. Parental standards are enforced to a degree unmatched in other collegiate living groups, with regard to public conduct, when escorted by men, and for dress "appropriate for a young lady." An elaborate calendar of parliamentary activities, committee meetings, confrontations with alumnae, and community projects such as student theatrical routines, must be carried out; the pressure to meet young men at social "exchanges," picnics, parties, co-operative building of floats for parades, etc., sometimes exceeds even the widespread desire to meet them; crowding is sometimes severe; the noise level is high; the esoteric rituals grow tedious and sophomoric; and most forms of privacy do not exist. Thus sororities are rather carefully designed to be far easier to enter, when the pleasures of membership are anticipated and youthful enthusiasm is high, than they are to leave later on, when alternatives to sororities have been discovered and their constraints have been directly experienced.

In short, the sorority protects its members against the stratum-dissolving standards of the larger university, and its potential for hypogamous love, simply by dominating their collegiate life. Time is encompassed completely, especially for the novitiates or "pledges," by compulsory activities planned in advance, so that little energy or time remains for events where inappropriate men might be encountered. The control is relaxed somewhat for accepted members, who by then have adequately learned the standards and taboos.

Sorority girls are especially limited in their opportunities to meet varieties of men. The typical arrangement is for each sorority to maintain traditional liaisons with one or more fraternities, matched closely on a basis of ethnicity or class level. Encounters and courtship are facilitated by parties and exchanges between sororities and fraternities, and by the untiring efforts of intermediaries, or "fixer-uppers," who arrange social engagements, or "dates," between those who might not otherwise meet, and on behalf of men too timid or unskilled to essay them directly. The efforts of the fixer-uppers greatly reduce the inconvenience, and more saliently the anxiety, in dating, and thus effectively raise its rate above what it would be otherwise. The control achieved in simple or traditional societies by parental arrangement of marriages is achieved in industrial society by these go-betweens, who in the case of the sorority operate within an organization controlled by interested ascriptive groups. The result is largely the same: marriage is timely, its rate is high, and exogamous and hypogamous combinations of partners are avoided. Then too the style and occasions of sorority dating tend to be expensive and time-consuming, and this discourages the attentions of poor and low-status men.

No organization with the characteristics described could depend for internal control on consensus among its active members; sororities are therefore effectively controlled by their alumnae. Control derives from alumnae ownership of the chapter house and from assumption of *in loco parentis* power over active members, most of whom are legal minors. But the principal basis for control is the recommendatory requirement for membership: no girl can be invited to join a sorority without recommendations (typically) from two or more alumnae. This procedure helps maintain standards of deportment, class position, reputations for sexual morality, and so on; and direct inheritance of membership, from mother to daughter, is given special consideration. This together with the active members' practical preference for congenial and accommodative persons who can be tolerated in constant interaction in close quarters effectively excludes from membership headstrong, enterprising, and innovative girls who, were they members, might be catalysts for organizational change. This is why sorority girls are so compliant in the face of alumnae dominance, and why, to academicians who often value novelty in ideas and a mild irreverence toward bourgeois conventions, they seem so consistently bland and uninteresting as students.

Although the day-to-day governing of the sorority is formally democratic, informally it is not. The broad outline of regulations is fixed by the national association, and much of the communication from national headquarters to local chapters, and from alumnae to active members, consists of efforts to explain and defend points of policy which are chronic sources of youthful complaint. The actual offices of control are filled by an elaborate process of coöptation of active members by alumnae and housemothers (who are appointed by alumnae). The ratio of officers to members is high, and the more demanding offices, or those entrusted to enforce unpopular standards, tend to be rewarded by special privileges or extra living space. And deviance on small matters, when discreet, is relatively unpunished; this draws attention from more important controls and provides a sense of independence to the deviants, keeps down the withdrawal rate, and permits for the sorority an economy of sanctions, the better that it can deploy those at its command against more serious transgressions.

To keep high the rate of engagement and marriage, sororities rely heavily on emotionally potent ceremonies and rituals to sanctify matrimony. Exposure to and dating of the right man are not enough; if endogamy is to be maintained the dates must lead to engagements and the engagements to marriage. Thus the sorority subculture, especially as sustained by the alumnae, define all dating encounters as prolegomena to marriage. Housemothers and alumnae do what they can to discourage truly casual and spontaneous dating and to encourage structured and organized involvement. "Pinning"—a pre-engagement relationship signifying reciprocal commitment and sexual prerogative—is solemnized by an elaborate ritual, often involving the participation of many students, witnessed by all the sorority sisters and attended, in its classic form, by a choir of fraternity men singing outside the sorority. This serves to reinforce progress toward engagement at its weakest point and to hinder withdrawal from the "pinned" commitment. The special status of the pinned and engaged is ceremonially reinforced in other ways too: where sorority functions are recorded in college newspapers, much attention is given to pinnings and engagements.

Sororities also encourage hypergamy by teaching a repertory of class-specific activities, especially where their members are from families of relatively low status (sororities are elaborately ranked among themselves, in ways correlative to stratification in their host society). Thus the lower-ranked sororities carefully teach the manners thought appropriate to the higher strata; e.g., "how to drink like a lady," always to order dry and sour mixed drinks, etc. Since the higher-ranked sororities are the reference groups for the lower (members of the latter being mainly girls who had hoped to be invited to join the former), in regard to distinctive sorority characteristics the lower sororities tend to be *plus royaux que le roi.*

A closing note: this analysis and illustration, necessarily brief and unqualified, has also been static, representing the sorority only at one point in time. Yet most of the factors that explain it are not constants but variables, and their values are changing over time. In a future paper I shall offer more empirical detail and discuss the future of the sororities in the light of changes in higher education.

22. DO "OPPOSITES ATTRACT" OR DOES "LIKE MARRY LIKE"?

Thomas and Virginia Ktsanes

§ This article will require and merits very careful reading. In the preliminary paragraphs the authors discuss what is known about similarity (homogamy) between husband and wife. They show that people tend to marry those with the same or similar occupational, educational, economic, and religious backgrounds. Homogamy, even when it exists,

SOURCE: Thomas and Virginia Ktsanes, "The Theory of Complementary Needs in Mate-Selection," in Robert F. Winch and Robert McGinnis, eds., *Selected Studies in Marriage and the Family* (New York: Holt, Rinehart and Winston, 1953), pp. 435–53. Reprinted by permission of the publisher.

The theory of complementary needs was first set forth by Robert F. Winch. Dr. Winch, whose doctorate is from the University of Chicago, is professor of sociology at Northwestern University. For a number of years he has carried on careful research on the basic factors that operate in mate selection. His publications

does not account for the individual choice. It simply defines the group within which each person will seek for a mate on personal grounds.

The main part of this article is a discussion of one important factor in the personal choice of a mate. The hypothesis is set forth that people love, and tend to marry, those who fulfill their needs. The perfect love match would be one in which each fulfilled the needs of the other while at the same time having his own needs fulfilled by the other. It follows that people, perhaps unconsciously, tend to fall in love with and marry those who gratify their needs. Research carried out after this article was written confirmed this hypothesis in part—mutual need gratification was one among other factors operating in mate selection.

The article ends with a long case, carefully analyzed to show how a husband and wife met each other's needs, while at the same time receiving satisfaction for their own needs.

Who Marries Whom?

The question of "who marries whom" is one which has aroused "common sense" as well as scientific interest. The common sense answer is paradoxical, for while everyone knows that "like marries like" and that "birds of a feather flock together," it is also equally clear that "opposites attract." As is frequently the case in folk wisdom, both assertions are probably true depending upon the characteristics considered. If by "like" one means similarity in regard to a variety of social characteristics such as ethnic origin, religion, occupation, residential location, and social status, then indeed the view that mates tends to be similar seems correct. If, on the other hand, "like" is used to denote similarity in a variety of psychological attitudes, traits, tendencies, or needs, then the situation is by no means clear. This being the case, it is in order to take a brief look at some studies which have attempted to answer the question of the degree to which homogamy or heterogamy prevails in marital choice. The tendency of persons to select mates who have certain characteristics similar to their own is called homogamy or assortative mating. Conversely, heterogamy refers to the selection of mates who are opposite or are merely different. We shall begin with a brief review of the research literature on homogamy. Later we shall present the theory of complementary needs as a special type of heterogamy.

include *The Modern Family, Mate-Selection,* and, as co-editor, *Selected Readings in Marriage and the Family.*

Thomas Ktsanes received his doctorate from Northwestern University; Virginia Ktsanes received an M.A. from Northwestern University. Both authors were associated with Professor Winch in the study of complementary needs from its beginning and carried out the interviewing of the men and women who were the subjects of the study. They are co-authors of a number of articles in professional sociological journals.

Homogamy in Social Characteristics

Interest in the problem of assortative mating is probably an analogical extension out of the field of biology where for lower animals there seems to be a trend toward similarity in size and vitality. On the human level also there is some slight evidence for homogamy in physical characteristics.[1] With human beings, however, physical similarity has not been the principal concern. Most work on assortative mating has concerned a variety of social characteristics. We shall now briefly examine some of this evidence.

In an early study by Marvin[2] it was noted that there was a greater than chance tendency for marriages to occur between persons with similar occupations. More recently Centers[3] has pointed out that there tend to be no wide differences in the occupational statuses of spouses. Burgess and Wallin[4] have shown that there is homogamy in educational level. Further, basing their conclusions on the ratings by the couple of the social status of their parents and on their report of the present income of their fathers, Burgess and Wallin state ". . . it is clear that there is a considerable excess over chance for young people to fall in love and become engaged to those in the same social and economic class."[5] Kennedy[6] has indicated that there is a strong trend toward homogamy in regard to religious affiliation and a tendency, though less marked, toward homogamy in ethnic origin.

Bossard,[7] in a study repeated by subsequent researchers, showed that people usually select their mates from those who live nearby. In Bossard's classic study more than half of the marriages in his sample were between persons living within twenty blocks of each other. However, the effect of this factor of mere spatial propinquity must not be over-emphasized for it overlaps with the factors discussed before. The various ecological areas of the city are characterized by heavy concentrations of certain socioeconomic classes, ethnic and religious groups; and these groups as noted above tend to be endogamous.[8]

[1] In Mary Schooley, "Personality Resemblance Among Married Couples," *Journal of Abnormal and Social Psychology*, 31 (1936), 340–47, some low positive correlations were found to exist between mates on height, weight, visual acuity, and appearance.
[2] Donald Marvin, "Occupational Propinquity as a Factor in Marriage Selection," *Journal of the American Statistical Association*, 16 (1918–19), 131–50.
[3] Richard Centers, "Marital Selection and Occupational Strata," *American Journal of Sociology*, 54 (1949), 530–35.
[4] E. W. Burgess and Paul Wallin, "Homogamy in Social Characteristics," *American Journal of Sociology*, 49 (1943), 109–24.
[5] *Ibid.*, p. 114.
[6] R. J. R. Kennedy, "Single or Triple Melting-Pot? Intermarriage Trends in New Haven, 1870–1950," *American Journal of Sociology*, 63 (1952), 56–59.
[7] J. H. S. Bossard, "Residential Propinquity as a Factor in Marriage Selection," *American Journal of Sociology*, 38 (1932), 219–24.
[8] Endogamy refers to marriage within the group.

In summary, the studies reviewed indicate that persons who marry tend to be similar in regard to a variety of characteristics such as social class, ethnic background, educational level, religion, occupation, and area of residence. However, these findings actually bear little direct relationship to our problem. They are of some interest in that they give us a notion of the limits within which another principle of selection may operate. As we interpret them, these factors tend to define a field of eligibles from which a mate may be selected on psychological grounds.

Homogamy in Psychological Characteristics

Psychological characteristics which have been studied with respect to homogamy include a long and varied list. Characteristics investigated by means of "paper-and-pencil" personality inventories include neuroticism, dominance, self-sufficiency, etc. One early study [9] found moderately high correlations between mates on neurotic tendency and dominance. Burgess and Wallin [10] in their more recent study of 1000 engaged couples found homogamy in regard to a few traits. Their correlations, however, were of a rather low order and are therefore not too convincing. In regard to various "content" attitudes, e.g., religious and political attitudes, there is some evidence for similarity.[11] These similarities, however, may have developed after marriage. The results in this area are thus considerably short of being definitive. Stagner in reviewing the studies on homogamy in psychological characteristics has pointed out that correlations indicating similarity are higher with respect to intellectual, interest, and attitude scores, but that measures of temperament do not show this tendency as clearly.[12] The measures of temperament referred to by Stagner are those estimates of various traits such as dominance, self-sufficiency, etc., which are arrived at by means of paper-and-pencil tests. Confidence in paper-and-pencil tests is vitiated by the fact that subjects can "fake" their responses and thereby create what they regard as favorable impressions.[13] When we try to get behind the picture of personality which the subject wants us to accept, and more particularly, when we want to understand a subject's motivational patterns of which he may be only partially aware, we find no systematic research on the question of

[9] E. L. Hoffeditz, "Personality Resemblances Among Married Couples," *Journal of Abnormal and Social Psychology*, 5 (1934), 214–27.
[10] E. W. Burgess and Paul Wallin, "Homogamy in Personality Characteristics," *Journal of Abnormal and Social Psychology*, 39 (1944), 475–81.
[11] T. M. Newcomb and G. Svehla, "Intra-family Relationships in Attitude," *Sociometry*, 1 (1937), 180–205.
[12] Ross Stagner, *Psychology of Personality*, New York, McGraw-Hill, 1948, p. 387.
[13] *Cf.* Albert Ellis, "The Validity of Marriage Prediction Tests" in Robert F. Winch and Robert McGinnis (eds.), *Selected Studies in Marriage and the Family*, New York, Holt, 1953, pp. 494–95.

homogamous *vs.* heterogamous mate-selection.[14] In the absence of experimental evidence various writers have been theorizing on this problem.

Toward a More Adequate Theory

Ideas about types of harmonic intermeshing of needs have been suggested by various theorists and researchers. Many of these owe a debt to Freud, who made a distinction between "anaclitic" and "narcissistic" love.[15] By the anaclitic type Freud meant a love which was expressed in attitudes of self-derogation and reverential admiration toward the love-object. In this type of love one is dependent on the loved one toward whom he can express his need to revere and admire. Narcissistic love is essentially self-love but the narcissist has a great need to be admired by others as well as by himself. Thus in his formulation of the narcissistic-anaclitic typology, Freud posited a type of complementary relationship, *i.e.*, the dependent person who has the need to revere and admire and is attracted to the narcissistic person who has a great need to be admired and receive adulation.

Following the suggestion that persons with complementary psychic make-ups are attracted to each other, several psychoanalysts have proposed that matching occurs between those who are complementarily neurotic.[16] According to this hypothesis, for example, a dependent male with unresolved emotional ties to his mother would be attracted to an aggressive and dominant woman burdened with conflicts over her sex role. As a general theory of mate-selection, however, this literature is inadequate because the writers have explained attraction only in terms of the highly individualized neurotic patterns of their patients. What we are seeking is a theory which will be generally applicable, not merely to Freud's anaclitic and narcissistic types of persons, not merely to dependent people who marry nurturant people, not merely to neurotics, but to all kinds of personalities.

Gray [17] had used a broader approach to this problem. He hypothesized

---

[14] A few individual cases have been reported at this "deep" level of analysis, but they have been neurotic patients and the authors' reports have lacked experimental control. *Cf.*, *e.g.*, C. P. Oberndorf, "Psychoanalysis of Married Couples," *Psychoanalytic Review*, 25 (1938), 453–57.

[15] Sigmund Freud, "On Narcissism: An Introduction," in *Collected Papers*, vol. 4, London, Hogarth, 1925, pp. 30–59.

[16] *Cf.*, *e.g.*, C. P. Oberndorf, *op. cit.*; Edmund Bergler, *Unhappy Marriage and Divorce*, New York, International Universities Press, 1946; and Bela Mittleman, "Complementary Neurotic Reactions in Intimate Relationships," *Psychoanalytic Quarterly*, 13 (1944), 479–91.

[17] *Cf.*, *e.g.*, H. Gray, "Psychological Types in Married People," *Journal of Social Psychology*, 29 (1949), 189–200; and "Jung's Psychological Types in Men and Women," *Stanford Medical Bulletin*, 6 (1948), 29–36.

that mate-selection would be complementary with respect to the types of personality formulated by Jung (extrovert-introvert, etc.). His empirical findings, however, were not convincing.[18]

Other theorists have tried to identify various motivation-linked aspects of interaction. Bernard, for example, suggests various dimensions of love.[19] She notes the usual dimension of dominance and also dwells upon the desire for response or acceptance and on the differential ability of persons to "give" as she calls it. As we shall see later, these are similar to some of the "needs" in our conceptual scheme. Bernard did not systematically state that attraction occurred between persons who were complementary in regard to these dimensions. Others, however, have come very close to this notion. Ohmann [20] stated this idea by saying that we are attracted to those who complete us psychologically. We seek in a mate those qualities which we do not possess.

Taking leads from all of the foregoing, Winch attempted to pull them together. He began by defining love in terms of needs:

> Love is the positive emotion experienced by one person (the person loving, or the lover) in an interpersonal relationship in which the second person (the person loved, or love-object) either (a) meets certain important needs of the first, or (b) manifests or appears (to the first) to manifest personal attributes (*e.g.*, beauty, skills, or status) highly prized by the first, or both.[21]

Then he hypothesized that mate-selection would take place according to what he called the theory of complementary needs:

> In mate-selection each individual seeks within his or her field of eligibles for that person who gives the greatest promise of providing him or her with maximum need gratification.[22]

Perhaps this can be phrased more simply by hypothesizing that the personality needs of marriage partners tend to be complementary rather than similar. Two points require further clarification: (a) What are personality needs and which needs are germane to our problem? and (b) What exactly is meant by the term "complementary"?

---

[18] Winch applied tests of significance to some of Gray's data. These tests showed that the selection of mates in terms of Jung's types was not significantly greater than might have been expected by chance.
[19] Jessie Bernard, *American Family Behavior*, New York, Harper and Brothers, 1942, pp. 435–56.
[20] Oliver Ohmann, "The Psychology of Attraction," in Helen Jordan (*ed.*), *You and Marriage*, New York, Wiley, 1942, chap. 2.
[21] Robert F. Winch, *The Modern Family*, New York, Holt, 1951, p. 333.
[22] *Ibid.*, p. 406. In the phrase "field of eligibles" Winch takes account of the previously noted homogamy with respect to such social characteristics as race, religion, and social class.

Needs

One can think of the term "need" as meaning a goal-oriented drive. Goal in this sense refers not only to such things as material objects and status in the social structure but more particularly to such things as the quality and kind of response desired in interpersonal situations. Examples of the latter are the desire to give help or adulation to others, the desire to take care of others, the desire to control, etc. When these goals are attained, the need is gratified. However, gratification is a dynamic process, and a need once gratified does not cease to function. Patterns of behavior which are tension-reducing tend rather to be reinforced. In a marriage, for example, a woman who finds in her interaction with her spouse gratification for a need to control will continue to want to control him. One further characteristic of needs should be noted. Needs function at both the conscious and unconscious levels. A person may be conscious, partly conscious, or not at all conscious of the goals he desires.

Henry A. Murray has defined "need" in a more formal way:

> A need is a construct . . . which stands for a force . . . which organizes perception, apperception, intellection, conation, and action in such a way as to transform in a certain direction an existing, unsatisfying situation.[23]

Further, he has elaborated an extensive list of emotional needs. However, because Murray's list is so detailed, we found it necessary to depart from it in a number of ways. The list of needs on page 203[24] is nevertheless based upon Murray's scheme.

A study to test this theory has been undertaken with a group of middle-class subjects. Because striving for upward mobility (or higher socio-economic status) is so central to the middle-class value system, it was decided to include two variables pertaining to status.

Complementariness

To explain this theory let us imagine two persons, A and B, interacting with each other. Let us assume that both are deriving gratification from this interaction. Then the interactional sequence will be in accordance with the theory of complementary needs if:

1. the need or needs in A which are being gratified are *different* from the *need* or needs being gratified in B; *or*
2. the need or needs in A which are being gratified are very *different* in *intensity* from the same needs in B which are also being gratified.

[23] H. A. Murray, *et al.*, *Explorations in Personality*, New York, Oxford University Press, pp. 123–24.
[24] R. F. Winch, *op. cit.*, pp. 408–409.

NEEDS

n Abasement [25]
To accept or invite blame, criticism or punishment. To blame or harm the self.

n Achievement
To work diligently to create something and/or to emulate others.

n Approach
To draw near and enjoy interaction with another person or persons.

n Autonomy
To get rid of the constraint of other persons. To avoid or escape from domination. To be unattached and independent.

n Deference
To admire and praise a person.

n Dominance
To influence and control the behavior of others.

n Hostility
To fight, injure, or kill others.

n Nurturance
To give sympathy and aid to a weak, helpless, ill, or dejected person or animal.

n Recognition
To excite the admiration and approval of others.

n Sex
To develop an erotic relationship and engage in sexual relations.

n Status Aspiration
To desire a socio-economic status considerably higher than one has. (A special case of achievement.)

n Status Striving
To work diligently to alter one's socio-economic status. (A special case of achievement.)

n Succorance
To be helped by a sympathetic person. To be nursed, loved, protected, indulged.

GENERAL TRAITS

Anxiety
Fear, conscious or unconscious, of harm or misfortune arising from the hostility of others and/or social reaction to one's own behavior.

Emotionality
The show of affect in behavior.

Vicariousness
The gratification of a need derived from the perception that another person is deriving gratification.

An example of (1) is found in the case of a person desirous of attention and recognition (n Recognition) who finds gratification in relationship with a person who tends to bestow admiration on the former (n Deference). Alternative (2) is illustrated in the interaction between a person who wants others to do his bidding (high n Dominance) and one lacking the ability to handle his environment who is looking for someone to tell him what to do (low n Dominance). It will be recognized that this definition of complementariness embraces two forms of heterogamy.

Points Requiring Further Elaboration

At present the theory of complementary needs is a hypothesis enunciating a general principle of mate-selection when both spouses are

[25] The notation "n" before the name of a variable is used as a shorthand form of the term "need," and where it is found on following pages, that is what it represents.

given some freedom of choice. (It is clear that the theory would not be applicable under such a system of arranged marriages as has been traditional in Japan.[26]) This principle is now under empirical investigation, but the results of this study will not be available for some time.[*]

There are a few points to be noted about the theory before the results of the research are known. First, although marriage is viewed as a major source of gratification, it is a matter of common observation that most married people derive gratification from social interaction with other persons as well as with their respective spouses. To the degree that this is true it is not necessary to hypothesize that marriage partners will be totally complementary in their need-patterns. The theory also hypothesizes, however, that if there is not a minimum degree of complementariness in the need patterns of the two persons, they will tend to regard the relationship as unsatisfactory. Their dissatisfaction would probably be registered as follows. Either the relationship would be broken during the dating or engagement periods, or if the couple should be married, their marriage would have more than the average probability of ending in divorce.

At this time the minimum degree of complementariness, referred to in the above paragraph, is unknown, and some criteria are required concerning the number of needs sufficient to hold a relationship together. Other questions which may be raised but which cannot yet be answered are as follows:

First, can matching which occurs only on one need in each spouse hold the marriage together? It seems logically possible that only one need of each member of the couple might be met in a relationship. This need, however, might be so important that it would set the tone of the whole relationship.

Second, when a person exhibits two needs which are in conflict, for which of these needs is gratification sought in marriage? For example, in the case of a woman who is upwardly mobile and is also very dominant, does she marry an aggressive type male who will get for her the status she desires but who will not submit to her domination, or does she marry a dependent male who will give in to her but who lacks the initiative to achieve status? It would be interesting to determine how frequently

---

[26] [Omitted.]

[*] [*Editor's note.* The research carried out by Professor Winch and his associates on mate-selection among twenty-five couples is reported in full in Robert F. Winch, *Mate-Selection* (New York: Harper & Brothers, 1958). Of the research, Winch concludes: ". . . it is my interpretation that the bulk of the evidence supports the general hypothesis of complementary needs in mate-selection, and I accept the hypothesis with the tentativeness usual in any scientific conclusion" (p. 119). He continues that not all variations in mate-selection are accounted for by complementariness but that this factor seems to be one of the determinants among middle-class urban groups in the United States.]

this type of problem is resolved by the individual's directing one need towards the marital partner and the other towards interaction with other persons. On the other hand, it may be that many persons with this type of conflict never achieve a satisfactory solution and that hence the intrapsychic conflict becomes a source of conflict in marital interaction.

Third, in persons who show a marked disparity between needs which are expressed overtly (or directly) and those which are expressed covertly (or indirectly), on which level does matching occur? Persons may behave overtly in a fashion quite different from, or even opposite to, their more basic wishes. We all have known insecure persons whose bold and aggressive exterior is an attempt to convince themselves and others that they are really unafraid. In this situation it may be that matching at the covert level would be more important than at the overt level, but this we do not know as yet.

Illustration of the Theory

To illustrate the theory of complementary needs we have chosen a case from a sample of middle-class married couples and have attempted to show how these two partners complement each other need-wise. It will be noted that in this case the male shows some dependent trends. We do not feel that this case is atypical of our middle-class sample. Dependent needs in the personality of the middle-class male are probably more frequent than is popularly supposed.[27] It is to be emphasized that the man and wife discussed here are a normally functioning couple.

The Case of Anne and Frank Hamilton [28]

Before we can understand how individual needs function for mutual gratification in a marital relationship, it is first necessary to present the

[27] For further elaboration on this point, cf., for example, Arnold Green, "The Middle Class Male Child and Neurosis," *American Sociological Review*, 11 (1946), 31–41; and Talcott Parsons, *The Social System*, Glencoe, Ill., The Free Press, 1951, esp. pp. 262–69.

[28] This case represents one of those being studied in a project under the direction of Dr. Robert F. Winch at Northwestern University. This investigation is supported by a research grant, MH-439, from the National Institute of Mental Health, U.S. Public Health Service.

The material upon which the case analysis was done consists of a case-history type interview, Thematic Apperception Test protocols, and a second type of interview designed to get at the more behavioral aspects of personality. The full case analysis was made by the research staff of this project which consists of Dr. Winch, Mrs. Sandra K. Oreck, Dr. Oliver J. B. Kerner, and the authors of this article. The present report is a synopsis of their findings, which cannot be presented in their entirety because the analysis runs to about two hundred pages of manuscript. Much of the documentation for generalizations must be omitted. All names and identifying characteristics have been changed in order to preserve the anonymity of the couple without impairing the crucial facts of the case. It is our desire to present the case as simply as possible for the purpose of illustrating the theory.

personalities involved. We shall consider first the wife and then the husband before we attempt to understand their relationship to each other.

Anne Hamilton is best described in build as "hefty." Her outstanding features facially are her large mouth and rather prominent teeth. That her mouth is so noticeable the interviewer attributes to the fact that "it never seems to be still." She talks loud and fast. She punctuates her words by dramatic use of her hands and facial expressions. Even when she is listening, her face does not relax. She smiles broadly or raises her eyebrows or in some other way responds aggressively to what is said.

Anne's energy is also evident in her capacity to work. To finish college in three years, she carried extra courses each term and still sailed through her undergraduate work. She earned most of the money to pay here college expenses even though her family was able and willing to pay them. But she just liked to keep busy, so not only did she work and keep up her grade average, but she also held responsible positions in numerous extra-curricular affairs. She was so efficient in getting ads for the school yearbook that for the first time that publication had a financial surplus.

Going along with this terrific need to achieve is a high need to dominate others, which Anne describes as "a certain element of bossiness in me." She feels that her way of doing things is best and she wants people to do things "in the manner I so designate." [29]

She does not like to be "stepped on" nor does she admire people who can be pushed around. Such people she cannot respect. "People that I cannot look up to, I have a tendency to shove out of my way or to trample on, just shove, push." Thus we see in Anne little need to feel sympathy for other persons (n Nurturance) but rather a hostile attitude towards them.

She tends to be critical of other people and apparently because of this she has encountered some difficulty in forming close friendships. She says that people usually like her if they can overcome their first impression which frequently is one of antagonism. She says on this point, "I'm very quick spoken and rarely stop to think that I may be hurting somebody's feelings or that they are not going to take it just the way I meant it." But she needs people and she wants them to like her.

The competitiveness and the need to manipulate people undoubtedly indicate compensatory behavior for feelings of insecurity at some level. There is some evidence to indicate that these feelings stem from her doubts about her being a feminine person. She tends to be jealous of pretty women. She is contemptuous towards them when their attractive-

---

[29] Shortly we shall note that this domination of others occurred very early in her life in her relationship to her parents and other members of the household.

ness and "poise" win them positions of prestige which they are not equipped to handle because of a lack of the "executive ability" that she possesses. All her life she states that she wanted to be like her mother who is pretty and sweet and "gives a lot, perhaps too much." She feels, however, that she has not succeeded in becoming this sort of woman. She regards herself as a person who is "quick, uneven-tempered and impatient, ambitious . . . ready to tell others how to do things." Evidence that she rejects this "masculine" component in her personality is her view that she would not want a daughter to be like herself, but "more like Mother."

The postulation of such a conflict helps to explain why Anne did not continue with her career plans. She took a master's degree in advertising the year following her undergraduate work. She then set out to make a career in this field, but there were no jobs immediately available. Employers did not want college graduates who had their own bright ideas about the business, and, according to her account, they were unwilling to employ her for menial jobs which she was willing to take because they felt she was too intelligent and soon would become disinterested.

At this point Anne's career drive began to fluctuate. She took a job in an office. While there and while formally engaged to another man, she met Frank. She and Frank were married six months after their meeting, and they moved to a city where she had obtained a good job and where he enrolled in college. At the end of a year she became pregnant and stopped working for a while. By the third month of her pregnancy, however, she became bored with "sitting around home" and took a job as a waitress, much against the doctor's orders. She lost the child three months later. She stated that she wanted the child very badly and that she was broken up over her loss. This wish would be consistent with the feminine desire to be a "mother." In addition to the conscious desire to be feminine, it seems probable that she had an unconscious wish to abort and to deny willingness to play a feminine (maternal) role.

Perhaps if we look into Anne's background for a moment we can see more clearly the circumstances which led to the development of her pattern of aggressive behavior and the confusion over appropriate sex-role behavior.

Anne was the only child in a family of four adults. Her father was a self-made man, one who built up a trucking business to the point where it netted him an income of around $700 monthly even during the depression years. She describes him as being a short man, one who was hot-tempered and stubborn. He was 30 when Anne was born and her mother was only 18. The mother is described as being even-tempered, calm, and dependent. The third adult was Anne's maternal grandmother who came to live with the family shortly after Anne was born.

She managed the house and Anne's mother and apparently Anne's father as well. Anne says her grandmother often warned the father against his outbreaks of wrath in front of the child. The grandmother brought with her one of her sons who was about the age of Anne's father who was similar to Anne's mother in temperament. He was very good to Anne and gave her everything she wanted. He married for the first time and left the household when he was 50 years old.

Anne was the center of attention for these four persons. What she could not get from one, she could get from another. This pattern of relationships was conducive to her manipulation of persons and the need for recognition from them which we have noted earlier.

Grounds for the competitiveness may also be found in this network of relationships. Anne's mother was very young and still dependent upon her mother who looked upon Anne as "her youngest child." Thus, the relationship between mother and daughter resembled sibling rivalry, not only for the "mutual mother's" love but for the husband-father's love as well. Here were two bases for Anne to dislike her mother, but her mother was such a sweet young thing that she never gave Anne any rationalization for hating her. This left Anne with an unexpressed hostility which apparently has been partially sublimated into an achievement drive and partially displaced onto "feminine" women like her mother. Her mother was better looking than she, so Anne could not compete with her on these grounds but had to seek other means of achieving superiority.

To strive in an aggressive manner was satisfactory in another way too because the father, who wanted a son, approved of such behavior in his little tomboy. Further, grandmother was a model of aggressive behavior. Anne's gratifying relationship with her fostered an identification. The aggressive pattern was fairly well set by the time Anne reached adolescence as is evident in her report that, in junior high school, teachers commented on it. One teacher advised her to change her ways or she would never get a husband. Father also changed his mind about what he wanted and began to look upon her as "feminine" and wanted her to become dependent on him while she was in college. These undoubtedly are the sources of some of the ambivalence we note in her picture, especially concerning career and motherhood.

Although she had doubts about her "feminine appeal," Anne apparently had little trouble in finding dating relationships. Though she confesses she was not the most popular girl on campus and that her weekend calendar was not always filled, she dated from the time she first entered high school. She had only one serious relationship before meeting Frank. This was an engagement to a man described as "suave and smooth . . . and with nice manners." It apparently was a stormy affair, off and on several times. The engagement was broken finally over the issue of whether or not there should be a formal wedding. Anne wanted one, but her fiancé's family did not.

Frank is unlike Anne in many ways. Whereas she gets much gratification from work and positions of responsibility, he much prefers just loafing and being with people. He is now in college, at Anne's request, and very much looks forward to the time when he will be through. College is just a means to an end for him; the less work he has to do to get through, the happier he will be. He wants the degree, however, because it will facilitate his getting a good job. He looks to the job to bring him status and prestige and to provide a large income so that he can buy sporty cars and a big house. Nevertheless, he does not like to work for such a position and is just as content if someone gets it for him.

Frank likes people and he gets along with them very well. It is important to him that they like him and give him attention. He loves to talk and to joke, and generally he is successful in winning friends. "I'm an easy person to get along with . . . I do a fair job of amusing people although I feel that people don't regard me as entirely full of nonsense." His physical appearance contributes to his acceptability for he is a good-looking man, tall and slightly heavy. His build is somewhat athletic but his muscles seem to lack the firmness and tonus of a well-developed athlete. He is light-hearted, pleasure-oriented, and loves to eat.[30]

To achieve acceptance Frank relates to people in a deferent manner. He consciously admires and accepts his allies almost uncritically. He shows no tendency to control them nor to compel them to do what he wants; in other words, he reveals no need to dominate. Though he likes very much to have the spotlight himself, he is willing to share it with others and even to concede it without resentment to people who are better attention-getters than he. He tends to establish friendships with such persons and to identify with them. Thus he receives vicarious gratification for his own for recognition. This is illustrated in the fact that he joined the fraternity to which most of the "big wheels" on campus belonged though he himself was not a big wheel. Merely through association he felt he was able to share in their glory.

It is interesting to note that Frank does not limit his struggle for recognition to a few fields or a select group of persons as mature adults generally do. He is almost child-like in his willingness to perform. Once when drunk, he paid the singer in a night club twenty-five dollars to let him sing with her in front of the microphone. He still wears the badge

---

[30] In terms of the Freudian stages of development, this aspect of his personality would place him at the "oral" stage, the stage at which the infant, for example, does little more than *receive* love, care, and attention from the mother. The passive-dependent trends which we note in Frank's personality are considered the psychological counterparts of this stage of development. We shall note, however, that this characteristic is by no means the whole picture and that he is considerably more active than is implied for this stage.

that he received when he was deputized a sheriff for a week in his home-town. The importance of this incident was shown when Frank flipped his lapel so the interviewer could see the badge.

In addition to recognition, Frank seems to want love and affection. He tells that he was the "mascot" of a sorority at the first college he at-tended, and he was chosen "king of the prom" one season. If he feels blue, which he says is rare, he can be cheered by having women, peers or the mothers of peers, tell him how handsome he is.

Apparently since high school Frank always got along well with women because he always had a girl. He tended to date one girl at a time and to go with her pretty "seriously." He expected the same of her, and as a result most of these relationships broke up by his becoming jealous when the girl would date another fellow. He became jealous he says because he wanted "all her attention." The girls he dated were all short and very attractive. They conformed to his "ideal" of "one other fellows thought highly of, a popular girl in other words." Apparently a girl of this type brought vicarious recognition to Frank in the same manner as did the "big wheels" in the fraternity.

Now let us consider Frank's background. Frank was the third son in a family of four boys, all of whom were born during a period of eight years. His father, who was 57 when Frank was born, was a successful salesman until the depression. After losing everything in the depression, the father stopped working. The major burden of supporting the family then fell upon his mother who was about 28 years younger than the father. In time this responsibility was shared by the oldest son. The mother was a petite and good-looking woman.[31] She was a very hard-working, efficient sort of person who, besides working at a full-time job, kept her house, herself, and her sons immaculately neat and also found time to participate in a few club activities. She had considerably more education than her husband in that she had a B.A. degree whereas he completed only the eighth grade. Frank remembers her as being un-demonstrative in her affections and as a reasonably impartial judge in the children's quarrels but with a tendency to side with the underdog. Frank had little to say about his father's personality. Though the man had died only two years before the interview, Frank gave the impression that his father had participated little in family affairs. Frank's few de-scriptive comments portrayed an opinionated man, harsh in his judg-ments.

Among the seemingly more important aspects of this family is the ab-sence of daughters. Having two sons already, both parents had desired that the next children be girls. Indeed Frank can remember the time

---

[31] It will be recalled that the girls he dated were of similar stature.

when his mother gave him a girl's haircut. It would appear therefore that this attitude on the part of his parents, and especially his mother, laid the groundwork for the passive-dependent trends we have noted in his personality. It seems logical that Frank wanted the love and attention that is given to the baby. At the age of two years, however, he could no longer be gratified in these desires because of the arrival of the fourth and final brother. It appears that Frank resented this brother greatly. In one two-hour interview he mentioned both of the older brothers but not this one. Undoubtedly as a consequence of this situation Frank has developed a fear of rejection to which he has responded by always doing what is expected of him and by endeavoring to please people in order not to be rejected by them. Frank did not react to his feelings of rejection by rebellion. Perhaps this was because the mother never actually rejected him; she just did not give him all the affection he desired. To avoid losing what he did receive and to try to get more he reacted by being a "good boy."

But Frank was not a sissy in the common use of the term. He was interested in athletics and became captain of his high school football team. He liked mechanics and cars. Currently he is studying mechanical engineering and hopes someday to become a salesman for some large engineering firm.[32]

These masculine interests are very important for understanding Frank's personality. We have shown the tendency towards dependency in his personality which culturally is considered "feminine." Generally, males in our culture who tend to be passive experience some conflict if they are not able to live up to the cultural imperatives that they be assertive and "masculine." Frank shows little anxiety on this score, however, and appears to be very well adjusted. His not having developed a conflict on this score may be due to his having achieved such successful identification with male authority figures that he consciously never questions his "maleness."

Undoubtedly, the oldest brother is a significant figure in understanding these identifications with males. Very early this brother became a counsellor to the mother. Frank felt ambivalent towards him. He was jealous because this brother played such an important role with the mother. On the other hand, if he hated his brother, then the mother would reject him completely; but if he were like his brother, he would get his mother's attention and at the same time establish a good relationship with the brother, who was moderately successful in his own business and popular with people. Thus, the brother became an ego-model

[32] It is not surprising that Frank wants to become a salesman because he enjoys so much talking with people and feels certain that he is able to get along with them well.

for him and at the same time was a person who could meet some of Frank's dependent needs.

Thus, we now see Frank as an amiable, non-anxious person who does not have a great deal of ambition but who has the knack of relating himself to people who can do things for him.

Up to this point we have attempted to describe both Anne and Frank with very little reference to each other. Now we shall discuss their case with relation to complementary need theory.

Frank says that he was attracted to Anne because "she's probably the smartest woman I've run into, and I admired her a great deal I think before I truly loved her." On the other hand, Anne admired his easy-going manner and his ability to get along with people. Knowing what we do about each of them individually, we can see in these two remarks alone some ground for their complementary matching. First of all, we have pointed out that Anne has had some difficulty in getting along with people and that she would like to be able to do so more easily. Frank's ability to attract friends and to keep them facilitates Anne's social relationships in that he attracts their mutual friends. For Frank, Anne's initiative and her ability to attain the financial and other goals she sets for herself complements his lack of drive. The question is open, however, whether or not this particular pattern of interaction which is now mutually gratifying will continue to be so if Frank becomes a successful salesman.

In their interaction with each other we note that Anne has the authority. She handles their finances, and she decided that he should go back to school. As we have seen, this is the way she likes to do things and we have also noted that Frank shows little need to dominate and he accedes quite willingly to her plans.

Anne tends to be a very emotional person who is easily aroused and upset. At such times Frank's calm and easy-going manner is consoling to her. He has a good shoulder to cry on and he is willing to listen to her problems. She feels that he is helping to calm her down.

About the only thing that disturbs Anne about Frank's personality is that he does not have as much ambition as she would like to see. Indeed she has been somewhat bothered by his rather lethargic attitude towards school work. She would prefer to see him as excited about it as she has always been, but she feels that she is learning to accept this attitude that graduation is the important thing and that the level of one's performance in school is soon forgotten.

Occasionally Frank is a little perturbed by Anne for sometimes he is embarrassed when she pushes ahead in a crowd and drags him along with her, but he goes along and says nothing about it. Undoubtedly he is ambivalent about her aggressiveness. On the one hand, her behavior and her drive facilitate the realization of such desires as the new car which they recently bought. On the other hand, Frank fears that the same aspects of Anne's personality may put him in a position of stepping on other people which might result in their rejecting him. However, this aggressiveness does not constitute one of the things he would change about her if he could push a button to change anything. He would want to modify only her quick temper and her heaviness.

Anne is very different from the girls that Frank dated. The other girls were like his mother in physical characteristics in that they were all short and attractive. Anne has none of these physical characteristics, but does resemble Frank's mother in her efficiency. Although very different from Anne's father, Frank tends to be more like Anne's uncle and Anne's mother who are calm, easy-going, and dependent.

Both Anne and Frank desire considerable recognition from other people. Frank is attentive to Anne and considerate of her. She undoubtedly regards his submissiveness to her as admiration. Anne does not pay as much attention to Frank as he would like. It would seem that although Frank would like more in the way of demonstrated "hero-worship," he does not feel too deprived because she facilitates his getting the symbols (*e.g.*, the new sports car) which enable him to attract attention from other persons.

There is one other thing about Frank which Anne finds gratifying and which is worthy of mention here. Frank's attractive appearance and engaging manner enable Anne to compete successfully on a feminine basis with other women. Although this appeal on his part is gratifying to her in one sense, in another sense it threatens her. She mentioned that she is jealous if he pays too much attention to other women at parties. He also becomes jealous when she has occasion to lunch with another man. This mutual jealousy is understandable in terms of the marked need for recognition which each of them exhibits. On Frank's part, it undoubtedly is a manifestation of his fear of rejection; and from Anne's point of view, the insecurity stems from doubts about her feminine ability "to hold a man."

The complementariness that is described in this couple can be summarized generally as a case of a passive-dependent male finding gratification in relationship with a striving, aggressive woman (and vice versa). Indeed, they are not complementary on all counts, *e.g.*, neither is willing to surrender his own desire for recognition in favor of the other. However, it would seem that the mutual choice that has been made satisfies the major, predominating trends within the personalities of each other.

23. FACTORS IN BROKEN ENGAGEMENTS

Ernest W. Burgess and Paul Wallin

§ Engagement is no longer considered the certain prelude to marriage. It has come to be considered, the authors say, "as the last stage in the selection process leading to the choice of a mate." The exclusive relationship of engagement is the last testing ground for the compatibility needed for marriage. Many engagements do not survive this last crucial test. Among one thousand engaged couples studied by Professors Burgess and Wallin, 24 per cent of the men and 36 per cent of the women reported that they had broken prior engagements; before the study closed, another 15 per cent of the couples had broken the engagements that they were partners in when the study began.

When the authors compared broken with unbroken engagements they found that they did not represent completely different types of relationships. However, the broken engagements more often than the unbroken ones were characterized by infrequent demonstration of affection, lack of confidence in the happiness of the marriage, short period of acquaintance, small amount of time spent together, parental disapproval, difference in religious affiliation, infrequent church attendance, disagreement on activities, desire to "be on the go," and failure to avoid arguments. These characteristics are perhaps symptoms of underlying personality traits or lack of compatibility.

From interviews, the researchers isolated five factors in broken engagements which are discussed and illustrated in the first part of the following excerpt. The latter part details the process by which engagements are broken.

Many concrete explanations are given by young people for broken engagements, such as falling in love with another person, interference of the man's or woman's mother, loss of interest, religious differences, or cultural conflicts. These, however, are frequently surface manifestations

SOURCE: Ernest W. Burgess and Paul Wallin, *Engagement and Marriage* (Philadelphia: J. B. Lippincott Company, 1953), pp. 273–82, 297–300. Copyright, 1953, by Ernest W. Burgess and Paul Wallin. Reprinted by permission of the publisher. *Engagement and Marriage* is the report of an extensive study of one thousand engaged couples.

Ernest W. Burgess' background is given in the footnote for article 3. Paul Wallin, professor of sociology at Stanford University, received his doctorate from the University of Chicago.

of more fundamental factors which need more intensive study than has as yet been given them.

The above, and other alleged "causes" of broken engagements, can be classified in five categories: (1) slight emotional attachment, (2) separation, (3) parental opposition, (4) cultural divergences, and (5) personality problems.

Slight Emotional Attachment

One or both parties to an engagement, as evident from case studies of broken engagements, may be in love to a slight or small degree if at all. Occasionally an engaged person is doubtful if he is in love, as in the following instance:

> Joan thinks she was very indifferent about her engagement to Frank. It did not impress her at all. She thinks now that she had no business ever to get engaged to him and that she is better off that the engagement is broken.

More often the youth has honestly believed himself to be in love only to realize later that his feelings were not deeply involved.

> Their real quarrels were about Ann being friendly with the men she knew before she became engaged. Her fiancé thought she should stop seeing them. She did not go out with them and could not see why he was so jealous of her. She did not consider that she gave him any reason to be jealous. The engagement was broken when she was nineteen. She thinks now she was too young to know what it was all about, and did not take it seriously enough.

A girl or youth may enter an engagement half-heartedly, not being too sure of keeping it.

> I never could get enthusiastic about the wedding because I felt that it would never take place. I never made any plans because I could not see myself married to Joe. Once during the engagement I danced with some friends when we were out together and Joe got angry. I had no respect for his opinions. I had compared him often with other men whom I met and he did not stack up very well. I felt sorry for him but that was all I felt.

Sometimes, the couple have been thrown together by circumstances, as during a summer vacation, without the presence of other eligible young people. Or, as in the following case, they kept company and were finally engaged as the result of the college dating and rating system which often emphasizes superficial characteristics like popularity and appearance rather than vital common interests and complementary personality needs.

> We were both the most popular in school for two years. I played football. She was vice-president of the class. We were both leaders in our respec-

tive groups. We took class after class together. My fraternity and her club had our marriage planned.

When the couple are held together only by a slight emotional attachment, the relation may easily be broken if one of them falls deeply in love with someone else. Of course, as seen in two of the above cases, one member of the couple may be more involved than the other.

Separation

Separation may be regarded as a special case of slight emotional involvement because it leads to the breaking of many engagements where love was not strong enough to hold the couple together.

But separation leads not only to the termination of relations based on a slight degree of emotional attachment. It also may result in the breakup of a certain proportion of engagements where there may have been rather strong mutual attraction. This takes place particularly among couples who have difficulty in maintaining their relationship by correspondence. One or the other is likely to drift into keeping company with a person who becomes a more emotionally significant object than the absent fiancé.

> When I met George at college I did not know about the girl back home. He did not tell me about her until after he let me know he loved me. I insisted that he write her breaking off the relation before we became engaged.

In other cases there has been insufficient association to establish a vital relationship. The effect of the separation of the couple from each other is illustrated in the case of Mr. A who lived in New York nearly a thousand miles away from his fiancée Miss N. In their nine months of acquaintance they were together two months before their engagement and only a total of five weeks afterwards.

> John used to write a letter each day. Then he wrote less often. He says that he just got tired of writing. There was never a quarrel. We just separated. When he was writing less often I became emotionally upset for two months or more. It was quite a blow to me. Later he was very anxious to renew our correspondence. I did not want to be hurt again. Whether I got over it completely, I don't know. I don't think I ever want to be engaged to him again.

Parental Opposition

Parents take a keen interest in the love affairs of their children. But the mores sanction arrangements for marriage by young people without parental interference. Consequently children tend to resent any direct control exerted by parents over pairing and engagement. In a study by Bates,[1] sons report that parental influence was brought to bear upon their courtship by fathers in 49.1 per cent and by mothers in 79.4 per cent of cases. Daughters stated that they had experienced more or less pressure by fathers in 68.7 per cent and by mothers in 97.1 per cent of the cases. Direct participation of parents was characterized by their children as generally moderate. In one-fifth of the cases extreme pressure by parents was reported. A very high proportion of elopements were by children of parents of this type. Parents with serious personality problems were those most likely to interfere arbitrarily in the love affairs of their children.

Parental influence may be exerted in favor of one suitor or in opposition to another. In general, parents tend to apply standards in which the economic and social status of the young man and his present or prospective earning ability are given the highest weight. They are likely to ignore or minimize considerations of romance and of compatibility of personality and of interests.

Parental influence on courtship and engagement may be direct or indirect, overt or subtle. A mother may openly oppose and criticize the defects in each girl in whom her son becomes interested. Or a mother who is ill or dependent upon a daughter may influence her, out of considerations of duty, to delay and postpone marriage until the young man breaks the engagement. Frequently, but not always, the son or daughter goes ahead with plans for the wedding in spite of the open disapproval of the parents.

The more intelligent parent is likely to be more subtle and often more effective in preventing a marriage. The wealthy father, disapproving of his prospective son-in-law, may take his daughter on a European trip, or plan for her to meet more "eligible" young men. The mother, instead of outwardly opposing her son's selection of a wife on the ground of her lower-class origin, may invite her to week-end events where her lack of social accomplishments is made evident to all, including her son. In the following case the girl's mother puts pressure upon her to become better acquainted with her fiancé.

> We were to be married in the fall and my mother insisted that I spend the summer visiting him in order to find out what he was like before we got married. By the end of the summer when I returned to the city I was sure we would never marry.

The parental expectation may be that the future son- or daughter-in-law will become a part of the family. This may be perceived and objected to by the prospective family newcomer.

[1] Alan Bates, "Parental Roles in Courtship," *Social Forces*, 20, 1942, pp. 483–486.

Tom was completely dominated by his mother. Both let me understand that she would live with us. It was not necessary, but he could not say "no" to her. So I broke the engagement.

To be frank, I am glad my engagement went on the rocks. The trouble was that I was marrying the family, not the girl.

Cultural Divergences

The term "cultural divergences" as used here covers a wide range of social differences. It includes differences in family background, in social class, in attitudes to the conventions, in habits such as drinking and smoking, and in interests, values, and ideals.

The cultural differences which most frequently lead to broken engagements are those involving religion, nationality stock, region of the country, rural-urban origin, and attitudes to sex, race, and interests and ideals.

In many engagements the initial interest of one or both has been on a superficial basis such as physical attraction, the personal prestige of the other, or association through the chance or romantic circumstances of propinquity. Or, as frequently happens, the couple were first attracted to each other by the novelty of their differences in cultural background.

Whatever the cause of their original interest in each other, cultural divergences often lead to difficulties in adjustment. The following case illustrates both the superficial nature of the mutual attraction which first brought the couple together and the cultural conflict which led to the break in the relationship.

We had little in common. Oh yes, we went to dances and movies together, to picnics and different sports and parties, but that was only entertainment. Intellectually we were worlds apart. I was interested in good books. Tom was only interested in how well he could play golf.

One is most acutely conscious of cultural divergence in a group of intimate friends. This leads to a reappraisal of the relation as in the next case.

He had always irritated her when they were with friends. His talk was so ponderous, he had such difficulty expressing himself and formulating his ideas. He was always dragging in highly intellectual subjects like semantics. He never understood my jokes or allusions to literature or current slang. He was just dumb.

Conflicts which sometimes break up an engagement are those arising out of religious differences. The most obvious of these are when the couple are of different religious faiths as in Protestant-Catholic or Protestant-Jewish unions. Sometimes even more important are differences in religious interest and devotion as in the following broken engagement:

> We had planned to be married in June. In May a shower was given for me, I bought a wedding dress and arrangements were made for a home wedding. We would have been married except that he began asking why we had to go to church Sunday mornings, the only morning we have? I think he would have liked it just as well if we had gone into the country and enjoyed the beauty. I agree with him perfectly but I thoroughly enjoy going to church. I don't go to church because someone says I must. I find it inspiring and it helps to make me a more cheerful person. I have never felt that it was keeping me from doing something that I would rather be doing. I just feel that he doesn't feel that way. He started to argue the point and tried to convince me that I shouldn't go to church Sunday mornings. Then he began talking very peculiarly about how he was on one side of the fence and I was on the other and couldn't I see that that was the case. So I began to think that religion was going to be an issue. I don't think any marriage can be successful where there is any issue that big.

Occasionally the cultural roots of the conflict are below the surface. In the following case the young man, according to his ex-fiancée's account, seemed determined to be the dominating one in the relationship, a role which she apparently did not concede.

> He was rather quiet. You had to get to know him before he'd open up. He was pretty set in some of his ideas. We used to fight all the time. We used to call it the Saturday-night session: that's when it usually happened. I think most of all he was afraid I was having my way too much.

This disagreement over the dominating role may be interpreted, of course, as due to personality conflict rather than cultural conflict since either factor, or both, may be involved.

Important divergences in values and interests may not be recognized until after engagement. The intimacy of this relationship gives an opportunity to discover if the couple have ideals and goals in life which will make for harmony or disharmony in marriage.

> She had one trait I did not like and that was her social ambition. She was interested in people for the sake of social aims. Her friends respected her very highly and thought she was a sincere, warm person. But I think she made friendships more of a business than she needed to.

Personality Problems

The terms "compatibility" and "incompatibility" are in popular use as an explanation of successful and unsuccessful personality adjustment in engagement and marriage. Where all other factors are favorable—

common interests, similarity in cultural backgrounds, congruent ideals and values—the couple may still have difficulties because of conflicts in temperament and personality traits.

First, there are persons with major personality problems which render them prone to break engagements. Men who are overly dependent upon their mothers, promiscuous in sexual relations, fearful of assuming marital responsibilities, or content with the irresponsibility and freedom of the bachelor state, may enter into, but often break, engagements.

Similarly, young women appear more likely to break engagements if they have idealized their fathers or have been attached to them to an extreme degree, if they are fearful of the physical aspects of marriage, or if their standards of mate selection are higher than the qualifications of their fiancés.

These and other attitudes may be symptomatic of underlying personality problems, such as feelings of inferiority, emotional insecurity, emotional instability, and emotional and social immaturity, which may have origins in the childhood family relationships of the person. The experience of a discordant home environment in childhood seems in some of the cases interviewed to be associated with the tendency to break engagements.

> In my interviews on broken engagements one factor has appeared frequently in a variety of forms which seems to be related, at least in part, to the breaking of the association in a large proportion of cases. This factor is the presence of a major personality problem in one or both of the partners to the engagement. A "major personality problem" is a problem important enough to color all social action undertaken by that individual. This usually manifests itself in some attempted behavior adaptation caused by consciously or unconsciously felt insecurity—generally emotional insecurity.
>
> A home environment which was markedly discordant for one reason or another seemed to be the most important cause of a major personality problem leading to the breaking of an engagement. A broken home, either through divorce or separation, not death; a home where the mother and father went their separate ways either with or without antagonism; a home where both mother and father were too concerned with their own affairs to bother with the children—either because of economic or temperamental difficulties—or a home where the children were taught to despise one parent, these were the types of discordant homes which have seemed to exert a significant influence in the formation of these personality problems.[2]

Since in our culture the engagement period is considered the final test of compatibility, the broken engagement is the recognition by one or both members of the couple of their lack of suitability. Incompatibility may take one or more of the following forms.

[2] Unpublished paper by Charlotte A. Cooper.

Incompatibility of temperament refers to clashes arising from the basic mood of the person. Two high-strung and tense individuals are likely to find difficulties in adjustment. So also are two people who are moody and pessimistic in their outlook on life. More often, one member of the couple has a temper or is emotionally unstable. Quarreling in the engagement period is the most frequent indication of temperamental incompatibility.

Jim had very much of a temper and was constantly at me whenever he wanted me to do something I didn't want to do. He liked to have his way all the time. In an effort to get this he would become very emotional and demonstrative. It made me sort of disgusted. We never quarreled before the engagement, but sometimes during the engagement. This was because of his gambling and his jealousy.

Every once in a while I used to break my engagement to Ned. I don't know why I did it. I would break it and make it up again. I think it gave me the jitters. I suppose it was just general emotional instability. I always wanted to marry him. The situations were not important to me; I can't even remember. I certainly was nasty. I would tell him I was not engaged. I used to get exasperated with Ned at times. Let me think. Most arguments we have had have been over subjects of a theoretical nature. We had no great disagreements but we were able to manufacture some. I don't remember anything over which we broke the engagement last summer.

Unsatisfied personality need is another source of incompatibility. The girl may wish for demonstration of affection and frequent verbal expressions of love which her fiancé does not supply. Or he may find that she does not give him the encouragement, understanding, and sympathy which he needs.

I did not measure our relations so much in terms of love as practical reality. Most important, she didn't understand me very well or my aims in life and what I hoped to achieve. She did not understand my intellectual interests, for example, my interest in religious theory. She was more of a motherly type of girl. She would make an excellent mother.

Unsatisfied personality need emphasizes two facts. First, liking is not the same as loving a person. There is a difference between love and friendship. Second, a sudden infatuation may represent only congeniality and not any emotional interdependence of the two, as is illustrated by the following case.

Well, he was just nice, real nice. The moment you met him you could tell he was just a swell person inside. About the third date, we had it all planned what we were going to do. Real fast and sudden. We had "now this is the real feeling." But it didn't last. I think if it had, the same thing would happen as before—the same sweet boy, but I'd get bored again.

The parental personality pattern which each member of a couple unconsciously seeks in the other may not match sufficiently to insure the happiness of the union. One requirement of a satisfying interpersonal adjustment appears to be that the love object have those personality characteristics of the parent of the opposite sex which had affectional significance for the person as a child. Concretely, this means that a young man will tend to fall in love and be emotionally satisfied with a girl who possesses those personality traits that were important to him as a child in his response relation to his mother. Conversely, a girl finds herself emotionally drawn to a young man who manifests in his association with her the traits which had meaning in her earlier relationships with her father.

In the following case the girl fell in love with a young man who looked like her father but who, as she found later, did not have his characteristics. The young man resented her efforts to change his traits to be more like those she admired in her father. Each recognizes the fact in their separate statements:

> Any time you are second choice to the girl's father! It doesn't click. She was always measuring me up to him and comparing me to him. When I marry I'm not going to be a person for her to make over to be her old man.

> Frank looked something like my father used to look, but my present fiancé acts more like him. He is very competent just as my father.

Frequently in the engagement period one member of the couple finds that the other one, who is entirely satisfied with the relationship, does not meet his or her personality needs.

> Mr. A fell deeply in love with Joan who had some of his mother's outstanding personality traits. But she broke their private understanding to be married as soon as she knew him better. She was greatly attached to her father who was an aggressive masculine type. She found that Mr. A needed emotional support and said, "He wanted someone to lean on, but I wanted a husband I could lean on."

The *career interest* of either the man or girl may be a decisive factor in the breaking of the affectional association. This is particularly true of young people entering or even in training for a profession. The ministerial student develops a conception of the characteristics appropriate for a pastor's wife. If he perceives that his fiancée falls short of these he begins to think about breaking the engagement especially if he becomes interested in a girl who corresponds to his ideal of a life companion. A somewhat parallel example is the girl who is engaged to a young man before he decides on the career of a minister. Previously she had pictured herself as the wife of a successful businessman. She finds she is unable to readjust to her conception of the role of a pastor's wife.

Frequently, other related factors enter into this type of broken engagement. The young man, beginning his professional career or preparing for it, enters a new social world. He finds that his ideas and values are changing, sometimes in ways that conflict with those of his fiancée. While he has been growing intellectually and socially she may have been vegetating in an unstimulating environment.

An illustration of this pattern of the disruption of an engagement may be taken from the profession of medicine. The medical student after his formal training is required to complete an internship in a hospital. Restricted in his social contacts, he falls in love and becomes engaged to a nurse who, besides her nurse's training, has had only a high school education. Her family background is of a lower social class than his. They have a common interest in medicine but in little else. He may realize before marriage that she will be unable to participate in other areas of his activities.

These different factors or conditions in broken engagements—slight emotional attachment, separation, parental opposition, cultural divergences, and personality problems—are seldom present independent of each other. Generally, two or more of them operate in conjunction. A given case of a broken engagement should be intensively studied to determine the actual interplay of factors which leads one or both members of a couple to seek the termination of their association.

· · · · ·

Breaking the Engagement

Two different techniques may be used by the person who wishes to end the engagement. One is the sharp complete break; the other is the tapering-off procedure. The advantage of the immediate clean break inheres in its aboveboard character; there is none of the camouflage of feelings of the cooling-off technique. Its disadvantage is the emotional shock to the jilted person and all the aggressive behavior it may set off. In our group of broken engagements there was no instance of the classic case where the rejected suitor kills the girl and then commits suicide in accordance with the frustration-aggression theory of directing hostility first outwardly and then toward oneself.

The advantage of the tapering-off procedure is that the rejected person, realizing gradually the defection of the other, is somewhat prepared and suffers less severe emotional turmoil and acute distress. Its disadvantage is that he may continue to hope against hope and so take a longer time to make an emotional readjustment and be psychologically ready to enter into a new relationship.

· · · · ·

The final break often occurs on the initiative of one member of the couple. The typical situation is that one wants the break and the other does not. Sometimes it comes as a "bolt out of the blue" to the jilted one. He has been oblivious, or so he claims, to the attitudes and intention of the other.

. . . . .

Reaction to the Broken Engagement

To the "jilted" person the broken engagement occasions an emotional crisis in something like direct proportion to its unexpectedness. The rejected individual is in a turmoil of conflicting impulses, feelings, and questionings. He is possessed by accusations against the errant lover about the reasons for the other's unaccountable and outrageous behavior, duplicity, and lack of frankness; by self-examination for failure in the engagement; and by real or imagined deficiencies. He considers any and all possible means of re-establishing the relationship. He may run the gamut of emotions from fantastic hope to deepest despair. He shrinks from the ordeal of meeting and informing relatives and friends. To himself and later to others he depreciates the qualities of his former inamorata, stressing defects where formerly he had seen only virtues. He may even reach the conclusion that she is morally irresponsible, mentally deranged, and may wonder why he had ever been attracted to her. A little later in a reversal of feeling he may affirm to himself and to others his willingness to forgive all if only she will consent to resume the relationship. Then his love, turning to hate, may lead to thoughts and threats of murder of the former loved one and even, in rare instances, to the act itself. Or he may contemplate, or attempt, or sometimes actually commit suicide. Literature includes instances of the murder of the loved one by the rejected suitor, followed by his suicide.

Later, however, the rejected person regains his emotional balance and when interviewed some months afterwards generally gives a less emotional account of the break.

. . . . .

Time, the comforting counsel of friends, the routine of life, new interests, and especially the formation of another attachment, gradually heal the injuries caused by the emotional wounding. Later, the person tends to minimize the degree of stress and strain experienced and to express satisfaction that the break occurred.

. . . . .

Engagement on the Rebound

Some persons pass rapidly from the emotional crisis of a broken engagement (or from an unsatisfactory love affair which has not reached this stage) to a new emotional involvement. This is particularly the case with persons with major personality problems, especially those with a history of rejections in family relationships in childhood. Even when there has been no childhood rejection, the need for emotional expression may impel the person into another close affectional relationship. Another contributing and sometimes decisive factor is the strength of the urge to regain status in one's intimate group of young people. These and other influences result in engagements and often marriages on the emotional rebound without the person making the discriminating choice he otherwise would be disposed to make.

> Our engagement was a rebound from an unhappy romance that I was trying to get over. The boy I had been going with suddenly married someone else and it upset me very much. I never felt that this second engagement would end in a marriage.

The following is a generalized case indicating some of the typical features in a group of instances of engagements on the rebound from a broken engagement.

> Polly was the pretty, charming, and intelligent daughter of a professional man of moderate means. She was pledged by one of the better sororities on entering a coeducational college. She was dated by several of the leading men of the campus and in her junior year was engaged to a young man who was able and ambitious. At the beginning of the second semester of the senior year he broke the engagement and before the school year was over the Sunday newspaper announced his engagement to the daughter of one of the wealthy and prominent families of the nearby metropolitan city. During the summer in her home town Polly met a high school acquaintance who had dropped his course in his high school sophomore year. She had previously paid little attention to him because he lived "across the tracks." But he was devoted and sympathetic and promised to go ahead with his education. They were engaged and married within a few months of the date of her former fiancé's wedding. After marriage, Polly soon realized that she and her husband were misfits psychologically, that they had no common interests, and that he had no serious intention of completing high school and preparing himself for a trade or profession. The situation became unbearable to both of them; she returned home and later secured a divorce.

Chapter 8: Love

24. ROLE OF LOVE IN HUMAN DEVELOPMENT

Daniel A. Prescott

§ Love is an emotion that almost everyone experiences in many different forms. Because love does take different forms it is hard to define. Dr. Prescott quotes what a number of different persons have to say about love and then presents his own analysis of the nature of love and its role in human development. He does not view loving or being loved as independent experiences but as two sides of one coin. The combined experience enriches life and facilitates adjustment.

This paper will address itself to three questions: (1) Is love a reality or a delusive romantic construct of our culture? (2) If love *is* a reality, what is its nature? (3) If love *is* a reality, what is its role in human development? In preparing this paper, I examined several dozen books in human development, educational psychology, cultural anthropology and sociology, psychiatry, and biography. In the majority of books in human development and educational psychology the word love did not occur. When it did occur, it was used without definitions for the most part. I feel that if love *is* a reality, we need seriously and scientifically to study its influence on human lives and to learn what conditions are favorable to its enhancement and fulfillment. If it is not a reality, we shall need to study the reasons for the emergence of so strong a myth, so frustrating an aspiration, so delusive a pretension. There is a remarkably small amount of scientific material now available about it.

A very brief review of the ideas found in the books examined comes

SOURCE: *Journal of Home Economics*, 44 (March, 1952), 173–76. Reprinted by permission of the publisher and the author.

The author, whose degree of Doctor of Education is from Harvard University, is professor of education and director of the Institute for Child Study at the University of Maryland. He is active in national and international educational organizations. He has contributed articles to professional journals and is the author of a number of books in education, including *The Child in the Education Process*.

first. Breckenridge and Vincent,[1] Strang,[2] and Barker, Kounin and Wright[3] all mention love as a reality. The general idea expressed is that love markedly influences behavior, development, and adjustment. One notes a vagueness about the nature of love as a positive force and finds much more specificity about the negative effects of lack of love and of inappropriate use of love relationships. Kluckhohn and Murray[4] give a great amount of material about sexual behavior and about family processes but no discussion of love as such.

James Plant[5] clearly regards love as a reality but does not define it. Love affords children a basic security, a sure feeling of belonging, he says. Insecure, unloved children show anxious, panicky symptoms that contrast with the aggressive overcompensation of inadequate children. He shows that confusion about their security often arises as children try to meet the learning and behavioral demands set for them by the authority of their parents and of society and again as they struggle for independence.

Harry Stack Sullivan[6] defines love: "When the satisfaction or the security of another person becomes as significant to one as is one's own security, then the state of love exists."

Overstreet[7] says,

The love of a person implies not the possession of that person but the affirmation of that person. It means granting him gladly the full right to his unique humanhood. One does not truly love a person and yet seek to enslave him—by law, or by bonds of dependence and possessiveness. Whenever we experience a genuine love we are moved by the transforming experience toward a capacity for good will.

Fromm[8] coins the term "productive love" because the word love as popularly used is so ambiguous. The essence of love, he contends, is the same whether it is the mother's love for a child, our love for man, or the erotic love between two individuals. Certain basic elements are characteristic of all forms of productive love. They are: care, responsibility, respect, and knowledge. He says,

[1] Breckenridge, Marian E., and Vincent, Elizabeth L. *Child Development.* Philadelphia: W. B. Saunders Company, 1943.
[2] Strang, Ruth. *Introduction to Child Study.* New York: The Macmillan Company, 1951.
[3] Barker, Roger G., Kounin, Jacob S., and Wright, Herbert F. *Child Behavior and Development.* New York: The McGraw-Hill Book Company, 1943.
[4] Kluckhohn, Clyde, and Murray, Henry A. *Personality in Nature, Society and Culture.* New York: Alfred A. Knopf, 1948.
[5] Plant, James. *The Envelope.* New York: The Commonwealth Fund, 1950.
[6] Sullivan, Harry Stack. *Conceptions of Modern Psychiatry.* Washington, D.C.: William Alanson White Psychiatric Foundation, 1947.
[7] Overstreet, Harry. *The Mature Mind.* New York: W. W. Norton & Company, Inc., 1949.
[8] Fromm, Erich. *Man for Himself.* New York: Rinehart & Co., Inc., 1947.

Care and responsibility denote that love is an activity, not a passion . . . the essence of love is to labor for something, to make something grow. . . . Without respect for and knowledge of the beloved person love deteriorates into domination and possessiveness. Respect . . . denotes the ability to see a person as he is, to be aware of his individuality and uniqueness. . . . Love is the expression of intimacy between two human beings under the condition of the preservation of each other's integrity. . . . To love one person productively means to be related to his human core, to him as representing mankind.

Fromm also contends that love of others and of ourselves are not alternatives.

The affirmation of one's own life, happiness, growth and freedom is rooted in one's capacity to love. . . . If an individual is able to love productively he loves himself too. . . . Selfishness and self-love, far from being identical, are actually opposites. . . . The selfish person does not love himself too much but too little, in fact he hates himself. . . . He is necessarily unhappy and anxiously concerned to snatch from life the satisfactions which he blocks himself from attaining. . . .

The recurring mention in the literature of the relatedness of love for self (self-respect), love for other individuals, and love for mankind led me to examine biographies and writings of three men who have lived lives of great devotion to mankind: Kagawa, Gandhi, and Albert Schweitzer.

Kagawa[9] says,

Love awakens all that it touches . . . creation is the art of life pursued for love. . . . Love is the true nature of God. . . . In social life human beings meet and love one another through a material medium. . . . Love spins garments for itself out of matter . . . through love economic life appears as the content of the spiritual. . . . Real reconstruction of society can be accomplished only through the operation of education through love. . . . If we view economics so, the study of it changes into a science of love. . . . Art must create externally beautiful objects and internally it is itself love.

The practical social and political application of love has worked several miracles in India during our times. Gandhi[10] said,

To be truly non-violent I must love my adversary and pray for him even when he hits me. . . . We may attack measures and systems. We may not, we must not attack men. Imperfect ourselves, we must be tender towards others . . . forgiveness is more manly than punishment.

Gandhi contended that God is love and can be known only through action. "Faith does not permit of telling. It has to be lived and then it is self-propagating."

[9] Kagawa, Toyokiko. *Meditations.* New York: Harper & Brothers, 1950.
[10] Fischer, Louis. *The Life of Mahatma Gandhi.* New York: Harper & Brothers, 1950.

Albert Schweitzer[11] is another extraordinary international figure who has accomplished the apparently impossible during the past 50 years. He has tremendous reverence for life and respect for the dignity of all human beings and believes that love is the great force of the universe. He says,

> By the spirit of the age the man of to-day is forced into skepticism about his own thinking in order to make him receptive to truth which comes to him from authority . . . [but] it is only by confidence in our ability to reach truth by our own individual thinking that we are capable of accepting truth from outside. . . . Man must bring himself into a spiritual relation to the world and become one with it. . . . Beginning to think about life and the world leads a man directly and almost irresistibly to reverence for life . . . the idea of love is the spiritual beam of light which reaches us from the Infinite . . . in God, the great first cause, the will-to-create and the will-to-love are one. . . . In knowledge of spiritual existence in God through love he [man] possesses the one thing needful.

Each of these three men was a man of action who accomplished the seemingly impossible during his lifetime in the first half of this our twentieth century. Each affirmed that love was a central dynamic in his accomplishment, love of other individuals, love of mankind, and love of God. Theirs certainly was "productive love." We may, therefore, regard our first question as answered in the affirmative. Love does exist. It is a potent reality.

The Nature of Love

Now what about the nature of love? On the basis of this little research, I have developed a number of theses about love. They will be presented with brief mention of the degree to which they seem to be supported by ideas in the material already cited.

1. Love involves more or less empathy with the loved one. A person who loves actually enters into the feeling of, and so shares intimately the experiences of, the loved one and the effects of experiences upon the loved one. Sullivan indicates something of how this comes about:[12]

> If another person matters as much to you as you do yourself, it is quite possible to talk to this person as you have never talked to anyone before. The freedom which comes . . . permits nuances of meaning, permits investigation without fear of rebuff which greatly augments the consensual validation of all sorts of things.

2. One who loves is deeply concerned for the welfare, happiness, and development of the loved one. This concern is so deep as to become one

11 Schweitzer, Albert. *Out of My Life and Thought.* New York: Henry Holt & Co., 1949.
12 Sullivan, Harry Stack. *Op. cit.*, p. 20.

of the major values in the organized personality or "self" structure of the loving person. All sources studied seem to agree on this proposition. It is especially validated by the lives of Kagawa, Gandhi, and Schweitzer. Each of them has shown by his actions that he values the human beings whom he serves not only as much as he values himself but even more.

3. *One who loves finds pleasure in making his resources available to the loved one*, to be used by the latter to enhance his welfare, happiness, and development. Strength, time, money, mind—indeed all resources—are happily proffered for the use of the loved one. This implies that a loving person acts with and on behalf of the loved one whenever his resources permit and the action is desired by the loved one. The loving person is not merely deeply concerned about the welfare, happiness, and development of the beloved; he *does* something to enhance them whenever possible. All sources seem to agree on this proposition, too.

4. *On the one hand the loving person seeks a maximum of participation in the activities that contribute to the welfare, happiness, and development of the loved one.* On the other hand, the loving one accepts fully the uniqueness and individuality of the loved one and accords him freedom to experience, to act, and to become what he desires. This thesis is agreed to by nearly all of our sources.

5. *Love is most readily and usually achieved within the family circle but can be extended to include many other individuals, or categories of people, or all of humanity.* For Schweitzer it also includes all living things and the Creative Force of the universe—God. In the same way a person can advantageously experience love from a limitless number of other human beings and living things. Of course, genuine full love is hard to achieve even with a few persons, as several of our sources pointed out. But this is not proof that with greater scientific understanding of its processes we cannot create conditions that will favor its broadening.

6. *The good effects of love are not limited to the loved one but promote the happiness and further development of the loving one as well.* Love is not altruistic, self-sacrificing, and limiting for the one who loves. On the contrary, it is a reciprocal dynamic which greatly enriches the lives of both. This idea is not too clearly stated in a number of our sources but seems implied where not stated in nearly all.

7. *Love is not rooted primarily in sexual dynamics or hormonal drives*, although it may well have large erotic components whether between parents and children, between children, or between adults. Fromm seems to support this position when he says that the essence of productive love is the same no matter who is concerned.

8. *Love affords many individuals fundamental insights into and basic relationships to humanity and to the Forces that organize and guide the universe.* It gives many persons a basic orientation in the universe and

among mankind. It can become the basis for faith in God. I was surprised to find support for this thesis from all sources. For example, Plant affirms that[13] "from early adolescence on the Church gives a great many children a sense of belongingness which has greater continuity and certainty for the individual than anything provided by his parents." The other sources also intimated that love is a great aid in the developmental tasks of orienting the self toward the rest of mankind and within the universe toward God.

These eight theses, I hope, may be of some aid in analyzing the nature of love and the processes by which it develops. Admittedly they represent only a first and faltering attempt. But if they are sufficient to focus more scientific attention and research on love, the purposes of this paper will have been accomplished.

The Roles of Love in Human Development

Now we address ourselves to the third question. Since love does exist, it potentially can become a reality in the life of every human being. Then, if our theses regarding the nature of love are true, what roles can love play in human development? This question will be answered during the next decade, I hope, by a whole series of researches. The findings should fill many monographs and some books. In the meantime, I should like to propose a series of hypotheses as to the probable findings of these researches, in the hope of suggesting profitable research leads.

The first hypothesis is that being loved can afford any human being a much needed basic security. To feel that one is deeply valued because one is, rather than because of the way one behaves or looks, is to feel fundamentally at home whenever one can be with the person who loves one so. From earliest infancy to most advanced age this feeling of being deeply valued is an important precondition to meeting life's challenges and expectations, to doing one's best without unhealthy stress.

The second hypothesis is that being loved makes it possible to learn to love oneself and others. The capacity of infants for empathy, before language development makes more explicit communication possible, permits the feeling of the nature of love very early in life. The closeness of mutual understanding among preadolescent peers makes its joyous expansion natural. The hormonal creation of unrest in the presence of peers of the opposite sex pushes its further development until it is stilled by intimate sexual sharing of vivid life in marriage. The mystery and the creative fulfillment that come with the first baby begin a cycle of nurturance and guidance of a rapidly developing new personality that brings tremendous fulfillment through the years. But this wonderful growth and enrichment of life by love seems possible only to those who

[13] Plant, James. *Op. cit.*, p. 26.

first were loved by others. Indeed we suspect that a person who has never been loved cannot fully respect and love himself but must always restlessly be reassuring himself as to his fundamental worth.

Our third hypothesis is that being loved and loving others facilitates winning belonging in groups. Of course, winning roles in group activities requires that the individual have knowledge and skills that are valuable in carrying on the activities of the group. Of course, conformity to group customs and codes is necessary to group belonging, and being loved contributes to none of these. But being secure through love and being able to give love, favors personality characteristics that are easy and attractive in group situations. Such a child or youth has no reason to lord it over others, to be aggressive and hostile, or to be shy and withdrawing. Such children do not need constantly to climb in status by calling attention to the failure and inadequacy of others.

A fourth hypothesis is that being loved and loving in return facilitates identifications with parents, relatives, teachers and peers by which the culture is internalized more readily and organizing attitudes and values are established easily. When one feels loved and loves in return, it is easy to learn that which is expected; it is easy to believe that which one's objects of love believe and to aspire in the directions encouraged by one's objects of identification. The unloved child feels so much insecurity that he scarcely dares try his wings in learning. Or he is so full of hostility that he tends to reject what he is told and to refuse to meet the expectancies that face him, as a way of demonstrating his power to himself. Obviously the readiness of loving persons to provide meaningful experiences and to aid them in the learning process are further facilitations that give great advantages to loved children.

Our fifth hypothesis is that being loved and loving facilitates adjustment to situations that involve strong unpleasant emotions. When a loved child fails at something, the failure does not cut so deep as to make him doubt his basic worth because he is still secure in that love relationship. Consequently he is more easily reassured and encouraged to try again and again. In contrast, the unloved child who fails is in double jeopardy. To his insecurity is added the feeling of inadequacy, and the world looks blacker and blacker. When a loved child is frightened, he can literally or figuratively take the hand of the person who loves him, approach and examine the terrifying situation, learn its true dimensions, and more readily find the courage to face it. But terror to the unloved child is unfaceable and overwhelming. Punishments, penalties, and the demands of authority are bearable for loved children because they do not imply rejection or fundamental lack of worth. Consequently they are analyzable by the loved child, who more easily can perceive their meaning and take them in stride. But to the unloved child these things may be taken as indicators of personal rejection or of unfavorable status.

Resentment, rebellion against authority, hostility against peers who seem more favored, or fundamental doubts of own worth ensue.

All of our hypotheses about the role of love in human development show it as a powerful facilitator of wholesome and full self-realization. As Bruno Bettelheim has so ably pointed out, *Love Is Not Enough* to cure badly maladjusted children. But it surely is a great aid to their adjustment and, best of all, it is a great preventive of maladjustment for the children who are fortunate enough to feel it constantly as they face their evolving developmental tasks.

25. EXPRESSIONS OF LOVE

Percival M. Symonds

§ In the first part of the selection. Dr. Symonds cautions that sexual expression and love, although they have much in common, are not identical. Sex, in a narrow sense, is physical; love, however, implies esteem of another's personality. The interweaving of sex and love is carefully analyzed. Love may also be expressed through friendship and cooperation.

Sex: Sex and Love Not Identical

The infrequent mention of sex in the foregoing discussion may seem to a number of persons to be strange inasmuch as love and sex are so commonly bracketed in most persons' minds. Love is almost universally used as a term to denote sex. When one picks up a book entitled The Art of Love, he expects to find a treatise on sex. Psychoanalysis in its early formulations was severely criticized because it was thought to overemphasize sex and to interpret all neurotic states as due to aberrations of the sexual impulse. It is true that psychoanalytic theory, being based mainly on extensive studies of neurotic persons, has failed to provide a wholly adequate analysis of love, which is in the main a characteristic of normal and stable individuals.

It is an interesting fact, however, that only recently in the history of the human race has love been considered an aspect of sexual activity. One does not speak of love in connection with the sexual activity of

SOURCE: Percival M. Symonds, *The Dynamics of Human Adjustment* (New York: D. Appleton-Century Company, 1946), pp. 547–50. Copyright, 1946, by D. Appleton-Century Company, Inc. Reprinted by permission of Appleton-Century-Crofts, Division of Meredith Corporation.

The author's background is given in the footnote for article 17.

lower animals, and primitive man by no means linked love and sex
together as one and the same thing. Anthropological studies of primitive
cultures will show that every conceivable emotional relationship can
accompany sexual relations. For instance, Margaret Mead[1] in studying
a New Guinea tribe found that a man gives all of his affection to his
sister and that his relations with his wife are to a high degree impersonal
and even antagonistic.[2]

Even in civilized countries where marriage is arranged between two
children by their parents, the marriage is not based on love but becomes
an economic and social transaction between families. Love may develop
in the marriage relationship, but sex is not accompanied by love at the
start. Indeed, romantic love as we know it in our own society has had a
late historical development. What seems so important and inevitable is
simply a product of our own culture. It is our way of conceiving sex.

Freud[3] has referred to love as "aim inhibited sex"; that is, he thinks
of love as the tender feelings that one has left after sex has been inhibited. Sex, which was originally present, has been subtracted from
these tender feelings. A libidinal concept of love was necessary for Freud
because he saw pleasure or sex as the ground-swell out of which all the
more mature emotions emerged. Freud's concept, however, fails to
comprehend the dynamic character of love, for he attempted to fit it too
narrowly into his libido theory. As we are discussing love in this chapter, it is more a function of the personality and its adjustments to the
people who are part of its world than it is a function of sex.

But Sex and Love Have Much in Common

Physiologically, love and sex have much in common. They both represent the operation of the parasympathetic nervous system. The preparatory stages of sexual excitement, including tumescence and a turgid
condition of the genital organs, represent a discharge of the parasympa-

[1] *Growing Up in New Guinea* (New York: William Morrow and Company, Inc.,
1930).
[2] "A man gives the allegiance of dependence to his father, occasionally to his mother,
mutual affection and feeling of reciprocity and co-operativeness to his sister, playfulness and easy give and take to his female cross cousin, anxious, solicitous, sedulous
care to his children. For his wife he reserves—what? Unrelieved by romantic fictions
or conventions of wooing, untouched by tenderness, unbulwarked by co-operativeness and good feeling as between partners, unhelped by playfulness, preliminary
play or intimacy, sex is conceived as something bad, inherently shameful, something
to be relegated to the darkness of night. . . . Married women are said to derive only
pain from intercourse until after they have borne a child."
[3] *Group Psychology and the Analysis of the Ego*, International Psychoanalytical
Library, No. 6 (London: The Hogarth Press, 1922; first published in German,
1921).
Civilization and Its Discontents. International Psychoanalytical Library, No. 17
(London: The Hogarth Press, 1929).

thetic. We have also seen that in a more general sense the discharge of the parasympathetic represents an essential condition for the expression of love. Both love and sex represent muscular relaxation, and freedom from inhibition and fear. They both represent pleasurable excitement. Both represent an outgoingness. Indeed, sex as a basic drive which demands the response of another person for its relief and satisfaction becomes a prime setting for the development of love. However, love must not be confused with sexual expression. There may be love of food and adventure in just as real and passionate a sense as the love which accompanies sex. On the other hand, sex must not be thought of too narrowly as the relief of physical tension. Indeed, most writers on sex would insist that the forepleasure and the personal relationship are important factors in the consummation of sexual pleasure. In this sense sexual love involves a confluence of two separate streams of expression and feeling, one purely physical, the other, emotional, based on human relationships. As these two come together, they result in a more profound and exalted experience than any other expression of love. Indeed, sexual expression depends for its highest satisfaction not only on the adequacy of the physical act but also on many other factors, just as the pleasures of eating are enhanced by refined appointments and entertaining company. The expectations of the culture determine in a large measure the quality of sexual expression. What custom permits and expects sets the stage for the quality of sexual pleasure. The vitality of the two partners also plays its part. The sexual temperaments of the man and woman as determined by their erotic experiences in infancy also determine the quality of sexual experience. Current discussions of sex put major emphasis on the adequacy of the sex act itself, but this is only one of a number of factors and not necessarily the most important one which contribute to the total satisfaction in sexual relations.

Sex in its narrow aspects is physical. Love implies, on the other hand, the esteem and recognition of another individual as a separate personality. For the most complete sexual relationships other persons must be acknowledged in a double way, first as persons and second as carriers of sex activities.

A disputed point for which conflicting arguments and evidence have been advanced is whether love or friendship must rest on a sensual and even a sexual basis. Some have asserted that any human relationship is to a degree sensual and ultimately will be found to invoke to some small degree an element of sex. One investigator[4] who collected many diaries and letters of adolescents believes that he has evidence to support the view that the feelings and expressions of friendship are different from, if not opposed to, those of sex. One cannot, perhaps, take a dogmatic posi-

[4] Iovetz-Tereschenko, N. M., *Friendship—Love in Adolescence* (London: George Allen and Unwin, 1936).

tion with regard to this issue at the present time, and it is not very important to do so. The fact of the matter is that even if there is a minute sensual basis to the most platonic friendships, it may be so minute as to be relatively unimportant. One knows, for instance, that there is moisture in unseasoned wood, because it will warp. However, in discussing wood the fact that it contains moisture within its pores would be a relatively unimportant characteristic.[5] There is a basic difference between sex and love in this respect. Sensual pleasure becomes extinguished when satisfied, whereas love continues unabated, indeed, is enhanced the more satisfaction a person derives from another. Actually, the satisfaction of the physical needs of sex occupies only a small, though necessary, part of life; whereas the emotional needs are all-embracing. To go back to Maslow's hierarchy of drives referred to in Chapter II, "Drive," the physical needs of sex are basic.* Generally they demand first satisfaction, but, unlike hunger, they can be widely displaced and sublimated. When the physical needs are met, the stage is set for the gratification of higher needs of safety, affection, recognition and self-realization.

Sex is one form of joint sharing and activity through which love may be expressed. Indeed, it is the most complete union and sharing of which men and women are capable. It represents the highest degree of intimacy; but it has been emphasized time and again that sex must not be thought of in its narrow physical aspects but in the whole circle of relationships, experiences, and responsibilities which accompany it.

Christian civilization, strangely enough, is opposed to sexuality while at the same time it endorses love. This inconsistent attitude makes all persons in our culture to a degree impotent and frigid. Love could receive a more widespread and deeper expression if society could take a less restrictive attitude toward sex.

Friendship

This long passage on the relation between love and sex would make it seem that sex is the only form of expression of object love. While it does occupy an important place, it is by no means the only form of expression. Indeed, friendship in which the sexual element is minimized or missing can serve as the expression of love quite as effectively as though sex expression were present. Friends can have many bases for

---

[5] Illustration from conversation with Theodor Reik.

* [*Editor's note.* Maslow gives five levels of needs as follows: first, the basic physiological needs of hunger, sex, and so on; second, the needs of safety from external dangers; third, the need for love; fourth, the need for esteem; fifth, the need for self-realization. Gratification of the lower levels frees a person for the higher social needs. A. H. Maslow, "A Theory of Human Motivation," *Psychological Review,* 50 (1943), 370–396.]

common interests, common pursuits, for sharing and helping one another, all of which foster love and serve as its expression. Reik points out that in friendship there is less overestimation of the object, less idealization, and a less intense possessiveness. Friendship usually involves certain qualities of the person and not the whole person himself. Reik sees the relationship in friendship as one of equality, but Fromm makes this equality a requisite of love. In friendship each of the two individuals keeps a stronger separate identity.

Cooperation

Love finds its social expression through various forms of cooperation. One of these is in the various modes of sharing. Husband and wife will find that love is enhanced to the degree in which they can share together in family life either their work or their play. A person feels that he is loved by another when he is invited to do intimate things. Sitting down to eat together is one form of intimacy and a valuable expression of love. The give and take of conversation is another form of sharing. One may give to another person his thoughts and feelings. To amuse him, to inspire him, to encourage him by the capacity to listen and to receive from the other person expresses fondness fully as much as the capacity to give. One must be ready to share grief as well as pleasure; and until one has shared hardships and trials, perhaps the bonds of love are not welded in their closest form. It is possible to establish love on a basis of interests as well as sex.

Helping another person and giving freely of one's time, energy, and wealth is another way of expressing love. The neglect of another person and the refusal to assist him is universally accepted as a refusal of love.

Exchanging gifts becomes an important token of love. A gift is a sign that the recipient is love-worthy. One gives freely objects such as food, toys, or clothing; his service or time; or erotic satisfaction only to a person whom he likes or admires.

Love also expresses itself through gentleness. The lover is considerate, is not brusque or importunate, and shows a quiet consideration of the other person.

Hart[6] has prepared the following tests of romantic love. (1) There is greater happiness in the presence of the loved partner than of any other person (this assumes a love that is exclusive and reciprocal). (2) There is a sense of unrest and dissatisfaction when they are separated. (3) The lovers find a wealth of things to say to each other. (4) There is an eagerness to share experiences. (5) Each is eager to give full consideration to his partner's opinions, judgments, and interest. (6) Plans and interests

6 Hornell Hart, *Personality and the Family* (Boston: D. C. Heath and Company, 1941), pp. 170ff.

keep organizing themselves around the partner. (7) The lover takes pride in his partner. (8) He is eager for the success of his partner.

Probably the best description of how love is expressed was given by Paul in the passage from Corinthians.

> Love suffereth long, and is kind; love envieth not; love vaunteth not itself, is not puffed up, doth not behave itself unseemly, seeketh not her own, is not provoked; taketh not account of evil; rejoiceth not in unrighteousness, but rejoiceth with the truth; beareth all things, believeth all things, hopeth all things, endureth all things. (I Corinthians, 13:4–7)

26. HETEROSEXUAL LOVE RELATIONSHIPS

Ira L. Reiss

§ Heterosexual love has connotations not found in other love relationships. Many writers have felt the challenge to try to distinguish heterosexual love from other types. In this article, it is analyzed into four sociological processes.

The heterosexual love relationship is one of the most vital and one of the most neglected aspects of courtship behavior. Recently the author examined the sociological literature, in particular the marriage and family textbooks, to discern the type of analysis present. In addition preliminary research was conducted on a new approach toward analyzing the love relationship. The purpose of this article is to put forth the basic findings of the above studies and, thereby, to propose a new direction for the sociological study of the heterosexual love relationship.

Textbook Treatment of the Love Relationship

An examination of twenty-six textbooks in marriage and the family revealed that twenty of these books took a rather limited or restricted approach to the heterosexual love relationship—that is, they most often focused on one type of love, which was usually described as the "best," "real," or "true" type. Other types, besides the preferred type, would

SOURCE: Ira L. Reiss, "Toward a Sociology of the Heterosexual Love Relationship," *Marriage and Family Living*, 22 (May, 1960), 139–45. Reprinted by permission of the publisher and the author.

For the author's background, see article 20.

commonly be viewed as not real forms of love or as inferior in quality to the true type of love. The following are several quotations from these marriage and the family textbooks which illustrate this restricted approach:

> Although one may fall precipitously into a condition of violent infatuation, it takes time for real love to develop. . . . Genuine love is centered on one person only.[1]

> Love at first sight is actually impossible, because love between two individuals is always a product of intimate and complex interaction, which depends upon varied types of experiences.[2]

> . . . love never makes the individual less effective, less fully functioning; rather it promotes growth and increases awareness of meanings, needs and opportunities in the world about one.[3]

> We can admit that young couples may be, and usually are, 'terribly infatuated' or 'awfully thrilled' with each other, but we hesitate to apply the word 'love' to such untested relationships [untested by many years of marriage] [4]

> Genuine love is possible only when couples know each other well. . . . Is it actually possible to 'fall in love at first sight'? The answer is 'no'. . . . If a person has serious doubts as to whether or not he is in love, obviously he is not.[5]

These textbook authors appear to have accepted one of our cultural beliefs: namely, that a "marriage type love" is the real form of love, and that such love is to be preferred over other emotional states such as romantic love or "infatuation." Although this restriction of analysis by a preferred type of love may afford insight into this preferred type, it does limit the objective investigation of other cultural forms of love in American society. In short, to the extent that this more restricted approach is emphasized, a more comprehensive sociological approach is minimized.

Other Conceptualizations

Even when we step outside the "textbook" area, this restricted approach is still operative. For example, this is how one sociologist defines love in an article in *Psychiatry*: "Love is that relationship between one person and another which is most conducive to the optimal development

[1] Henry A. Bowman, *Marriage for Moderns*, New York: McGraw-Hill, 1954, pp. 32–37.

[2] J. L. Hirning and Alma L. Hirning, *Marriage Adjustment*, New York: American, 1956, p. 125.

[3] Judson T. Landis and Mary G. Landis, *Building a Successful Marriage*, New Jersey, Prentice-Hall, 1958, p. 169.

[4] E. E. LeMasters, *Modern Courtship and Marriage*, New York: Macmillan, 1957, p. 61.

[5] Rex A. Skidmore and Anthony S. Cannon, *Building Your Marriage*, New York: Harper, 1951, pp. 57–61.

of both."[6] Here, too, one finds a particular kind of love as the center of focus rather than an objective analysis of all cultural types of love.

Winch's work on love relationships has been quite suggestive.[7] However, his efforts so far seem to be more fully in the realm of psychology than in sociology. Heavy reliance on psychoanalytic concepts in his analysis of love relationships, focusing on the individual relationship, and emphasis on the complementary needs of the particular couple without reference to possible cultural sources, all indicate greater concern with what the personality system has to contribute to love relationships rather than what the social or cultural systems may have to contribute to such relationships. Nevertheless, Winch does not by any means totally ignore the cultural background. He brings it in partly when he mentions that his theory applies only to societies where marriages are for love. He also makes up four major types of complementariness, but he fails causally to relate these types to any cultural variables.[8]

Winch's effort is of importance to sociologists, but unless he brings the social and cultural system into more central focus, there will be a serious gap in the sociological approach to the heterosexual love relationship. As sociologists we must know what kinds of social and cultural factors are related to particular types of love relationships. Whether the personality needs that individuals are satisfying are complementary or homogamous does not seem to be as important in a sociological analysis as the discernment of the socio-cultural factors which are causally related to these personality needs.

In addition to Winch's formulations the work of Burgess and Wallin is important for a sociological conception of love.[9] In particular, their efforts in dealing with homogamy seem quite relevant, for here the emphasis is on common cultural factors, such as religion and education, which are to be found in love relationships.[10] Burgess and Wallin also deal with personality needs, but they, like Winch, fail to tie this level to relevant causal background factors in the social and cultural systems. Even when dealing with homogamy, no complete effort is made to show why such background factors as religion and education are similar in many love relationships. In short, a correlational rather than a causal approach is taken. Thus, although Winch and Burgess and Wallin have contributed to our sociological knowledge of the love relationship, none of these individuals has related the personality-need level of the love

[6] Nelson N. Foote, "Love," *Psychiatry*, 16 (August 1953), p. 247.
[7] For the most recent statement of Winch's work see Robert F. Winch, *Mate Selection, A Study of Complementary Needs*, New York: Harper, 1958.
[8] See Winch, *op. cit.*, Chapters 7–10 and 14.
[9] Ernest W. Burgess and Paul Wallin, *Engagement and Marriage*, New York: Lippincott, 1953. Especially Chapters 6 and 7.
[10] *Ibid.*, Chapter 6.

relationship to its cultural sources—to put it another way, we are lacking a basic framework for a sociological theory of love.

There are interesting works on the love relationship such as those by Caplow, Kirkpatrick, Ellis and others.[11] However, these works, though valuable, are not directly relevant to the question of a basic over-all sociological approach to the love relationship; rather they are researches dealing with specific aspects of such relationships.

A Sociological Theory of Love

The above examination of the literature gives one the impression that what is needed in our approach to love is a frame of reference which is more fully on the sociological level. As a step toward this goal, a general theoretical approach to the heterosexual love relationship has been formulated which, it is believed, takes account of the psychological level but brings into central focus the social and cultural levels. As will be shown, this formulation is in accord with the research evidence in this area, and interviews of numerous students also seem to support this conceptualization. The following theory is put forth only as a first attempt to formulate the broad outlines of a sociological theory of the heterosexual love relationship.

First, it is important to describe the processes through which it is proposed all of our major cultural types of love develop. In American society young people meet under a variety of informal conditions such as at a party, a dance, or in school. After meeting, these two people become aware of the presence or lack of a feeling of rapport. That is, they may feel quite at ease and relaxed and be willing and desirous to talk about themselves and learn more about the other person, or they may feel quite ill at ease and watch the clock until the evening ends. To the sociologist the vital question is *not* just whether such a couple feels rapport because they complement each other or are similar to each other in their personality needs. Such information certainly can be valuable, as Winch has shown; but the crucial sociological question is: What are the social and cultural background factors which make this type of couple capable of feeling rapport—what social and cultural variables are related to particular personality needs? Certainly, if cultural backgrounds differ too sharply the people involved would be unable to communicate at all. However, if cultural backgrounds differ in some

[11] Included here are some of the classic researches into the love relationship: Clifford Kirkpatrick and Theodore Caplow, "Courtship in a Group of Minnesota Students," *The American Journal of Sociology*, 55 (May 1950), pp. 550–558. See also the interesting study of romantic love notions in our communication media: Albert Ellis, *The American Sexual Tragedy*, New York: Twayne, 1954, Chapter 5 especially.

particular ways they may still be compatible; while the same amount of difference in other directions makes compatibility most unlikely.

Thus, it is one of the sociologist's tasks to discern what role cultural background plays in heterosexual love relationships. This can be done on a more precise level than just seeing if the two people are of the same religion or education group. The latter has been done for us by Burgess and Wallin—but one must also see what cultural factors made these two particular people, who are of the same religion and education group, feel rapport for each other. The specific way each views and defines his social roles may be a fruitful area to examine. For example, within the same religious, educational, and income group there are divisions regarding how equalitarian the female role should be, and those people whose definitions of the female role are alike may well be more apt to feel rapport for each other. As a preliminary testing of this approach, seventy-four students were asked to select from ten personality needs which ones they felt to be the most important in their best love relationship. Table 1 shows some of the results of this pilot study.

These results are surely not conclusive but they are suggestive. In need number 9, for example, only 22 per cent of the boys stated that they

TABLE 1 *Personality Needs Which College Students Consider to Be Most Important in Their Best Love Relationship**

Personality Needs for Someone:	Boys (Percentage)	Girls (Percentage)
1. Who loves me	87	95
2. To confide in	60	65
3. Who shows me a lot of affection	40	53
4. Who respects my ideals	50	74
5. Who appreciates what I want to achieve	32	28
6. Who understands my moods	36	23
7. Who helps me in making important decisions	16	28
8. To stimulate my ambition	16	7
9. I can look up to very much	22	70
10. Who gives me self-confidence in my relations with people	32	19

* Each student was allowed to check as many of the ten as he thought were "most important." These ten needs are the same as Anselm Strauss used; see "Personality Needs and Marital Choice," *Social Forces*, 25 (March 1947), pp. 332–335. The questionnaire was administered by R. Wayne Kernodle and the author in 1958 to 74 of our "marriage" students (43 girls, 31 boys). A more rigorous testing is planned for the future.

felt it most important in their love relationships to have "someone to look up to." Seventy percent of the girls checked this response. This large difference seems to reflect the double standard in our society which brings girls up with more of an orientation to want to love someone they can "look up to." A girl who felt this need would, it seems, blend well with a boy who did *not* feel this need, and both of these attitudes are traceable to our double-standard culture. This is one way in which we may connect personality needs with cultural background. Other needs in Table 1 suggest cultural variables, e.g., the higher percentage of men who need their ambition stimulated and the higher percentage of girls who need help in decisions.

It should be emphasized that this is but a pilot study and much further work is needed to refine this method of analysis and test some of the above interpretations. The effort here is merely aimed at showing that one can analyze the rapport aspect of a relationship in terms of the cultural background which makes such rapport possible.

The feeling of rapport seems to be the first step in the development of heterosexual love relationships. Concomitant with such rapport is a second process which may be labeled "self-revelation." When one feels at ease in a social relationship he is more likely to reveal intimate aspects of his existence. He is, under such conditions, more likely to tell of his hopes, desires, fears, and ambitions. He is also more likely to engage in sexual activities, according to recent studies on college students.[12] Here, too, the sociologist need not focus on the psychological aspects—he can, instead, look at the cultural backgrounds of the participants. The cultural background of each person should help determine what he feels is proper to reveal, i.e., whether petting is acceptable, whether talking about one's personal ambitions is proper, or whether discussing religion is right. The person's cultural background will define what and how much one should reveal when a certain amount of rapport is present.

The above process of self-revelation is vital to the development of love, and it is through this that a third process occurs: namely, the development of mutual dependencies, or, more technically put, of interdependent habit systems. One becomes dependent on the other person to fulfill one's own habits: e.g., one needs the other person to tell one's ideas or feelings; one needs the other person to joke with; one needs the other person to fulfill one's sexual desires. When such habitual expectations are not fulfilled, loneliness and frustration are experienced. Thus, such habits tend to perpetuate a relationship. The type of habits which

---

[12] Winston Ehrmann's study of students at the University of Florida is the source of this statement. Ehrmann found that coitus was three times as likely to occur when love was involved. Winston Ehrmann, *Premarital Dating Behavior*, New York: Henry Holt, 1959.

are established are culturally determined, in large measure, for these habits are outgrowths of the revelations, and the type of revelation is culturally regulated.

Finally, a fourth process is involved, and that is personality need fulfillment. The needs referred to here are needs such as the basic needs in Table 1, which were examined in relation to feelings of rapport. As has been shown, these needs seem to vary with cultural background. These four processes are in a sense really one process, for when one feels rapport, he reveals himself and becomes dependent, thereby fulfilling his personality needs. The circularity is most clearly seen in that the needs being fulfilled were the original reason for feeling rapport. In summary, then, the cultural background produces certain types of personality needs in particular groups of people, and when these people meet other groups which have similar or complementary backgrounds they feel rapport, reveal themselves, become dependent, and thereby fulfill these personality needs.

Since these four processes turn one into the other and are constantly occurring, the above formulation concerning the development of love will be called the "Wheel Theory." This is, of course, merely a label for the above four processes—one which was chosen because the term has explanatory value and helps emphasize the circularity and unity of these four processes. As has been mentioned, the key interest for the sociologist would be in the cultural and social factors underlying these four processes as they occur between various types of young people. The diagram on page 245 is a graphic representation of this theory.

Of course, the "wheel" can turn in a negative direction and "unwind"; that is, the relationship can weaken when an argument or competing interest, or such, occurs. Such an event can lessen rapport and that, in turn, decrease self-revelation, mutual dependency, and need fulfillment. This decrease further lessens rapport and can thus continue to "unwind" the relationship. The wheel can also continue to turn indefinitely in a positive direction as long as the four processes continue to be activated. In this fashion the rapport, revelation, dependency and fulfillment processes can continue to "turn" for as long and as intensely as the cultural backgrounds of the people involved will allow.

Upon inspection it can be seen that the four spokes of the wheel are processes which universally occur in any primary relationship, i.e., the general description would apply to the development of a friendship relationship or a parent-child relationship. The four wheel processes would be involved in a primary relationship in Samoa as well as in New York. Thus, heterosexual love in America is the cultural development and elaboration of *one* type of primary relationship.

We give a specific meaning and content to this type of heterosexual love relation that distinguishes it from all other types of primary rela-

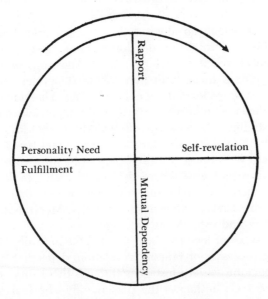

FIGURE 1. Graphic Presentation of the Wheel Theory of the Development of Love

tions. For the last thousand years the Western world has singled out the heterosexual type of primary relationship for special attention. Some other cultures have people who fall in love, but usually they do not use such love feelings as the basis for marriage. Such feelings most often develop after marriage and they lack the "romantic" aura ours possess. Goode has recently put forth evidence on the relative potentiality and actuality of love relationships in other cultures.[13]

Love in America is culturally defined regarding how intense the feelings should be before one calls it "love," and how one should behave when he believes he is in love. Although such cultural definitions are widely shared there still are some people who will apply the label "love" to a relationship quite freely, and some others who require so much that they may never believe a relationship is intense enough to be love. There may possibly be variation by social classes as to what is required

[13] William J. Goode, "The Theoretical Importance of Love," *American Sociological Review*, 24 (February 1959), pp. 37–48. Our explanation of love as a type of primary relationship fits in with Goode's findings that heterosexual love is more common than once thought and that many cultures set up specific controls to prevent its occurrence. For if heterosexual love develops as do other primary relationships, then it is more of an ever-present possibility, and one would expect to find it more widespread or to find specific controls set up against it. This is precisely what Goode found.

before using the term "love" to describe a heterosexual primary relationship.

The symptoms which go along with love vary from the Hollywood variety of walking into doors and losing one's appetite to the more "rational" type of symptoms which involve knowing the person thoroughly and wanting to be with him. These symptoms are learned in much the same way we learn other cultural forms. The kind of symptoms one displays depends in large measure on the type of love one accepts. The author's studies of college love affairs indicate that love in American culture may be hypothetically classified into several types, which have varying degrees of support in our society: (1) ultra romantic love at first sight, (2) sexual love where the sexual factor is dominant, (3) rational love where the intellectual appraisal of the affair is important, and (4) probably several other mixed varieties. Much more research is needed to verify and extend this typology.

All of these types of love can be explained theoretically as developing via the wheel processes of rapport, revelation, dependency, and fulfillment. The romantic variety just goes through these processes in rapid order and one feels he knows the person fully—he feels the rapport, reveals himself, becomes dependent and feels fulfilled, all sometimes in the course of one evening! The sexual type of love merely emphasizes one way around the wheel—one way of revealing oneself. The rational type of love emphasizes the need to know each other under a variety of circumstances and to evaluate the relationship before allowing oneself to become too involved. This type of love seems to be increasingly popular among college students.[14] It involves a larger number of rapport, revelation, dependency, and fulfillment factors than do the other love types.

Final Comments

With the Wheel Theory, one can distinguish and describe the development and maintenance of the major types of love relationships. Love, thus, can be viewed as a type of primary relationship which our culture has singled out for special attention. The problem becomes to discern what cultural forms have been given to this primary relationship and what cultural backgrounds tend to promote the possibility of this type

---

[14] Burgess and Wallin, *op. cit.*, p. 170. Over two-thirds of the engaged couples in this study refused to call their relationship "head-over-heels in love," because that phrase smacked too much of ultra-romantic love notions. The author's interviews with college students also tends to support this popularity of a "rational" type love. However, there are quite strong emotional attachments to some of the older romantic love notions, even among those who are intellectually "liberated."

of primary relationship. In this fashion one can avoid the more restricted approaches referred to above. Instead one can analyze the characteristics and consequences of each type of love in various segments of our culture and society. Goode's recent analysis suggests that love attitudes may differ considerably by social class.[15] The Wheel Theory thus affords a broad over-all conception which can encompass all the heterosexual love relationships.

Furthermore, the Wheel Theory does not depend on the truth or falsity of the complementary needs of homogamy conceptions. Rather, if one desires he may incorporate Winch's notion of complementary mating as well as the homogamy and personality-need views of Burgess and Wallin and Strauss.[16] Such explanations are compatible with the Wheel Theory and future research can resolve any competing conceptions which exist among these explanations.

In addition the Wheel Theory seems to be capable of accounting for and integrating much of the available specific field research evidence on love relationships. For example, some of the key findings in this area by Strauss show that 100 per cent personality need fulfillment is had by only a minority of the couples in his sample (18 per cent); Burgess and Wallin in their study of 1000 engaged couples showed how very common doubt and conflict were in engaged love relationships; Ellis in his study of 500 college girls points out that about a quarter of them had experienced simultaneous loves.[17] These are representative findings and they all are explainable by the Wheel Theory: e.g., if love does develop through the culturally directed processes of a primary relationship involving rapport, revelation, dependency, and need fulfillment, then one would expect that there would be wide differences in the amount of needs which were fulfilled in any one relationship; that the very common failure to fully satisfy one's needs might well make one have some doubts and conflicts concerning the value of the relationship; and it also follows that although one has fulfilled some of his needs in one love relationship, he may fall simultaneously in love with another person who is capable of fulfilling different combinations of needs.

Of course, the fact that the Wheel Theory is compatible with the major theoretical approaches and research findings in this area is not

[15] Goode, *op. cit.*, p. 46.

[16] Burgess and Wallin do not speak of homogamy alone—they emphasize personality need fulfillment as vital in love. Even though they do not stress the necessity for getting behind personality needs to their social and cultural correlates, their approach is still quite compatible with the Wheel Theory. See Burgess and Wallin, *op. cit.*, pp. 202–204, 212.

[17] Anselm Strauss, "Personality Needs and Marital Choice," *Social Forces*, 25 (March 1947), p. 333; Burgess and Wallin, *op. cit.*, pp. 179–182, 247; Albert Ellis, "A Study of Human Love Relationships," *The Journal of Genetic Psychology*, 75 (September 1949), pp. 61–71.

in itself conclusive evidence of its worth. The analysis here should serve mainly as a spur to further research testing of the Wheel Theory. It is believed that a new direction for study of the love relationship is needed. This paper is put forth only as a step toward filling the gaps in the sociological conceptualization of the heterosexual love relationship in America.

Chapter 9: Intimacies before Marriage

27. HELPING CHILDREN GROW UP SEXUALLY: HOW? WHEN? BY WHOM?

Eleanore Braun Luckey

§ In this selection, the goals of sex education for the individual and for society, as well as the more practical aspects of giving information and developing attitudes, are explored. A serious handicap to the formulation of goals is the lack of consensus on what values or types of sexual behavior should be taught. Instead of the teaching of specifics on sexual goals, the author suggests a wider concept of morality that would include the total personality and also social morality.

Today many parents who themselves were reared by mothers and fathers afraid to educate their children in sexual matters are now afraid *not* to educate their own children regarding sex. Social pressures on young people different from the kind they experienced when young, prevalent attitudes toward sex that reflect a changing value system in society as a whole, and behavior among many young people that they do not understand have left today's parents perplexed and anxious. As a result they are eagerly seeking help for themselves and for their children, whom they want to achieve "normal sexual maturity."

Community agencies, youth organizations, churches, and schools are all scurrying to initiate programs of sex education—sometimes called family life education, boy-girl relationships, or interpersonal development. Inservice training programs, workshops, and institutes are being

SOURCE: *Children*, 14 (July-August, 1967), 130–35. Published by the U.S. Department of Health, Education, and Welfare, Social and Rehabilitation Service, Children's Bureau.

A special consultant to the Children's Bureau on family life education, Dr. Luckey is a professor at and head of the Department of Child Development and Family Relations, University of Connecticut.

organized for nurses, social workers, clergymen, teachers, counselors, health educators, community youth leaders, and parents. After a long period of being treated with silence or half-truths, blushes and snickers, the subject of sex can openly be talked about in "respectable" society. Young people's attitudes and behavior toward the opposite sex—and the consequences—are the subject of serious concern not just to adolescents and their parents but also to persons in the teaching and helping professions.

Nevertheless, the goals of sex education are not altogether clear. Nor is it clear just whose responsibility it is to give sex information to children and adolescents and to try to shape the attitudes that determine their moral values and sexual behavior. Dealing with the sexual problems of young people is especially difficult for adults brought up in a society confused about sex, one that has been filled with sexual stimuli and at the same time with harsh taboos against sexual expression. Social scientists are not surprised that the combination of stimulation and repression has resulted in a demand for a "better way" of dealing with sex.

In response to the demand, persons who work professionally with children, adolescents, and parents are seeking *the* way (if there is *one*) or *a* way (if there are *many*) to help children grow toward "sexual maturity." This goal in itself is difficult to define, and to chart a course leading to its achievement is even more challenging.

Sexual behavior among men and women and sexuality as it is manifested in masculinity and femininity vary from culture to culture. Anthropologists tell us that there is no sexual practice that has been universally sanctioned or prohibited; even incest, the sexual behavior that comes nearest to being universally tabooed, has been approved in some societies in some periods of history.

In any culture, what is "normal" depends upon the practices of the majority. Many behavior patterns that are quite objectionable in our society are sanctioned in others; for example, homosexual practices, sexual relationships between children, premarital sexual promiscuity, and wife swapping and borrowing are approved forms of behavior in some societies. It is not possible to speak of what is or is not "normal" unless we specify the society to which we refer.

Normality? Maturity?

Even in this country alone the wide range of sexual behavior and values existing today make "the norm" impossible to define. At one extreme are those people who advocate complete sexual freedom amounting to anarchy; at the other extreme are those who condone the use of sex only for reproduction. Between these extremes lies immense variation in attitude and practice. For example, chastity before marriage is held to be a supreme value; it is considered "a good thing"; it is thought not to be very important; it is valued not at all; it is considered a poor thing. Masturbation is valued as a means of releasing sexual tension; it is considered an acceptable adolescent pastime; it is thought to be a shameful practice or a sin. Marital practices vary: there is no consensus on how frequently coitus should take place, nor on the appropriate position, nor on the amount or kind of foreplay that is acceptable. Most social scientists agree that it would be difficult if not impossible to define the norm of sexual behavior in contemporary American society. Even if such a norm could be defined, the definition would be meaningless, for sexual expression is a highly individual matter, an integral part of the total personality.

Sexual maturity rather than sexual normality may be a better goal for sex education. Even so, we must make assumptions that cannot be validated about the nature of man and the patterns of his maturing. By careful measurement and observation we have learned a great deal about the physical growth and development of boys and girls; we know about many of the factors that contribute to or detract from soundness and roundness of body; we have been able to trace general developmental patterns from the prenatal period to maturity and then to decadence. Intellectual growth has been more difficult to discover and predict in a sequential pattern, but in general we know a good deal about such aspects of growth as language development, concept development, learning, and creativity.

What we know of emotional growth is still largely theory or educated guesses; and social patterns that propel a child on to becoming a socially mature adult are known to vary from generation to generation. Even so, through keen observation, crude but persistent evaluation, and creative speculation, we can draw at least some tentative conclusions about the emotional and social development of the human being.

When we realize that sexual growth includes factors that are physical, intellectual, emotional, and social, it becomes clear that with the incompleteness of our knowledge it is impossible to trace a sequential pattern of sexual development and to predict maturity with any degree of precision. This is a task to be explored by scientific research. We cannot wait for the results, however, to define our social goals in broad terms and to plan the practical steps toward their achievement.

The Goals

As with other social goals, the consideration of educational goals requires two foci: the individual and the group in which he lives. Managing these two compatibly is a constant challenge for a democratic society. It is a greater challenge today than ever before, for in our rapidly changing society young people are demanding greater freedom in individual behavior than in any previous generation.

Our society has not yet provided an adequate way of caring for children born out of wedlock; it is therefore desirable today to discourage out-of-wedlock births. This is one social goal on which we can secure a great deal of agreement. Another is the elimination of venereal disease. So far, we have found no medically satisfactory way of preventing venereal infection. Both of these goals are served when premarital, promiscuous intercourse is avoided. Thus, at this point in our social development, it is reasonable to want to restrict premarital coitus.

However, with the increased effectiveness and availability of contraceptives and with the possible future development of immunizations against venereal diseases, the social consequences of promiscuous premarital sexual relationships will change. Insofar as morality is based on social consequences, when the consequences change the moral values change. What is immoral in today's society may be moral in tomorrow's. And what is right for today's generation of young people may be wrong for a generation to come.

One way to avoid getting hopelessly involved in dilemmas is to go beyond what is presently called "sexual morality" to a broader concept of morality, one based on the use of self and one's personal freedom for the benefit of others.

Broader definitions of goals are appropriate, too, in considering the individual's personal growth and satisfaction. Here the goal is not only a sexually fulfilled person but also one who accepts and values his total self—a person who understands himself, his behavior, and his value system and who has the integrity to defend his principles. The ultimate goal is a person who can communicate with others without fear, who can reveal himself, and who can listen to and be concerned about the welfare of others.

Sexuality can never be separated from personality, nor can sexual morality be separated from social morality. For this reason the term "sex education" tends to be misleading. By emphasizing sex it pulls the subject out of a total context. Unfortunately, our culture has for a long time treated a sexual relationship as a special and separate part of personal and social relationships rather than a normal, natural use of self in relating meaningfully to a person of the opposite sex.

Now, because of the need to provide information, to correct misconceptions, and to break the spell of silence, it will be hard for any program of sex education to avoid further isolating and emphasizing the sexual components of personality and interpersonal relationships. Nevertheless, the real goal of any program must be to help in the total development of young people so that they will become the kind of secure persons described above. If we can achieve this goal, we will not have to worry about sexual behavior.

How and When?

The questions of *how* and *when* are better dealt with together, because, except for always giving children frank, honest answers and explanations, the most important point about sex education is to provide the information in a normal context. Sexual matters need to be dealt with as the natural part of a total picture, whatever that picture may be. When children are curious about their own bodies—hands, feet, elbows, and "tummies"—they are also interested in their genitals and need to know proper terms for them. When children are interested in what happens to food in the human body and in why and how we breathe, they are also interested in the excretory functions and need proper explanations about them.

Most of a child's early questions about sex are occasioned by exposure to a situation that is new to him. He sees an adult body and notes that it is different from his own; he wants to know more about it. He sees a child of the other sex and notes that the genitals are different; he wants an explanation. He sees a pregnant woman and wants to know why her stomach is swollen, and he also may want to know how this came about. The child usually brings these questions to his mother because they occur to him before he reaches school age.

The way in which these early questions are answered largely determines what other questions the child will ask, how he will feel about asking them, and how he will feel about the answers. A parent reveals his own feelings about sex through common, everyday events in many ways. His attitudes will be regarded by his child as those of all adults, so that what questions the child asks or does not ask the teacher at school depend a great deal on the kind of reception they would get if asked at home.

In the school the teacher has continuous opportunities to answer questions bearing on sex that come up in the ordinary events of the day and in the content of every subject. From kindergarten through 12th grade, the child can be encouraged to develop a normal progression of interest in and an increasing body of information about family relationships and sex differences and functions and, in doing so, to form values and make decisions about behavior. In the elementary grades imparting information about animal and human reproduction is becoming a routine part of instruction. However, helping children understand their own developing masculinity or femininity is more difficult for the teacher because it involves a personal concept that can be discussed more naturally in the home than in the schoolroom; nonetheless, much thought about the meaning to oneself of one's sex can be stimulated at school through units in self-understanding and personality growth.

Many persons believe that the school has a better opportunity than the home to present the child with *information* regarding sex. This is partly true, at least, because teachers tend to be more knowledgeable than many parents about physiology, anatomy, health, psychology, and social problems. It is true, also, because as the child progresses through the grades the teaching becomes concentrated into subject areas, many of which relate specifically to sex and reproduction, to social-sexual-psychological development, and to social problems and health. Thus information about sex is not only a normal part of the subject matter in junior and senior high schools but is also an integral part that has to be conspicuously avoided if it is *not* to be included.

Every school subject, even one not directly concerned with sex information, has its contribution to make in helping children and young people understand interpersonal relationships, familial roles, and the relation of one's sex to these. Literature, music, art, history, and the social sciences especially offer such opportunities.

The home and the school are not alone in having opportunities to help the child develop a mature understanding of sex. Groups such as the Boy Scouts, Boys Clubs, Girl Scouts, Girls Clubs, Camp Fire Girls, Young Men's Christian Associations, Young Women's Christian Association, and 4–H Clubs are dedicated to helping young people develop healthy bodies and well-rounded personalities. Most of these organizations work informally with adolescents or preadolescents in small groups over a span of a few years. They offer the young person an excellent opportunity to develop a self-confident personality, including an acceptance of his sexual identity; they also offer him practice in forming intimate, meaningful relationships with others, both of his own and the opposite sex. The sexual aspects of interpersonal relationships become especially important during adolescence when cultural expectation pushes young people toward dating, and their own heightened sex drive urges them toward exploration.

It is not possible to give information without at the same time conveying attitudes, and the attitudes of adults determine the values of the young, which in turn determine their behavior. The values that young people hold are those that have been demonstrated by the persons they respect.

The churches, of course, are specifically concerned with the values in our society and more than any other institution except the home are expected to take responsibility for the development of attitudes in keeping with their religious and moral precepts. However, such value positions are only meaningful to young people if they are clearly enunciated and are demonstrated as useful in today's society.

Perhaps the most consistent informers about adult attitudes and builders of young people's ideals today are not the traditional institutions that purposefully outline and pursue programs or policies of education but rather the mass media of communication: the television that the child watches from the time he is too small to respond to much more than the movement and the sound to the time he is able to sit for several hours absorbed in its entertainment programs and its advertisements that use sexual appeal to sell products; the magazine illustrations, the comic strips, the paperback book covers, the films that make the sparsely clad body a common sight and the seductive female or male an appealing personality. The child exists so constantly in the midst of these stimuli that as his own understanding grows they become increasingly meaningful to him. This is sex education in the context of commercialism, of entertainment, and the message it conveys, while often indirect, is powerful.

All these agencies of society—the home, the school, the community agency, the church, the mass media—bring their messages to the child in one way or another almost from infancy. Some of the messages are direct, some are subtle; they are seen, heard, felt. Some of them are quiet, some loud; some are conspicuous chiefly because of their absence. Some are true; some, half-true; some, false. Altogether they are very inconsistent. As a result our children come to adolescence confused, curious, and often determined to find out on their own.

If the adults who touch the lives of children could determine what their own values are, if they could know beyond question why they hold these values, and if they could demonstrate them in their daily living, children would get their message. If adults themselves could put sexual matters into the normal context of living, young people would be better able to do the same. The ultimate problem for adults is not so much how to educate children and adolescents as how to work out their own problems and how to convey their attitudes to the young people whose lives they influence. That adults who are significant for them do not readily have all the solutions will not distress the children nearly so much as people seem to think. Children will not feel confused about seeking many of their own answers to the problems of interpersonal, intersexual relations if they realize that adults too are honestly seeking solutions.

By Whom?

Who it is that is responsible for sex education becomes clearer when we recognize that sex education is a segment of an individual's total preparation for living in a complex world of interrelatedness, and that information and attitudes specifically regarding sex are normal parts of knowledge and of a social value structure. Every adult who deals with children or adolescents in any way is likely at some time or another, in some way, to influence significantly the attitudes that help determine how a child will use himself—sexually as well as in other ways—in relation to other people.

Because most adults today have not had the advantage of growing up in a society in which the kind of sex education advocated here was available, many adults find it difficult to deal with their own attitudes and to communicate them in an open way to children and adolescents. Some adults, however, are able to do this better than others, and those who *can*, must! The opportunity that adults have to do so will largely be determined by their role in relation to the young. The parent has the longest and most intense relationship with the child and so the greatest opportunity; the teacher, the school nurse, the school counselor, and the principal each has significant opportunities from time to time, as does the youth leader, the clergyman, and the religious educator. So, too, does the advertising man, the sales manager, the editor, the journalist, the filmmaker, the television or radio director.

Where to Begin?

In a wilderness that seems so vast, adults who are concerned with helping children and adolescents grow up sexually are likely to feel that it is all but a hopeless task. This, it is not. In addition to setting his own house in order and examining his own values and behavior and being open about them, the person who works professionally with young people can take a number of steps toward furthering a program of education that will make for mature sexual behavior in our society:

1. He can help other professional workers define their values and learn how to convey them to others. One of the most helpful tools for this kind of learning is the sensitivity group, sometimes called the T-group. Composed usually of about 10 persons with a professionally trained leader, the group is designed to encourage its members to explore their feelings and to interact in such a way that insight and self-understanding develop.[1]

2. He can take part in inservice training sessions, workshops, and institutes that provide the participants not only with information but also with an opportunity to clarify their own attitudes for themselves. Because acquiring information is usually accomplished much more quickly than acquiring insight into one's own feelings, the emphasis in the most effective groups is on the exploration of the participants' attitudes.

[1] Bradford, L. P.; Gibb, J. R.; Benne, K. D. (eds.): T-group theory and laboratory method. John Wiley & Sons, New York, 1964.

Many universities and colleges are now offering such courses, and many more would set them up if requested.

3. He can focus much of his educational efforts on parents, especially parents of infants and very young children. Because the parental influence is so constant and so intense, what parents believe, what they convey, and what they know are crucial influences in the development of the child's sexual attitudes.

Parents, however, often have uncertainties and fears about their own sexuality that inhibit their ability to help their children—for example, a mother who does not value her femininity will find it hard to help her daughter grow up to accept and value herself as a woman.

Parents also often need some of the skill that persons in the helping professions have in giving direct answers to questions about sex, and often they also need the information itself. Some parents, for example, have misconceptions about the effects of masturbation on the developing child; some do not understand the physiology of menstruation; and some have fears and apprehensions about their own sexual functions, the use of contraceptives, the effects of menopause, or their marital compatibility.

Thus many parents might benefit from the same kind of sensitivity group suggested for professional persons. The opportunity for parents to discuss such problems in a safe, accepting group of other adults could help them clarify their own feelings and thinking and learn how to deal with intimate matters openly and frankly. Such groups might be formed through a neighborhood house, an elementary-school guidance program, a parent-teacher association, a church, or any other local organization. A trained professional leader, however, is a *must*.

4. He can make known to the molders of the mass media his convictions regarding the use—and misuse—of sexual stimuli, particularly in advertising and in entertainment. If he finds that young people are being given a false or unclear picture about the meaning of sexual maturity through any form of mass communication, he can protest.

More important than all these steps, however, is the professional person's way of dealing directly with young people. Can he be open and willing to share his time, thoughts, and knowledge with the questing young? Anything less is not enough. The young have the right to honest answers—even when the adult's answer must be that he does not know or is himself confused.

And So—

Helping children grow into sexual maturity is not easy for a generation of adults who have grown up in a society frightened of sex. It can only be done by breaking through the silence and half-truths that have obscured their own knowledge and feeling and by establishing a broader objective than mere "sex education." This means striving for the development of the whole personality, for producing a man or woman able to feel genuine concern for the welfare of others, eager and able to establish intimate relationships with others, desirous of parenthood, and capable of assuming the responsibility of his own freedom.

Professional workers concerned about young people need to clarify their own attitudes and values and to develop ways of communicating them to others. When they do, they can be of special help to parents and to other professional workers—teachers, nurses, school counselors, principals, social workers, youth leaders, clergymen. They can influence the mass media's interpretation of sex and interpersonal relationships. They can help young people with the problems troubling them, always keeping sexual information in the context of the whole person, being honest and frank, and admitting that along with the young people, they, too, are *seeking*.

28. UNDERSTANDING ADOLESCENT SEX BEHAVIOR

Marian D. Hall

§ The author identifies three types of premarital sex behavior. The most overt type is the result of character disorders that lead to an impulsive shallow relationship. A second type, chiefly among girls, is a search for tenderness which they have not experienced from their parents. The third, and newer, type is part of a conscious search for a new morality, in which love, sex, and marriage are not necessarily inevitably linked together.

One of the challenging, tormenting aspects of our decade is the fact that we are all too often aware that we are living through a time of revolution—social, racial, sexual—but that we cannot define it. We are *in* it but not *of* it; and we feel peripheral, out of communication with something we know is going on just outside our office door. We

SOURCE: *Mental Hygiene*, 50 (July, 1966), 371–73. Reprinted by permission of the publisher and the author.

Dr. Hall is an associate professor at the University of Minnesota and assistant director of the School Psychology Training Program.

This paper was presented at the 1965 Annual Convention of the National Association of Woman Deans and Counselors, Minneapolis, Minn., April, 1965.

have sense enough to distrust our self-report surveys and to question routine interview information. We identify the retrospective fallacies of comparisons with a past generation. We fail, frequently, to attempt an overview, to synthesize research data, interview material, and day-to-day observations into a frame of reference that can be subjected to critical examination. The purpose of this paper is to attempt such an overview of contemporary adolescent sexual behavior.

When we look at referrals and adolescent self-report data, three patterns of sexual behavior seem to emerge, similar in their present symptomatology but significantly different in their history and predictive implications. Any of the three patterns can, and does, result in personality dysfunction, pregnancies out of wedlock, unwanted children, abortion, precipitate marriage, psychologic consequences of long-lasting importance, and social impact. The similarity, however, is limited to these phenotypic signs. In intrapsychic genesis and implications for current coping ability and future ego-integration the three types of sexual behavior are markedly different. Two of the patterns of behavior, the impulse disorders and the need-determined identification conflicts, are those we have always had with us (at least since mankind "invented" adolescence!). The third type of behavior, characterized by a conscious and concerned effort to redefine premarital relationships between the sexes, appears and is given new expression in this generation.[1-3]

Impulse Disorders and Character Disorders

The most overt and active of adolescent behavior problems are the character disorders. Redl and Wineman [4] have described the defective inner controls and Johnson and Szurek,[5] the superego lacunae that are characteristic of adolescents with character disorders. Frequently coming from an environment in which promiscuity and family instability are the prevailing pattern, these youngsters have internalized the model they have seen and have made partial identification with a long series of transient adults whose lives have touched theirs superficially. For them, sex is only another fast ride, and the partner is as insignificant as the seat-mate on a plane ride; the kicks are in the moment of takeoff, and the danger is estimated only after the crack-up. This kind of adolescent sexual behavior (which is by no means limited to high-school students) is part and parcel of the general impulsivity, paucity of ego

[1] Freedman, M. B.: Merrill-Palmer Quarterly, 11:33, 1965.
[2] Glassberg, B. Y.: Journal of Marriage and the Family, 27:190, 1965.
[3] Walters, P. A., Jr.: American Journal of Orthopsychiatry, 35:670, 1965.
[4] Redl, F., and Wineman, D.: Children Who Hate. Glencoe, Ill., Free Press, 1951.
[5] Johnson, A. M., and Szurek, S. A.: Psychoanalytic Quarterly, 21:323, 1952.

controls, and shallowness of feeling characteristic of the whole array of character disorders. The aim of such behavior is to ward off closeness, with its dangerous memories from a repressed past, and to foreclose the possibility of a durable relationship, which is equally threatening because it lays claims on the future.

Identity Confusion

The second group of adolescents who present signs of dyscontrol and disjunction in the area of sexual behavior is the group that rushes *into* intimacy rather than away from it. These youngsters have arrived at physiologic adolescence with many of the early pregenital developmental tasks poorly resolved. Many of them, particularly the girls, are seeking tenderness and caretaking unknown in their own lives. They are actively in search of closeness and continuity. These girls may be seen to run toward pregnancy in order to fill nurturing needs that were never fulfilled for them by their own mothers. Frequently they are driven, by long exposure to their own hostile mothers and by anger against fathers who have not rescued them, to turn to the first postpubertal love-object, no matter how inappropriate. The feelings of isolation and alienation are then both lessened and increased. Instead of being alone, the person is now one of two in the capsule; and the two are, in a real sense, encapsulated from the outside world.

This first sexual conquest is more a conquest of self than of the other. Traditionally linked with initiation rites, it brings, in our culture as in primitive cultures, many accolades of coming of age. The pressure on both boys and girls to join the initiate, to avoid the humiliation of being alone among the children while the others drive off in pairs, is more intense than we realize—or remember. There are also internal pressures—flight from homosexual fears, from incest fantasies, from threats to the security of the parental marriage and home. All of these are forces that drive the adolescent toward sexual behavior along a path of development that is universal and essential to the maturing of the individual but that is, nevertheless, ringed around with hazards and roadblocks, some that are culturally imposed and some that are intrinsic to the human conflict between impulse gratification and ego integration.

The New Search

Both of the above patterns of behavior are old and familiar stories. They are part of a picture of evolving sexual mores. The third pattern, one we have more difficulty defining because we are not always allowed in the "high councils" of its proponents, is a more revolutionary one.

It differs from the second primarily in that it is a *conscious* mode of behavior. In the privacy of the in-groups there is long and painful searching into their own needs and feelings. There is a new openness in conversation between boys and girls. There is questioning of old shibboleths. Conscious and searching, this new approach to youthful sexual expression is as closely tied to a thought-out morality as is the traditional and church-based morality of an earlier generation, and it involves as genuine a commitment; but it is more individualized and more personally and verbally communicated. The young people of college age and, following our "seepage" system of cultural exchange, also of high-school age, are seriously rethinking and making decisions about love and sex and marriage. And they are acting upon their decisions; they are not just "falling" into them—to use the tell-tale expression of an older generation. They haven't bought the package deal that love, sex, and marriage are identical and inseparable. This conscious re-evaluation brings with it strengths as well as dangers. Its dangers are well known. Its strengths are too frequently underestimated: straight and self-aware thinking, clear communication between the sexes, a challenge to outworn sexual restrictions, an open, risk-taking attitude, and the substitution of responsibility and fidelity for prohibition and chastity as the desiderata of intimate relationships between the sexes.

If the varieties of adolescent behavior patterns are to be understood, it will be increasingly important to look beneath the surface phenomena. The three types of sexual experimentation mentioned here are infrequently discriminated, either in research tallies or in counselors' judgments. The extent of the divergence among the three patterns and the significance of the differences for the individual and for society are not made clearer if the traditional nosology is applied. In fact, the limitations of such labels as "psychopathic" or "schizoid" personality are nowhere more sharply apparent. Application of basic, unitary measures such as, for example, Erikson's [6] qualities of ego identity or Menninger's [7] orders of personality dysfunction is more helpful in assessing the extent of the divergence. If the wide range of behavior that is presently disguised behind a mask of similarity is to be understood and dealt with, it will demand more than collecting, counting, and classifying information under old labels.

[6] Erikson, E. H.: Journal of the American Psychoanalytic Association, 4:56, 1956.
[7] Menninger, K.: The Vital Balance. New York, Viking Press, 1963.

29. SEXUAL CODES IN TEEN-AGE CULTURE

Ira L. Reiss

§ This article demonstrates that teen-agers do not act erratically in sexual behavior that differs from adult standards, but subject themselves to codes developed among themselves. Several codes exist, including the double standard for boys and, especially among girls, approval of coitus when the pair is bound together by bonds of affection. Limits are set, which differ from one social class to another.

Teen-age sexual codes reflect quite clearly the bold outlines of adult sexual codes. The high degree of conformity in teen-age culture increases the observability of teen-age beliefs and adds to our understanding of adult beliefs. The teen-ager exists in a world somewhere between youthful idealism and adult realism, and his sexual codes reflect this state of being. In a very real sense, he is a marginal man with one foot in the world of the child and the other foot in the world of the adult.

The teen-ager is at the stage at which it is vitally important for him to learn how to exist in society independent of his parents. For this reason, he transfers his dependence to his peers and strives to learn from them the secrets of entrance into the adult world. One would think that this vaguely defined status of "almost adult" would lead to confusion and weak statements of belief. To a large extent, this is the case, but, nevertheless, it is equally true that it leads to dogmatic statements of belief and a search for conviction through conformity. Teen-agers translate and adapt the sexual codes of adults to fit their particular circumstance and state of mind.

Going Steady

When unchaperoned dating gained prevalence in the early part of this century, it involved a much more rapid change of dating partners than occurs today. Nevertheless, by the time of World War II, going steady had taken root, and, today, it seems that slightly more than half of the high school students have some going-steady experience. Even among the early teen-agers, possibly one quarter go steady.

SOURCE: *Annals of the American Academy of Political and Social Science*, 338 (November, 1961), 53–62. Reprinted by permission of the publisher and the author.
    The author's background is given in the footnote for article 20.

Class differences are important in examining the going-steady complex. It seems that those high school people who go steady and plan to go to college are not likely to marry their high school steadies, and those who are from lower economic classes and who do not plan to go to college are much more likely to marry their high school steadies.[1] Thus, in looking at the custom of going steady, one must realize that there are different subtypes and that the consequences differ for each type.

Although a psychologist may point to the security of going steady as its chief reason for being, as a sociologist, I would point out how Western society has, for centuries, been developing an association of sexual behavior with mutual affection. This association is hard to achieve in casual dating; but, in steady dating, sex and affection can quite easily be combined, and, in this way, a potential strain in the social system is reduced. Another area of strain which is reduced by going steady is the conflict a girl may feel between her desire for sexual experience and her desire to maintain her reputation. For many, sexual behavior is made respectable by going steady.[2] In these ways, one may say that no other dating custom is quite as central to the understanding of teen-age sexual codes as going steady.

Girls' Sexual Codes

One of the most popular sexual codes among teen-age girls is petting-with-affection. This code is a modern day subtype of our formal abstinence standard. This subtype of abstinence seems extremely popular among high school couples who are going steady. Such couples feel it is proper to engage in heavy petting if they are going steady, the justification being that they are in love or at least extremely fond of each other. The petting-with-affection sex code probably grew along with the going-steady custom; they both illustrate adaptations of our dating institution to the newer unchaperoned dating circumstances.

What evidence do we have for such petting behavior among teen-agers? Though surely not perfect, the most extensive study of sexual behavior is that done by the Institute for Sex Research, formerly headed by Alfred C. Kinsey and now run by Paul H. Gebhard. It should be noted that the Kinsey studies are most valid for urban, white, northeastern, college-educated people, and, thus, great care must be taken when applying the results to other groups. The reader should keep in mind the tenuousness of any such generalizations made in this paper.

Kinsey's data show that, of the females who were twenty years old or

---

[1] Robert D. Herman, "The Going Steady Complex: A Re-Examination," *Marriage and Family Living*, Vol. 17 (February 1955), pp. 36–40.
[2] For evidence on this point, see Winston W. Ehrmann, *Premarital Dating Behavior* (New York, 1959), p. 141.

older when interviewed, about one fifth to one fourth admitted they had petted to orgasm while still in their teens. Most of this behavior occurred between the ages of sixteen and twenty. About three-quarters of all the girls twenty years old or more admitted being aroused by some form of petting or kissing in their teens, and approximately 90 per cent stated they had at least been kissed during their teens.[3]

Those girls who marry in their teens start their petting and kissing behavior earlier than those who marry later. In general, the few years previous to marriage are by far the most sexually active for girls. Lower class females marry earlier, and, thus, they are more active in their teens and are more likely to marry their teen-age steadies.

The above rates are averages for Kinsey's entire sample of several thousand females; were we to take only the females born in more recent decades, the rates would be considerably higher. For example, of those females born before 1900, only 10 per cent ever petted to orgasm in their teens, whereas, of those girls born in the 1920's, almost 30 per cent, or three times the proportion, petted to orgasm by age twenty.[4]

It seems clear that we have developed not only new dating forms such as going steady but also, as we have seen, new sexual codes to go with them. These new codes allow females much more freedom in heavy petting, provided affection is involved. Of course, other girls, particularly in the early teens, adhere to standards which only permit kissing, and a few others adhere to standards which allow full sexual relations, but, by and large, petting-with-affection seems the increasingly popular sex code for high school girls.

The most recent evidence of the nature of teen-age sex codes also supports these contentions. This evidence comes from research which the author is engaged in at present.[5] Some preliminary reports on this study were made in the author's book *Premarital Sexual Standards in America*. The study involves 1,000 high school and college students, most of whom are teen-agers. Although final analysis of the study has not been completed, it is clear that petting-with-affection is an extremely popular code with teen-age girls, particularly with the teen-agers who are high school juniors and seniors.

Finally, one should note that, in my own study and in the Kinsey study, religion was another key factor affecting girls' sexual beliefs and behaviors. Those girls who were devout in their religion were much more conservative in their sexual behavior and belief. Religion was not as strong a factor for boys and did not control their behavior as much.

[3] Alfred C. Kinsey and Others, *Sexual Behavior in the Human Female* (Philadelphia, 1953), Chap. 7.
[4] *Ibid.*, p. 244.
[5] This investigation is supported by a Public Health Service research grant (M-4045) from the National Institute of Mental Health, Public Health Service.

As we shall see, amount of education was the key determination for male sexual behavior.

Boys' Sexual Codes

Among the teen-age boys, we find a quite different code dominant. Abstinence is given some form of lip service, particularly among the more highly educated classes, but, by and large, it is not an operational code; it is not adhered to in the behavior of the majority of the teen-age boys. Even among the males destined for college, about 40 per cent have coitus in their teens; among those who stop their education in high school, about three-quarters have coitus in their teens, and, among those whose education stops before high school, about eight-tenths have coitus in their teens. Thus, it is clear that the majority of all males, in this sample of Kinsey's, at least, experienced full sexual relations before reaching twenty years of age.[6]

For teen-age girls, the rate of nonvirginity appears to be considerably lower. Kinsey reports approximately 20 per cent nonvirginity for females by age twenty. Of course, the greater liberality of the boys does not involve a single standard; that is, they are predominantly adherents of the double standard which allows boys to have coitus but condemns girls for the same thing. This is an ancient standard reaching back many thousands of years in Western culture. It is by no means a universal standard, however, for we do find many cultures where the sexes are treated equally.[7]

Although in recent generations, due to our greater equalitarianism and the evolving nature of the dating institution, the double standard seems to have been weakened sharply, it is still quite dominant among teen-age boys. The greater freedom allowed the male child in almost all areas of life constantly buttresses this standard and makes it seem obvious to teen-agers. Teen-agers are not sufficiently objective or sophisticated to be bothered by the contradictions in this or any other sexual code. For example, if all women abided fully by the double standard, then no men could, for the men would have no partners! Thus, this code operates only to the extent that someone violates it.

Some of these double standard teen-age boys will condemn a girl who accepts petting-with-affection, for they believe heavy petting is improper for girls. However, my own data indicate that most of these teen-age males will accept heavy petting in a going-steady relationship. They, of

[6] Alfred C. Kinsey, *Sexual Behavior in the Human Male* (Philadelphia, 1948), p. 550.
[7] For a full discussion of this standard, its historical sources and reasons for being, see Ira L. Reiss, *Premarital Sexual Standards in America* (Glencoe, Ill., 1960), Chap. 4.

course, allow themselves to go further and may try to have coitus with a steady in order to see if she is a "good" girl. It is not unusual to find a relationship either broken up or its affectionate nature altered if a girl gives in to her double standard steady. Such condemnatory behavior on the part of double standard males keeps many girls from going as far sexually as they might want to. Thus, the double standard male eliminates many potential sex partners because of the attitude he takes toward such sex partners.

Teen-age double standard males are often stricter than their older brothers who accept coitus for a girl when she is in love and/or engaged. These teen-age males are supported in this rigidity by the conformity of their peer group. Double standard males typically view the act of coitus as a conquest, as a source of peer group prestige. Thus, they are quite prone to tell their friends all of the details of any affair. This characteristic tends further to discourage females from yielding to double standard males. Instead, the girl is encouraged to be, in part at least, a tease, that is, to show just enough sexual activity to keep the male interested but not enough to arouse his condemnation. Sexual behavior in this sense involves a great deal of the aspect of a game. Sex comes to be used as a power leverage to control the relationship. Under such circumstances, sexual desire is developed so sharply in the male and so differently in the female that the male wants the female to be both sexually active and sexually pure. Under such conditions, sexual behavior can only with great difficulty relate directly to feelings of affection. This is particularly true for the act of coitus. In fact, one finds very often an inverse relation, in that boys prefer to have coitus with girls they do not care for, because they regard the girls they do care for as "too good" for such behavior. Girls, too, may control their sexual reactions, particularly with someone they care for, until they are sure they will not be condemned for their sexual response.

Thus, in the area of coitus among teen-agers, the double standard does seem to block the association of sex and affection. However, one should quickly add that, on the level of petting, sex and affection can more easily be combined, for this behavior is much more likely to be accepted for both sexes by both males and females.

Minor Standards

There are minor teen-age standards which are more permissive than petting-with-affection or the double standard. For the older teen-ager, the most popular minor standard is what I shall call permissiveness-with-affection. This standard accepts full sexual intercourse for both boys and girls, provided they are involved in a stable, affectionate relationship. The degree of stability and affection required varies among adherents from feeling strong affection to being in love and engaged. Some teen-age couples who are going steady have coitus in accord with this standard. The situation here is quite different from that of the double standard boy and his girl friend, for, in permissiveness-with-affection, both the boy and girl accept for each other what they are doing. They combine sex with affection and use affection as one of the key justifications of the sexual act.

There is a class difference in sexual standards among boys. My evidence indicates that the lower classes are more likely to be strong supporters of the double standard, while the upper classes, though still mostly double standard, contain a large proportion of boys who are not so dogmatic in their beliefs and a minority who accept permissiveness-with-affection. In general, the upper classes seem to stress equality of the sexes and the importance of affection more than the lower classes. A permissiveness-without-affection code seems more widespread at the lower levels.

Age is a crucial factor among teen-agers. Teen-agers under sixteen are much more likely to accept only kissing than are older teen-agers, who may accept petting or coitus. As noted earlier, religion does not restrict sexual behavior as much among boys as it does among girls. Education is a more important factor, with the more highly educated groups being the most conservative.

Promiscuity

The newspapers from time to time pick up stories of high school "sex clubs" and other forms of promiscuous teen-age sexual behavior. The available evidence indicates that promiscuous coitus is common predominantly for double standard males and a few females. Promiscuous coitus is not common on an equalitarian basis, that is, where both male and female accept the behavior as right for each other. Our culture has stressed the association of sex-with-affection to such an extent that it is difficult, at least for many females, to violate this association in coitus. In the case of petting, one finds more likelihood of violation of this norm by both men and women, but, in the case of coitus, it is much more often violated by males. Ehrmann's study of 1,000 college students supports this difference between male and female sexual activity and attitudes.[8] Females, in addition to associating love with sexual behavior more than males, also have more nonsexual motives for sexual behavior, such as the desire to please the boy or to cement a relationship.

During the teens, the sexual outlets of boys and girls differ considerably. The chief outlet for girls seems to be masturbation and petting,

[8] Ehrmann, *op. cit.*, pp. 263–266.

whereas for boys the chief outlets include coitus at the fore. In Kinsey's sample, about one third of the girls masturbated to orgasm in their teens, while over 90 per cent of the boys have so masturbated in their teens.[9] Despite their high rate of masturbation, males also have a high rate of coitus. The lower class boys rely less on masturbation and petting and more on coitus for their sexual outlets than do those boys who go to college.

The teen-age girl today is still typically the much more conservative partner and the guardian of sexual limits. However, she appears increasingly to be a half-willing guardian who more and more seeks her self-satisfaction and strives to achieve sexual equality.

There is a general trend in American society toward more equalitarian and more permissive sexual codes in all areas. This is true for teen-age sexual codes, too. The growth within abstinence of petting-with-affection is one sign of this increasing equalitarian and permissive force. Also, within the double standard, one finds increased willingness by males to accept some coitus on the part of females, especially if it occurs when the girl is in love and/or engaged. Finally, in the minor standard of permissiveness-with-affection, one sees this trend in the increased strength of this standard among teen-agers, particularly among older, college teen-agers. And these trends toward equalitarianism and permissiveness seem even stronger among older dating couples in their twenties. The teen-agers are relatively new at sexual behavior, and they, at first, grab the basic outlines of the older couples' codes. With the passage of time, they come to behave in a somewhat more equalitarian and permissive manner.

In my current research, there is evidence that the real change-over in a teen-ager's sexual code is more one of integrating attitudes and changing overt behavior than of changing basic attitudes. In short, it seems that a person holds his basic sexual attitudes in rudimentary form in his teens, but he is not fully ready to act upon them and has not fully learned how to combine the values into a coherent code of living. As he learns to do this, his behavior changes and so does his awareness of his beliefs and their unity, but his basic beliefs may well remain the same. This entire area of how our sexual beliefs are formed and how they change is in need of more careful study. My own research is aimed at probing some aspects of this problem.

Parents are prone to be most aware of what they consider excessive sexual behavior, for they are concerned about the consequences of such behavior as they may affect their children. Thus, parents complain about sexual acts of which they become aware, and they often believe teen-

---

[9] Kinsey, *Sexual Behavior : . . Female, op. cit.*, p. 173. See also William R. Reevy, "Adolescent Sexuality," in A. Ellis and A. Abarbanel, *The Encyclopedia of Sexual Behavior* (New York, 1961), pp. 52–67.

agers are sexually promiscuous. Actually, according to our best estimates, the real increases in teen-age sexual behavior over the last generation are not in the area of sexual intercourse but rather in the area of petting and in the public nature of some petting behavior.[10] Thus, these parents of today have probably had similar rates of coitus but perhaps lower rates of petting. In addition, one should note that the petting behavior today very often is not promiscuous but occurs in a stable affectionate relationship.

Youth Culture: Tame or Wild?

About twenty years ago, Kingsley Davis and Talcott Parsons wrote of a youth culture and of a parent-youth conflict and in doing so, implied in part that youth culture was largely irresponsible, impulsive, and anti-adult.[11] Many people have come to share this view and to expect rather extreme sexual behavior from teen-agers. I myself formerly accepted this view of the teen-ager as valid. However, after examining the evidence in the key areas of teen-age sexual behavior, I must admit that I can no longer accept such a conception of youth culture without serious modification and qualification. I would submit that the vast majority of our approximately twenty million teen-agers are not only not extreme but are quite conservative and restrained in the area of premarital sexual codes and behavior when we compare them to their older brothers and sisters.

There is evidence to show that teen-agers are unsure of how far to go sexually, that they feel ill at ease on dates, and that they are concerned with such "tame" issues as whether one should kiss good night on a first date.[12] A recent study showed that teen-agers rate themselves lower in comparison to adults than adults rate them. Teen-agers in this study rated adults considerably higher than themselves on most all "good" qualities.[13] These are hardly the attitudes of an arrogant or anti-adult youth. They seem more those of a group desirous of becoming like adults and striving toward that goal.

Further, when we look at the rates of female petting to orgasm in the Kinsey studies, we find considerably more of this behavior among girls in their twenties than among girls in their teens. The coitus rate for

[10] Kinsey, *Sexual Behavior . . . Female, op. cit.*, pp. 275, 339 *passim*.
[11] Kingsley Davis, "The Sociology of Parent Youth Conflict," *American Sociological Review*, Vol. 5 (October 1940), pp. 523–535; Talcott Parsons, "Age and Sex in the Social Structure of the United States," *American Sociological Review*, Vol. 7 (December 1942), pp. 604–616.
[12] H. H. Remmers and D. H. Radley, *The American Teen-Ager* (Indianapolis, 1957), pp. 83, 225–236.
[13] R. D. Hess and I. Goldblatt, "The Status of Adolescents in American Society," in Jerome M. Seidman, ed., *The Adolescent: A Book of Readings*, rev. ed. (New York: Holt, Rinehart and Winston, 1960), pp. 321–333.

females doubles between the ages of twenty and twenty-five. Masturbation rates also increase considerably after the teens.[14] In all these ways, the teen-agers seem more conservative than those individuals who are in their twenties.

August Hollingshead's excellent study of a midwest community also gives evidence on the conservatism of youth. He found a very close correspondence between social class of parents and social class of teen-agers' dating partners. In this study, too, we are given a picture of youth culture that is very much like adult culture in its status consciousness. Hollingshead and others have also noted the fact that a large proportion of the teen-age population is virtually not involved in any dating. A good estimate for the high school age group would be that about one third of the boys and one fifth of the girls are not involved in dating.[15]

Venereal Disease and Pregnancy

Let us now examine two key indices, venereal disease and pregnancy, which should give us additional insights into the behavior of teen-agers. Teen-agers do have significant rates of venereal disease and illegitimacy. However, the press has largely exaggerated such rates. The teen-age rate of venereal disease for ages fifteen to nineteen is only about a third of the rate for the twenty to twenty-four age group and is also lower than that of the twenty-five to twenty-nine age group.[16]

There has been a slight rise in the number of teen-age venereal disease cases in recent years, and this has received much publicity. It is quite likely that the actual rates for teen-agers are not higher and that this slight increase is due to the greater number of teen-agers today. More than 80 per cent of the venereal disease reported is from older groups of people. Finally, the rate of venereal disease among teen-agers is not evenly distributed in the teen-age group. As far as we can tell from reported cases, it is highly concentrated in the lower social classes.[17]

When one examines the national figures for unwed mothers, one finds that 40 per cent are teen-agers. Here, too, several qualifications are needed. First, most of these reported cases are Negro, and class status in general is low. The upper classes, according to Paul Gebhard's recent study, are much more willing to resort to abortion.[18] The upper classes,

---

[14] Kinsey, *Sexual Behavior . . . Female, op. cit.*, Chaps. 5, 7, 8.

[15] August B. Hollingshead, *Elmtown's Youth* (New York, 1949), p. 227. See also Maxine Davis, *Sex and the Adolescent* (New York, 1960), p. 136.

[16] T. Lefoy Richman, *Venereal Disease: Old Plague—New Challenge* (Public Affairs Pamphlet No. 292; New York, 1960), p. 7. For more technical data, see T. Lefoy Richman (ed.), *Today's Venereal Disease Control Problem* (New York: American Social Health Association, 1961), especially pp. 36–43.

[17] Richman, *Venereal Disease . . . , op. cit.*, pp. 6, 20.

[18] Paul H. Gebhard and Others, *Pregnancy, Birth, and Abortion* (New York, 1958), pp. 45, 160.

also, have a greater ability to stay out of public statistics and may, thus, show lower rates. According to Clark Vincent's study, when upper class females become pregnant before marriage, it is more likely to be the result of a love affair, whereas, when lower class females become pregnant, it is more likely to be a result of a casual affair.[19] Thus, there are important class differences here, too.

When we compare teen-age unwed motherhood with that for girls in their twenties, we find that the older girls have about the same proportion of the illegitimate children. We also find that the teen-age rates are not increasing as much as the rates for older groups. For example, in 1940 teen-age mothers were 46 per cent of the total; in 1957 they were 40 per cent.

Thus, from the evidence of national figures, it seems reasonable to conclude that it is a small and specific segment of the teen-age population that becomes involved with venereal disease or premarital pregnancy. Furthermore, the people in their twenties seem somewhat more likely to be involved in such circumstances. Also, these older couples are much more involved in adult culture in terms of their occupations and their nearness to marriage, and yet their sexual behavior is less conservative.

A warning must be added at this point concerning the venereal disease rates and unwed motherhood rates. They are far from perfect indices and, as mentioned, many higher class people manage to be excluded from them because they can afford more private means of coping with their problems. However, to the extent that we use these rates, we fail to find support for the charges made about teen-agers. It is no doubt true that teen-agers are irresponsible in the sense that they seek "to have a good time," but I would suggest that, in the area of sexual codes and behavior, the evidence shows more conservatism and responsibility than one might otherwise suspect. It may be well to avoid the over-all impressions given by a general use of the term "youth culture" as described by Parsons. Here, as elsewhere, qualification and specific research is a step toward better theoretical formulation and better understanding.

A Final Overview

What has occurred in teen-age sexual codes in recent generations is a working out of sexual practices acceptable to teen-agers. Many of these practices are at the level of petting. In short, as unchaperoned dating came into vogue and as adolescence became more prolonged due to our specialized industrial culture, young people worked out additional sexual codes to supplement and modify the older codes of abstinence and

[19] Clark E. Vincent, "Illegitimacy in the United States," in Duvall (eds.), *op. cit.*, p. 143.

the double standard. There always were people who engaged in coitus; today there are more, but, for girls in their teens, it is still a minor activity. When we look at petting, we note something different, for here we see a much more continuous and current change among teen-agers— it is here in this middle ground that teen-agers have come to accept a petting-with-affection standard. The equalitarian and permissive aspects of this standard in many cases lead at later ages to acceptance of the more radical permissiveness-with-affection standard. However, during the teens, petting-with-affection is probably the major standard involved in stable affectionate relationships at middle and upper class levels.

At the present time, it is impossible to predict precise changes in sexual codes. This is especially true because as we have seen, there are differences according to social class, religion, educational level, and so forth. But one can say that all the signs indicate a continued trend toward equalitarian and permissive codes. The trend seems to be toward that which now obtains in the Scandinavian countries, with the inclusion of sex education in the schools and with permissive attitudes on the formal as well as covert levels. This does not forebode the end of the double standard, for the double standard is still deeply rooted in our male dominant culture, but it does mean a continued weakening of the double standard and more qualifications of its mandates.

Teen-agers are a paradoxical group. They are not as wild as their parents or they themselves sometimes think. Teen-agers do want independence. But, judging by their sexual codes, they want independence from their parents, not from the total adult culture.

30. ADOLESCENTS AND THE PILL CULTURE

Miriam Birdwhistell

§ In this provocative article, the author states that the contraceptive pill has introduced a new element into male-female relationships. Sex and reproduction may be completely separated in what the author terms the "pill culture." The unmarried girl need no longer fear pregnancy. The author points to the need for a public policy to determine the use

SOURCE: *The Family Coordinator*, 17 (1968), 27–32. Reprinted by permission of the publisher and the author.

The author is clinical instructor, chief medical social work consultant, Children and Youth Project, Department of Pediatrics, University of Virginia School of Medicine.

and issuance of the pill to unmarried girls. She also discusses probable future discoveries in the field of contraception, as well as new types of marriage that may result.

Since the public is concerned with the question of illegitimacy and especially illegitimately pregnant, teenage girls, a few statistics are germane. An estimated seven million people in the United States today are of illegitimate birth. They represent four percent of the total population, and include four percent of the nation's children under 18 years of age. There is a slow but steady increase in illegitimate births (from 3.8 percent of all live births in 1940 to 5.6 percent in 1961). The illegitimacy rate is highest among women between 25 to 29 years of age, rather than among teenagers. Although there have been increases in the number and proportions of teenage girls (15 to 19 years of age) in the total child population, in recent years there has been a slight decrease in the percentage of all unmarried mothers who were teenagers. This may be a commentary on social pressure toward forced marriages for pregnant teenagers. Parenthetically, it is noted that estimated abortions range between 200,000 and 1,200,000 a year (HEW, 1963).

It should be noted that the statistics presented were mostly "pre-pill," in that the contraceptive pill was first available in the United States for prescription use in 1960. Current figures frequently quoted are that in 1966 approximately ten million women throughout the world were taking contraceptive pills (Parade Magazine, 1967). Of these, six million were American. The Planned Parenthood Association predicts that by 1980 at least 80 million women will be using oral contraceptives.

These data set the stage for discussing contraception and adolescent morality in the light of the so-called sexual revolution. This may be viewed in the perspective of the progress toward equality of the sexes. (Here we hasten to add that "equality of the sexes" should not imply "negation of sexuality.")

Changes one thinks of, instantly, in the recent past toward greater equality of the sexes include the industrial revolution which allowed women to leave the domestic world and go to work in factories; passage of the law that gave them the right to vote; acceptance of the idea that women have a right to be educated as well as men; inheritance laws that recognized women's rights. Perhaps not in the same category, but very significant in the area of women's rights, was the crusade of Margaret Sanger which resulted in some recognition of the right of married women to plan for their children.

Now we have entered the Space Age and there is a Cybernetic, Demographic, and Sexual Revolution. At the time when there is push for sexual equality (different from equality of the sexes, and maybe this is really what we are describing when we say "sexual revolution,") our scientific advances have brought us "the pill." Physiological control of the population is now possible at the very moment that the need to do so is critical for survival of the species.

What does this mean in terms of re-molding our traditional view of women's reproductive role? Historically, women's central role and primary responsibility has been the bearing and rearing of children. Dr. Rhoda Metraux, anthropologist, has pointed out that now, in a reversal of all human history, we are proposing to ask women to accept the chief responsibility for *not* having and *not* rearing children as part of a public social responsibility for assuming that earth will remain a livable planet. She observes that principal responsibility must be carried by the very young who have as yet a minimum of life experience and who are in the midst of developing a personal, out of cultural, style of heterosexual relationships, including (but not limited to) sexual relationships. Cultural acceptance of "the pill" places the immediate responsibility for population control on the girls and women. This anthropologist points out that the young people (male and female) must, together, develop a new style within societies for the organization of their interaction, with the knowledge that the older generation will probably not "approve" of their innovations (Metraux, 1967).

We are asking the young to assume these new responsibilities while they are surrounded by their parent generational members (the current adult leadership) exhibiting their own confusion in meeting their life crises with a good deal of social disorganization.

What, then, are some of the pieces of the milieu we have handed the youth, out of their own inheritance, in which to shape their sexual behavior and some of the practical "here and now" questions?

Fathers have indicated to boys that they were supposed to "get experience," and mothers have responded, in effect, "but not with our daughters." Here was the double standard in its most callous form: some girls were necessarily the object of such "experience getting" and yet contraceptive devices "across the counter" were available only to boys. If the girl became pregnant it was she, not the boy, whom society shamed. Society was not judging the morals of the two people involved, only the girl's lack of luck, so euphemistically and so aptly described as "some boy got *her* in trouble." Society's unequal blaming system also is so clearly demonstrated by the established concept of "the unwed mother," whereas the phrase "the unwed father" is used only by a few professionals.

The girl has been expected to be the keeper of the morals for both sexes. The boy was supposed to try to "go as far as he could," and the girl was supposed to "keep him from going too far." The maternal instruction to the girl has been "now you know how you are supposed to behave." She was to be supra-human in the dating and courtship period, to be able to control chemistry and passion for both sexes through the ever-present fear of the consequences, namely, pregnancy. Then with the saying of the marriage vows, she was supposed to push another control button, do a right-about-face and become the responsive, non-frigid, compliant sexual partner.

So we come to the philosophical moment of truth: "the pill" is here, the means of separating sex and reproduction. Do we make the pill available to every female, regardless of marital status and at what age? Now that the means is possible, we believe women will demand that they have equal rights with men to decide their actions as regards sex without consideration of reproductivity. They will demand, that, like the male, they be allowed the right of individual choice in this area; that, like him, their choice now can be made with regard to what is moral for them, not what are the procreative consequences. We do not believe that the moral fiber of girls will suddenly crumble en masse or that they will become different people by swallowing the pill. The issue of equal rights in this area, though, is a moral one and should be prominent in any discussion of morality.

There is the further moral proposition that it is every child's right to be a wanted child. We must consider this when we are deciding whether to give the pill to all females of child-bearing age or only to females who are married or have born one child. Do we guard this right of the child to be wanted or do we wait to sacrifice one child as a test to find out which girls need the pill? In Baltimore, an attempt is being made to anticipate and forestall such pregnancies by establishing a clinic for "sexually active" girls in which birth control information and counseling is given.

Mothers should scarcely be asked to make this decision for society, in isolated instances, of giving or not giving the pill to their daughters. In such isolated settings there is the implied sanction of this mother for this daughter to pursue a behavior that is not sanctioned by the society as a whole. Neither should our society endorse promiscuity among the young. Without any implied moralizing or lack of moralizing, physicians could prescribe hormones, the micro-dose (with the "side effects" issue resolved) perhaps, at the onset of menses, to be taken every day just as the daily vitamin is commonly taken to supplement infant feedings, teenage and adult diets. If such medical planning were instituted, concomitant planning would have to be made for courses of sex instruction in the schools. This education would be simultaneous with adult courses in sex education, teaching respect for individuals that could thus be implemented in the home, and having a pervasive effect in the lives of the members of the society.

If this is not aggressively planned for, there may be unevenness in the timing at which various institutions in society accept "the pill culture." Our official health agencies may be way ahead of our educational agencies, even now. Some modern countries are passing laws about teenagers' rights in this area. Denmark passed a law in 1966 to provide contraceptives to teenagers, by age 16, without parental consent. Currently, a United States Senator is proposing, in legislation being prepared, that birth control information should be available to girls beginning at 14 years of age.

Even without a public policy, many adolescent girls have access to the pill through borrowing of prescriptions, or through knowing the acceptable things to present to physicians—engagement to be married, or erratic and/or painful menses that need to be adjusted.

Even with complete accessibility, this does not mean that all females will want or take the pill. We are all familiar with descriptions of the rebellious girl who strikes out at her parents by becoming pregnant; the insecure girl who hopes pregnancy will lead to marriage; the girl whose father does not give her positive response at the appropriate developmental point and so she seeks substitute male love and becomes pregnant; the girl who knows she will be rewarded for her "mistake" by her parents who will give her a lavish church-masqueraded wedding. Recently there came to us a young girl with a very deprived emotional background who said she intended to take "the pill" just long enough to increase her fertility so that when she stopped taking it she would become pregnant.

But, if there had been doubt about the acceptance of, or ability to use, the newer methods of contraception (the oral pill and the intrauterine device) by the so-called "clinic population," there is adequate documentation now that persons of low education readily accept, and use successfully, both methods. Dr. Donald Bogue, Professor of Sociology and Director of the Community and Family Study Center at the University of Chicago, has contributed major research in this area and has stated that the cost of the pill and the tardiness of national medical groups to authorize its use have been the major impediments to the spread of the oral pill—not inability to use it correctly, or rejection by the masses (Bogue, 1966). Clinical experience in the Pediatric Clinic at the University of Virginia Medical Center, has given us a personal verification of this statement. In our clinic we have interviewed many women who have been deterred from seeking "the pill" because they think their husbands' permission is required (as in the sterilization) and they are acutely aware that he fears any such magical potion "will take his power away from him." It has been our experience also that the women are pleased to have the subject of family planning initiated by our medical team in the context of our concern for optimal family health.

This bears out Rainwater's findings about the desire of patients for medical assertiveness in this area (Rainwater, 1965).

It is quite possible that before the public arbiters decide what the official policy shall be for all unmarried women, the scientific discoveries will have again outstripped the mores. The "morning after pill" is being clinically tested throughout Sweden. That nation's Judiciary Committee recommended approval of a government proposal that clinical tests of drugs stopping the development of a fertilized ovum be permitted (Washington Post, 1967). Note that we have referred to it as "the morning after pill," when the Swedish report refers to it as "the abortion pill." In the reference to the development of such a pill here in our country, it *has* been called "the morning after pill" and the implication is that it would be taken on an undifferentiated basis.

Before that pill is marketed, we may have the long lasting (up to 20 years) contraceptive capsule, or the immunization against fertility. Then the reversal of the anti-fertility status would involve taking some kind of neutralizer or birth pill. This taking of a "birth pill" to *have* a child, rather than a "birth-control pill" *not* to have a child would have the appeal of taking positive action for conception rather than negative action against it (Segal, 1966). We may think of this as a kind of science-fiction world where, at puberty, the pediatrician would give contraceptive immunization along with the regular booster shots, with the obstetrician then giving the neutralizer when a baby was desired.

We are already living in the science fiction world of several short years ago. The wisest skill of social planners is needed to meet the scientific advances. We who exert some influence in these areas must be actively thinking about how we are to use that influence. For instance, how will it be decided when and to whom that neutralizing pill should be given? The young are space-age oriented and do not label as "far out" the idea of non-sexual production of offspring by vegetative reproduction, gene banks of the future, or manipulation of who are permitted to have which children with what genetic endowment. There must be a public discussion of the social consequences to man's increasing ability to manipulate genetics. A call for such a discussion was issued by the geneticist, Dr. James Crow, last year at a scientific conference in California (Crow, 1966).

The educators, the social scientists, the medical scientists have an opportunity to assist the youth (the parents of the next generation) in developing a personal integrity and adaptive behavior that will assist them in meeting the changes that scientific advances will precipitate. The educators can teach knowledge in such a way that boys and girls will respect the integrity of each other as individuals, and will respect the roles each must play to become responsible young people and adults. The medical scientists are showing concern about developmental life crises that the individual meets throughout adulthood, and can influence the shape of the lives of these adults who are the parents with whom the young have to cope, and who provide the role models. For instance, some physicians are prescribing perpetual oral hormonal intake for women, pre-menopausally, to continue through the rest of their lives, recognizing that it is important to anticipate this chemical imbalance and thus prevent its side effects in emotional stresses. It is particularly important for the adolescent children whose mothers they are, and for the women themselves at a critical time in their life when they need all their adaptive ability to meet the crises of the end of their reproductive period, their children's leaving home, their picking up the strands of their careers or inventing careers. Hopefully, similar concern will be shown for the male in his middlescent physiological and emotional changes in this transition period for him, family-wise and career-wise. The growing breakdown in family organization in this period of life provides poor models for the young. In their preventive roles, the educators and the physicians with their teams, can assist in the preparation of individuals in our society for predictable maturational crises even beyond the secondary school years such as: the higher education and/or career decision, first job with economic independence, marriage, parenthood, first child enters school, last child enters school, first child marries, last child leaves home, menopause, climacteric, retirement, death of parents, death of marital partner. We must educate in a planned way to prepare men and women to recognize these crisis points and to achieve the adaptive mechanism required. We must meet these current societal needs, at the same time fashioning new ways to meet our "pill culture." We must understand its implications for present-day family organization, and, as Dr. Metraux pointed out, we must know something about how members of various cultures think about the relations of adults of both sexes to children and about the interpersonal relations of adults with and without children (Metraux, 1967).

Dr. Metraux has noted that in every on-going society of which we know, sex has been subordinated to family organization. And in our culture, it seems that men have recently been using the rearing of children as a means to the maintenance of relatively permanent heterosexual adult relationships rather than as the end for which such relationships were established. She indicates that this should lead us to explore what other human potentialities are protected and fostered by the long term association of a man and woman within a family constellation. This is where we must struggle with new social inventions. She asks the questions, can we, in part, link more people to fewer children? Can we discover other imperative responsibilities besides children to serve to continue the long tradition we have of linking men and women? Can we invent ways to help women carry the evolution of their roles a step farther by better combination of their care-taking and responsive capacities, and to help men to share in these in ways that will foster long-term relations between men and women?

Dr. Margaret Mead has responded to the need for new social inventions in this day of family disorganization by proposing a new model for marriages which she calls the "two-step marriage," (also physiologically possible now with the reality of "the pill"). She conceives of this as being stylized so that an adequate investment in and commitment to the individual marriage would give it proper weight and chance to succeed, to evolve into the parental marriage (Mead, 1966). In her column, she discusses, in detail, the hazards of our present marriage forms, our emphasis on the nuclear family unit, and the prevalent practice of "fathers" marrying "mothers" and the goals that she personally hopes we may reach. These goals provide the framework of her thinking about new forms of marriage. She advances her ideas in this article as one contribution to what she says she hopes will be an on-going discussion. I think our wisest social scientists should take up this challenge.

These observations about adolescents and social symptoms may be closed with a reference to the comments about youth of one of our currently most "mod" social scientists, Marshall McLuhan (McLuhan, 1967). We seem to be caught up in some sort of "instant McLuhanism," as a result of his ability to speak directly to the adolescents, in an idiom immediately perceived by them, even if not intellectually completely understood. He describes this as "the Electric Age," and "plugs in" to the needs of the youth in this "Age," their button mania, their need to explore LSD and existentialism and a host of other needs. He makes some very pertinent observations about the generational conflict and about privacy: "As the electronic revolution gathers momentum, it will overturn all traditional patterns of thought and behavior. This situation accounts for the peculiar urgency of the current generational conflict. One generation has mistrusted another since Adam; but the gap between generations has rarely been so intensely perceived as today. The first generation to be reared in an electronic culture, instinctively understands the new environment, shucks off the rational-vision past, lives mystically, and in depth. Young people do not look for detached patterns for ways of relating themselves to the world, they demand, instead, a 'participation mystique.' It is this situation, too, which has created the contemporary assault on privacy and the very serious dilemma between our claim to privacy and the community's need to know" (McLuhan, 1967, p. 100). A parallel may be drawn, here, between the adolescents' claim to privacy and the parents' need to know. McLuhan attempts to explain history and predict the future in terms of alterations in the means of communication, to use the subliminal effects of the communication media to give insight into the dynamics of change. This is one approach, and we need to use all the approaches that enlighten.

We must be receptive to new ways of patterning interaction between generations, so that we can better communicate with each other. We must see technical advances of every kind ("the pill" included) not as threats to traditional modes of behavior but as new tools in shaping human behavior. A sense of urgency about these concerns stems from professional contact with people struggling with daily decisions about procreation, not able to wait for the culture to catch up and give guidance.

References

Bogue, D., Jr. The Demographic Moment of Truth. Paper presented at Pacific Service Congress, Tokyo, August 1966.

Crow, J. F. Paper presented at Scientific Progress and Human Values Conference, Pasadena, October 1966.

Health and Welfare Indicators, Illegitimacy and Dependency, Washington, D.C.: Bureau of Family Services, Welfare Administration, HEW, September 1963.

Mead, M. Personal Communication, November 25, 1966, monthly column in *Redbook*, July 1966.

Metraux, R. Cultural Implications of Modern Methods of Control of Conception, Symposium on the Physiological Control of Conception and Its Implications. Paper presented at 1965 Annual Meetings of AAAS, Berkeley.

McLuhan, M. & Fiore, Q. *The Medium Is the Massage: An Inventory of Effects.* New York: Random House, 1967.

Parade, 1967, Mar. 19, 15.

Rainwater, L. *Family Design.* Chicago: Aldine, 1965.

Segal, S. J. & Tietze, C. Papers presented at the National Academy of Sciences, Duke University, Durham, 1966.

Tappan, P. *Juvenile Delinquency.* New York: McGraw Hill, 1949.

Washington Post, anonymous article datelined Stockholm, Sweden, March 15, 1967.

Chapter 10: Unmarried Parents

31. UNMARRIED MOTHERS: SOME QUESTIONS TO BE ANSWERED AND SOME ANSWERS TO BE QUESTIONED

Elizabeth Herzog

§ The material in this article stems from two sources: extensive reading of research on unmarried mothers; and discussion with a number of research people interested in births out of wedlock, referred to in the article as "respondents." Many assumptions commonly made about unmarried mothers are questioned, and an emotional approach is replaced by an analysis of the facts.

For purposes of this paper, we are talking about unmarried mothers and illegitimate births. I shall refer to them as unmarried mothers, even though a considerable number of illegitimate pregnancies occur during marriage, between marriages, and after marriage.

The survey of experts brought out three main questions that serious researchers would most like to have answered—three questions, each of which trails a host of others. These three are:

1. How big is the problem?
2. Who are the unmarried mothers?
3. What factors contribute to, or are associated with, births out of wedlock?

I will try to indicate under each question some of the reasons they thought we should learn more about it.

SOURCE: *Child Welfare*, 41 (October, 1962), 339–50. Reprinted by permission of the publisher and the author.

The author is chief of the Child Life Studies Branch, Division of Research, Children's Bureau, Department of Health, Education, and Welfare.

282   *Unmarried Parents*

Question One: How Big Is the Problem?

The first question can be studied from two viewpoints: How big is the problem in absolute numbers and how big is it relative to other numbers? Our galloping publicity makes us more familiar with the absolute than with the relative picture. We are constantly being reminded that the number of births out of wedlock has risen radically. In the twenty years between 1938 and 1958 it has more than doubled—from less than 100,000 to more than 200,000.[1] And if we look at birth rates rather than the absolute numbers, the increase is even more striking.

. . . . .

Those who dwell on the alarming aspect of the increase sometimes forget that it is part of an over-all increase in the total number of live births and also in the birth rates. These rates, in turn, reflect changes in the number of women of childbearing age, in their age distribution, and in changes in marriage rates and in average family size. Marriage rates and family size, in their turn, respond to economic conditions, war and peace, and perhaps other more elusive influences.

If we look at illegitimate births as part of all live births, we see them in a context of general increase. . . . The rate of increase among illegitimate births has been a little faster than the over-all rate. In 1958 out-of-wedlock births represent about one percentage point more than in 1938, as a proportion of all live births. How much of this increase is real and how much is merely apparent is a moot question. But one point to be recognized for the moment is that the main increase is part of a total picture. It is not that suddenly and erratically illegitimate births have shot up, and that this is an isolated phenomenon to be dealt with as a crisis. It is rather that gradually, over a considerable period, births out of wedlock have shown the same tendency to increase that characterizes all births. We are trying to cope, not with a crisis, but with a long-term trend.

There are, of course, disagreements about interpreting the togetherness of birth rates in and out of wedlock. People ask, why *should* the two rates stay neck and neck? Why should the things that make total births go up also affect illegitimate births? The question is not unreasonable. Nevertheless, a gradual increase in these rates, which is of a piece with rates for all live births, is a different phenomenon from a sudden spurt that represents a *departure* from the rates for other live births. It seems more accurate to view it as part of an over-all picture and then to

[1] No figures later than 1960 were available, and some go back to 1957. Unless otherwise specified, figures quoted are from the Bureau of the Census or the National Office of Vital Statistics.

consider how we can *make* it diverge from the over-all trend than to view it out of context as a lonely and somewhat monstrous phenomenon. What forces cause the rise or fall in all birth rates is a grand and challenging question, beyond the scope of our present discussion.

Another point to be recognized is that the problems arising from births out of wedlock are not due to the increase. They are due to the phenomenon itself, which has been with us for a long time, and of which the increase per se is only a fraction. . . .

This point seems worthy of consideration because the crisis view invites reactions of fear and hostility. Not only are these emotions destructive in themselves, but they often constitute blocks to communication and problem-solving.

One point a good deal more prominent in the minds of my respondents than in the daily press is that our national figures on births out of wedlock are estimates, based on reports from thirty-five states. The tendency to forget this is no fault of the National Vital Statistics Division (more familiar under its former name, National Office of Vital Statistics). In addition to performing a remarkable job of reporting and analysis, this office continuously supplies us with model statements of limitation. If every news story about statistics on unmarried mothers carried one of these excellent paragraphs at its head, probably—well, probably—they would sell fewer papers. It would be well, however, for those of us who are concerned with understanding this explosive complex of problems to ponder these limiting statements.[2]

My respondents were not inclined to view the present figures as overestimates. Some of them, however, question the magnitude of the reported *increase* in rates. The reasons are probably familiar. Despite careful estimates we are not sure about the effects of the constant improvement in reporting. It seems possible that accurate allowance for changes in reporting would substantially reduce—and perhaps even eliminate—that one percentage point by which illegitimate births have outstripped total live births in amount of *increase* during the last twenty years.

This, of course, would not reduce the current illegitimacy rate. It would merely put the rate in line with the picture of total live births, or perhaps show it increasing at a slower pace. Thus, the rate of increase would be converted from an alarming rise to a more gradual and therefore presumably less alarming one.

Doubts about the rise have been with us for a long time. About seventy years ago a study of illegitimate births in Massachusetts reported a gradual increase in rates of illegitimacy over the preceding forty years,

---

[2] *Illegitimate Births: Fact Sheet* (Washington, D.C.: U. S. Department of Health, Education, and Welfare, Public Health Service, National Office of Vital Statistics, April 15, 1960).

but warned that the increase might be more apparent than real and might, in fact, be due to improvements in reporting.

The crisis view of our subject is often associated with reminders that the number of teenage unmarried mothers has increased greatly, that they represent 40 per cent of all unmarried mothers, and that this is the largest proportion for any age group. All three statements are true. . . . In 1959, 40 percent of the unmarried mothers were under twenty—the largest proportion for any five-year age span.

It is also true, for many reasons, that perhaps we need to be more concerned about the teenage unmarried mother than about any other, no matter what proportion of the whole she represents. That proportion, however, is not in itself the reason for concern. To view it without alarm might help to view it without hostility—which, in turn, might help communication and understanding between generations.

The Teenage Unmarried Mother

Four points help to put in perspective the teenage unmarried mother as a statistic. One is that the majority of unmarried mothers are *not* teenagers. . . . The so-called "older mothers"—that is, those above twenty—account for 60 percent, as compared with 40 percent for the teenagers. It might perhaps be added that in 1938 the proportion was not 40 percent, but 48 percent. In other words, the teenager accounts, not for a larger, but for a smaller proportion of the unmarried mothers than before.

A second point for perspective is that, although teenagers do not constitute a majority of unmarried mothers, they do constitute a majority of unmarried women of childbearing age. . . . In 1960 teenagers represented 68 percent of our unmarried female population of childbearing age, while unmarried women between twenty and forty-four represented 32 percent.[3] Thus, the teenager—as she surely should be—is underrepresented in the population of unmarried mothers. Not as much underrepresented as we would like to see her, and as we should surely try to make her. But the implications of the frequently quoted figure seem unfair.

A third point for perspective is that, although rates of illegitimate births have increased since 1938 for all women of childbearing age, they have increased least of all for the teenager. . . . These increases, it should be repeated, represent rates rather than numbers—that is, they show the number of children born out of wedlock per 1000 unmarried women of childbearing age. In 1938, the rate for teenagers was higher than for

[3] Joseph Schachter and Mary McCarthy, *Illegitimate Births: United States, 1938–57* (Washington, D.C.: U. S. Department of Health, Education, and Welfare, Public Health Service, National Office of Vital Statistics, 1960), Table F, p. 231.

any age group except those twenty to twenty-four years old. According to our latest figures, however, the rate among teenagers is lower than for any age group under thirty-five.

My last point for perspective is perhaps the most important of the four. This is that in the last few years for which we have figures—1956 to 1958—the teenager represents the one age group that has shown *no* increase in rates of illegitimate births. . . .

Question Two: Who Are the Unmarried Mothers?

. . . . .

Describing Unmarried Mothers

Who are the unmarried mothers? Four familiar answers have influenced assumptions about who they are.

The first of these concerns mentality. Time was when it was commonly said that low intelligence was significantly related to unmarried motherhood. Perhaps there has been a real change in this correlation. Or perhaps we have become more alert to the limitations of certain intelligence tests for people not proficient in the language or the mores. Or perhaps we are more alert to sampling problems. A study of the twenties, for instance, described the unmarried mothers who had been sent to a psychiatric clinic for testing as representative of those known to social agencies—apparently without considering that the very reasons for wanting them tested might constitute a difference between them and the others. In any case, recent studies do not encourage an assumption that inferior intelligence is especially associated with, and may contribute to, unmarried motherhood.

The second stock answer concerns broken homes. Here again, sophisticated sampling raises doubts. It is probably true that a large proportion of unmarried mothers do come from broken homes. However, the incidence of broken homes is very high among the groups with high out-of-wedlock birth rates—that is, the low-income groups, both white and nonwhite. It has yet to be established, however, that the broken home is more characteristic of unmarried mothers than of other women in these groups. In fact, some studies explicitly absolve it.[4] This is a point on which more evidence is needed.

The third answer concerns geographic mobility. It is often said that unwed motherhood is most frequent among the newest migrants from the South to the North or from rural to urban environment. The explanations offered are persuasive. A few recent studies, however, show less illegitimacy among very recent arrivals than among those who have

---

[4] F. Ivan Nye, "Child Adjustment in Broken and in Unhappy Unbroken Homes," *Marriage and Family Living,* XIX (1957), 356–361; and Virginia Wimperis, *The Unmarried Mother and Her Child* (London: Allen and Unwin, 1960).

been longer exposed to urban influences.[5] Until this point is resolved, one can no longer with any comfort put the onus on the newcomer.

The fourth familiar answer is often the only one given to the question: Who are the unmarried mothers? The terms used vary among emotional disturbance, psychological disturbance, disturbed parent-daughter relations—usually mother-daughter. Most frequently this answer involves the assumption that out-of-wedlock pregnancy is the unmarried mother's solution to her intra- and inter-personal problems, that her pregnancy is not accidental but quasi-deliberate, and that her personality and problems conform to a regularly recurring—in fact almost invariable—pattern. Often there is a lip-service recognition that unmarried mothers are not all psychological identical twins. Yet a doctoral dissertation published as late as 1958 can declare roundly that all unmarried mothers show the same traits and have become pregnant through the same psychological mechanism; and a serious article dated 1956 can declare that pregnancy out of wedlock is never really accidental and that these girls can become pregnant almost at will—even though failure to use contraception may help a little.

A root of conflict in testimony about who the unmarried mothers are seems to be that, through the years, the most available subjects for study have been the clients of social agencies, and generalizations about *the* unmarried mother have typically reflected the characteristics of agency or clinic clientele.

The evidence supports at least one unqualified statement. So far no single trait or condition—physical, intellectual, or emotional—stands up as *the* overwhelming constant characterizing *the* unmarried mother—except, of course, bearing a child out of wedlock. Nor is there convincing evidence that, among those who do suffer from emotional and inter-personal disturbances, one pattern is overwhelmingly preponderant. To those whose business is the assessment of evidence, it is surprising that statements as sweeping as the one cited can still be made.

Clark Vincent is the investigator who in recent years has most emphatically and convincingly pointed out the distortions in our notions of who the unmarried mothers are, and some of the consequences of these distortions. When he presented evidence that some unmarried mothers are relatively mature, upstanding, and economically self-sufficient, he added an essential and long-lost piece to our picture—a piece consistent with the neglected message of our national statistics. The results of his studies, and of his thinking about them, are brought together in his recent book, *Unmarried Mothers*, which offers our field something

[5] Jane Collier Kronick, "An Assessment of Research Knowledge Concerning the Unmarried Mother," *Research Perspectives on the Unmarried Mother* (New York: CWLA, 1962).

like a shot of iron and vitamins.[6] He asked a simple question: Who are the *other* unmarried mothers—the ones who do not form our captive populations for study, in agencies and on relief rolls; the ones who are over twenty and supplied with cash and able to leave home to bear their out-of-wedlock children, whom they then place—all secretly and without benefit of agency? This question he proceeded to begin answering, and in doing so he began sketching in the lines of a more balanced and realistic picture than had been accepted before.

The neglected group he added to our ken represents a minority of unmarried mothers, but an important one. They are white girls and women, chiefly of the middle- and upper-income levels. It is generally conceded that the great majority of unmarried mothers come from low-income brackets. We do not know exactly how large a proportion, but my respondents agree that we would do well to find out.

We do know how large a proportion are nonwhite, according to the national estimates. The overrepresentation of nonwhites among births out of wedlock is a familiar theme. Moreover, our national figures show the rates for nonwhites increasing more than the rates for whites.[7]

Sources of Difference

Some of my respondents voiced skepticism about the size of the differences between illegitimate birth rates for whites and for non-whites—differences in present rates and also differences in the rate of increase. Almost no one doubted the existence of a difference. Several suspected, however, that if relevant factors could be controlled, the difference in rate at a given time would be radically reduced and the difference in amount of increase might be wiped out.

The difference in amount of increase has undoubtedly been affected by improved reporting of all births, an improvement far greater for non-whites than for whites, as estimated by the National Office of Vital Statistics.[8] Thus, a considerable portion of the apparent nonwhite increase does seem attributable to improved reporting.

An unknown element in reported difference is represented by the fact that the states which do not report illegitimacy are the very ones to which white unwed mothers are most likely to travel, in order to give birth secretly and place the child in adoption, with the illegitimacy reported neither in the state of birth nor in the mother's state of residence.

[6] Clark E. Vincent, *Unmarried Mothers* (New York: The Free Press of Glencoe, 1961).
[7] Nonwhite is the classification used in our national figures. About 92 percent of the nonwhite population is Negro.
[8] *Vital Statistics of the United States, 1959* (Washington, D.C.: U. S. Department of Health, Education, and Welfare, Public Health Service, National Office of Vital Statistics, 1961), Section 3, Natality Statistics, Table 3-D.

These states include, among others, New York, California, and Massachusetts.

One source of real disparity between white and nonwhite rates is that the over-all rate is higher for nonwhite births than for white births, and has increased more. . . .

Another source of real difference between white and nonwhite rates is socioeconomic status. We have no national figures directly relating unmarried motherhood to social-economic level. One of the few unchallenged statements that can be made on this subject, however, is that the overwhelming majority of reported births out of wedlock are to mothers on the low-income levels. A recent study in New York City, for example, estimated that less than one in twenty of the illegitimate births during the study period occurred to private patients.[9]

The extent to which births out of wedlock are concentrated in the lower economic levels has been computed by a sociologist, drawing on the data of the Kinsey group and some other investigators. According to his computation, out of 100 middle- or upper-class white girls who have premarital coitus, one will have an illegitimate child; while out of 100 lower-class Negro girls who follow this course, seventeen will bear children.[10]

This proportion is in large measure a result of the fact that, according to available evidence, fewer middle- and upper-class white girls will conceive because most of those who have coitus will use contraception; and fewer who conceive will bear children because 90 percent will have abortions, as compared with 30 percent of the low-income Negro girls.[11]

There is ample evidence that contraception is disliked and feared by lower-class whites as well as by lower-class Negroes, and far more by males than by females. Many find abortion too expensive or too frightening, and to many it is so unthinkable that they do not reach the stage of fear.

If the small segment of unmarried mothers above the lower socioeconomic level were deducted, it would be appropriate to base the rates only on the low-income population. But that part of the population represents a much larger fraction of the whole for the nonwhites than for the whites. . . . The peak of nonwhite family income is between $1000 and $2000 per year. The largest proportion of white families fall

[9] Jean Pakter, Henry J. Rosner, Harold Jacobziner, and Frieda Greenstein, "Out-of-Wedlock Births in New York City: I—Sociological Aspects," *American Journal of Public Health*, LI (1961), 683–697; "II—Medical Aspects," *American Journal of Public Health*, LI (1961), 846–865.

[10] Howard Stanton, unpublished manuscript.

[11] H. Paul Gebhard, Wardell B. Pomeroy, Clyde E. Martin, and Cornelia V. Christenson, *Pregnancy, Birth and Abortion* (New York: Harper & Bros. and Paul B. Hoeber, Inc., 1958).

between $5000 and $6000. If we arbitrarily accept $3000 as our cutting point, almost one-half of the nonwhite population falls below it, as compared with not quite one-fifth of the white. If we cut at $1500, 24 percent of the nonwhite and 7 percent of the white family incomes fall below it—over three to one. If our rates of illegitimacy could be figured against the base that produces most births out of wedlock, that base would include a much smaller proportion of whites than of nonwhites, and the difference in rates would be reduced by a sharp rise in the white rates.

Question Three: What Factors Are Associated with Births Out of Wedlock?

Our first two questions concerned my respondents' urge to check assumptions about the dimensions of a problem and the identity of those most involved. Question three concerns their wish to check assumptions about factors contributing to, or associated with, unmarried motherhood. The main challenges to widely accepted ideas cluster about those two iffy factors, cultural background (specifically the Negro-white distinction) and socioeconomic status. . . . It seems clear that some often-heard statements and assumptions about them require modification in the light of available evidence.

A frequent feature of such statements is their absolute quality. When historical and cultural factors began to be mentioned as throwing light on current behavior, it was by way of counteracting stereotypes. An effort was made to introduce additional considerations that might help to explain behavior in all its complexity. But these additional considerations have somehow become new means to oversimplification. A pat phrase—"it's the culture"—is used, not to help explain, but to brush aside the need for explanation. And so in its turn the culture reference becomes a sort of neostereotype that blurs rather than sharpens our picture.

This rubber-stamp substitute for thought fails to do justice to the complexities of culture itself. Among those who have been most explicit in reminding about and illustrating these complexities are John Rohrer and his co-author.[12] I recommend their discussion as an antidote to the oversimplifications I perpetrate here.

I have said that the two factors—or factor complexes—most compelling to my respondents are the cultural and the socioeconomic. In our society, however, the culture constellation of each individual is

[12] John H. Rohrer and Munro S. Edmonson, *The Eighth Generation* (New York: Harper & Bros., 1960).

vastly affected by his social-economic position. The interest of my repondents in the relation of this position to unwed motherhood is largely, in fact, an interest in the "culture of poverty." [13]

Under question three I shall concentrate on cultural influences—ethnic or socioeconomic—partly because they cover so many facets and partly because they represent the outstanding interest of my respondents. And I shall comment on only two of the several statements and assumptions they challenged or qualified.

1. High on the list comes the slavery-specific culture thesis: that is, the proposition that illegitimacy rates among low-income Negroes derive primarily from a "Negro culture" produced by the situation under slavery. One difficulty with this proposition is that slavery is a hundred years behind us—crowded years, during which many influences have affected the family life and sex patterns of us all. Another is that some characteristics lumped under the slavery-legacy label are characteristically found also among low-income whites.

This convergence is the less surprising when we consider that much of what is ascribed to the culture of slavery is—and always was—inherent in the culture of poverty. If Negroes had not been slaves in a plantation setting but had been in as depressed an economic situation as the majority of them have been during and since slavery, the behavior of the low-income segment would probably show some of the elements now ascribed to slavery.

In discussing the culture of poverty, the grinding elements of physical insecurity and deprivation are occasionally neglected—though not by those who have actually lived among the very poor. Aside from these, a characteristic often noted in reports on the culture of poverty is lack of command over one's own destiny. The poor, be they deserving or undeserving, are on the whole more at the mercy of circumstances they cannot control than are the rich. This fact is frequently linked to a short, rather than a long, time perspective. If you feel—and to a considerable extent are—the pawn of circumstance, there is little inducement to planfulness and future orientation. You make the best you can of the moment. This lack of autonomy is at least as native to slavery as to poverty.

Associated with a tendency to present rather than future orientation, in reports on the culture of poverty, are a high degree of family disorganization and a lack of commitment to the norms and values accepted by the great society. I do not wish to belabor or even to explore the point here. I will merely report that a number of my respondents

[13] Oscar Lewis, "The Culture of Poverty," presented at the National Conference on Social Welfare, Minneapolis, Minn., 1961; and Thomas Gladwin, "The Anthropologist's View of Poverty," *The Social Welfare Forum* (New York and London: Columbia University Press, 1961).

think the influence of ethnic identification has been overemphasized and that of social-economic status has been underemphasized. This is not to deny that both exist.

The habit of analyzing data by color rather than by income level has helped to support the slavery-specific thesis. Since a much larger proportion of Negroes than of whites are on the lowest income levels, what look like statistically significant differences between Negroes and whites may also look like significant differences between different social-economic levels. But if the figures are presented only in one way, we don't find out about the other.

A few studies have done it both ways, with illuminating results. Clark Vincent, for example, found differences both by class and by race in the way unmarried mothers described their relationships with the putative father—whether love, friendship, or (much less often than is commonly assumed) a casual and transitory relation. The income level appeared to be the stronger in this study, but the color influence did not by any means disappear.[14] This may mean that both are significant, and I know of few investigators who would deny that both are, although a good many consider income level the more important—as it appears to be in Vincent's data and in some other studies.[15]

At the same time, almost no study of unmarried mothers so far has succeeded in an adequate breakdown by income level. There is sometimes a tendency to assume that the low-income level is homogeneous. Yet it has its own layers, and a much larger proportion of Negroes than of whites occupy the lower ones. A number of investigators have succeeded in documenting—though not in exploring fully—the existence of these layers within layers, as well as their crucial significance.[16]

Current evidence, then, indicates that neither a Negro culture nor an income level can be used as a tag to wipe away the need for looking closer. The label alone will never tell what we need to know about just which elements derive from each, how they manifest themselves, and how they interact.

2. A corollary of the slavery cliché is the often-heard statement that no stigma attaches to illegitimacy among low-income Negroes. This statement usually carries the implication that no stigma means no penalty and that this means it doesn't matter whether one is born in or out of wedlock. Here is the catch. The evidence does indicate that the social stigma for the low-income Negro is nothing like that suffered by the

[14] Vincent, *op. cit.*
[15] Henry J. Meyer, Wyatt Jones, and Edgar F. Borgatta, "The Decision by Unmarried Mothers To Keep or Surrender Their Baby," *Social Work*, I, No. 2 (1956), 103–109; and Henry J. Meyer, Edgar F. Borgatta, and David Fanshel, "Unwed Mothers' Decisions About Their Babies," *Child Welfare*, XXXVIII, No. 2 (1959), 1–6.
[16] See, for example, Gebhard, *et al., op. cit.*

middle- or high-income Negro or white person. But to be born in wedlock and to have your children born in wedlock is a decided social plus,
and a gratification; and if it is part of a stable marriage, it can be a
tremendous source of emotional support and pride. An interviewer in a
Chicago study told about the unwed mother of several children who
kept in the honor place of her room a large picture of her sister in full
wedding regalia. She quickly made an opportunity to call attention to
the picture, with the greatest pride and gratification, as if her relationship to a regularly married woman was a status symbol worth displaying.

Apparently the plus value of regular marriage is stronger in some circles than the minus value of no marriage. There is an old Yiddish
proverb that says: Money is not so good as the lack of money is bad.
Here one might say: Lack of marriage is not so bad as having a marriage
is good.

Yet the lack is by no means a matter of indifference. Some low-income
mothers pray for boys in order to avoid "trouble" for their daughters,
and when trouble comes there is grief and anger, even though there is
also the strong conviction that you stick to your own, take care of your
own, never turn them away. There is also a revulsion against forcing a
marriage between a girl pregnant out of wedlock and the putative
father, unless they really love each other. Apparently the stigma is not
enough to make an unhappy marriage more desirable than an out-of-
wedlock birth. On the contrary, a girl may take pride in waiting until
she is "sure she loves him"—even though this assurance comes after the
baby is born. (Some of these contrasts between high- and low-income
attitudes toward marriage offer interesting food for speculation about
the function of marriage for different groups.)

Our purpose here is to note what is challenged, and on what grounds,
rather than to provide the intricate answers required. Some answers are
available, however, and some are being supplied or reinforced by studies
already published or still in process. Among the latter, the study of low-
income families in the District of Columbia, directed by Hylan Lewis,
is one source of challenge to easy generalizations and of information to
fill the gaps left when they topple.[17] For me it is a major source, on
which I am drawing heavily right now.

Among the complex of reasons for the distortion implicit in the stigma
cliché, one is a prevailing assumption that people have a single, consistent set of values, directly mirrored in their daily lives. Most of us
know this is not necessarily so. In relation to illegitimacy, we have
abundant evidence that prevailing middle-class norms may represent an
approved pattern, but one considered unattainable by people who com-

[17] Hylan Lewis, "Child-Rearing Practices Among Low-Income Families," *Casework
Papers, 1961* (New York: Family Service Association of America, 1961), pp. 79–92.

fortably continue to act as if those norms did not exist. "Beggars can't be choosers," is the way one unwed mother put it. The existence of a dual set of values must be recognized in order to make sense. One observer comments that "the lower class subscribes to the general values of the society and also has values unique to itself. . . ." ". . . legal marriage and a non-legal union . . . are two types of acceptable marital patterns. . . . This is not to say that these two patterns are equally valued."[18] A realistic picture of the relation between value preference and actual behavior must recognize both the acceptability of patterns that violate middle-class norms and the higher values put on those norms.

· · · · ·

Summary

I have mentioned a number of points in an effort to make only a few. What I have been trying to say can be summed up under three statements:

1. Seen in context, the rise in illegitimacy rates is substantial but not alarming, merits concern rather than panic or rage, and can be coped with best if viewed without alarm.

2. The behavior patterns responsible for most out-of-wedlock births are related both to the culture of poverty and to the culture of an ethnic group, but the socioeconomic factors are probably more significant.

3. If we want to bring about change we must be clear about what we want to change from and what we want to change to, we must demonstrate the value and the feasibility of change to those whose behavior we want to modify, and we ourselves must want it enough to put in what it takes.

[18] Hyman Rodman, "On Understanding Lower-Class Behavior," *Social and Economic Studies*, VIII (1959), 441–450. See also William J. Goode, "Illegitimacy in the Caribbean Social Structure," *American Sociological Review*, XXV (1960), 21–30.

32. UNMARRIED FATHERS

Clark E. Vincent

§ This article examines the popular conception of the unmarried father as a sexual exploiter of some unsophisticated girl. The author finds the conception to be false and continues his examination to include various attitudes toward both the man and the woman involved in unmarried parenthood.

Unmarried fathers are, so to say, half the biological cause of illegitimacy, yet the ratio of studies of them to studies of unwed mothers is approximately one to 25. This disproportionate ratio provided the initial stimulus for the present examination of the normative and research significance of the label "sexual exploiter" as affixed to the unmarried father.

A very brief consideration of several folkways, social practices, and values which serve to define the unwed mother as a more important social problem and research subject than the unmarried father may help to explain this disproportionate ratio, as well as to provide a background for the data and discussion that follow. Thus: (1) The traditional double standard effects a harsher judgment of the female than of the male for sexual misbehavior during courtship, for involvement in an extra-marital affair, and for an unwanted pregnancy within marriage. (2) The "presumption of innocence until guilt is proven" provides far less protection for the unwed mother, whose maternity becomes self-evident, than it does for the unmarried father whose paternity must be proven. (3) The "principle of legitimacy"[1] is maintained by censuring primarily the unwed mother; for since it is she whose evidence of sexual misbehavior overtly threatens the mores supporting legitimacy her behavior is censured as an object lesson to prevent these mores from "dying-out in the conscience of the society." (4) Public and research interest in a given social problem is in part a function of the financial burden which that problem imposes on taxpayers; and it is the unwed mother, rather than

SOURCE: "Unmarried Fathers and the Mores: 'Sexual Exploiter' as an Ex Post Facto Label," *American Sociological Review*, 25 (February, 1960), 40–46. Reprinted by permission of the publisher and the author.

Clark E. Vincent, who received his doctorate from the University of California, is on the staff of the Bowman Gray School of Medicine. He is the editor of *Readings in Marriage Counseling* and the author of *Unmarried Mothers*, as well as numerous professional articles.

[1] Kingsley Davis, "Illegitimacy and the Social Structure," *American Journal of Sociology*, 45 (August, 1939), pp. 215–233.

the unmarried father, who needs a maternity home, financial aid, and casework services. (5) With limited time and research funds, it is more economical to study *groups* of unwed mothers from maternity homes and welfare agency files than to study *individual* unmarried fathers who remain anonymous in the population at large.

That these social attitudes and practices influence research on illegitimacy is evident in the present study of unmarried fathers. I did not obtain the data directly from them, nor did I ascertain their marital status—a datum recognized as crucial for defining unwed mothers, but overlooked in this study of their male counterparts.

Population and Sample

Data on 736 out-of-wedlock births were obtained from three sources in Alameda County, California, throughout 1954: the Salvation Army Maternity Home, the Alameda County Hospital, and physicians' private practice. These 736 cases represent 3.2 per cent of the total live births, and the three sample sources included all the discernible outlets for the delivery of babies during 1954 in Alameda County—a metropolitan area with an estimated population of 838,900 at the time of the study.

These 736 cases were reduced to 201. The 387 non white unwed mothers were excluded because over four-fifths of them were attended at the county hospital where very few of the non whites reported any data on unmarried fathers. Also excluded were 148 of the original 349 white unwed mothers (93 were divorced, separated, or married to a man other than the unmarried father; 23 did not report the identity of the unmarried father; 21 had had a previous out-of-wedlock pregnancy; six were pregnant as the result of rape or incest; and five had a Negro sexual mate). The sample for the present study, then, consists of the sexual mates of the 201 white unwed mothers who remained after these exclusions. An abbreviated socio-economic description of this sample is provided by the data in Table 1.

How representative of white unmarried fathers in general are these 201 sires described in Table 1? Unfortunately, survey data are not available on unmarried fathers in the general population, and data from regional or institutional studies are not reported by multiple sample sources and unmarried father-unwed mother pairs—as is done in the present study. Moreover, the temporary migration of unwed mothers during pregnancy makes them a tenuous basis for ascertaining the population source and representatives of any given sample of unmarried fathers.

The lack of information on the distribution of unmarried fathers in the general population and the tendency to overgeneralize from "social-

TABLE 1   *Age, Educational, and Occupational Distribution of 201 White Unmarried Fathers*

Age Groups	Per Cent	Educational Groups	Per Cent	Occupational Groups	Per Cent
15–18	15.9	College graduate	11.4	Professional and technical	12.4
19–22	22.4	Attended college	21.9	Business and managerial	7.0
23–26	18.4	High school		Sales and services	11.4
27–30	12.9	graduate	33.8	Skilled tradesman and	
31–34	14.4	Less than 12th		craftsman	11.9
35 and		grade	28.9	Protective services	14.9
over	5.5	No data	4.0	Semi-skilled services	7.0
No data	10.5			Unskilled laborer	7.0
			100.0	Students	20.9
	100.0			Unemployed and no data	7.5
					100.0

problems" research data justify the precaution of repeating in summary form the sampling procedure used in the present study. The *initial population* of 736 included all the unwed mothers reported as attended in a maternity home, the county hospital, and private practice, in Alameda County during 1954. The *sample* of 201 white unmarried fathers included the sexual mates of all the unwed mothers in this population who were white, single-never-married, pregnant for the first time, and who were not impregnated by a non white, a relative, or by force. Thus, the data and interpretations presented below are not held to be applicable to unmarried fathers who are non white, or who impregnate Negro, divorced, widowed, married, or recidivous unwed mothers.

Unmarried Father–Unwed Mother Mating Patterns

The notion that unmarried fathers are much older and much better educated than the females they impregnate is not supported by the data in the present study. This notion has not been seriously challenged as long as descriptions of unwed mothers were derived primarily from institution-type samples and as long as descriptions of unmarried fathers were either unavailable or were not reported on an unmarried father-unwed mother pair basis. For the emphasis on the age and educational superiority of the unmarried father has received support from and represents the obverse of earlier conventional descriptions of unwed mothers. These descriptions, which emphasize the extreme youth, poverty, and lack of education of unwed mothers, were derived primarily from studies of unwed mothers in maternity homes, welfare agencies, and county hospitals—where youth and low socio-economic status were socially imposed criteria for admission.[2]

Education

In Table 2, the educational attainment of the unmarried fathers is seen to be quite similar to that of the respective unwed mothers they impregnated. In Table 3, educational differences between the unmarried father-unwed mother pairs are seen to approximate educational differences between husband-wife pairs in a given census population.

Age

Comparison of their ages with the ages of the respective unwed mothers they impregnated shows that 17 per cent of the 201 unmarried fathers were seven or more years older, 21 per cent were from four to six years older, and 56 per cent were within three years of the same age (6 per cent did not provide information). These age differences would appear to approximate husband-wife age differences in the general population. Census reports do not permit rigorous comparisons of data on this point, but the following distribution was computed from data on 1,763,400 white wives between the ages of 14 and 22 who were married less than three years at the time of the 1950 census: 16 per cent of the husbands were seven or more years older than their wives, 31 per cent were at least four to six years older, and 53 per cent of the husbands were within three years of their wives' ages.[3]

TABLE 2   *Education of 193 Unmarried Fathers and 193 Unwed Mothers, as Reported by the Unwed Mother**

	UNMARRIED FATHER'S EDUCATION			
Unwed Mother's Education	College Graduate (N = 23)	Attended College (N = 44)	High School Graduate (N = 68)	Less than 12 years (N = 58)
College graduate	69.6%	6.8%	1.5%	—
Attended college	17.4	72.7	5.9	1.7%
High school graduate	8.7	18.2	58.8	19.0
Less than 12 years	4.3	2.3	33.8	79.3
	100.0	100.0	100.0	100.0

* Eight of the 201 respondents did not report complete information on education.

[2] See Clark E. Vincent, "The Unwed Mother and Sampling Bias," *American Sociological Review*, 19 (October, 1954), pp. 562–567, for a partial bibliography of these earlier studies.

[3] Computed from *1950 U. S. Census of Population, Special Report P-E, No. 2E,* Washington, D.C.: U. S. Government Printing Office, 1955, Table 3, pp. 2E-12, 2E-13.

TABLE 3   *Median Years of School Completed, for Husbands and Wives Who Entered First Marriages Between 1947 and 1954, by Educational Level of Spouse: United States**

Educational Level of Spouse (Sexual Mate)		MEDIAN YEARS OF SCHOOL COMPLETED			
		Husbands	(Unmarried Fathers)	Wives	(Unwed Mothers)
Elementary	0 to 7 years	6.5	(6.0)	8.6	(8.7)
	8 years	8.8	(7.2)	9.6	(10.0)
High School	1 to 3 years	10.7	(10.6)	11.7	(10.6)
	4 years	12.4	(12.3)	12.4	(11.4)
College		13.9	(14.6)	12.7	(13.5)
	1 or more	16.+	(17.+)	14.8	(15.1)
Total Group		12.1	(12.1)	12.2	(11.9)

* As compared with median years of school completed, for 193 unmarried fathers and 193 unwed mothers, by educational level of sexual mate. Adapted from Paul C. Glick and Hugh Carter, "Marriage Patterns and Educational Level," *American Sociological Review*, 23 (June, 1958), pp. 294–300, Table 3.

The age data were then compiled as shown in Table 4. The unmarried fathers who had the greatest age seniority were found to be mated predominantly with older or with college-educated unwed mothers, while those with the least age seniority were mated predominantly with the youngest unwed mothers or with those who had not completed high school.

"Sexual Exploiter" as an Ex Post Facto Label

The following discussion has some of the characteristics of a strawman argument, inasmuch as it is based on an assertion for which evidence is not provided. The assertion is that the label of "sexual exploiter" has frequently been affixed to unmarried fathers and used implicitly, at least as a partial explanation of the "cause" of illegitimacy. No attempt is made to substantiate this assertion, since space limitations preclude citing the several hundred references from among which it was derived and since selectively quoting from only a few such sources is a misleading substitute for the systematic study (content analysis or attitude survey) needed to confirm or to negate adequately the assertion. Moreover, the primary intention of the present discussion is to clarify the normative content of the label, rather than to examine the extent of its usage.

The term sexual exploiter (or its conceptual equivalent) is interpreted here as representing an ex post facto label for unmarried fathers—a label that is affixed *after* the female has become pregnant. This interpretation is derived from the foregoing data, which fail to show any overwhelming

TABLE 4 *Age and Education of Unwed Mothers by Age Differences Between Unmarried Fathers and Their Respective Unwed Mothers, as Reported by the Unwed Mothers***

	AGE DIFFERENCE CATEGORIES			
Unwed Mothers' Ages	UF [1] was 7 years older than UM [2] (N = 34)	UF was 4–6 years older than UM (N = 33)	UF was 2–3 years older than UM (N = 41)	UF was within 1 year of UM's age (N = 70)
26 and older	17.6%	9.1%	2.5%	2.9%
25–22	55.9	48.5	7.3	2.9
21–18	17.6	27.3	63.4	41.3
17 and younger	8.9	15.1	26.8	52.9
	100.0	100.0	100.0	100.0
Unwed Mothers' Education	(N = 33)	(N = 32)	(N = 39)	(N = 68)
College graduate	48.5%	6.2%	5.1%	—
Attended college	36.4	50.0	18.0	4.4%
High school graduate	12.1	34.4	51.3	22.1
Less than 12 years	3.0	9.4	25.6	73.5
	100.0	100.0	100.0	100.0

* Age data for 23 and education data for 29 cases were not reported.
[1] UF = unmarried father.
[2] UM = unwed mother.

or one-sided age and educational superiority of the unmarried fathers over the unwed mothers in the present study, as well as from additional questionnaire data for over 500 unwed mothers and from individual interviews and counseling sessions with 82 unwed mothers and 32 unmarried fathers (to be reported in a separate paper).

That this term is an ex post facto label in many if not the majority of cases in which it is applied becomes more understandable when it is viewed within a normative framework; for the notion that unmarried fathers tend to mate sexually with and thereby exploit females who are much younger, less-educated, and poorer, is in one sense a logical projection of folkways and attitudes which form a part of mate-selection patterns in general. For example, the traditional view of the male as being somewhat superior or dominant in male-female relationships is still reflected in the tendency of females to marry males who in comparison with themselves are taller, older, have more education, and possess the potential for higher occupational status. Thus, the same age, educational, and socio-economic superiority of the male over the female that is accepted and encouraged as normative in dating, courtship, and marriage is viewed as the basis for and as evidence of sexual exploitation when illegitimacy is involved.

Any "exploitation" present in the relationship during the time when illicit sexual unions are occurring is as likely to be reciprocal as one-sided. This relationship has some of the characteristics of an informal and implicit contract, and it is usually only after one party loses too much that the other party is viewed as an exploiter. The unwed mother is as likely as the unmarried father to be "exploiting" during the time their relationship is active, but with a different focus. She tends to use *sex* (or sexual enticements in the larger sense) *as a means*—to dates, companionship, an expense account, upward mobility, and possible marriage. He reverses this. He tends to date, provide companionship, pay the bills, court, and express love—*as a means to sex*.

This is not to say that they view each other or sex in any deliberate or even conscious manner as representing only a means, nor is it to say that sexual experience is the main motivation of and focus for their relationship. Rather, it is to state (and thereby overemphasize) only one of many orientations, and only one of many points on a means-end continuum, in male-female relationships. Given this limited context, to say that the unwed mother tends to use sex as a means to other goals is only to explicate what is implied when being erotically attractive and enticing (short of acquiescence, if unmarried) receives normative sanction as a part of female role-expectations in general, as evidence of femininity, and as a "typically feminine" means of achieving a variety of goals. Within this same context, to say that the unmarried father tends to use dating as a means to sex is but to isolate (and thereby oversimplify) one of many implications of current male role-expectations. For when masculinity is a socially sanctioned goal for the male and when the pursuance of sexual favors is sanctioned as evidence (means) of masculinity, dating will represent one of the potential means to the goal of sexual experience which, in turn, is a means (evidence) to the goal of demonstrated masculinity.

Consistent with these normative sanctions, is the fact that the label of "exploiter" is rarely applied to the male involved when the female's skill and performance in her expected role result in marriage—even though the male is considerably older, better educated, and of higher socio-economic status than the female. (In fact, the female is sometimes

thought to have "exploited" her sexual means when a premarital pregnancy is associated with her marriage to a male of much higher socio-
economic status.) There is also little use of the label in a relationship
in which sexual intercourse occurs without pregnancy and without marriage—presumably, because each of the parties has incurred either some
benefit or no serious loss from the temporary relationship.

It is when pregnancy without marriage occurs that he is labeled the
exploiter, she the exploited. His superiority in age, education, and socio-
economic status, which would have been viewed as evidence of her desirability and as a rightful reward for her feminine skills if marriage had
occurred, is now pointed to as evidence of his exploitative position—of
which he took advantage.

Two Double-Standards in Sexual Behavior

Thus, we come full-circle with reference to mores associated with not
one but two double-standards in sexual behavior: females are judged
more harshly than males for sexual misbehavior. An illicit pregnancy is
judged more harshly than is an illicit sexual union.

As to the first double-standard, the harsher judgment of the female can
be understood within the following context: mores which ascribe to the
female the traditional role of "maintainer and upholder of morality";
mores which sanction feminine skill in sexual enticement; and mores
which serve to define the female's sexual misbehavior as containing the
potential for a more serious social problem (unwed motherhood) than
is represented by the male's sexual misbehavior (unmarried fatherhood).
The softer judgment of the male is related to his traditional role of pursuing sexual favors as evidence of his masculinity, his lack of evidence
of sexual misbehavior that would overtly threaten cherished family
values, and social practices and attitudes that preclude his identification
as a burden on taxpayers.

The second double-standard, the tendency to judge the *result* (illicit
pregnancy) more harshly than the *cause* (illicit sexual union), is illustrated by such folk-sayings as "what they don't know won't hurt them"
and "out of sight, out of mind." The unwed mother's changing profile
makes her sexual misbehavior public knowledge, thereby threatening to
weaken traditional sex mores if left uncensured; whereas, the single
female who remains discreet and nonpregnant while engaging in illicit
sexual unions poses no overt threat to these mores. Also, as noted above,
the financial costs of an illicit pregnancy pose a very tangible problem
for public taxpayers, while (with the exception of V. D. Clinics) the
"costs" of an illicit sexual union usually remain the private problem of
the participants. Thus, the harsher judgment of an illicit pregnancy than
of an illicit sexual union is in large part a function of the greater

normative and financial threats which the former represents. Censure of the unwed mother and her behavior is one of the oldest methods used to decrease these threats.

It is at this point that humanitarian values come to the fore to soften the censure of the unwed mother by labeling the unmarried father as an exploiter. She now can be seen more as a violated victim and less as a violator. Diverting some of the censure from her to the unmarried father is also a way of rewarding her for reinforcing that aspect of traditional motherhood which places the welfare of the unborn child ahead of the fears and solitariness of the mother.

Within this context the ex post facto labeling of the unmarried father as an exploiter is less a censuring of his *sexual misbehavior* (since it is primarily the female's responsibility to avoid illicit sexual unions), and more a censuring of his *role misbehavior*—his failure to assume the traditional masculine role of protecting the female. Having illicit sexual relations and becoming pregnant are primarily the female's "areas of fault." Failing to protect and to shield her from shame (by marrying her) when she becomes pregnant is primarily the male's "area of fault."

In this sense the male passes the "masculinity test" when he pursues and obtains sexual favors from the female, but fails the test when he refuses to protect her from shame and to provide for her when she becomes pregnant. The female tends to fail one aspect of the "femininity test" when she acquiesces to an illicit sexual union, but passes another aspect of this test when she accepts the role of motherhood and completes her pregnancy in a traditionally heroic manner—alone and faced with censure. In so doing she partially diverts the censure from herself to the missing father who traditionally should protect her and provide for the baby.

Current efforts to censure and to counter this weakening of the traditional protective role of the male consist primarily of name-calling—affixing the ex post facto label of sexual exploiter to the unmarried father. Although such efforts may appear to be weak deterrents to the breakdown of the traditional protective role of the male, they are consistent with the mores noted at the beginning of this paper and consistent with the current disclarity concerning male and female roles in general.

Summary and Implications

On the basis of the present study of white unmarried father–unwed mother pairs, whose educational and age differences approximate those sanctioned in dating and mate-selection patterns in general, the term sexual exploiter is interpreted as an ex post facto label for the unmarried father.

The significance of this interpretation is not as an explanation of the cause of illegitimacy, but as a clarification of the mores from which the label is derived and to which it gives support. Within the larger normative setting, this ex post facto label serves humane values by modifying the blame or censure of unwed mothers who lend support to the heroic aspect of the traditional role of motherhood by bringing their pregnancies to fruition. This label also serves to sanction the traditional protective role of the male by censuring males who fail to protect females from shame, and serves to support cherished family values by censuring any father who leaves a mother in an unwed status whereby she overtly threatens the traditional family system.

This interpretation of sexual exploiter as primarily an ex post facto label can also serve to broaden the base for research in illegitimacy, inasmuch as it suggests the need to examine the following matters: the study of unmarried parents by pairs; the reciprocal exploitation involved in illicit sexual unions that do not result in pregnancy; and the differential goals involved in, and the social practices that provide normative sanction for, the instrumental use of illicit sexual relations.

Chapter 11: Laws Regulating Marriage and Family Life

33. LEGAL REGULATION OF MARRIAGE

Ruth Shonle Cavan

§ One of the problems of discussing the legal aspects of marriage in the United States is that laws pertaining to marriage and the family are state laws; therefore there are as many different sets of laws as there are states. Nevertheless, a general pattern runs through the laws due to the fact that almost without exception the basic laws have grown out of the English common law. This common root gives a similarity to the state laws but has not prevented deviations based on regional differences of thought and belief and on the difference in time of the passage of laws from the earliest laws of the Atlantic Seaboard to the relatively recent laws of some of the western states. This summary attempts only to give the general pattern, from which there are individual state deviations. In the reports available, the District of Columbia is included but not Alaska or Hawaii.

Although marriage is sometimes referred to as a civil contract, it differs greatly from other civil contracts. For instance, it often can be entered into at an earlier age than other contracts, and in this sense the marriage law is more liberal than that governing civil contracts. However, marriage cannot be terminated without appeal to the proper court, which may or may not grant the appeal; in this the law is more strict for marriage than for many other kinds of contract./Legally, marriage is regarded as a relationship of supreme importance for the well-being of the whole society and for the careful rearing of children. The popular trend in the United States has been for marriage to be regarded more and more as the personal affair of husband and wife, to be entered or

SOURCE: A summary of some factual material in *The Legal Status of Women in the United States of America*, Women's Bureau Bulletin 157 (rev. 1956; Washington, D.C.: United States Department of Labor, 1956 and later announcements; supplemented from Harriet F. Pilpel and Theodora Zavin, *Your Marriage and the Law* (New York: Rinehart & Company, Inc., 1952); interpretation is the author's.

The author's background is given in the footnote for article 13.

left at will, sometimes without much regard for the effect on children. The law takes another stand; marriage creates duties and obligations which the couple cannot neglect at will. Each state has numerous laws to regulate marriage.

Common Law and Written Law

The complexities of laws governing marriage are easier to understand when the distinction between common law and written law is made clear. Marriage is an old institution and the English common law still controls or influences some aspects of American marriage in the 1960's.

The basis for the laws of the various states lies in the English common law as it was at the time of the American Revolution and, in a few states settled by French or Spanish people, in French and Spanish civil codes. These early imported rules have been modified by constitutional provisions, colonial and state statutes or laws, and court decisions. The common law is known as unwritten law and the statutes and court decisions as written law. If no written law applies to a specific situation, the principles of the old English common law apply. The written law may simply repeat the common law or may change it or discard it altogether.

When the common law still operates in regulation of marriage, this fact will be pointed out. Often its continued use indicates that marriage laws are very much out of step with current social conditions. In other instances, the common law has only recently been replaced by more appropriate statutes, often after persistent efforts of determined women and their male supporters in the state legislatures.

Trend of Laws

In general, the trend of laws and court decisions has been in four directions.

First, laws have liberated married women from the subordinate status imposed by the feudal common law. According to this body of law, a woman's legal identity was destroyed by marriage. Her property and earnings belonged to her husband and her personal conduct was subject to his control. This concept was in keeping with the feudal hierarchy of control that placed strong leadership in the hands of men, who also carried heavy responsibilities. Gradually, laws in the United States have established economic and personal independence for married women. Many of the changes have come recently.

Second, although laws pertaining to marriage have not changed much in the past 75 years and in some respects have become stricter, court decisions have tended to interpret the laws leniently, especially those pertaining to divorce. Stricter regulation can be seen in laws requiring freedom from venereal disease or requiring a waiting or thinking-over period between application for the marriage license and its issuance.

Third, some old laws clearly out of step with the times and often now a means of exploitation are slowly, state by state, being discarded. Two examples are the right to bring breach of promise suits and recognition of common-law marriages.

Fourth, laws not thought of as marriage laws often indirectly affect the privileges or duties of marriage. Fathers are obligated to support their minor children; but laws granting aid to dependent children lighten the earlier obligations for ill or absent fathers. Old-age assistance (grants to old people in need) and Medicare have lifted some of the burden of supporting old parents from their adult children who may be having a difficult time meeting the expenses of rearing a family. School attendance laws have relieved parents of the supervision of children for many hours during the week through most of the adolescent period; these laws also often increase the length of time during which parents must support their children.

With these various trends in mind, let us turn to specific areas of legal regulation.

Breach of Promise

Breach of promise refers to the breaking of an engagement. The engagement is regarded as a binding contract to marry, the breaking of which by one party may injure the other. Under common law, the injured party could sue in court the one who broke the engagement and claim money payment for damages. Gradually state laws have been passed abolishing this common-law right.

Breach of promise suits usually are started by women. At an earlier period, the engagement was regarded in a sense as the beginning of marriage. If the man broke the engagement, the woman's reputation, and therefore her chances of future marriage to someone else, was often damaged. If the engagement was broken by mutual consent, neither man nor woman could bring suit.

At present an engagement is regarded by most young people as a private arrangement to permit them to test their compatibility for each other. It is a stronger relationship than steady or serious dating, but lacks legal connotations. Engagements, even after being publicly announced, are often broken. Regardless of feelings of frustration or rejection, neither man nor woman feels that either owes money to the other in payment of damages.

Breach of promise suits now are often abused. A wealthy man may be sued by an ex-fiancée who is perhaps more interested in acquiring a large sum of money than in remedying any actual damage to her reputation or previous financial status. The threat of a suit may force a man to make a money settlement to avoid unfavorable publicity. However, if the woman has invested money from which the man benefits or has given up some lucrative employment which she cannot regain, courts are inclined to require the man to reimburse her to the extent of actual money loss.

Who May Not Marry

The law does not compel anyone to marry, but it does regulate eligibility for marriage. Laws tend to rule out types of persons whom public opinion or the legislators have thought unsuitable for marriage. The laws do not set up positive standards which would tend to lift the quality of marriage. The laws set formal minimum standards for mate selection.

Age

In general, in the United States, children may not marry. According to the table of Marriage Laws, prepared by the Women's Bureau, which follows this article, in the majority of states the minimum age for a legal marriage, even with the consent of parents, is eighteen for males and sixteen for females. However, a few states permit girls as young as fourteen and boys as young as fifteen to marry when the parents consent.

Without parental consent, the most usual minimum age is eighteen for girls and twenty-one for men. In actual practice, these ages are more nearly representative of the lower age of marriage than are the minimum ages with parental consent. In 1966 the median age for first marriages contracted by men was 22.8 years and for women 20.5 years. These figures mean that half of all men married when over 22.8 years and half of all women when over 20.5 years. Of course, half marry below these ages, but few reach down into the years when parental consent is required.

The old common-law rule placed the minimum age at about the age of puberty, at a time when educational attainments were also completed by about this same period. Present laws and customs allow not only for sexual maturity but for general bodily maturity, completion of secondary education, and some experience in economic independence.

When a person under the minimum age does marry, the marriage usually stands unless court action is taken to dissolve it. Thus young people may lie about their ages and marry. If no one (for example, parents) brings a suit in court to have the marriage annulled, the marriage stands.

Degree of Kinship

Members of an immediate family related by blood may not marry. The "marriage" or sexual relations between a parent and his or her child or between brother and sister is called incest. Public abhorrence as well as laws exact heavy penalties from adult offenders.

First cousins may not marry each other in more than half of the states and in a few states somewhat more remote relatives—sometimes including ones related by marriage—are forbidden to marry.

Prohibitions of marriages between close relatives are old and widespread. Almost the only exceptions are found in certain royal lines, where few people are of sufficient status to be able to marry a member of the royal family. An extreme example is the Ptolemies of Egypt who sometimes followed an Egyptian custom of brother-sister marriages.

Reasons for the prohibitions are not always clear. Some of them undoubtedly reduce tension and conflict in family and kinship groups. The prohibition of first-cousin marriages has certain implications for heredity, although it is obvious that this is not the primary reason, since such marriages are forbidden in groups which do not have a science of genetics. A defective family strain might be carried by both cousins and thus increase the probability that children of the marriage might inherit the defect. A favorable characteristic might similarly come to a child in double measure.

Whatever the reason for the origin of these laws, we now have ingrained attitudes of abhorrence against sexual relations, in or out of marriage, between closely related persons.

Other Prohibitions

Various states have selected certain physical grounds for prohibiting marriages, declaring them void if they occur. These conditions and the number of states using each as grounds for forbidding marriage are listed below:

Unsound mind	24 states
Epilepsy	14 states
Venereal disease in communicable stage	9 states
Habitual drunkenness	3 states
Tuberculosis in a communicable stage	1 state
Any communicable disease	1 state
Communicable disease if unknown to the other party	1 state
Drug addiction	1 state
Impotency	1 state

People with unfavorable behavior records may also be forbidden to marry. Three states have some type of prohibition of marriage by criminals. Two states forbid the marriage of a male who has been an inmate of a home for indigents unless he can show he is able to support a family.

Many of these prohibitions (all aimed at protecting the marriage partner or the children) are difficult to enforce, as it is not customary to require a certificate that these conditions do not exist and often the officer issuing the marriage license would have only the assertion of the applicant to guide him. True, many of the marriages are illegal or could be annulled—but often no one takes the step to bring about court action so that functionally the marriages may continue through the years and be accepted as legal.

Getting Married

Physical Examination

Forty-five states require a physical examination whose purpose is to determine whether the person has a venereal disease (see table on Marriage Laws). A few states require a certificate of freedom from certain other diseases or physical defects. The nature of the examination is not always adequate; in fact, in a few states the applicants for a license to marry simply affirm that they are not infected. In different states, the examination must be taken within seven to forty days prior to the date of application for a license. The requirements are enforced by the refusal of the licensing officer to issue a license when a certificate is not presented. When the person who has had the disease later is able to present a certificate to show he no longer has it, he may secure a license. Most states provide for some exceptions, for instance, if the infected woman is pregnant. In a few such states the infected woman must undergo treatment after marriage. Since not all states require the certificate, a couple may evade the law in one state by traveling for their marriage to a state without the requirement.

When these laws were first passed, many people objected to the examination as a violation of their right of privacy in personal matters. However, the danger of one infected partner infecting the other is so great that public opinion has gradually moved to support the laws. Another danger is that a woman with venereal disease may infect her child before birth, in which case it requires special treatment for cure. Sometimes an infected child is born with some serious mental or physical defect. Venereal disease is not inherited. Its control lies in the hands of the man and woman who marry.

License

In most states, the couple desiring to marry must secure a license from a legally designated officer, usually the county clerk or a judge. The license becomes a matter of public record. Unless common-law marriages are permitted, a marriage ceremony must take place, with exchange of vows. In general, either a religious or a civil ceremony is sufficient; Maryland, West Virginia, and Delaware, however, require a religious ceremony.

Most states require witnesses to the marriage and also require that the marriage be recorded. The public record establishes the status of the man and woman as married people and is a later safeguard if husband or wife denies the marriage and disregards his or her obligations; it also protects the child against a charge of illegitimacy (unless the husband charges and proves that he is not the father). The license and the record of marriage remove marriage from the realm of purely personal and private relationships and make of it a socially responsible relationship.

Common-Law Marriage

Fifteen states recognize common-law marriages and enforce the rights and obligations of husband and wife in them. Common-law marriages are ones in which a marriage ceremony has not been performed and usually in which a license has not been secured. They were not recognized in the common law of England but are a vestige from our own past when on the frontier judge and minister were often miles distant or passed through a given community perhaps once a year on their circuits. Meanwhile men and women fell in love, set up a home, and perhaps had a child. Sometimes they were married when the opportunity came; but often they indefinitely postponed the ceremony, although they performed all the obligations of a married couple and established a loving and protective home for their children.

Nowadays there seems little excuse not to have a marriage in compliance with the laws. A common-law marriage is a weak marriage. The man may desert, claiming he was never married. Many complications and possibilities for fraud can arise when one of the couple dies and someone, perhaps fraudulently, appears, claiming to be a common-law spouse and demanding rights of inheritance. Legitimacy and inheritance rights of children may also be questioned if the parents have not been legally married. Many states, therefore, have passed laws invalidating common-law marriages, sometimes continuing to recognize those contracted before a specified date.

In states that still recognize common-law marriages, the requirements stated above for a license and ceremony are merely directive and their disregard does not make marriage (common-law) invalid.

Waiting Period

More than half the states require a waiting period of one to five days, usually between the time of applying for a license and its issuance. A few states place the waiting period between issuance of the license and the time of the marriage.

The waiting period is aimed at the prevention of elopements, marriages on the spur of the moment, or marriages by people who are intoxicated. The waiting period gives the couple time for a second thought about their plans; it does not permanently prevent anyone from marrying.

Rights and Responsibilities of Husband and Wife

The laws outlining rights and responsibilities of husbands and wives to each other and to their children are minimum requirements. A marriage which did not rise above these laws would be a very meager relationship. Nevertheless, some marriages do not rise—in fact, sink below —and therefore laws are necessary to define the lowest limits of marriage.

Personal Relations

On the personal side, each partner has the right to live with the other, to have normal sexual relations, and to have the other's love, society, and assistance. The husband is obligated to support his wife in a manner appropriate to his income, even though she may have property or income of her own. The wife is obligated to make a home for her husband without demanding to be paid by the husband. If the husband does not support his wife when he is able to do so, she may sue him in court in most states, or often she may use nonsupport as the grounds for a legal separation or divorce. The husband has the right to choose where the couple will live, but the wife has the right to a home of her own, under her management. Thus there is a balancing of rights and obligations between husband and wife in establishing and maintaining a home.

Property Adjustment

On the property side, the trend has been to give women greater freedom in control of their property. The common law of England and older laws in the United States specified that, at marriage, all the personal property that a woman had at the time of marriage passed to her husband, who could also take over ownership of bonds and corporate stock and could control her real estate. She could not enter into contracts and all her earnings belonged to her husband.

Under statutes passed by the various states, the married woman now retains ownership of all property, both real estate and personal, belonging to her at the time of her marriage. (Louisiana has a somewhat more restrictive law.) The wife also has broad powers in making contracts and in most states controls her earnings. In eight states (community-property states), husband and wife own everything jointly, regardless of who brought it to the marriage or who has earned or inherited it. Since most property and income originate with the husband, the wife acquires considerable authority through this joint ownership. The states differ in the details of the community-property law.

It may be pointed out that whereas formerly the wife was at a disadvantage, now the husband may be, since he may be required to support his wife regardless of her earnings. However, twelve states require that the wife support her husband out of her property if he has no separate or community property and is too infirm to support himself.

All women received increased economic security and status with the passage of the Civil Rights Act of 1964, which bans all types of discrimination in private employment involving interstate commerce, including discrimination on the basis of sex.

Parents and Children

Support of Children

Just as the husband is charged with the support of his wife, so is he responsible for the support of his minor children. Many states place a secondary responsibility on the wife for the support of children. Parents are required to send their children to school or otherwise educate them to the age of compulsory school attendance of the state. Children in turn are obligated to give service to their parents; a child's earnings legally belong to his parents.

These relationships of parent and child end when the child becomes of age or marries at a younger age or is conceded by the parents to be self-supporting. In some states, however, adult children are obligated to contribute to the support of indigent parents.

Illegitimate Children

An illegitimate child is one whose parents are not married to each other. The parents may not be married at the time of conception, but if they are married at the time of the child's birth, the child is legitimate. Several limited studies have shown that about 20 per cent of first babies born to married couples were conceived before the marriage. These children are legitimate. In twenty-two states, parents may also legitimatize their children by marrying after the birth of the child; in an additional ten states the husband must also acknowledge his parenthood. In a few states the child may be declared legitimate without marriage of the parents by the acknowledgement of the father that the child is his.

In general, the trend has been for a slow improvement in the status of an illegitimate child. Under early common law, an illegitimate child was considered no one's child and neither parent was held responsible for its support. Under present common law, the mother is held responsible since she is considered to have custody or care of the child; the father is not responsible for its support. However, in most states laws have been passed to compel the father to contribute to the support of his illegitimate child. However, if the mother has had sex relations with more than one man, she may not be sure who the father is. Men tend to deny paternity. Proof of paternity is therefore difficult to establish in court. Moreover, many women do not want to force the issue because of unfavorable publicity. Therefore, few fathers actually contribute to the support of illegitimate children and when they do, the amounts are small. Often the problem is solved by the mother agreeing to the adoption of the child.

Abortions

For many years, abortions were a criminal offense in all states, with the exception of abortions to preserve the life of the pregnant woman (and on occasion other exceptions). Such abortions were termed therapeutic to distinguish them from spontaneous abortions (usually called miscarriages) and from "criminal abortions," or those performed for reasons other than to save the woman's life. After much agitation, Colorado passed a law in 1968 making abortions legal whenever pregnancy results from incest or rape, threatens grave damage to the woman's physical or mental health, or is likely to result in the birth of a child with a severe mental or physical defect. A board is required to certify that one of these grounds exists. Other states have passed similar laws, and it seems probable that a trend has been established toward passage of similar or more liberalized laws permitting abortions on a number of grounds.

Ending a Marriage by Legal Means

There are two ways in which a marriage may be terminated by law and the husband and wife set free to marry someone else (or to remarry each other): annulment and divorce.

Annulment

By an annulment decree, a marriage is voided, that is, it is as though the marriage had never existed so far as property or other rights incident to the marriage are concerned. Annulment is granted when the marriage violated some law prohibiting marriage or when it was against some established public policy. Since annulment was not recognized by common law, it exists because of laws passed by the various states.

Almost every state has some provision for annulment. The most common grounds for annulment are as follows:

Nonage, that is one or both parties to the marriage are below the legal age, or parental consent has not been secured
Mental incapacity
Fraud or misrepresentation by one party

Degree of kinship makes marriage illegal

Use of force or threats

Physical incapacity to enter into the marriage relationship, such as impotence at the time of marriage

Interracial marriages

One party has an undivorced spouse still living (such marriages do not really exist but an annulment is often used to clear the record)

Annulments are not granted automatically. Either one party to the marriage or, in the case of nonage, the parents or guardian must bring a suit in court asking to have the marriage annulled. If the couple have lived together for some time or have children the judge may be reluctant to grant an annulment even though technically a cause for annulment exists. Since the marriage is wiped out, children become illegitimate. Recognizing the unfairness of this status, most states provide by law for legitimatization of children and Georgia and New Jersey will not annul a marriage when a child has been born or is likely to be born.

Divorce

Divorce is a legal termination of a valid marriage. At the time of the American Revolution, English common law did not include divorce, which could be granted only by an Act of Parliament in special cases. In the United States, divorce was granted at first only by a special act of a state legislature for each divorce. Gradually, however, laws were passed providing for divorces and setting up the grounds that would justify a divorce. All states now grant divorces, although provisions differ from state to state. The table of Divorce Laws, which follows this article, gives many of the details.

State laws vary greatly on the grounds for divorce. The only ground recognized by all states is adultery. Other very common grounds are cruelty, desertion, alcoholism, impotency, neglect to provide support, conviction of a felony or imprisonment, and insanity. Many other grounds are included by some states. People who live in states with few grounds for divorce are not deterred from terminating their marriages. They may sometimes find some cause for annulment, falsely claim some legal ground, or move temporarily to a state with more liberal laws and a short period of required residence before a divorce suit may be filed. States with short period of required residence are Idaho and Nevada (42 days), Arkansas and Wyoming (60 days), and Utah (90 days).

Many states require a period of time to elapse between the granting of a divorce and remarriage. But in many other states a new marriage may follow immediately after the divorce.

The high rate of divorce has caused many people to feel that laws are constantly becoming more lenient. Actually, divorce laws change slowly. The attitude toward divorce, however, has changed radically in the past fifty years. It is no longer regarded as the disgrace it was once felt to be and the divorced person is no longer doomed to a single life. In fact, by far the majority of divorced persons remarry.

Although law is not involved, the stand of the Catholic Church should be noted. This Church has maintained a firm stand against divorce. A Catholic who secures a divorce is no longer considered a member of the Church. Under certain limited conditions, a Catholic may secure a church annulment to his marriage. This annulment is distinct from the legal annulment discussed above and must be followed by a civil or legal annulment or divorce in order to terminate the marriage.

Women usually file suit for divorce. Men are not necessarily responsible for creating the grounds that justify a divorce, but it has become a custom or perhaps a matter of courtesy for the wife to bring suit. The husband is thus presented to the public as the "guilty" party, the wife as "innocent" of wrongdoing.

Divorce frees husband and wife from many of their obligations and destroys many of their rights. Sexual relations, common habitation, and mutual care and companionship granted by marriage can no longer be expected or claimed. However, not all obligations are destroyed.

The husband's obligation to support his wife remains, subject to adjustment by the court which grants the divorce decree. This payment to the wife is called alimony. It was originally justified by the fact that married women did not earn money or what they earned became the property of the husband. They were thus dependent upon the husband for support after divorce as well as before. Nowadays the feeling is growing that alimony is justified chiefly when the divorced wife will be occupied with the care of small children or is unable to earn a suitable living because of age, lack of training, or illness, or has become accustomed in marriage to a standard of living that she cannot maintain by her own efforts. If the wife receives alimony and remarries, her former husband is no longer liable for her support. If property has been accumulated, some division must be made of it also. Since most divorces are granted in the early years of marriage, usually there is not a large accumulation of property.

The husband also retains his obligation for the financial support of his children. Many complications arise as the attempt is made to stretch the father's salary to cover the needs of his children and former wife in one household and also his needs in another household, especially if he remarries. A second marriage for his former wife does not relieve him of the support of his children.

Legal Separations

Without formality husband and wife may separate and renew marriage at will. But state laws also provide for various types of separation in which husband or wife applies for some form of legal separation and a defining of responsibilities. Usually the court decides upon the amount of alimony and child-support to be paid and upon the custody of any children. The couple do not thereafter live together and cannot make personal demands on each other. They are not free, however, to marry anyone else. They are neither completely married nor completely free. These arrangements are often made by people who find it intolerable to continue living as husband and wife but who do not believe in divorce. If they wish to renew their marriage to each other, they often must ask the court to dispose of the legal separation arrangement.

Custody of Children

Even in divorce, children remain the responsibility of both parents. The judge must arrange for the support of the children, with the heavier part of the burden usually falling upon the father.

Arrangements must also be made for the actual daily care of the children. Since the father is usually employed and the mother already accustomed to the major care of the children, the children are usually placed in the custody of the mother. An exception comes when the mother is clearly unfit to be in charge of the children. Usually the parent who does not have custody of the children has specified visiting privileges. The policy of having the child live some portion of the year with one parent and the remainder with the other is often criticized as placing too great a burden on the child in making a complete transition several times a year in home, parents, school, and friends.

34. MARRIAGE AND DIVORCE LAWS

§ The carefully prepared tables on marriage and divorce laws are included for ready reference by the reader who wishes to learn at a glance the general tenor of these laws across the United States, or who wishes to know the laws of a specific state.

SOURCE: Women's Bureau, U. S. Department of Labor.

Marriage Laws as of July 1, 1965

State or other jurisdiction	AGE AT WHICH MARRIAGE CAN BE CONTRACTED WITH PARENTAL CONSENT		AGE BELOW WHICH PARENTAL CONSENT IS REQUIRED		Common-law marriage recognized	PHYSICAL EXAMINATION AND BLOOD TEST FOR MALE AND FEMALE		WAITING PERIOD	
	Male	Female	Male	Female		Maximum period between examination and issuance of marriage license	Scope of medical examination	Before issuance of license	After issuance of license
Alabama	17(a)	14(a)	21	18	★	30 da.	(b)	.....	.....
Alaska	18(c)	16(c)	21	18	.....	30 da.	(b)	3 da.	.....
Arizona	18(c)	16(c)	21	18	.....	30 da.	(b)	.....	.....
Arkansas	18(c)	16(c)	21	18	.....	30 da.	(b)	3 da.	.....
California	18(a,d)	16(a,d)	21	18	.....	30 da.	(b)	.....	.....
Colorado	16(d)	16(d)	21	18	★	30 da.	(b)	.....	.....
Connecticut	16(d)	16(d)	21	21	.....	40 da.	(b)	4 da.	(e)
Delaware	18(c)	16(c)	21	18	.....	30 da.	(b)	.....	.....
Florida	18(a,c)	16(a,c)	21	21	★	30 da.	(b)	3 da.	.....
Georgia	18(c,f)	16(c,f)	19	19	★★	30 da.	(b)	3 da.(g)	.....
Hawaii	18	16(d)	20	20	.....	30 da.	(b)	3 da.	.....
Idaho	15	15(d)	18	18	★	30 da.	(b)	.....	.....
Illinois	18	16	21	18	.....	15 da.	(b)	3 da.	.....
Indiana	18(c)	16(c)	21	18	.....	30 da.	(b)	3 da.	.....
Iowa	18(c)	16(c)	21	18	★★	20 da.	(b)	3 da.	.....
Kansas	18(d)	16(d)	21	18	★★	30 da.	(b,h)	3 da.	.....
Kentucky	18(a,c)	16(a,c)	21	21	.....	15 da.	(b)	3 da.	.....
Louisiana	18(d)	16(d)	21	21	.....	10 da.	(b)	.....	72 hrs.
Maine	16(d)	16(d)	21	18	.....	30 da.	(b)	5 da.	.....
Maryland	18(c)	16(c)	21	18	.....	.....	.....	48 hrs.	.....

Marriage Laws as of July 1, 1965 (continued)

State or other jurisdiction	AGE AT WHICH MARRIAGE CAN BE CONTRACTED WITH PARENTAL CONSENT		AGE BELOW WHICH PARENTAL CONSENT IS REQUIRED		Common-law marriage recognized	PHYSICAL EXAMINATION AND BLOOD TEST FOR MALE AND FEMALE		WAITING PERIOD	
	Male	Female	Male	Female		Maximum period between examination and issuance of marriage license	Scope of medical examination	Before issuance of license	After issuance of license
Massachusetts	18(d)	16(d)	21	18	.....	30 da.	(b)	3 da.	.....
Michigan	(i)	16(c)	18	18	.....	30 da.	(b)	3 da.	.....
Minnesota	18(a)	16(i)	21	18	.....	.....	.....	5 da.	.....
Mississippi	17(d)	15(d)	21	21	.....	30 da.	.....	3 da.	.....
Missouri	15(d)	15(d)	21	18	.....	15 da.	(b)	3 da.	.....
Montana	18(d)	16(d)	21	18	★	20 da.	(b)	5 da.	.....
Nebraska	18(c)	16(c)	21	21	.....	30 da.	(b)	.....	.....
Nevada	18(a,d)	16(a,d)	21	18	.....	.....	(b)	.....	.....
New Hampshire	(k)	(k)	20	18	.....	30 da.	(b)	5 da.	.....
New Jersey	18(d)	16(d)	21	18	.....	30 da.	(b)	72 hrs.	.....
New Mexico	18(c)	16(c)	21	18	.....	30 da.	(b)	.....	.....
New York	16	16(d)	21	18	.....	30 da.	(b)	(n)	24 hrs.(l)
North Carolina	16	16(c)	18	18	.....	30 da.	(m)	.....	.....
North Dakota	18	15	21	18	.....	30 da.	(o)	.....	.....
Ohio	18(c)	16(c)	21	21	★	30 da.	(b)	5 da.	.....
Oklahoma	18(c)	15(c)	21	18	★	30 da.	(b)	72 hrs.(p)	.....
Oregon	18(i)	15(i)	21	18	.....	30 da.(q)	(r)	7 da.	.....
Pennsylvania	16(d)	16(d)	21	21	★	30 da.	(b)	3 da.	.....
Rhode Island	18(d)	16(d)	21	21	★	40 da.	(s)	.....	(t)

State	Age, male (with consent)	Age, female (with consent)	Age, male (without consent)	Age, female (without consent)	Common-law	Wait before license	Blood test note	Wait after license	
South Carolina	16(c)	14(c)	18	18	★	.....	.....	24 hrs.	.....
South Dakota	18(c)	16(c)	21	18	.....	20 da.	(b)	.....	.....
Tennessee	16(d)	16(d)	21	21	.....	30 da.	(b)	3 da.(u)	.....
Texas	16	14	21	18	★	15 da.	(b)	3 da.(p)	.....
Utah	16(a)	14(a)	21	18	.....	30 da.	(b)	.....	5 da.
Vermont	18(d)	16(d)	21	18	.....	30 da.	(b)	.....	.....
Virginia	18(a,c)	16(a,c)	21	21	.....	.....	(b)	.....	.....
Washington	17(d)	17(d)	21	18	.....	30 da.	(o)	3 da.	.....
West Virginia	18(a)	16(a)	21	21	.....	30 da.	(b)	3 da.	.....
Wisconsin	18	16	21	18	.....	20 da.	(b)	5 da.	.....
Wyoming	18	16	21	21	★	30 da.	(b)	.....	.....
Dist. of Columbia	18(a)	16(a)	21	18	.....	.....	.....	3 da.	.....

(★) Indicates common-law marriage recognized.

(a) Parental consent not required if minor was previously married.

(b) Venereal diseases.

(c) Statute establishes procedure whereby younger parties may obtain license in case of pregnancy or birth of a child.

(d) Statute establishes procedure whereby younger parties may obtain license in special circumstances.

(e) Residents, 24 hours; nonresidents, 96 hours.

(f) If parties are under 19 years of age, proof of age, and the consent of parents in person required. If a parent is ill, an affidavit by the incapacitated parent and a physician's affidavit to that effect required.

(g) Unless parties are 21 years of age or more, or female is pregnant, or applicants are the parents of a living child born out of wedlock.

(h) Feeblemindedness.

(i) No provision in law for parental consent for males.

(j) Parental consent and permission of judge required. In Oregon, permission of judge required for male under 19 years of age or female under 17.

(k) Below age of consent parties need parental consent and permission of judge.

(l) Marriage may not be solemnized within 3 days from date on which specimen for serological test was taken.

(m) Uncontrolled epileptic attacks, idiocy, imbecility, mental defectiveness, unsound mind, infectious tuberculosis, and venereal diseases.

(n) Forty-eight hours if both are nonresidents of Pamlico county.

(o) Feeblemindedness, imbecility, insanity, chronic alcoholism, and venereal diseases. In Washington, also advanced tuberculosis and, if male, contagious venereal disease.

(p) If one or both parties are below the age for marriage without parental consent.

(q) Time limit between date of examination and expiration of marriage license.

(r) Venereal diseases, feeblemindedness, mental illness, drug addiction, and chronic alcoholism.

(s) Infectious tuberculosis and venereal diseases.

(t) If female is nonresident, must complete and sign license 5 days prior to marriage.

(u) Unless parties are over 21 years of age.

Divorce Laws as of July 1, 1966

State or other jurisdiction	Residence required before filing suit for divorce	GROUNDS FOR ABSOLUTE DIVORCE				
		Adultery	Mental and/or physical cruelty	Desertion	Alcoholism	Impotency
Alabama	(a)	*	*	1 yr.	*	*
Alaska	1 yr.	*	*	1 yr.	*	*
Arizona	1 yr.	*	*	1 yr.	*	*
Arkansas	2 mos.	*	*	1 yr.	*	*
California	1 yr.	*	*	1 yr.	*	..
Colorado	1 yr.(j)	*	*	1 yr.	*	*
Connecticut	3 yrs.(j)	*	*	3 yrs.	*	..
Delaware	2 yrs.(j)	*	*	2 yrs.	*	..
Florida	6 mos.	*	*	1 yr.	*	*
Georgia	6 mos.	*	*	1 yr.	*	*
Hawaii	2 yrs.	*	*	6 mos.	*	..
Idaho	6 wks.	*	*	1 yr.	*	..
Illinois	1 yr.(j)	*	*	1 yr.	*	*
Indiana	1 yr.(t)	*	*	2 yrs.	*	*
Iowa	1 yr.	*	*	2 yrs.	*	..
Kansas	1 yr.(w)	*	*	1 yr.	*	..
Kentucky	1 yr.	*	*	1 yr.	*(x)	*
Louisiana	(aa)	*	..	......	..	..
Maine	6 mos.(j)	*	*	3 yrs.	*	*
Maryland	1 yr.(ad)	*	..	18 mos.	..	..
Massachusetts	5 yrs.(j)	*	*	3 yrs.	*	*
Michigan	1 yr.(j)	*	*	2 yrs.	*	*
Minnesota	1 yr.(j)	*	*	1 yr.	*	*
Mississippi	1 yr.	*	*	1 yr.	*	*
Missouri	1 yr.(j)	*	*	1 yr.	*	*
Montana	1 yr.	*	*	1 yr.	*	..
Nebraska	2 yrs.(j)	*	*	2 yrs.	*	*
Nevada	6 wks.(j)	*	*	1 yr.	*	..
New Hampshire	1 yr.(j)	*	*	2 yrs.	*	*
New Jersey	2 yrs.(j)	*	*	2 yrs.	..	..
New Mexico	1 yr.	*	*	*	*	*
New York	1 yr.	*	*	2 yrs.	..	..
North Carolina	6 mos.	*	..	......	..	*
North Dakota	1 yr.(t)	*	*	1 yr.	*	..
Ohio	1 yr.	*	*	......	*	*
Oklahoma	6 mos.(w)	*	*	1 yr.	*	*
Oregon	1 yr.	*	*	1 yr.	*	*
Pennsylvania	1 yr.	*	*	2 yrs.	..	*
Rhode Island	2 yrs.	*	*	5 yrs.(al)	*	*
South Carolina	1 yr.	*	*	1 yr.	*	..
South Dakota	1 yr.(j)	*	*	1 yr.	*	..
Tennessee	1 yr.	*	*	1 yr.	*	*
Texas	12 mos.	*	*	3 yrs.	..	..
Utah	3 mos.	*	*	1 yr.	*	*
Vermont	6 mos.(ar)	*	..	3 yrs.	..	..
Virginia	1 yr.	*	..	1 yr.	..	*
Washington	1 yr.	*	*	1 yr.	*	*
West Virginia	2 yrs.(j)	*	*	1 yr.	*	..
Wisconsin	2 yrs.	*	*	1 yr.	*	..
Wyoming	60 days(j)	*	*	1 yr.	*	*
Dist. of Columbia	1 yr.	*	..	1 yr.	..	..

(*) Indicates ground for absolute divorce.
(a) No specific period, except 1 year when ground is desertion or defendant is nonresident or 2 years if wife sues husband for nonsupport.
(b) To wife, living separate and apart from husband, as resident of the State for 2 years before suit and without support from him during such time.
(c) May be enlarged into an absolute divorce after expiration of 4 years; in Connecticut, any time after decree of separation; Hawaii, 2 years after decree for separate maintenance or from bed and board; Michigan, 5 years after decree of limited divorce.
(d) Crime against nature.
(e) Except to each other.
(f) Incompatibility.
(g) Crime before marriage.
(h) Also to husband in certain circumstances.
(i) Final decree is not entered until 1 year after interlocutory decree.
(j) Under certain circumstances a lesser period of time may be required.
(k) Female under 16, male under 18, if complaining party under age of consent at time of marriage has not confirmed the marriage after reaching such age.
(l) In the discretion of the court.
(m) Habitual violent and ungovernable temper.
(n) Defendant obtained divorce from plaintiff in another State.
(o) Relationship within prohibited degrees.
(p) Mental incapacity.
(q) Under decree of separate maintenance.
(r) Loathsome disease.
(s) Attempt on the life of the spouse by poison or other means showing malice.

GROUNDS FOR ABSOLUTE DIVORCE

Non-support	Insanity	Pregnancy at marriage	Bigamy	Separation or absence	Felony conviction or imprisonment	Drug addiction	Fraud, force or duress
*(b)	5 yrs.	*	..	......	*	*	..
*	18 mos.	..	..	......	*	*	..
......	......	*	..	5 yrs.	*	..	..
*(h)	3 yrs.	..	*	3 yrs.	*	..	..
*	3 yrs.	..	..	......	*	..	..
*	3 yrs.	..	..	3 yrs.	*	*	..
..	5 yrs.	..	..	7 yrs.	*	..	..
*	5 yrs.	..	*	3 yrs.	*	..	..
..	......	..	*	......	..	*	..
..	2 yrs.	*	..	......	..	..	*
*	3 yrs.	..	..	2 yrs.(q)	*	*	..
*	6 yrs.	..	..	5 yrs.	*	..	..
..	......	..	*	......	*	..	..
*	5 yrs.	..	..	......	*	..	..
..	......	*(v)	..	......	*	..	..
*	5 yrs.	..	..	......	*	..	..
..	5 yrs.	*	..	5 yrs.	*	..	*
..	......	..	..	2 yrs.	*	..	..
*	3 yrs.	..	..	18 mos.	*	..	..
*	......	..	..	......	*	*	..
*	......	..	..	......	*	..	..
..	5 yrs.	..	..	2 yrs.(q)	*	..	..
..	3 yrs.	*	*	......	*	*	..
*	......	..	..	......	*	..	..
*	5 yrs.	..	..	......	*	..	..
*	5 yrs.	..	..	......	*	..	..
*	2 yrs.	..	..	3 yrs.	*	..	..
..	......	..	..	2 yrs.	*	..	..
*	5 yrs.	*	..	......	*	..	..
..	......	..	..	2 yrs.(q)	*	..	..
*	5 yrs.	*	..	1 yr.	*	..	..
*(h)	5 yrs.	..	*	......	*	*	..
*	5 yrs.	*	..	1 yr.	*	..	*
..	2 yrs.	..	..	......	*	..	*
*	......	..	*	......	*	..	*
*	......	..	..	10 yrs.	..	*	..
*	5 yrs.	..	..	......	*	..	..
*	......	*	*	2 yrs.(ap)	*	..	..
..	5 yrs.	..	..	7 yrs.	*	..	..
*	*	..	..	3 yrs.(q)	*	..	..
*	5 yrs.	..	..	3 yrs.	*	..	..
..	......	*	..	2 yrs.	*	..	*
*	2 yrs.	..	..	2 yrs.	*	..	..
*	......	..	..	......	*	*	..
*	......	..	..	5 yrs.	*	..	..
*	2 yrs.	*	..	2 yrs.	*	..	..
..	......	..	..	1 yr.	*	..	..

(t) Five years if on ground of insanity.
(u) Two years where service on defendant is only by publication.
(v) Unless at time of marriage husband had an illegitimate child living, which fact was not known to wife.
(w) Five years if on ground of insanity and insane spouse is in out-of-State institution.
(x) If on part of the husband, accompanied by wasting of husband's estate to the detriment of the wife and children.
(y) Joining religious sect disbelieving in marriage.
(z) Unchaste behavior on part of wife after marriage.
(aa) No statutory requirement for adultery or felony conviction; 2 years when ground is separation.
(ab) Limited divorce may be enlarged into absolute divorce after 6 months for the party who obtained the limited divorce and after nine months for the other spouse.
(ac) When divorce is granted on ground of adultery, guilty party cannot marry the accomplice in adultery during lifetime of former spouse.
(ad) No specific period required, except 1 year if cause occurred out of State and 2 years if on ground of insanity.
(ae) Any cause which renders marriage null and void from the beginning.
(af) Not more than 2 years in court's discretion.
(ag) When divorce is granted on ground of adultery, court may prohibit remarriage. After 1 year, court may remove disability upon satisfactory evidence of reformation.
(ah) Husband a vagrant.
(ai) Wife's absence out of State for 10 years without husband's consent.
(aj) When husband is entitled to a divorce and alimony or child support from husband is granted, the decree may be delayed until security is entered for payment.

Divorce Laws as of July 1, 1966 (continued)

	GROUNDS FOR ABSOLUTE DIVORCE			PERIOD BEFORE PARTIES MAY REMARRY AFTER FINAL DECREE	
	Infamous crime	Prior decree of limited divorce	Other	Plaintiff	Defendant
Alabama	..	(c)	(d)	60 days (e)	60 days(e)
Alaska	..	..	(f)	....	....
Arizona	*	..	(g)	1 yr.	1 yr.
Arkansas	*	..	......		
California	..	..	......	(i)	(i)
Colorado	..	..			
Connecticut	*	(c)	......	....	....
Delaware	..	..	(k)	3 mos.(l)	3 mos.(l)
Florida	..	..	(m,n,o)	....	....
Georgia	..	..	(o,p)	(l)	(l)
Hawaii	..	(c)	......	(i)	(i)
Idaho	..	..			
Illinois	*	..	(r,s)		
Indiana	*	..	......	(u)	....
Iowa	..	..	......	1 yr.(e,l)	1 yr.(e,l)
Kansas	..	..	......	60 days	60 days
Kentucky	..	..	(r,y,z)		
Louisiana	..	(ab)	......	wife, 10 mos.	wife, 10 mos.(ac)
Maine	..	..			
Maryland	..	..	(ae)	....	....
Massachusetts	..	..	......		
Michigan	..	..	(n)	....	(af)
Minnesota	..	(c)	......	6 mos.	6 mos.
Mississippi	..	..	(o,p)	....	(ag)
Missouri	*	..	(g,ah)		
Montana	..	..	......	6 mos.	6 mos.
Nebraska	..	..	......	6 mos.	6 mos.
Nevada	*	..	......	....	....
New Hampshire	..	..	(y,ai)		
New Jersey	..	..	......	3 mos.(l)	3 mos.(l)
New Mexico	..	..	(f)	....	....
New York	..	..			
North Carolina	..	..	(d)		
North Dakota	..	(c)	......	(l)	(l)
Ohio	..	..	(n)	(aj)	....
Oklahoma	..	..	(f,n)	6 mos.	6 mos.
Oregon	..	..	......	6 mos.	6 mos.
Pennsylvania	..	..	(o,ak)	....	(ac)
Rhode Island	..	..	(am,an)	6 mos.	6 mos.
South Carolina	..	..	......		
South Dakota	..	..	......	....	(ao)
Tennessee	*	..	(s,ak)	....	(ac)
Texas	..	..	......	(aq)	(aq)
Utah	..	..	......	3 mos.(l)	3 mos.(l)
Vermont	..	..	(as)	6 mos.(l)	2 yrs.(l)
Virginia	*	(at)	(d,au)	(av)	(av)
Washington	..	..	(aw)	6 mos.	6 mos.
West Virginia	..	..	......	60 days	60 days(ax)
Wisconsin	..	(ay)	......	1 yr.	1 yr.
Wyoming	*	..	(g,ah)	....	....
Dist. of Columbia	..	(az)	......	6 mos.	6 mos.

(ak) Incapable of procreation.
(al) Or a lesser time in court's discretion.
(am) Void or voidable marriage.
(an) Gross misbehavior or wickedness; loss of citizenship rights of one party due to crime; presumption of death.
(ao) When divorce is for adultery, guilty party cannot remarry except to the innocent person, until the death of the other.
(ap) To husband for wife's refusal to move with him to this State without reasonable cause, and willfully absenting herself from him for 2 years.
(aq) When divorce is granted on ground of cruelty, neither party may remarry for 12 months except to each other.
(ar) One year before final hearing, and 2 years if on ground of insanity.
(as) Intolerable severity.
(at) A limited divorce granted on the ground of cruelty or desertion may be merged with an absolute divorce after 1 year.
(au) Wife a prostitute prior to marriage.
(av) When divorce is granted on ground of adultery, court may decree the guilty party cannot remarry. After 6 months the court may remove disability for good cause. Remarriage of either party forbidden pending appeal.
(aw) Want of legal age or sufficient understanding.
(ax) In court's discretion, guilty party may be prohibited from remarrying for a period not to exceed 1 year.
(ay) Living entirely apart for 5 years pursuant to a judgment of legal separation.
(az) Limited divorce may be enlarged into absolute divorce after 1 year. Also, absolute divorce may be granted for any cause arising after a divorce from bed and board, sufficient to entitle complaining party to an absolute divorce.

Chapter 12: Adjustment between Husband and Wife

35. RECIPROCAL INTERDEPENDENCE
Robert O. Blood, Jr., and Donald M. Wolfe

§ In order to test and clarify time-worn assumptions about who decides and who does what in the American family, the authors interviewed 731 city wives and 178 farm wives living in Metropolitan Detroit, selected to give a cross-section sample. From the book-length report, summaries of four chapters are reprinted here that point up how husband and wife specialize in certain tasks and share others in decision-making, economic functions, companionship, and mental hygiene functions.

The Power to Make Decisions

The power to make decisions stems primarily from the resources which the individual can provide to meet the needs of his marriage partner and to upgrade his decision-making skill. Because it is based on such tangible and relevant criteria, the balance of power may be said to be adapted to the interpersonal relationship of the two partners involved.

Contemporary married couples are freed from the "dead hand" of patriarchal tradition to work out their own destiny in the way best suited to them. This does not mean that they can work out their decision-making pattern in any fashion whatever, but that they are not bound by any "cake of custom" which arbitrarily installs one sex in power.

SOURCE: Robert O. Blood, Jr., and Donald M. Wolfe, *Husbands and Wives: The Dynamics of Married Living* (New York: Free Press, 1960), pp. 44–46, 113–14, 172–74, 218–20. Reprinted by permission of the publisher and the authors.

Robert O. Blood, Jr., whose doctorate is from the University of North Carolina, is on the faculty of Pendel Hill, Wallingford, Pa. He is the author of *Marriage*, a textbook, *Love Match and Arranged Marriage: A Tokyo-Detroit Comparison*, and numerous articles.

Donald M. Wolfe received his doctorate from the University of Michigan and teaches at Case Institute of Technology. He is the author of several articles dealing with the family.

Whereas in the past, custom often dictated that all families should be patriarchal, today the rise of women produces considerable variation between families (and even within families with the passage of time). With less sex-linked cultural norms, such variation incurs less penalty than it once would have. Indeed, the emerging norm may not be a particular pattern of male-dominance or equalitarianism but, rather, the idea of appropriateness. If a wife is working today, it is appropriate that she should have more voice in decisions, rather than be subjugated to an arbitrary standard.

Only at the wife-dominant extreme is there evidence of deviance from the norm today. It may be appropriate for the wife who is the sole support of her family to make most of the decisions, but it certainly is not normal for the marital roles to be reversed in this way. We will find throughout this study dissatisfaction associated with wife-dominance. This is not, however, simply a reflection of breaking social rules. Rather, the circumstances which lead to the wife's dominance involve corresponding inadequacies and incompetencies on the husband's part. An inadequate husband is by definition unable to make a satisfactory marriage partner. So the dominant wife is not exultant over her "victory," but exercises power regretfully by default of her "no good" or incapacitated husband.

Within the range from husband-dominance to extreme equalitarianism, appropriateness appears to be linked with satisfaction. A wife who doesn't get to make many decisions does get to have her needs met by a resourceful husband and the husband who "has to" share his power with his wife has the compensation of her greater contributions to the marriage.

Under these circumstances, power in American marriages is not a matter of brute coercion and unwilling defeat so much as a mutual recognition of individual skills in particular areas of competence and of the partners' dual stake in areas of joint concern. Given such a natural working out of particular decisions under varying circumstances, it is no wonder that most wives cannot say *why* they make decisions at home the way they do. All they are aware of is that somehow their balance of power "just growed" and that it is right.

Only when American marriages are looked at *en masse* is it clear why power is patterned the way it is—and why it seems right to the couples involved. The answer lies in the tangible resources and skills which the two partners pool in marriage. Today's marriages have a variable balance of power which is not determined by the assignment of authority to one sex, but by the interplay of dynamic forces which affect the marriage from within and without.

·   ·   ·   ·   ·

The Economic Function

The economic function in today's urban marriages differs sharply from what it still does on contemporary farms and what it once did in the average American family. Moving off the land has separated the work place from the family residence. As a result, the city family cannot function as an economic team except in those few families which operate a family business. By and large, the economic system has been divorced from the family system with remarkable thoroughness.

As a result, the economic function of the family depends primarily on the efforts of the husband who goes out of the family to participate in the economic system. His occupational success determines the economic resources available to the family. Whether the wife is satisfied with these resources depends, however, on how they compare with her frame of reference. Despite the "leveling-up" influence of the mass media and modern advertising, special family origins or ethnic communities can provide higher than average norms resulting in dissatisfaction with even substantial economic resources.

A dissatisfied wife has two main alternatives. She can put pressure on her husband to do better—but if he hasn't got what it takes, that won't do much good. Or she can go to work herself. If family finances had been strained to a great extent, her work may increase the family income so much that everybody feels better. If not, her work may only irritate the husband and strain the marriage. At the beginning of marriage, however, work is taken for granted by most wives—so great is the need for getting off to a good financial start, and so unnecessary the wife's remaining at home when there are no children. Later in life, after the children grow up, re-employment is more optional for the wife, an option which more and more women are taking up.

Quite unimportant, today, is the production of goods at home like grandmother used to make—so unimportant that home production has hardly any economic meaning today and is largely an art instead. It, too, is optional.

More significant, however, for the wife who stays home is her attitude toward her husband's work. Few men start out at the peak of their careers and almost every young bride hopes her man will progress beyond his starting job or pay. As time goes on and those hopes are fulfilled or proven empty, her feeling for him changes correspondingly. Either he comes to be appreciated all the more for his achievements in life, or he is resented a bit for disappointing her. In any case, the relationship between the husband and the wife is affected by the way he plays his economic role. If he plays it well, the economic function is a source of strength to the marriage, with the wife an applauding audience to her husband's performance. If he plays it badly, he retires in disgrace behind a curtain of silence and she turns her attention to her own role in life.

The economic function of the family is therefore primarily the husband's function. Even when the wife works, the reasons why she works and the relative permanence of her work reflects his career. He is the one whose main job and permanent job it is to provide for the economic needs of the family. Her job uniquely is to bear the children. . . .

. . . . .

Companionship between Husbands and Wives

Companionship has emerged as the most valued aspect of American marriage today. In this sense, the family has undergone a transition "from institution to companionship." But what is meant by companionship is not necessarily what sometimes comes to mind. The primary emphasis is on companionship in leisure-time activities, not on merging every aspect of married life. In this respect, a wife can be enthusiastic about companionship even though she stays home while her husband goes to work, does most of the housework without his help, and in general plays a quite different role in life. In other words men and women don't have to be identical in order to have a good time together.

On the other hand, couples must take time to do things together if companionship is to exist. Such time is short if the husband works overtime, if he is obsessed with getting ahead in life, and if the wife is tied down with a large number of children.

Just having time available to spend is not enough. The enjoyment of leisure is heightened by education which may enlarge one's sphere of appreciation in life. Similarity in education provides the two partners with a common outlook on life, and common tastes for leisure-time activities. Similarity in religion furnishes an important leisure-time activity in itself—going to church together. Moreover, most churches are the focus of a host of auxiliary activities which provide companionship to joint members which is lacking in interfaith marriages.

Even with similar tastes and common backgrounds, however, companionship is not universal. Primarily it is characteristic of young couples, but even more so of newlyweds, regardless of age. This may be because companionship in marriage carries over from premarital dating. Indeed, Englishmen sometimes refer to marital companionship itself as dating, though the term sounds a bit strange to American ears. Couples discover each other through dating and look forward to the sense of mutual acceptance and response gained in dating situations. Their appreciation of each other's company reaches a peak in the honeymoon— a time of pure companionship. In subsequent years, satisfaction declines as the two partners come to take each other for granted, to deplete the stock of new experiences which they can share together, to find companionship vicariously in children repeating the cycle of romance—or even less directly in TV.

The ebb tide of companionship can be reversed in second honeymoons when the kids depart, and in second honeymoons when people remarry. This is one reason why some couples divorce—because leisure together has lost its kick—and why second marriages, too, sometimes end in boredom.

However, these are tendencies, not iron laws. As life's end approaches, one wife in four is still enthusiastic about the companionship she finds in marriage and a second is still quite satisfied. For the individual couple, companionship doesn't have to lose its savor. But for American marriages as a whole, the trend is unmistakable: during the childbearing years, husbands and wives often cease doing things together, and grow apart from each other. When they are left with only each other again for company, their losses are only partially recouped. For many couples, the estrangement is permanent and the second opportunity comes too late to catch fire. Such couples live the later years as relative strangers under the same roof, searching elsewhere for companionship or resigned to a life of increasing loneliness.

This is the loneliness that marriage is designed to prevent. This is the need that companionship is supposed to meet. Companionship is above all what marriage is supposed to provide—but the wedding ceremony does not guarantee it. Companionship is available for the taking—for all except the most badly mismatched couples. But companionship requires taking time and making a little effort. Most couples do—but not all.

. . . . .

The Mental-Hygiene Function in Marriage

Companionship may wane and love may wither but the typical American wife can count on more lasting understanding from her husband. The passing years sap the energy which joint activities require and calm the fires of passionate love—but sheer living together provides the basic condition for understanding another person. The longer a man lives with a woman, the greater his accumulated store of memories of how she behaves, what upsets her, and what will make her feel better. The wisdom of experience enables him to read her facial expressions more accurately, to sense her silences, to interpret her sighs. Hearing her troubles becomes less necessary, since he can read her thoughts without words.

Similarly for the wife, the sense of being understood and accepted depends less and less on words—though words never become completely superfluous. As long as the wife faces the same problems, the memory of previous sympathy from her husband is reassuring. New problems require fresh feedback, however, to be sure the ego still has its partner. Especially is this true when new problems involve the ego's vehicle—the human body. When that vehicle begins to show signs of wear and tear, the threat to the ego is acute. Old cars are junked—why not old wives? The fact that some American wives *are* replaced with newer models heightens the anxiety. Fortunately for the wife, most are not. Fortunate, because there is no companion for the older years who compares with an equally aging one.

Second wives in polygynous societies may renew the old man's sex life and rejuvenate the female work force. But it is hard for the young to empathize with the problems of the old. Old men and old women need each other for mutual understanding and that companionship of the spirit which revives the drooping ego.

Old people are not the only ones with problems. Life always has its downs as well as its ups. Young wives quite rightly tell their troubles often to their husbands, for they are news to him and help him get acquainted with her. As time goes on, most wives become more selective and many cease sharing their burdens altogether.

It seems doubtful that complete withholding can ever be considered therapeutic. Where silence is prolonged, it usually signifies failure for this aspect of marriage. Selectivity, on the other hand, seems to be the mark of maturity. A mature wife is able not only to consider her need for therapy but to predict her husband's ability to give it. If he seems depressed or preoccupied with other things, it may be wise to leave him alone. More than that, a mature wife considers not only her own needs but his, and not only his needs but his responsibilities elsewhere. If he has important duties outside the family, they deserve to be balanced against the wife's problems. High-status men have more taxing outside responsibilities and high-status women tend to have the ability—learned in childhood and perfected in marital interaction—to refrain from telling all their troubles, waiting instead until their gain will exceed the price asked of the husband.

Once the wife has revealed her need, the husband's responsibility is to do whatever he can to meet it. How much time he can devote to ego repair depends on the other pressures he is under. The least he can do— if his own emotional resources are adequate—is to listen sympathetically to her statement of the problem. Better yet, he can discuss it with her, help her find new insights, communicate to her the knowledge that he still loves and respects her. Most effective of all is taking time to solve the problem, contributing his own strength to make up for her deficiencies. Then he really makes his marriage work to the best of his ability.

If he is inadequate in other respects, however, the chances are he won't be much of an ego-repairman either. Men whose egos are incapacitated may be familiar with the feelings afflicting the wife but too wrapped up in their own problems to be able to say so. Just as psychiatrists need to be freed of their own problems through didactic analysis, husbands must have emotional resources of their own to be able to respond therapeutically to their wives.

In most marriages, therapy for bruised feelings is provided by the husband on request (and presumably by the wife in return). Perhaps more than ever before in the history of the human race, the average man meets this particular need. Not that men have suddenly become angels, but marital therapy has been facilitated by the American Federation of Labor and the American Psychological Association—one providing the necessary leisure time, and the other improved understanding.

As modern marriages restrict their functioning in other respects, ego therapy for the participants becomes more possible and more salient. Today, the mental-hygiene function is valued enough to be recognized as an important family function and effective enough to be a source of genuine satisfaction to most wives.

36. HELPING THE COLLEGE WOMAN CHOOSE HER ROLE

Clark E. Vincent

§ Many articles on the contemporary married woman's choice of roles oppose homemaking to job holding, implying that the woman must choose between the two. Other articles suggest a series of roles, employment immediately after marriage, followed by childbearing and rearing, and a return to employment in middle age. Professor Vincent does not lay down any fixed rules in the matter. He probes into the background pressures on young women and explores the implications of different choices. He gives helpful suggestions for clarification of roles.

Although investigators may not agree as to the seriousness of the disclarity in the role of the college-educated woman of today, it has become a truism that her role is indecisive. The average library with its 25 to

SOURCE: Clark E. Vincent, "Role Clarification for the Contemporary College-educated Woman," *Journal of Home Economics*, 45 (October, 1953), 567–70. Reprinted by permission of the publisher and the author.

The author's background is given in the footnote for article 32.

50 references dealing with women's roles to every one reference concerned with men's roles, substantiates such a truism.

The threefold emphasis of this discussion is to indicate that, if we consider the social context of personality formation and individual behavior, (1) there are some very real pressures operating to make it extremely difficult for the contemporary college-educated female to clarify, and make decisive choices concerning, her own role; (2) the educational efforts to clarify her role are frequently misdirected, as evidenced by the failure to take into account the social sources of her role ambiguity; (3) some suggestions for role clarification are possible.

While the following may be applicable to other than college-educated females, the impressions were derived primarily from counseling sessions with college girls contemplating marriage and with college-educated mothers experiencing marital difficulties.

The Illusion of Three Alternatives

Theoretically, the dilemma of the college-educated female comprises the choice between a "homemaking career" and what we shall refer to as a "commercial career," or employment outside the home. Superficially, it would appear that such a decision would be relatively easy to make by either selecting one of the two alternatives or by combining both alternatives. However, such a choice is frequently an illusion for the college-educated female.

Suppose she chooses homemaking? A college girl cannot make this choice too explicit, for it assumes success in obtaining a husband, and there is the possibility that she may be the one woman out of every ten who will never marry. To her, emotionally, the risk is far greater than it appears statistically. Thus, in part for this reason, she may hesitate to major in home economics but select a major involving a higher male enrollment. But after four years of journalism, history, or home economics, the ideas expressed in textbooks as well as the emphasis upon scholastic achievement and the professional expectations of instructors may have indoctrinated her with goals in addition to or other than those associated with her original decision to be a homemaker.

If she successfully meets a husband during college, friends and instructors may actually reveal, or, she may interpret, verbal or facial hints of disappointment when she informs them that she is going to be a full-time homemaker after graduation. If she has not obtained a husband during her four years of college, she has little choice but to find employment—but not as a homemaker.

Suppose she decides initially to have a commercial career? She plans, dreams, studies, and after college spends a few years becoming established in her chosen career. But by the time she is prepared to receive professional recognition, the prospective husband—or the concern because there is no husband—intervenes. For, she lives in a society permeated with the values and the desirability of marriage and a family. However, there is also the realization that if she marries, marriage and especially children, if they are to arrive before she is "too old," are going to take her away from the competitive arena just at the time when her education and experience were going to bring her the long-sought recognition. What was once a clear-cut decision to have a commercial career becomes blurred.

What appears theoretically as a simple choice between two alternatives gives evidence upon closer scrutiny of being an illusion of a choice. *This is true not only prior to marriage but perhaps even more so after marriage.* The following are only some of the subtle pressures which cause the college-educated female constantly to rethink her decision and question her role regardless of her initial choice.

1. The average, middle-class husband desires a clean, well-kept home in which the children are reared in the latest scientific fashion. He expects his wife to be a perfect hostess and sensitive to the importance of "social status" for his professional advancement.[1] He assumes that she will continue to be an intelligent and witty conversationalist who is interested in and able to understand his business and professional transactions, despite the fact that she has been surrounded all day with the conversations of a six-year-old, a three-year-old, and an infant.

However, this husband also appreciates the income of a working wife, and he may imply quite innocently on occasion that his wife has little to do all day since he compares her with the neighbor who "manages her home" in addition to her outside occupation.

2. The woman who has mastered the "gospel" according to various women's magazines is instructed—frequently within a single issue—how to be the perfect hostess, an ideal wife and mother; how to be a frugal economist, a painter, plumber, mechanic, and practicing psychologist; how to be the model of civic participation, have a hobby, and work part or full time for "self-expression"; and how to remain eternally young.

Many of these articles imply that her life isn't complete as a homemaker and entice her with success stories of glamorous mothers who have careers in addition to homemaking. Still other articles tacitly assume that if she is only a career woman she is missing the greatest joys of womanhood.

3. There is currently an attempt to convince "housewives" that they are more than "just housewives." The homemaker is informed that she

---

[1] Whyte, W. H., Jr. The wives of management. *Fortune*, 44, No. 4 (Oct. 1951), pp. 86–88+; Whyte, W. H., Jr. The corporation and the wife. *Fortune*, 44, No. 5 (Nov. 1951), pp. 109–111+; and McLemore, E. W. Manifesto from a corporation wife. *Fortune*, 45, No. 3 (March 1952), pp. 83+.

is involved in an art, a science, and the most worth-while profession. However, the average woman knows that domestic helpers are among the lowest paid workers and that they occupy one of the bottom rungs on the occupational prestige ladder.

She may be exhausted at the end of the day from giving "proper" psychological answers to the children's questions, repairing the electric mixer, making countless decisions on where and how much to buy, and encountering the hazards of traffic in shopping as well as in taking family members to and from work and school. However, she receives neither the prestige nor the status of the psychologist, the mechanic, the economist, or the taxi driver. Lacking such recognition, she repeatedly questions her homemaker's role and looks elsewhere for more rewarding roles. For she is made aware that for some reason filing letters and folding boxes bring more prestige than filing recipes and folding diapers.

4. If she works outside the home and leaves her children at a child-care center or nursery, she may be labeled as a delinquent mother by educators, ministers, and neighbors. However, if she remains home, psychiatrists may suggest that she is "too close" to her children and that such closeness is causally related to the fact that nearly 3,000,000 men were emotionally or mentally unfit for military service during World War II.[2]

5. She is told that motherhood is her responsibility, and she is reminded of her sacred duties and sacrifices as a mother. However, she is led to believe that she is incapable of motherhood and that she must rely on the child-rearing and infant-care "experts." This in spite of the fact that the "experts" have changed their opinions twice in three decades.[3]

Thus, although the college-educated female may have made an initial decision between the first two alternatives, *the implication is always present that a combination of both is the test* of a "successful woman." Many homemakers see a commercial career as the solution to their problems in the counseling situation, whereas many of the women employed outside the home have as their major goal to be able to "quit work and be with my family."

Suppose she chooses both a homemaking and a commercial career? It would appear that this is the decision reached by an increasing number of married women. The percentage of married women in the labor force increased 10 per cent—from 16.7 per cent to 26.7 per cent—between 1940 and April 1951, whereas "the labor force participation rate for single women and for widowed and divorced women has shown no

[2] Strecker, E. A. *Their Mothers' Sons.* Philadelphia: J. B. Lippincott Co., 1946.
[3] Vincent, C. E. Trends in infant care ideas. *Child Devel.*, 22 (1951), pp. 199–209. [For a discussion of influence upon mothers of professional and technical advice, see "Emotional and cultural impacts on contemporary motherhood" by L. Kanner, *J. Child Psychiatry*, 2 (1951), pp. 168–175.]

significant change during recent years."[4] In April 1951 there were 10.2 million married women in the labor force, which was 1.6 million more than the highest number during World War II.[5]

But if she does select this third alternative, she finds it a decision involving many difficulties. Census figures indicate a 10 to 15 per cent decrease in the number of domestic workers between 1940 and 1950; her husband may not be willing for her to work outside their home; she may not live in an area where both she and her husband can find their specialized fields of employment; she may not have the physical energy for both careers; and she may develop guilt feelings over neglect of the children. There is also the suggestion by some writers that the two roles are contradictory since one requires "drive, self-assertion, competitiveness, and assertion," while the other necessitates traits that are "protective or nurturing, passive and receptive."[6]

It may well be that in society's emphasis upon the third alternative for women, "female emancipation" becomes a misnomer. It is recognized that a part of the dilemma is related to the self-expectations which college-educated females have of themselves,[7] but these are not unrelated to the social context in which they are learned.

Misdirected Emphasis in Role Clarification

It is interesting that the books and articles concerning women's roles are frequently written for and to women, implying that it is the women who are to clarify their roles and that it is the female's role which needs clarifying. In reality it may be the male's role which needs clarification. Men still expect to work as they have always expected to work; and while their role has remained somewhat constant, their responsibilities may actually have decreased. Increasingly, we expect women to assist in breadwinning, politics, civic affairs, in the professions, in education, *and* we still expect them to be *the* homemakers.

Whether women should or should not work outside the home is beside the point in our present discussion. *The point is that if society continues to expect women to share many of the male's responsibilities, then society may need to expect men to share more of the female's responsibilities. The contemporary indecision in the college-educated female's role is as much related to overexpectation as it is to indecision between alterna-*

---

[4] Marital status of women in the labor force: April 1951. U. S. Bur. Census, Current Population Repts., Ser. P-50, No. 37 (Dec. 26, 1951), p. 1.
[5] Annual report on the labor force: 1951. U. S. Bur. Census, Current Population Repts., Ser. P-50, No. 40 (May 19, 1952), p. 1.
[6] Farnham, M. Battles won and lost. *Ann. Am. Acad. Pol. & Soc. Sci.*, 251 (1947), pp. 113–119.
[7] Rose, A. The adequacy of women's expectations for adult roles. *Soc. Forces*, 30, No. 1 (Oct. 1951), pp. 69–77.

tives. To clarify her role, we need to direct our educational emphasis toward those expecting so much of her and re-examine the role of the male in our society in relation to the added expectations we have of the female.

We may agree with Shakespeare that

> All the world's a stage,
> And all the men and women merely players:

but if we view personality formation and the learning process within the social context, we are made aware that we seldom write our own scripts. Contemporary women attempt to play the part or act the role being written for them by their husbands, ministers, women's magazines, and economic society, the rules of occupational competition, and professors' expectations. To clarify the contemporary woman's role our educational emphasis might more fruitfully be directed toward those writing her script.

Suggestions for Role Clarification

1. *Accept social reality.* Whether we believe that women should or should not work outside the home, the fact remains that almost 11 million married women are doing so and our economy could hardly withstand their withdrawal from the labor force even if it were desirable. The fact also remains that an increasing number of women who are receiving college educations and being trained in the same classrooms with men will want to work outside the home. If an increasing number of married women are to work outside the home, if available domestic help is decreasing, and if the standards for the successful wife, mother, and homemaker are continually raised, something or someone has to give.

2. *Conceive of homemaking as a "husband-wife" role, not as a "wife only" role.* This involves having home economics courses more applicable to male students. The sharing of homemaking frequently enables the husband to understand better the manual labor involved in the statement "the woman's place is in the home." We still retain an interesting concept of masculinity which regards sitting at an office desk all day as being more masculine than scrubbing floors, cleaning house, and disciplining youngsters. Conversely, the wife who works outside the home is frequently better able to appreciate the demands and strains in her husband's working world. Their area of interests-in-common is increased immeasurably when homemaking as well as breadwinning is shared.

It is to be recognized that males have lost some prestige in giving up their patriarchal throne and that some males experience a feeling of inadequacy in not being *the* breadwinner. Even though scrubbing floors and washing diapers may enable him to appreciate the lack of prestige associated with homemaking, it may also threaten his ego-security. However, the historical and social source of this ego-threat needs to be recognized. For when sharing breadwinning and homemaking roles is viewed as an ego-threat to the male, it usually implies the retention of the patriarchal conception of the husband-wife relationship as a dominant-submissive relationship.

With homemaking as a "we" role, it may be easier to appreciate that the wife who works outside the home also needs a psychological retreat from her work as does her husband, and that as a homemaker she needs a psychological retreat from *their* children. Some studies have indicated that the children having the best parent-child adjustment are those whose mothers are away from the home for from 10 to 30 hours a week.[8] If we view child-rearing as a mother *and* father role, then the 3,000,000 men rejected for World War II service were as much caused by an absent or disinterested father as by a too-close and too-interested mother.

3. *Appreciate the therapeutic nature of physical work.* At a time when the best-sellers are prescriptions on how to prevent worry and acquire peace of mind in the alleged stress and strain of modern living, too little attention is given to the therapeutic benefit of expending physical energy in homemaking tasks. Dirt may never be glamorous to the college-educated female, but *getting rid of it* may be therapeutic.

4. *Examine the self-image being given to college-educated females by their professors.* What kind of a script are college professors and especially home economics professors writing for their female students? Do they tend to assume that all their female students are interested in becoming a professional historian, sociologist, or home economist as the professor is? Are professors' self-images projected onto the female students through values which rate a commercial career higher than a homemaking career? Are courses offered which permit the female student to become a homemaker without being indoctrinated with professional data and methodology? Is there a recognition that homemaking courses are not necessarily "easier" or "softer" than other professional courses but are of a different kind and perhaps for that reason more difficult for the professionalized instructor to teach? Does the professor tend to increase the future homemaker's feeling of inadequacy by implying reliance upon the "experts" in child-rearing, husband-wife relationships, and homemaking skills?

5. *Examine whether women contribute to their own dilemma of "homemaking being just homemaking"* by continued low wages and servant relationships to their domestic help.

6. *Eliminate some of the role conflict for women by educating them*

[8] Nye, I. Adolescent-parent adjustment: age, sex, sibling number, broken homes, and employed mothers are variables. *Marriage & Family Living*, 14 (1952), pp. 327–332.

for both a homemaking and a commercial career. It appears realistic to do so since 90 per cent of them will at some time in their lives be home-makers and from 50 to 75 per cent will at some time be working outside the home.

7. *Enable the college-educated female to appreciate better the social sources of her self-image and role expectations.* With such an appreciation, it may be easier to redirect more fruitfully educational efforts in role clarification for both the college-educated female and male. With increased awareness of the social source of her role expectations, it may be easier for her to take greater confidence in her own ability as a wife, mother, and homemaker as well as in her ability to set her own individual limits on the demands society makes of her. With less incorporation of these "generalized others" of contemporary society, she need not be so confused in her role and so absorbed in the conforming "participating, lubricating, integrating and communicating" struggle.[9]

37. LONG-RANGE CAUSES AND CONSEQUENCES OF THE EMPLOYMENT OF MARRIED WOMEN

Robert O. Blood, Jr.

§ The remarkable postwar increase in the employment of married women will be intensified by the eventual decline of the American birth rate, the earlier completion of child-rearing, and the decreasing work week. However, automation will require renewed attention to professional education for women, especially "continuing" education following the child-rearing period. Maternal employment is producing a more symmetrical family structure with greater equality between husbands and wives and between sons and daughters. Short-run effects frequently differ for sons vs. daughters, the masculine side of the family appearing demoralized as a result of the father's relative loss of status.

The increase in the number of married women (and mothers in particular) who work outside the home is one of the most startling social

[9] *Fortune*, XLIV, 5 (November, 1951), 76.—Ed.

SOURCE: *Journal of Marriage and the Family*, 27 (February, 1965), 43–47. Reprinted by permission of the publisher and the author.

For the author's background, see article 35.

changes in American history. Hardly any other social phenomenon in the United States has undergone so rapid a change.

This change was quite unpredicted. During World War II, when much was made of the fact that "Rosie" was riveting, everybody assumed that after the war she would go back home and never rivet again. But the number of working mothers today is greater than the wartime peak when a shortage of men in the labor force and the urgent demands of the war machine created practical and patriotic motives for working. Now, under ordinary peace-time conditions, voluntarily, and in full competition with men, millions of married women have gone back to work.

Not only has this change been rapid and extensive, but it involves a major reallocation of energies. When a woman shifts from full-time housework to full-time outside work, her talents are so drastically redistributed that both the family and the economic system are profoundly affected.

Forces Affecting Maternal Employment

Few Americans other than sociologists are aware that a *population explosion* is occurring in the United States.[1] The current rate of increase in the American population is so great that this blithe innocence will soon pass. In a few decades, the American people will realize that our population explosion creates many problems for American society. We have already been made aware of this on a small scale by the freshmen pounding on the doors of our colleges and universities. We will be increasingly concerned about the shortage not only of universities, public schools, parks, and all other public facilities, but (especially in the northeastern part of the United States) about the fact that we are running out of space. Already the statisticians are predicting how soon there will be only one square foot of land left for each American. Their predictions are not so far in the future as one might think. As long as we go on having three and four children per family, we will double our population every second generation and then, by a kind of compound interest, double it again. Since we are marrying younger and having our children sooner, the time lapse from generation to generation is shortening, which further speeds up the process.

Gradually but increasingly, Americans will become concerned about slowing down and halting the growth of the American population. When the social pressure gets to be strong enough, the birth rate will drop from its present postwar high. Young women will be considerably emancipated from their present preoccupation with childbearing and child-

---

[1] For a recent discussion, see Philip M. Hauser, *The Population Dilemma*, Englewood Cliffs, N.J.: Prentice-Hall, 1963.

rearing. The two children considered permissible will grow up so fast
that their mothers will be left with major amounts of time on their hands.
Therefore, work will be even more attractive.

Secondly, *automation* will have major implications for the employment of women.[2] Already it is disastrously affecting the employment of
Negroes and of young people fresh out of high school, especially those
who dropped out before finishing school. The unemployment problem
for people with little skill or experience is already beginning to include
women. Unemployment rates for women are higher than for men, and
automation is one of the reasons.

Automation will have its major impact on factories and offices
(especially large-scale offices, such as the headquarters of insurance
companies and national corporations). Computers sometimes displace
as much as 90 per cent of the clerical staff of large offices, and automated
machinery similarly affects some factories. Factories and offices are two
of the chief places where women have worked in the past. In factories
they have manned machines, and in offices they have held typing and
filing jobs requiring little skill. Women enjoyed the opportunity to move
into a job that required little skill. They did not want to stay in college
very long, dropped out to have children, and then could leave their
children behind to pick up an easy job. But the days when women could
hope to find such jobs whenever they wanted to are rapidly passing.

Women without special training who want to go back to work will be
handicapped in the future. Up to now, their marginal commitment has
enabled them to drift into the occupational world and out of it whenever
they felt like it or circumstances seemed to require it.[3] Women have had
high rates of absenteeism. They work for one company for a few months
or years and then quit for awhile or work for another company. High
turnover means low seniority. In a tightening labor market, to be last
hired is to be first fired. Women, like other "marginal men," will have
to commit themselves to a serious career or to forego working at all.

Soon women will be divided into two categories. One category will
be the noncareer women who have too little education to break into the
occupational system. They will be trapped in domesticity with no way
out. In families with large numbers of children closely spaced together,
mothers may be eager to earn multiple tuition costs. But women who
never got an adequate education in the past and do not manage somehow to pick one up in the future will be unable to find a job. The second
category will be a growing group of career women. More college girls
will be interested in a foundation for future work. They will not earn a

[2] See, for example, Ida R. Hoos, *Automation in the Office*, Washington: Public
Affairs Press, 1961.
[3] Alva Myrdal and Viola Klein, *Women's Two Roles*, London: Routledge and Kegan
Paul, pp. 90–115.

teacher's certificate simply as a "life insurance policy" against the husband's premature death. They will want to put their education to good use.

American women are discovering that domesticity is no longer a sufficient life-long role. The declining *age at marriage* means that when the last child leaves home, the woman still has 15 or 20 years of potentially productive life ahead of her. It is already common and socially acceptable for her to go back to work when she has finally emptied her nest. And at younger ages, more women are entering the labor force when their children are still in the nest.

A great deal of the vocational preparation of such women for skilled and professional work will have to be gained after the children come rather than before. The age at marriage has dropped so far that it is interfering with college education. Many girls drop out of college to get married and have children.[4] As the unemployment problem for women increases, we will become concerned about women dropouts from college as we already are about boys who drop out of high school.

Even a girl who completes a bachelor's degree before having children will find her education obsolete by the time she gets ready to go back to work ten or 20 years later. The tempo of change and progress in American life is accelerating. We already recognize that a ten- or 20-year-old education is old-fashioned. But 20 years from now, the pace of change and improvement in knowledge and technology will have increased still further. It took thousands of years for the world's store of knowledge to double, then hundreds of years for it to double again, then only 20, and now it redoubles every ten years. Anyone with a ten-year-old education who has been out of touch with his field has only half an education left. Even men who work continuously have an increasing problem keeping up. Doctors find it difficult to master all the new drugs and diagnostic and therapeutic techniques that are invented. This is only an extreme case of what is happening to all professions and what will happen to women in the kinds of jobs that will be available in the future. Therefore, continuing education will become important not only for women but for men as well.

Continuing education will require more flexibility from academic institutions in the time limits for completing graduate study. At the moment, relatively few women secure a Ph.D. degree. American women are falling farther and farther behind the men in professional study. The proportion of advanced degrees earned by women is less today than it was 30 or 40 years ago.[5] But this educational regression cannot last

[4] Mabel Newcomer, *A Century of Higher Education for Women*, New York: Harper, 1959, p. 215.
[5] John B. Parrish, "Professional Womanpower as a National Resource," *Quarterly Review of Economics and Business*, 1 (February 1961), pp. 54–63.

much longer. After the unskilled jobs for women vanish, there will have to be an upgrading of the female labor force. When the birth rate starts dropping, women will become interested in Ph.D.'s again, the way they were during the feminist revolt of the 1920's. But those who do not get their doctorate before having children will find it difficult to finish an entire graduate program in the traditional seven years. Increased flexibility will enable women to prepare themselves for the work which they want and which our society will need. Our unemployment problem in the United States is paradoxically counterbalanced by an acute shortage in the upper reaches of our occupational system. There are not nearly enough psychiatrists, social workers, or college professors. When women begin to fill these gaps in our occupational system, the men will be glad to share the heavy loads involved in these responsible positions.

The fourth social force at work in America is the rising *productivity* of our economic system (which is closely linked in turn with automation). One consequence is a long-term decrease in the number of working hours per week. Professional people may ask, "What decrease"; but for other segments of the labor force, it is happening.[6] As men become able to turn out the same products in a shorter period of time, the 40-hour week will eventually shorten still further. This has already been seriously proposed by Walter Reuther as one of the few ways in which job opportunities can be spread among uneducated or half-educated people who are unable to fill the jobs which are in short supply. As the work week drops to 35 hours, to 30 hours and, foreseeably, to 25 or even 20, full-time jobs will be converted into part-time jobs.

This is music to the ears of women who would like to work but have a hard time finding part-time jobs. It is difficult to combine full-time work with being a housewife and mother. A shorter work week will make it easier for women to combine motherhood with being employed and will reduce the role conflicts of working women.

Part-time jobs are not only easier on the mother but have a superior effect on adolescent children, particularly daughters.[7] A girl whose mother is working part-time is better off than one whose mother is working full-time (and is not available when needed) and is also better off than one whose mother is not working at all. This reflects the fact that adolescents may receive too much mothering. Danger lies at both extremes. One can have either too little mothering (from a full-time working mother) or too much mothering (from a full-time mother). Therefore, it is socially advantageous to have more part-time jobs available.

[6] Harold L. Wilensky, "The Uneven Distribution of Leisure: The Impact of Economic Growth on Free Time," *Social Problems*, 9 (Summer 1961), pp. 32–56. It should be emphasized that this trend is a very long-range one.

[7] Elizabeth Douvan, "Employment and the Adolescent," in *The Employed Mother in America*, ed. by F. Ivan Nye and Lois W. Hoffman, Chicago: Rand McNally, 1963.

Shorter working hours will benefit family life by reducing the number of hours the husband has to work. If both partners work at different times of the day, the husband will be able to stay home and babysit with the children while the wife is off working. Many student parents arrange their college schedules this way.

More women will be able to have the kind of work schedule which only school teachers do now: to work at 8:30, home at 3:30, Christmas vacation off, and summer vacation off. Such an employment schedule resembles the children's school schedule. Mothers and children will leave home together and return together.

Not only will mothers have such hours—fathers will, too. As fathers come home from work early and have longer vacations, a new symmetry will be introduced into family living. There will be new opportunities for togetherness in leisure because the working and studying schedules of both sexes and both generations will coincide. The more women go to work, the more they make it possible for men to reduce their work. As the work week generally shrinks, more women will go to work. This beneficent cycle will equalize the roles of men and women in the occupational system.

Besides shortening the work week, increased productivity is raising family incomes. This will affect working women by raising the minimum wage level. Already the national minimum wage has risen from $1.00 an hour to $1.25 an hour. Increased affluence will also enable us to raise the amounts of money we make available to families in desperate straits. Therefore, fewer women will work because they *have* to, because that is the only way the family can make ends meet. Reduced economic pressure will benefit both the women themselves and their children. When poverty forces women to work, they are liable to resent it and to take their resentment out on their husband and children. They are not very nice people for any members of the family (including themselves!) to live with. As the employment of women becomes optional, women will work only if they want to and when they want to. This will be happier for everybody concerned.

Effects of the Employment of Women on the Family

Opportunities for togetherness will be just one impact on family life. Families are also changing their "shape" as a result of the employment of women. In the feudal, patriarchal family, woman's place was in the home. She got no education and was completely subordinate to the husband. Sex roles were rigidly segregated. Men never did what women did and vice versa. This placed women in as inferior a position as American Negroes had under slavery. In almost the same year that the emancipation movement began to concern itself with freeing Negroes from slavery, women became concerned about freeing themselves from their own servitude. Many of the same women were active in both the emancipation movement and the feminist movement.[8]

The feminist revolt finally succeeded with the granting of women's suffrage in 1920. During the following decade, pioneering women were anxious to go to college, get Ph.D.'s, become doctors and lawyers—and do all the things women had never done before. The fact that they were pioneers led many of these women to decide not to marry. Others could not have married if they had wanted to because the men of the generation refused to have them. They were mannish and aggressive: they had to be in order to throw off the shackles of the patriarchal family. These Ph.D. spinsters were few, but they were important symbols in proving the equality of the sexes.

After World War II, the pendulum swung back to neo-traditionalism. It did not go all the way back to patriarchy. Women did not surrender the right to vote either in public elections or in family elections; but they did go home and began having children in large numbers, re-emphasizing family life and discounting educational and occupational achievements. The symbols of the postwar period have been the station wagon overflowing with children and the suburb where women reigned while the men went off to work in the city.

Today, however, we may be on the verge of a new phase in American family history, when the companionship family is beginning to manifest itself. One distinguishing characteristic of this companionship family is the dual employment of husband and wife. The woman need not work continuously throughout her life span. But her phased employment consolidates and extends the long-term trends which have been at work in American family life.

Employment emancipates women from domination by their husbands and, secondarily, raises their daughters from inferiority to their brothers (echoing the rising status of their mothers). The employment of women affects the power structure of the family by equalizing the resources of husband and wife. A working wife's husband listens to her more, and she listens to herself more. She expresses herself and has more opinions. Instead of looking up into her husband's eyes and worshipping him, she levels with him, compromising on the issues at hand. Thus her power increases and, relatively speaking, the husband's falls.[9]

This shift in the balance of power is echoed in the children. Many

---

[8]Eleanor Flexner, *Century of Struggle*, Cambridge, Mass.: Harvard U. Press, 1959, pp. 62–70.
[9] For a review of the literature on the effects of the wife's employment on the structure of marriage, see Robert O. Blood, Jr., "The Husband-Wife Relationship," in *The Employed Mother in America, op. cit.*, pp. 282–305.

studies show that maternal employment currently affects boys and girls differently. For example, boys are often more dependent—on their mothers and on mother substitutes like school teachers.[10] They are more succorant; i.e., they like to be taken care of more. And they are more obedient. These differences reflect a lower status for the masculine side of the family. The father has less status—the sons see it and slump too. By contrast, daughters of working mothers are more independent, more self-reliant, more aggressive, more dominant, and more disobedient.[11] Such girls are no longer meek, mild, submissive, and feminine like "little ladies" ought to be. They are rough and tough, actively express their ideas, and refuse to take anything from anybody else. In short, they act as little boys are supposed to do. This is not to suggest that the two sexes actually switch positions. These are simply the directions in which things change. If we had precise measures, we would probably find that the girls become less girlish and the boys less boyish. The classic differences between masculinity and femininity are disappearing as both sexes in the adult generation take on the same roles in the labor market.

In the division of labor, there is a similar parallel between what happens to parents and to children. Husbands get drafted into the domestic service when their wives leave home. They have to fill the gap unless, as in the deep South, there happen to be Negro women available to take the husband's place.[12] In the North, where cheap labor is not available, husbands get pressed into service washing dishes and doing other kinds of work that ordinarily the housewife does if she is home all the time. Once she takes a full-time job outside the home, it is physically impossible for her to do all the housework. Naturally and spontaneously, the division of household tasks shifts, depending upon the changed amount of time that the husband and wife have available to do the work.[13] To be sure, the pattern does not shift as far as justice might suggest. The husband seldom shares 50-50 in the housework.[14] Nevertheless, he generally does substantially more housework than before.

[10] Lois W. Hoffman, "Mother's Enjoyment of Work and Effects on the Child," in *Ibid.*, pp. 95–105. Ivan Nye points out that these differences are accentuated when the mother's employment is motivated by her own superior education and by her husband's inferior occupational achievement, characteristics which, quite apart from maternal employment, would create a mother-dominated home and correspondingly passive sons. However, as employment becomes normative for middle-aged women, such accentuating factors will become less influential, to be replaced by role convergence as the long-run consequence.

[11] Alberta E. Siegel, Lois M. Stoltz, Ethel A. Hitchcock, and Jean Adamson, "Dependence and Independence in Children," in *Ibid.*, pp. 67–81.

[12] Kathryn S. Powell, "Family Variables," in *Ibid.*, pp. 231–340 (from Tallahassee, Florida data).

[13] Blood, *op. cit.*

[14] Robert O. Blood, Jr. and Robert L. Hamblin, "The Effect of the Wife's Employment on the Family Power Structure," *Social Forces*, 36 (May 1958), pp. 347–352.

Sons share in these feminine household tasks as well.[15] Theoretically, the father might take over the mother's work and the boys take over the father's, but this does not happen. Rather, both fathers and sons become more domesticated in feminine spheres. The girls do not do any less housework under these circumstances. They too share the mother's work.

In the division of labor outside the home, there is a curious difference between what happens to sons and daughters.[16] In addition to increasing their housework, daughters take more jobs outside the home. Because their mothers have set an example, the daughters get up the courage and the desire to earn money as well. They take more part-time jobs after school and more jobs during summer vacation. So the whole feminine contingent in the family starts bringing home more money. Meanwhile, the sons often work less. They are somehow demoralized by the fact that the women have suddenly achieved equality with them. In a sense, they are following their father's example—not that fathers actually quit work, but that their *share* of the financial responsibility for the family decreases.

In such ways, the shape of the American family is being altered by the exodus of women into the labor market. The roles of men and women are converging for both adults and children. As a result, the family will be far less segregated internally, far less stratified into different age generations and different sexes. This will enable family members to share more of the activities of life together, both work activities and play activities.

The old asymmetry of male-dominated, female-serviced family life is being replaced by a new symmetry, both between husbands and wives and between brothers and sisters. To this emerging symmetry, the dual employment of mothers as well as fathers is a major contributor.

[15] Prodipto Roy, "Adolescent Roles: Rural-Urban Differentials," in *The Employed Mother in America, op. cit.*, pp. 165–181.
[16] *Ibid.*

38. SHOULD MEN MARRY OLDER WOMEN?

Albert Ellis, with Lester David

§ Public opinion holds definite ideas about the relative age of husband and wife—the husband should be older. Is this idea simply tradition and custom? Or are there sound reasons for it? This article reviews the situation pro and con and comes to an interesting conclusion.

There is a surprising and little-noted trend in this country that would make Grandpa and Grandma raise their eyebrows more than a little.

One in every seven new husbands is younger than his bride.

And of this group nearly half of the husbands are younger than their brides by three years or more.

Almost as many more are the same age. The two groups together add up to a quarter of the nation's marrying couples.

In Victorian days, it wasn't rare for a man to take a bride ten or even 20 years younger than himself. How things have changed! And the trend seems to be continuing, according to latest census figures.

Well, what about it? Is it good or bad? Are we throwing away a wise piece of folklore, or merely ridding ourselves of the deadening weight of tradition? My own reaction is hooray! I think at long last we are on the way to eradicating a foolish taboo, one as outdated as the hard and fast rule of the past that no nice girl works.

And I am not the only one who thinks so. At least a half dozen famous sociologists, following intensive investigations, have discovered that these marriages are often the happiest.

Dr. Judson T. Landis, of the University of California, studied 4,000

SOURCE: *This Week* magazine (July 6, 1958), pp. 8–9. Copyright 1958 by the United Newspapers Magazine Corporation. Reprinted by permission of the publisher and the authors.

Dr. Ellis is a clinical psychologist who now carries on psychotherapy and marriage counseling independently (after having had experience with several kinds of institutions). He received his doctorate from Columbia University. His professional writings deal primarily with problems of sex, love, marriage, and family relations. He has written *The Folklore of Sex* and *The American Sexual Tragedy* and many professional articles; he has also edited several books in his field of interest.

Mr. David, who has a Master's degree from Columbia University, is a journalist who specializes in articles on marriage and family relations. He has lectured on magazine writing in this area at New York University and The New School for Social Research. His many articles appear in nationally known magazines.

couples and found the lowest divorce rates among marriages in which the wife was older! Dr. Harvey J. Locke, of the University of Southern California, reports that age difference is not a major factor in good marital adjustment. And the late Dr. Lewis M. Terman, of Stanford University, went so far as to assert, on the basis of his investigations, that the happiest wives married men four to ten years younger.

Despite all this, many young people continue to be influenced by tradition and prejudice. I know one young man who broke up with his fiancée after two years because she was 34 and he 27. He finally decided the social pressures would be too much for him.

Obviously, this man should neither marry nor date older women if the age factor bothers him. But what bothers me is why the difference should matter to anybody in the first place.

Why does it, actually? Just suppose you were one of a couple planning a marriage in which the bride was older than the groom. Let's see how the commonest arguments against your plans would stack up:

1. Other People Will Scoff. Valid, but can be overcome. Many persons will look askance and remarks along the lines of "She's robbing the cradle" will be made. The man won't escape being talked about either. He'll be accused of immaturity in comments such as: "He doesn't want a wife, he needs a second mother." The woman, too, can expect the parlor psychiatrists to diagnose her motives: "She didn't marry him for love, it's just her mothering instinct."

However, as the marriage proves itself, the whispers will fade and most people will simply get used to it.

2. When She Gets Older, He Will Start Roaming. Very little validity. In most cases if a man is going to be unfaithful he will be—regardless of his wife's age. He may offer her age as a reason to himself, but it's only camouflage. If she were younger and prettier, he'd find another excuse.

If a deeply satisfying relationship is built up through the years, instead of crumbling as time goes on, it can grow stronger.

3. Her Sex Desires Will Wane before His. Completely invalid. Studies by the Kinsey Institute, confirmed by other researchers, prove conclusively that a woman's sexual interest continues virtually unabated until the 60's.

4. Girls Mature Earlier and Need Older Men. Invalid. During the teens, girls are often more mature, but in the twenties, the gap between the sexes vanishes.

5. Friends of the Couple Will be of Different Ages. Valid. A five- or six-year gap could produce some noticeable effects. For instance, a 33-year-old teacher had difficulty adjusting to a marriage with an accountant of 26 for this reason.

Her friends, averaging 35, were mainly interested in their pre-teen children's problems, schools and running suburban homes. His friends were either unmarried or had much younger children, and the talk was still about formulas, nursery school, and the plan to buy a house.

There can be trouble if friends don't mesh, but time brings adjustment. After all, there's much less difference in outlook between 35 and 45 than between 25 and 35.

6. He'd Be More Active, She'd Prefer a Quiet Life. Not valid unless the age gap is extremely large. A few extra years do not put a wife in the rocking-chair class.

Thus, although some reasonable objections are apparent, the majority of arguments against reversing "tradition" wither when analyzed closely.

On the other hand, there are a number of decided advantages for both parties. Let's start with women:

A significant benefit which marriage with a younger man offers is the lessened likelihood of prolonged widowhood. According to life-expectancy tables, even if a man and wife were the same age on their wedding day, she would face an average of 5.5 years without him. These could be made fewer or even eliminated entirely, depending on the age balance at marriage.

Even more important, eradication of the taboo would offer many who face lifelong spinsterhood a second chance at finding husbands. Currently, there are about 1,200,000 single women in the U.S. between 30 and 44 who have never wed. The likelihood that they ever will is estimated at less than ten per cent, chiefly because the pool of available men diminishes sharply. There are plenty of single males, though, in younger age groups.

A third advantage for women lies in this simple but significant fact: A younger man can have a hard day at the office and still say to his wife: "Let's do something tonight." Often, only an act of Congress can budge an older man from his easy chair in the evening.

Finally, a younger man is less habit-hardened than a bachelor of some years' standing. The latter would tend to insist that married life conform to his old living patterns, while the former can change his ways readily and make a smoother adjustment to marriage.

Now how about the advantages to the men?

First, things will be easier for them. Let's be practical and let's be honest: No marriage counselor in his right mind would say that money doesn't matter in a marriage. It does! A woman better established financially can ease those early struggling years.

I am not in the least advocating that a young man turn to an older woman solely because of her job and bank balance. I'm a strong champion of love as a foundation-stone for marriage, but if a bride can help the family financially at the start, a great many problems will be solved even before they arise. Love is important, but it's also important to be realistic. I may believe in love, but I am a realist, too.

From this point stems another advantage for men. Many put off marriage because they can't afford a wife and family. If they turn their eyes to older women, the economic barrier may be eliminated. Thus instead of remaining single until they get on their feet, they can wed and enjoy more years of married life.

Finally, a man who picks an older woman usually selects her for solid wifely virtues and not because he is entranced by moonlight and roses. A more mature woman has lived long enough to be aware of life's everyday realities. She won't storm off to Mother quite so readily because married life didn't turn out as it was in her dreams or on television.

Add it all up and the conviction hardens: There is no sense in this unwritten law and it ought to be repealed. I am not saying all men should henceforth take unto themselves older brides—frankly, I myself did not. I am saying that a man should marry the woman he loves, and a few years plus or minus should make not one jot of difference in his mind, in her mind, in anyone's mind.

39. WHY ALL THESE YOUNG MARRIAGES?

Harold T. Christensen

§ Teen-age marriages are a symptom of a changing pattern of marriage, about which there is a good deal of concern on the part of teachers, parents, and social workers. Dr. Christensen analyzes some of the reasons for early marriages, among young college students as well as high-school students.

Within the United States for more than a half century the average age at first marriage has been going down. In 1890, men and women married

SOURCE: *The PTA Magazine*, 52 (April, 1958), 4–5. Reprinted by permission of the publisher and the author.

The author is head of the Department of Sociology at Purdue University. He received his doctorate from the University of Wisconsin. His interest in the processes of marital adjustment has led to a number of research projects and publication of articles, as well as to leadership in organizations concerned with marriage adjustment. He is the author of a college textbook, *Marriage Analysis* and editor of *Handbook on Marriage and the Family*.

at the approximate ages of twenty-six and twenty-two respectively. In 1956 the corresponding ages were about twenty-three and twenty. Thus, on the average, men are now marrying about three years younger and women about two years younger than they were some sixty or seventy years ago.

In 1956 there were approximately 12,000 married males and 284,000 married females under the age of eighteen. Furthermore, by the age of eighteen some 12,000 to 15,000 additional young people (mostly girls) had become either widowed or divorced.

It used to be that people waited until they were out of school before they got married. About the only exceptions were a few advanced students doing graduate and postgraduate work in the colleges and universities. But today the picture is different. Scattered studies reveal that perhaps 15 to 20 per cent of all *undergraduate* college students are now married and that the practice is rapidly filtering down to the high school level.

Consider, for example, these findings—which may be somewhat typical—from a recent study of senior high schools in California. Of the 205 schools studied, 90 per cent reported one or more student marriages during a one-year period. Nearly ten times as many girls had married as had boys, and most of those girls married out-of-school youths. Most of the marrying boys, however, had teamed up with girls still in school. The percentages of married students increased with each year in school. Among girls, 2.4 per cent of the sophomore class were married; 4.0 per cent of the junior class; and 5.7 per cent of the senior class. Nearly three fourths of the girls dropped out of school following their marriage as contrasted with very few of the married boys.

This high drop-out rate for girls may have been encouraged by the ill-defined and rather negative attitudes of some school officials toward student marriages. Many administrators have the fear (probably unfounded) that married students will talk about marital sexual experiences to unmarried students. Then, too, when a student wife becomes pregnant she is frequently requested or pressured to withdraw. If more schools offered effective courses in family life education, they could help prepare youngsters for the future and prevent some premature and usually ill-advised marriages. But too many of our high schools make only halfhearted efforts—or no attempts at all—in that direction.

It is natural for parents, teachers, school officials, and others to worry over today's wave of teen-age marriages. But is their worry well founded? The answer is *yes*—though, as will be shown, we need to move from the unproductive level of mere worry to that of seeking to understand and solve the problem.

Virtually all the research shows lower marital-happiness scores and higher divorce rates for those who marry quite young. Statistically speaking, the best time for marriage seems to be the early and middle twenties, not the late teens. There are at least three good reasons for this.

In Defense of Deferment

In the first place, teen-agers are not usually mature enough, in their emotions and judgment, for marriage. They are likely to choose their mates impetuously and to be nervous and unsure in their later adjustments. As a result they make very unstable husbands, wives, and parents. Moreover, pediatricians testify that the extremely young mother is most likely to be tense and anxious about motherhood and then to transfer this insecurity to the child.

Second, the younger a couple are at marriage, the shorter, generally speaking, has been their courtship—which means that there wasn't time to test the relationship and to prepare for the marriage. In other words, the relationship itself suffers from immaturity.

In the third place, it is likely that the circumstances may not be right. The boy and girl may not have finished school. He may still be facing his period of military service. Or the two of them may be unprepared in other ways to assume the social and economic responsibilities that marriage normally entails. These are reality factors outside the individual and outside the relationship. Because of them it seems likely that, given the same degree of maturity and involvement, success in marriage will be more probable at ages twenty-one to twenty-five than, say, at ages fourteen to eighteen.

Of course there are exceptions. Some couples who marry early do achieve real happiness, just as certain of those who wait longer do fail. Age in itself is not the primary consideration. But since many young people are, by virtue of their youth, immature, the chances of failure are greater in very youthful marriages.

It is probably no accident that the increasing divorce rate in the United States is paralleled by a decreasing age at marriage. The causes of divorce are many, to be sure, but marrying too young is definitely one of them.

Why the Rush into Matrimony?

Reasons for a trend toward youthful marriage seem to group themselves into three large clusters, which it may be worthwhile to examine.

There is the increasing *encouragement from contemporary culture.* Many of today's musical, literary, and dramatic presentations are designed to stimulate romantic and sexual interests. In consequence, marriage is made to appear as something glamorous, the answer to all problems. This unrealistic overvaluation gives rise to early and steady dating, which can lead to emotional and sexual involvement and eventually to premature marriage. Indeed growing-up has been so speeded up that in this modern day young people are permitted and even expected to do many things formerly reserved for adults. Going steady and getting married tend to fall in this category. They are avenues by which the youngster comes to feel that he can demonstrate his maturity and gain adult status. Finally, early dating, going steady, and marriage are "the style" today. Many teen-agers follow this course not because they particularly want to but because of social pressure—because it is "the thing to do."

Youthful marriages are, in part, a reflection of the *insecurities of our time.* The rapid tempo of living, the confusion arising from a complex and changing culture, the tensions of modern war—hot or cold—all tend to propel young people in the direction of steady dating and then marriage. Having less to cling to in the culture they cling more to each other. Not far from central in all of this are the interruptions of military service and the almost constant threat of war.

Equally important is the growing number of unsettled and broken homes, which may leave children feeling rejected and "so alone." Also, along with the increasing divorce rate has come an increasing irresponsibility and laxness on the part of parents toward the care and guidance of their children. And parental rejection or abuse, real or imagined, tends to drive children out of the home. It is the insecure and unhappy youngster who is most apt to turn to marriage as an escape. Unfortunately this kind of marriage is often without a solid foundation, so that the same unfavorable conditions are passed on to the next generation.

No Need for a Nest Egg

Another reason for the rush into matrimony is that the *economic risk is smaller* today than it was in earlier generations. This country has enjoyed two full decades of prosperity, with a constantly rising standard of living, and most young people now find it easier to get jobs that pay well. More and more women are working, and the "two-job family" emerges as the norm, especially for the period immediately after marriage. Among many young couples it is customary for both husband and wife to work until they get established; hence lack of financial preparation is less of a deterrent to an early marriage.

Parents, too, often lessen the economic risk by their willingness to help support the young couple for a while after marriage, especially if the boy and girl are still in school. Along with this, social security under government sponsorship has reduced many of the economic risks inherent in marrying and rearing a family.

Related to these three social trends is the ever present and perhaps increasing phenomenon of premarital pregnancy. Some girls get married, or do so sooner than they otherwise would, because they find themselves pregnant. My own research has demonstrated that early marriages are associated with abnormally high rates of both premarital pregnancy and divorce.

The Path of Best Resistance

The $64,000 question, of course, is "What can be done about it all?" There is no easy answer. Perhaps part of the answer is for us to understand what is happening so that we can be tolerant and somewhat philosophic about the matter. There are fashions in dating and marriage as well as in dress, and these change from time to time. There is no point in taking a completely hostile position or in being continually miserable about what cannot be changed.

But this does not mean that we must be fatalistic and make no attempt to steer youth into a wiser course. With an understanding of the social currents of our times, parents, teachers, and others can do much to shape the features in the environment that influence behavior. As citizens they can work for such things as community betterment and world peace. As teachers they can impart the insight and impetus necessary for control. And as parents they can make their children feel secure, loved, and happy.

In the end it all boils down to the necessity for doing a better job of *family life education*—in the home largely by example and in the school largely by instruction. It must be an education that not only imparts facts but shapes attitudes, that builds values and provides incentives. And it must be an education that comes early enough to do some good, starting in elementary school and continuing through college.

If we are worrying about high school marriages, why not start by initiating good family life education at the high school level? This would have two desirable results: It would delay or prevent many of the early marriages now taking place; and to those few youthful marriages that are probably bound to occur in any event—human nature being what it is—it would give a better foundation.

Chapter 13: Nuclear Family and Kinship Web

40. KIN FAMILY NETWORK

Marvin B. Sussman and Lee Burchinal

§ This article carries the family beyond the boundaries of the nuclear family and relates it to other kin units. The nuclear family appears as a voluntarily reciprocating unit in service and companionship with other kin units. A number of earlier studies in the field are reviewed.

Introduction

Most Americans reject the notion that receiving aid from their kin is a good thing. The proper ideological stance is that the individual and his family should fend for themselves. The family in this instance is nuclear in structure and consists of husband and wife and children. Further investigation would probably reveal that most of these rejectors are receiving or have received financial and other types of aid from their kin long after the time they were supposed to be on their own. After marriage many are involved within a network of mutual assistance with kin, especially with parents. Moreover, one would find that independence of the nuclear family of procreation is being maintained. Where independence is threatened, it is probably due to other causes. The rejection of the idea of receiving aid from kin and actually being helped by them is another case of discrepancy between belief and practice.

SOURCE: "Kin Family Network, Unheralded Structure in Current Conceptualization of Family Functioning," *Marriage and Family Living*, 24 (August, 1962) 231–40. Reprinted by permission of the publisher and authors.

The article is Journal Paper No. J-4197 of the Iowa Agricultural and Home Economics Experiment Station, Ames, Iowa, Project No. 1370.

Marvin B. Sussman, who received his doctorate from Yale University, is at Western Reserve University. Lee Burchinal, who received his doctorate from Ohio State University, is with the Bureau of Research, United States Office of Education. Both authors have been active in research, publications, and such organizations as the Groves Conference on Marriage and the Family and the National Council on Family Relations. Sussman is the author of *Community Structure and Analysis*.

Discrepancies between belief and practice of "ideal" and "real" behavior are common in our society. In family sociology the reason is "academic cultural lag"; the lag between apparently antiquated family theory and empirical reality. The theory stresses the social isolation and social mobility of the nuclear family while findings from empirical studies reveal an existing and functioning extended kin family system closely integrated within a network of relationships and mutual assistance along bilateral kinship lines and encompassing several generations.

The major purpose of this paper is to reduce the lag between family theory and research insofar as it concerns the functioning of the American kin family network and its matrix of help and service among kin members. The procedure is to review relevant theory and conclusions derived from research on kin family networks completed by sociologists and anthropologists. Appropriate modifications of existing theory which posits the notion of the isolated nuclear family are then suggested.

Nuclear Family Theory

Durkheim, Simmel, Toennies and Mannheim have stressed that the family in urban society is a relatively isolated unit. Social differentiation in complex societies requires of its members a readiness to move, to move to where there are needs for workers and where there are opportunities for better jobs.

American social theorists such as Linton,[1] Wirth,[2] and Parsons[3] support this position. Parsons suggests that the isolated nuclear family system consisting of husband and wife and offspring living independent from their families of orientation is ideally suited to the demands of occupational and geographical mobility which are inherent in modern industrial society. Major obligations, interactions and nurturance behavior occur within the nuclear family. While bonds exist between the nuclear family and other consanguineous relatives and affinals of the kin group, these lack significance for the maintenance of the individual conjugal family.

Family sociologists generally accept the isolated nuclear theory as promulgated above. They report the changes in the structure and func-

---

[1] Ralph Linton, "The Natural History of the Family," in Ruth N. Anshen, *The Family: Its Function and Destiny* (New York: Harpers, 1959), pp. 45–46.

[2] Louis Wirth, "Urbanism As a Way of Life," *American Journal of Sociology*, 44 (July, 1938), pp. 1–24.

[3] All by the same author, see Talcott Parsons, "The Kinship System of the Contemporary United States," *American Anthropologist*, 45 (January-March, 1943), pp. 22–38; "Revised Analytical Approach to the Theory of Social Stratification," in R. Bendix and S. M. Lipset, eds., *Class, Status, and Power* (Glencoe, Illinois: Free Press, 1953), p. 166 ff.; "The Social Structures of the Family" in Ruth Anshen, *op. cit.*, p. 263 ff.; Parsons and Robert F. Bales, *Family, Socialization and Process* (Glencoe, Illinois: Free Press, 1955), pp. 3–33.

tions of the American family system which have occurred as the system has adapted to the demands of a developing industrial society. There is general agreement that the basic functions reserved for the family are procreation, status placement, biological and emotional maintenance, and socialization. However, these functions are generally analyzed in the context of the "isolated" nuclear family. The functions of intergenerational and bilateral kin family networks regarding the processes of biological and emotional maintenance or socialization are given little attention by theorists or analysts. The conclusion reached is that demands associated with occupational and geographical mobility have brought about a family pattern in urban areas consisting of relatively isolated nuclear family units which operate without much support from the kinship system.

The textbooks are written by family sociologists. Few among them, either texts on the sociology of the family or those written for marriage and family preparation courses, give theoretical or empirical treatment to the maintenance of the family system by the mutual assistance activities of the kin group. Among the texts examined, only one considers in any detail financial arrangements among kin members. One result of the review of basic family and preparation for marriage texts regarding current knowledge of the functioning of the kin network and its matrix of help and service is that the theory of the isolated nuclear family prevails.

Discussion of the Theoretical Argument

The lack of research until the 1950's and the almost complete omission of the topic, kin family network and its matrix of help and services, in family texts are closely related. If the generalized description of the American family system as atomistic and nuclear were valid, there would be very little exchange of financial help or services within the kin family network. Parental support of married children or exchange of services and other forms of help among kin members would be comparatively rare and hence, unimportant. Research would be unnecessary and discussion of the subject, except in crisis situations, could be safely omitted from textbook discussions. However, accepting this theory as essentially valid without considerable empirical substantiation has contributed to errors in descriptions of kin family networks and aid patterns among families. A new empiricism emerging in the late 1940's questioned the persistence of the isolated nuclear family notion and presented evidence to support the viability of kin family network in industrial society.

The ideal description of the isolated nuclear character of the American family system cannot be applied equally to all segments of American society. Regional, racial, ethnic, and rural and urban, as well as socioeconomic status differences in modified extended relations and family continuity patterns are known to exist. Family continuity and inheritance patterns of families in several social strata have been described.[4] Among upper class families direct, substantial and continuous financial support flows from the parents, uncles, aunts, and grandparents to the children both before and after marriage. Only by receiving substantial kin support can the young high-status groom and his bride begin and sustain their family life at the financial and social level which is shared by their parents, other relatives and their friends. This support frequently includes obtaining a position for the husband in his or his in-law family's economic enterprise.

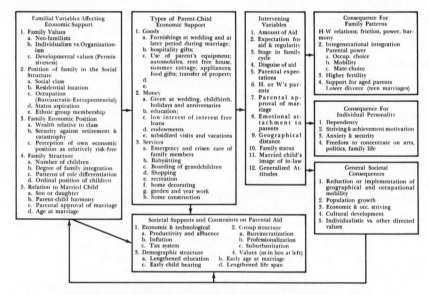

Functional Analysis of Parental Aid to Married Children

Members of lower class kin groups generally have few financial resources with which to assist married children. Among certain European ethnic groups some effort is made to assist the young couple at marriage; the notion of a dowry still persists. Generally, however, there is little knowledge, tradition or tangible forms of assistance transmitted to children which directly aids children in establishing or enhancing their

[4] W. Lloyd Warner and Paul S. Lunt, *The Social Life in a Modern Community* (New Haven, Connecticut: Yale University Press, 1941). See also Cavan, *The American Family, op. cit.*, pp. 119–87, for a review of other studies of social status differentials in family behavior.

socioeconomic status. Kin support in this class most frequently takes the form of providing services and sharing what financial resources are available at the time of crisis or of exchanging nonmonetary forms of aid. Marginal financial resources and the impact of unemployment hits all kin members alike.

The description of the isolated, nuclear American family system, if valid, is most suited to the white, urban, middle class segment of American society. Presumably, the leisure time of the members of these families is absorbed in the activities of secondary, special interest social groups. Since urban, lower class family members participate less than middle class family members in voluntary organizations, it is believed that social activities of adult lower class family members are restricted to informal visiting patterns. Visiting with relatives would be a significant proportion of all of their social relations. However, prevailing sociological theory suggests that the disparities between an extended kin family system and the requirements of a mobile labor force and intergenerational family discontinuities generated by social mobility should be reflected in the lack of continuity among lower class families as well as among middle class families.

The degree to which urban lower or middle class families function as relatively isolated from their extended kin family systems is critical for all subsequent discussions of the question of kinship network and its matrix of help and service. Unless there is a reasonably frequent occurrence of primary group interaction among kin members, very likely there will be an insignificant help pattern.

The emphasis on the atomistic character of urban families has contributed to incorrect assumptions concerning interaction within the kinship matrix. It has led family sociologists to incorrectly assume that assistance among kin members was comparatively rarely sought or offered. A reconsideration of these assumptions is necessary. The bases of reconsideration are logical constructs and empirical realities set forth in the following data.

Family Networks and Mutual Aid: Conceptualization and Research

A theory is here considered to be composed of logically interrelated propositions which explain phenomena. Concepts are elements of a theory, defining what is to be observed. Concepts by themselves cannot be construed as a theory. They require integration into a logical scheme to become a theory.

The existence of a modified extended family with its intricate network of mutual aid in lieu of the isolated nuclear family notion is probably more of a conceptualization than a theory. However, it approaches the state of being a theory since it is not an isolated concept but is integrated with other propositions concerned with the maintenance over time of the family and other social systems of the society.

Family networks and their patterns of mutual aid are organized into a structure identified as a "modified extended family" adopted to contemporary urban and industrial society. This structure is composed of nuclear families bound together by affectional ties and by choice. Geographical propinquity, involvement of the family in the occupational placement and advancement of its members, direct intervention into the process of achieving social status by members of nuclear family units, and a rigid hierarchical authority structure are unrequired and largely absent. The modified extended family functions indirectly rather than directly to facilitate the achievement and mobility drives of component families and individual members. Its tasks complement those of other social systems. By achieving integration with other social systems, concerned with the general goals of maintenance and accomplishment of these systems, the extended family network cannot be considered as an isolated or idiosyncratic concept. Its elements require organization as logically interrelated propositions and whereupon it should emerge as a theory replacing the prevalent one of the isolated nuclear family.

Our concepts die hard and one way to speed their demise is to examine the evidence supporting the new ones. Evidence and measurement are difficult terms to define. When do you have evidence and when have you achieved a measurement? The reader will have to judge. The approach here is to examine the writings and research emerging from several disciplines. In some cases the work is focused on testing hypotheses or describing relationships relevant to the new conceptualization. In others, the discussions and findings emerge incidentally to the major purpose of the study. There are cases of serendipity. They occur more frequently than one would expect and add to the uncertainty of the notion of the isolated nuclear family.

One assumption of the isolated nuclear family conceptualization is that the small nuclear family came into existence in Western Europe and the United States as a consequence of the urban-industrial revolution. Furthermore its small size is ideally suited for meeting requirements of an industrial society for a mobile workforce. The effect of the urban-industrial revolution is to produce a small-sized family unit to replace the large rural one. This assumption can be challenged. A study of different societies reveals that industrialization and urbanization can occur with or without the small nuclear family.

If household size reflects in any way the structure and characteristics of the joint extended family in India, then little changes have occurred in this system during the period of industrialization in India from 1911 to 1951.

The uprooting of the rural family, the weakening of family ties, and the reshaping of the rural family form into a nuclear type as a consequence of the industrial revolution are disclaimed for one Swiss town in a recent investigation. On the contrary many fringe rural families were stabilized and further strengthened in their kin ties from earning supplementary income in nearby factories. Able-bodied members obtained work nearby and no longer had to leave the family unit in search of work. Families which moved closer to their place of employment were accommodated in row houses; these units facilitated the living together of large family groups. These findings question the impact of industrialization upon the structure and functioning of the pre-industrial family.

It is difficult to determine if the conditions of living during the transition from a rural to an industrial society ended the dominance of the classical extended family and replaced it with a modified kin form, or if it was replaced by the nuclear one. The question is whether the modified extended family has existed since industrialization occurred; is it a recent phenomenon or an emergent urban familism, a departure from the traditional nuclear form; or is it nonexistent? The evidence to support either of these positions is inconclusive. It remains however that the family network described variously as "an emergent urban familism" or "modified extended family" exists and functions in the modern community.

The family network and its functions of mutual aid has implications for the functioning of other social systems. With the growth of large metropolitan areas and concomitant occupational specialization, there is less need for the individual to leave the village, town, city or suburb of the urban complex in order to find work according to his training. Large urban areas supply all kinds of specialized educational and occupational training. The individual can remain in the midst of his kin group, work at his specialty and be the recipient of the advantages or disadvantages preferred by the kin family network. If individuals are intricately involved within a kin family network, will they be influenced by kin leaders and be less amenable to influence by outsiders; will they seek basic gratifications in kin relationships in lieu of the work place or the neighborhood; will they modify drastically current patterns of spending leisure time thus affecting current leisure forms and social systems?

Empirical evidence from studies by investigations in a variety of disciplines substantiate the notion that the extended kin family carries on multitudinous activities that have implications for the functioning of other social systems of the society. The major activities linking the network are mutual aid and social activities among kin related families. Significant data have been accumulated on the mutual aid network between parents and their married child's family in a number of separate and independent investigations. The conclusions are:

TABLE 1 *Direction of Service Network of Respondent's Family and Related Kin by Major Forms of Help*

	DIRECTION OF SERVICE NETWORK				
Major Forms of Help and Service	Between Respondent's Family and Related Kin Per Cent°	From Respondents to Parents Per Cent°	From Respondents to Siblings Per Cent°	From Parents to Respondents Per Cent°	From Siblings to Respondents Per Cent°
Any Form of Help	93.3	56.3	47.6	79.6	44.8
Help During Illness	76.0	47.0	42.0	46.4	39.0
Financial Aid	53.0	14.6	10.3	46.8	6.4
Care of Children	46.8	4.0	29.5	20.5	10.8
Advice (Personal and Business)	31.0	2.0	3.0	26.5	4.5
Valuable Gifts	22.0	3.4	2.3	17.6	3.4

° Totals do not add up to 100 per cent because many families received more than one form of help or service.

SOURCE: Marvin B. Sussman, "The Isolated Nuclear Family: Fact or Fiction," *Social Problems*, 6 (Spring, 1959), 338.

1. Help patterns take many forms, including the exchange of services, gifts, advice and financial assistance. Financial aid patterns may be direct as in the case of the young married couples Burchinal interviewed; or indirect and subtle, such as the wide range of help patterns observed by Sussman and Sharp and Axelrod.

2. Such help patterns are probably more widespread in the middle and working class families and are more integral a feature of family relationships than has been appreciated by students of family behavior. Very few families included in available studies reported neither giving nor receiving aid from relatives. However, these relationships until recently have not been the subject of extensive research.

3. The exchange of aid among families flows in several directions, from parents to children and vice versa, among siblings, and less frequently, from more distant relatives. However, financial assistance generally appears to flow from parents to children.

4. While there may be a difference in the absolute amount of financial aid received by families of middle and working class status, there are

insignificant differences in the proportion of families in these two strata who report receiving, giving or exchanging economic assistance in some form.

5. Financial aid is received most commonly during the early years of married life. Parents are probably more likely to support financially "approved" than "disapproved" ones, such as elopements, interfaith and interracial marriages. Support can be disguised in the form of substantial sums of money or valuable gifts given at the time of marriage, at the time of the birth of children, and continuing gifts at Christmas, anniversaries or birthdays. High rates of parental support are probably associated with marriages of children while they are still in a dependency status; those among high school or college students are examples.

6. Research data are inadequate for assessing the effects of parental aid on family continuity and the marital relations of the couple receiving aid. Few studies report associations between the form and amount of aid given with the parents' motivations for providing aid. Additional studies on these points are necessary before the implications of aid to married children can be better known.

Social activities are principal functions of the kin family network. The major forms are inter-family visitation, participation together in recreational activities, and ceremonial behavior significant to family unity. Major research findings are:

1. Disintegration of the extended family in urban areas because of lack of contact is unsupported and often the contrary situation is found. The difficulty in developing satisfactory primary relationships outside of the family in urban areas makes the extended family *more important* to the individual.

2. Extended family get-togethers and joint recreational activities with kin dominate the leisure time pursuits of urban working class members.

3. Kinship visiting is a primary activity of urban dwelling and outranks visitation patterns found for friends, neighbors, or co-workers.

4. Among urban middle classes there is an almost universal desire to have interaction with extended kin, but distance among independent nuclear related units is a limiting factor.

5. The family network extends between generational ties of conjugal units. Some structures are identified as sibling bonds, "occasional kin groups" family circles and cousin clubs. These structures perform important recreational, ceremonial, mutual aid, and often economic functions.

Services performed regularly throughout the year or on occasions are additional functions of the family network. The findings from empirical studies are:

1. Shopping, escorting, care of children, advice giving and counselling, cooperating with social agencies on counselling and welfare prob-

lems of family members, are types of day-to-day activities performed by members of the kin network.

2. Services to old persons such as physical care, providing shelter, escorting, shopping, performing household tasks, sharing of leisure time, etc. are expected and practiced roles of children and other kin members. These acts of filial and kin responsibility are performed voluntarily without law or compulsion.

3. Families or individual members on the move are serviced by units of the family network. Services range from supplying motel-type accommodations for vacationing kin passing through town, to scouting for homes and jobs for kin, and in providing supportive functions during the period of in-migration and transition from rural to the urban pattern of living.

4. Services on occasions would include those performed at weddings or during periods of crisis, death, accident, disaster, and personal trouble of family members. A sense of moral obligation to give service or acknowledgement of one's kin appropriate to the occasion is found among kin members. The turning to kin when in trouble before using other agencies established for such purposes is the mode rather than the exception.

5. General supportive behavior from members of the kin family network facilitate achievement and maintenance of family and community status. Supportive behavior of kin appears to be instrumental in affecting fertility rites among component family members.

A convergence of many of these findings occurs in the work of Eugene Litwak. In an extensive study of a middle class population. Litwak tests several hypotheses on the functional properties of the isolated nuclear family for an industrial society: (a) occupational mobility is antithetical to extended family relations; (b) extended family relations are impossible because of geographical mobility. His findings summarized briefly are: 1) The extended kin family as a structure exists in modern urban society at least among middle class families; 2) Extended family relations are possible in urban industrial society; 3) Geographical propinquity is an unnecessary condition for these relationships; 4) Occupational mobility is unhindered by the activities of the extended family, such activities as advice, financial assistance, temporary housing, and the like provide aid during such movement; and 5) The classical extended family of rural society or its ethnic counterpart are unsuited for modern society, the isolated nuclear family is not the most functional type, the most functional being a modified extended kin family.[5]

[5] Eugene Litwak, "The Use of Extended Family Groups in the Achievement of Social Goals: Some Policy Implications," *Social Problems*, 7 (Winter, 1959–60), pp. 177–87; *op. cit.*, "Occupational Mobility and Extended Family Cohesion"; *op. cit.*, "Geographical Mobility and Family Cohesion."

Conclusions

There exists an American kin family system with complicated matrices of aid and service activities which link together the component units into a functioning network. The network identified by Litwak as extended family relations is composed of nuclear units related by blood and affinal ties. Relations extend along generational lines and bilaterally where structures take the form of sibling bonds and ambilineages, i.e., the family circle or cousin club.

As a consequence of limited historical work and particularistic developments in theory and research in sociology there is uncertainty concerning the impact of industrialization upon the structure and function of the pre-industrial family. Was the extended classical type found in rural society replaced by a nuclear one, or did it evolve into the modified kin form described in this paper? It is suggested that the notion of the isolated nuclear family stems from theories and research on immigrant groups coming into the city to work during the period of urbanization in Western society. Anomie in family behavior resulted from individual and institutional failure to make appropriate adjustments required by this migration. The coldness and indifference of the workplace and the city as a steel and concrete bastion contributed to a feeling of aloneness and isolation. The basic concern of the in-migrant was survival in an unknown man-made jungle. Survival was related to dependence upon small family units. These could make quicker and more complete adjustments to the new ways of urban life. The ethos of a competitive and expanding industrial society supported the flexibility of movement now possible by an atomistic unit. Every man is for himself, every man should be unencumbered by ties that will hinder his economic or social progress, and every man should seize opportunities to better himself. One assumption of this position is that early urban man had little time for concern or activity with kinsmen. A more logical assumption is that isolation, a depressive workplace, and uncertainty produced greater reliance upon kin. Once new immigrants became established in the city they served as informants, innkeepers, and providers for later kin arrivals. Once these followers arrived the kin family network then functioned most effectively to protect and acculturate their members into urban ways.

Major activities of this network are that members give to each other financial aid and goods of value, and a wide range of services at specific times and under certain conditions. The aid and service provided within the network supplement rather than displace the basic activities of nuclear family units. Kinship behavior assists more than negates the achievement of status and occupational advance of component families and their members.

The main flow of financial aid is along generational lines, from parents to young married children and from middle-aged parents to aged parents. Such aid is not restricted to emergencies, but may be given at various occasions such as support for education, to start a family, at time of marriage, to begin a career, and the like.

The network is used among middle class families as a principal source of aid and service when member families or individuals are in personal difficulty, in times of disaster and crisis, and on ceremonial occasions. There are some indications that established working class families are following the same pattern. Some situations cannot be handled by the nuclear unit alone, e.g., destruction of the family home by a tornado; while other situations involve more than one nuclear family or individual member, e.g., the death of an aging parent. In such situations there are mutual expectations of going to the aid of kin. Aid is sought from the most immediate kin chiefly along sibling or generational lines. Then it is followed by help from more distant kin.

In many instances everyday or weekly activities link together the members of the kin family network. Joint participation in leisure time activities are possible because of reduction of the work week. Visiting among kin is facilitated by high speed highways and other conveyances of a modern transportation system. Constant communication among kin members is possible by the widespread adoption on all class levels of the telephone as a household necessity.

The feasibility of the kin network in modern society is due to the existence of modern communication and transportation systems which facilitate interaction among members; a bureaucratic industrial structure suited to modern society which removes the responsibility for job placement from the network will still permit the network to concentrate on activities intended to aid the social and economic achievement of network members; and expansion of metropolitan areas in which individuals can obtain educational, occupational and status objectives without leaving their kin area. Kin members can live some distance from each other within the metropolitan area and still have relationships within the network. Nuclear units function autonomously. Decisions on what and when to act are responsibilities of the nuclear family. Influence may be exerted by the kin group upon the nuclear units so that the latter may make the "right" decision. However the kin group seldom directs the decision or action of the nuclear family in a given situation. Immunity from such control is guaranteed by legal and cultural norms which reaffirm the right and accountability of the nuclear family in such situations. The role of the family kin network is supportive rather than coercive in its relationship with the nuclear family.

Understanding of the family as a functioning social system interrelated with other social systems in society is possible *only by rejection of the isolated nuclear family concept.* Accepting the isolated nuclear family as the most functional type today has led to erroneous conclusions concerning the goals and functions of these other social systems. In social service fields, for instance, institutions establish goals and programs concerned with caring for individuals and families who are unable to fend for themselves. Institutions assume that the family unit is a small and isolated unit easily injured and upset by the many problems it faces in contemporary society. The therapeutic approach is to treat the individual or at best the members of the nuclear family. The kin network is overlooked. Often nuclear families respond hesitantly to the overtures of these institutions; the nuclear unit prefers to find solutions to its problems within the family kin network. When such solutions are impossible then the specialized service institution may be used. How the operations of the kin family network affect the functioning of other social systems is yet to be established. Their positive or negative effects are unknown. Some beginning research on this problem is now underway.

41. MARRIAGE MAKES IN-LAWS

Evelyn Millis Duvall

§ A marriage is never really limited to the relationship between husband and wife. Even if they are both orphans or live across the continent from their parents, the influence of early family experiences stays with them. Religious beliefs, basic values, unconscious emotional likes and dislikes, fears and enthusiasms often are based upon childhood training or early informal experiences. Most couples are not orphans and many live in or near the community where their parents or other close relatives live. In-laws cannot be disregarded; they are part of the family group, through the effect they have had in molding the personality of husband and wife and often as frequent visitors.

In-laws are often referred to as a problem. But need they be? Dr. Duvall's book, *In-laws, Pro and Con,* is based upon an intensive study of information contributed by over five thousand men and women in individual and group interviews and in letters written in response to a network radio contest soliciting letters on "Why I Think Mothers-in-

SOURCE: Evelyn Millis Duvall, *In-laws, Pro and Con* (New York: Association Press, 1954), pp. 276–80, 293–96. Reprinted by permission of the publisher and the author. The author's background is given in connection with article 13.

Law Are Wonderful People." Her book goes beyond mothers-in-law and covers the entire situation. The brief selections that follow analyze the in-law situation and give a general framework for understanding specific in-law experiences.

He was stationed at Great Lakes. She was living with the children at her parents' home in Michigan. Their separation was not easy for either of them, and he called home every week to talk with her—just to hear the sound of her voice, he said. One night her voice was heavy with tears as she begged:

"Try to find a place near you for the children and me. I can't stand this living with in-laws any more!"

Touched and baffled, he replied:

"What in-laws are you talking about? You're living with your own folks, aren't you?"

Her response was a poignant—

"Everybody's in-laws when you're married."

That young wife put her finger on a sore point in the relationships of the married couple and either set of parents. Once a man and woman marry, they are faced with the challenge of identifying with each other. This means making new loyalties in which they both come first in each other's eyes. It necessarily involves breaking away from both sets of parents. Old identifications with the members of both families now must undergo a change to the place where "everybody is an in-law when you are married."

But old loyalties and responsibilities carry on in the lives of both the husband and the wife. They still are adult children of the parents who knew them when. . . . They still are and want to be part of the families they came from and married into. At the same time, their own new family unit must and should come first.

· · · · ·

When a man marries, he may try to tell himself that he is not marrying her family, he is marrying the girl. But let the first holiday come along, or the first baby, and he will find out whom he married. As will his wife. The marriage of the two people unites the two families from which they both have come, as inexorably as it binds the couple.

Every married couple belongs to three families. They belong first of all to themselves. They are the WE of the new family they are founding together. But, at the same time they also belong to *his* family, and to *hers*. If they are to establish a strong family unit of their own, they must inevitably realign their loyalties to the place where *our* family comes before either *yours* or *mine*.

This is the elemental triangle of married living. Unless the cohesive force in the new family unit is stronger than that which ties either of the couple to the parental home, the founding family is threatened, as we see in the figures.

In Figure 1a, "YOU" have in-law trouble because "MY" family is too close. It may be because I am still immature and not ready to emancipate myself from my parental home. It may be that one or more members of my family is possessive and finds it difficult to let me go. It may be that circumstances within my family require from me more loyalty and attention than I can comfortably give at the time that I am involved in building my own home and marriage. Whatever the reason, if the forces pulling me/us toward loyalties to "MY" home are too strong, the development of "OUR" common sense of identity is delayed or weakened.

In Figure 1b, "YOUR" family is too close, and so "I" have in-law trouble. Because "YOU" are bound so tightly to "YOUR" family, I am pulled away from mine, and "WE" make little progress in establishing "OURS."

In Figure 1c, "OUR" family unit comes first in our joint loyalties. We are threatened neither by the ties that bind us to "YOUR" family, nor by the bonds that unite us to "MINE." We are able to make progress as a new family because the force of our common identification pulls us out and away together into a home of our own. Now we can share in the common heritage of both your family and mine because we are not threatened by the pull from either. Only thus are WE free to enjoy being members of the entire extended family, without the stress of in-law strains.

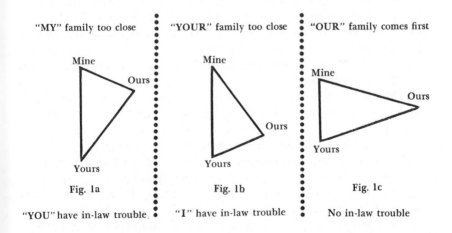

"MY" family too close   "YOUR" family too close   "OUR" family comes first

Mine   Mine   Mine

Ours   Ours   Ours

Yours   Yours   Yours

Fig. 1a   Fig. 1b   Fig. 1c

"YOU" have in-law trouble   "I" have in-law trouble   No in-law trouble

The basic task in the early years of marriage is to cement the marriage bonds to the place where the two feel, behave, and fundamentally *want to be* ONE. This is the explicit commitment of the marriage ceremony in which the man and wife promise, "Forsaking all others, keep Ye only to him/her as long as Ye both shall live."

Any intrusion or threat from either his family or hers may be considered an in-law problem. The autonomy of the married pair is so imperative for the solidity of the union that there is a peculiar sensitivity to any conflicting force emanating from either parental home. For this reason, anything that a member of his family or hers does that imperils the independence of the pair may be construed as an in-law difficulty.

· · · · ·

Identifications Shift at Marriage

For twenty years, more or less, a girl is identified with her childhood family. She is known as their girl. She carries their name. She thinks of herself as a member of that family. Her loyalties are to them. Her sense of who she is, is in terms of who they are, where they live, what they do, how they look at life.

Then she marries, and must evolve a new set of identifications. She changes her name. But more than that, she changes her sense of who she is and to whom she belongs. She is no longer her parents' little girl. She is now her husband's wife. Where once her loyalties were to her father and mother and to their way of life, now her loyalties must shift to center in those held in common with her husband.

· · · · ·

Marriage adjustment involves the sorting out of older loyalties and developing new patterns of identification. These consist not only of practices and ways of living, but most basically of concepts of self. As we marry, we must re-examine our sense of self, and rediscover what it means to be a wife, a mother, a husband, a father. These concepts have been in the process of building throughout our early experience with ourselves and with others.

By the time we marry we have a vast miscellany of concepts and pictures in our heads of the way things should be and how we should conceive of ourselves. The more powerful of these conceptions of role have come out of former identifications with those important to us—father, mother, siblings, and the other special people of childhood and youth. Some of these ways of life, picked up in our association and identification with those close to us, carry over unchallenged through the rest of life, as do language patterns and personal hygiene and table manners for most of us. But some of these earlier identifications must undergo extreme shifts as the new sense of self as husband or wife develops.

The implications of shifting identifications from the childhood home to the extended family that comes into being at marriage are many. . . . At the moment, one more question is pertinent.

In-laws by definition are those relatives that one gains in marriage. The question is: How can we feel the same love and acceptance for the mate's family that we have for our own flesh and blood? Through two decades, more or less, we develop tender, special love feelings for our own primary family group and the people in it. Then, with the pronouncement as man and wife, we are expected to love the other's people as our own. Granted that warm acceptance is a strong unifying factor in in-law relationships, how is it attained?

The simplest answer seems to be that to the extent to which we have learned to love in our childhood homes, we have developed the capacities of affection and acceptance in ever widening relationships. This is therefore a matter of relative maturity, a factor of great importance in the business of living with others.

Chapter 14: Husband and Wife in the Middle and Later Years

42. SOCIALIZATION FOR POSTPARENTAL LIFE

Irwin Deutscher

§ Husband and wife are often described as desolate when their children leave home. The term "empty nest" has been attached to this situation. In his research, Deutscher found little of the anticipated feeling of isolation. Parents accepted the departure of their children with equanimity— sometimes with a measure of relief. Seeking the reasons for this acceptance, Deutscher concluded that the generational rupture in family life did not come with surprise or lack of preparation. A measure of anticipatory socialization had already taken place.

Theoretically, it might be expected that the transition to postparental life would be a difficult one for the middle-aged spouses to make. Since this is an emerging phase of the family cycle, few of those entering it can find role models: in most cases one of their own parents was dead before the last of their own siblings was launched. This lack of anticipatory socialization—the absence of an opportunity to take the role of a postparental spouse, to rehearse the part before having to play the role themselves—ought theoretically to make for an extremely difficult situation after the children leave home. Much of the descriptive literature indicates that this, indeed, is a dangerous time of life. *Nevertheless, despite expectations based on both theory and clinical experience, when urban middle-class postparental couples describe their life, the hurdle*

SOURCE: Arnold M. Rose, ed., *Human Behavior and Social Processes* (Boston: Houghton Mifflin Company, 1962), pp. 508–23, with certain omissions. Reprinted by permission of the publisher.

The author received his doctorate from the University of Missouri. Formerly Director of the Division of Research in Health and Welfare of Community Studies, Inc., Kansas City, he is now Director of the Youth Development Center, Syracuse University.

does not appear to have been insurmountable and the adaptations are seldom pathological.[1]

In discussing postparental life, middle-aged spouses clearly reveal that it is not sound to assume that anticipatory socialization is absent because this is a new stage of the family cycle—that is, because middle-aged couples of today have not had the experience of observing their parents make such a transition. In spite of the fact that the identical situation could not be observed and rehearsed—that there was no opportunity to learn to take the role of the other by observing others— *analogous* situations exist in one's own life. Sussman recognizes this when he suggests that "most parents are gradually prepared to some degree for the day when their children marry and leave home by their periodic absences away at school or elsewhere."[2] Such periodic absences do not, however, represent the full extent to which such socialization by analogy can occur.

Situations such as these provide an opportunity for the parent to rehearse in his own mind what life will be like when his children are gone. Anomalously, he himself becomes the "other" whose role he has an opportunity to take. Even though these practice situations may not be considered as permanent, important, or serious (they are more nearly instances of "playing-at-roles" than "role-playing") it will be seen that they provide the continuity in role conditioning—the socializing opportunity—that is needed. The word "opportunity" is used advisedly. Individuals react to the socialization process in different ways; on some it "takes" and on others it doesn't. The simple fact that an individual is provided with a potentially socializing experience does not necessarily result in his defining it as such or in his being socialized as a result of the experience. The remainder of this paper will be devoted to an examination of what these socializing opportunities are and the manner in which they appear to facilitate the transition to postparental life.

Opportunities for Anticipatory Socialization

Change as a Culture Value

One of the underlying cultural values of our contemporary society is the focus on change for its own sake. In a sense all Americans are social-

[1] Observations made and materials cited below are derived from intensive interviews with 49 urban middle-class postparental spouses. The investigator gathered sufficient data on family characteristics from approximately 540 middle-class households to determine whether or not they met his criteria of postparental. Those selected were between 40 and 65 years of age, had from one to four children all of whom had been launched, and both parents were alive and living together. Self-selection occurred in only two cases where the family refused to be interviewed.
[2] Marvin B. Sussman, "Parental Participation in Mate Selection and Its Effect upon Family Continuity," *Social Forces*, 32 (October, 1953), 76–77.

ized from early childhood to believe that change is both inevitable and good. The notion that things will not remain the same—politically, economically, or socially—is an integral part of our national ethos. Otherwise there could be no Horatio Alger myth. Otherwise the political slogan "It's time for a change" could not have been so effective as it obviously was in 1952. Otherwise Southern segregationists would not concede that the best they can do is fight a *delaying* action against integration. Change apparently is accepted as something both natural and inevitable by the vast majority of the members of our society. Such a value provides a general conditioning for the acceptance of new and different situations regardless of their specific nature.

In our interviews, we find evidence that middle-class urban Americans have internalized this value and are able logically to relate it to the family cycle. One mother observes philosophically that "it seems like life spaces itself. You look forward to finishing up one space but then another space always pops up. When this is accomplished something else comes along." The clearest statements, however, come from two of the fathers. One of them, when asked how it felt to become a grandfather responded that "like most things in my life, it's just a matter of course. Things can be expected, like you expect changes in jobs and expect children to be married. Natural events come afterward and you take those things as a matter of course." This process, felt to be "natural" in our society, is described in full detail by the other father:

> Of course you hate to give up your daughter, but I think we all understand that is the way of life; you can't stand still; you can't be the same forever. Life moves on and that is the most natural thing. You see them grow. You see them graduate from high school. Then you see them graduate from college—you follow along. It is changing all the time. First it is childhood. You hold them on your lap then you go walking with them. Then you see them through high school. I was her chauffeur, all the time taking her to social functions. She went through music school, then she got a bachelor of arts, then we sent her for four years to Juilliard and she got her bachelor's and master's there. Then she comes out and teaches in college for one year and then she gets married and settles down.

It is clear that at least some people are aware of a life cycle and a family cycle and are resigned (if not committed) to a philosophy of change. Whether or not one is willing to accept the conditioning effect of a basic cultural emphasis on change *per se*, there remain several more specific types of experiences which provide parents with an opportunity for anticipatory socialization.

The Temporary Departure of Children

Opportunities for middle-class parents at least to play at a postparental role frequently occur when the children leave home for college. However, such opportunities are exploited to varying degrees, or, to put it another way, the experience is defined differently by different couples. Some parents make no mention of the possibility of college as a socializing experience for themselves. Presumably many of these do not see that possibility. On the other hand, there are others who see clearly what is happening. A mother claims that "The breaking point is when your children go away to college. After that you grow used to it. By the time they get married you're used to the idea of their being away and adjust to it."

The question "Do you think your child was ready to marry when he did?" brought out the functionality of the college experience. One father responded, "Yes, I thought she was. She had already gone through college—those five years of college and two years working. She was ready to get married." More important is that the college experience meant that he was now ready for her to get married. This kind of projection—the notion that college is training for the child to get away rather that training for the parent to release him—is expressed most clearly by a mother:

> It's only natural, when you have a family of three without any relatives near by, to notice a gap when she gets married. Of course, the first adjustment is when they go away to school; that's the first break. It's healthy for an only child to go far away to school. It makes them more self-sufficient. She had been in school away from home since she was sixteen and I think she was very well adjusted. Being away like that she learned to be independent, and make her own decisions and take responsibilities on her own. It was a sort of training period which prepared her [*sic*; "us"?] for leaving us [*sic*; "her"?].

Another mother says of her recently married son, "We had gotten used to just being by ourselves while he was in the Navy and away at college." This brings us to another frequently occurring opportunity for parents to play at the postparental role: the departure of children for military service. Life experiences tend to be evaluated in comparison with other experiences. They are not just good or bad; they are better or worse. Apparently it is better to lose a child through marriage than through war: "My most unhappy time was around the war years when my boy was in service. I worried over him coming back; he was missing several times." This is the kind of socialization that gives a parent a sense of relief to have a child home and married. We learn from another mother that, "When he was sent overseas, I was so worried about him over there that it was a relief when he got married and settled down." The importance of this as a learning experience is illustrated by the mother whose three children are now married, but who says of the time when her son went into service and she still had two others at home, "I think that the lonesomest part of my life I ever had was when my son was in service. We missed our boy." Her husband, interestingly enough, explicitly states that the Army experience serves as preparation for marriage. When asked if he thought his children were mature enough to get married, he responded: "Well, I thought more so about the boy because he was in the Army, but I did think that she (the daughter) should have waited."

Being in the armed forces serves both to wean the parents away from the children and the children away from the parents. Still another mother reports that:

> After he came out of the service he had aged a lot. He used to confide in us about life and to tell us about everything that was happening in school. But after he went into service he changed. We always spent the afternoons together—both the children. We'd go out for drives or picnics or something like that. But after he came home from service he didn't do that anymore. He wasn't content to be at home.

But then, after the anguish of wartime separation, another woman implies that it is good to know that the child is safe and is in this country:

> He was in the Second World War and he was overseas. And after having been so far away from home he feels like he's practically right here, because we can telephone and it's just 50 miles. After having been in Europe a couple of years, you know 50 miles away is "at home."

There are other experiences which, like college or service in the armed forces, give parents an opportunity to practice living without their children. Nearly a quarter of the families interviewed had parted with their children for extended periods of time while they were still in their teens. For example, there is the son who couldn't get along with his father: "My son used to say that as much as he would like to stay here, he couldn't take things off of his dad any longer. So I never insisted on him staying. He left a couple of times and would come back." Then there is the child with the wanderlust: "That boy wasn't interested in anything except to hitchhike—just to get as far as he could and to see what he could see. He was walking when he was eight months old and has been walking ever since." More common than either of these two experiences is the departure of children prior to marriage in search of work. Although this sometimes occurs with daughters, it is more frequently the sons who leave for this reason.

> (Do you remember how you felt when you first found out he was going to get married?) Yes, he was the first one. Both of them are married now. It was all right. He was able to take care of himself. He was away from home a lot. He and the oldest boy were up in Detroit on defense work. They have really been away from home a long time—ever since 1940.

(How did you find it when the children left? Did you have a lot of time on your hands?) Well, that came gradually. The war had something to do with that. They were both in the war before they got married and we were alone then. And the youngest one went to aviation school. He was just barely 18 when he got his first job in Texas. Then he went to Phoenix and then he came home and then he went into service. And the other boy was at home for a while and then he had to go. So with their coming and going it kinda eased off gradually.

Finally, in connection with these temporary departures of children prior to marriage, a word should be said about the modern middle-class urban high school complex. In some cases it results in the home being little more than a place to sleep and certainly in infrequent contacts with the parents. This reaction was obtained only from fathers. Possibly mothers maintain closer contacts with their children—especially with daughters—during the high school years. Be this as it may, one father reports that:

> There is a difference when they grow older—particularly when they went to high school. Naturally they got their own friends and you saw less of them than you did before. They'd come home from school late and then they'd have a game or maybe the girl would have a date and you might see them at dinner time, but you probably wouldn't see them until breakfast— or maybe after the game or date.

Another father stated that the "best years" were when his boys were around nine or ten: (When they started to grow up did you feel that they were growing away from you?) "No, but when they go to high school they have different ideas and interests than the people at home have." There is, however, another side to this coin. The proud father of a high school athlete was asked when was the happiest time of his life: "Oh—that kid of mine—the things he did when he was in high school. It was like living your life over again. I guess I really enjoyed that period."

On the basis of such observations, there is reason to believe that there are bridges—transitional learning experiences which aid parents in adapting themselves to postparental life. These appear to provide continuity in role conditioning. Such "rehearsals" are not as difficult as "opening night," the real and permanent departure of the children which will come later. They are defined as temporary and are broken by regular visits home or the expectation that the children will at some time again return to live at home. But the "temporary" can gradually shift into the permanent without any traumatic transition. "My daughter went to California, to Berkeley, to go to school. Then she decided to work there a while and then she got married out there and she has lived there ever since." The fact that these socializing experiences occur at a time when the parents are still extremely active with their own affairs should not be ignored. It is probably easier to prepare for and accept such a transition in early middle age than in later years when it will actually occur. When one mother was asked how she made out at home with the children all off to college, she shrugged off the question with "Oh, I don't know. I was just too busy to be bothered about anything."

Life without Father

If there are temporary departures of the children which provide parents with an opportunity to practice the post-parental role, there is also a combination of recent historical events and cultural expectations which have provided middle-class fathers with an additional opportunity to practice this role. The historical events are the Great Depression and the Second World War; the cultural expectations are those related to the middle-class notion of "work." Unlike some of the temporary departures of children mentioned in the preceding section, a temporary shattering of the family constellation due to the exigencies of war, work, or economic depression can be rationalized as beyond the control of those involved—attributed to immitigable external forces. Such rationalization is not always possible when the family break-up results from a unilateral decision on the part of a child to leave home for reasons related to education or work. When opportunities to engage in these pursuits are locally available, the parents may view the child's decision as a rejection of themselves. Such a definition of the situation (whether accurate or inaccurate) is hardly conducive to promoting a smooth transition into postparental life.

Some fathers, owing to the press of circumstances, have lived for extended periods of time away from their wives and children.

> I was having a rough time. I was six months or a year on WPA and when I got off that I couldn't find anything. But I had a brother in Portland, Oregon, so I went out there and it seems I was away from mother (wife) and the kids for close to a year and a half.

> During the war my husband was on a swingshift and worked nights and then he was in the Hawaiian Islands for a year working for the Navy.

> Let me tell you how it was. On a certain day I had $50,000 in the bank and a $25,000 home paid for and all the trimmings to go with it. Three months later I borrowed $25 to send my wife and children up to Kansas City (from Oklahoma). It was months before I got things straightened out enough to join them.

> My husband was 38 and the company sent us to Ottawa (Kansas). The draft board there just had a high quota and they scraped the bottom of the barrel. That's how they got him.

Nearly one in every five of the families interviewed was broken for extended periods of time under circumstances similar to those described above. It is relevant that these experiences most often were narrated in response to questions about how close the father was to the children when they were growing up.

A somewhat more common experience (also usually discussed in relation to that same line of questioning) is the detachment of the father from his growing children and his lack of involvement in their activities as a result of his being "on the road." One third of these middle-class fathers found it necessary to travel regularly during some phase of their work career, and in all but one case this was defined as alienating the father from the children. When asked if she felt that she was closer to her children than her husband, one wife answered, "I think I was, definitely, because my husband is a traveling man. I really reared the children; most of the time he was only home Saturdays and Sundays." Other wives of traveling men tend to respond in like manner:

> He travels from Monday to Thursday and he's in Thursday evening until Monday morning. (Do you think this had anything to do with his relationship with the children when they were growing up?) Yes, quite a bit! They didn't have the companionship with their dad that I thought they should have had.

This is not a one-sided "mama's" point of view. As the following couplets excerpted from husband and wife interviews reveal, the husbands are in essential agreement on this matter:

> (1) WIFE: (Do you think your husband's occupation kept him away from the boys?) Very definitely! It was unfortunate too. He felt he was just not able to devote the time to them and it was not up to me to say what he should and should not do. (He was out of town a good part of the time?) Yes, when they were young he was gone a great deal. Then later on he had so much responsibility in the office. He was the kind that went early and stayed late. You see he had had considerable trouble when he was younger, seeing his mother working and slaving while his father was ill and he didn't want me to have to do the same thing. *That* result has been fine. But as for the boys, he never did have much time for them.

> HUSBAND: (Did you feel that your job kept you away from your children— that you didn't have enough time to spend with them?) I didn't have enough time to spend with them. When I was traveling I was away a great deal, and then when I went into the office my job there kept me on the job from early in the morning until dinner time and then I worked a good many nights at home. So I didn't have too much time with them.

> (2) WIFE: (Which one of you was closer to the children when they were younger?) I would say I was. For one thing, he was gone so much. He

would only see them on weekends. So I would definitely say they were closer to me. They respect their father and think a lot of him, but they wouldn't bring their problems to him as much as they would to me.

HUSBAND: (Tell me how your work affects your family life?) Well, like the average man gets up and goes to work every morning. *I* am out for a week! Now that we have better highways and faster cars you can make most all your territory in a week's time. I used to make a lot of two and three weeks' trips because we had slower cars and not very good highways and it took just that much longer.

Although improvements in transportation may have reduced the periods of absence, they still exist. However, simply because a man travels does not mean that he has become detached from his children and family. A railroader and his wife demonstrate how a family can be tightly knit because his absence for short periods results in his being home for five or six day "weekends." This traveling man had the opportunity to be closer to his family than most who do not travel:

(Do you think it took you away from your family too much to be on the road?) Well, I was away from the family. Like a trip from here to Omaha and Colorado it was two nights and one day away and come in and sleep a day and then go right back out again when I had to make two round trips. So I was four nights off on the road, but then I'd come in and I'd have five days off one time and six the next.

And from his wife:

Yes, he was on the road a lot. He was on the Super Chief on the Santa Fe Main Line. He was on that train for eleven years. (Would you rather he worked at something that kept him home?) Oh my no! He liked his work. He was on the railroad for 44 years. (Do you think his being away from home affected his relationship with the children?) No, no, they were always regular companions—all of them. He knew the children as well as I did.

As has been indicated in some of the passages cited, even when father is at home, he may be so in body only, being engrossed in his work day and night whether on the road or in town. When this kind of commitment to work evolves, men whose work never takes them out of town may see less of their families than some who, like the railroader, travel a great deal. One mother generalizes: "I think most men are so occupied with their work that they sort of leave that (rearing of children) to the mother." A father whose work has never taken him out of town concurs: "I'm afraid I left most of bringing him up to his mother. Lots of times when he was growing up I had to work late. I wouldn't get home till 9:30 or 10:00 at night and I'd be out to the office at 5:00 in the morning."

It is important, however, that this parental detachment not be over-emphasized. Not all middle-class fathers orient themselves to the work role so strongly. There are certainly some who leave their work at the office: "I have no night work. My work is at the office and when I leave the office I'm through until the next day, regardless of what I've got. I've never made a practice of bringing work home." There are others who emphasize that, in spite of many temptations, they have steadfastly refused to take their work out of the office.

It would seem that there are a good many cases among urban middle-class families where life goes on without father during the years when the child is growing up. As dysfunctional as this may be to the family at that stage, it does provide the fathers with continuity in role conditioning which can stand them in good stead at the later postparental stage when the time comes for the children to depart permanently.

The Mother-in-Law Myth as a Conditioning Device

If the work role helps to condition fathers for the departure of their children, at least some mothers appear to be provided with a conditioning device which is the distinctive property of their sex. That device is the cultural myth of the mother-in-law: "As soon as my youngsters were born I made up my mind that I was not going to be a mother-in-law like you read about." Such a resolution, if intended seriously, could go far in preparing a mother to accept the departure of her children. In addition to the folklore on the mother-in-law, there is the reality of experience:

> My son got married before he even finished his education. He was only seventeen years old, but I did not say a word! I don't think it's good policy. That can be a very tender spot. I know because I went through it. I had a mother-in-law—well, she was just butting into everything all the time. I just resolved never to act like that myself. The Bible says something about to hold your peace. And that's not prose. That's just the way it should be. People when they get married should get away from relatives. Far enough away so that it takes three days for a postcard to get to them and three more for it to get back.

The following mother expresses the same opinion even more vehemently:

> I'll go to the county home before I'll live with any of my children. I have very definite ideas on that. Because I had his mother with us every winter for 20 years whether I had room for her or not and it *doesn't* work and I very *definitely* will *not* do a thing like that! I have to take a dose of strychnine first, I won't!

Humor is, of course, an effective form of social control—especially in an increasingly other-directed society. Mothers, like everyone else, are sensitive to the pleas of the mass media for conformity. They want to be "good" mothers-in-law and Evelyn Duvall's study indicates that they are—that the mother-in-law is not nearly the center of conflict in America that she is often thought to be. It is very possible that a more accurate statement would be that the mother-in-law is not nearly the center of conflict that she *used* to be. The pressures of experience and folklore as indicated in the passages cited above may have brought about a shift in the self-conception of mothers-in-law and in the role which they play. In any event, at least in some cases, these myths and experiences provide an opportunity for mothers to anticipate and prepare themselves for postparental life—a socializing opportunity.

Survivals of an Older Family Pattern

The postparental phase of the family cycle was described earlier as a newly emerging phenomenon resulting from increasing longevity and decreasing fertility. No longer is it true, as it was at the turn of the century, that both parents will have died before the last of their children was launched. However, as with any emerging phenomenon, fragmentary survivals of the earlier pattern remain. In such cases, there is, in effect, no transition to make—these people have no postparental period. Take, for example, the couple with six children ranging in age from 31 to 44, with three of them married and residing in the metropolitan area and a fourth divorced and living at home. Their daily life remains essentially the same as it has always been, although the work is somewhat lighter and the economic situation somewhat more secure:

> (Tell me just how you spend a typical day nowadays?) Well, I do my housework in the morning and then I get meals again, and the children will come in once in a while and sometimes I go down to one of my daughters'. That is all I do. I have a fine family. They are all good Christian children and I am just as proud of them as I can be.

Life has changed so little for this couple that they even argue about the same kinds of trivialities they did thirty years ago:

> . . . take that rug there in the dining room. I didn't like the color but he bought it anyway because it was a good buy. It was a remnant. But it seemed to me that a rug is something that you have to live with for a long time and it ought to satisfy you. But he said that I had had my way with the wallpaper so he went ahead and bought it.

An extended family need not be one of procreation; even with few children, postparental couples may refer themselves to a large family of orientation. This older pattern manifests itself in the case of a couple one of whose two married children is now living in Minneapolis. In spite of this, there is a plethora of parental siblings, in-laws, nephews, nieces, and grandchildren—all part of a second- and third-generation Irish clan residing in the Kansas City area:

(Tell me what you do with your time these days?) Well, we are quite home people, that is, with the grandchildren, the daughter, and his (husband's) people. He has seven brothers and they are all living in Kansas City, and we are very close to one another—the husbands and wives. We have picnics, and we go from home to home for little parties and then I have my sisters too and they live here. You know, we just enjoy family. I have brothers and sisters and he has all brothers. So that gives me a lot of sisters-in-law too. So we are very family people—very home people.

This kind of extended family support appears to lessen the trauma of the disintegration of the family of procreation. Most families, however, find themselves far more isolated from "kin-folk" in the modern American city.

Summary and Conclusion

We have seen that several conditioning situations present themselves as potential aids in the socialization of parents for postparental life. These situations provide an opportunity to anticipate postparental roles, not by taking the role of the other in the usual sense, but by experiencing analogous situations which are quasi-postparental and which enable the parents to play-at anticipated roles. There is the underlying value in our society on change for its own sake—a value which can be applied to the particular case of change in the family structure; there are the temporary departures of children during the adolescent years for college, service in the armed forces, and a variety of other reasons; there is the modern complex of urban high school life, which can move the children into a world which is foreign to their parents; there are the exigencies of the work situation which often remove the middle-class father from the family during the years when the children are growing up; there is the myth and the reality of the mother-in-law which some mothers internalize as lessons for themselves. In addition, remnants of the older extended family pattern which tend to reduce the impact of the transition cannot be ignored.

It was stated earlier that *theoretically* this could be assumed to be a difficult transition to make, largely because of the absence of role models —the absence of socialization to play postparental roles. However, middle-aged couples whose children have left home indicate that there are opportunities for them to learn these new roles before they are thrust upon them.

It was also stated earlier that much of the descriptive literature indicates that this is a difficult period of life. By and large such observations are based on clinical experiences with persons who have so much difficulty in making the transition that they must seek outside help. The small group of postparental spouses interviewed by the present writer represent a random sample of such people who discussed their lives in their own living room. Although definite conclusions cannot be drawn from the responses of this small fragment of the population, they have managed to provide us with some notion of the variety of alternative modes of anticipatory socialization available to their ilk. It would appear from their comments that it is reasonable to assume that people do have opportunities to prepare for postparental life and, in addition, that most of them take advantage of these opportunities.

This phase of the family cycle is seen by the majority of middle-aged spouses as a time of new freedoms: freedom from the economic responsibilities of children; freedom to be mobile (geographically); freedom from housework and other chores. And, finally, freedom to be one's self for the first time since the children came along. No longer do the parents need to live the self-consciously restricted existence of models for their own children: "We just take life easy now that the children are grown. We even serve dinner right from the stove when we're alone. It's hotter that way, but you just couldn't let down like that when your children are still at home."

43. THE COUPLE IN OLD AGE

Ruth Shonle Cavan

§ In this article, old age is analyzed in terms of changes in or loss of the close associations wherein adult roles were first formed and played (work for the husband, home for the wife). In old age, compensating group associations are difficult to find to replace the earlier ones and usually offer little outlet for earlier roles and often no opportunity for new roles of equal status. With changes in roles come also changes in self-concepts, which often are of a character that the old person finds hard to accept.

The concepts of self-conception, role-taking, and role-playing have possibilities for a significant analysis of adjustment to old age. They are here applied, first, to retirement from occupation, which is commonly accepted as the most acute adjustment that the older man has to make.

SOURCE: Arnold M. Rose, ed., *Human Behavior and Social Processes* (Boston: Houghton Mifflin Company, 1962), pp. 526–35, with certain omissions. Reprinted by permission of the publisher. This paper was read at the Twentieth Groves Conference on Marriage and the Family, May 1, 1957, East Lansing, Michigan.

The author's background is given in the footnote for article 13.

The concepts are further tested in brief analyses of the adjustment of the retired man to his family, the adjustment of the widow, and adjustment to grandparenthood. These situations should be regarded as illustrative of the way in which the three concepts may illuminate adjustment in old age.

Retirement

Both self-conceptions and the social roles through which they find expression are culturally determined. Moreover, some conceptions and roles have higher public esteem than others. For example, the "ideal" male self-conception is the mature adult who is at the height of his powers in a position that he has reached competitively through his own efforts. The self-made man in general is more highly respected than the one who steps in at the top because of family contacts; the employed man outclasses the unemployed or the retired; the self-supporting man has a higher status than the one who depends upon some form of assistance or pension, unless he has earlier contributed to the pension. These different valuations are extremely important at the time of retirement.

At the point of retirement, we may make a generalized picture of the male. He has a well-ingrained self-image as competent, successful at some level of work, usefully productive, self-supporting, and able to provide for his family. This image has been built up over years of time by the favorable reactions of his family, friends, co-workers, and those segments of society whose opinion he values. He has, moreover, found a kind of work—a social role—that permits him to express his self-image satisfactorily, and he is firmly incorporated into a physical environment and a group of co-workers which make it possible for him to carry out his role.

Using the concepts employed above, let us consider what happens at the point of compulsory retirement. First, the means of carrying out the social role disappears: the man is a lawyer without a case, a bookkeeper without books, a machinist without tools. Second, he is excluded from his group of former co-workers; as an isolated person he may be completely unable to function in his former role. Third, as a retired person, he begins to find a different evaluation of himself in the minds of others from the evaluation he had as an employed person. He no longer sees respect in the eyes of former subordinates, praise in the faces of former superiors, and approval in the manner of former co-workers. The looking glass composed of his former important groups throws back a changed image: he is done for, an old-timer, old fashioned, on the shelf. Fourth, he cannot accept this new evaluation for several reasons. He has had the old self-image for so many years that it has become part and parcel of him and is no longer dependent upon the current reflection of himself that he sees in the words and gestures of others. Long ago he internalized satisfying group reflections which now form a kind of independent self-conception. His self-image therefore is in conflict with the reflection he now finds in the attitudes and actions of others. Any movement toward solving the conflict is made difficult because the new self-image offered by those around him is of lower valuation than his internalized self-image.

Therefore at retirement we have a man still motivated by his old self-conception, but separated from his previous roles and many of his previous evaluative groups. He is a true social isolate. Moreover, the faint traces of a new self-image that he sees reflected in old and perhaps new groups is distasteful and unrewarding. His emotional reactions are likely to be distressing.

We will not go into the changes in this general sequence made by such factors as ill health, voluntary retirement, or retirement of the person who dislikes his work.

Let us look rather at what would be necessary to give a retired person a satisfying adjustment experience. The same concepts are involved as in the original building up of a self-image. First, there would need to be a culturally approved set of values for old age as the basis for a new self-conception. At present, old age is more or less of a vacuum; culturally, it has few real values. Second, these values would have to be accepted and respected by society itself and by the specific groups to which the retired person belonged. Without these two steps the retired person is almost helpless to change his self-image in a constructive manner. His new self-image will develop as his original self-image developed —through finding in others an evaluation of himself as a retired person which he can internalize. Third, new roles are needed through which the retired person may find expression for his new self-image.

Two difficulties exist at present. (a) To be satisfying, the new self-image offered by society should be the equivalent in respect of the one he has lost through retirement. A solution is found in partial retirement or in the transition from active worker to consultant. The old self-image may then be retained. Other solutions are less happy. One new self-conception offered to the retired man is the man of leisure who makes a career of leisure-time activities. While recreation has a definite value, to make a career of recreation, hobbies, and the like goes against deeply instilled values. The playboy has never held the respect given to the industrious producer. Another new conception offered by society is the image of oneself as old—that is, identification with old age itself. The names of clubs often suggest simply an old age self-conception: Golden Age Club, Borrowed Time Club, Three-Quarter Century Club, Senior

Citizens, and so on. Thus the lawyer, doctor, philanthropist, shop superintendent, and foreman are all invited to stop being their former selves and to become generalized old age selves.

(*b*) The second difficulty is that many retired men have no real social group to replace their former co-workers. Many recreational and other programs are offered to the retired by social welfare or recreational workers, who make up a group in which the retired man does not have membership. Recall that the self-image is created by the evaluation of a group in which the person has membership. In time, the recreational club may form its own social group exclusive of social workers and may create some new self-conceptions. Such self-conceptions are often limited, however, in that they may not be capable of expression in any group except the club itself.

The present rush to find activities to fill leisure time for old people will not solve the problem of retirement adjustment satisfactorily. The two basic ingredients for adjustment are a culturally approved concept of an old age self held in respect by groups that are meaningful to the old person, and provision to express overtly the implications of the self-image. These elements usually are not present in the present programs devised for the old.

Adjustment of the Retired Man to His Family

An important adjustment that the retired man has to make is to his family. At the time a man retires his immediate family usually consists only of his wife. The wife, like the husband, has a long established self-image. For a woman now in her sixties, the basic self-image is usually that of wife, mother, homemaker, with a peripheral self of church or community worker, which is in reality but an extension of the homemaker self. Her image has been reflected with approval by family, friends, and community. Her overt role has consisted in establishing the tone of the home, doing or managing the housework, planning and purchasing, giving her husband sympathy and support in his work, and in earlier years rearing children. She has already made one change in her self-image when her children married and left home. Although this change is difficult for some women, it actually is less difficult than the retirement adjustment of the husband. The wife still receives a favorable reflection of herself from those around her, for her married and self-supporting children are a credit to her; and she retains much of the old self-conception and attendant role in continuing as homemaker and companion for her husband. Moreover, society has provided a new self-image for the woman who finds her life too constricted after children leave. The middle-aged employed woman now is socially accepted, and many types of work are open to her. She may devise some mixture of the old and new selves or she may discard the old homemaker self-image and develop a new employed-woman self-image. However, with the present group of retired husbands, the percentage of working wives is low, and the self-image usually is that of wife, homemaker, and retired mother.

Before the retirement of the husband, the self-images and the social roles of husband and wife were neatly dovetailed. It was conceded that the husband's role had slightly higher social status and that he was the head of the family. In her own home, however, the wife reigned supreme. Her self-conception included her queenship in the dominion of the home.

When the retired husband finds himself without his usual means of expression of his self-conception through his work role, he may try to work out a new role at home, without materially changing his self-image. Like a bull in a china shop, we have a man whose self-conception tells him to be competent, decisive, and productive, electing to express this self in a situation in which the available roles are already well filled by his wife, who, within her home, visualizes herself as competent, decisive, and productive. The husband's entrance into the situation tends to create tension in the former coordination between himself and his wife with respect both to their self-images and their roles. The husband sometimes attempts to express his superior status by assuming the decision-making roles in the home; or he may become a self-appointed expert, either criticizing or making suggestions regarding the way in which his wife manages the home. In thus attempting to give expression to his self-conception, he threatens his wife's image of herself. The wife is not opposed to having help in her housekeeping, but her self-conception calls for subordinates who take directions from her. Here, then, is a serious conflict between husband and wife in terms of their self-conceptions and roles. The problem is not one of what housework the husband will do, but of how the self-conceptions of husband and wife will be readjusted. If she retains her superior status and its self-image, his self-conception is damaged; if the husband takes control, the wife's self-conception is damaged.

Often husband and wife go through a period of incipient or actual conflict while self-images and roles are adjusted to a new orientation. Often these adjustments work out very well, especially if increasing age diminishes the desire of both husband and wife for full-time work. In other families, however, little change occurs in the self-images. Accommodation may be made only in roles, as some functions are assigned to the husband and the two overtly carry out coordinated roles. But each may feel dissatisfied and frustrated, with the result that there is bickering between the two.

Widowhood

Eventually each family dwindles to one person, and this person is more likely to be the wife than the husband. Only the widow will be discussed.

Instead of looking at widowhood only in terms of loneliness and lack of support, it is helpful to consider it also in terms of self and role. As we have just seen, the self-conceptions as well as the roles of husband and wife become well coordinated during the period when the husband is working; after the husband's retirement, and a transitional period of tensions, the coordination may become even closer with a new orientation. The death of the husband therefore severely disturbs the self-image of the wife. In a sense the two self-images have come to form one unit, a kind of family self-conception carried out jointly by husband and wife. Must the widow expand her self-image to include that of her husband, or must the family concept shrink to match her self-image? One may surmise that sometimes one thing happens and sometimes the other. Some widows seem to acquire the attributes of their former husbands; other widows never seem to recover from the bisecting blow of death. The widow may assume the overt roles or tasks of her husband, but this move may be because of necessity. It is in the intangible adjustment of self-image that the heart of the problem of adjustment lies.

If the widow is to modify her self-image, we must go back again to the conditions under which new self-images arise—the culturally acceptable pattern for self-conceptions, and groups of which the widow is a member which will help her achieve a new self-image through their approving evaluation of her change. Fortunately in the case of widowhood, the culture has devised several appropriate self-conceptions. It is important also to recall that the widow usually retains at least some of her old group memberships. She will receive a favorable reflection from her groups if she is courageous, if she attacks practical problems realistically, if she increases her civic or church work, and so forth.

It is at the point of widowhood that adult children often enter the picture, sympathetically offering the mother a home with the family of one of them. If the shock of death has been severe or if there are not sufficient financial resources for continued independence, such a move may be wise. It involves, however, some serious changes in self-conceptions for all concerned. We will consider primarily the situation of the widow. She is now very much in the position of the man who has experienced compulsory retirement. She retains her former self-image as competent housekeeper, companion to her husband, and so forth. But she has no way in which to enact the appropriate roles to give expression to this self-image. As in any well-coordinated household, the members of the younger family have developed self-images and roles that fit together to produce a unified family. It often seems impossible for such a unified family to open to admit an old relative in any except a subordinate— and, to the old person, almost disgraceful—status. Moreover, if the move has carried the widow into another city, she loses her supporting group of friends. Her children's friends are kind to her but do not accept her as an important person with a self of her own. She is Charlie's aunt or Ida's mother. Hence the widow who moves into a younger functioning family in a new community has none of the elements for the construction of a satisfying new self-image. Unless the family is wise enough to help her find a new and respected self-image and accompanying role, she is likely to deteriorate rapidly in personality or to become chronically complaining and disgruntled. It should be emphasized here that the step needed is not to provide love and activities alone, but also to provide a new and valued self-conception which will receive approval and which may be appropriately expressed.

Grandparenthood

Finally, a word about the grandparent self-conception. Often this self-conception has been absorbed into the personality during the fifties or early sixties, especially on the part of women. In fact, some women visualize themselves as grandparents before a child is born and eagerly await the birth of a grandchild so that they may express the grandmother self-image in an appropriate role.

During middle age, men may be proud of their grandchildren, but perhaps do not savor the role completely until after retirement. At first, the man may have some difficulty in accepting the grandfather self as the culture defines it. In the patriarchal and to some extent in the patri-centered family, the grandfather self-image was one of authority and responsibility. Now, however, change has swept away this often satisfying self-image. As the culture defines the grandfather self-image and social role they are maternal in nature. The approved grandparent self is really a grandmother self-conception, whether the holder is the grandfather or the grandmother. Unless the child's own father is dead or not functioning in his role, the grandfather has little opportunity to function in the father role, which is one of financial supporter and source of authority as well as teacher and friend. The child's father guards his self-image and role jealously because they contribute to his conception as head of his family. The maternal role is less precisely defined and may be filled concurrently or successively by a number of different people, each of whom may develop some degree of maternal self-image. In this array of people who fill a maternal role toward the child the retired grandfather takes his place. He must see himself in relation to his grandchild not as a secondary father but as a minor form of mother. His role is to baby-sit, spoon in food, and trundle the baby around in its carriage. If he resents the role, he may arouse some resentment in turn from the baby's mother, who is often pressed for a responsible subordinate. If he accepts the role and develops a slightly masculine grandmother self-image, he may receive an emotional experience that he missed when his own children were young and his time was absorbed in earning a living for them. But to enjoy it he must genuinely be able to acquire a grandparent conception of himself and discover the values in the conception, for the self-image and the role differ widely from the man-of-affairs self and role which dominated his earlier years. Fortunately, the elements for developing a grandparent self are present in the culture. Since children are highly valued in the United States, the mere possession of a grandchild brings respect (or even envy) from friends and from society in general. Since the maternal type of grandparent image is virtually the only one in existence in the United States, the retired man trundling the baby carriage does not feel out of place. The baby comes to love the kindly man who helps to care for it, and the hurried mother adds her thanks. Thus the members of the man's social group approve of the self-image and he sees himself reflected on all sides as a good grandfather filling a valued position.

Conclusion

This essay has attempted to point out the way in which the concepts of self-conception based upon role-taking and social role-playing can be helpful in analyzing certain kinds of adjustment in old age and in suggesting how better adjustment could be manipulated. The necessary elements for forming, maintaining, or modifying self-conceptions are socially approved self-images and social roles for their expression, and a group that supports these self-images and roles. To achieve or modify a self-image, the person must be a member of one of these groups and must value the group's evaluation of himself. He will then incorporate within himself the self-image approved by the group. He will need continued membership and the opportunity to enact an appropriate role. These elements are all present at the point of original formulation of self-images in youth, but are partially or completely lacking at the point of reformulations in old age.

Chapter 15: Severe Stresses on the Family

44. ALCOHOLISM AND THE FAMILY

Joan K. Jackson

§ A personal and family problem now receiving intensive research is alcoholism. In this article Dr. Jackson, who has carried on extensive research in this field, discusses some alternative theories of the relation of the wife of an alcoholic to his alcoholism. She also treats the situation as a family crisis and shows the process that the family follows in attempting to adjust to the situation. The reader will find the discussion of how the crisis is handled useful also in connection with other kinds of critical disorganization.

Until recently it was possible to think of alcoholism as if it involved the alcoholic only. Most of the alcoholics studied were inmates of publicly supported institutions: jails, mental hospitals, and public general hospitals. These ill people appeared to be homeless and tieless. As the public became more aware of the extent and nature of alcoholism and that treatment possibilities existed, alcoholics who were still integral parts of the community appeared at clinics. The definition of "the problems of alcoholism" has had to be broadened to include all those with whom the alcoholic is or has been in close and continuing contact.

At present we do not know how many nonalcoholics are affected directly by alcoholism. However, an estimate can be derived from the available statistics on the marital histories of alcoholics. The recurrently arrested alcoholic seems to affect the fewest nonalcoholics. Reports range from 19 per cent to 51 per cent who have never married—this is,

SOURCE: *Annals of the American Academy of Political and Social Science*, 315 (January, 1958), 90–98. Reprinted by permission of the publisher. Several footnotes have been omitted.

The author is a sociologist who received her doctorate from the University of Washington. The research here reported was supported in part by the National Institute of Mental Health, U.S. Public Health Service. Her findings have been reported in a number of professional journals in addition to the *Annals*, e.g., *Marriage and Family Living* and the *Quarterly Journal of Studies on Alcohol*.

from slightly more than the expected number of single men to three to four times the expected rate. The vast majority who had married are now separated from their families. Alcoholics who voluntarily seek treatment at clinics affect the lives of more people than jailed alcoholics. While the number of broken marriages is still excessive, approximately the expected number of voluntary patients have been married. Any estimate of nonalcoholics affected must take into consideration not only the present marital status of alcoholics, but also the past marital history. About one-third of the alcoholics have been married more than once. Jailed alcoholics had multiple marriages less frequently than clinic alcoholics.

There has been no enumeration of the children and other relatives influenced by alcoholism. From the author's studies it can be estimated that for each alcoholic there are at least two people in the immediate family who are affected. Approximately two-thirds of the married alcoholics have children, thus averaging two apiece. Family studies indicate that a minimum of one other relative is also directly involved. The importance of understanding the problems faced by the families of alcoholics is obvious from these figures. To date, little is known about the nature of the effects of living with or having lived with an alcoholic. However, there is considerable evidence that it has disturbing effects on the personalities of family members.

Once attention had been focussed on the families of alcoholics, it became obvious that the relationship between the alcoholic and his family is not a one-way relationship. The family also affects the alcoholic and his illness. The very existence of family ties appears to be related to recovery from alcoholism. Some families are successful in helping their alcoholic member to recognize his need for help and are supportive of treatment efforts. Yet other types of families may discourage the patient from seeking treatment and may actually encourage the persistence of alcoholism. It is now believed that the most successful treatment of alcoholism involves helping both the alcoholic and those members of his family who are directly involved in his drinking behavior.

The Alcoholic and His Children

The children are affected by living with an alcoholic more than any other family member. Personalities are formed in a social milieu which is markedly unstable, torn with dissension, culturally deviant, and socially disapproved. The children must model themselves on adults who play their roles in a distorted fashion. The alcoholic shows little adequate adult behavior. The nonalcoholic parent attempts to play the roles of both father and mother, often failing to do either well.

The child of an alcoholic is bound to have problems in learning who he is, what is expected of him, and what he can expect from others. Almost inevitably his parents behave inconsistently towards him. His self-conception evolves in a situation in which the way others act towards him has more to do with the current events in the family than with the child's nature. His alcoholic parent feels one way about him when he is sober, another when drunk, and yet another during the hangover stage.

What the child can expect from his parents will also depend on the phase of the drinking cycle as well as on where he stands in relation to each parent at any given time. Only too frequently he is used in the battle between them. The wives of alcoholics find themselves disliking, punishing, or depriving the children preferred by the father and those who resemble him. Similarly, the child who is preferred by, or resembles the mother is often hurt by the father. If the child tries to stay close to both parents he is caught in an impossible situation. Each parent resents the affection the other receives while demanding that the child show affection to both.

The children do not understand what is happening. The very young ones do not know that their families are different from other families. When they become aware of the differences, the children are torn between their own loyalty and the views of their parents that others hold. When neighbors ostracize them, the children are bewildered about what *they* did to bring about this result. Even those who are not ostracized become isolated. They hesitate to bring their friends to a home where their parent is likely to be drunk.

The behavior of the alcoholic parent is unpredictable and unintelligible to the child. The tendency of the child to look for the reasons in his own behavior very often is reinforced inadvertently by his mother. When father is leading up to a drinking episode, the children are put on their best behavior. When the drinking episode occurs, it is not surprising that the children feel that they have somehow done something to precipitate it.

Newell[1] states that the children of alcoholics are placed in a situation very similar to that of the experimental animals who are tempted towards rewards and then continually frustrated, whose environment changes constantly in a manner over which they have no control. Under such circumstances experimental animals have convulsions or "nervous breakdowns." Unfortunately, we still know very little about what happens to the children or about the duration of the effects.

Yet some of the children appear undisturbed. The personality damage appears to be least when the nonalcoholic parent is aware of the problems they face, gives them emotional support, keeps from using them

[1] N. Newell, "Alcoholism and the Father Image," *Quarterly Journal of Studies on Alcohol*, Vol. 11, March 1950, pp. 92–96.

against the alcoholic, tries to be consistent, and has insight into her own problems with the alcoholic. It also appears to mitigate some of the child's confusion if alcoholism is explained to him by a parent who accepts alcoholism as an illness.

The Alcoholic and His Wife

The wives of alcoholics have received considerably more attention than the children. The focus tends to be on how they affect the alcoholic and his alcoholism, rather than on how alcoholism and the alcoholic affect them. Most writers seem to feel that the wives of alcoholics are drawn from the ranks of emotionally disturbed women who seek out spouses who are not threatening to them, spouses who can be manipulated to meet their own personality needs. According to this theory, the wife has a vested interest in the persistence of the alcoholism of her spouse. Her own emotional stability depends upon it. Should the husband become sober, the wives are in danger of decompensating and showing marked neurotic disturbances.

A complementary theory suggests that prealcoholic or alcoholic males tend to select certain types of women as wives. The most commonly reported type is a dominating, maternal woman who uses her maternal role as a defense against inadequate femininity.

Any attempt to assess the general applicability of this theory to *all* the wives of alcoholics runs into difficulties. First, the only wives who can be studied by researchers are those who have stayed with their husbands until alcoholism was well under way. The high divorce rate among alcoholics suggests that these wives are the exception rather than the rule. The majority of women who find themselves married to alcoholics appear to divorce them. Second, if a high rate of emotional disturbance is found among women still living with alcoholics, it is difficult to determine whether the personality difficulties antedated or postdated the alcoholism, whether they were partly causal or whether they emerged during the recurrent crises and the cumulative stresses of living with an alcoholic. Third, the wives who were studied were women who were actively blocking the treatment of their husbands, who had entered mental hospitals after their husbands' sobriety, who were themselves seeking psychiatric care, or who were in the process of manipulating social agencies to provide services. It is of interest that neither of the studies which deal with women who were taking an active part in their husbands' recovery process comment upon any similarities in the personality structures of the wives.

It is likely that the final test of the hypotheses about the role of the wives' personalities in their husbands' alcoholism will have to await the accumulation of considerably more information. No alcoholic personality type has been found on psychological tests; no tests have been given to the wives of alcoholics. Until we know more about the etiology of alcoholism and its remedy, the role of the wives' personalities in its onset, in its persistence, and in its alleviation will remain in the realm of speculation.

No one denies that the wives of active alcoholics are emotionally disturbed. In nonthreatening situations, the wives are the first to admit their own concerns about "their sanity." Of over one hundred women who attended a discussion group at one time or another during the past six years, there was not one who failed to talk about her concerns about her own emotional health. All of the women worry about the part which their attitudes and behavior play in the persistence of the drinking and in their families' disturbances. Although no uniform personality types are discernible, they do share feelings of confusion and anxiety. Most feel ambivalent about their husbands. However, this group is composed of women who are oriented towards changing themselves and the situation rather than escaping from it.

The Impact of Alcoholism on the Family

When two or more persons live together over a period of time, patterns of relating to one another evolve. In a family, a division of functions occurs and roles interlock. For the family to function smoothly, each person must play his roles in a predictable manner and according to the expectations of others in the family. When the family as a whole is functioning smoothly, individual members of the family also tend to function well. Everyone is aware of where he fits, what he is expected to do, and what he can expect from others in the family. When this organization is disrupted, repercussions are felt by each family member. A crisis is under way.

Family crises tend to follow a similar pattern, regardless of the nature of the precipitant. Usually there is an initial denial that a problem exists. The family tries to continue in its usual behavior patterns until it is obvious that these patterns are no longer effective. At this point there is a downward slump in organization. Roles are played with less enthusiasm and there is an increase in tensions and strained relationships. Finally an improvement occurs as some adjustive technique is successful. Family organization becomes stabilized at a new level. At each stage of the crisis there is a reshuffling of roles among family members, changes in status and prestige, changes in "self" and "other" images, shifts in family solidarity and self-sufficiency and in the visibility of the crisis to outsiders. In the process of the crisis, considerable mental conflict is engendered in all family members, and personality distortion occurs. These are the elements which are uniform regardless of the type of family crisis. The phases vary in length and intensity depending on the nature of the crisis and the nature of the individuals involved in it.

When one of the adults in a family becomes an alcoholic, the over-all pattern of the crisis takes a form similar to that of other family crises. However there are usually recurrent subsidiary crises which complicate the over-all situation and the attempts at its resolution. Shame, unemployment, impoverishment, desertion and return, nonsupport, infidelity, imprisonment, illness and progressive dissension also occur. For other types of family crises, there are cultural prescriptions for socially appropriate behavior and for procedures which will terminate the crisis. But this is not so in the case of alcoholism. The cultural view is that alcoholism is shameful and should not occur. Thus, when facing alcoholism, the family is in a socially unstructured situation and must find the techniques for handling the crisis through trial and error behavior and without social support. In many respects, there are marked similarities between the type of crisis precipitated by alcoholism and those precipitated by mental illness.

Attempts to Deny the Problem

Alcoholism rarely emerges full-blown overnight. It is usually heralded by widely spaced incidents of excessive drinking, each of which sets off a small family crisis. Both spouses try to account for the episode and then to avoid the family situations which appear to have caused the drinking. In their search for explanations, they try to define the situation as controllable, understandable, and "perfectly normal." Between drinking episodes, both feel guilty about their behavior and about their impact on each other. Each tries to be an "ideal spouse" to the other. Gradually not only the drinking problem, but also the other problems in the marriage are denied or sidestepped.

It takes some time before the wife realizes that the drinking is neither normal nor controllable behavior. It takes the alcoholic considerably longer to come to the same conclusion. The cultural view that alcoholics are Skid Row bums who are constantly inebriated also serves to keep the situation clouded. Friends compound the confusion. If the wife compares her husband with them, some show parallels to his behavior and others are in marked contrast. She wavers between defining his behavior as "normal" and "not normal." If she consults friends, they tend to discount her concern, thus facilitating her tendency to deny that a problem exists and adding to her guilt about thinking disloyal thoughts about her husband.

During this stage the family is very concerned about the social visibility of the drinking behavior. They feel that they would surely be ostracized if the extent of the drinking were known. To protect themselves against discovery, the family begins to cut down on their social activities and to withdraw into the home.

Attempts to Eliminate the Problem

The second stage begins when the family defines the alcoholic's drinking behavior as "not normal." At this point frantic efforts are made to eliminate the problem. Lacking clear-cut cultural prescriptions for what to do in a situation like this, the efforts are of the trial and error variety. In rapid succession, the wife threatens to leave the husband, babies him during hangovers, drinks with him, hides or empties his bottles, curtails money, tries to understand his problem, keeps his liquor handy for him, and nags at him. However, all efforts to change the situation fail. Gradually the family becomes so preoccupied with the problem of discovering how to keep father sober that all long-term family goals recede into the background.

At the same time isolation of the family reaches its peak intensity. The extreme isolation magnifies the importance of all intrafamily interactions and events. Almost all thought becomes drinking-centered. Drinking comes to symbolize all conflicts between the spouses, and even mother-child conflicts are regarded as indirect derivatives of the drinking behavior. Attempts to keep the social visibility of the behavior at the lowest possible level increase.

The husband-wife alienation also accelerates. Each feels resentful of the other. Each feels misunderstood and unable to understand. Both search frantically for the reasons for the drinking, believing that if the reason could be discovered, all family members could gear their behavior in a way to make the drinking unnecessary.

The wife feels increasingly inadequate as a wife, mother, woman, and person. She feels she has failed to make a happy and united home for her husband and children. Her husband's frequent comments to the effect that her behavior causes his drinking and her own concerns that this may be true intensified the process of self-devaluation.

Disorganization

This is a stage which could also be entitled "What's the use?" Nothing seems effective in stabilizing the alcoholic. Efforts to change the situation become, at best, sporadic. Behavior is geared to relieve tensions rather than to achieve goals. The family gives up trying to understand the alcoholic. They do not care if the neighbors know about the drinking. The children are told that their father is a drunk. They are no longer required to show him affection or respect. The myth that father still has an important status in the family is dropped when he no longer supports them, is imprisoned, caught in infidelity, or disappears for long periods of time. The family ceases to care about its self-sufficiency and begins to resort to public agencies for help, thereby losing self-respect.

The wife becomes very concerned about her sanity. She finds herself engaging in tension-relieving behavior which she knows is goalless. She is aware that she feels tense, anxious, and hostile. She regards her pre-crisis self as "the real me" and becomes very frightened at how she has changed.

Attempts to Reorganize in Spite of the Problem

When some major or minor subsidiary crisis occurs, the family is forced to take survival action. At this point many wives leave their husbands.

The major characteristic of this stage is that the wife takes over. The alcoholic is ignored or is assigned the status of the most recalcitrant child. When the wife's obligations to her husband conflict with those to her children, she decides in favor of the children. Family ranks are closed progressively and the father excluded.

As a result of the changed family organization, father's behavior constitutes less of a problem. Hostility towards him diminishes as the family no longer expects him to change. Feelings of pity, exasperation, and protectiveness arise.

The reorganization has a stabilizing effect on the children. They find their environment and their mother more consistent. Their relationship to their father is more clearly defined. Guilt and anxiety diminish as they come to accept their mother's view that drinking is not caused by any behavior of family members.

Long-term family goals and planning begin again. Help from public agencies is accepted as necessary and no longer impairs family self-respect. With the taking over of family control, the wife gradually regains her sense of worth. Her concerns about her emotional health decrease.

Despite the greater stabilization, subsidiary crises multiply. The alcoholic is violent or withdraws more often; income becomes more uncertain; imprisonments and hospitalizations occur more frequently. Each crisis is temporarily disruptive to the new family organization. The symbolization of these events as being caused by alcoholism, however, prevents the complete disruption of the family.

The most disruptive type of crisis occurs if the husband recognizes that he has a drinking problem and makes an effort to get help. Hope is mobilized. The family attempts to open its ranks again in order to give him the maximum chance for recovery. Roles are partially reshuffled and attempts at attitude change are made, only to be disrupted again if treatment is unsuccessful.

Efforts to Escape the Problem

The problems involved in separating from the alcoholic are similar to the problems involved in separation for any other reason. However, some of the problems are more intense. The wife, who could count on some support from her husband in earlier stages, even though it was a manipulative move on his part, can no longer be sure of any support. The mental conflict about deserting a sick man must be resolved as well as the wife's feelings of responsibility for his alcoholism. The family which has experienced violence from the alcoholic is concerned that separation may intensify the violence. When the decision is made to separate because of the drinking, the alcoholic often gives up drinking for a while, thereby removing what is apparently the major reason for the separation.

Some other events, however, have made separation possible. The wife has learned that the family can run smoothly without her husband. Taking over control has bolstered her self-confidence. Her orientation has shifted from inaction to action. The wife also has familiarity with public agencies which can provide help, and she has overcome her shame about using them.

Reorganization of the Family

Without the father, the family tends to reorganize rather smoothly. They have already closed ranks against him and now they feel free of the minor disruptions he still created in the family. Reorganization is impeded if the alcoholic continues to attempt reconciliation or feels he must "get even" with the family for deserting him.

The whole family becomes united when the husband achieves sobriety, whether or not separation has preceded. For the wife and husband facing a sober marriage after many years of an alcoholic marriage, the expectations for marriage without alcoholism are unrealistic and idealistic.

Many problems arise. The wife has managed the family for years. Now her husband wishes to be reinstated as head of the house. Usually the first role he re-establishes is that of bread-winner. With the resumption of this role, he feels that the family should reinstate him immediately in all his former roles. Difficulties inevitably follow. For example, the children are often unable to accept his resumption of the father role.

Their mother has been mother and father to them for so long that it takes time to get used to consulting their father. Often the father tries to manage his change overnight, and the very pressure he puts on the children towards this end defeats him.

The wife, who finds it difficult to believe that her husband is sober permanently, is often unwilling to relinquish her control of family affairs even though she knows that this is necessary to her husband's sobriety. She remembers when his failures to handle responsibility were catastrophic to the family. Used to avoiding any issues which might upset him, the wife often has difficulty discussing problems openly. If she permits him to resume his father role, she often feels resentful of his intrusion into territory she has come to regard as her own. If he makes any decisions which are detrimental to the family, her former feelings of superiority may be mobilized and affect her relationship with him.

Gradually the difficulties related to alcoholism recede into the past and family adjustment at some level is achieved. The drinking problem shows up only sporadically—when the time comes for a decision about permitting the children to drink or when pressure is put on the husband to drink at a party.

Personality Disturbances in Family Members

Each stage in the crisis of alcoholism has distinctive characteristics. The type of problems faced, the extent to which the situation is structured, the amount of emotional support received by individual family members, and the rewards vary as to the stage of the crisis. Some stages "fit" the personalities of the individuals involved better than others.

Although each stage of the crisis appears to give rise to some similar patterns of response, there is considerable variation from family to family. The wife whose original personality fits comfortably into denying the existence of the problem will probably take longer to get past this phase of the crisis than the wife who finds dominating more congenial. The latter will probably prolong the stage of attempting to eliminate the problem. Some families make an adjustment at one level of the crisis and never seem to go on to the next phase.

With the transition from one stage to another, there is the danger of marked personality disturbance in family members. Some become their most disturbed when drinking first becomes a problem; others become most disturbed when the alcoholic becomes sober. In the experience of the author, there has been little uniformity within families or between families in this respect. However, after two or three years of sobriety, the alcoholics' family members appear to resemble a cross section of people anywhere. Any uniformities which were obvious earlier seem to have disappeared.

Therapy and the Family

The major goal of the families of most alcoholics is to find some way of bringing about a change in father's drinking. When the alcoholic seeks treatment, the family members usually have very mixed feelings towards the treatment agency. Hope that father may recover is remobilized and if sobriety ensues for any length of time, they are grateful. At the same time, they often feel resentment that an outside agency can accomplish what they have tried to do for years. They may also resent the emotional support which the alcoholic receives from the treatment agency, while they are left to cope with still another change in their relationship to him without support.

Most families have little awareness of what treatment involves and are forced to rely on the alcoholic patient for their information. The patient frequently passes on a distorted picture in order to manipulate the family situation for his own ends. What information is given is perceived by the family against a background of their attitudes towards the alcoholic at that point in time. The actions they take are also influenced by their estimate of the probability that treatment will be successful. The result is often a family which works at cross purposes with therapy.

Recently there has been a growing recognition that the family of the alcoholic also requires help if the alcoholic is to be treated successfully. An experiment was tried at the Henry Phipps Psychiatric Clinic of Johns Hopkins Hospital. Alcoholics and their wives were treated in concurrent group therapy sessions. The Al-Anon Family Groups provide the same type of situation for the families of AA members and have the additional asset of helping the families of alcoholics who are still not interested in receiving help for themselves. Joint treatment of alcoholics and the members of their family aims at getting a better understanding of the underlying emotional disturbance, of the relationship between the alcoholic and the person who is most frequently the object and stimulus of the drinking behavior, and of the treatment process.[2]

Joint treatment of the alcoholic and his family has other assets, as Gliedman and his co-workers point out.[3] Joint therapy emphasizes the marriage. In addition, with both spouses coming for help, there is less likelihood that undertaking treatment will be construed as an admission of guilt or that therapy will be used as a weapon by one against the other. The wife's entrance into therapy is a tacit admission of her need to change too. It represents a hopeful attitude on the part of both the

[2] L. H. Gliedman, D. Rosenthal, J. Frank, H. T. Nash, "Group Therapy of Alcoholics with Concurrent Group Meetings of Their Wives," *Quarterly Journal of Studies on Alcohol*, Vol. 17, December 1956, pp. 655–70.
[3] *Ibid.*

alcoholic and his wife that recovery is possible and creates an orientation towards working things out together as a family unit.

The members of an Al-Anon group with which the author is familiar receive understanding of their problems and their feelings from one another, emotional support which facilitates change in attitudes and behavior, basic information about solutions to common problems, and information about the treatment process and about the nature of alcoholism as an illness. Shame is alleviated and hope engendered. The nonalcoholic spouses gain perspective on what has happened in their families and on the possibilities of changing towards greater stability. Anxiety diminishes in an almost visible fashion. As they gain perspective on the situation, behavior tends to become more realistic and rewarding. By no means the least important effect derived from membership in the group is a structuring of what has seemed to be a completely unstructured situation and the feelings of security which this engenders.

45. UNEMPLOYMENT: CRISIS OF THE COMMON MAN

Ruth Shonle Cavan

§ Four kinds of external stresses that disturb family life are common in the United States: economic recessions and depressions, death of a family member, natural disasters, and wars. Other countries may have some or all of these and may have others. The United States has not suffered the effects of bombing, as some European and Asiatic countries have during recent wars; nor are we subject to famines as in some parts of Asia, nor to devastating plagues.

Recessions and depressions bring widespread unemployment, which not only affects the standard of living of a family but, perhaps more disastrous, disturbs the status of the husband relative to that of other members of the family and often calls for a new alignment of roles. Individual unemployment when there is no recession may have much the same effect. Such unemployment may result from chronic illness, the development of a handicap, removal of an industry to a new location, introduction of automation, or the difficulty of finding a satisfactory position immediately after graduation. Whatever the cause, unemploy-

SOURCE: *Marriage and Family Living*, 21 (May, 1959), 139–46. Based on a paper read at the Groves Conference on Marriage and the Family, Washington, D.C., April 15, 1958. Reprinted by permission of the publisher and the author.

The author's background is given in the footnote for article 13.

ment often has the quality of a crisis—it is unexpected and the family is not adequately prepared to meet it. If it becomes permanent, drastic readjustment is necessary.

Any period of widespread, prolonged unemployment raises the specter of possible family disorganization and even disintegration. The Great Depression of the 1930's led to a number of studies of family reactions to unemployment and lowered income. These studies can lay the foundation for current studies and even for current methods of alleviation, with some consideration for the differences between the 1930's and the late 1950's.

In order to sharpen our view of the impact of unemployment on family life, this review of the depression studies is organized according to social class, so far as such a classification is possible in studies made before the concept of social class was well defined.[1]

The social classes discussed here are as follows:

1. The lower-lower class family:
   a. with long-term or permanent unemployment
   b. with regular repetitive unemployment
   c. usually employed, except in time of personal or economic emergency;
2. The family of the "common man," that is, upper-lower and lower-middle class, regularly employed except in time of great economic emergency;
3. The upper-middle class.

The family of the common man is discussed first, since the traumatic impact of unemployment seems most acute in this social class.

The Common Man, Upper-Lower and Lower-Middle Classes

The conditions imposed by unemployment and lowered income are most significant when seen against a backdrop of what the common man wants, expects, and has partially achieved. One of the chief values of the common man is to be self-supporting at all times, with a backlog of moderate savings. Often the family prides itself on "getting ahead," with a goal of upward mobility, if not for the parents, at least for their children. Wives may work regularly or intermittently and older children work, but the husband is the chief and most steady worker and makes the largest contribution to the family budget. Typically, his status is recognized as the highest in the family. The effort toward upward mobility is chiefly in the acquisition of rather expensive equipment, not always paid for, or in moving into a better neighborhood than the one

---

[1] Family life according to social class is discussed in Ruth Shonle Cavan, *The American Family*, 4th ed., New York: Thomas Y. Crowell Company, 1969.

in which the family originally lived. Culturally and socially, the family may not have established itself in the next higher class. Hence, considerable emphasis is placed on visible material possessions which are symbols of status.

Four depression studies that concentrated on the common man are:[2] Cavan and Ranck, whose study of one hundred Chicago families included sixty-eight of common-man status; Komarovsky who concentrated on fifty-nine cases; Bakke, *The Unemployed Worker*, based on a number of studies made between 1932 and 1939; and *Citizens without Work*, by the same author, an eight year study of twenty-four families suffering prolonged unemployment.

Reaction to Unemployment

A loss of or reduction in employment and hence in income among these families poses a many-sided threat: loss of the symbols of social class status; eventual probable application for relief; disorganized personal reactions; disorganization and rearrangement of roles within the family; downward social mobility.

First came the financial adjustment. At least at the beginning of the depression, there was disbelief that the situation was anything except a normal short lay-off. Men therefore were inclined to speak of deserving a short vacation. When no recall came, they sought employment first in their special skill, then in a less specialized and lower paid type of work, finally in any work, and eventually at odd jobs. [Cavan and Ranck, Bakke (2)] This devaluation of job status was a long-drawn out procedure. For as long as six months, skilled workers held out for the old wages, but by the end of twelve months, 85 per cent were willing, although often resentful, to take any kind of job. [Bakke (1), ch. 8]

If other members of the family found work, their employment eased the financial strain, but often produced interpersonal strains.

As unemployment was prolonged, resources (symbols of status) were used with the following order of frequency: credit, small savings, loans, selling or pawning goods, and cashing of insurance policies. [Bakke (1), ch. 8; Cavan and Ranck, p. 84] Expenses were reduced by having the telephone removed, not taking summer vacations, dropping club memberships, and the like. Some families moved to less expensive living quarters; others moved in with relatives. As long as possible, invisible reductions were made; but eventually it was not possible to conceal the

[2] Ruth Shonle Cavan and Katherine Howland Ranck, *The Family and the Depression*, Chicago: University of Chicago Press, 1938; Mirra Komarovsky, *The Unemployed Man and His Family*, New York: Dryden Press, 1940; E. Wight Bakke, *The Unemployed Worker, A Study of the Task of Making a Living without a Job*, New Haven: Yale University Press, 1940, No. 1; and Bakke, *Citizens without Work*, New Haven: Yale University Press, 1940, No. 2. No. 1 and No. 2 are used in the text to distinguish Bakke's two books.

financial condition from neighbors. The final and most difficult financial adjustment was in applying for relief. For these self-supporting and often upwardly mobile families, relief was regarded as a personal disgrace. It was also the end of their hopes for upward mobility and often was preceded by definite downward mobility, partly because personal resources had to be reduced to a very low point before the family would be accepted by most relief agencies.

During this period of declining employment and exhaustion of resources, three types of reaction occurred.

1. Emotional reactions of husband and wife. The period preceding application for relief was a harrowing one as the family resisted the change in self-conception that relief made necessary. Worry, discouragement, and despondency were common emotional reactions. When forced to apply for relief, husband and wife cried at the agency. Definitely neurotic symptoms occurred in a minority of cases, as extreme insomnia, hysterical laughter, burning spots on the body, and suicide threats. However, out of the total of one hundred Chicago cases there were only two suicides, neither attributable solely to the depression. Husband and wife often shared equally in the emotional tension. In some families, one member, often the husband, became more disturbed than the others. A few drank heavily and several had "nervous breakdowns." [Cavan and Ranck, pp. 55–66; Komarovsky, pp. 36 ff., 66 ff.]

2. Changes in roles within the family. Although the husband is the chief earner in the family of the common man, it is accepted that the wife works when necessary, and that older children have an obligation to work part or full time as soon as they reach the legal age for employment. It was less true in the early 1930's than now that the wife works as a matter of choice and not simply from necessity. But even in the 1930's the employment of the wife was not taken as a threat to the husband's superior status, so long as it was conceded that the wife's employment was temporary.

The unemployment of the husband affected roles in three ways. First, when the husband could not find any work, his role suffered in the eyes of other members of the family. Wives sometimes lost their respect or accused their husbands of not trying to find work. Unless the husband could work out some role in the household (difficult to do), he really had no role to play. [Cavan and Ranck, Komarovsky, various items]

Second, when some members of the family usurped the role of the husband as chief wage earner, interpersonal relationships became strained. Apparently actual reduction in dollars earned was less devastating than change in roles; or, dire poverty was easier to bear than the husband's loss of status to some previously subordinate member. It seems to make little difference what members worked or how much or how little each earned, provided that the husband remained the largest contributor to the family purse. Tension was increased by the custom of children contributing their money to the family through the mother, who then often became the bursar for the family. [Cavan, Komarovsky, Bakke]

Third, when the family finally applied for relief and was accepted as a client further rearrangement of roles became necessary. The relief worker assumed a role superior to that of the husband. Since the relief worker was usually a woman, and dealt primarily with the wife, the husband now found himself subordinate both to his wife and to the woman relief worker. [Bakke (2)]

3. Change in social class status. In the hierarchy of social class levels, families on relief are relegated to lower-lower class status. Especially for upward mobile families, their descent to lower-lower class was embittering. When these families were forced to move, the search for lower rent sometimes brought many relief families into the same neighborhood. Bakke (1) speaks of entire neighborhoods of relief families.

As the depression progressed, certain cushions were devised. One of these was the Works Progress Administration (WPA), established in 1935, which provided work relief. At first, WPA workers were contrasted with persons still on relief; their self-respect increased and their social status was slightly improved. But in time, WPA workers were identified with relief cases and contrasted with persons privately employed. Their status and self-respect then again declined. [Bakke (1), ch. 12]

Another cushion was unemployment compensation, established in 1938, and by now a customary way to tide over short periods of unemployment. The implications of unemployment compensation are discussed later in this paper.

Readjustment of Family

Emotional disturbance usually continued until the family reached a level, however low, of stability. As soon as the family accepted this level as probably permanent, reorganization began as the family adjusted itself to its new level. As the depression decreased and various members of the family found work, upward mobility sometimes began again; however older members of the family often were unable to regain their former personal status, so that the family status might be organized around the older children as the chief earners.

Bakke (2) divides the readjustment process into experimental and permanent. He says that few families remained disorganized for a very long period of time. In experimental readjustment, the husband accepted his lowered status and a new hierarchy of statuses began to develop, with the wife granted the authority to manage finances and each child assigned a status relative to earning capacity. New interests and new plans for children developed, appropriate to the new social class status.

The family drew together again with new roles that fitted together into an integrated pattern. Permanent readjustment came when the family stopped comparing the meager present with the more comfortable past, accepted rationalizations for the lowered status, and renewed a full round of family activities although of a different type than formerly.

In other families, the disarrangement of roles and lowering of statuses were less severe and consequently readjustment came more quickly. When the family did not have to make a residential move, loss of social status was less noticeable. Avoidance of relief through reduced expenses or help from relatives saved the family from the greatest humiliation. Activities and goals could be modified without great disorganization. [Cavan and Ranck, ch. 7]

Pre-unemployment Factors

Two studies, Cavan and Ranck, and Komarovsky, emphasized the previous family organization as a factor in the way in which families of the common man reacted to the depression.

Cavan and Ranck used the concept of well organized family, defined as a family with a high degree of unity and reciprocal functioning. Although well and poorly organized families varied in their reactions to unemployment, in general well organized families fared better than the poorly organized. They suffered emotionally as they approached the relief status, but also attempted to adjust realistically. The family group remained intact and as the lower status was accepted, family goals of a new type evolved. The family group worked together to overcome their problems.

Families disorganized prior to the depression tended to become more disorganized. Previous latent tensions between husband and wife or between parents and children came into the open under the increased tension of unemployment and low income. In a few cases the parents separated, adolescent children ran away from home, or the family broke into several small units. In some of these families, stability increased with the entrance of a relief agency whose worker helped to hold the family together by permitting the members to become dependent upon her. [Cavan and Ranck, ch. 7]

Komarovsky limited her research to a study of the relation between the husband's role as the economic provider of the family and his authority in the family. In forty-five out of fifty-nine cases, all on relief one or more years, the husband did not lose his authority in the family. In these families the authority of the husband was based either on love and respect, or on the traditional semi-patriarchal organization of the common-man family. Unemployment was not interpreted as a reflection on the husband.

When the authority of the husband was based on fear of the husband or was maintained for utilitarian purposes, his unemployment was followed by loss of respect and loss of authority. In some of these families, the wife did not respect her husband prior to the unemployment. When unemployment freed her from economic dependence upon him, the thin veneer of submission cracked. The husbands attempted to force respect from wife and children, psychologically or physically, or selected a few areas of dominance about which they would not yield; some sought compensation in alcohol or religion.

Summary of the Common Man and Unemployment

In general the upper-lower and lower-middle class families suffered greatly from prolonged unemployment which violated deeply revered values of the common man: relief substituted for self-support; transfer of the highest family status from the husband to some previously subordinate member of the family; and downward social mobility. The lengthy period of downgrading to relief status was the most difficult and was marked by severe emotional reactions. Readjustment came with acceptance of the condition of poverty and reorganization of the family in harmony with the reality of the situation. The well organized family with unity of purpose and reciprocal functioning of members in which the husband held his status on the basis of love and respect or tradition weathered the adjustment better than poorly organized families or those in which fear and utilitarian motives were at the basis of the hierarchy of statuses.

The Upper-Middle Class

The upper-middle class was less affected by the depression than the common man, and very few persons became relief clients.[3] Most upper-middle workers remained in their accustomed positions, sometimes at higher incomes than prior to the depression. The few whose businesses failed or who became unemployed tended to re-establish themselves by their own efforts.

However, one study concentrated on families, primarily upper-middle class, which had suffered a decrease of at least 25 per cent in their income, often accompanied by total or partial unemployment.[4] The reaction of these families was severe but was related chiefly to changes of personal status within the family. With a few exceptions, the families were able to remain in their homes and thus were saved one of the

[3] W. Lloyd Warner and Paul S. Lunt, *Social Life of a Modern Community*, New Haven: Yale University Press, 1941, pp. 277–279; Winona L. Morgan, *The Family Meets the Depression*, Minneapolis: University of Minnesota Press, 1939.

[4] Robert Cooley Angell, *The Family Encounters the Depression*, New York: Charles Scribner's Sons, 1936.

drastic steps in downward social mobility. They also managed to get along without applying for relief.

Angell's main focus was on the effect of reduced income on interpersonal relationships among family members. The two elements of family life found most significant in type of adjustment were integration and adaptability. Angell applied these concepts to the way in which families accepted changes in relative status of family members, especially to lowered status of the husband. The most severe test came when the husband yielded his dominant status to someone else, for example, to the wife who became the chief wage earner. When the husband was able to retain his previous status or modified it only slightly, adjustment was easier. Successful adjustment to modified or markedly changed status called for a change of roles and acceptance of the change by all concerned.

Readjustment of roles without personal or familial disorganization was accomplished most readily by integrated, adaptable families. Unadaptable families, regardless of the degree of integration, experienced personal and/or family disorganization. Unintegrated families with a low degree of adaptability made unpredictable responses.

It was also found that adaptability increased with a non-materialistic philosophy of life, freedom from traditionalism, and responsibleness of the parents.

One may summarize Angell's study of upper-middle class families by saying that adaptability is more important than integration in adjusting to lowered income, but that the unstructured, unintegrated, and unadaptable family tends to increase in disintegration.

The Lower-Lower Class Family

Although lower-lower class families experience more unemployment than any other class, they are least affected by it. They may earlier have suffered from it, but in time they tend to accept unemployment as a normal way of life. These families contrast sharply with the unemployment families in the common man class and the upper-middle class.

Long Term or Permanent Unemployment

Permanently unemployed families are relief clients year in and year out, in prosperity as well as in depression; or they have found some unrespectable way to live without working. By the time unemployment is reached, there are usually physical and personality deficiencies, such as disease, vagrancy, petty thievery, alcoholism, unstable emotional reactions, or inability to work with others or to accept authority. Which of these conditions are causes and which effects of unemployment, it seems impossible to say. These deficiencies become a permanent part of the situation and often are used to manipulate relief agencies or the public into giving aid. They become assets rather than disintegrating elements in the family.

These families tend to accept their impoverished status and to stabilize family life at a dependency level. Some members may have been reared in similar families and thus have been socialized into this type of family from birth. Others, however, have slipped downward. With time, some kind of adjustment is made and the family develops rationalizations or a philosophy of life, appropriate family roles, and relationships with the outside world that enable it to function.

In his study, *The Beggar*, Gilmore describes a family in which begging set the mode of life through sixty years and five generations.[5] Beggars not reared in begging families sometimes reach this status after intermittent periods on relief. When all private resources have been exhausted and relief is unavailable or inadequate, these families turn to begging. Soon they have developed a philosophy that they cannot or should not work in ordinary occupations; they refer to begging as work. Even though all members of the family may not beg, the whole family shares the begging philosophy since the social status of the family is determined by even one begging member. Society places the begger at one of the lowest social levels, but the beggar himself is protected from feeling debased by his philosophy.

Begging is a family project, which helps to unify the family. Whichever members of the family can make the greatest appeal for sympathy go out to beg, with the family as a whole sharing the proceeds. Parents who thus provide well for their children have family roles of authority and respect.

Studies of families permanently on relief also show how unemployment is accepted as a normal status. The function of the relief agency is important. The longitudinal study of one hundred Chicago families made in 1934–35 by Cavan and Ranck yielded twelve families that had been wholly or partially on relief prior to the depression. In time of high employment, they nevertheless lived in the social world of the permanently unemployed. Many of these families included at least one disorganized person, often the husband, whose disabilities gave justification for the relief status in the eyes of the family. The families held together, having adjusted family roles to the personalities of their members, sometimes in unorthodox ways. Important in the family organization was the relief agency, which often assumed functions typical of a husband. The agency supplied money, sometimes managed the budget-

[5] Harlan W. Gilmore, *The Beggar*, Chapel Hill: University of North Carolina Press, 1940, pp. 168–182; Chapter 5 on "Urban Beggardom" also is pertinent to family reactions.

ing, helped the family plan, and in general gave stability and security in many areas other than financial.

A third report throws light on mobile unemployed families.[6] When the Atomic Energy Commission established a plant in southern Ohio, many mobile families were drawn into the area for employment. Social services were approached by six mobile families who were not seeking employment, but whose histories showed that their mode of life was constant migration back and forth across the country in battered automobiles, their means of support whatever they could get from relief agencies. The husbands as a rule were very infantile and dependent in personality type; the wives were docile. They wanted to be cared for by the agency. The family units were closely organized and void of conflict. The men maintained their family status through the skill with which they could manipulate the relief workers or community sentiment in their favor. Although the means were unconventional, the husband still held high status as the good provider. As with public begging, the technique of appeal was well developed. The man made the appeal for sympathy, playing up the needs of his family, and ingratiating himself with the relief worker or others in the community who might help him. As a rule, the men were at first successful in arousing interest and securing aid. As soon as efforts were made to provide employment, the family quietly disappeared, to turn up later in some other city. As with the dependent families in the Chicago study, already cited, the relief agency tended to assume many of the functions normally held by the husband.

It seems to be possible to conclude from studies of permanently unemployed people that permanent unemployment is not a traumatic, disorganizing experience. It is accepted as the customary way of life. The family devises ways to support itself without work and builds up a supporting philosophy and integrated family roles.

Regular, Repetitive Unemployment

The seasonal worker who follows a yearly routine of alternating periods of employment and unemployment typifies the above category. According to Hathaway's 1934 study of the migratory family, and other fragmentary sources, these families often are not rooted in any community and the standard of living tends to be low.[7] The families are not,

[6] Martha Bushfield Van Valen, "An Approach to Mobile Dependent Families," *Social Casework*, 37 (April, 1956), pp. 180–186.

[7] Studies of migrant workers usually are focused on conditions of work, health problems, and lack of education for the children. Few give very much information on family organization, roles, or reaction to unemployment. Some insight can be gleaned from Marion Hathaway, *The Migratory Worker and Family Life*, Chicago: University of Chicago Press, 1934. *The American Child*, published bi-monthly, November to May by the National Child Labor Committee, contains numerous articles regarding the handicaps of migratory life for children.

however, disorganized. They have accepted the mobile life and the rotation of employment and unemployment as normal for themselves. Often a regular route is followed year after year and the family knows in advance where it is likely to be throughout the working season. The off-season often finds each family in the same city every year. If the family has not been able to save sufficient money for the off-season, relief is sought. The whole yearly pattern can be foreseen. There is therefore no shock, no crisis, when seasonal unemployment comes; and there is a technique for handling the lack of funds.

The families are organized with the father as head. He makes the arrangements for work for the family as a unit. He therefore has authority and respect. Once the family has accepted migrancy as a way of life, the husband fulfills his role if he makes good contacts for work during the working seasons; he is not considered a failure if the family must apply for relief in the off-season.

The seasonal working family, like the permanently dependent family, illustrates adjustment to unemployment, the maintenance of roles within the family, and as a consequence little personal or family disorganization is a result of unemployment. Since both types of family tend to be at a bare subsistence level with or without relief, there is no question of downward social mobility. These two types of unemployment are cited to illustrate that unemployment is not necessarily disorganizing, when it is part of the customary way of life, when roles are integrated, and when the family has developed techniques acceptable to itself for securing maintenance when there is no earned income.

One or More Members Usually Employed

These families are marginal between self-support and dependence on relief agencies—between the common man and the permanently unemployed.

They are usually able to meet their own expenses, but any emergency that either throws the chief wage earner out of work or increases expenses leads the family to some source of temporary help. These temporary lapses from financial self-sufficiency are recognized as emergencies beyond personal control. They do not cause the family to change its conception of itself as self-supporting, nor do family roles change, although one member of the family may temporarily carry out the functions of another member.

A few such families appeared among the one hundred Chicago families studied by Cavan and Ranck. The long-continued unemployment of the depression came as a crisis with which the families could not cope. They could not understand the cause of the depression unemployment, as they had been able to understand previous short periods of distress. They were forced to apply for relief for an indefinite period of time.

They were also compelled to change their conception of themselves as self-supporting, and to adjust roles and sometimes class status to conform to their relief status. The reactions of these families were similar to the reactions of common man families who had never been on relief prior to the depression.

Conclusions

Briefly, one may conclude that the following reactions to prolonged unemployment may be expected:

1. The common man struggles to maintain personal status, family integration, and social class status.

2. The upper-middle class family (when affected at all) struggles to maintain personal roles, especially of the father, within the family.

3. The permanently or seasonally unemployed accept their position as normal, adjust personal statuses and roles, and integrate relief agencies or public donors into the family.

4. Even when family disorganization is marked, the family tends to reorganize once the downward decline in personal and class status reaches a stable point.

5. Characteristics facilitating good adjustment are a well organized family prior to unemployment, adaptability, responsibleness, and a non-materialistic and non-traditional philosophy of life.

Applicability of the 1930 Research to the 1950 Family

A higher percentage of married women work now than in the early 1930's, a situation that gives more economic security. We assume that the family is more equalitarian in its functioning. Do these two facts, taken together, mean that the unemployed husband could yield the dominant role (which he still retains) more gracefully to his wife than he could in the early 1930's? If so, his emotional disturbance should be less.

The great number of cars, summer homes, electrical household equipment, suburban homes, and college educations that have been bought since World War II suggest increased upward mobility, or at least the collection of material symbols of upward mobility. Many of these are being bought on the installment plan and therefore are insecurely owned. Would prolonged unemployment bring a great downward movement in social class status? Such a movement would increase bitterness and disappointment.

Do families of the common man category have the same aversion to relief that they had in the 1930's? To anything called "relief," probably they have. But the nation-wide forms of relief instituted by the federal government in the 1930's operate under sugar-coated names such as pension, aid, insurance, and compensation. The fact that employees pay into Old Age and Survivor's Insurance has created a wide-spread idea that they also pay into other forms of aid, such as Old Age Assistance or Pensions and Unemployment Compensation. Actually, they have not done so, but their belief that they have makes it easier for them to apply. The eligibility rules for public assistance programs have been widely publicized and people are urged to apply when eligible; they are not urged to be strong, independent, and self-sufficient. Nor does the public agency probe into family relationships or violate the feeling of privacy of the family. When eligibility rules have been met, the applicant receives a check which he may spend as he chooses. It seems probable, therefore, that the unemployed person today accepts Unemployment Compensation as his due and not as charity.

Unemployment Compensation is designed to tide a family or worker over a short period of unemployment. It is much less than the person's wages and it runs for only a few months. If the person becomes re-employed soon, he does not lose social class status and probably family roles are not disturbed. However, if he has no other income, he must reduce expenses and if he has private resources he must dip into them. With long term unemployment, the Unemployment Compensation runs out along with the private resources. At this point, the person is in the same position that the 1930 unemployed person was when he had exhausted his resources; Unemployment Compensation has simply postponed or prolonged the decline to relief status.

It seems probable that the socio-psychological trends and adjustments of the 1930's would be found in the 1950's, but that the conditions under which these trends and adjustments would work themselves out have changed.

46. ADJUSTING TO THE DEATH OF A LOVED ONE

Thomas D. Eliot

§ One of the inevitable experiences that people face is death of members of the family. The better health and prolonged length of life of the present period reduce the probability of death of husband, wife, or children in the early years of marriage. Nevertheless, even these first years sometimes bring death, if not in the immediate family, then of parents, other close relatives, or friends. As the years of marriage increase, the probability of death does also. Many people shrink from the thought of death and dislike facing the types of adjustments that must be made when a death occurs.

Dr. Eliot, who began to study bereavement some thirty years ago, here traces the series of reactions that typically follow a death and also gives some suggestions for adjustment.

Bereaved families experience a sequence of fairly distinguishable stages according to objective studies. These include: cognizance of the actual approach of actual death, immediate reactions to actual death, pre-funeral period, funeral and disposal, mourning period, and recovery or stabilization period. These "stages" overlap, or blend to some extent. There are infinite variations within the range of the non-pathological or "normal."

Cognizance of the Approach of Death

Death itself usually occurs so quietly that it is not necessarily recognized until a physician declares it. Probably death itself, for most of those dying, is not a difficult experience. If the patient is in pain, death is relief, and not the cause of pain. If the patient is unconscious or unaware of approaching death, he is spared the fears of the unknown or of extinction. Such fears are presumed to have a biological basis in survival-

SOURCE: Abstracted and adapted from parts of "Facing Instantaneous Wholesale Abolition and Bereavement," a paper delivered at the 1958 Annual Meeting of the Groves Conference on Marriage and the Family. By permission of the author.

The author is Professor Emeritus of Sociology at Northwestern University. He received his doctorate in social economics from Columbia University and has written extensively in the family field, the latest production being a study with Arthur Hillman of families in the Norwegian culture, carried on while on a Fulbright research professorship in Norway.

value, but are characteristic of humans as beings of conscious observation, and such fears are sometimes complicated by certain theological beliefs and guilts.

Immediate Reactions

The writer once listed various observed or reported immediate effects of bereavement as follows: (1) denial or rejection of the facts, a natural but only temporary defense, including dissociation of emotion, sense of unreality, or "feeling no grief"; (2) preternatural or detached calm; (3) shock, in a physiological sense; (4) exaltation or preternatural cheerfulness; (5) self-injury or suicidal impulses; (6) blame of self or others, revenge; (7) suppression of grief; (8) intense longing; (9) abandoned weeping. One should add (10) sense of relief and (11) rationalization—whether naive or intelligent. Some of these, of course, can be noted in sequence or combination.

The impulse to die, with or instead of the deceased, whether in order to save the deceased, to join the deceased, or to escape unbearable grief, is occasionally reported, with or without overt expression. It may have a guilt component, or an element of faith in future reunion.

Despite sincere love and sorrow, the circumstances of many deaths, especially of some incurable and of the aged, are a relief to the survivors as well as to the deceased. Such attitudes need not be guiltily suppressed: others can understand them. They are often rationalized: God had mercy on her suffering; it was better so; it is in the course of nature; Death is sometimes a friend.

The Pre-funeral Period

Usually, following the immediate reactions at the instant of bereavement, there are more or less quick readjustments, often stimulated by recognition that there are "things to be done." If the bereaved do not do them the bereaved are worked upon by those who are less involved or better controlled. Fulcomer recognized five types of responses in the post-immediate stage, in which he includes the funeral episode.[1]

(1) The acquiescent type: behavior being as nearly usual as circumstances permit. The facts are recognized and at least intellectually accepted. The conventions are fulfilled or tolerated. There is self-direction and responsibility. There is a touch of the stoic.

(2) The excited type: characterized by overstimulation, talkativeness, an urge to constant activity, active interest in the formalities, and rest-

---

[1] David M. Fulcomer, *The Adjustive Behavior of Some Recently Bereaved Spouses: A Psycho-Sociological Study,* unpublished Ph.D. dissertation, Northwestern University, 1942.

lessness. The self-control and cheer seem artificial, perhaps a matter of pride or of defense against the inner pain, or of admirable courage fostered by some code or standard.

(3) *The protestive or blaming response:* characterized by violent crying, moaning, and/or weeping, the "Why?" pattern—the "why" of cause, of purpose, or of resented injustice. The tendency is to blame self, others, fate, God. These persons are self-centered, not sharing in the arrangements. They show no self-control at funeral or grave.

(4) *The detached type:* displaying little weeping, but impassive or apparently indifferent. These persons take no active role in necessary arrangements but do some unimportant or irrelevant acts. Habitual routines are gone through in some sort of daze, as are the funeral rites. There is lack of direction and almost lack of orientation, or partial dissociation.

(5) *The despondent type:* depression rather than active weeping occurs. There is self-centered suffering, wish to be alone, lack of energy, compliance with ritual but minimum participation, and a loss of appetite and sleep.

Fulcomer notes that while the predominant behavior is usually of one of these five types, there may also be episodes in which one or more of the other type-behaviors emerge. He notes also that acquiescent and despondent responses are more frequent among men; protestive responses are more frequent among women.

Other patterns of behavior frequently reported in the post-immediate period are: dependence on others, consoling others, praising the deceased (possibly from over-compensatory guilt), active efforts to deny the fact of death, revulsion against funeral conventions and theological doctrines, a feeling that the world has stopped, and numerous others. A grieved person is especially helpless when it is precisely the deceased who would normally be the confidant consoling the bereaved.

During this period the bereaved's attention is turned inward because of the struggle between the actualities of the outer world forced into his consciousness, and the organized, more or less unconscious resistance of his wishes and habits against the acceptance of the outer facts.

There may be a continuity or consistency between the types of response shown in the immediate and post-immediate stages, as, for example, from stoicism to acquiescence, weeping to despondency, or dazedness to detachment. On the other hand, there may be (especially for cyclothymic temperament) a sharp shift of mood as from dazed to excited, or from lacrimose to revengeful. Many of the behaviors and feelings noted in this whole section recur or continue into the later "stages" of mourning and recovery.

We have no way of measuring depths of grief, but there is tentative evidence that the more the status, role, and affectional habits of the bereaved have depended upon and been organized around the role of the deceased, the greater is the disturbance and disequilibrium to be readjusted. In general, parents may grieve more painfully over the loss of their children than *vice versa*. Loss of spouse tends to be worse than loss of parents, especially if the child has been "weaned" of his early dependence.

One may trace these types of response to bereavement back to corresponding and recognizable types of emotional habits and temperament which probably would appear in the person's total response to other kinds of family crises.

Funerals as a Family Service

The funeral is an ordeal for the family, and many deplore its elaboration for mere security of status or competitive display. Yet there are social-psychological values and functions which funerals serve. Family pride may be traditionally and symbolically represented and satisfied. The death which is thus publicly recognized, is made more real. It begins to be accepted as actual and to that extent is adjusted to by the bereaved.

Mourning, Grief-Work, and Readjustments

In the period after the funeral, difficult transitions to new, socially durable roles are made, for better or for worse. Responsibilities have to be assumed or rearranged. Properties are to be redisposed. Decisions are to be made, or the family drifts. For some, there is a definite turning-point stage between the funeral and stable readjustment. The behavior of the bereaved, however, often is experimental: several types of distraction, defense, compensation, or projection may be attempted before the life situation process is gradually repatterned or channelized again. The moody person especially may start out on a depressed, despondent level (insomnia, no appetite, inactivity, silence) but be drawn by habit or necessity into the participation of a job. It is during this period that family contacts and guidance are most influential.

Our culture gives to men more than to women opportunities or necessities for return to normal roles and duties. Women often receive ego-satisfaction from receiving attention rather than through action. A person who has always been a seeker of attention, and who has suddenly found satisfaction in being noticed because of bereavement, may crave such attention or fear to give it up. Friends are flooded with talk about the deceased and the misery of the bereaved. Without verbalizing such a purpose, the bereaved seeks to make others weep for and with her.

The process of mourning is paralleled by the process of recovery. During mourning, the bereaved person recalls the loved one: but, for episode after episode, he comes to realize that the reality is no longer the same. Gradually, emotions and energies, habitually attached to the deceased, are free to be dispersed or transferred to other objects. As the late Willard Waller pointed out, memories of the deceased will recur until all significant events of the relationship have been recalled. If these memories are repressed, they will tend to obsess the personality. But if they are permitted to come into conscious memory and are reviewed and revalued, they can be placed among other memories of one's past and tensions will relax. The working over of memories and reorientation of roles during the mourning stage have been called the "grief-work" by Rogers. These processes are necessary for adjustment.

The period of mourning also permits the relaxing or releasing of any resentments the bereaved may have felt toward the deceased (however sincerely loved), and the expiation, self-punishment, or other accommodation or assimilation, of any guilts felt on account of previous grudges or spites. Hate and love are often ambivalent attitudes. The bereaved, in order to avoid or offset a feeling of guilt, may constantly need to demonstrate to himself and to others his role as mourner.

In the period of mourning there may be a strong wish to be alone. This is at least natural, if the situation is confusing or jarring, or has been exhausting in activity and details. One needs rest and time to reorient. But if social withdrawal, seclusion, despondency or silence threaten to become a habit, crippling to the usefulness or happiness of the bereaved, then family or friends should create situations which make it easy for them to outgrow the desire for seclusion and to re-enter accustomed or new social roles. On the other hand, lonesomeness may be feared and avoided by the bereaved.

The wish for reunion with the loved one may, of course, find expression in beliefs in immortality. Such beliefs (whether unquestioned or accepted as a last resort against intolerable despair and grief) are of course an important element in the attitudes of many bereaved persons.

All the reaction-patterns of grief-work are compensatory, that is, they are the organism's efforts to restore equilibrium. They should be tolerated as such by friends, counselors, and by the bereaved themselves. Only if the reactions threaten to become habitual, repressive, or over-compensatory do they need to be re-corrected by advice or self-guidance.

Recovery and Stabilization

In the later readjustment period, we normally get the relaxation of personal tensions, fixations, and obsessions, along with the habituation of whatever shifts of role were precipitated by the event. Fulcomer classifies the type of stabilized adjustments during this period into five types:

(1) Transfer or displacement of attachments from the deceased to some other person, who may be another member of the family or a new member acquired through "adoption."

(2) Participation in organizations and causes, whereby the grief is sublimated through some type of activity, perhaps of a welfare nature.

(3) Identification with the deceased by means of assumptions of the roles of the dead, fulfilling the wishes of the dead, carrying on his life values, or living up to his expectations.

(4) Memory fantasy of the deceased. Memories may become a fixation, with a regressive effort to relive or to glorify the dead person's life.

(5) Repressive-seclusive. After preliminary responses on dazed, protestive, and attention-seeking levels, Fulcomer's Case 8, refusing to move from a large home, resisted help, and indulged in memories by elaborate settings, reminders, and fantasies. But she withdrew from all her social clubs and was cold or resistant, despite friendly warnings. She was childless. The typical repatterning is deliberate holding aloof from normal interaction; solitary living; fixation on painful private mementoes as a satisfying symbol of continuity; resistance to others' efforts to modify the pattern or the attitude. Such persons are masochistic voluptuaries of grief.

Suggestions for Adjusting to Bereavement

In summarizing the foregoing discussion, some suggestions may be drawn out to aid in adjustment.

1. Adjustment can be expected to be a long, slow process. The first reactions can be expected to change several times before final adjustment is reached. It is of little use to try to hurry the process. It is therefore of little use to try to fill time completely full of activity; this may simply result in repressing or delaying the normal process of adjustment.

2. First reactions may be expected to be intense, although one cannot predict what form they will take.

3. The funeral often has a beneficial effect: it forces the bereaved person to face the fact of the death, gives opportunity to pay honor to the deceased, and provides activity. Friends and relatives gather and the general spirit is one of cooperation and consolation.

4. A more difficult phase of adjustment comes after the funeral when the normal responsibilities and tasks of everyday living must be resumed. Among the adjustments usually necessary, are modifications in the roles played, changes in sources of emotional satisfaction, and often the restructuring of finances. Although the person should not try to crowd

out his normal feeling of grief, these necessary adjustments should be made as soon as feasible and a new pattern of living established.

5. Although the roles, personal relationships, and emotional responses of living will never be quite the same after bereavement as before, since one person of the constellation has been removed, new roles, new personal relationships, and new emotional responses will develop. They should be allowed and encouraged to develop. The deceased one becomes part of a welcome memory, but life must be lived in the active present.

Chapter 16: Conflict, Divorce, and Readjustment

47. RESOLVING FAMILY CONFLICTS

Robert O. Blood, Jr.

§ This article presents some of the characteristics that contribute to potential conflict, mechanisms for prevention, and the processes of resolving conflict.

How does it happen that conflict afflicts so many families?

Sources of Family Conflict

Families everywhere tend to have certain characteristics which lay them open to potential conflict.

Compulsion

For one thing, a family is not a voluntary organization (except for the husband and wife). Children do not choose their parents. When the going gets tough, they cannot resign their membership. Even the parents are under heavy pressure to stick with the group no matter what.

Such involuntary participation tends to intensify conflict, once it originates. Because they have to continue living in the same house year in and year out, family members can develop deep antipathies for one another. What began as a mere conflict of interest easily turns into emotional hatred through the accumulation of grievances between two family members. Once such hostility has arisen, conflict becomes self-perpetuating.

Intimacy

The conflict potentialities inherent in the involuntary membership of the family are accentuated by the intimacy of contact within the family.

SOURCE: *Conflict Resolution*, 4 (June, 1960), 209–18, with certain omissions. Copyright 1960 by the Editorial Board. Reprinted by permission of the publisher.

The author's background is given in the footnote for article 35.

In school or church or business physical distance and social formality are maintained at some minimum level. Moreover, contact is restricted to a limited range of relationships, such as teacher-pupil, priest-parishioners, or boss-secretary.[1]

By contrast, relationships within the family are functionally diffuse. Family members lay all sorts of claims on one another for economic maintenance, recreational companionship, sexual responsiveness, sympathetic understanding, love and affection, etc. The comprehensiveness of these claims points to additional potential sources of conflict.

When conflict does occur within the family, it lacks the restraint imposed by concern for public opinion. If a man's home is his castle, it is also the place where his dungeons of despair are. A man who would never strike a woman in public finds his fury uncontrollable when goaded by a nagging wife behind closed doors. A child who would be patiently admonished in a public park needs a pillow in his pants for the same behavior at home. The very privacy which makes possible the most uninhibited embrace within the bedroom permits an equally uninhibited tongue-lashing. Intimacy of contact, therefore, contributes to both the extensity and the intensity of conflict within the family.

Smallness

While families everywhere are characterized by compulsory membership and intimate contact, the American family's small number of children further magnifies the problem of conflict, especially between siblings. In a large family, one child's share of his mother's attention and affection is so limited that it matters little whether he has it or not. In a two-child family, however, one child can monopolize the parent simply by vanquishing his sole sibling. Under these circumstances sibling rivalry becomes acute.

Similarly, among three siblings, the inherent instability of the triad typically leads the two older children to battle for the pawn. Again limited size dictates who the potential enemy shall be, makes him highly visible in the small group, and leads to the development of long-term feuds.

Change

The above family features would not be so bad were it not for the rapidity with which the family situation changes. Given fixed ingredients, a stable equilibrium might be sought. But families change so fast that a moving equilibrium is the best that can be hoped for.

Families change rapidly in size. Census figures show that newlyweds

---

[1] This is what Talcott Parsons calls "functionally specific relationships" in his "The Social Structure of the Family." In Ruth Nanda Anshen, ed., *The Family: Its Function and Destiny* (New York: Harper & Bros., 1949).

typically have hardly more than a year in which to work out their marital relationship before it is altered by the nausea of pregnancy. Then the children come every two years—bing, bing, bing. A decade and a half later they leave for college or its working-class equivalents with similar rapidity.[2]

Meanwhile the family may have maintained the same size, but the needs of its members were rapidly changing. Every time a new child starts to crawl, to climb, to wander across the street, to go to school, to experience puberty, or to drive a car, the pattern of family living must be readjusted. The changing "developmental tasks" of growing individuals create corresponding "family developmental tasks." Even parents' needs change as, for example, when the mother loses her figure or the father fails to get the raise he expected. Since the American family specializes in personality development and personal need fulfilment, such individual changes tend to disrupt the family equilibrium.

Given so many potentialities for conflict, what mechanisms exist for preventing the total disruption of what is so often called the "basic unit" in society?

Normative Mechanisms for Preventing Family Conflict

No society can afford to turn its back on family conflict. The family is too indispensable a unit of social structure and too necessary a means for the transmission of culture to the oncoming generation to be allowed to fall apart.

Consequently, every society tends to develop patterned ways of inhibiting the emergence of conflict. With the passage of time, these mechanisms tend to acquire the force of norms. That is, social pressures are mobilized to increase the likelihood that these mechanisms will be utilized, and social sanctions are imposed on those who violate them.

Different preventive mechanisms are found in various societies, depending partly on the points at which their family system is especially vulnerable to conflict. The following analysis classifies particular taboos and requirements in broad categories of general interest.

1. Avoidance of Probable Sources of Conflict

Many societies have devices for keeping apart potential or actual family members who otherwise would be likely to come into conflict with each other. By "potential family members" are meant couples who are not yet married. Societies have many ways of screening out those most predisposed to conflict. The traditional "publishing of the banns" allowed triple opportunities for objections to be raised to an inappro-

[2] Paul Glick, "The Life Cycle of the Family," in *Marriage and Family Living*, XVII (1955), 3–9.

priate partnership. The formal engagement notifies parents and friends of the couple's intentions, providing a last opportunity for pressures to be brought to bear in disapproved cases. Studies of broken engagements show that such pressures often successfully prevent what would presumably be conflict-laden marriages.[3]

Studies of "mixed marriages" of many sorts show a greater incidence of conflict due to the contrasting cultural values, expectations, and behavior patterns of the partners.[4] Church organizations mobilize their resources to discourage interfaith marriages, and informal social pressure tends to prevent heterogamous marriages across racial, national, or class boundaries. Although a majority of all mixed marriages succeeds, such social pressures presumably break up in advance those mixed marriages which would be least likely to succeed.

New preventive mechanisms in our society are marriage education and premarital counseling. An estimated 10 per cent of American college students now take a course in preparation for marriage, one of whose main purposes is to rationalize the process of mate selection through emphasizing numerous ways of testing compatibility.[5] Most such courses operate on the premise that young people are liable to contract incompatible marriages if they are not careful. Hence the chief value of compatibility testing is to detect which relationships are incompatible.

One of the main functions of premarital counseling, similarly, is to provide couples in doubt with an opportunity to look objectively at the conflicts already apparent in their relationships and to provide them with emotional support as they go through the process of deciding to avoid each other in the future.

Two legal moves designed to avoid domestic difficulties are almost universal among the fifty states. One of these is the five-day waiting period between the time of applying for a marriage license and the date of the wedding. This provides an opportunity for those intoxicated with wine or perfume to sober up and reconsider. Similarly, the age at which couples can marry without the blessing of their parents has been increased to eighteen for the bride and twenty-one for the groom. Since teen-age marriages have a conspicuously higher divorce rate, raising the minimum age probably reduces the number of marriages which get off to a bad start.

Once the marriage has been contracted, one of the widespread sources of difficulty is the in-law relationship. Since marriage involves a drastic shift in allegiance from parents to spouse, newlyweds often have ambiva-

---

[3] Ernest W. Burgess and Paul Wallin, *Engagement and Marriage* (Philadelphia: J. B. Lippincott Co., 1953), pp. 275–76.
[4] Judson T. Landis, "Marriages of Mixed and Nonmixed Religious Faith," in *American Sociological Review*, XIV (1949), pp. 401–7.
[5] Henry A. Bowman, *Marriage Education in the Colleges* (New York: American Social Hygiene Association, 1949).

lent feelings which are reflected in interspousal jealousy and conflict. This marital tension makes it correspondingly difficult for couples to get along with their parents-in-law.

Our society reduces friction in this area by warning couples not to move in with their in-laws if they can possibly avoid doing so. Some societies prescribe even stricter avoidance by restricting or prohibiting social intercourse with the mother-in-law. Especially taboo is the familiarity of joking with the mother-in-law. Reserve and formality are frequently required. Sometimes complete avoidance is the rule—one must neither talk with nor even look at the mother-in-law.[6] Although there may be social losses, such mechanisms of avoidance effectively rule out the possibility of conflict between potentially hostile individuals.

2. Allocation of Rights and Duties to Particular Roles

A second way in which societies prevent conflict is by distributing the authority, privileges, and responsibilities of family members according to a fixed pattern. In so doing, these societies predetermine the outcome. In fact, they short-circuit the conflict process completely because they take the issue out of the area of legitimate controversy. Henceforth, only in socially deviant families does conflict ever occur over the allocated matters. For example, the incest taboo allocates sexual privileges exclusively to the husband and wife. Murdock and other anthropologists believe that the reason why this allocation pattern is found universally is because it is essential to family harmony.[7] It functions to prevent sexual jealousy and rivalry within the family which would exist if more than one member of the family were allowed access to the same sexual partner.

Similarly, authority in the family is seldom distributed evenly among family members or (vaguer yet) left to each new family to decide for itself. Almost every society centralizes legitimate power in one role, usually that of the father. This is not to say that the wife and children are necessarily excluded from consultation in the decision-making process. Indeed, consideration for the wishes of the members of his family may be enjoined on the patriarch. However, a patriarchal family system specifies that in a showdown—when husband and wife cannot agree on mutually exclusive alternatives—the husband's wishes should prevail. The beauty of this system lies not in male superiority but in the fact that a ready out is available from any deadlock which may arise. It could as easily be the wife (and is in a few societies). It is handy, however, to have a way of avoiding prolonged crises within the family.

Authority need not be allocated entirely to one role. Each partner

---

[6] Most of the cross-cultural examples in this paper are drawn from George P. Murdock, *Social Structure* (New York: The Macmillan Co., 1949).
[7] *Ibid.*, pp. 295–96.

may have certain areas of family living in which he has autonomous jurisdiction. For example, most Detroit husbands make the final decision about what car to buy, while the typical wife decides how much money to spend on food for the family.[8] Whenever people grow up expecting the husband or the wife to make decisions on their own in the "proper" areas, those areas are effectively removed from the domain of conflict.

Herein lies the problem of the democratic family. Whenever two or more family members believe they ought to share in making a certain decision, they have added another potential conflict to their portfolio. The American family has been drifting in the direction of a "companionship" ideology, which specifies that an increasing number of decisions should be made jointly. A good example is the family vacation, which 66 per cent of all Detroit housewives report is planned fifty-fifty. In the long run, mutual planning is likely to produce results which at least partly please both partners. And, according to our democratic philosophy, this is an improvement over the old system of fully pleasing one partner at the expense of the other.

But the process may be painful. The trend "from institution to companionship" has opened a whole Pandora's box of potential new conflicts. These do not necessarily materialize; under the classical patriarchate, they could not.

The blurring lines in the division of labor similarly open the way to more conflict. In a time when women did the dishes without question, dish-washing was not a topic for cartoons (symptoms of sore spots in any society). But, as men and women alike begin to wonder whether and how much men should help out in the kitchen, a new area of controversy is added to the list. Thus a clearly defined division of labor, like a clear-cut allocation of authority, may be a social device for preventing conflict.

3. Equality of Treatment within the Family

The allocation of authority to particular members of the family does not mean the right to wield it arbitrarily. Despotic power creates unrest within the body domestic just as much as in the body politic. To prevent such unrest, the centralization of authority must be coupled with a bill of rights for the weaker family members to protect them from discriminatory treatment.

The exercise of power within the family takes two forms: (1) influencing or forcing the individual to alter his behavior (either by doing

---

[8] All references to Detroit families are drawn from the writer's 1955 interview study of 731 housewives (a representative sample of the Detroit Metropolitan Area). Robert O. Blood, Jr. and Donald M. Wolfe, *Husbands and Wives: The Dynamics of Married Living* (Glencoe, Ill.: The Free Press, 1960).

something he does not want to do or by stopping what he would like to do) and (2) granting or withholding favors. Even though the ability to exercise both types of power may be vested primarily (or ultimately) in the father, it is well to remember that the mother is a powerful figure for her children, especially when they are small. Indeed, every member of the family has the power to grant or withhold his attention, love, and respect regardless of how weak he may be in other respects. Therefore, when we speak of the necessity of equal treatment, we are not referring to the father alone.

How does equal treatment manifest itself in the family? The illustrations are endless. If Johnnie gets a story before he goes to bed, so must Jane. If he has to pick up the livingroom floor, she has to be forced to do her share. If Tom gets to use the family car on Friday, then Dick has a right to it on Saturday. Children and parents alike recognize the justice of such claims and can appeal to the moral value of fair play to secure equality. Insofar as equality is achieved, conflict tends to be avoided.

The administrative problem is complicated, however, by the fact that siblings are rarely of the same age. As a result, the principle of equality cannot always mean uniformity of treatment at any particular time. If John stays up until 9:00 P.M., that does not mean Jane can—being two years younger, she must have extra sleep. Accepting such seeming discrepancies is not easy for younger children. However, parental emphasis on the idea that, "when you are ten years old, you will be able to stay up until 9:00 P.M. too" is often effective.

Age-graded equality is likely to prevent conflict especially well when the system for moving from one notch to the next is clearly understood by all concerned. For instance, if every child's allowance automatically increases a nickel on his birthday, the younger siblings can feel confident that they will receive their "just deserts" when the proper time comes.

In the light of what was said earlier about the conflict-preventing function of the incest taboo, it is apparent that the custom of polygyny presents very serious problems. When there are several wives but only one husband, the danger of jealousy and conflict among the wives is very acute. It is not surprising, therefore, that polygynous societies have devised all three types of measures for preventing the outbreak of such conflict. (1) Avoidance is achieved by placing each wife and her children in a separate hut. (2) Authority over subsequent wives is usually allocated to the first wife—her position is thereby less threatened, and the loss of exclusive wifehood is offset by the addition of maid service. (3) More important for our present purposes is the common requirement that the man treat his wives equally, that he not play favorites among them. This often takes the form of requiring the husband to follow a strict schedule of rotation among his wives, spending an equal number of nights with each in turn. No society can effectively control the warmth or coolness with which he treats an unpopular wife; however, this merry-go-round rule at least spares her the humiliation of public knowledge of her husband's disfavor.

Equality of treatment is not an easy achievement, especially where intangibles like affection and attention are involved. Only the childless couple can completely avoid conflict from this source. As soon as the first child arrives, competition for the time and interest of the mother is created. Since she does not have enough time to go around, she must be prepared to say to her son, "I played with you last night, so tonight you should not object to my going out with your father." Even the child whose oedipal wishes have not been effectively resolved may accept such a statement if the norm of family equality has been adequately learned.

Avoidance, allocation, and equality—not separately but in combination—are the inventions which cross-cultural research shows to have been practical ways by which societies have prevented family conflict.

Instrumental Mechanisms for Resolving Family Conflicts

Despite the existence of preventive mechanisms, and wherever those mechanisms do not exist, conflict occurs. The means of ending those conflicts seem far less often culturally prescribed. Rather there seem to be a number of optional procedures, in the United States at least, which are available to families as ways out of their dilemmas. These mechanisms are instrumental in the sense that they can be employed as means to achieve certain ends, if the family so desires.

1. Increased Facilities for Family Living

When conflict results from scarce facilities, it is sometimes possible to satisfy both the conflicting parties by increasing the resources at the family's disposal. For example, sibling jealousy often originates from the mother's preoccupation with the new baby on her return from the hospital. An extra "mother" in the form of grandmother or nurse relieves the real mother of part of her workload so that she can give more attention to her displaced child.

Those societies with an extended family system have built-in grandmothers, aunts, and cousins who flexibly replace the mother when her attention is unavailable. Ethnographers report a general lack of sibling rivalry under this multiple mothering.

Conflict in the American home often centers around the use of scarce physical facilities. The current trends to a second car, a second television set, and a second telephone result not only in increased profits for the corresponding manufacturers but in decreased tension for family personnel who can now use parallel facilities simultaneously instead of having to compete for control of single channels. Similarly, the new-fangled recreation room provides the rest of the family with a retreat when daughter decides to throw a party in the living room, taking the tension off competition for "the only room in the house where I can entertain my friends."

2. Priority Systems for the Use of Limited Facilities

When enlargement of facilities is impossible, family conflict often becomes chronic—there is perpetual tension between family members, perennial jockeying for position, and fear that the competitor is getting ahead or taking advantage. Such feuding can often be seen among young children and is difficult to end by rational means. With older family members, war weariness may eventuate in a desire for peace at any price. Conflict may then be ended by facing the issues and arriving at decisions in some fashion or other.

The product of such decision-making is often a priority system governing the use of the scarce facility. If the bone of contention is the television set, a schedule for the whole week, born of a major showdown, may take the place of petty conflict "every hour on the hour." If the scarcity has been financial, the record of decisions takes the form of a budget. Here the mutual recriminations sparked by overdrawn bank accounts can be obviated by advance planning about where the money is to be spent.

The beauty of a budget, as of any other system, is that personal control ("I say you must") is replaced by impersonal control ("The budget says you must"). The process of agreeing on a budget is still liable to plenty of conflict, but, once formulated, a budget tends to divert attention from the hostile antagonist to the operational code.

3. Enlargement of Areas of Autonomy

Analogous in many ways to the method of effecting an absolute increase in the facilities available to family members is the chopping-up of existing facilities into smaller units which can then be made available exclusively to different members of the family. This results in a relative increase in the facilities at the disposal of the individual without the necessity of securing the consent of other family members. Hence potential conflict is avoided. For example, some couples plague themselves with difficulty by trying to arrive at joint decisions about the disposition of the scarce commodity of money. Worse yet, each partner may endlessly reproach the other for the petty expenditures he has already made. Such bickering can be ended by granting each partner an allowance to be spent as he sees fit without the necessity of accounting to the other for his whims and fancies. This innovation correspondingly restricts the area in which decision-making (and potential conflict) must occur to more critical areas of financial management.

The method of granting autonomy is not limited, however, to the use of scarce facilities. The problem of adolescent-parent conflict may be resolved by judicious increases in the amount of autonomy granted the teenager. Some parents clash head-on with their high-school sons and daughters in attempting to curb their adoption for the latest fads in dress and speech. Certainly, the easiest way out of this dilemma is to recognize that teenagers are old enough to decide for themselves what to wear and how to talk.

Similarly, conflict may result from undue stress on total-family activities. The mother who worries about finding recreation which both her four-year-old and her fourteen-year-old will enjoy may be troubling herself unduly, since almost anything she chooses evokes dissent from one child or the other. Autonomy under such circumstances need not mean a complete atomization of the family but simply a willingness of a subgroup within the family to enjoy singing nursery rhymes without feeling the necessity of compelling disinterested members to join.

4. Safety Valves for Reducing Tension between Family Members

Insofar as conflict within the family is precipitated or accentuated by accumulated interpersonal resentment, various means are available for reducing the level of this tension. Vacations are one such resource. Of course, a family may find plenty of things to quarrel about on a vacation, but at least they are new issues. As far as the old problems are concerned, a change of scenery makes it possible to forget about them for a while, and on return they may even have lost their power to provoke antagonism.

A change in personnel may be just as effective. Adding a pal or two for the morning play period may so restructure relationships within the sibling group that the old feuds are disrupted at least for the time being.

For some purposes, however, it is most effective to get away from the family group completely. One reason we speak of harried housewives but not of harried husbands is that wives (and especially mothers) are so often tied down to the four walls and the four faces of the home. The piling-up of petty irritations into peaks of tension results in perennial irritability and conflict-proneness. Then little issues provoke major crises because of the loading of accumulated tension.

Under these circumstances escape mechanisms are not childish but sensible. Getting out of the house produces a sense of relief. A television farce or romance produces the right kind of distraction. Even "going home to mama" may be useful provided mama does not take daughter's troubles too seriously.

There may be corresponding value in masculine and children's expeditions. The husband's "night out with the boys" may be resented by his wife but is likely to result in a new look in marital relations. And the children need not always be on the receiving end of personnel changes but may find welcome escape from the network of conflict by visiting their friends in return.

There is also what the psychologists call "catharsis"—the reduction of tension through telling one's troubles to someone else. There is little doubt that "unloading" one's difficulties on someone else genuinely lightens the burden of conflict for most people. In so doing, it reduces the necessity for purposeless vindictiveness which prolongs the conflict. In effect, catharsis (like the other safety valves) helps to break the vicious circle of attack and retaliation which so often characterizes families with a long history of conflict.

The only problem involved in the use of catharsis is the selection of the target. Among the shoulders which might conveniently be cried on are those of the husband (provided he is not the antagonist in the conflict), the mother, and the neighbor. Providing a sympathetic ear for the spouse is one of the major steps in accomplishing what I like to call the "mental hygiene function" of marriage. Mothers and neighbors can usually be counted on to be sympathetic—but sometimes too much so, tending to jump into the conflict, too, starting a mobilization race on both sides.

Because of these dangers in lay friendships, couples in serious conflict sometimes find it useful to turn to a professional third party, for instance, a clergyman, doctor, or family counselor. These functionaries are accustomed to providing people with discreet opportunities for catharsis.

Whatever the specific safety valve opened, the reduction of the head of steam facilitates the tolerance of frustration and a patient approach to finding satisfactory solutions to the basic sources of conflict.

Processes of Resolving Family Conflict

So far we have been ducking the main issue of what happens when two parties to a family conflict collide head-on. To treat this problem, it is necessary to assume that the two partners (for it is most often the husband and wife who find themselves in this position) think of each other as equals. Hence the problem cannot be solved by appeal to differential authority.

One obstacle to resolving family conflict is that it is often dyadic in nature. Hence voting is impossible. Or at least there is no way to break the inevitable tie. Some families have found that conflicts of limited importance can be settled by ordinary voting procedures—especially if there is an odd number of children in the family. But this easy way out is available at best during a small fraction of the total family life-cycle.

What, then, to do in case of deadlock?

Discussion

The natural first step is to talk things over, to outline the various possible solutions, to weigh the pros and cons in an attempt to arrive at some sort of solution. This process of decision-making has been studied and analyzed too well elsewhere to need detailed treatment here.[9] Suffice it to say that there are three major types of solutions which can be reached: (1) *consensus*—that is, mutual agreement by both partners that a vacation at the lake would be best for both of them; (2) *compromise*—one week at the lake and one week in the mountains so that both partners gain part and lose part of their objectives; (3) *concession*—two weeks in the mountains, not because the wife is convinced that that would be most enjoyable, but because she decides to end the conflict by dropping her own demands.

Most families solve most of their problems by such processes of communication followed by decision-making.

Mediation

Occasionally, couples need outside help in arriving at a decision. Here relatives and friends can seldom qualify because they are usually more closely aligned with one partner than the other. Hence professional personnel are almost the only resort.

The function of the third party in this case is seldom to take over the decision-making process. Rather he acts as a catalytic agent, enabling the couple to become more objective and more rational by his very presence. If conflict is serious and hostile feelings have accumulated, he may work with each partner separately for a long time. Only after self-insight and mutual empathy have been achieved might it be productive for the couple to be seen jointly. Meanwhile the couple may discover on their own that they have already acquired the ability to settle their conflict, aided by the new skills and understandings gained in counseling. Even when only one partner turns to a third party, the beneficial repercussions of the counselor's collaboration may be felt throughout the family.

Accommodation

In one sense, accommodation might be listed as a type of decision. More accurately, however, it represents the recognition of a failure to agree. In the classic phrase, we "agree to disagree" or to "live and let

[9] Robert O. Blood, Jr., *Anticipating Your Marriage* (Glencoe, Ill.: Free Press, 1955), pp. 225–51.

live." In the specific case of the summer vacation, this could mean separate vacations for husband and wife (though so much autonomy runs heavily counter to American mores).

It is not always possible for the parties to a family conflict to go their separate ways. If the issue at hand is the need for a new car, one either gets one or one does not. But if John likes to play tennis while Mary likes to go to concerts, Mary could accommodate herself to going it alone while John finds a different partner.

Essentially, accommodation involves adopting a philosophical attitude of resignation—coming to the conclusion that further attempts to influence the partner are just not worth the conflict they provoke. Hence expectations of mutuality are abandoned in favor of accepting the partner as he is.

Separation

If neither discussion, mediation, nor accommodation succeeds in settling family conflict, the last resort is separation. In a sense, separation does not really settle conflict at all, but it usually does end it. If the antagonists are no longer within shooting distance of each other, their attention is soon likely to be diverted from the point at issue.

The term "separation" is usually applied to husband and wife. If they cannot live together in peace, few there are who would force them to go on living in conflict. Even those groups who are most opposed to divorce and remarriage recognize that separating the marriage partners is sometimes preferable to prolonging the agony.

Separation can also occur between parents and children. The military academies of this country are populated by boys whose parents were unable to arrive at peace treaties with them. And the older adolescent who leaves home for college, job, or marriage sometimes only thus terminates his or her revolutionary war.

Separation is the most drastic way out of family conflict, yet those who have tried it often say that peaceful loneliness is an improvement over perpetual conflict.

48. HOLY DEADLOCK: A STUDY OF UNSUCCESSFUL MARRIAGES

E. E. LeMasters

§ Not all cases of marital maladjustment arise from major crises and not all end in divorce. This article traces the history of thirty-six couples, caught in a chain of conflict situations that had extended over at least ten years' time. The study covers such items as degree of personal disorganization, effect on children, and reasons that held the couple together.

Introduction

Some years ago Waller demonstrated that divorced persons in our society suffer personal disorganization as the price of marital failure.[1] More recently, in a careful study of divorced women, Goode has shown again that divorce is no bed of roses, sociologically speaking.[2]

In the present study a somewhat different problem has been posed: what happens to married couples whose marriages have failed but who *don't* separate or divorce? More specifically, the study attempts to answer the following questions: (1) Do the couples who don't separate or divorce escape personal disorganization, as measured by such indices as alcoholism, mental illness, etc.? (2) Do couples with a long history of marital conflict (ten years minimum in this study) ever "solve" their marital problems? (3) What are the effects of such marriages on the children?

In an attempt to discover some tentative answers to these questions, 36 marriages characterized by chronic husband-wife conflict were analyzed. To be included in the sample, the cases had to meet three requirements: (1) both spouses had to regard the marriage as unsuccessful; (2) this condition must have persisted for at least ten years; and (3) the marriage had to be intact—that is, they were still living together. No case which met these requirements was excluded.

The couples were located through friends, attorneys, physicians, min-

SOURCE: *Sociological Quarterly*, 21 (1959), 86–91. Reprinted by permission of the publisher and the author. This paper was read at the meeting of the Midwest Sociological Society, Lincoln, Nebraska, April, 1959.

The author's background is given in the footnote for article 16.

[1] Willard Waller, *The Old Love and the New*, New York: Liveright, 1930.
[2] William J. Goode, *After Divorce*, Glencoe: The Free Press, 1956.

isters, and marriage counselors. An average of three hours was spent interviewing each couple. With four exceptions, both spouses were seen.

The sample is basically white, urban, Protestant, and middle-class, with scattered cases falling into diverse socio-economic categories. No claim is made for the representativeness of the sample. In view of the limited nature of the study, the findings are presented as being suggestive rather than conclusive.

The Findings

Data bearing on the three questions posed for the study will be presented first. Other material which might be of interest to research persons and practitioners in this field will be discussed later.

1. *Do the couples who don't separate or divorce escape personal disorganization?* The evidence from these cases is that they don't. Of the 36 married couples, objective evidence of personal disorganization could be demonstrated for one or both spouses in 27 cases (75%).[3] The most frequent types of disorganization were alcoholism, chronic psychosomatic illness, neurotic or psychotic behavior, occupational disorganization, extramarital affairs, and a syndrome of patterns best described by Schulberg's term, "disenchantment."[4] The table below summarizes the distribution of these types of personal disorganization.

Types of Personal Disorganization in 36 Unsuccessful Marriages

Type	Husbands	Wives
Alcoholism	14	6
Psychosomatic illness	5	12
Neurotic-psychotic behavior	8	10
Occupational disorganization	17	0
Extramarital affairs	12	6
Disenchantment	18	22

It is not known, of course, what these persons would have been like had they married someone else (or not married at all). Nor is it possible to know what their adjustment would have been had they separated or divorced. Keeping these limitations in mind, it still seems well established that these couples did not escape the destructive impact of marital failure by avoiding separation or divorce.

2. *Do couples with a long history of marital conflict ever "solve" their marital problems?* A recent follow-up of these couples revealed that of

---

[3] For a discussion of the concept of personal disorganization, see Marshall B. Clinard, *Sociology of Deviant Behavior*, New York: Rinehart and Company, 1957.
[4] Budd Schulberg, *The Disenchanted*, New York: Random House, 1950.

the 29 still living together, not one couple had been able to work out what seemed to them to be a satisfactory marriage. The implications of this finding will be presented later.

3. *What are the effects of such marriages on the children?* One would assume a high incidence of disorganization in the children of these couples. The data, however, do not seem to support such an assumption. Of the 76 children in these marriages, only 7 have ever been referred to a child guidance clinic or school psychologist for diagnosis or therapy for emotional or behavioral problems. And only 3 children in the sample have ever been booked for a juvenile offense. Furthermore, of the male children who have served in the armed forces (17), none has been rejected or discharged for psychiatric reasons or behavioral problems.

It is recognized that the above "tests" are very crude and that a psychiatric screening might prove these children to have been damaged emotionally in various ways. Most certainly they have not had an optimum opportunity to develop their capacities as human beings. But using such crude measuring devices as school and community adjustment, plus performance in the armed forces, these children appear to be a relatively "normal" group.

This finding does not agree with that of Despert,[5] who concludes that chronic marital conflict is often more damaging to children than separation or divorce. It is also not entirely in line with the findings of Goode, whose divorced women felt their children to be better adjusted after the divorce.[6]

If other studies should support our finding in this point, how could one explain the ability of these children to be well organized in spite of their negative home environment? The writer suggests several possible interpretations: (1) the conclusion of Orlansky that children are tougher emotionally than has generally been thought;[7] (2) the possibility that children are not as aware of parental conflict as child psychiatrists have supposed—for example, the finding of Burchinal and his co-workers that the relationship between parental acceptance of children and the adjustment of the children was negligible;[8] (3) that modern society permits the child enough contacts with other human beings that the parents are custodians of personality rather than its shapers;[9] (4) that genetic factors are crucial in personality disorganization and that these operate

[5] J. Louise Despert, *Children of Divorce*, New York: Doubleday, 1953.
[6] See Goode, *op. cit.*, ch. 21.
[7] Harold Orlansky, "Infant Care and Personality," *Psychological Bulletin*, 46 (1949), 1–48.
[8] Lee G. Burchinal, Glenn R. Hawkes, and Bruce Gardner, "The Relationship Between Parental Acceptance and Adjustment of Children," *Child Development*, 28 (March, 1957), 65–77.
[9] This is partly implied in Cohen's analysis of the impact of the peer group on gang behavior. See Albert K. Cohen, *Delinquent Boys, The Culture of the Gang*, Glencoe: The Free Press, 1955.

independently of parental conflict—for example, the findings of Kallmann on schizophrenia.[10] The work of Sewell in which infant care techniques did not correlate significantly with later school adjustment might also be fitted into this analysis.[11]

Regardless of the interpretation of this finding, it could be maintained with some logic that the results of this study support the argument that parents should continue their marriage "for the benefit of the children."

Other Observations on the Cases

Differential Reaction Patterns of Husbands and Wives

The husbands and wives in this sample utilized quite different substitute satisfaction patterns to soften the blow of marital failure. The men tended to turn to (a) their job, (b) liquor, (c) other women. With the wives, however, the major substitute satisfactions were (a) their children, (b) a job, (c) religion, and (d) community service.

As Kinsey would have predicted, extramarital affairs were reported for twice as many husbands as wives.[12] It is interesting to note that the extramarital affairs tended to follow rather than precede the marital failure, thus raising the question whether this so-called "cause" of marital difficulty may be an effect instead.

Of the two sets of substitute satisfactions, it appears that those of the husbands are potentially more destructive. The writer has the distinct impression from these cases that husbands are more likely to be severely damaged by chronic marital failure than are the wives. This is contrary to the old saying that "the woman pays," but it may be true nevertheless. Unfortunately, the best study available on divorced persons, that cited by Goode, did not cover the post-divorce adjustment of the husbands, hence gives us no comparable data.

If it is true that men do suffer more damage than women from marital failure, the interpretation would seem to be that the substitute satisfactions of the women are more in line with the basic values of the society —increased interest in their children, greater participation in church affairs, etc.

The Process of Disenchantment

Given the romantic approach to marriage in American society, it would seem logical to expect some degree of trauma in these couples.

[10] Franz J. Kallmann, "The Genetic Theory of Schizophrenia," in *Personality in Nature, Society, and Culture*, edited by Clyde Kluckhohn and Henry A. Murray, New York: Alfred A. Knopf, 1949.
[11] William H. Sewell, "Infant Training and the Personality of the Child," *American Journal of Sociology*, 58 (1952), 150–159.
[12] Alfred C. Kinsey *et al.*, *Sexual Behavior in the Human Male*, Philadelphia: W. B. Saunders, 1948.

Of the 72 husbands and wives in the sample, 40 (56 per cent) exhibited what we have chosen to call "disenchantment." These persons have lost their faith in romance and are cynical (if not bitter). In the most severe cases they refer to love as "a joke"; some perceive themselves as "suckers." They also use the expression "kid stuff" in referring to the romantic complex.

Careful study of these 40 persons reveals a process of disenchantment: (a) the feeling of concern that the marriage has not gone as they had expected; (b) a stage of determined effort to be brave and to solve their problems; (c) this is followed by a stage of hostility toward the partner for not "cooperating" in the effort to save the marriage; (d) and then resignation and perhaps bitterness.

It is worthwhile to note that these couples do not exhibit a stage (e) described by Waller and Goode—namely, the therapeutic excitement of a new love affair and the possibility of another marriage. If it is true that the best treatment for a broken love affair is a new one, as the above studies seem to indicate, then one of the prices paid by these couples for not terminating their marriages is their inability to form new meaningful love relationships. With a very few exceptions, the extramarital affairs reported by the couples failed to be deep enough to heal the wounds from the marital failure.

Counseling Efforts with These Couples

Marriage counselors, ministers, and psychotherapists consulted by this sample (14 had consulted at least one of the above) seem in general to have been committed to keeping these couples together. In view of the fact that not one of the couples eventually succeeded in building what they regarded as an adequate marriage, one wonders why more effort was not directed at helping the couples dissolve what was for most of them essentially a destructive relationship. It would seem that professional practitioners working with such couples may be reflecting a cultural bias in their counseling efforts—that the function of the counselor is to keep the marriage intact no matter what the cost.

It is undoubtedly true that the counselor who suggests separation or divorce is open to the charge of "undermining" marriage and of not being able to "save marriages." It is also true, however, that the counselor who fails to consider separation or divorce for marriages such as these must face the fact that some of these couples will deteriorate seriously if the relationship is continued for any length of time. Actually, not even the Catholic moral code demands that destructive marriages be continued. And as Gold says, divorce (with or without remarriage) can be therapeutic for some persons.[13]

---

[13] Herbert Gold, "Divorce as a Moral Act," *The Atlantic Monthly*, November, 1957.

How Did Some of the Couples Escape Disorganization?

It will be remembered that of the 36 couples disorganization could not be demonstrated for nine (25 per cent) of the couples. If marriage is so crucial in our society in meeting basic needs, how is one to explain the fact that one-fourth of these husbands and wives apparently succeeded in living constructive lives in spite of what might have been a disastrous marital relationship?

It is suggested that the following interpretations may be helpful in understanding these cases: (1) Differential ability to tolerate frustration. It is well recognized in psychiatry that humans vary widely in their ability to absorb physical or psychic punishment. World War II supplied ample evidence of this for the men in the armed forces. Sociologists who specialize in crime, alcoholism, and the entire field of deviation are well aware of the fact that what drives one man to murder (or drink) will scarcely upset another man (or woman). (2) Displacement of hostility and other forms of negative emotion. Some persons express their hostility directly onto the marriage partner, others turn the emotion back on themselves, whereas still others displace the feeling onto the outside world—employees working under them, employers, minority groups, the economic system, etc. Whatever the device, the emotion which might damage the married partners is not released within the primary group, thus minimizing the destructive effects within the family itself. It could be maintained that these nine marriages did produce damage but that it was to persons outside the intimate circle. As one wife said of her husband: "He doesn't get ulcers—he gives them to *other* people." (3) The development of separate worlds for the husband and wife. Difficult as it may be to believe, it is possible in modern society to live as man and wife and hardly interact with each other. One man, for example, seeing that his marriage was unsuccessful, arranged to be assigned a wide territory which kept him away from home six weeks at a time. Another case was more ingenious: the man would arise about five A.M., prepare his own breakfast and leave for work. He lunched downtown (although he could easily have come home for lunch), had an early dinner in the evening and went to bed about seven. His wife, on the other hand, always stayed in bed until her husband had gone to work, and she usually stayed up until two or so in the morning. As this pattern developed, it became possible for them to live together while spending only about two hours together in the evening (from 5 to 7). They each slept with one of the children, so that part of the day or night did not involve interaction either. In a very pragmatic way, this couple worked out a style of life which held to the barest minimum their opportunity to express hostility.

A more common pattern involving separate worlds finds the husband becoming increasingly absorbed in his career, while the wife immerses herself in the children, community service, the church, etc. This sort of behavior represents what has been called "sublimation" in the redirection of sexual drives—the energy which might normally go into husband-wife interaction is expressed through other channels which meet with society's approval. Thus these couples minimize the potential destructiveness of the marriage and are actually industrial and community leaders in many cases. Sloan Wilson describes such a marriage in *Man in the Gray Flannel Suit*.[14] Oddly enough, society and the community often do benefit from such marriages—in these cases there was one children's hospital and one low cost housing project which owe their existence to a poor marriage.

In view of the above, it appears that there are various ultimate reactions to an unsuccessful marriage, some of which are more socially desirable than others.

Why Did They Stay Together?

In a few cases only psychiatric theory would appear to explain why some of these couples continued living together. In perhaps the "worst" case, the man and wife seemed to hate each other, yet were unable to separate. They had no children, nor did their religious beliefs prevent separation. Yet they lived on together for over twenty years. One might say that they were locked together in a deadly struggle to see which one would break first. The man finally became an invalid, at which point the wife seemed to feel that she had "won." In such cases there seems to be a desire to "get even" with the partner. The reasoning (if such it can be called) seems to be like this: you have ruined my life by marrying me, and the only way I can pay you back is by living with you and ruining your life too. Separation, it seems, is too good for the partner: he or she must be made to pay. Oddly enough, such marriages are recorded statistically in our society as being "successful," since no separation, desertion, or divorce is ever recorded. It should be said that only a small number of cases (three) exhibited such psychopathic characteristics.

A more typical reason for continuing the relationship was the desire to give the children a normal home life. And in these cases, there seems to have been some reality content in this desire. This reason for living together was mentioned by 24 of the couples (66%).

There was also the hope, at least in the early years of discord, that matters would improve. Then by the time it became clear that the problems were not being solved, there were children to think of, community position to consider, financial complications, etc.

---

[14] Sloan Wilson, *Man in the Gray Flannel Suit*, New York: Simon and Schuster, 1955.

How Did They Choose Each Other?

Although it is beyond the scope of this paper to attempt to answer this question, two observations can be made: (1) lengthy dating and courtship in themselves do not necessarily prevent unsuccessful marriages in our society—14 of these couples (39%) had gone together for over three years before marrying. This supports Goode's finding that the divorces in his sample could not be explained by this variable. It appears that we need some way to measure the depth and intensity of courtship rather than just its duration in time. (2) Winch's theory of the unconscious nature of psychodynamic attraction between future marital partners merits further attention.[15] Some of the most incompatible couples in this sample seemed to be pulled toward each other by forces of which they had no real understanding.

Conclusion

The sample and the research design in this study are not adequate to support any definitive generalizations. But as suggestions for further research two findings seem of special interest: (1) that marital failure not terminated by separation or divorce has a differential impact on the two sexes, with the male suffering the more severe damage. (It is unfortunate that the best study we have of divorce, that by Goode, focused on wives exclusively, thus providing no comparable data on this finding.) (2) that the adjustment of the children in these marriages did not seem to reflect that of the parents. Although the indices of adjustment used in this study are admittedly very crude, their direction is so impressive that the matter merits systematic study. Furthermore, they are not entirely unsupported by more carefully designed research published in recent years.[16]

It is hoped that these two findings in particular will be subjected to further analysis by other sociologists.

[15] Robert Winch, *Mate-Selection*, New York: Harper and Brothers, 1958.
[16] See references 7, 8, 9, 10, and 11.

49. DIVORCE AS AN ESCAPE MECHANISM

William J. Goode

§ The author starts with the premise that family conflict and personal unhappiness are inevitable in all cultures, although each culture tends to define how much conflict is permissible, how to avoid conflicts, and how to solve them. Divorce, then, is "one kind of mechanism for dealing with the pressures and problems inevitably caused by marriage." Of course, there are other mechanisms as well.

After discussing the way divorce is handled in some other societies, the author shows that in the United States divorce is only partially accepted, is condemned by some groups, often arouses feelings of guilt on the part of the divorced persons, and fails to provide ways for individuals after divorce to receive help or make a new place in society.

This theoretical discussion is an excellent background for the understanding of some of the specific problems of divorce, as discussed in articles 33 and 34 (laws), 52 (remarriage), and 61 (custody).

The Norms of Marital Stability and Expression of Conflict

We insist, then, that happiness is not, and cannot be, built into any family system as either a statistical average, or as a moral norm. As members of the society, we can *not* be morally required to be happy or unhappy. Family *stability*, on the other hand, can be the focus of major value complexes, and often is. Just as marital happiness can not be a moral prescription in any society, so can marital unhappiness or conflict not be morally proscribed. Social or physical inevitabilities are rarely, if ever, prohibited.

Of course, such matters are not left socially unstructured. Hostility or conflict can not be allowed to develop without check, for any such lack of harmony may become overt and thus disrupt existing and approved role relations. There are moral and ethical norms to prohibit many kinds of behavior which might tend to excite or intensify hostility and conflict. (Thus, it is wrong for me to sneer often at my wife.) We are also socialized to accept many *common* values so that *grounds* for con-

SOURCE: William J. Goode, *After Divorce* (New York: The Free Press, 1956), pp. 7–15, with omission of several footnotes. Reprinted by permission of the publisher.

For the author's background, see the footnote to article 1.

flict are lessened. (E.g., both my wife and I have been socialized to believe that we ought to live together, that we shall have sexual access to one another, etc.) Moreover, we are taught to regard many differences and difficulties as *unimportant*, so that we can overlook, or live comfortably with, potential sources of conflict. This is reinforced by values which state that we are "immature," "petty," etc., if we base our conflict on such differences. (Thus, I may not base my conflict with my wife on her failure to butter my toast properly.)

We need not outline these types of patterns systematically. We merely illustrate the fact that values and norms *do* proscribe conflict *indirectly*, by defining as improper various kinds of actions that might *lead* to conflict and hostility.

Correspondingly, the moral structure will not prohibit falling in love with someone who is not one's spouse, but it can and does define as improper those activities of married people which have a good chance of leading to outside love relationships: dating, courtship, being alone with the outsider, especially in situations culturally defined as romantic, and so on.

We therefore assert that some marital conflict is inevitable in any society so long as husband and wife are two different people, and their actions are important to one another.

Correspondingly one may surmise it to be an uncorrectable error in historical reconstruction and nostalgia to believe that our Victorian (or any other) ancestors lived in marital placidity. Doubtless they were stable, but their *stability* is no reliable index of happiness or of absence of conflict, and we have no objective data for exploring that traditional reconstruction adequately. We can accept neither the sketches of avant-garde literary men who for many reasons concentrated upon deviations, nor the preachments of latter-day moralists and rootless urbanites who seek a calm in the past which can be no part of their present lives.

Variation in Conflict Intensity, Acceptance of Conflict and Solutions for It

This is not to say (1) that cultures do not vary in the *degree* of such marital conflict. Undoubtedly, for example, in periods of great change in the role of definitions of the sexes there is (a) far *more* disagreement and conflict between spouses, and (b) certainly more expression of this conflict in *overt behavior*. We are merely asserting the inevitability of family conflict and personal unhappiness in all cultures, and the impossibility of there being meaningful, *direct* moral proscriptions against them.

Moreover, (2) what the culture defines as a *bearable* level or degree of conflict will also doubtless vary from one epoch or society to another;

and (3) what the society or culture defines as an *appropriate solution* for conflict also varies. The first of these three propositions is borne out by general observations and some theory, although intensity of marital conflict has not been measured in any culture. With reference to the second, there are beginnings of systematic theory in the structural-functional hypotheses of the past decade, specifically those dealing with mechanisms for alleviating and preventing conflict. Here, let us simply note, once more, the possibility of analyzing various elements in any kinship system by reference to their effect upon the *stability* of marriage. The universal nuclear family is to be viewed as one type of boundary-maintaining social unit, under various internal and external pressures toward boundary dissolution and maintenance. Marital unhappiness is only a resultant of various factors that predispose toward marital instability. Among these factors, there are also various mechanisms which (1) *prevent* the building of tensions or external forces; (2) alleviate or deflect such forces; (3) define various difficulties as bearable; (4) and offer various solutions for changing the structure or direction of these forces, or even for removing them.

Within such a view, divorce is to be seen as one kind of mechanism for dealing with the pressures and problems inevitably caused by marriage. Divorce is in a basic sense "caused" by marriage.

A typical set of preventive mechanisms was found in pre-revolutionary China. According to traditional descriptions of this "classical" family, the roles of husband and wife were *clearly* defined. Respect and not romantic love was demanded between husband and wife. There was an extended family system, so that intimate emotional interaction between husband and wife was less continuous or intense than in our own system. Extended deviations from proper marital patterns were prevented in part by the continuous supervision by other, older relatives. If the wife built up any large reservoir of hatred and fear, it was more likely to be aimed at the mother-in-law, rather than at the husband, who was only rarely the most powerful member of the family in the first decade of a marriage.

When conflict *does* reach high limits, there are different solutions in different cultures. One rare solution is that of Dobu, where overt conflict is viewed as standard. There are, however, many outlets for aggression. There is an alternation of family residence each year, from the village of wife's family to that of husband's family. Thus, each of the two spouses may look forward to a period in which great freedom of unchecked, mostly unilinear aggression is permitted.[1]

Perhaps the most common solution is that of divorce, the extended families of each spouse offering at times the necessary help. *Divorce is, then, an institutionalized element of certain kinship systems.* It is not

[1] Reo Fortune, *The Sorcerers of Dobu* (London: Routledge, 1932).

always a kind of excrescence, a sort of pathology or unpredictable deviation. This does not ignore or minimize the difficulties that individuals experience in divorce, or the devastation that may occur in their private lives when a divorce conflict occurs. Rather, we are noting that *all* family systems have *some* kinds of escape mechanisms built into them, to permit individuals to survive the pressures of the system, and one of these is divorce.

Nor is this solution confined to industrial societies. As Murdock has shown, and as Hobhouse began to show earlier, divorce is very common in many pre-literate societies. Even without a complete set of data, it is clear that the rate of divorce is often higher than in our own, or than in the other few nations that have at various times had still higher rates than the U.S.[2]

It is then an error to think that, because primitive societies are mostly "rural," they are therefore to be identified with the classical family of Western nostalgia, an idealized picture of the rural family in America at some unspecified period prior to the 1900's.

Theoretical Importance of Divorce

We do not have, unfortunately, any adequate analysis of the values relating to divorce in these societies. We know that in our own, divorce has been a possible, but disapproved, solution for marital conflict. That is, it seems that divorce is not as yet fully *institutionalized* in our own cultural structure. Certainly among some groups of our society it is still disapproved strongly. It is equally certain that this attitude is *changing*. Thus, although a rise in our divorce rate can not be viewed as a simple index of social pathology or even of personal disorganization, it is without question an index of social change.

In the light of these hypotheses, divorce as a phenomenon and as an experience is theoretically very interesting. It is closely tied to several sets of strong value patterns relating to the family and to marital conflict. It is an index of interpersonal strain, and within our own society it is also an index of strain in the social structure, in that (a) there are many strong, if gradually weaker, moral proscriptions against it; but (b) in spite of these proscriptions, the divorces continue to occur and the rate of divorce continues to rise as a mass phenomena. Moreover, (c) since marital stability in our society is morally approved, since the roots of this attitude are to be found in the three major sects of the Judeo-Christian religious tradition, and since divorce is also judged to be an act of self-seeking or of moral failure, it is likely that few couples divorce

[2] George P. Murdock, "Family Stability in Non-European Cultures," *Annals,* 272 (1950), 195–201; also J. L. Hobhouse *et al., The Material Culture and Social Institutions of Primitive Peoples* (London: Chapman and Hall, 1930), pp. 159 ff.

in our culture without a guilt component on both sides with specific reference to the divorce (aside from guilts with other sources). Thus on both the psychodynamic and the socio-structural levels there are interesting ramifications.

Furthermore, (d) divorce as a large-scale solution for marital conflict is a relatively recent reappearance in the cultural history of Western society (for Rome in its "decline," as for Athens, the rate must have been high), yet it has been an always *potentially* institutionalized element in the social structure because of its many Semitic religious antecedents (both Arab and Hebrew, of course). Since these potentialities did not become actual, divorce as a social deviation is in certain respects not like crime or juvenile delinquency, treason or sacrilege.

These latter and other violations are like divorce in that they can be predicted to some extent on the basis of individual characteristics, and to a very great extent on a mass basis. However, they are very different in that prescribed modes of official and unofficial behavior exist for dealing with such deviations. We are socialized to react against these deviations with a fairly specific behavioral and emotional set, and we are even told to some extent how they ought to be punished.

This is not the case for divorce. Neither the participants nor their close friends and relatives have been taught to react in a culturally approved fashion with respect to divorce. We are all taught how to grieve at the death of a relative. We are not taught how we should behave as a divorcee. We are given many culturally approved rationalizations for failing to achieve high status in our occupation, but we are not taught how to solve or to adjust to the failure of our marriage. The general preferences in our culture for rationalistic approaches to problems fail us in this area of great emotionality. Consequently, we should expect to find a set of social phenomena of considerable interest for understanding the family patterns in our culture. Finally, since divorce is a personal and often familial crisis, study of it should add to our knowledge about how individuals adjust to crises.

Numerical Importance of Divorce

A rather substantial segment of the population has, at one time or another, been involved in the divorce process. We do not have an exact figure for the segment composing all who have ever divorced. However, even allowing a substantial amount of cohort mortality, this group must number nearly ten million. Kingsley Davis has estimated that 150,000 to 200,000 children are affected by divorce each year in this country, and calculates further that for the year 1940 the total number of children, then under the age of 18 years, whose parents had ever been divorced, numbered 1,533,000.[3] The figure has certainly not declined. In addition, although the divorce rate fluctuates somewhat from one year to the next, it is clear that the secular trend of divorce is still upward. It seems a conservative estimate to assert that the experience of divorce is likely to occur to one-fifth to one-sixth of the men and women in this country who live out an average life span.[4]

On the other hand, as we have noted before, several countries have exhibited a *higher* rate of divorce than even the United States. Burgess and Locke have assembled these rates for several countries, and show that under the old family system in Japan, there were approximately 367 divorces per 1,000 marriages for the years 1884–1888.[5] Russia, Palestine, and Egypt had higher rates than the United States for the period in or about 1938. As we also noted previously, many primitive societies have relatively high divorce rates. At any given time, approximately 2% of the adult population of the United States is in the marital status "still divorced."[6] Finally, we must remember that death still dissolves more marriages than does divorce.[7]

The Structural Importance of Divorce

Whether or not we judge this segment of the population or this rate to be large, it seems at least likely that in our society the group impact of divorce is much greater than in most others. We have elsewhere noted some of the behavioral indices of this concern. They may be summarized as follows: (1) A widespread condemnation of the extent of divorce and of its increase; (2) the emotional difficulties suffered by the individuals in the divorce; (3) the number of panaceas offered as general solutions for the problem; (4) its frequency as an object of clinical research; and (5) the development of organizations and experts whose aim is to ameliorate this distress.

The kinship structure fails to define clearly an acceptable behavior

[3] "Child of Divorced Parents: A Sociological and Statistical Analysis," *Law and Contemporary Problems*, Summer, 1944, p. 713.
[4] Such an estimate rests on two rough but reasonable assumptions: that 80% to 90% of the population living out an average life span will marry, and that the ratio of marriages to divorces over this period would be from one in four, to one in five. Kingsley Davis suggests that the rate will level off. *Annals* [272, 1950], pp. 9–22.
[5] Ernest W. Burgess and Harvey J. Locke, *The Family* (New York: American Book Co., 1945), pp. 627–8.
[6] *Current Population Reports, Population Characteristics*, "Marital Status and Household Characteristics, March 1950," Series P-20, No. 33 (Washington, D.C.: Bureau of the Census, February 12, 1951), pp. 10–11.
[7] Paul H. Jacobson, "Total Marital Dissolutions in the United States: Relative Importance of Mortality and Divorce," in *Studies in Population*, ed. George Mair (Princeton: Princeton University Press, 1949), p. 7; and *Statistical Bulletin*, 30, No. 11 (New York: Metropolitan Life Insurance Company, 1949), pp. 1–3.

pattern for this experience in the life history of a substantial segment of the population. The kinship system fails to furnish unambiguous arrangements for the following kinds of problems.

1. There are no ethical imperatives for relatives or friends that would make them feel constrained to furnish material support during the crisis and afterwards to the divorcees *as* divorcees. This is a period of dissolution of certain household arrangements. Most often, the two spouses separate from one another, and at least one of them must set up a new abode. There are new problems of purchasing food and housing, and, of course, there are various legal fees. These costs cannot usually come out of existing income. There is no room for such added expenses. In addition, of course, one or both spouses may lose their jobs, and there is only rarely enough money for both to continue their usual activities without need for added funds.

2. Similarly, there are no ethical imperatives for friends and relatives to furnish *emotional* support during this period. There is a general ethical imperative to furnish support to close friends during any kind of crisis, and to some extent this is applicable to the divorce situation. It is not comparable, however, to the kind of crisis created by an emergency operation or sudden illness, death, loss of job, etc. In the event of divorce, the friend must make an adjustment among several other imperatives, such as whether he *should* support the break-up of a family, whether he approves his friend's conduct, or how friendly he is to the other spouse. What we are distinguishing here is the difference between a crisis situation in which the imperatives are clear and one in which they are not clear. As we shall show later, friends and relatives actually do help in this situation, but this is not the crucial point at issue. Whether a given individual gives such support is the resultant of many factors, but he cannot, in our society, base his action upon a simple rule of the kinship or friendship structure. The most striking contrast, of course, is with death of the spouse, for in this case the relative or friend who is unwilling to provide economic or emotional support is viewed with disapproval by all within the group.

3. A further point of ambiguity centers around the *readmission* of participants into their former kinship structure or into a new one. The importance of this ambiguity is not to be underestimated, and it is indeed the base on which other ambiguities rest. By contrast, among the Zuñi, for example, the kinship is matrilineal, divorce is relatively common, and it is accompanied by little public concern and attention. This is the case generally, as it happens, for merely private matters of marital conflict and even marriage. In this society the property in land is owned by the woman's side of the family and descends through her line. In one sense, divorce means that the man is "dismissed." We are not, however, concerned with the personal impact of this situation, but with the fact

that in the case of a divorce, all the parties concerned know what they are supposed to do. The man returns to his mother's household, where there is a known place for him. He is part of her family line, and marriage has not changed that fact. He does not carry away the corn he has raised, and there is no argument about the ownership of real property, for that remains in the possession of his wife's lineage. There can be no argument about the children, since the children belong to his wife's line. Whether she herself rears the children or they are given to one of her male relatives to rear, the children are nevertheless part of her family, and it is the right of her family to make decisions about the children's welfare. There is no alimony and no child support, since both sides are simply reabsorbed into an existing and usually extended familial network. These provisions exist whether or not either family approves the behavior of either spouse. There may, of course, be some deviations from these rough rules laid down here, for in no society does everyone live up to the ideal. Nevertheless, these are the general moral imperatives, and the individual or family who failed to live by them would be criticized.

In our own society, by contrast, we are not at all clear as to where the members of the divorcing family ought to go. Indeed, in our society the emphasis is so much on the single family unit, the nuclear family, with only rather tenuous and increasingly vague connections with the older generation or with collateral relatives, that often there is almost no other family cell to which the members of the divorced family *can* go. This is a somewhat exaggerated statement, but it does describe the *norms*. The husband's original family has no moral imperative to take him back. He has made a claim to adulthood and independence, having founded his new family. He has left the family nest. There is no room for him, not alone spatially as is so often the situation in our time, but in kinship terms. It is assumed that if he divorces he will continue to work and support himself, together with perhaps his divorced spouse and children, but this is not a necessary concern of the family from which he originally came. Again, we must emphasize that, concretely, his original family may help him and be friendly to him, but there is no moral injunction that *as divorcé* he has such rights.

The wife is in an even more ambiguous position. Our own society is patrilineal, and patriarchal to a degree. By the Judeo-Christian traditions of the Western world, the wife leaves her original family and becomes a member of the husband's family. Actually, because of the pattern of small nuclear families in our generation, husband and wife simply form a new family unit. In any event, she is considered to be part of that new unit, and no longer part of her family of orientation. This is emphasized by the fact that she takes her husband's name and, if she has children, usually keeps her husband's name even after the divorce. The children also have her husband's name, so that even if she returns with her children to her own family's home, her name and kinship designation lie with the family of her husband. To this degree, then, the divorce asserts a legal cleavage which is only partially carried out in institutional fact.

In any event, for all the family members involved in the divorce, there is some ambiguity about the family status and role to which each must *return* when a divorce is made final. Neither of the two families of orientation is given clear definitions of the approved kinship status to be reassumed by the two married children.

4. As an almost necessary consequence of these ambiguities, the kinship structure does not point out avenues for the *formation of new families*. In some strata, after what is considered an appropriate period of emotional recovery, the divorced wife gradually forms new male friendships. In others, this behavior is considered vaguely or definitely improper. What is certain, however, is that the family's obligation to help her form a new family is not clear. This is in contrast with the moral imperatives families feel for helping the younger generation find a first husband or wife. Daughters are admonished by both parents that they must look for the right kind of husband, and parents usually make at least token gestures toward helping in this process. Even the most protective mother gives at least lip service to the notion that she must help her son find a wife. The push toward marriage is strong in our culture, and it affects both generations. The family has, however, discharged its obligations when the child is married. The unhappiness and disorganization of the divorced spouse may lead in time to the parent family offering help in moving toward a second marriage. However, this is a result of the personal affection of family members for one another and the distress caused by the other's suffering, and is not so much due to a socially recognized obligation to offer this type of aid to a divorced child.

5. Correlative with these gaps is a further ambiguity concerning the proper behavior and emotional attitudes of the spouses most directly concerned. We have just noted the failure to specify the proper behavior for various activities which might be carried out by relatives or even friends. However, the other side of all such sets of definitions is a specification of the appropriate role behavior of the two spouses. There is no clear definition as to whether they should be grieved or relieved. They are in some sense now "single," but the role behavior of the never married is much more definitely specified. Having *once* been defined as adult and married, a status which is in turn defined as being chronologically later than the status of "never married," neither the spouses nor their families have a simple definition of an in-between state: they are neither old nor young, adult nor child, married nor single. Lacking such a specification, the divorced spouse is subject to criticism by some,

no matter what she or he does. Behavior and emotion may seem inappropriate to some members of the family or to some friends. In particular, the proper relationship *between the divorced spouses* is not clearly defined.

These ambiguities do not necessarily create great emotional distress and, as we shall see later on, many women may adjust to divorce with relatively little anguish. However, social behavior is simplified in all societies by role definitions, accepted and known to almost all participants, and morally approved. When these definitions are lacking, the necessary decisions must be made on a more individual basis, and the people concerned can not count on general social approval, whether or not their previous behavior has been proper.

50. STRUCTURAL PROBLEMS OF THE ONE-PARENT FAMILY

Paul Glasser and Elizabeth Navarre

§ Death or divorce automatically creates a one-parent family which may continue until the death of the parent or may be converted into a step-parent family; it will never return to the status of a family with two natural parents unless a divorced couple remarries. As compared with a two-parent family, the one-parent family changes structure in performance of tasks, channels of communication, power hierarchy, and affectional relationships. In most one-parent families, it is the mother who remains with the children. Poverty is often an added problem with which the lone parent must contend.

Introduction

Recent concern about the problems of people who are poor has led to renewed interest in the sources of such difficulties.[1] While these are

SOURCE: *Journal of Social Issues*, 21 (January, 1964), 98–109. Reprinted by permission of the publisher and the authors.

Paul Glasser is with the University of Michigan School of Social Work; at the time of the preparation of the article, Elizabeth Navarre was a doctoral candidate in sociology at the University of Michigan. The conceptualization in the article grew out of work on Project D-16, financed by a grant from the Children's Bureau.

[1] The conceptualization in this paper grew out of work on Project D-16, "Demonstration of Social Group Work With Parents," financed by a grant from the Children's Bureau, Welfare Administration, Department of Health, Education and Welfare. The authors are indebted to Professor Edwin Thomas for his suggestions.

manifold and complexly related to each other, emphasis has been placed upon the opportunity structure and the socialization process found among lower socio-economic groups. Relatively little attention has been paid to family structure, which serves as an important intervening variable between these two considerations. This seems to be a significant omission in view of the major change in the structure of family life in the United States during this century, and the large number of one-parent families classified as poor. The consequences of the latter structural arrangements for family members, parents and children, and for society, is the focus of this paper.

One-parent families are far more apt to be poor than other families. This is true for one-fourth of those headed by a woman. Chilman and Sussman summarize that data in the following way:

> About ten percent of the children in the United States are living with only one parent, usually the mother. Nonwhite children are much more likely to live in such circumstances, with one-third of them living in one-parent families. Two-and-a-quarter million families in the United States today are composed of a mother and her children. They represent only one-twelfth of all families with children but make up more than a fourth of all that are classed as poor. . . .
>
> Despite the resulting economic disadvantages, among both white and nonwhite families there is a growing number headed only by a mother. By 1960 the total was 7½ per cent of all families with own children rather than the 6 per cent of ten years earlier. By March 1962 the mother-child families represented 8½ per cent of all families with own children (4, p. 393).

When these demographic findings are seen in the context of the relative isolation of the nuclear family in the United States today, the structural consequences of the one-parent group takes on added meaning. It may be seen as the culmination of the contraction of the effective kin group.

> This "isolation" is manifested in the fact that the members of the nuclear family, consisting of parents and their still dependent children, ordinarily occupy a separate dwelling not shared with members of the family of orientation. . . . It is, of course, not uncommon to find a (member of the family of orientation) residing with the family, but this is both statistically secondary, and it is clearly not felt to be the "normal arrangement" (9, p. 10).

While families maintain social contact with grown children and with siblings, lines of responsibility outside of the nuclear group are neither clear nor binding, and obligations among extended kin are often seen as limited and weak. Even when affectional ties among extended family members are strong, their spatial mobility in contemporary society isolates the nuclear group geographically, and increases the difficulty of giving aid in personal service among them (2, 6).

Associated with the weakening of the extended kinship structure has been the loss of some social functions of the family and the lessened import of others. Nonetheless, reproduction, physical maintenance, placement or status, and socialization are still considered significant social functions of the modern American family although they often have to be buttressed by other institutions in the community. At the same time, however, the personal functions of the family including affection, security, guidance and sexual gratification have been heightened and highlighted (3, 9). These functions are closely and complexly related to each other but can serve as foci for analysis of the consequences of family structure. In the one-parent family neither reproduction nor sexual gratification can be carried out within the confines of the nuclear group itself. But more importantly, the other personal and social functions are drastically affected also, and it is to these that this paper will give its attention. A few of the implications for social policy and practice will be mentioned at the end.

While it is recognized that all individuals have some contact with others outside the nuclear group, for purposes of analytic clarity this paper will confine itself to a discussion of the relationships among nuclear family members primarily. Two factors will be the foci of much of the content. The age difference between parent and children is central to the analysis. Although it is understood that children vary with age in the degree of independence from their parents, the nature of their dependence will be emphasized throughout. The sex of the parent and the sex of the children is the second variable. Cultured definitions of appropriate behavior for men and women and for girls and boys vary from place to place and are in the process of change, but nonetheless this factor cannot be ignored. Since the largest majority of one-parent families are headed by a woman, greater attention will be given to the mother-son and mother-daughter relationships in the absence of the father.

Structural Characteristics of One-Parent Families and Their Consequences

Task Structure

The large majority of tasks for which a family is responsible devolve upon the parents. Providing for the physical, emotional, and social needs of all the family members is a full-time job for two adults. If these tasks are to be performed by the nuclear group during the absence or incapacity of one of its adult members, the crucial factor is the availability of another member with sufficient maturity, competence, and time to perform them. The two-parent family has sufficient flexibility to adapt to such a crisis. Although there is considerable specialization in the traditional sex roles concerning these tasks, there is little evidence that such specialization is inherent in the sex roles. It is, in fact, expected that one parent will substitute if the other parent is incapacitated and, in our essentially servantless society, such acquired tasks are given full social approval. However, in the one-parent family such flexibility is much less possible, and the permanent loss of the remaining parent generally dissolves the nuclear group.

Even if the remaining parent is able to function adequately, it is unlikely that one person can take over all parental tasks on a long term basis. Financial support, child care, and household maintenance are concrete tasks involving temporal and spatial relationships, and in one form or another they account for a large proportion of the waking life of two adult family members. A permanent adjustment then must involve a reduction in the tasks performed and/or a reduction in the adequacy of performance, or external assistance.

In addition to limitations on the time and energy available to the solitary parent for the performance of tasks, there are social limitations on the extent to which both the male and the female tasks may be fulfilled by a member of one sex. If the remaining parent be male, it is possible for him to continue to perform his major role as breadwinner and to hire a woman to keep house and, at least, to care for the children's physical needs. If, however, the solitary parent be a female, as is the more usual case, the woman must take on the male role of breadwinner, unless society or the absent husband provides financial support in the form of insurance, pensions, welfare payments, etc. This is a major reversal in cultural roles and, in addition, usually consumes the mother's time and energy away from the home for many hours during the day. There is little time or energy left to perform the tasks normally performed by the female in the household and she, too, must hire a female substitute at considerable cost. The effect of this reversal of the sex role model in the socialization of children has been a matter of some concern, but the emphasis has been upon the male child who lacked a male role model rather than upon the effect of the reversal of the female role model for children of both sexes. In both cases, the probability seems great that some tasks will be neglected, particularly those of the traditionally female specialization.

The wish to accomplish concrete household tasks in the most efficient manner in terms of time and energy expenditure may lead to less involvement of children in these tasks and the concomitant loss of peripheral benefits that are extremely important to the socialization process and/or to family cohesion. Some tasks may be almost completely avoided, especially those which are not immediately obvious to the local community, such as the provision of emotional support and attention to children. A third possibility is to overload children, particularly adolescents, with such tasks. These may be greater than the child is ready to assume, or tasks inappropriate for the child of a particular sex to perform regularly.

Females are often lacking in skills and experience in the economic world, and frequently receive less pay and lower status jobs than men with similar skills. The probability of lower income and lower occupational status for the female headed household are likely to lower the family's social position in a society which bases social status primarily upon these variables. If the family perceives a great enough distance between its former level and that achieved by the single parent, it is possible that the family as a whole may become more or less anomic, with serious consequences in the socialization process of the children and in the remaining parent's perception of personal adequacy.

Communication Structure

Parents serve as the channels of communication with the adult world in two ways; first as transmitters of the cultural value system which has previously been internalized by the parents; and secondly, as the child's contact with and representative in the adult world. Except for very young children, the parents are not the sole means of communication, but for a large part of the socialization process, the child sees the adult world through the eyes and by the experience of his parents, and even his own experiences are limited to those which can be provided for him within whatever social opportunities that are open to his parents. More importantly, to the extent that the child's identity is integrated with that of the family, he is likely to see himself not only as his parents see him but also as the world sees his parents.

Since sex differences have been assumed in the ways men and women see the world and differences can be substantiated in the ways that the world sees men and women, the child can have a relatively undistorted channel of communication only if both parents are present. Therefore, whatever the interests, values, and opinions of the remaining parent, the loss of a parent of one sex produces a structural distortion in the communications between the child and the adult world and, since such communication is a factor in the development of the self-image, of social skills, and of an image of the total society, the totality of the child's possible development is also distorted.

The type and quality of experiences available even to adults tend to be regulated according to sex. In the two-parent family not only is the child provided with more varied experiences, but the parent of either sex has, through the spouse, some communication with the experiences typical of the opposite sex. Thus, the housewife is likely to have some idea of what is going on in the business or sports worlds even if she has no interest in them. The solitary parent is not likely to be apprised of such information and is handicapped to the extent that it may be necessary for decision making. The female who has taken on the breadwinner role may be cut off from the sources of information pertinent to the female role as she misses out on neighborhood gossip about the symptoms of the latest virus prevalent among the children, events being planned, the best places to shop, etc.

Finally, the solitary parent is likely to be limited in the social ties that are normal channels of communication. Most social occasions for adults tend to be planned for couples and the lone parent is often excluded or refuses because of the discomfort of being a fifth wheel. Her responsibilities to home and children tend to never be completed and provide additional reasons for refusing invitations. Lone women are particularly vulnerable to community sanctions and must be cautious in their social relationships lest their own standing and that of the family be lowered. Finally, the possible drop in social status previously discussed may isolate the family from its own peer group and place them among a group with which they can not or will not communicate freely.

Power Structure

Bales and Borgatta (1) have pointed out that the diad has unique properties and certainly a uniquely simple power structure. In terms of authority from which the children are more or less excluded by age and social norms, the one-parent family establishes a diadic relationship, between the parent and each child. Society places full responsibility in the parental role, and, therefore, the parent becomes the only power figure in the one-parent family. Consequently, the adult in any given situation is either for or against the child. Some experience of playing one adult against the other, as long as it is not carried to extremes, is probably valuable in developing social skills and in developing a view of authority as tolerable and even manipulable within reason, rather than absolute and possibly tyrannical. In the one-parent family the child is more likely to see authority as personal rather than consensual, and this in itself removes some of the legitimation of the power of parents as the representatives of society.

Even if benevolent, the absolutism of the power figure in the one-parent family, where there can be no experience of democratic decision making between equals in power, may increase the difficulty of the adolescent and the young adult in achieving independence from the family, and that of the parent in allowing and encouraging such development. Further, the adult, the power, the authority figure, is always of one sex, whether that sex be the same sex as the child or the opposite. However, in contemporary society where decision making is the responsibility of both sexes, the child who has identified authority too closely with either sex may have a difficult adjustment. The situation also has consequences for the parent, for when the supportive reinforcement or the balancing mediation which comes with the sharing of authority for decision making is absent, there may be a greater tendency to frequent changes in the decisions made, inconsistency, or rigidity.

Affectional Structure

The personal functions of the family in providing for the emotional needs of its members have been increasingly emphasized. There is ample evidence that children require love and security in order to develop in a healthy manner. Although there is nearly as much substantiation for the emotional needs of parents, these are less frequently emphasized. Adults must have love and security in order to maintain emotional stability under the stresses of life and in order to meet the emotional demands made upon them by their children. In addition to providing the positive emotional needs of its members, the family has the further function of providing a safe outlet for negative feelings as well. Buttressed by the underlying security of family affection, the dissatisfactions and frustrations of life may be expressed without the negative consequences attendant upon their expression in other contexts. Even within the family, however, the expressions of such basic emotions cannot go unchecked. The needs of one member or one sub-group may dominate to the point that the requirements of others are not fulfilled, or are not met in a manner acceptable to society. To some extent this danger exists in any group, but it is particularly strong in a group where emotional relationships are intensive. Traditionally, the danger is reduced by regulating the context, manner, and occasion of the expression of such needs.

Family structure is an important element both in the provision and the regulation of emotional needs. The increasing isolation of the nuclear family focuses these needs on the nuclear group by weakening ties with the larger kin group. Thus, both generations and both sexes are forced into a more intensive relationship; yet the marital relationship itself is increasingly unsupported by legal or social norms and is increasingly dependent upon affectional ties alone for its solidity. Such intense relationships are increased within the one-parent family, and possibly reach their culmination in the family consisting of one parent and one child.

In a two person group the loss of one person destroys the group. The structure, therefore, creates pressure for greater attention to group maintenance through the expression of affection and the denial of negative feelings, and in turn may restrict problem solving efforts.

In a sense, the one-parent family is in this position even if there are several children because the loss of the remaining parent effectively breaks up the group. The children have neither the ability nor the social power to maintain the group's independence. Therefore, the one-parent family structure exerts at least some pressure in this direction.

However, where there is more than one child there is some mitigation of the pattern, though this in itself may have some disadvantages. In a group of three or more there are greater possibilities for emotional outlet for those not in an authority role. Unfortunately, there are also greater possibilities that one member may become the scapegoat as other members combine against him. In spite of the power relationships, it is even possible that the solitary parent will become the scapegoat if the children combine against her. This problem is greatest in the three person family as three of the five possible sub-groups reject one member (Figure 2). The problem is also present in the four person family, although the possible sub-groups in which the family combines against one member has dropped to four out of twelve (Figure 1). The relation of group structure to emotional constriction has been clearly expressed by Slater:

> The disadvantages of the smaller groups are not verbalized by members, but can only be inferred from their behavior. It appears that group members are too tense, passive, tactful, and constrained, to work together in

Sub-Group Choices Among Groups of Varying Sizes *

FIGURE 1: THE FOUR PERSON GROUP

1. A,B,C,D	5. B,C,D	9. B,D
2. A,B,C	6. A,B	10. A,D
3. A,B,D	7. C,D	11. B,C
4. A,C,D	8. A,C	12. All persons independent; no sub-group

FIGURE 2: THE THREE PERSON GROUP

1. A,B,C	3. A,B	5. All persons independent; no sub-group
2. B,C	4. A,C	

FIGURE 3: THE TWO PERSON GROUP

1. A,B	2. Both persons independent; no sub-group.

* Persons designated by letter.

a manner which is altogether satisfying to them. *Their fear of alienating one another seems to prevent them from expressing their ideas freely.* (Emphasis is ours.)

These findings suggest that maximal group satisfaction is achieved when the group is large enough so that the members feel able to express positive and negative feelings freely, and to make aggressive efforts toward problem solving even at the risk of antagonizing each other, yet small enough so that some regard will be shown for the feelings and needs of others; large enough so that the loss of a member could be tolerated, but small enough so that such a loss could not be altogether ignored (11, p. 138).

Interpersonal relationships between parents and children in the area of emotional needs are not entirely reciprocal because of age and power differences in the family. Parents provide children with love, emotional support, and an outlet for negative feelings. However, while the love of a child is gratifying to the adult in some ways, it cannot be considered as supporting; rather it is demanding in the responsibilities it places upon the loved one. Support may be received only from one who is seen as equal or greater in power and discrimination. Nor can the child serve as a socially acceptable outlet for negative emotions to the extent that another adult can, for the child's emotional and physical dependency upon the adult makes him more vulnerable to possible damage from this source. The solitary parent in the one-parent family is structurally deprived of a significant element in the meeting of his own emotional needs. To this must be added the psychological and physical frustrations of the loss of the means for sexual gratification. In some situations involving divorce or desertion, the damage to the self-image of the remaining parent may intensify the very needs for support and reassurance which can no longer be met within the family structure.

The regulation of emotional demands of family members is similar in many ways to the regulation of the behavior of family members discussed under power structure. As there was the possibility that authority might be too closely identified with only one sex in the one-parent family, there is the similar danger that the source of love and affection may be seen as absolute and/or as vested in only one sex. Having only one source of love and security, both physical and emotional, is more likely to produce greater anxiety about its loss in the child, and may make the child's necessary withdrawal from the family with growing maturity more difficult for both parent and child. Again, as in the power structure, the identification of the source of love with only one sex is likely to cause a difficult adjustment to adult life, particularly if the original source of love was of the same sex as the child, for our society's expectations are that the source of love for an adult must lie with the opposite sex.

One of the most important regulatory devices for the emotional needs of the group is the presence and influence of members who serve to deter or limit demands which would be harmful to group members or to group cohesion, and to prevent the intensification of the influence of any one individual by balancing it with the influence of others. Parental figures will tend to have greater influence in acting as a deterrent or balance to the needs and demands of other family members because of their greater power and maturity. The loss of one parent removes a large portion of the structural balance and intensifies the influence of the remaining parent upon the children, while possibly limiting the ability of this parent to withstand demands made upon her by the children. There is also a tendency for any family member to transfer to one or more of the remaining members the demands formerly filled by the absent person (8). There would seem to be a danger in the one-parent family that:

1. The demands of the sole parent for the fulfillment of individual and emotional needs normally met within the marital relationship may prove intolerable and damaging to the children, who are unable to give emotional support or to absorb negative feelings from this source, or

2. The combined needs of the children may be intolerable to the emotionally unsupported solitary parent. Since the emotional requirements of children are very likely to take the form of demands for physical attention or personal service, the remaining parent may be subject to physical as well as emotional exhaustion from this source.

When emotional needs are not met within the family, there may be important consequences for the socialization of the children and for the personal adjustment of all family members. Further, fulfillment of such needs may be sought in the larger community by illegitimate means. The children may exhibit emotional problems in school or in their relations with their play group. A parent may be unable to control her own emotions and anxieties sufficiently to function adequately in society. When there are no means for the satisfaction of these demands they may well prove destructive, not only to the family group and its individual members, but to society as well.

The consequences of the problems discussed above may be minimized or magnified by the personal resources or inadequacies of the family members, and particularly the solitary parent in this situation. But, the problems are structural elements of the situation, and must be faced on this level if they are to be solved.

Implications for Social Policy and Practice

The Introduction describes the growth of the number of one-parent families during the last generation. Chilman and Sussman go on to describe the financial plight of many of these families.

> The public program of aid to families with dependent children (AFDC) that is most applicable to this group currently makes payments on behalf of children in nearly a million families. Three out of every four of these families have no father in the home. Less than half of the families that are estimated to be in need receive payments under the program and, ". . . with the low financial standards for aid to dependent children prevailing in many states, dependence on the program for support is in itself likely to put the family in low-income status. . . . The average monthly payment per family as reported in a study late in 1961 was only $112. . . .
>
> "The overall poverty of the recipient families is suggested by the fact that, according to the standards set up in their own states, half of them are still in financial need even with their assistance payment" (4, p. 394; 10).

There is increasing evidence that both the one-parent family structure and poverty are being transmitted from one generation to the next.

> "A recently released study of cases assisted by aid to families with dependent children shows that, for a nationwide sample of such families whose cases were closed early in 1961" more than 40 per cent of the mothers and/or fathers were raised in the homes where some form of assistance had been received at some time. "Nearly half of these cases had received aid to families with dependent children. This estimated proportion that received some type of aid is more than four times the almost 10 per cent estimated for the total United States population . . ." (4, p. 395; 10).

If poverty and one-parent family structure tend to go together, providing increases in financial assistance alone may not be sufficient to help parents and children in the present and future generation to become financially independent of welfare funds. Under the 1962 Amendments to the Social Security Act states are now receiving additional funds to provide rehabilitation services to welfare families, and these programs have begun. Creative use of such funds to overcome some of the consequences of one-parent family structure is a possibility, but as yet the authors know of no services that have explicitly taken this direction.

A few suggestions may serve to illustrate how existing or new services might deal with the consequences of one-parent family structure:

1. Recognition of the need of the mother without a husband at home for emotional support and social outlets could lead to a variety

of services. Recreation and problem focused groups for women in this situation, which would provide some opportunities for socially sanctioned heterosexual relationships, might go a long way in helping these parents and their children.

2. Special efforts to provide male figures to which both girls and boys can relate may have utility. This can be done in day-care centers, settlement house agencies, schools, and through the inclusion of girls in programs like the Big Brothers. It would be particularly useful for children in one-parent families to see the ways in which adults of each sex deal with each other in these situations, and at an early age.

3. Subsidization of child care and housekeeping services for parents with children too young or unsuitable for day-care services would provide greater freedom for solitary mothers to work outside the home. Training persons as homemakers and making them responsible to an agency or a professional organization would reduce the anxiety of the working parent, and provide greater insurance to both the parent and society that this important job would be done well.

More fundamental to the prevention of poverty and the problems of one-parent family status may be programs aimed at averting family dissolution through divorce, separation and desertion, particularly among lower socio-economic groups. Few public programs have addressed themselves to this problem, and there is now a good deal of evidence that the private family agencies which provide counseling services have disenfranchised themselves from the poor (5). The need to involve other institutional components in the community, such as the educational, economic and political systems, is obvious but beyond the scope of discussion in this paper (7). Increasing the number of stable and enduring marriages in the community so as to prevent the consequences of one-parent family structure may be a first line of defense, and more closely related to treating the causes rather than the effects of poverty for a large number of people who are poor.

Summary

One-parent families constitute more than a fourth of that group classified as poor, and are growing in number. Family structure is seen as a variable intervening between the opportunity system and the socialization process. The task, communication, power and affectional structure within the nuclear group are influenced by the absence of one parent, and the family's ability to fulfill its social and personal functions may be adversely affected. Some of the consequences of this deviant family structure seem related to both the evolvement of low socio-economic status and its continuation from one generation to the next. Solutions must take account of this social situational problem.

References

1. BALES, R. F. AND BORGATTA, E. F. Size of group as a factor in the inter-action profile. In Hare, Borgatta and Bales (Eds.) *Small Groups*. New York: Knopf, 1955.
2. BELL, W. AND BOAT, M. D. Urban neighborhoods and informal social relations. *Amer. J. Soc.*, 1957, 43, 391-398.
3. BERNARD, J. *American Family Behavior*. New York: Harper, 1942.
4. CHILMAN, C. AND SUSSMAN, M. Poverty in the United States. *J. Marriage and the Family*, 1964, 26, 391-395.
5. CLOWARD, R. A. AND EPSTEIN, I. Private social welfare's disengagement from the poor: the case of family adjustment agencies. Mimeographed, April 1964.
6. LITWAK, E. Geographic mobility and extended family cohesion. *Amer. Soc. Rev.*, 1960, 25, 385-394.
7. LUTZ, W. A. Marital incompatability. In Cohen, N. E. (Ed.) *Social Work and Social Problems*. New York: National Association of Social Workers, 1964.
8. MITTLEMAN, B. Analysis of reciprocal neurotic patterns in family rela-tionships. In V. Eisenstein (Ed.) *Neurotic Interaction in Marriage*. New York: Basic Books, 1956.
9. PARSONS, T. AND BALES, R. F. Family socialization and interaction proc-esses. Glencoe, Illinois: The Free Press, 1954.
10. *Poverty in the United States*. Committee on Education and Labor, House of Representatives, 88th Congress, Second Session, April 1964, U. S. Government Printing Office, Washington, D. C.
11. SLATER, P. E. Contrasting correlates of group size, *Sociometry*, 1958, 6, 129-139.

51. REMARRIAGE OF THE WIDOWED AND THE DIVORCED

Jessie Bernard

§ Marriage may terminate by the death of husband or wife or by divorce. In each case, people must adjust to the dissolution of the marriage. In each case, also, many husbands and wives marry another time, and are faced with types of adjustment not found in a first marriage. Dr. Bernard

SOURCE: Jessie Bernard, *Remarriage: A Study of Marriage* (New York: Holt, Rine-hart and Winston, 1956), pp. 199–207. Reprinted by permission of the publisher.

The author received her doctorate from Washington University and is now Re-search Scholar, *Honoris-Causa*, Pennsylvania State University. Among her publica-tions are *American Family Behavior* and *Marriage and Family among Negroes*.

comments that "there are at least three or four persons involved in every remarriage. One or two, the previous spouses, may not be living in the flesh, but their memory may be very much alive." When the former spouse is alive, formidable problems may need solution before a happy remarriage is assured.

Former Spouses of the Widowed

When at least one partner to a remarriage is a widowed person, there are three chief areas of potential difficulty to which the couple must adjust: (1) the tendency of the widowed spouse to idealize the deceased mate; (2) the knowledge of the other spouse that the partner's first marriage was not terminated voluntarily; and (3) the feeling of friends and relatives that the new spouse is an intruder. An additional source of difficulty may be an underlying sense of guilt on the part of one or both spouses. The attitudes of children by the former marriage may further complicate the situation, especially if there is property involved. Children tend to keep the memory of the former spouse active in the new relationship.

The widowed person's tendency to idealize his first mate may constitute an unconquerable obstacle to the new marriage. (Since it is more common for widowed men than for widowed women to remarry, we shall carry through our discussion in terms of a man whose previous marital status was widowhood.) When such idealization exists, the present wife is at a great disadvantage in competition with the former wife. She cannot prove to her husband that her cooking is better, her housekeeping more competent, her budgeting more efficient, or her sexual appeal greater than that of her rival, and she herself has no way of knowing whether or not she is superior to the first wife. She must always box with a phantom. The rules of etiquette and good taste are all on the side of the deceased. There may be pictures, mementoes, a score of reminders of the first wife, especially if the second wife has come to live in the widowed man's home. And the husband may, consciously or unconsciously, play upon his advantage. His manner may imply that his former marriage set a high standard which the present marriage is not achieving. Without saying anything at all, he may communicate an invidious contrast between his former and his present wife. If there is a considerable difference in age between the widowed man and his bride—as there might well be if she were previously unmarried—he may wistfully recall the comfort of having a partner whose biological pace suited his own.

A woman who marries a widowed man steps into a situation that is the result of an event which was not deliberately brought about. If the former wife had not died, presumably her husband would not have sought his freedom, and the present marriage would not have taken place. This fact introduces an element of insecurity which is not so likely to be present in remarriage to a divorced man. If the widowed man had known both his first and his second wife at the time he first married, the second wife may feel—perhaps with some justification—that she was not his first choice.

Perhaps a more important problem is the remarried couple's adjustment to the social world in which the marriage must function. The new wife may be considered an intruder into a long-established social pattern. No matter how much she may be liked personally, she represents a change, something new that must be assimilated, a break in an accustomed routine. Widowed persons and their friends are likely to be in the older age brackets, and the necessary readjustments are more difficult to make among this group than among younger men and women. Friends who share common memories may speak of the former wife as though she were still alive. "Do you remember the time you and Mary drove with us to Chicago and . . .?" "Wasn't it funny the time you and Helen gave that party where . . .?" "Did Margaret ever tell you about the time she and I . . .?" Comments of this nature may serve to render a marriage psychologically bigamous.

If the new wife is herself secure in the marriage, she may be able to take all this in stride. "Yes, I remember that too. And Jack tells me that once she. . . ." "Mary must have been an awfully resourceful person. Tom has told me about the time she. . . ." In brief, instead of permitting outsiders to wall her off from her husband, she may use such occasions to reaffirm her ties with him, establishing them as more intimate and comprehensive than those of his friends. She shares more memories with her husband, even of his first wife, than others do. But if she is insecure in her new marriage, she may feel cut off, as though the first wife were preempting her position.

The remarried man and his new wife may or may not refer to former spouses. In at least one remarriage in Utopolis, the first wife was never mentioned at all; in another, conversely, she was referred to as though she were an actual, still-present member of the household. In one remarriage, involving two previously married persons, the husband sometimes called his present wife by his first wife's name, but neither seemed even to notice it.

The children and former in-laws of widowed men may have a motive in keeping the memory of the first wife alive. "Poor Mama," one adult daughter of a widowed man was overheard to say in the presence of her father and his new wife, "she worked so hard all her life to help Dad save his money, and now She comes in to spend it." The purpose, often poorly concealed, is to create guilt feeling in the father so that he will attempt to buy a free conscience from the children by remembering them generously in his will. They are, in effect, blackmailing him.

Younger children too can keep the first spouse alive. Although, as we shall see presently, most children of widowed men and women want their parents to remarry, not all of them do. And a child who wishes to do so can make the life of a new mother or father extremely difficult. "Mother never did it that way," one child kept repeating. No matter how conciliatory his new mother was, the resentful child continued to make invidious comparisons between her and his "real mother." It has often been said that there is no room for two women in one home; this may be as true when one of the women is a memory as when she is present in the flesh.

If the first marriage was unsuccessful, despite the fact that it had remained intact until the death of one of the partners, the surviving spouse may suffer from guilt feelings which keep the first spouse alive in his memory. He may have often wished to be free, and although the death of his partner may have been wholly natural, the fact that it coincided with his unconscious wishes may color his memory. He may expiate his "sin" by overdoing his grief for her death. The second wife in such a case can do little but try to understand her husband's behavior.

Fortunately, the problems discussed above occur only infrequently and are usually handled satisfactorily, for the marriages of widowed persons, as reported in the Utopolis data, seem to outside informants to be extremely successful.

Former Spouses of the Divorced

Difficult problems are likely to be introduced into a remarriage when the former spouse of one or both partners is still alive. The unremarried divorced woman, perhaps because she is less likely to remarry than the divorced man, is more likely to constitute an obstacle to the success of her ex-husband's remarriage than is the divorced man to his ex-wife's remarriage.

Even without the remarriage of a former husband or wife, divorce can be an extremely ego-wounding experience—and one which, paradoxically, unremarried divorced men and women are probably least capable of handling. These persons were selected into the divorced population in many cases because they were incapable of achieving good human relations; they were probably selected out of the remarried population for the same reason. Their death rates are high, and they are more prone to mental illness and suicide than the married population, which includes, of course, the remarried population.

The adjustment problems of these people, may of whom are social misfits, are compounded many times by the role divorce has imposed upon them. No matter how bitter they are, how much they still love their former mates, how defeated they feel, they are obliged by convention to behave as though they were indifferent to it all. One student describes the position of the young, urban divorced woman as follows:

> The divorcee . . . may be very unhappy about the marital failure, and even be attached to the former husband, but must instead show little sorrow or continued affection. As a consequence, whenever the divorcee is permitted, she is likely to give a stereotyped answer, one in conformity with public social expectations. She will describe her feelings toward the former spouse as those of indifference. Exactly half of the pilot group gave this response. Only one out of ten expressed strong affection. One out of four admitted a desire that their husbands be punished. Yet side comments and answers to open-ended questions revealed considerable emotion, sometimes strongly negative, of course. Further, all gave some main cause for the divorce, and only one out of ten indicated an unemotional recognition of fault on both sides. Finally, almost one out of four admitted that under certain circumstances they might be willing to remarry the former spouse.[1]

The position of the divorced woman is made still more difficult if her former husband remarries. It was bad enough to lose him; it is unbearable that someone else should win him. In a certain sense, it may be said that the cost of a successful second marriage after divorce is often borne by the unremarried first spouse. If the first marriage had been preserved, the husband (assuming that he was the instigator of the divorce) would have paid in frustration and marital unhappiness; the wife would have won in terms of security, status, and face. When the first marriage is dissolved, the divorced woman has lost everything; the remarrying husband has won. There seems to be no way short of remarriage for each in which both can win. The community usually fails to appreciate the cost of keeping unsuccessful marriages intact; hence there is not much reward for the spouse who remains married for the sake of his partner. But the community is likely to appreciate fully the costs of divorce; the divorced spouse may make them very clear.

Jealousy, paranoia, and desire for revenge are, of course, as typical of men as of women in such situations. Jealousy may become extremely intense, especially in the partner who did not seek the divorce. It may lead him to constant checking-up on the former spouse.[2]

Closely associated with jealousy is near-paranoia—the feeling that "People are ganged up against me. It's not my fault. There's no justice in it. . . ." The paradox of "justice" in human relations constitutes one

---

[1] William J. Goode, "Problems in Postdivorce Adjustment," *American Sociological Review*, 14 (June, 1949), p. 400.

[2] See, for example, Morris Ernst and D. G. Loth, *For Better or Worse* (Harper, 1951), pp. 32–33, 160–164.

of the most difficult problems in the adjustment of many divorced persons. A divorced woman may be, at least in the legal sense, wholly "innocent." She has never committed adultery, she was not—deliberately, at any rate—cruel, she has never deserted her mate, she has acquiesced to his sexual demands, she is neat and trim about her person, she has been a good housekeeper, she has been thrifty and economical, she has reared clean, polite children. . . . Now her husband has discarded her and married someone else. It isn't fair! If the woman has been taught that virtue is always rewarded and evil punished, she cannot understand why her virtue is now being punished and the evil of others rewarded. If she is unable to view the situation objectively, she may be able to explain it only as a conspiracy against her. Everyone, especially the new wife, seems to be mocking her. Such paranoid reactions, in men as well as women, may, along with grief and despondency, contribute to the high mental-illness rate so characteristic of the unremarried divorced.

Further, such paranoid behavior may constitute a hazard to the former spouse's second marriage, especially if the disturbed person should become extremely vindictive and retaliatory. The former wife may spread venomous gossip about her former husband or his new wife; she may make outrageous financial demands or constant appeals in behalf of their children. She may continue to treat him possessively. She may in countless ways attempt to drive a wedge between her former husband and his new wife. Even if she does not succeed in breaking up the second marriage, she may make it difficult for the couple to remain in the community, by stirring up adverse community pressures.

The devoted spouse may take quite another tack, with equally devastating effects. She may decide sweetly to wait for her husband to return, to "come to his senses." She may, with relative—and cruelly calculating—equanimity, wait ten or twenty years, like Patience on a rock smiling at grief. In short, she makes a career of her martyrdom. This role of the wronged-wife-forgiving-all confers on her the only distinction she has.

What, actually, is the impact of this kind of situation on the second marriage? It may, as we have remarked, tend to isolate the remarried persons socially because the friends and acquaintances wish to remain uninvolved. It may, in fact, drive the remarried persons out of the community to start over without this incubus.

But its subtlest effect is the guilt feeling it arouses in the remarried spouse, especially if his second marriage is relatively successful. Although he knows that his first marriage was a failure for both parties, he knows also that if he had been willing to keep it intact his wife would have been better off than she is now. Because she has made him realize that he has by far the better of the bargain, he feels compelled to accede to her demands, no matter how outrageous they may be. Her weaknesses are her greatest strength, for pity and guilt forge a powerful chain linking him to her.

If the man's second spouse feels secure in her marriage, this common enemy may actually contribute to increased solidarity. The more intolerable the first wife is, the better the second seems by contrast. But if the new wife feels resentment, she can place an added burden on her husband. He becomes torn between his guilt-generated sense of responsibility for his first wife and his desire to please his second wife.

In quite another way, the distress of the first marriage may contribute toward the success of the husband's second marriage. Feeling guilt and remorse for having caused his first wife unhappiness, he may try much harder to be a good husband in his second marriage.

The fact that there are relatively fewer successful remarriages reported among the divorced as compared with the widowed may be explained in part by the problems which arise when a former spouse is still alive. Failure in remarriage for some divorced persons may be caused by neuroticism not in the remarried spouse but in the spouse who did not remarry.

Types of Attitudes Toward Former Mates

The problems introduced into all areas of marital adjustment by the existence of a former spouse are formidable; but quite remarkably, in a large number of cases, the new partners seem to be able to take them in their stride. For example, relatively few of the informants in Utopolis reported cases of negative attitudes toward former spouses. The Utopolis data comparing widowed and divorced persons and their present spouses with respect to attitudes toward former mates are summarized in Table 1.

Unfriendly attitudes toward the first spouses were, as expected, reported as almost nonexistent among the widowed men (2.2 percent) and women (.9 percent), and, perhaps because of idealization or perhaps because of a genuine history of successful marriage, most remarried widowed persons seemed to show positive attitudes toward their former spouses.

Not so, of course, among the divorced. Only about a fourth of the remarried divorced men (26.9 percent) and a fifth of the women (21.9 percent) were reported to have a friendly attitude toward their former mates. The interesting fact here is not the relative absence of friendly attitudes, for they are virtually precluded by the divorce; rather, it is the relatively small proportions of the remarried divorced—18.7 and 26.8 percent for men and women, respectively—who were reported as having *un*friendly attitudes toward their former spouses. Most of them

TABLE 1   *Reported Attitudes of the Widowed and Divorced toward Own and Spouse's First Partner in Utopolis*

| | I. TOWARD OWN FIRST PARTNER | | |
	Friendly	Indifferent or No Attitude	Unfriendly
Widowed men (273)	65.6%	32.2%	2.2%
Divorced men (675)	26.9	54.4	18.7
Widowed women (224)	61.6	37.5	.9
Divorced women (684)	21.9	51.3	26.8

| | II. TOWARD SPOUSE'S FIRST PARTNER | | | |
	Friendly	Indifferent	Jealous or Resentful	Other
Husbands of widowed women (212)	38.7%	44.8%	8.0%	8.5%
Husbands of divorced women (576)	21.7	59.5	14.8	4.0
Wives of widowed men (253)	46.6	36.4	5.1	11.9
Wives of divorced men (420)	27.6	46.6	19.8	6.0

at least feigned indifference (54.4 percent for men and 51.3 percent for women). A study of young divorced women in Detroit corroborates this reported indifference among approximately half of the divorced toward former spouses.[3] But the interviewers detected strong negative feelings in side comments and in answers to open-ended questions. The reported attitudes of indifference both in Utopolis and in the Detroit study should, therefore, probably be taken with a grain of salt. Indifference toward former spouses, as we have previously pointed out, is a culturally imposed attitude for those in the role of divorced persons.

Virtually all of the new spouses of remarried widowed persons in Utopolis were reported as indifferent or friendly toward the first mates of their partners; only a very small proportion—8.0 percent of the husbands and 5.1 percent of the wives—were reported as jealous or resentful. In the case of the divorced, however, a much larger proportion—14.8 percent of the husbands of the new spouses and 19.8 percent of the

[3] One out of four in the Detroit study admitted a desire that her husband be punished; in Utopolis, 26.8 percent were reported as unfriendly. One in four in the Detroit study admitted that she might wish to remarry her former husband; in Utopolis, 21.7 percent were reported as friendly.

wives—were reported as jealous or resentful. The proportion of spouses of divorced men with unfriendly attitudes toward their husband's first wife was thus almost twice as great as the proportion of wives of widowers with similar attitudes. The differential was twice as large in the case of husbands of divorced and widowed women. Almost 60 percent of the husbands of divorced women were reported to be indifferent to their wife's first husband; but only 46.6 percent of the women married to divorced men were reported to be indifferent to their husband's first wife. This disparity may reflect a greater tolerance on the part of the men, or it may be due to the fact that the men had less contact with their wife's previous spouse—a hypothesis supported by the likelihood that the wife's first husband was himself remarried and thus out of the picture. The former wives of the divorced men, on the other hand, may have made themselves too active, as we have seen, to permit indifference.

Chapter 17: Family Planning and the First Baby

52. SOME MATERNAL ATTITUDES TOWARDS CONCEPTION

W. Godfrey Cobliner

§ Attitude toward motherhood has a preliminary stage in attitudes toward conception. After observing marked differences in the way in which mothers handled their newborn babies, the author systemically studied factors associated with whether the mothers were happy or unhappy about conception of the child. Only slightly more than half of the mothers were happy without reservations. Factors associated with happiness (though sometimes only slightly) were first pregnancy, Catholic religion, minimum interference with life plans, marriage, and practically no morning sickness. None of the factors was sufficiently distinctive of the unhappy mothers to afford a clear explanation. Dr. Cobliner's results indicate that further research is needed.

Most babies in industrial societies these days are born in hospital maternity wards. Here interaction between a mother and her newborn is initiated in the presence of trained nurses during the feeding episodes. The prevailing atmosphere is one of efficiency and standardization, where the major concern is the fleeting commodity of time. Many mothers (especially primiparas) seem unprepared for such an experience. Most mothers lack the skill of "mothercraft." This includes the art of initiating a satisfactory interaction between the mother and her newborn baby. It used to be passed on from one generation to the next through watching, modeling and an apprenticeship lasting months

SOURCE: *Mental Hygiene*, 49 (1965), 550–57. Reprinted by permission of the publisher and the author.

Grateful acknowledgement is hereby made to Joseph P. Donnelly, M.D., Medical Director of the Margaret Hague Maternity Hospital, for permission to conduct the interviews.

Dr. Cobliner teaches in the Department of Psychiatry, Division of Behavioral Science, New Jersey College of Medicine and Dentistry.

472

and often years. The locus was the home of the extended family, which included several experienced mothers. Today such regular transmission of mothercraft is non-existent. A fragment of it is imparted to an already pregnant woman in an atmosphere of haste and pressure in the lecture halls of maternity clinics or the out-patient divisions of general hospitals; this is done in a few sessions through a process of rapid indoctrination. The interested, the curious, the perfectionist, the anxious and the doubtful mothers-to-be (among countless other categories) supplement this recently acquired "information" on the subject by consulting the writings of Dr. Spock, by questioning friends who are already mothers and perhaps by the absorption of dramatic "knowledge" printed haphazardly in women's magazines picked up at the check-out counter of our supermarkets. The exchange of knowledge between a mother-to-be and her own mother is rare. Chances are that the grandmother-to-be has little to offer. In the absence of any further determining influences, one would therefore expect mother-neonate interaction observable in the maternity ward to show a certain uniformity and standardization. But such expectation would seem unwarranted.

In an extended observation of mother-neonate interaction on the wards of a large maternity hospital in Jersey City, N.J., the mothers in residence showed remarkable differences among one another in regard to handling their babies during the feeding episodes. These were the only times the mother spent with her newborn. Typically, a mother retained her characteristic way of handling the baby throughout her stay at the hospital. The ethnic backgrounds of these women varied considerably, but the differences in baby handling were too striking and extreme to stem solely from a collective element, ethnic, cultural or regional. Since the social backgrounds of these mothers were similar, the possibility of a link between maternal handling of her neonate and more *personal* factors (maternal attitudes towards the baby) seemed worthy of investigation.

A pilot study on mother-neonate interaction was begun in July, 1962, with residents of the Margaret Hague Hospital in Jersey City. Our mothers were systematically observed and filmed while feeding their newborn babies during the first 96 hours of the neonates' lives, which coincided with the stay at the hospital.

Concurrently, a survey was undertaken of maternal attitudes and related subjects among the observed (and filmed) mothers, and also among a larger group of mothers who were in residence at the Margaret Hague Hospital between July, 1962, and March, 1963.

All interviewed mothers were in the low-income group. Most, indeed, were from families living on a subsistence level. The head of the family was usually an unskilled worker. He and his wife (the interviewed mother) typically had less than a high school education.

Jersey City is a medium-sized community with 276,000 inhabitants. Unlike developments in the rest of the U.S.A., its population declined by about 8 per cent between 1950 and 1960. Besides this actual loss in sheer numbers, many residents spend part of the day away from the city. Indeed, some 45 per cent of the working population seek gainful employment outside the city boundaries. The centrifugal tendency is heightened by internal circumstances. About 12 per cent of the population are foreign-born (Italian, Irish, Polish, Puerto Rican). Another 24 per cent came from foreign-born parents of similar ethnic affiliation who more or less cling to the old ways.

The Site and the Sample

The Margaret Hague Maternity Hospital in Jersey City is one of the largest and finest institutions of its kind on the Eastern seaboard. The mothers coming in for delivery represent a fair cross-section of the lower-income stratum of the population of Hudson County and the city. On the average, between 900 and 1,000 children are delivered here every month. At the time of this study, the hospital's obstetric and pediatric division was affiliated with the New Jersey College of Medicine and Dentistry.

In this pilot study, 215 mothers were interviewed. The selection of subjects was random, within certain limitations. Mothers who could not communicate in English, or who were not yet strong enough to talk, were excluded. It could happen, therefore, that by the time the next interview period took place a mother originally selected as a subject had left the hospital. (It is not unusual for a mother to sign herself out of the hospital 48 hours after giving birth.) But those excluded for linguistic difficulties and other reasons did not exceed ten per cent of those available for sampling.

In the clinic wards of the Margaret Hague Hospital, four mothers share a room. Average stay these days is about 80 hours. They spend about four hours daily with their newborns during four feeding episodes of one hour each; at night, at 2 A.M., the babies are fed by the nursing personnel.

There was a wide range of variation in the way the mothers fed, burped and handled their newborns; similarly there were significant differences in the phenomena that accompanied these activities. For example, while feeding, some mothers carried on a continued "conversation" with their babies, pinched their mouths, handled their heads, rocked their bodies, rhythmically or arhythmically, up and down or sidewise, and played with them after the feeding. Other mothers remained apathetic and listless, regardless of the child's temperament, and seemed generally uninterested. A sizeable group of mothers seemed anxious to expedite the pace of the feeding. Many women, regardless of their other behavior patterns, were frequently seen to interrupt the feeding process, taking the bottle out of the baby's mouth, often unexpectedly, to check the milk level. Apparently they did this in accordance with the instruction that, after the ingestion of a specified quantity of milk, burping the baby is imperative. Other mothers, however, dispensed with the checking and burped their babies periodically without disturbing the feeding. Apparently they intuitively sensed individual needs. Thus a wide spectrum of the mother's general behavior was here revealed in the process of handling the newborns. One is tempted to interpret the meaning of the behavior severally, that is, in isolation as a manifestation of the mother's specific personality. Yet clinical observations suggest that the way a given mother handles her child in the first few weeks is often unique, and in many details unlike the treatment she accords, or has accorded, her other children. There is then no fixed relationship between the handling of a baby and the underlying motives. Practically speaking, the relationship of mother-baby, the interactional framework, is more likely to provide understanding of the observed behavior than the framework of individual psychology.

In line with this reasoning, a set of questions was directed to the mothers, yielding data presented here in the form of tables.

The Results of the Survey

1. How did you feel when you first became aware of your pregnancy?

TABLE 1   *Attitude towards the Baby at Time of Conception*

N = 215		
Happy	50%	
Happy (delayed affirmation)	3	53%
"It came too soon"	3	
Mixed feelings	2	5%
Not looking forward to baby	11	
Not happy	27	38%
Indifferent	1	
No answer	3	4%
	100%	

Thus only slightly more than half of the mothers were happy without reservations when they became aware of their pregnancy. Five per cent had reservations, 38 per cent were unhappy, and four per cent were neutral about the coming baby. The size of the group with negative feelings towards their conception is impressive. The implication of these figures for the child's prospective emotional and physical well-being cannot be ignored. It is therefore interesting to explore to what extent the maternal attitudes derive from external or situational circumstances.

The answers to the next question—how many children had they borne—served to qualify the findings of Table 1 which, for purposes of simplification, are now condensed into two major categories "happy" and "other than happy."

TABLE 2   *Attitude towards Motherhood and Parity*

	PRIMIPARA	MULTIPARA	UNKNOWN
	(N = 66)	(N = 146)	(N = 3)
Happy	84%	36%	—
Other than happy	16	64	100
	100%	100%	100%

It can be seen that the large majority of women who had their first child welcomed their pregnancies (84 per cent) while among the multiparas only slightly more than one third (36 per cent) were happy about the event. The age factor (see appendix) did not alter this. In what way do multiple pregnancies influence the maternal attitudes towards further conception?

Table 3 suggests that the connection between maternal attitudes

TABLE 3   *Attitude towards Motherhood and Multiparity*

	SECOND CHILD	THIRD CHILD	FOURTH CHILD	FIVE OR MORE CHILDREN
	(N = 59)	(N = 27)	(N = 24)	(N = 36)
Happy	46%	34%	44%	31%
Other than happy	54	66	56	69
	100%	100%	100%	100%

towards conception and the number of previous births is curvilinear; the proportion of mothers with negative attitudes does not rise in relation to previous pregnancies. Thus more mothers (44 per cent) are happy carrying their fourth child than those who carry their third child (34 per cent). But the sample is too small to allow a definite conclusion. Perhaps the mother's background will shed more light on this phenomenon. (See Table 4.)

In the group of Catholic mothers, the proportion of those who did *not* welcome their current pregnancy is substantial (40 per cent) but remains a good deal below that of Protestant mothers (57 per cent). In the absence of further information, one is tempted to attribute this difference to religious beliefs. It is therefore important to mention here that in the group of Catholic mothers there was a fairly large segment of women of Puerto Rican parentage with whom it was not possible for the interviewers to achieve optimum rapport within the few minutes of the interview. Had these mothers been interviewed in their native tongue (possible in only a few instances) many would have disclosed their negative attitudes towards their pregnancies. It is fair to say then that the "other than happy" figures for Catholic women perhaps understates the actual size of that segment. For technical reasons, it was not possible to determine the actual number of mothers of Puerto

TABLE 4   *Attitude towards Motherhood and Religion*

	CATHOLICS (N = 82)	PROTESTANTS (N = 128)	OTHER (N = 5)
Happy	60%	43%	60%
Other than happy	40	57	40
	100%	100%	100%

Rican extraction. By combining data contained in the last three tables, we obtain Table 5, which sheds light on the link between maternal attitudes, religion and parity.

Bearing in mind the smallness of this sample when broken down into the subgroups, one can only point to a *trend* suggesting that in general Catholic mothers are more consistent, which indicates that the number of pregnancies co-determines their attitudes. Generally speaking, they are more favorably disposed to conception than their Protestant counterparts, up to their fourth child.

Protestant mothers show a more "negative" attitude, but the fluctuation as the number of pregnancies increases suggests a conflict of motives which cannot be confirmed or disproved by the data collected in this project.

To what extent is the mother's attitude toward the pregnancy influenced by her life plans? Is the negative attitude generated by the feeling that the pregnancy interfered with her long-range plans?

Attitudes towards motherhood are not closely connected with the

TABLE 5 *Attitude towards Motherhood, Religion and Parity*

	CATHOLICS (N = 82)				
	First child	Second child	Third child	Fourth child	Five or more children
	(N = 25)	(N = 28)	(N = 10)	(N = 8)	(N = 11)
Happy	92%	50%	50%	50%	34%
Not happy	8	50	50	50	66
	100%	100%	100%	100%	100%
	PROTESTANTS (N = 125)*				
	(N = 38)	(N = 32)	(N = 16)	(N = 16)	(N = 23)
Happy	66%	38%	25%	44%	30%
Not happy	34	62	75	56	70
	100%	100%	100%	100%	100%

* Unknown parity reduces the number of Protestant mothers.

realization of long-range life plans; the proportion of mothers who feel that the pregnancy prevented them from carrying out these plans remains below 15 per cent among both the "happy" and the "other than happy" group. To what extent does the marital status provide a motive for these expressed attitudes? (See Table 7.)

Marital status seems to have little bearing on attitudes towards motherhood. Indeed, the proportion of unmarried mothers is so negligible (14 per cent in the "other than happy" column) that it hardly influences the over-all picture. However, if one looks at this table for

TABLE 6 *Pregnancy and Long-Range Life Plans*

	HAPPY (N = 108)	OTHER THAN HAPPY (N = 107)
Pregnancy interfered with life plans		
Yes	7%	13%
No	93	84
No answer	—	2
	100%	100%

TABLE 7 *Attitude towards Pregnancy and Marital Status*

	HAPPY	OTHER THAN HAPPY
	(N = 108)	(N = 107)
Married	90%	83%
Separated or widowed	3	3
Never married	7	14
	100%	100%

a moment horizontally—that is, across the first and last rows—one notes a striking (though not surprising) difference between the married and unmarried mothers. Slightly more married mothers are happy about their pregnancy than otherwise, but the proportion of unmarried mothers who are unhappy about the event is twice as large as that of the happy ones (fourteen against seven per cent).

A painful pregnancy may generate a negative attitude towards the coming baby and so may other experiences connected with the pregnancy. These experiences may well have shaped the maternal attitudes towards conception, even though the mother asserted that she reported only attitudes already crystallized at the time she became aware of her pregnancy. Tables 8, 9, and 10 examine this contingency.

All mothers in this sample were in fairly good health and very few had somatic illness. The only "suffering" the subjects reported was caused by morning sickness. The figures in the table suggest that it had no appreciable influence on attitudes towards the babies. It is true, though, that as a group the "happy" mothers-to-be felt somewhat better than the "other-than-happy" group (62 vs. 47 per cent, the sum of the last two rows).

TABLE 8 *Attitude towards Pregnancy and Morning Sickness*

	HAPPY	OTHER THAN HAPPY
	(N = 108)	(N = 107)
Extensive morning sickness up to 3rd month	32%	43%
Morning sickness after 3rd month	6	10
Practically no morning sickness	56	46
Felt better than ever during pregnancy	6	1
	100%	100%

Worry (according to the figures in Table 9) can be ruled out as a generator of negative attitudes towards motherhood. A further analysis of Table 9 (see Table 13) shows that the "happy" mothers are more worried about the baby's intactness and his and their own health (65 vs. 53 per cent) while the "other-than-happy" mothers are more preoccupied with economic problems and the baby's care (31 vs. 14 per cent).

A final element requires examination. In view of the low standard of living of the interviewed mothers, whose families existed on the

TABLE 9   *Attitude towards Motherhood and Worries*

	HAPPY	OTHER THAN HAPPY
	(N = 108)	(N = 107)
Worried during pregnancy	44%	42%
Not worried	55	57
No answer	1	1
	100%	100%

subsistence level, family planning may play an important role. In Jersey City the idea of family planning is no longer uniformly rejected among Catholics and the rhythm method is not banned. Puerto Rican immigrants, too, are likely to be familiar with contraceptive methods widely publicized in their homeland.

To avoid any complications that could arise by a frank exploration of the topic, an indirect question was addressed to the mother, "Were you surprised when you became aware of your current pregnancy?" This phrasing, it was hoped, would disclose the relevant information.

TABLE 10   *Attitude towards Motherhood and Expectation*

	HAPPY	OTHER THAN HAPPY
	(N = 108)	(N = 107)
Expectation		
Surprised	71%	62%
Not surprised	19	25
No answer	10	13
	100%	100%

If one accepts the notion that the surprise of the mother indicates that she did not expect to get pregnant at the time, then the figures suggest that the unexpectedness of the pregnancy had little if any bearing on the rejection of motherhood. In fact, the percentage of those who are surprised is higher among the "happy" mothers.

Summary and Conclusions

1. Only slightly more than one-half of the mothers said that they welcomed their babies without reservations at the time of conception. These figures are conservative and would seem to maximize the actual number of those wanting their children. The data further reveal that among multiparas, those wishing to have a baby at that particular time exceed only slightly one-third of the total sample. These figures refer to mental attitudes at the *time of conception* and do not necessarily hold true for the time of delivery. Many readers may wonder at this point whether another question dealing with maternal attitudes at the time of delivery might not clear up the matter. This is erroneous. In fact, such a question was asked. Many "other-than-happy" mothers volunteered the information that they eventually "accepted" the baby, became more favorably disposed towards it and so on. However, this was a lengthy change with many fluctuations. The writer feels that this is in the nature of a process, the study of which requires a prospective rather than a reconstructive approach. Consequently, it would call for a series of interrogations during the course of the pregnancy.

2. It was established, as far as this sample goes, that the religious affiliation of the mother, her marital status or economic hardship cannot fully explain the high rate of rejection of motherhood. Moreover, the suffering connected with intensive morning sickness and worries of any kind do not engender these attitudes, which the mother then would tend to date back to the moment of the conception.

A state of affairs in which about one-half of the children born are unwelcome at the time of conception can certainly not be ignored by a society which strives to provide optimal opportunities and care for its members and makes a major effort to insure the well-being of its children, whether in the area of health, education or economic security. It is felt that an unwanted child has a chip on his shoulder right from the day of his birth; he is bound to be victimized in some respect by this very circumstance. A society which is concerned with population policies should make sure that those who are born are also wanted in this world. The first step in the implementation of such a policy is to detect the reason or reasons that make so many mothers oppose their pregnancies.

Appendix

TABLE 11   *Age Distribution*

Age	
Under 15 years	1%
16–20	38
21–25	28
26–30	17
31–35	10
36–40	5
Over 41	1
	100%

TABLE 12   *Race and Religion*

	PROTESTANTS	CATHOLICS	OTHER
Race	(128)	(82)	(5)
White	17%	86%	100%
Non-white	83	14	—
	100%	100%	100%

TABLE 13   *Breakdown of "Worry" Category among Pregnant Women (Elaboration of Table 7)*

	HAPPY	OTHER THAN HAPPY
	(48)	(45)
Baby's intactness		
Health		
Prematurity		
Fear of losing baby	44%	38%
Own Health		
Survival		
Labor	21	15
Financial concern	12	22
Own and baby's health	2	7
Health and financial concerns	—	7
Baby's care	2	9
Miscellaneous	19	2
	100%	100%

53. TRANSITION TO PARENTHOOD

Alice S. Rossi

§ In this selection, the transition to parenthood is pinpointed as a more difficult stage than adjustment to marital or occupational roles. In cultural expectations, parenthood may not be rejected nor an unwanted pregnancy terminated. Guidelines to adjustment are lacking when the abrupt transition comes at childhood. The transition affects the paternal as well as the maternal role. The distinctive and the overlapping qualities of the two parental roles are examined.

The Problem

The central concern in this sociological analysis of parenthood will be with two closely related questions. (1) What is involved in the transition to parenthood: what must be learned and what readjustments of other role commitments must take place in order to move smoothly through the transition from a childless married state to parenthood? (2) What is the effect of parenthood on the adult: in what ways do parents, and in particular mothers, change as a result of their parental experiences?

To get a firmer conceptual handle on the problem, I shall first specify the stages in the development of the parental role and then explore several of the most salient features of the parental role by comparing it with the two other major adult social roles—the marital and work role. Throughout the discussion, special attention will be given to the social changes that have taken place during the past few decades which facilitate or complicate the transition to and the experience of parenthood among young American adults.

From Child to Parent: An Example

What is unique about this perspective on parenthood is the focus on the adult parent rather than the child. Until quite recent years, concern

SOURCE: *Journal of Marriage and the Family*, 30 (1968), 26–39. Reprinted by permission of the publisher and the author.

This paper was presented to the American Orthopsychiatric Association, Washington, D.C., March 22, 1967. The work was sponsored by the National Institutes of Health, under a Research Career Development Award (USPHS-K3-MH23768).

Alice S. Rossi is the research associate in the Department of Social Relations, The Johns Hopkins University.

in the behavioral sciences with the parent-child relationship has been confined almost exclusively to the child. Whether a psychological study such as Ferreira's on the influence of the pregnant woman's attitude to maternity upon postnatal behavior of the neonate,[1] Sears and Maccoby's survey of child-rearing practices,[2] or Brody's detailed observations of mothering,[3] the long tradition of studies of maternal deprivation[4] and more recently of maternal employment,[5] the child has been the center of attention. The design of such research has assumed that, if enough were known about what parents were like and what they in fact did in rearing their children, much of the variation among children could be accounted for.[6]

The very different order of questions which emerge when the parent replaces the child as the primary focus of analytic attention can best be shown with an illustration. Let us take, as our example, the point Benedek makes that the child's need for mothering is *absolute* while the need of an adult woman to mother is *relative*.[7] From a concern for the child, this discrepancy in need leads to an analysis of the impact on the child of separation from the mother or inadequacy of mothering. Family systems that provide numerous adults to care for the young child can make up for this discrepancy in need between mother and child, which may be why ethnographic accounts give little evidence of postpartum depression following childbirth in simpler societies. Yet our family system of isolated households, increasingly distant from kinswomen to assist in mothering, requires that new mothers shoulder total responsibil-

[1] Antonio J. Ferreira, "The Pregnant Woman's Emotional Attitude and its Reflection on the Newborn," *American Journal of Orthopsychiatry*, 30 (1960), pp. 553–561.
[2] Robert Sears, E. Maccoby, and H. Levin, *Patterns of Child-Rearing*, Evanston, Illinois: Row, Peterson, 1957.
[3] Sylvia Brody, *Patterns of Mothering: maternal influences during infancy*, New York: International Universities Press, 1956.
[4] Leon J. Yarrow, "Maternal Deprivation: Toward an Empirical and Conceptual Re-evaluation," *Psychological Bulletin*, 58:6 (1961), 459–490.
[5] F. Ivan Nye and L. W. Hoffman, *The Employed Mother in America*, Chicago: Rand McNally, 1963; Alice S. Rossi, "Equality Between the Sexes: An Immodest Proposal," *Daedalus*, 93:2 (1964), pp. 607–652.
[6] The younger the child, the more was this the accepted view. It is only in recent years that research has paid any attention to the initiating role of the infant in the development of his attachment to maternal and other adult figures, as in Ainsworth's research which showed that infants become attached to the mother, not solely because she is instrumental in satisfying their primary visceral drives, but through a chain of behavioral interchange between the infant and the mother, thus supporting Bowlby's rejection of the secondary drive theory of the infant's ties to his mother. Mary D. Ainsworth, "Patterns of Attachment Behavior shown by the Infant in interaction with his mother," *Merrill-Palmer Quarterly*, 10:1 (1964), pp. 51–58; John Bowlby, "The Nature of the child's tie to his mother," *International Journal of Psychoanalysis*, 39 (1958), pp. 1–34.
[7] Therese Benedek, "Parenthood as a Developmental Phase," *Journal of American Psychoanalytic Association*, 7:8 (1959), pp. 389–417.

ity for the infant precisely for that stage of the child's life when his need for mothering is far in excess of the mother's need for the child.

From the perspective of the mother, the question has therefore become: what does maternity deprive her of? Are the intrinsic gratifications of maternity sufficient to compensate for shelving or reducing a woman's involvement in non-family interests and social roles? The literature on maternal deprivation cannot answer such questions, because the concept, even in the careful specification Yarrow has given it,[8] has never meant anything but the effect on the child of various kinds of insufficient mothering. Yet what has been seen as a failure or inadequacy of individual women may in fact be a failure of the society to provide institutionalized substitutes for the extended kin to assist in the care of infants and young children. It may be that the role requirements of maternity in the American family system extract too high a price of deprivation for young adult women reared with highly diversified interests and social expectations concerning adult life. Here, as at several points in the course of this paper, familiar problems take on a new and suggestive research dimension when the focus is on the parent rather than the child.

Background

Since it is a relatively recent development to focus on the parent side of the parent-child relationship, some preliminary attention to the emergence of this focus on parenthood is in order. Several developments in the behavioral sciences paved the way to this perspective. Of perhaps most importance have been the development of ego psychology and the problem of adaptation of Murray[9] and Hartmann,[10] the interpersonal focus of Sullivan's psychoanalytic theories,[11] and the life cycle approach to identity of Erikson.[12] These have been fundamental to the growth of the human development perspective: that personality is not a stable given but a constantly changing phenomenon, that the individual changes along the life line as he lives through critical life experiences. The transition to parenthood, or the impact of parenthood upon the adult, is part of the heightened contemporary interest in adult socialization.

[8] Yarrow, *op. cit.*

[9] Henry A. Murray, *Explorations in Personality*, New York: Oxford University Press, 1938.

[10] Heinz Hartmann, *Ego Psychology and the Problem of Adaptation*, New York: International Universities Press, Inc., 1958.

[11] Patrick Mullahy (ed.), *The Contributions of Harry Stack Sullivan*, New York: Hermitage House, 1952.

[12] E. Erikson, "Identity and the Life Cycle: Selected Papers," *Psychological Issues*, 1 (1959), pp. 1–171.

A second and related development has been the growing concern of behavioral scientists with crossing levels of analysis to adequately comprehend social and individual phenomena and to build theories appropriate to a complex social system. In the past, social anthropologists focused as purely on the level of prescriptive normative variables as psychologists had concentrated on intrapsychic processes at the individual level or sociologists on social-structural and institutional variables. These are adequate, perhaps, when societies are in a stable state of equilibrium and the social sciences were at early stages of conceptual development, but they become inadequate when the societies we study are undergoing rapid social change and we have an increasing amount of individual and subgroup variance to account for.

Psychology and anthropology were the first to join theoretical forces in their concern for the connections between culture and personality. The question of how culture is transmitted across the generations and finds its manifestations in the personality structure and social roles of the individual has brought renewed research attention to the primary institutions of the family and the schools, which provide the intermediary contexts through which culture is transmitted and built into personality structure.

It is no longer possible for a psychologist or a therapist to neglect the social environment of the individual subject or patient, nor is the "family" they are concerned with any longer confined to the family of origin, for current theory and therapy view the adult individual in the context of his current family of procreation. So too it is no longer possible for the sociologist to focus exclusively on the current family relationships of the individual. The incorporation of psychoanalytic theory into the informal, if not the formal, training of the sociologist has led to an increasing concern for the quality of relationships in the family of origin as determinants of the adult attitudes, values, and behavior which the sociologist studies.

Quite another tradition of research has led to the formulation of "normal crises of parenthood." "Crisis" research began with the studies of individuals undergoing traumatic experiences, such as that by Tyhurst on natural catastrophes,[13] Caplan on parental responses to premature births,[14] Lindemann on grief and bereavement,[15] and Janis on surgery.[16] In these studies attention was on differential response to stress—how and

---

[13] J. Tyhurst, "Individual Reactions to Community Disaster," *American Journal of Psychiatry*, 107 (1951), pp. 764–769.

[14] G. Caplan, "Patterns of Parental Response to the Crisis of Premature Birth: A Preliminary Approach to Modifying the Mental Health Outcome," *Psychiatry*, 23 (1960), pp. 365–374.

[15] E. Lindemann, "Symptomatology and Management of Acute Grief," *American Journal of Psychiatry*, 101 (1944), pp. 141–148.

[16] Irving Janis, *Psychological Stress*, New York: John Wiley, 1958.

why individuals vary in the ease with which they coped with the stressful experience and achieved some reintegration. Sociological interest has been piqued as these studies were built upon by Rhona and Robert Rapoport's research on the honeymoon and the engagement as normal crises in the role transitions to marriage and their theoretical attempt to build a conceptual bridge between family and occupational research from a "transition task" perspective.[17] LeMasters, Dyer, and Hobbs have each conducted studies of parenthood precisely as a crisis or disruptive event in family life.[18]

I think, however, that the time is now ripe to drop the concept of "normal crises" and to speak directly, instead, of the transition to and impact of parenthood. There is an uncomfortable incongruity in speaking of any crisis as normal. If the transition is achieved and if a successful reintegration of personality or social roles occurs, then crisis is a misnomer. To confine attention to "normal crises" suggests, even if it is not logically implied, successful outcome, thus excluding from our analysis the deviant instances in which failure occurs.

Sociologists have been just as prone as psychologists to dichotomize normality and pathology. We have had one set of theories to deal with deviance, social problems, and conflict and quite another set in theoretical analyses of a normal system—whether a family or a society. In the latter case our theories seldom include categories to cover deviance, strain, dysfunction, or failure. Thus, Parsons and Bales' systems find "task-leaders" oriented to problem solution, but not instrumental leaders attempting to undercut or destroy the goal of the group, and "sociometric stars" who play a positive integrative function in cementing ties among group members, but not negatively expressive persons with hostile aims of reducing or destroying such intragroup ties.[19]

---

[17] Rhona Rapoport, "Normal Crises, Family Structure and Mental Health," *Family Process*, 2:1 (1963), pp. 68–80; Rhona Rapoport and Robert Rapoport, "New Light on the Honeymoon," *Human Relations*, 17:1 (1964), pp. 33–56; Rhona Rapoport, "The Transition from Engagement to Marriage," *Acta Sociologica*, 8, fasc, 1–2 (1964), pp. 36–55; and Robert Rapoport and Rhona Rapoport, "Work and Family in Contemporary Society," *American Sociological Review*, 30:3 (1965), pp. 381–394.
[18] E. E. LeMasters, "Parenthood as Crisis," *Marriage and Family Living*, 19 (1957), pp. 352–355; Everett D. Dyer, "Parenthood as Crisis: A Re-Study," *Marriage and Family Living*, 25 (1963), pp. 196–201; and Daniel F. Hobbs, Jr., "Parenthood as Crisis: A Third Study," *Journal of Marriage and the Family*, 27:3 (1963), pp. 367–372. LeMasters and Dyer both report the first experience of parenthood involves extensive to severe crises in the lives of their young parent respondents. Hobbs's study does not show first parenthood to be a crisis experience, but this may be due to the fact his couples have very young (seven-week old) first babies and are therefore still experiencing the euphoric honeymoon stage of parenthood.
[19] Parsons' theoretical analysis of the family system builds directly on Bales's research on small groups. The latter are typically comprised of volunteers willing to attempt the single task put to the group. This positive orientation is most apt to yield the empirical discovery of "sociometric stars" and "task leaders," least apt to sensitize the researcher or theorist to the effect of hostile nonacceptance of the

Parsons' analysis of the experience of parenthood as a step in maturation and personality growth does not allow for negative outcome. In
this view either parents show little or no positive impact upon themselves of their parental role experiences, or they show a new level of
maturity. Yet many women, whose interests and values made a congenial
combination of wifehood and work role, may find that the addition of
maternal responsibilities has the consequence of a fundamental and
undesired change in both their relationships to their husbands and their
involvements outside the family. Still other women, who might have kept
a precarious hold on adequate functioning as adults had they *not* become
parents, suffer severe retrogression with pregnancy and childbearing,
because the reactivation of older unresolved conflicts with their own
mothers is not favorably resolved but in fact leads to personality deterioration [20] and the transmission of pathology to their children.[21]

Where cultural pressure is very great to assume a particular adult
role, as it is for American women to bear and rear children, latent desire
and psychological readiness for parenthood may often be at odds with
manifest desire and actual ability to perform adequately as parents.
Clinicians and therapists are aware, as perhaps many sociologists are
not, that failure, hostility, and destructiveness are as much a part of the
family system and the relationships among family members as success,
love, and solidarity are.[22]

A conceptual system which can deal with both successful and unsuccessful role transitions, or positive and negative impact of parenthood
upon adult men and women, is thus more powerful than one built to
handle success but not failure or vice versa. For these reasons I have
concluded that it is misleading and restrictive to perpetuate the use of

---

group task. Talcott Parsons and R. F. Bales, *Family, Socialization and Interaction
Process,* New York: The Free Press, a division of the Macmillan Co., 1955.

Yet the same limited definition of the key variables is found in the important
attempts by Straus to develop the theory that every social system, as every personality, requires a circumplex model with two independent axes of authority and
support. His discussion and examples indicate a variable definition with limited
range: support is defined as High $(+)$ or Low $(-)$, but "low" covers both the
absence of high support and the presence of negative support; there is love or
neutrality in this system, but not hate. Applied to actual families, this groups
destructive mothers with low-supportive mothers, much as the non-authoritarian
pole on the Authoritarian Personality Scale includes both mere nonauthoritarians
and vigorously anti-authoritarian personalities. Murray A. Straus, "Power and Support Structure of the Family in Relation to Socialization," *Journal of Marriage and
the Family,* 26:3 (1964), pp. 318–326.

[20] Mabel Blake Cohen, "Personal Identity and Sexual Identity," *Psychiatry,* 29:1
(1966), pp. 1–14; Joseph C. Rheingold, *The Fear of Being a Woman: A Theory of
Maternal Destructiveness,* New York: Grune and Stratton, 1964.

[21] Theodore Lidz, S. Fleck, and A. Cornelison, *Schizophrenia and the Family,* New
York: International Universities Press, Inc., 1965; Rheingold, *op. cit.*

[22] Cf. the long review of studies Rheingold covers in his book on maternal destructiveness, *op. cit.*

the concept of "normal crisis." A more fruitful point of departure is to build upon the stage-task concepts of Erikson, viewing parenthood as a developmental stage, as Benedek[23] and Hill[24] have done, a perspective carried into the research of Raush, Goodrich, and Campbell[25] and of Rhona and Robert Rapoport[26] on adaptation to the early years of marriage and that of Cohen, Fearing *et al.*[27] on the adjustments involved in pregnancy.

Role Cycle Stages

A discussion of the impact of parenthood upon the parent will be assisted by two analytic devices. One is to follow a comparative approach, by asking in what basic structural ways the parental role differs from other primary adult roles. The marital and occupational roles will be used for this comparison. A second device is to specify the phases in the development of a social role. If the total life span may be said to have a cycle, each stage with its unique tasks, then by analogy a role may be said to have a cycle and each stage in that role cycle, to have its unique tasks and problems of adjustment. Four broad stages of a role cycle may be specified:

1. Anticipatory Stage

All major adult roles have a long history of anticipatory training for them, since parental and school socialization of children is dedicated precisely to this task of producing the kind of competent adult valued by the culture. For our present purposes, however, a narrower conception of the anticipatory stage is preferable: the engagement period in the case of the marital role, pregnancy in the case of the parental role, and the last stages of highly vocationally oriented schooling or on-the-job apprenticeship in the case of an occupational role.

2. Honeymoon Stage

This is the time period immediately following the full assumption of the adult role. The inception of this stage is more easily defined than its termination. In the case of the marital role, the honeymoon stage extends from the marriage ceremony itself through the literal honeymoon and on through an unspecified and individually varying period of time. Raush[28] has caught this stage of the marital role in his description of the "psychic honeymoon": that extended postmarital period when, through close

[23] Benedek, *op. cit.*
[24] Reuben Hill and D. A. Hansen, "The Identification of a Conceptual Framework Utilized in Family Study," *Marriage and Family Living*, 22 (1960), pp. 299–311.
[25] Harold L. Raush, W. Goodrich, and J. D. Campbell, "Adaptation to the First Years of Marriage," *Psychiatry*, 26:4 (1963), pp. 368–380.
[26] Rapoport, *op. cit.*   [27] Cohen, *op. cit.*   [28] Raush *et al.*, *op. cit.*

intimacy and joint activity, the couple can explore each other's capacities and limitations. I shall arbitrarily consider the onset of pregnancy as marking the end of the honeymoon stage of the marital role. This stage of the parental role may involve an equivalent psychic honeymoon, that post-childbirth period during which, through intimacy and prolonged contact, an attachment between parent and child is laid down. There is a crucial difference, however, from the marital role in this stage. A woman knows her husband as a unique real person when she enters the honeymoon stage of marriage. A good deal of preparatory adjustment on a firm reality-base is possible during the engagement period which is not possible in the equivalent pregnancy period. Fantasy is not corrected by the reality of a specific individual child until the birth of the child. The "quickening" is psychologically of special significance to women precisely because it marks the first evidence of a real baby rather than a purely fantasized one. On this basis alone there is greater interpersonal adjustment and learning during the honeymoon stage of the parental role than of the marital role.

3. Plateau Stage

This is the protracted middle period of a role cycle during which the role is fully exercised. Depending on the specific problem under analysis, one would obviously subdivide this large plateau stage further. For my present purposes it is not necessary to do so, since my focus is on the earlier anticipatory and honeymoon stages of the parental role and the overall impact of parenthood on adults.

4. Disengagement-Termination Stage

This period immediately precedes and includes the actual termination of the role. Marriage ends with the death of the spouse or, just as definitively, with separation and divorce. A unique characteristic of parental role termination is the fact that it is not clearly marked by any specific act but is an attenuated process of termination with little cultural prescription about when the authority and obligations of a parent end. Many parents, however, experience the marriage of the child as a psychological termination of the active parental role.

Unique Features of Parental Role

With this role cycle suggestion as a broader framework, we can narrow our focus to what are the unique and most salient features of the parental role. In doing so, special attention will be given to two further questions: (1) the impact of social changes over the past few decades in facilitating or complicating the transition to and experience of parenthood and (2) the new interpretations or new research suggested by the focus on the parent rather than the child.

1. Cultural Pressure to Assume the Role

On the level of cultural values, men have no freedom of choice where work is concerned: They must work to secure their status as adult men.

The equivalent for women has been maternity. There is considerable pressure upon the growing girl and young woman to consider maternity necessary for a woman's fulfillment as an individual and to secure her status as an adult.[29]

This is not to say there are no fluctuations over time in the intensity of the cultural pressure to parenthood. During the depression years of the 1930's, there was more widespread awareness of the economic hardships parenthood can entail, and many demographic experts believe there was a great increase in illegal abortions during those years. Bird has discussed the dread with which a suspected pregnancy was viewed by many American women in the 1930's.[30] Quite a different set of pressures were at work during the 1950's, when the general societal tendency was toward withdrawal from active engagement with the issues of the larger society and a turning in to the gratifications of the private sphere of home and family life. Important in the background were the general affluence of the period and the expanded room and ease of child rearing that go with suburban living. For the past five years, there has been a drop in the birth rate in general, fourth and higher-order births in particular. During this same period there has been increased concern and debate about women's participation in politics and work, with more women now returning to work rather than conceiving the third or fourth child.[31]

2. Inception of the Parental Role

The decision to marry and the choice of a mate are voluntary acts of individuals in our family system. Engagements are therefore consciously

[29] The greater the cultural pressure to assume a given adult social role, the greater will be the tendency for individual negative feelings toward that role to be expressed covertly. Men may complain about a given job but not about working per se, and hence their work dissatisfactions are often displaced to the non-work sphere, as psychosomatic complaints or irritation and dominance at home. An equivalent displacement for women of the ambivalence many may feel toward maternity is to dissatisfactions with the homemaker role.

[30] Caroline Bird, *The Invisible Scar*, New York: David McKay Company, 1966.

[31] When it is realized that a mean family size of 3.5 would double the population in 40 years, while a mean of 2.5 would yield a stable population in the same period, the social importance of withholding praise for procreative prowess is clear. At the same time, a drop in the birth rate may reduce the number of unwanted babies born, for such a drop would mean more efficient contraceptive usage and a closer correspondence between desired and attained family size.

considered, freely entered, and freely terminated if increased familiarity decreases, rather than increases, intimacy and commitment to the choice. The inception of a pregnancy, unlike the engagement, is not always a voluntary decision, for it may be the unintended consequence of a sexual act that was recreative in intent rather than procreative. Secondly, and again unlike the engagement, the termination of a pregnancy is not socially sanctioned, as shown by current resistance to abortion-law reform.

The implication of this difference is a much higher probability of unwanted pregnancies than of unwanted marriages in our family system. Coupled with the ample clinical evidence of parental rejection and sometimes cruelty to children, it is all the more surprising that there has not been more consistent research attention to the problem of *parental satisfaction*, as there has for long been on *marital satisfaction* or *work satisfaction*. Only the extreme iceberg tip of the parental satisfaction continuum is clearly demarcated and researched, as in the growing concern with "battered babies." Cultural and psychological resistance to the image of a nonnurturant woman may afflict social scientists as well as the American public.

The timing of a first pregnancy is critical to the manner in which parental responsibilities are joined to the marital relationship. The single most important change over the past few decades is extensive and efficient contraceptive usage, since this has meant for a growing proportion of new marriages, the possibility of and increasing preference for some postponement of childbearing after marriage. When pregnancy was likely to follow shortly after marriage, the major transition point in a woman's life was marriage itself. *This transition point is increasingly the first pregnancy rather than marriage.* It is accepted and increasingly expected that women will work after marriage, while household furnishings are acquired and spouses complete their advanced training or gain a foothold in their work.[32] This provides an early marriage period in which the fact of a wife's employment presses for a greater egalitarian relationship between husband and wife in decision-making, commonality of experience, and sharing of household responsibilities.

The balance between individual autonomy and couple mutuality that develops during the honeymoon stage of such a marriage may be important in establishing a pattern that will later affect the quality of the parent-child relationship and the extent of sex-role segregation of duties between the parents. It is only in the context of a growing egalitarian base to the marital relationship that one could find, as Gavron has,[33] a tendency for parents to establish some barriers between themselves

[32] James A. Davis, *Stipends and Spouses: The Finances of American Arts and Sciences Graduate Students*, Chicago: University of Chicago Press, 1962.
[33] Hannah Gavron, *The Captive Wife*, London: Routledge & Kegan Paul, 1966.

and their children, a marital defense against the institution of parenthood as she describes it. This may eventually replace the typical coali-
tion in more traditional families of mother and children against husband-
father. Parenthood will continue for some time to impose a degree of
temporary segregation of primary responsibilities between husband and
wife, but, when this takes place in the context of a previously established
egalitarian relationship between the husband and wife, such role segregation may become blurred, with greater recognition of the wife's need
for autonomy and the husband's role in the routines of home and child
rearing.[34]

There is one further significant social change that has important implications for the changed relationship between husband and wife: the
increasing departure from an old pattern of role-inception phasing in
which the young person first completed his schooling, then established
himself in the world of work, then married and began his family. Marriage and parenthood are increasingly taking place *before* the schooling
of the husband, and often of the wife, has been completed.[35] An important reason for this trend lies in the fact that, during the same decades
in which the average age of physical-sexual maturation has dropped,
the average amount of education which young people obtain has been
on the increase. Particularly for the college and graduate or professional
school population, family roles are often assumed before the degrees
needed to enter careers have been obtained.

Just how long it now takes young people to complete their higher

[34] The recent increase in natural childbirth, prenatal courses for expectant fathers,
and greater participation of men during childbirth and postnatal care of the infant
may therefore be a *consequence* of greater sharing between husband and wife when
both work and jointly maintain their new households during the early months of
marriage. Indeed, natural childbirth builds directly on this shifted base to the
marital relationship. Goshen-Gottstein has found in an Israeli sample that women
with a "traditional" orientation to marriage far exceed women with a "modern"
orientation to marriage in menstrual difficulty, dislike of sexual intercourse, and
pregnancy disorders and complaints such as vomiting. She argues that traditional
women demand and expect little from their husbands and become demanding and
narcissistic by means of their children, as shown in pregnancy by an over-exaggera-
tion of symptoms and attention-seeking. Esther R. Goshen-Gottstein, *Marriage and
First Pregnancy: Cultural Influences on Attitudes of Israeli Women*, London: Tavistock Publications, 1966. A prolonged psychic honeymoon uncomplicated by an
early pregnancy, and with the new acceptance of married women's employment,
may help to cement the egalitarian relationship in the marriage and reduce both the
tendency to pregnancy difficulties and the need for a narcissistic focus on the
children. Such a background is fruitful ground for sympathy toward and acceptance
of the natural childbirth ideology.

[35] James A. Davis, *Stipends and Spouses: The Finances of American Arts and Sci-
ences Graduate Students, op. cit.;* James A. Davis, *Great Aspirations,* Chicago:
Aldine Publishing Company, 1964; Eli Ginsberg, *Life Styles of Educated Women,*
New York: Columbia University Press, 1966; Ginsberg, *Educated American Women:
Self Portraits,* New York: Columbia University Press, 1967; National Science
Foundation, *Two Years After the College Degree—Work and Further Study Pat-
terns,* Washington, D.C.: Government Printing Office, NSF 63-26, 1963.

education has been investigated only recently in several longitudinal studies of college-graduate cohorts.[36] College is far less uniformly a four-year period than high school is. A full third of the college freshmen in one study had been out of high school a year or more before entering college.[37] In a large sample of college graduates in 1961, one in five were over 25 years of age at graduation.[38] Thus, financial difficulties, military service, change of career plans, and marriage itself all tend to create interruptions in the college attendance of a significant proportion of college graduates. At the graduate and professional school level, this is even more marked: the mean age of men receiving the doctorate, for example, is 32, and of women, 36.[39] It is the exception rather than the rule for men and women who seek graduate degrees to go directly from college to graduate school and remain there until they secure their degrees.[40]

The major implication of this change is that more men and women are achieving full adult status in family roles while they are still less than fully adult in status terms in the occupational system. Graduate students are, increasingly, men and women with full family responsibilities. Within the family many more husbands and fathers are still students, often quite dependent on the earnings of their wives to see them through their advanced training.[41] No matter what the couple's desires and preferences are, this fact alone presses for more egalitarian relations between husband and wife, just as the adult family status of graduate students presses for more egalitarian relations between students and faculty.

3. Irrevocability

If marriages do not work out, there is now widespread acceptance of divorce and remarriage as a solution. The same point applies to the work world: we are free to leave an unsatisfactory job and seek another. But once a pregnancy occurs, there is little possibility of undoing the commitment to parenthood implicit in conception except in the rare instance of placing children for adoption. We can have ex-spouses and ex-jobs

---

[36] Davis, *Great Aspirations, op. cit.*; Laure Sharp, "Graduate Study and Its Relation to Careers: The Experience of a Recent Cohort of College Graduates," *Journal of Human Resources*, 1:2 (1966), pp. 41–58.

[37] James D. Cowhig and C. Nam, "Educational Status, College Plans and Occupational Status of Farm and Nonfarm Youths," U.S. Bureau of the Census Series ERS (P-27). No. 30, 1961.

[38] Davis, *Great Aspirations, op. cit.*

[39] Lindsey R. Harmon, *Profiles of Ph.D.'s in the Sciences: Summary Report on Follow-up of Doctorate Cohorts, 1935–1960*, Washington, D.C.: National Research Council, Publication 1293, 1965.

[40] Sharp, *op. cit.*

[41] Davis, *Stipends and Spouses: The Finances of American Arts and Sciences Graduate Students, op. cit.*

but not ex-children. This being so, it is scarcely surprising to find marked differences between the relationship of a parent and one child and the relationship of the same parent with another child. If the culture does not permit pregnancy termination, the equivalent to giving up a child is psychological withdrawal on the part of the parent.

This taps an important area in which a focus on the parent rather than the child may contribute a new interpretive dimension to an old problem: the long history of interest, in the social sciences, in differences among children associated with their sex-birth-order position in their sibling set. Research has largely been based on data gathered about and/or from the children, and interpretations make inferences back to the "probable" quality of the child's relation to a parent and how a parent might differ in relating to a first-born compared to a last-born child. The relevant research, directed at the parents (mothers in particular), remains to be done, but at least a few examples can be suggested of the different order of interpretation that flows from a focus on the parent.

Some birth-order research stresses the influence of sibs upon other sibs, as in Koch's finding that second-born boys with an older sister are more feminine than second-born boys with an older brother.[42] A similar sib-influence interpretation is offered in the major common finding of birth-order correlates, that sociability is greater among last-borns [43] and achievement among first-borns.[44] It has been suggested that last-borns use social skills to increase acceptance by their older sibs or are more peer-oriented because they receive less adult stimulation from parents. The tendency of first-borns to greater achievement has been interpreted in a corollary way, as a reflection of early assumption of responsibility for younger sibs, greater adult stimulation during the time the oldest was the only child in the family,[45] and the greater significance of the first-born for the larger kinship network of the family.[46]

Sociologists have shown increasing interest in structural family variables in recent years, a primary variable being family size. From Bos-

---

[42] Orville G. Brim, "Family Structure and Sex-Role Learning by Children," *Sociometry*, 21 (1958), pp. 1–16; H. L. Koch, "Sissiness and Tomboyishness in Relation to Sibling Characteristics," *Journal of Genetic Psychology*, 88 (1956), pp. 231–244.
[43] Charles MacArthur, "Personalities of First and Second Children," *Psychiatry*, 19 (1956), pp. 47–54; S. Schachter, "Birth Order and Sociometric Choice," *Journal of Abnormal and Social Psychology*, 68 (1964), pp. 453–456.
[44] Irving Harris, *The Promised Seed*, New York: The Free Press, a division of the Macmillan Co., 1964; Bernard Rosen, "Family Structure and Achievement Motivation," *American Sociological Review*, 26 (1961), pp. 574–585; Alice S. Rossi, "Naming Children in Middle-Class Families," *American Sociological Review*, 30:4 (1965), pp. 499–513; Stanley Schachter, "Birth Order, Eminence and Higher Education," *American Sociological Review*, 28 (1963), pp. 757–768.
[45] Harris, *op. cit.*   [46] Rossi, "Naming Children in Middle-Class Families," *op. cit.*

sard's descriptive work on the large family[47] to more methodologically sophisticated work such as that by Rosen,[48] Elder and Bowerman,[49] Boocock,[50] and Nisbet,[51] the question posed is: what is the effect of growing up in a small family, compared with a large family, that is attributable to this group-size variable? Unfortunately, the theoretical point of departure for sociologists' expectations of the effect of the family-size variables is the Durkheim-Simmel tradition of the differential effect of group size or population density upon members or inhabitants.[52] In the case of the family, however, this overlooks the very important fact that family size is determined by the key figures *within* the group, i.e., the parents. To find that children in small families differ from children in large families is not simply due to the impact of group size upon individual members but to the very different involvement of the parent with the children and to relations between the parents themselves in small versus large families.

An important clue to a new interpretation can be gained by examining family size from the perspective of parental motivation toward having children. A small family is small for one of two primary reasons: either the parents wanted a small family and achieved their desired size, or they wanted a large family but were not able to attain it. In either case, there is a low probability of unwanted children. Indeed, in the latter eventuality they may take particularly great interest in the children they do have. Small families are therefore most likely to contain parents with a strong and positive orientation to each of the children they have. A large family, by contrast, is large either because the parents achieved the size they desired or because they have more children than they in fact wanted. Large families therefore have a higher probability than small families of including unwanted and unloved children. Consistent with this are Nye's finding that adolescents in small families have better

[47] James H. Bossard, *Parent and Child*, Philadelphia: University of Pennsylvania Press, 1953; James H. Bossard and E. Boll, *The Large Family System*, Philadelphia: University of Pennsylvania, 1956.
[48] Rosen, *op. cit.*
[49] Glen H. J. Elder and C. Bowerman, "Family Structure and Child Rearing Patterns: The Effect of Family Size and Sex Composition on Child-Rearing Practices," *American Sociological Review*, 28 (1963), pp. 891–905.
[50] Sarane S. Boocock, "Toward a Sociology of Learning: A Selective Review of Existing Research," *Sociology of Education*, 39:1 (1966), pp. 1–45.
[51] John Nisbet, "Family Environment and Intelligence," in *Education, Economy and Society*, ed. by Halsey *et al.* New York: The Free Press, a division of the Macmillan Company, 1961.
[52] Thus Rosen writes: "Considering the sociologist's traditional and continuing concern with group size as an independent variable (from Simmel and Durkheim to the recent experimental studies of small groups), there have been surprisingly few studies of the influence of group size upon the nature of interaction in the family," *op. cit.*, p. 576.

relations with their parents than those in large families [53] and Sears and Maccoby's finding that mothers of large families are more restrictive toward their children than mothers of small families.[54]

This also means that last-born children are more likely to be unwanted than first- or middle-born children, particularly in large families. This is consistent with what is known of abortion patterns among married women, who typically resort to abortion only when they have achieved the number of children they want or feel they can afford to have. Only a small proportion of women faced with such unwanted pregnancies actually resort to abortion. *This suggests the possibility that the last-born child's reliance on social skills may be his device for securing the attention and loving involvement of a parent less positively predisposed to him than to his older siblings.*

In developing this interpretation, rather extreme cases have been stressed. Closer to the normal range, of families in which even the last-born child was desired and planned for, there is still another element which may contribute to the greater sociability of the last-born child. Most parents are themselves aware of the greater ease with which they face the care of a third fragile newborn than the first; clearly, parental skills and confidence are greater with last-born children than with first-born children. But this does not mean that the attitude of the parent is more positive toward the care of the third child than the first. There is no necessary correlation between skills in an area and enjoyment of that area. Searls [55] found that older homemakers are *more* skillful in domestic tasks but experience *less* enjoyment of them than younger homemakers, pointing to a declining euphoria for a particular role with the passage of time. In the same way, older people rate their marriages as "very happy" less often than younger people do.[56] It is perhaps culturally and psychologically more difficult to face the possibility that women may find less enjoyment of the maternal role with the passage of time, though women themselves know the difference between the romantic expectation concerning child care and the incorporation of the first baby into the household and the more realistic expectation and sharper assessment of their own abilities to do an adequate job of mothering as they face a third confinement. Last-born children may experience not only less verbal stimulation from the parents than first-

[53] Ivan Nye, "Adolescent-Parent Adjustment: Age, Sex, Sibling, Number, Broken Homes, and Employed Mothers as Variables," *Marriage and Family Living*, 14 (1952), pp. 327–332.

[54] Sears *et al., op. cit.*

[55] Laura G. Searls, "Leisure Role Emphasis of College Graduate Homemakers," *Journal of Marriage and the Family*, 28:1 (1966), pp. 77–82.

[56] Norman Bradburn and D. Caplovitz, *Reports on Happiness*, Chicago: Aldine Publishing, 1965.

born children but also less prompt and enthusiastic response to their demands—from feeding and diaper-change as infants to requests for stories read at three or a college education at eighteen—simply because the parents experience less intense gratification from the parent role with the third child than they did with the first. The child's response to this might well be to cultivate winning, pleasing manners in early childhood that blossom as charm and sociability in later life, showing both a greater need to be loved and greater pressure to seek approval.

One last point may be appropriately developed at this juncture. Mention was made earlier that for many women the personal outcome of experience in the parent role is not a higher level of maturation but the negative outcome of a depressed sense of self-worth, if not actual personality deterioration. There is considerable evidence that this is more prevalent than we recognize. On a qualitative level, a close reading of the portrait of the working-class wife in Rainwater,[57] Newsom,[58] Komarovsky,[59] Gavron,[60] or Zweig [61] gives little suggestion that maternity has provided these women with opportunities for personal growth and development. So too, Cohen [62] notes with some surprise that in her sample of middle-class educated couples, as in Pavenstadt's study of lower-income women in Boston, there were more emotional difficulty and lower levels of maturation among multiparous women than primiparous women. On a more extensive sample basis, in Gurin's survey of Americans viewing their mental health,[63] as in Bradburn's reports on happiness,[64] single men are less happy and less active than single women, but among the married respondents the women are unhappier, have more problems, feel inadequate as parents, have a more negative and passive outlook on life, and show a more negative self-image. All of these characteristics increase with age among married women but show no relationship to age among men. While it may be true, as Gurin argues, that women are more introspective and hence more attuned to the psychological facets of experience than men are, this point does not account for the fact that the things which the women report are all on the negative side; few are on the positive side, indicative of euphoric sensitivity and pleasure. The possibility must be faced, and at some point

[57] Lee Rainwater, R. Coleman, and G. Handel, *Workingman's Wife*, New York: Oceana Publications, 1959.
[58] John Newsom and E. Newsom, *Infant Care in an Urban Community*, New York: International Universities Press, 1963.
[59] Mirra Komarovsky, *Blue Collar Marriage*, New York: Random House, 1962.
[60] Gavron, *op. cit.*
[61] Ferdinand Zweig, *Woman's Life and Labor*, London: Camelot Press, 1952.
[62] Cohen, *op. cit.*
[63] Gerald Gurin, J. Veroff, and S. Feld, *Americans View Their Mental Health*, New York: Basic Books, Monograph Series No. 4, Joint Commission on Mental Illness and Health, 1960.
[64] Bradburn and Caplovitz, *op. cit.*

researched, that women lose ground in personal development and self-esteem during the early and middle years of adulthood, whereas men gain ground in these respects during the same years. The retention of a high level of self-esteem may depend upon the adequacy of earlier preparation for major adult roles: men's training adequately prepares them for their primary adult roles in the occupational system, as it does for those women who opt to participate significantly in the work world. Training in the qualities and skills needed for family roles in contemporary society may be inadequate for both sexes, but the lowering of self-esteem occurs only among women because their primary adult roles are within the family system.

4. Preparation for Parenthood

Four factors may be given special attention on the question of what preparation American couples bring to parenthood.

A. PAUCITY OF PREPARATION. Our educational system is dedicated to the cognitive development of the young, and our primary teaching approach is the pragmatic one of learning by doing. How much one knows and how well he can apply what he knows are the standards by which the child is judged in school, as the employee is judged at work. The child can learn by doing in such subjects as science, mathematics, art work, or shop, but not in the subjects most relevant to successful family life: sex, home maintenance, child care, interpersonal competence, and empathy. If the home is deficient in training in these areas, the child is left with no preparation for a major segment of his adult life. A doctor facing his first patient in private practice has treated numerous patients under close supervision during his internship, but probably a majority of American mothers approach maternity with no previous child-care experience beyond sporadic baby-sitting, perhaps a course in child psychology, or occasional care of younger siblings.

B. LIMITED LEARNING DURING PREGNANCY. A second important point makes adjustment to parenthood potentially more stressful than marital adjustment. This is the lack of any realistic training for parenthood during the anticipatory stage of pregnancy. By contrast, during the engagement period preceding marriage, an individual has opportunities to develop the skills and make the adjustments which ease the transition to marriage. Through discussions of values and life goals, through sexual experimentation, shared social experiences as an engaged couple with friends and relatives, and planning and furnishing an apartment, the engaged couple can make considerable progress in developing mutuality in advance of the marriage itself.[65] No such headstart is possible in the case of pregnancy. What preparation exists is confined to reading, con-

[65] Rapoport, "The Transition from Engagement to Marriage," *op. cit.*; Raush *et al.*, *op. cit.*

sultation with friends and parents, discussions between husband and wife, and a minor nesting phase in which a place and the equipment for a baby are prepared in the household.[66]

C. ABRUPTNESS OF TRANSITION. Thirdly, the birth of a child is not followed by any gradual taking on of responsibility, as in the case of a professional work role. It is as if the woman shifted from a graduate student to a full professor with little intervening apprenticeship experience of slowly increasing responsibility. The new mother starts out immediately on 24-hour duty, with responsibility for a fragile and mysterious infant totally dependent on her care.

If marital adjustment is more difficult for very young brides than more mature ones,[67] adjustment to motherhood may be even more difficult. A woman can adapt a passive dependence on a husband and still have a successful marriage, but a young mother with strong dependency needs is in for difficulty in maternal adjustment, because the role precludes such dependency. This situation was well described in Cohen's study [68] in a case of a young wife with a background of co-ed popularity and a passive dependent relationship to her admired and admiring husband, who collapsed into restricted incapacity when faced with the responsibilities of maintaining a home and caring for a child.

D. LACK OF GUIDELINES TO SUCCESSFUL PARENTHOOD. If the central task of parenthood is the rearing of children to become the kind of competent adults valued by the society, then an important question facing any parent is what he or she specifically can do to create such a competent adult. This is where the parent is left with few or no guidelines from the expert. Parents can readily inform themselves concerning the young infant's nutritional, clothing, and medical needs and follow the general prescription that a child needs loving physical contact and emotional support. Such advice may be sufficient to produce a healthy, happy, and well-adjusted preschooler, but adult competency is quite another matter.

In fact, the adults who do "succeed" in American society show a complex of characteristics as children that current experts in child-care would evaluate as "poor" to "bad." Biographies of leading authors and artists, as well as the more rigorous research inquiries of creativity among

---

[66] During the period when marriage was the critical transition in the adult woman's life rather than pregnancy, a good deal of anticipatory "nesting" behavior took place from the time of conception. Now more women work through a considerable portion of the first pregnancy, and such nesting behavior as exists may be confined to a few shopping expeditions or baby showers, thus adding to the abruptness of the transition and the difficulty of adjustment following the birth of a first child.

[67] Lee G. Burchinal, "Adolescent Role Deprivation and High School Marriage," *Marriage and Family Living*, 21 (1959), pp. 378–384; Floyd M. Martinson, "Ego Deficiency as a Factor in Marriage," *American Sociological Review*, 22 (1955), pp. 161–164; J. Joel Moss and Ruby Gingles, "The Relationship of Personality to the Incidence of Early Marriage," *Marriage and Family Living*, 21 (1959), pp. 373–377.

[68] Cohen, *op. cit.*

architects [69] or scientists,[70] do not portray childhoods with characteristics currently endorsed by mental health and child-care authorities. Indeed, there is often a predominance of tension in childhood family relations and traumatic loss rather than loving parental support, intense channeling of energy in one area of interest rather than an all-round profile of diverse interests, and social withdrawal and preference for loner activities rather than gregarious sociability. Thus, the stress in current child-rearing advice on a high level of loving support but a low level of discipline or restriction on the behavior of the child—the "developmental" family type as Duvall calls it [71]—is a profile consistent with the focus on mental health, sociability, and adjustment. Yet, the combination of both high support and high authority on the part of parents is most strongly related to the child's sense of responsibility, leadership quality, and achievement level, as found in Bronfenbrenner's studies [72] and that of Mussen and Distler.[73]

Brim points out [74] that we are a long way from being able to say just what parent role prescriptions have what effect on the adult characteristics of the child. We know even less about how such parental prescriptions should be changed to adapt to changed conceptions of competency in adulthood. In such an ambiguous context, the great interest parents take in school reports on their children or the pediatrician's assessment of the child's developmental progress should be seen as among the few indices parents have of how well *they* are doing as parents.

System and Role Requirements: Instrumentality and Integration

Typological dichotomies and unidimensional scales have loomed large in the search by social scientists for the most economical and general principles to account for some significant portion of the complex human behavior or social organization they study. Thus, for example, the European dichotomy of *Gemeinschaft* and *Gesellschaft* became the American

[69] Donald W. MacKinnon, "Creativity and Images of the Self," in *The Study of Lives*, ed. by Robert W. White, New York: Atherton Press, 1963.
[70] Anne Roe, *A Psychological Study of Eminent Biologists, Psychological Monographs*, 65:14 (1951), 68 pages; Anne Roe, "A Psychological Study of Physical Scientists," *Genetic Psychology Monographs*, 43 (1951), pp. 121–239; Anne Roe, "Crucial Life Experiences in the Development of Scientists," in *Talent and Education*, ed. by E. P. Torrance, Minneapolis: University of Minnesota Press, 1960.
[71] Evelyn M. Duvall, "Conceptions of Parenthood," *American Journal of Sociology*, 52 (1946), pp. 193–203.
[72] Urie Bronfenbrenner, "Some Familial Antecedents of Responsibility and Leadership in Adolescents," in *Studies in Leadership*, ed. by L. Petrullo and B. Bass, New York: Holt, Rinehart, and Winston, 1960.
[73] Paul Mussen and L. Distler, "Masculinity, Identification and Father-Son Relationships," *Journal of Abnormal and Social Psychology*, 59 (1959), pp. 350–356.
[74] Orville G. Brim, "The Parent-Child Relation as a Social System: I. Parent and Child Roles," *Child Development*, 28:3 (1957), pp. 343–364.

sociological distinction between rural and urban sociology, subfields that have outlasted their conceptual utility now that the rural environment has become urbanized and the interstices between country and city are swelling with suburban developments.

In recent years a new dichotomy has gained more acceptance in sociological circles—the Parsonian distinction between *instrumental* and *expressive*, an interesting dichotomy that is unfortunately applied in an indiscriminate way to all manner of social phenomena including the analysis of teacher role conflict, occupational choice, the contrast between the family system and the occupational system, and the primary roles or personality tendencies of men compared to women.

On a system level, for example, the "instrumental" occupational system is characterized by rationality, efficiency, rejection of tradition, and depression of interpersonal loyalty, while the "expressive" family system is characterized by nurturance, integration, tension-management, ritual, and interpersonal solidarity. Applied to sex roles within the family, the husband-father emerges as the instrumental rational leader, a symbolic representative of the outside world, and the wife-mother emerges as the expressive, nurturant, affective center of the family. Such distinctions may be useful in the attempt to capture some general tendency of a system or a role, but they lead to more distortion than illumination when applied to the actual functioning of a specific system or social role or to the actual behavior of a given individual in a particular role.

Take, for example, the husband-father as the instrumental role within the family on the assumption that men are the major breadwinners and therefore carry the instrumentality associated with work into their roles within the family. To begin with, the family is not an experimental one-task small group but a complex, ongoing 24-hour entity with many tasks that must be performed. Secondly, we really know very little about how occupational roles affect the performance of family roles.[75] An aggressive courtroom lawyer or a shrewd business executive are not lawyers

[75] Miller and Swanson have suggested a connection between the trend toward bureaucratic structure in the occupational world and the shift in child-rearing practices toward permissiveness and a greater stress on personal adjustment of children. Their findings, however, are suggestive rather than definitive, and no hard research has subjected this question to empirical inquiry. Daniel R. Miller and G. Swanson, *The Changing American Parent*, New York: John Wiley & Sons, 1958.

The same suggestive but nondefinitive clues are to be found in von Mering's study of the contrast between professional and nonprofessional women as mothers. She shows that the professionally active woman in her mother role tends toward a greater stress on discipline rather than indulgence and has a larger number of rules with fewer choices or suggestions to the child: the emphasis is in equipping the child to cope effectively with rules and techniques of his culture. The nonprofessional mother, by contrast, has a greater value stress on insuring the child's emotional security, tending to take the role of the clinician in an attempt to diagnose the child's problems and behavior. Faye H. von Mering, "Professional and Non-Professional Women as Mothers," *Journal of Social Psychology*, 42 (1955), pp. 21–34.

and businessmen at home but husbands and fathers. Unless shown to be in error, we should proceed on the assumption that behavior is role-specific. (Indeed, Brim [76] argues that even personality is role-specific.) A strict teacher may be an indulgent mother at home; a submissive wife may be a dominant mother; a dictatorial father may be an exploited and passive worker on the assembly line; or, as in some of Lidz's schizophrenic patients' families,[77] a passive dependent husband at home may be a successful dominant lawyer away from home.

There is, however, a more fundamental level to the criticism that the dichotomous usage of instrumentality and expressiveness, linked to sex and applied to intrafamily roles, leads to more distortion than illumination. The logic of my argument starts with the premise that every social system, group, or role has two primary, independent, structural axes. Whether these axes are called "authority and support," as in Straus's circumplex model,[78] or "instrumental and expressive" as by Parsons,[79] there are tasks to be performed and affective support to be given in all the cases cited. There must be discipline, rules, and division of labor in the nation-state as in the family or a business enterprise *and* there must be solidarity among the units comprising these same systems in order for the system to function adequately. *This means that the role of father, husband, wife, or mother each has these two independent dimensions of authority and support, instrumentality and expressiveness, work and love.* Little is gained by trying to stretch empirical results to fit the father role to the instrumental category, as Brim [80] has done, or the mother role to the expressive category, as Zelditch has done.[81]

In taking a next logical step from this premise, the critical issue, both theoretically and empirically, becomes gauging the *balance* between these two dimensions of the system or of the role. Roles or systems could be compared in terms of the average difference among them in the direction and extent of the discrepancy between authority and support; or individuals could be compared in terms of the variation among them in the discrepancy between the two dimensions in a given role.

An example may clarify these points. A teacher who is all loving, warm support to her students and plans many occasions to evoke integrative ties among them but who is incompetent in the exercise of authority or knowledge of the subjects she teaches would be judged by any school principal as an inadequate teacher. The same judgment of inadequacy would apply to a strict disciplinarian teacher, competent and informed

---

[76] Orville G. Brim, "Personality Development as Role-Learning," in *Personality Development in Children*, ed. by Ira Iscoe and Harold Stevenson, University of Texas Press, 1960.
[77] Lidz *et al., op. cit.*   [78] Straus, *op. cit.*   [79] Parsons and Bales, *op. cit.*
[80] Brim, "The Parent-Child Relation as a Social System: I. Parent and Child Roles," *op. cit.*
[81] Parsons and Bales, *op. cit.*

about her subjects but totally lacking in any personal quality of warmth or ability to encourage integrative and cooperative responses among her students. Maximum adequacy of teacher performance requires a relatively high positive level on both of these two dimensions of the teacher role.

To claim that teachers have a basic conflict in approaching their role because they are required to be a "bisexual parent, permissive giver of love and harsh disciplinarian with a masculine intellectual grasp of the world," as Jackson and Moscovici [82] have argued, at least recognizes the two dimensions of the teacher role, though it shares the view of many sociologists that role *conflict* is inherent wherever these seeming polarities are required. Why conflict is predicted hinges on the assumed invariance of the linkage of the male to authority and the female to the expressive-integrative roles.

It is this latter assumed difference between the sexes that restricts theory-building in family sociology and produces so much puzzlement on the part of researchers into marriage and parenthood, sex-role socialization, or personality tendencies toward masculinity or femininity. Let me give one example of recent findings on this latter topic and then move on to apply the two-dimension concept to the parental role. Vincent [83] administered the Gough Femininity Scale along with several other scale batteries from the California Personality Inventory to several hundred college men and women. He found that women *low* on femininity were higher in the Class I scale which measures poise, ascendancy, and self-assurance, and men *high* in femininity were higher in dominance, capacity for status, and responsibility. Successful adult men in a technological society are rarely interested in racing cars, soldiering, or hunting; they are cautious, subtle, and psychologically attuned to others. So too, contemporary adult women who fear windstorms, the dark, strange places, automobile accidents, excitement, crowded parties, or practical jokes (and are therefore high on femininity in the Gough scale) will be inadequate for the task of managing an isolated household with neither men nor kinswomen close by to help them through daily crises, for the assumption of leadership roles in community organizations, or for holding down supplementary breadwinning or cakewinning jobs.

When Deutsch [84] and Escalona [85] point out that today's "neurotic"

[82] Philip Jackson and F. Moscovici, "The Teacher-to-be: A Study of Embryonic Identification with a Professional Role," *School Review*, 71:1 (1963), pp. 41–65.
[83] Clark E. Vincent, "Implications of Changes in Male-Female Role Expectations for Interpreting M-F Scores," *Journal of Marriage and the Family*, 28:2 (1966), pp. 196–199.
[84] Helene Deutsch, *The Psychology of Women: A Psychoanalytic Interpretation*, Vol. 1, New York: Grune and Stratton, 1944.
[85] Sibylle Escalona, "The Psychological Situation of Mother and Child Upon Return from the Hospital," in *Problems of Infancy and Childhood: Transactions of the Third Conference*, ed. by Milton Senn, 1949.

woman is not an assertive dominant person but a passive dependent one, the reason may be found in the social change in role expectations concerning competence among adult women, not that there has been a social change in the characteristics of neurotic women. In the past an assertive, dominant woman might have defined herself and been defined by her analyst as "neurotic" because she could not fill the expectations then held for adequacy among adult women. Today, it is the passive dependent woman who will be judged "neurotic" because she cannot fill adequately the expectations now set for and by her. What is really meant when we say that sex role definitions have become increasingly blurred is that men are now required to show more integrative skills than in the past, and women more instrumental skills. This incurs potential sex-role "confusion" only by the standards of the past, not by the standards of what is required for contemporary adult competence in family and work roles.

Once freed from the assumption of a single bipolar continuum of masculinity-femininity,[86] authority-integration, or even independence-dependence,[87] one can observe increased instrumentality in a role with no implication of necessarily decreased integration, and vice versa. Thus, an increasing rationality in the care of children, the maintenance of a household, or meal planning for a family does not imply a decreasing level of integrative support associated with the wife-mother role. So, too, the increased involvement of a young father in playful encounters with his toddler carries no necessary implication of a change in the instrumental dimension of his role.

The two-dimensional approach also frees our analysis of parenthood on two other important questions. Brim has reviewed much of the research on the parent-child relationship [88] and noted the necessity of

[86] Several authors have recently pointed out the inadequacy of social science usage of the masculinity-femininity concept. Landreth, in a study of parent-role appropriateness in giving physical care and companionship to the child, found her four-year-old subjects, particularly in New Zealand, made no simple linkage of activity to mother as opposed to father. Catherine Landreth, "Four-Year-Olds' Notions about Sex Appropriateness of Parental Care and Companionship Activities," *Merrill-Palmer Quarterly*, 9:3 (1963), pp. 175–182. She comments that in New Zealand "masculinity and femininity appear to be comfortably relegated to chromosome rather than to contrived activity" (p. 176). Lansky, in a study of the effect of the sex of the children upon the parents' own sex identification, calls for devising tests which look at masculinity and femininity as two dimensions rather than a single continuum. Leonard M. Lansky, "The Family Structure also Affects the Model: Sex-Role Identification in Parents of Preschool Children," *Merrill-Palmer Quarterly*, 10:1 (1964), pp. 39–50.

[87] Beller has already shown the value of such an approach, in a study that defined independence and dependence as two separate dimensions rather than the extremes of a bipolar continuum. He found, as hypothesized, a very *low* negative correlation between the two measures. E. K. Beller, "Exploratory Studies of Dependency," trans., *N.Y. Academy of Science*, 21 (1959), pp. 414–426.

[88] Brim, "The Parent-Child Relation as a Social System: I. Parent and Child Roles," *op. cit.*

specifying not only the sex of the parent but the sex of the child and whether a given parent-child dyad is a cross-sex or same-sex pair. It is clear from his review that fathers and mothers relate differently to their sons and daughters: fathers have been found to be stricter with their sons than with their daughters, and mothers stricter with their daughters than with their sons. Thus, a two-dimensional approach to the parent role is more appropriate to what is already empirically known about the parent-child relationship.

Secondly, only on a very general overview level does a parent maintain a particular level of support and of discipline toward a given child: situational variation is an important determinant of parental response to a child. A father with a general tendency toward relatively little emotional support of his son may offer a good deal of comfort if the child is hurt. An indulgent and loving mother may show an extreme degree of discipline when the same child misbehaves. Landreth found that her four-year-olds gave more mother responses on a care item concerning food than on bath-time or bedtime care and suggests, as Brim has,[89] that "any generalizations on parent roles should be made in terms of the role activities studied."[90]

Let me illustrate the utility of the two-dimensional concept by applying it to the parental role. Clearly there are a number of expressive requirements for adequate performance in this role: spontaneity and flexibility, the ability to be tender and loving and to respond to tenderness and love from a child, to take pleasure in tactile contact and in play, and to forget one's adultness and unself-consciously respond to the sensitivities and fantasies of a child. Equally important are the instrumental requirements for adequate performance in the parental role: firmness and consistency; the ability to manage time and energy; to plan and organize activities involving the child; to teach and to train the child in body controls, motor and language skills, and knowledge of the natural and social world; and interpersonal and value discriminations.

Assuming we had empirical measures of these two dimensions of the parental role, one could then compare individual women both by their levels on each of these dimensions and by the extent to which the discrepancy in level on the two dimensions was tipped toward a high expressive or instrumental dimension. This makes no assumptions about what the balance "should" be; that remains an empirical question awaiting a test in the form of output variables—the characteristics of children we deem to be critical for their competence as adults. Indeed, I would predict that an exhaustive count of the actual components of both the marital and parental roles would show a very high proportion of instrumental components in the parental role and a low proportion in the marital role and that this is an underlying reason why maternal role

[89] *Ibid.*   [90] Landreth, *op. cit.*, p. 181.

adjustment is more difficult for women than marital role adjustment. It also leaves as an open, empirical question what the variance is, among fathers, in the level of expressiveness and instrumentality in their paternal role performance and how the profile of fathers compares with that of mothers.

It would not surprise many of us, of course, if women scored higher than men on the expressive dimension and men scored higher on the instrumental dimension of the parental role. Yet quite the opposite might actually result. Men spend relatively little time with their children, and it is time of a particular kind: evenings, weekends, and vacations, when the activities and mood of the family are heavily on the expressive side. Women carry the major burden of the instrumental dimension of parenting. If, as Mabel Cohen [91] suggests, the rearing of American boys is inadequate on the social and sexual dimension of development and the rearing of American girls is inadequate on the personal dimension of development, then from the perspective of adequate parenthood performance, we have indeed cause to reexamine the socialization of boys and girls in families and schools. Our current practices appear adequate as preparation for occupational life for men but not women, and inadequate as preparation for family life for both sexes.

However, this is to look too far ahead. At the present, this analysis of parenthood suggests we have much to rethink and much to research before we develop policy recommendations in this area.

[91] Cohen, *op. cit.*

54. ADOPTION: UNITED STATES PHILOSOPHY AND TEAM APPROACH

Katherine Bain

§ The basic philosophy of child-rearing in the United States is that ideally it takes place in a nuclear family of two parents and, usually, brothers and sisters. When a child is deprived of such a family through the death of his parents or their inability to care for him, a substitute family is sought through adoption. Because of the importance of the

SOURCE: Multigraphed and distributed by the Department of Health, Education, and Welfare, Social and Rehabilitation Service, Children's Bureau. This paper was read at a panel on Adoption at the XI International Congress of Pediatrics, Tokyo, Japan, November 6–13, 1965.

The author, who is a Doctor of Medicine, is Assistant Chief for International Cooperation for the Children's Bureau.

family in the child's development, safeguards are needed to protect the child from haphazard placement. Some of these safeguards, and the way in which a qualified social agency is able to provide them, are discussed in this article.

Certain fundamental principles of child care and protection, applicable to all societies and accepted by most cultures, are embodied in the Declaration of the Rights of the Child unanimously adopted by the United Nations General Assembly in 1959. One of these principles states, "He [the child] shall, wherever possible, grow up in the care and under the responsibility of his parents. . . ." All persons who deal with children would, I believe, accept this as a fundamental principle.

The Declaration further states, "Society and the public authority shall have the duty to extend particular care to children without a family." Again, all of us would probably agree with this principle. On the implementation of this principle, however, we might not agree. How to provide for the child deprived of normal home life is our problem for discussion today.

During different eras in history, different cultures have had different solutions for the homeless child, such as destroying the child, selling him into slavery, making him an apprentice to an artisan, requiring the extended family to assume his care, giving him shelter by a religious order, or providing special creches or orphanages for his upbringing.

In the United States during its early years, as in most developed countries, institutional care was the method used to provide for children deprived of normal home life. Gradually as the physical danger of institutional life to infants and young children—the danger of infection—was recognized, and later the psychological damage to the development of children living in inadequate institutions, the use of foster homes and adoption came to the fore. Social and psychological research have shown that the institutionalized child, even though he may grow and develop physically, is nevertheless often badly handicapped in his mental and social growth.

Ample evidence exists today that a good family is the best environment in which a child can grow and develop normally. Since this is so, it follows that every effort should be made to strengthen and preserve family life so that each child may grow up with his own parents. This is the ideal situation, but unfortunately modern life is not ideal. When efforts to salvage the home fail and the child is deprived of a normal home, some substitute for his family must be found.

In the past, children were deprived of parental care largely because of death of the parents. Today, with the very low mortality rate, few children in the United States lose both their parents through death. Often those who are orphans are taken care of by relatives and supported by social security benefits. It is the child of the inadequate home, of neglectful or incompetent parents, incapable of providing the right kind of home life, and of the unmarried mother who frequently requires care in a family other than his own.

On the basis of the belief that the best place for a child to grow up is within a family, the present system of adoption has been developed in the United States. Adoption is designed to provide a permanent substitute family for a child deprived of his natural family, and by family we mean the nuclear family: mother, father, and brothers and sisters. Adoption in the United States is child-centered. True, it has certain side advantages, such as providing a child for a childless couple, but its central focus is on the needs of the child. It is in this framework that our laws and our practices have developed.

The adoption process is not a simple one and requires the cooperation of the legal, medical, and social-work professions. The skills of these three professions are essential to a successful adoption, and no one of the three can operate adequately without the others. Clearly, adoption is not a hit-and-miss process—something that anyone with good will and good intentions can do. It is a job for a team of professionals who can carry out the necessary steps in a logical and orderly manner.

The first step in the process of adoption relates to the termination of the rights and the responsibilities of the natural parents. Sometimes children are taken from their parents by the court because of neglect or mistreatment, and the court then may terminate the right of the parents to these children.

If the child is born out of wedlock, the mother makes the decision to keep the baby or to give him up. She must be given every opportunity to come to a firm decision with assistance from a social worker as to what she wants to do about her baby. Many of the tragedies in adoption occur when the mother has been hurried or pushed into giving up the child and later changes her mind. This may happen when individuals pressure her in order to secure a child or offer her needed money.

An effort is made to give counseling service to the unmarried mother all through her pregnancy so that at the time of delivery she can make a sound and lasting decision to keep or to give up the child. If she gives up the child, her rights must be terminated by the court and custody of the child given to a qualified social agency that will make plans for the adoption.

We believe very firmly that the job of selecting a home for the child and making the placement is the job of a qualified social agency. There are many reasons why a doctor or a lawyer or a friend should not undertake this delicate task. An agency is a stable institution which is responsible to the community and can be held responsible for its acts, as an individual cannot. An agency also has staff with the necessary social-work skills to provide the service essential in this part of the adoption. The agency also has available to it a large selection of prospective parents from which to select the particular couple most desirable for a particular child. And finally, if something goes wrong with the adoption, the agency is available to take the child back and care for him until other suitable arrangements can be made.

A good agency makes a very careful study of the adoptive home and decides whether a child will fit into this environment satisfactorily. Within the agency, it is not one person who makes the final decision but a group of people considering all the facts before them. The child is then placed in the home and lives there for a number of months prior to court action. In some States, this may be six months, in some nine months, and in some a year. But in all instances, there should be an adjustment period during which the social worker helps the child and family to grow into a family unit and during which she evaluates the success of the adoptive placement. The agency makes its recommendation to the court and the judge, after considering all aspects of the placement, makes a decision to approve or deny the adoption petition. When an adoption decree is issued by the court, there is provision for the appropriate agency to issue a new birth certificate giving the names of the adoptive parents as the parents of the child. All the court procedures and the social agency records are confidential.

It is clear that the social agency has a central role in the adoption process, but the doctor and the lawyer have functions, equally important though different from those of the social worker. The three professions work together as a team, and each carries out his functions in relation to the other two.

The physician has a very definite responsibility, first in providing the unmarried mother with good maternity care and in caring for her infant. He must examine and evaluate the infant or child and determine insofar as possible his potential and his handicaps. And finally he must carefully appraise the health of the adoptive couple. Of course, these various steps may be performed by different physicians, but they are all medical activities which must be performed by skilled medical practitioners.

The physician contributes a great deal to successful adoption through the skill with which he makes a referral to the proper social agency. He does not make an adoptive study of the home and does not place the child, but he does prepare the way for the social worker who has the professional education, the experience, and the function necessary to provide good adoptive services.

The lawyer functions in relation to the termination of parental rights by making sure that the child is free for adoption, and by determining that the court adoption decree is in order to protect the child and the adoptive parents. The lawyer also has responsibility to help the family or the child to secure the benefits of the service of a good social agency. Similarly, since the social worker has neither the education, the experience, nor the function to prescribe medically or to represent her client in court, she in turn seeks the services of the physician and lawyer in planning for adoption. When each member of the three professions recognizes his own skills, his own responsibility and limitations, and respects those of the other two, then a successful adoption can be carried through.

Since laws relating to adoption in the United States are State rather than Federal laws, they are not all alike and some contain many inadequacies. For example, some of these laws do not give sufficient protection to the placement of the child since they allow an interested person rather than a social agency to make a placement. In some States, a social study prior to judicial disposition of the adoption petition is not mandatory. Some States do not require a period of supervised residence in the adoptive home. In some States, the confidential nature of the record is not protected. However, a growing number of States are introducing all of these protections into State adoption laws. To facilitate enactment of good and uniform legislation in the States, the Children's Bureau issued a pamphlet [1] which outlines the principles of adoption and suggests the specific provisions of an adoption law. This guide has proved most effective in helping the States bring about improvement in the laws.

Adoption is popular in the United States. Many childless couples wishing to have children obtain them through adoption. In the past, in many communities there were more couples wishing to adopt white infants than there were infants available. Consequently there were long waiting periods and a number of applications were not accepted. However, the situation is somewhat changed in many parts of the United States, since more infants have become available. On the other hand, it is difficult to locate sufficient adoptive homes for older children, for children with handicaps, or for children of minority groups or of mixed parentage.

It is the current belief in the United States that any child who could profit from home life is suitable for adoption. Even for those with physical or mental handicaps, homes can often be found if adequate attention is given to the problem. Social agencies recognize that they

---

[1] *Essentials of Adoption Law and Procedure*, now out of print, replaced by *Legislative Guides for the Termination of Parental Rights and Responsibilities and the Adoption of Children*, Children's Bureau Publication 394. Washington, D.C., 20402: U.S. Government Printing Office, 1961. 61 pp.

cannot find a perfect child for a perfect adoptive couple, but through the social study, they make every effort to find for each child parents who can grow to love him and accept him as their own. Rigid requirements are no longer the basis upon which placement is made. Though at one time only young couples would be considered as adoptive parents, now many agencies will consider couples who are in their forties. At one time also, a home was not considered suitable if the adoptive mother worked. This is no longer true in many agencies. The economic position of the family also does not have to be high. Many families living in very simple circumstances are considered acceptable if they are capable of providing good and loving care for a child.

The number of adoptions continues to grow each year in the United States. Since 1951, more than a million children have been adopted. In 1963, 127,000 children were adopted legally, a little more than half of them being adopted by non-relatives. About 75,000 of the 127,000 were illegitimate.

Some families have turned to foreign countries in their quest for a child to adopt. During the past 15 years, 20,000 children of alien birth were adopted by United States citizens. The reasons for seeking children from other countries have varied but include kinship ties, emotional appeal felt by military personnel located in foreign countries, or availability of greater numbers of children. In recent years the legislation permitting adoptions of foreign children has been tightened. Proxy adoptions of foreign children are no longer permissible. An adequate social study of the adoptive home is now required before a visa will be issued for a child.

Physicians, especially pediatricians in the United States, have become increasingly interested in the question of adoption. The American Academy of Pediatrics has had a committee dealing with this question. This committee developed a manual for physicians relating to adoption. Many pediatricians have become interested in adoption because they see adopted children in their practice and have come to realize some of the problems which adopted children may have as they grow up. Though controversy still lingers around the emotional and behavior problems which adopted children may develop as they grow older, relative to their adoptive status and their background, there is general agreement that an adoptive home usually offers a child who cannot be cared for by his own parents the best opportunity for normal development. But this can only hold true if the adoption is well planned and the services of skilled people from the three professions are used. Unfortunately, we do not always have enough adequate social agencies with well-trained staff to carry out all the steps necessary in adoption.

For a truly effective system of protection for children deprived of normal home life, a country should have, first, good laws which protect the rights of the child, the natural parents, and the adoptive parents; second, adequate social agencies with trained staff to deal with individual cases; third, enlightened legal and medical professions willing to work in harmony with the social agencies, and, finally, understanding by the public of the purpose of adoption and of what constitutes good practice for all concerned, but especially for the child.

55. HELPING ADOPTING COUPLES COME TO GRIPS WITH THEIR NEW PARENTAL ROLES

Edith M. Chappelear and Joyce E. Fried

§ After the formal adoption proceedings have ended, the process of adjustment between adoptive parents and their child begins. Recognition of the special qualities of adoptive parent-child adjustment led one department of public welfare to institute a special program to help the parents. The discussion indicates not only what was done but also the special aspects of adoptive parenthood as distinct from biological parenthood.

When a husband and wife learn that their application to adopt a child has been approved, it is for them as though their fondest dream has come true. But when the child is actually placed with them, questions that ought to have been resolved through the home study process may arise. However, their reluctance to share anxiety with a caseworker after placement often makes it difficult to help them prepare for the special problems they may face as parents of adopted children. The Montgomery County (Md.) Department of Public Welfare has found the group discussion method an effective way of breaking through such reluctance.

The agency has had professionally trained social workers on its adoption staff for the past 4 years. During this time it has emphasized the preparation of applicant couples during the home study for the problems they may face as adoptive parents.

SOURCE: *Children*, 14 (November–December, 1967), 223–26. Published by the U.S. Department of Health, Education, and Welfare, Social and Rehabilitation Service, Children's Bureau.

Both Edith M. Chappelear and Joyce E. Fried were on the staff of the Montgomery County (Md.) Department of Public Welfare when they wrote this article, Mrs. Chappelear as adoption supervisor and Mrs. Fried as a caseworker in the adoption unit.

Over the years, the agency found that the early period of placement is the most crucial to the quality of parent-child and child-parent adjustment. Unfortunately, it also found that this was the period when social workers face the greatest difficulty in finding a meaningful relationship with adopting parents. At this point, parents were usually most unwilling to discuss or come to grips in any way with the problems they might have with their children. The caseworkers felt effectively shut out by couples who had participated actively during the home study and preplacement period. For the adopting parents, once they had the baby, the focus seemed too narrow to include only themselves and the child. In talking with the caseworker, they tended to gloss over their problems and to make only platitudinous observations such as "It is as though he had been with us always."

Knowing that initial parent-child adjustment is rarely so idyllic, the adoption unit considered the following possible reasons for the failure to get a true picture of what was going on in these homes.

1. The worker's visits in the supervisory period seemed threatening to adoptive parents. The couples felt that since the agency still retained guardianship over the child it might use its authority to remove the child if the social worker thought the placement was not proceeding satisfactorily. Parents, therefore, felt a great need to emphasize the positive.

2. The couples unconsciously felt that discussion of the strangeness, fears, and changes involved in the new experience of adoptive parenthood would sharpen their awareness of the differences between adoptive and natural parenthood. They preferred to avoid the pain of speaking of something they would like not to exist. It is easier to deny an unpleasant fact than to face it, particularly in talking to a person vested with authority.

Realizing that both these reasons were probably operating to a certain extent, we wondered whether the parents might be able to help one another. We, therefore, instigated the program of group meetings to supplement the social workers' individual interviews with the parents. Under the plan each couple was to attend two group meetings in the office in the supervisory period: one, 6 weeks to 2 months after the placement, and the other, 1 week after that. One home visit was made by the caseworker within 2 weeks after placement.

The new program got underway in October 1965. Each meeting was attended by five or six couples and lasted about an hour and a half. Discussion was led by a caseworker, who encouraged the couples to participate and gradually turned the meeting over to them as much as possible, intervening only with occasional guidance. No two meetings were exactly alike. They varied with the group's composition and the leader's experience in stimulating discussion.

The only bases for membership in specific groups were the date the couple had received a child and the age of the child. Parents who were adopting children over 4 years of age met in separate groups. Some couples were having their first experience with parenthood; some already had one or more adopted children; some had children who had been born to them in addition to one or more adopted children. The age range among the couples was wide: from the early twenties to the forties.

The only common denominator among the couples was the similar situation they were in: they had all undergone a home study and had a child placed in their home by an agency—usually the Montgomery County Department of Public Welfare, but sometimes an out-of-State agency for whom the department was carrying the supervisory responsibility.

The discussions were always concerned with the adjustment involved in becoming an adoptive parent, the kinds of problems that could be anticipated, and how they might be met.

The Meetings

The first of the two meetings each couple attended was focused on the subject "Being Adoptive Parents"; the second, on "Being an Adopted Child." The discussions covered the following aspects of adoption:

1. The difference between adoptive and biological parenthood.
2. Helping a child to an acceptance and understanding of his adoptive status.
3. The adoptive parents' feelings toward the child's biological parents.
4. The adoptive parents' feelings about illegitimacy.
5. Letting persons outside the family know that the child has been adopted.

The group leader always opened the first of the two meetings by explaining the purpose of having them—giving the couples an opportunity to discuss a common experience and problems of common concern. She pointed out that the agency's workers were always ready to be of help, but that in a way they were on the outside looking in and that the agency believed the participants as new adoptive parents might have something to say to each other. In almost every group, the parents in their first meeting began to discuss questions their friends, relatives, and acquaintances had raised—questions they resented and did not know how to answer. Almost all had been asked what they knew of the child's background. To this, may of them had given angry, evasive answers such as "none of your business." Some had even been asked if they could really love an adopted child as they would a child of their own.

Often during the first meeting a parent would express concern about how his adopted child would look on him and whether the child would feel he had no need to respect or obey him because adoptive parents are not "real" parents. In discussing this possibility, the group members usually decided that it might happen, but then some one—sometimes the group leader, sometimes one of the parents—would point out that even children living with their "real" parents often had moments of rebellion, and examples would be cited of such children who had accused their parents of not being their "real parents."

The parents were nearly always unanimous in feeling that they would have difficulty in discussing the subject of adoption with their child. In the first meeting, the group leader did not usually make specific suggestions in regard to this problem but, rather, suggested that the parents think a lot about what they might do, read about what others had done, and plan to discuss the subject again in the second meeting.

The second meeting usually started with a reading of the minutes of the previous meeting after which the group leader would ask whether the participants had any questions they would like to discuss further. Often the first question raised was whether it is important to discuss the fact of adoption with the child. All of the parents had been encouraged to explore the subject in their individual interviews with the social worker before a child had been placed with them. The questions of "when" and "how" usually elicited much difference of opinion. In one group, for example, a man who had adopted four children from different agencies said he felt he could tell them all that their parents were dead.

"To me," he said, "they are dead. If the children believe they are living they will go to the ends of the earth to find them."

His wife did not agree with him. Other couples said they understood his wish to "bury the parents" but tried to explain to him why this would not "work." They said that they could not in good conscience falsify the facts, that it would be easier for them to help a child face and accept the facts behind his placement than to live with a lie. Some parents said they felt that "truth will out" anyway, that as the child got older and learned more about the frequent association between illegitimacy and adoption, he would begin to wonder if his adoptive parents had been entirely truthful with him. All of the parents in the group indicated they felt they could not comfortably repeat an earlier falsification, nor did they wish to jeopardize their relationship with the child by admitting they had lied originally to protect him.

The group leader always encouraged the participants to talk about why it would be difficult for them to bring up the subject of adoption with their child. Usually it turned out that their difficulty was closely related to their feelings about the child's out-of-wedlock birth. As one participant expressed it: "It's hard enough to talk to a child about sex without having to talk about birth out of wedlock." Some parents tried to reassure themselves that out-of-wedlock birth would have no stigma by the time their children were old enough to ask questions.

The leader would then encourage the participants to discuss their feelings about illegitimacy in general, how these feelings were affecting their feeling about the natural mother of their child, and what other feelings they had about this "unknown" (as far as they were concerned) woman or girl. The reactions were as varied as the personalities of the participants. There was usually at least one parent who said the mother "didn't care" that she had "dumped the baby with the welfare." This was always countered by others with compassion—"She will always remember," "The birthday will be terrible for her," "She tried to give the baby what she couldn't give by herself—a family."

When the discussion revealed the parents' negative feelings about unmarried mothers and even some fear that their adopted children might become as "irresponsible" as the women who bore them, the group leader would ask the parents why they themselves had come to the agency and then would try to help them see that an unmarried mother who has released her baby to an agency for adoption has shown the same sort of responsible concern for the child's future as has the couple who has come to a social agency to secure a child for adoption. When the group leader asked what kind of information about the mother of their child might be helpful to them, the parents would usually respond that they did not want to know very much.

While the major part of both meetings was spent discussing the effects of adoption on the parent-child relationship, the group leader would always make a point of bringing the discussion around to the danger of overemphasizing the fact of adoption both in the parents' direct dealings with the child and in their search for causes of whatever behavior difficulties may arise.

The leader always closed the second meeting by expressing the agency's belief in the ability of adoptive families to become closely knit, loving families.

Because only two postplacement meetings were held with each group, we did not attempt to do anything more in these meetings than to raise questions and to help adoptive parents talk about them together so that they might become more comfortable in their new parental role.

After nine series of meetings, we sent a letter and a questionnaire to the 44 couples who had attended them in an attempt to evaluate the program. The couples were not asked to sign the questionnaire. The letter explained that the meetings had grown out of the agency's desire to help the parents discuss problems of concern to all of them. Thirty of the couples filled out and returned the questionnaires.

Parents' Opinions

The following is a list of the questions with a summary of the parents' responses:

1. We did (or did not) find the postplacement group meeting helpful—21, did; 7, did not; 2, "somewhat helpful."
2. Did the meeting evoke any new questions in your minds concerning adoption? If yes, what are they?—1, yes; 25, no; 4 returns showed no response to this question. A specific question was not mentioned.
3. Did you find the subject matter stimulating?—14, yes; repetitive?—5, yes; moderately interesting?—7, yes; not pertinent?—2, yes; a waste of time?—none; no response—2.
4. Did the questions raised cause you to worry? If yes, which ones?—1, yes; 28, no; 1, no response. (The respondent who answered "yes" did not explain.)
5. Please check which, if any, of the following subjects seemed appropriate to your present experience and worth talking over in a group: (a) Adjustments involved in becoming a parent—7; (b) difference between adoptive and biological parenthood—4; (c) helping a child to an acceptance and understanding of his adoptive status—23; (d) adoptive parents' feelings toward child's biological parents—5; (e) adoptive parents' feeling about illegitimacy—3; (f) sharing knowledge of child's adoption with outsiders—12.
6. Did you feel free to express your opinions and feelings at the meetings? —26, yes; 4, no response.

Twenty couples offered suggestions of topics they would like to discuss in future meetings. Most frequently mentioned was the desire to speak with a couple who had been adoptive parents for some time.

The four caseworkers who conducted the meetings regarded them as varying in their effectiveness. In some of the sessions, the discussion was very lively; in others, the leader was hard put to stimulate any kind of discussion. In general, we found that couples whose ages and family situations were analogous and whose adoptive children were of similar ages seemed to have more to say to each other than to couples whose family situations were markedly different from their own. We found, too, that the couples were often more interested in exchanging pictures of and pleasant anecdotes about their children than in thinking out loud about the problematic and emotional aspects of adoption. Several parents said at the meetings that the problems seemed "so far in the future" that they found it difficult to theorize about how they would meet them when and if they occurred.

Nevertheless, the answers to the questionnaire showed that 23 of the 30 responding couples found topic 5c—helping a child to an acceptance and understanding of his adoptive status—the most "appropriate to their present experience and worth talking over in a group." This, of course, is the crux of the problem.

What of the 14 couples who did not answer? Since we did not require the returns to be signed, we have no way of knowing who responded and who did not. Perhaps in some instances the questionnaire was not received because of changes of address. For the majority of those who did not respond, however, one or the other, or both, of the following assumptions may apply:

1. The couple was reluctant to indicate a negative response and, therefore, did not reply.
2. The child seems to have become so much a part of the adoptive family that the parents have not wanted to be reminded of the adoptive status.

In either case, it is difficult if not impossible to tell whether the meetings were of value to these couples.

Some of the agency's caseworkers who have not been directly involved in the group meetings have expressed some skepticism about their value. They have not relished the possibility of being exposed to criticism from a group of parents who by and large have resisted their efforts to be of service in individual interviews. The agency has, however, come to the conclusion that it is better to help adoptive parents in a group situation than in a one-to-one relationship. It is, therefore, continuing to carry on group meetings, and at the same time it is seeking ways to improve its service to adoptive parents through a combination of individual and group approaches.

Chapter 18: Children and Parents

56. ADOLESCENT PROBLEMS: SYMPTOMS OF FAMILY DYSFUNCTION

Rae B. Weiner

§ The adolescent launches himself into development toward maturity from the family situation in which he has been living. In some poorly adjusted families, a child is often made a scapegoat for the family's ills, and in time accepts the role. This article illustrates one such situation and shows how casework treatment with the entire family helped the family members to readjust roles and free the child for a normal adolescence.

It is known that family maturational tasks arising out of the necessity to make major shifts—from the early years of marriage to the child-bearing years, for example—frequently become transitional crises. This paper deals specifically with one such critical period: a child's entering adolescence. I plan to describe this period in the framework of the family; to discuss family treatment as a method that can be used when difficulties relate to adolescents; and to outline the processes involved in selecting and applying this treatment method.

When a family applies for help in coping with the behavior of an adolescent, we can agree that the adolescent is a problem. We can view his behavior primarily as the representation of a problem in individual adjustment or primarily as a reaction to parental handling. The first opinion would lead us to focus treatment on the adolescent; the latter, on the parents. A shift from this traditional way of thinking is evident, however, when we view the adolescent's behavior as only the most obvious symptom of a disorder in the family's life—the mother, the

SOURCE: *Social Casework*, 47 (June, 1966), 373–77. Reprinted by permission of the publisher and the author.

Rae B. Weiner is a caseworker, Family Service of Delaware County, Media, Pennsylvania. Her paper was presented at the Biennial Meeting of the Family Service Association of America held in Detroit, Michigan, November 10–13, 1965.

father, the designated client, and the "well" siblings all being involved in a shared psychopathology.

The Maturational Process of Adolescence

Adolescence is generally described as a critical phase in growth, a period when there is eruption into consciousness of the unresolved problems of the earlier phases of development. It is a time of physiological changes, of preoccupation with one's body and physical attributes, and of an emerging sex drive. The specific task of the adolescent is to become self-governing and to achieve a firm sense of self. He must stabilize his identification with his family and build a personal identification uniquely his own.

The adolescent does not move consistently forward as he endeavors to accomplish this task. He vacillates between being a child and being an adult. He is buffeted by confusions stemming from his conscious strivings for independence coupled with his unconscious need to maintain dependence on his family. His inner turmoil manifests itself in erratic social behavior, in mood swings, in vacillating moral standards, in poor impulse control, and in shifting concepts of himself and the world around him. The adolescent needs help from his family in his growth toward maturity, for it is the family that must provide the setting in which he can ultimately resolve his struggle in a positive way. The appropriate environment can only be successfully achieved when the parents themselves have resolved their own identity crises, when they have been able to separate from their own parents, and when they have assumed the parenting role from the time of the child's birth, unencumbered by unresolved problems from their own past. The daily bombardment of the adolescent's behavior, a reawakening for the parents of the pain experienced during their own adolescence, the threatened loss in parental status as the child becomes, in a sense, a rival to them—these experiences are not easily tolerated under any circumstances. In a healthy situation, however, the family can take such pressures in its stride; it will not be devastated by them or feel faced with extinction.

The Rationale of Family Treatment

Contrast this kind of situation with what happens in a disordered family, one that cannot tolerate growth and individuation in the family members. In a disordered family, separation of the generations is lacking; children are cast in the role of parents, and parents see themselves as children; immature symbiotic attachments of parents to children and parents to grandparents persist. Such parents cannot see their children as they really are, but project onto them their own hurts, longings, and distress, stemming from earlier experiences with their own families.

Such families operate by certain rules that are not easily broken and are enforced by the implied threat of abandonment or loss of love. Such families require a scapegoat, someone who will sacrifice his autonomy in order to fill the gaps and the voids in the past lives of the parents or in the parents' marital relationship, to conform to the parents' preconceived idea of what he should be, or to preserve the parents' stability. The reasons for which a particular child is chosen for this role are not always clear. They may be related to the time in the family's life when the child was born, to the pressures to which the parents are currently subjected, or to the roles the family assigns to the different children— like "the good one," "the smart one," or "the wild one." When the role of scapegoat is imposed on a child, which may be at birth or even before, he is helpless and dependent and unable to fight back. As time goes on, there is a shift: The child is no longer only a victim; he becomes a half-willing partner. Certain benefits may come to him because he is the scapegoat. For example, in a situation in which the parents have resigned themselves to an unhappy marriage, one of the parents may over-invest himself emotionally in the child. No one outside the family offers the child so much gratification as the parent does. This ties the child to the family; it ensures his not looking outside for a love object. Another benefit may be that he receives mothering. If his symptoms are severe enough, he may get the attention he would never have obtained otherwise. It is not real mothering that he receives; it is more a promise, but it is enough to keep him tied, in the hope that at some future time he may be given more.

When the child who is the scapegoat reaches adolescence, he, like any other adolescent, struggles to grow. He is immediately disadvantaged, however, because he is burdened with special unresolved problems. In addition, the family cannot support his strivings. The family has been able to function through the years through the scapegoating of this child. His separation from the family group would tip the balance and reveal the underlying pathology in the family. Thus, the changing situation is seen by the family members as a threat rather than an enhancement, and in its anxiety the family seeks to reinforce the scapegoat relationship. In the adolescent himself the striving toward maturity produces guilt. It is true that the role he plays in the family is painful to him; however, by then he, too, has a stake in maintaining the family system, and he offers himself as a sacrifice to protect the family equilibrium.

It follows that, to be most helpful to the family, the worker will have to treat *not* the adolescent *alone* but the whole family. The entire family system is disordered, and it is with this interpersonal organization that the caseworker must endeavor to establish a relationship. His task is to look at the over-all balance of the family; to explore directly the intra-familial interaction; to understand its patterning, roots, and dynamics;

to help the family members recognize the reciprocal nature of the inter-action—all toward the goal of improving the adjustment and health of all the family members. With this as a frame of reference, how do we embark on helping in this way, and how can we select families for whom this method is appropriate? From my experience, family interviews are suitable in any situation in which the problem manifested by the adoles-cent seems related to the transactional patterns of the family. The follow-ing case is an example.

Mr. and Mrs. K applied for help in behalf of their son Gary, aged seventeen, who showed aggressive and sometimes violent behavior toward his parents and two younger siblings. The boy, a high school senior, was an outstanding student, determined to win a scholarship so that he could attend college. He was not a problem in school, nor had he ever been in trouble in the community. In the family, however, he was completely out of control. He tried to dominate everyone; he provoked arguments at every opportunity; and when he felt threatened in any way, he would lash out, hit his parents, attack his brother and sister, and become for a time like "a madman." The parents said that the physical attacks had been going on for a long time; they explained that now that Gary was growing up they were afraid he would hurt someone seriously.

In the first interview with the parents, the worker observed that they seemed animated only when they were describing Gary's behavior. Other-wise, they seemed depressed and defeated. They described themselves as "good parents" who had tried their best to cope with a difficult son, without success. They both said that Gary had been a problem since birth. He was "a pest," who always wanted his own way, while ignoring the rights of everyone else. His mother could never control him successfully. His father managed him by beating him. Now this method no longer worked, for Gary was big and strong and quite capable of hitting back. Mr. K. had suffered a heart attack several years previously, and he had no strength to endure such scenes.

The family was in financial straits, not only because of Mr. K.'s heart attack but also because he had never been able to earn a living. He blamed this, rather defensively, on "hard luck." He saw himself as a failure, and his own feelings about himself were reinforced by Gary, who held him in contempt and regularly told him so. Mrs. K. was also distressed about her husband's lack of success. She had given up saying much about it directly; instead, she talked about the shabby appearance of the house. The K's tended to pass over the problems between them, stating they would get along "like any other couple" if only Gary would behave and not upset them so much. The K's described their other two children in positive terms. They had minor faults, not to be compared with Gary's. Judy, fourteen years of age, was nervous "because of Gary" and required medication. Jim, twelve years of age, was clearly the preferred child of both parents. He was not intimidated by Gary, and when everyone else felt helpless against Gary's onslaught, Jim would still fight him. The K's stated proudly: "Jim will probably be a district attorney; he has such a gift of gab."

From the first interview the worker had clues that Gary's aggressive behavior was closely interwoven with the family pathology. He questioned why the parents had finally come for help with a problem they said had existed since Gary's birth. Their fear that he could hurt someone because he was seventeen did not seem a valid reason. Perhaps the real reason lay closer to the fact that, as a high school senior desperately trying to win a scholarship, Gary might soon leave his home. Why should this disturb the family? Other questions had to be considered. Could it be that Gary's behavior served a purpose for the family? What purpose did it serve? Without Gary's behavior, would the problems in the marriage or the father's failure as a breadwinner come into sharper focus? Was Gary really going to be able to win a scholarship and leave the family, or was he trying to create a situation that would prevent his leaving the home, perhaps by provoking his parents to request legal action against him? What gratification did Gary derive from his behavior? Did he succeed in getting his mother's undivided attention? Did he want to continue a possible homosexual gratification in his father's beatings? What was the adjustment of the younger children? Was Jim really well adjusted, or had he adjusted well to a pathological family system? Was Judy reacting only to Gary, or was she suffering other stresses?

The interview with the parents revealed that everyone in the family was in some kind of trouble, that all were suffering in some way. No family member was untouched or standing on the outside looking in; all were enmeshed, entangled, and involved in their own internal problems and with each other. The significance of the family interaction had to be pointed out to the parents in the initial interview so that they would understand the necessity for holding a conjoint family interview to explore the appropriateness of family treatment.

It has been my experience that a family usually agrees to a suggestion of a family interview. Parents will say, as the K's said, that they are willing to do anything if it will help their child. Prior to the interview, however, someone in the family often telephones the worker to explain that some complication prevents the family from keeping the appointment: the adolescent will not come; one of the other children has too much homework; the husband must work late. This first struggle is an indication of the deep anxiety the family members have about revealing what is really operating in their situation. It is often helpful, at this time, for a worker to suggest another interview with the parents to help allay some of the anxiety. Most families will agree to at least one conjoint family interview, if they can be reassured regarding the handling of the exposure of their problems.

Casework Method in the Family Interview

In the interview with the family, the worker explores and clarifies the nature and sources of family difficulty. He hopes to get the family members to agree that there are more problems inherent in their situation than just those of the adolescent about whom they came to the agency. A direct or verbal acceptance of the worker's approach is not necessarily asked for, although it may be requested in some situations.

It is more important for the worker to engage the family in discussing areas of family functioning not directly related to the presenting problem. Were he to start the interview by dwelling on the adolescent, a situation would undoubtedly develop in which the parents would turn to the youngster and say, in effect, "Talk! This is your chance to present your viewpoint." The adolescent might well respond, "You talk. You brought me." The parents could then launch an attack on the adolescent, with siblings joining in. On the other hand, if the adolescent should talk and attack the parents in any way, they could turn to the worker and say, "See, what did we tell you! See how he treats us."

Questions should be phrased in general terms: "Tell me about yourselves. What is your family like?" A question may be directed to the group, or if no one answers, to a particular person. There may follow other questions, such as, "Who is the boss in the family? How do you settle a fight?" Immediately, as the family members struggle to answer the questions, there are interruptions, disputes, and reactions. Often, for the first time, family members begin to have an awareness of how others in the family see them, which may be very different from the way in which they see themselves. Sometimes the worker may ask for a history of the marriage or the past life of the parents. Children may hear facts they have never heard before; secrets may be revealed. The "gospel truth" is not important at this time. In continuing interviews there will be many opportunities to check and recheck the facts. What is important is that the worker open up areas for discussion that will lead to an understanding of the problems in the family and begin to uncover the deeper psychological elements that are operating to keep all the family members bound in conflictive relationships.

In the K case the interview with the family revealed that the parents felt deep disappointment in the marriage; that they had early accepted the lacks in their relationship and that, from his birth, Mrs. K. had dedicated her life to making Gary happy and was deeply distressed by the fact that he had never appreciated her efforts. The worker learned that Gary, like his parents, had no friends. After school he came home, and all his energy seemed to be discharged in compulsive attention to schoolwork and in arguments with the family. Mr. K, too, came home directly from work. He had a hobby related to clipping and organizing crossword puzzles into book form, an activity that took all his attention and interest. The K's had no form of recreation together. They led a dead existence, enlivened only by Gary's violent behavior.

Other areas of interaction were noted. The worker observed, for example, that Jim took a parental role toward his parents. He comforted and supported them and attacked Gary for them. During the interview he spoke for them. The worker learned also that the relationship between Judy and Gary was not such as the parents described it to be— that Gary often helped Judy with her schoolwork. The anger between them seemed to be related to the issue of who would be allowed to use the desk in the parents' room, which was the one room that afforded protection from noise and interruptions. This explanation led to additional information: that there was no privacy in the family, that everyone was in and out of everyone else's room.

In the discussion, a somewhat dramatic reference was made to the fact that Gary did not seem to fit into the family—that he was not like anyone else. Gary raised the question whether he was actually his father's son. He said he doubted it because his father beat him so severely he was covered with scars. The father did not reply to Gary's question, but he became defensive and suggested that Gary had probably arranged for someone else to beat him to make the father "look bad."

In the process of treating such family groups, the worker observes the family carefully. He listens to the interchange between the family members. He may bring what he sees and hears to their attention. He offers help to all the family members, assessing at the same time whether they can recognize their need for help. He uses the immediate, ongoing transactions as the starting point of his observations. There are many patterns of response from different families. Some families are intellectual and reasonable, and everyone seems to have remarkable insight into the family's interaction. Some are entirely out of control, rife with fights, accusations, and counteraccusations. In some instances the parents are willing to come to the sessions, whereas the children grumble and complain. If the worker takes at face value what he sees, he may be misled. He must always question whether the behavior, no matter what it is, serves a purpose for the family as a whole. He should try to determine whether it is the family's way of warding him off or, perhaps, swallowing him up. He should try to discover whether the family's behavior in the interview is similar to its behavior in other situations with "outsiders." The worker's subjective experience with the family is an important lever that can be used throughout the treatment process.

It may be that after a first family interview the worker will decide that a particular family cannot continue with ongoing conjoint family interviews. The current constellation of the family, the system of defenses, or the family's motivation may require other treatment methods.

Once the decision is made by the worker and the family to continue family sessions, the intensive phase of family treatment begins. In this phase of treatment the worker helps the family understand and work through current destructive agreements and the unresolved problems of the past that interfere with present functioning. The techniques used by the worker vary, depending on the needs of the particular family.

Reactions to Treatment

Without going into a detailed discussion of the treatment process, one fact is important to note. When family treatment has begun to be effective, the problems of the designated client, which were the exclusive preoccupation of the family when it came to the agency, begin to recede. At times during this period—when new issues arise, when destructive patterns are uncovered, when projections are revealed, and when connections are made between past and present behavior—it is not uncommon for the family in its anxiety to try to focus back on the adolescent. Sometimes the adolescent will say in the family's behalf that he does not think family treatment is helpful, that his problems have nothing to do with the family. At times, if the children feel the parents are suffering as they deal with their own unresolved past, the adolescent or his siblings may develop new symptoms or act out outside the sessions to "save" the parents.

In general, however, as the family members become involved in the the treatment process—as they learn to become aware of their behavior and to communicate with each other in a more meaningful way, as they begin to take on their appropriate roles—old forms of gratification no longer satisfy them. They begin to find new ways of relating to each other, new ways of living together—ways that maintain the family unity and still allow individualization of the members. The adolescent can begin to achieve freedom from parental authority with a minimum degree of emotional tension. He can begin to establish his own identity. His expanded ego can enable him to cope with the various pressures inherent in his current situation, and he will be able to take the first step toward becoming a mature adult.

57. SHIFTING PATTERNS OF AFFECTION: TRANSITIONAL FIGURES

R. V. Heckel

§ Adolescents normally make the transition from childhood dependence on parents to adult independence by transferring affection from parents to a series of intermediary adults before forming an adult love relationship that leads to marriage. Some adolescents are unable to make the transition; some attach themselves to deviant persons. When the transitional persons are well adjusted themselves, the development of the adolescent proceeds smoothly.

All those who deal with the developmental aspects of affectional behavior have recognized the necessary turning outward from the family in normal development for mature fulfillment of these needs.

Also recognized has been the transitional nature of this response. It has never been regarded as a simple switching from parental attachments to an adult love relationship.

Ausubel (1) describes and discusses the transitional social sex role which occurs in normal adolescent development, but he confines his discussion to describing expected roles and the social pressures which force both males and females to follow them.

Mead (2) describes the training offered to the young in other cultures by persons outside the primary family group (mother, father, siblings). This training was described as occurring on a formalized basis prescribed by the culture. There was no attempt to draw parallels to our culture where such interaction occurs in the development of extra-familial affectional behavior, though on an informal basis. Other writers have indicated the universality in normals of the outward directing of affectional impulses in adolescence, but they have not described the transitional persons who serve as catalytic agents in the shifting of affection from the family to the peer group.

This paper is a summary of observations on a series of individuals, both normals and patients, and their affectional patterns during child-

SOURCE: *Mental Hygiene*, 48 (July, 1964), 451–54. Reprinted by permission of the publisher and the author.

Dr. Heckel is co-ordinator, Research and Training, Psychology Service, Veterans Administration Hospital, Augusta, Ga.

hood, adolescence and early adulthood. The article will also deal with perhaps the most important and least understood shifts which take place in development. This is important to both parents and their offspring. It occurs when there is a shifting from the primary source of love and affection—parents—to other figures in the environment. Characteristically, in normal development this movement is away from parents as love objects to other environmental figures—both male and female— around them. In some cases this transition may occur as early as childhood. When it occurs in this period, the shift continues for a long period, in which initially peripheral figures are perceived to take on some of the characteristics and roles of the parents, even if for very brief periods of time.[1]

For example, the child may spend the night or several days with relatives or close friends who will be permitted to fulfill all the roles normally carried out by the parent. Active play during this period also takes on the character of "trying on" a more advanced personal role for the child.

Sometimes the shift is not gradual and young persons are observed to make what appears to be a sudden and often traumatic (for both the parent and himself) separation from the primary family constellation.

Evaluation of families in which this has occurred reveals that two factors have occurred: First, the young person has implicitly acted out through fantasy, play and, in some cases, constructive planning, a new role for himself which his family could not or would not tolerate. Thus, a gradual separation was not possible. This required that the break be sudden or not at all.

Since the movement from the primary family constellation represents only a phase in the total emergence of the mature adult personality pattern, it too is subject to distortions and the fixating of behavior at this level. For those who have sought out transitional figures of the same sex, such arrestation may lead to homosexual behavioral manifestations and consequent rejection of the typical male role.

Another, very tentative in his interactions, may fear to go beyond this dependency on a transitional figure and thus he becomes one of a familiar and well-identified type in the American culture—the adult individual who is attached to a married family as a friend, who associates closely with the family unit, serves as a companion when the oppositely sexed family member is out of town, is the person invited as a date or escort at parties and functions when someone needs an extra partner but who lacks sufficient ego strength to establish a marriage or home of his own.

[1] Unlike introjection and identification wherein the child, adolescent or young adult takes on the behaviors or values of the peripheral figure, with transitional figures, these values and behaviors are projected onto or perceived in them.

Fortunately, for the majority of persons this aspect of their development does not represent a terminal point. It is an anxiety-reducing introduction into the extrafamilial world. It is also a safe medium for the transferring of strong affectional needs away from the parent. This occurs before these persons feel sufficiently mature, secure and self-assured in being able to convey these feelings to an intended mate.

No attempt will be made here to deal in detail with those abnormal aspects of development in which the child may not make or is not permitted to make a separation from the primary family constellation, nor will it attempt to deal with other semisymbiotic relationships and ties which may prevent a more global affectional pattern on an extrafamilial basis.

It is possible to take a strictly analytic viewpoint and speak of early affectional sources as developing from the oedipal relationship or, if preferred, it is possible to speak in more general terms regarding the positive love relationship which a child may have with the parent of the opposite sex. The theoretical orientation does not appear to be crucial to the description of the complex love relationships which are a part of the family group and should not affect the discussion of transitional figures.

It is generally agreed that in the normal development of the child there is an affectional bond built up between the child and one or both parents. As part of growing up, these relationships undergo change. It is necessary for the individual to shift away from the family to other affectional sources in the environment who can more nearly satisfy his needs, which are developing and partially unfilled.

In cases where *all* affectional needs are met, the child probably would not turn away from the home to other figures; rather he would be content to remain in this more primitive state of emotional development.

But what of the figures to whom these children turn in adolescence when they leave the secure (in the cases of normal children) or affectionally distorted (in the case of disturbed individuals) relationships and seek other sources of gratification?

The term chosen to describe this individual is that of transitional figure. This has been done because rarely, if ever, is affection transferred from the primary family constellation to a love object who is accessible for the more dramatic and independent role of love, marriage, and complete independence of the family, except in cases of a traumatic shifting of affectional sources.

More characteristic is the transfer of affection to an intermediary figure. An example is to be found in the transfer of affections away from the mother to the teacher by students who see her not only as a mother figure but as a love object as well. She is external to the home, in frequent and close proximity, yet she is nearly as inaccessible as the mother.

This is perhaps more dramatically brought out in observing teenagers in their relationships with married persons of the opposite sex with whom they share a great deal on a nonsexual or emotional basis. In general, the individual chosen is sufficiently older than the teenager so that many of the possible complexities and potential for acting out are obviated. There can, however, develop quite complex and traumatic situations if the figure chosen for this transitional stage is not sufficiently mature to handle the attachment which has developed.

In the community there are a number of individuals with whom this transition is made quite easily. Both male and female, they are active in providing a strong source of identification in some cases, or in serving as a love object for the young person. In most instances these men and women who attract young persons to them are warm, outgoing, emotionally healthy individuals who, because of a lack of children of their own, the fact that their children are grown, or based on the need to be of service to others, devote a portion of their time to young persons in the community around them. They tend also to possess some of the characteristics of the parent and other characteristics which make them unique, exciting and interesting. They also appear to be sufficiently mature, in most instances, to be able to maintain the emotional distance that is required by the young person if he is to feel safe and secure.

There are other instances where young persons have turned, because of emotional distortions in their development, to less healthy figures. These are adult individuals who act out needs through their contacts with young persons. In many instances these persons are sought out by young persons seeking support for their hostile and asocial impulses.

These impulses cannot be easily acted out with or in the presence of healthy individuals, either in their own age group or with those who play the role of transitional figures.

The negative transitional figures, having many unresolved problems of their own, consciously or unconsciously attract to themselves the young person who is uncertain in his identification and unsure of the acceptability of his patterns of behavior.

It is characteristic of disturbed young persons that they seek out transitional figures of the same sex. This is done because of the unresolved conflicts they have experienced in the realm of identification and in the establishing of their basic sexual role. This is not a manifestation of recent trauma or difficulties; rather, it is evidence of a process having its inception in the very earliest years of life.

In effect, these persons are functioning on a pre-oedipal level in their feelings and are seeking to establish a basic relationship which was lacking in their home. Unfortunately, their needs for identification, affection and attention from an older person make them much more vulnerable to seduction or exploitation by older individuals.

Many learn that their rewards from older persons come from either acting out or behaving like some of the more poorly adjusted adults they have turned to for this relationship. They are not able to make the more mature contact with transitional figures which other, more healthy young persons have made.

In normals, the movement of affectional needs to transitional figures may not always provide a smooth and easy course of action. Many young persons, in discussing these attachments, describe feelings of acute (but temporary) depression and hopelessness. However, it is this very hopelessness of their feelings of affection and attachment for the unattainable person—the teacher, the older married woman or man down the street—that permits them to serve this transitional purpose. It is not totally unlike the hopelessness of marrying the parent but it does contain the turning outward of the emotional need and a seeking for avenues of expression for emotional needs with others.

The inherent danger in these behaviors is small because were the transitional figure to attempt to use this attachment for purposes of seducing the young person or otherwise distorting this relationship, the original defensive need for establishing the relationship would be destroyed and the young person, except in instances where a serious emotional need or deficiency exists, would, and has, fled from the more intimate level of interaction.

Summary

This article attempted to shed light on one aspect of the developing of social behavior which is seen to occur in normal development, the use of a transitional figure on whom to center affectional needs prior to their emergence in an adult pattern. Some distortions of this pattern were described and discussed.

References

1. AUSUBEL, D. P., *Theory and Problems of Adolescent Development* (New York: Grune & Stratton, Inc., 1954).
2. MEAD, MARGARET, *Male and Female: A Study of the Sexes in a Changing World* (New York: William Morrow & Co., Inc., 1949).

58. CHILDREN OF WORKING MOTHERS

Elizabeth Herzog

§ This article gives a competent summary of the situation of employed mothers and of the care they provide for their children. The increasing percentage of mothers of small children who are employed has brought into sharp focus the effect of employment on children and the need to evaluate provisions for the care of children. The findings of numerous research projects in this area are presented in succinct fashion.

Effects on Children and Families

A working mother's children and family life are affected by her absence while she works, by the accommodations she makes in child rearing and homemaking to the fact of her absence (including arrangements for child care), by the effects on her—physical and psychological—of carrying two jobs, and by the fact that she is augmenting the family income. To say that her working makes a difference, however, does not tell the nature, degree, or consequences of that difference.

It is appropriate, then, to raise the question: What do we know about the social and psychological effects on children and families of the mother's employment outside the home?

This question has often been asked as if any effects discovered are bound to be crucial and unfavorable. We are learning, however, to ask: Are they major or minor; are they favorable, unfavorable, mixed or neutral? We are also tending more and more to recognize that the effects will be different for different kinds of mothers, children, and families; and that "different kinds" may refer to age, income, individual temperament, social setting, and a number of other variables.

· · · · ·

Effects on Preschool Children (Psychological and Emotional)

To begin with, it is usually assumed—and this assumption is not challenged by any studies we have found—that a loving mother who wants to take care of her own child and is reasonably well equipped to do so is likely to be the best caretaker, especially in the early years. Moreover, for such a mother to be with her children when they are very young

SOURCE: Children's Bureau, No. 382 (Washington, D.C., 1960), pp. 16–31.
The author's background is given in the footnote for article 31.

533

is a profound gratification and to be separated from them a profound deprivation. We have seen, in fact, that most mothers of young children are not in the labor force. Our figures make it clear that *most* mothers of preschool children do not work unless they feel compelled to do so. However, it is no secret that some mothers are not loving, and some who are not do not want to devote themselves exclusively to infant or child care. There is a strong and growing conviction among psychiatrists and social workers that some women are better mothers if their mothering activities are part time rather than full time; and that their children may suffer adverse effects if the mother is constrained *not* to work. This belief merits research investigation. We also know all too well that some mothers are forced by circumstances to entrust their children to the care of others for the working hours of the day; and that, whether by preference or by necessity, a growing proportion of mothers of young children are in the labor force. What, then, of their children?

Our evidence suggests:

That the effects of being apart from the mother during work hours are not to be equated with the effects of losing her entirely.

That the effects of care by warm and friendly adults, in addition to their own mothers, are probably not as damaging to most infants and very young children as is often assumed—*if* the care provided for the children is adapted to their needs. To spell out the requirements for meeting their needs is beyond the scope of this paper. It is generally agreed, for example, that the needs of very young children cannot be met adequately if one adult is responsible for more than a small number of children.

There is among many who work with children a strong conviction that it is damaging to an infant or a very young child to have more than one "mother figure" at a time, or in sequence. This principle has been challenged by some anthropologists who point to the frequency of "assistant mothers" in primitive societies, and the absence of evidence that children, or the adults they become, are harmed by it. Mothers often leave children to be cared for by other adults or older children, while they work in the fields. Since the custom is universal in the groups that practice it, say the anthropologists, one would have to conclude either that the society itself is "sick" or that the children survive the mother's daily absence without perceptible damage.

According to Margaret Mead, "anthropological evidence gives no support at present to the value of such an accentuation of the tie between mother and child (as occurs in the United States). On the contrary, cross-cultural studies suggest that adjustment is most facilitated if the child is cared for by many warm friendly people."[1]

Who the people are and how the child is cared for are obviously

[1] Mead, 1954.

crucial considerations. The one point to be made here is that the belief in a child's need for care *only* by his own mother or by one constant surrogate mother—like so many other beliefs—appears to be a cultural rather than a universal human belief.

Even in occidental culture, the insistence on this need is recent and far from universal. The "nannie" or governess raised a great many children in Europe and the United States. A good many solid American citizens have also been the children of working mothers. Possibly the constant care of a loving mother would have been better for these and possible some were maladjusted who otherwise might not have been. However, this kind of experience raises questions about the prevailing harmfulness of having young children cared for part of the time by others in addition to the mother.

A salient concern among child-care workers has been lest early separation of the child from his mother should inflict irreversible damage on his general development and especially on his capacity for interpersonal relations. To some extent this concern has been stimulated by oversimplification of the conclusions Bowlby drew from his compilation of studies relating to maternal deprivation.[2] Subsequent studies have shown the damage caused by maternal deprivation to be less frequent, and less permanent when it occurred, than many had believed.[3] More important for our purposes, however, our evidence offers no basis for believing that the sweeping and often traumatic maternal deprivation to which he gave major attention is equivalent to separation during the working hours of the day and return to the parents at night.

A number of studies indicate that separation from the mother during part of the day is not *in itself* necessarily damaging to the child.[4] That the impact will be different for different children goes without saying; and that it will be conditioned by the kind of care the child receives during this period. According to the Children's Bureau study, 121,000 preschool children whose mothers worked full time were given group care during her work hours (as of 1958). What we do not know is the *quality* of that care, and how much—if at all—it differs for children in different economic groups. We also lack any over-all picture of the quality of care given by relatives, neighbors, and others. We do know something about those daytime foster homes that are licensed—but many day-care arrangements are made informally and individually without agency assistance. As I have already explained, I cannot even begin to discuss this large question of daytime care. I must comment, however, that its quality is crucial and we know too little about it.

Assuming that the substitute care is adequate—and this is a large

[2] Bowlby, 1952.   [3] Bowlby *et al.*, 1956.
[4] A few relevant studies are: Rabin, 1958; Glass, 1949; Simonson, 1947; Heinicke, 1956. See also Rheingold and Bayley, 1959; Maccoby, 1958; Lewis, 1954.

assumption—the impact on the child of his mother's working is likely to be influenced by the attitudes and practices of the community in which he lives, especially as he grows older. If it is usual for mothers to go to work, he is probably more likely to accept the daily absence as a fact of life than if his mother is the exception among those he knows. The impact is also likely to be influenced, as he grows older, by his perception of her reasons for working, by her own attitude and that of the father toward her working, and by her devices for counteracting the sense of separation. These in turn depend on a number of other factors, among which the personality of the mother is paramount.

No studies have been found directly relating to the effects of care of very young children at home or in another family while the mother works. However, we do have a large body of evidence about the kind of care that is helpful or harmful to any child, whether his mother works or not. Wherever the child is cared for, he needs warm and consistent supervision that is in keeping with the developmental needs of his age.

It is unfortunately true that in our society, with its increasing tendency to small family units, including parents and children but not grandparents or other relatives, the middle-income mother may find it easier than the low-income mother to arrange for adequate substitute care. True, extended households are more common among the low-income groups than in the middle- or upper-income levels. Nevertheless, the glib statement that supervision is crucial (a statement to which I shall return later) may be as useless to some low-income working mothers as a physician's advice to go south for a 6-month rest.

A number of studies have attempted to investigate the extent to which the fact of the mother's working outside the home is related to various aspects of child adjustment and behavior.

One of these studies, which deals with preschool children, is an investigation into the effect of maternal employment on the child's dependency. As the authors explain, "it seemed reasonable to believe that if maternal employment is indeed a significant factor in the constellation of psychological and social factors which provide a background for the mother-child relation and thus for personality development in the young child, its implications will be greatest for the child's development with respect to dependence and independence. Development in this respect may be presumed to relate to the consistency of the care the child receives, the frequency of his contacts with the caretaker, the number of different people who assume caretaking responsibility for him, the diversity of their child-rearing techniques and the diversity of their attitudes toward the child. All of these conditions may be quite different for the child of a working mother than for the child of a full-time homemaker."[5]

[5] Siegel *et al.*, 1959; p. 534.

Using a carefully conceived and executed matched-pairs design, they failed to find significant differences between the children of working and nonworking mothers with respect to behavior related to dependence and independence. Their conclusion from their data is that "maternal employment per se is not the overwhelmingly influential factor in children's lives that some have thought it to be." They did, however, find hints that the implications of maternal employment may differ for the two sexes, and they suggest the need for further research concerning maternal employment and the process by which children become familiar with and grow into their own sex roles.

Effects on School-age Children

The finding of Siegel and her colleagues is in line with the growing evidence that identification processes are different in the two sexes.[6] Hand also found evidence that the mother's working might affect boys and girls differently. Although he discovered no significant over-all relationship between the adjustment of children of working and nonworking mothers, he found the percentage of working mothers slightly larger for maladjusted boys than for the well-adjusted boys in a group of elementary school children. The reverse was true for the girls, although neither difference was statistically significant.[7]

Two other studies have failed to find evidence that children of working mothers were less well adjusted generally than children of nonworking mothers.[8] A third shows less favorable parent-child relations among the daughters of working than of nonworking mothers.[9] However, the groups were not matched by socioeconomic status and may reflect this difference rather than the effect of the mother's working. The working mothers were probably concentrated in the low-income families; and the kinds of problems indicated by the girls are those that several investigators have found to be more characteristic of working-class than of middle-class families.[10]

With respect to school performance, the studies reviewed showed no difference between children of working and nonworking mothers, with one exception. Ivan Nye found that adolescent children of working mothers did better than the children of nonworking mothers. Here again, that obstreperous variable, socioeconomic status, raises doubt about the results. In this sample (2,350 high school students, in 3 communities) the working mothers were, on the whole, better educated than the others, and it is well established that the children of well-educated

[6] Hartley, 1959–60.   [7] Hand, 1957.   [8] Blood and Hamblin, 1958; Nye, 1958.
[9] Essig and Morgan, 1946.
[10] Bronfenbrenner, 1958; Sears *et al.*, 1957; Kohn, 1959.

parents tend to do better at school than the children of parents with less education.[11]

The most explosive topic discussed in relation to maternal employment is juvenile delinquency. A typical comment is that of an Ohio judge who announced that among juvenile delinquents, both parents are employed twice as often as in the general population, and urged that families restrict themselves to the father's income and keep the children at home. This statement, like many others, was based on cases coming before the court, with no control group to determine in what way the backgrounds of delinquent children resemble or differ from those of nondelinquents. Most adjudged delinquents come from relatively low socioeconomic groups, where—as we have seen—the proportion of working mothers is relatively high.

A much-publicized article by Sheldon and Eleanor Glueck is based on data taken from a study conducted in the 1940's [12] and reanalyzed with an eye to the working mother. The Gluecks do not say that the mother's working causes delinquency. They found, in fact, that the children of regularly employed mothers were no more likely to be delinquent than the children of nonworking mothers, but that the children of sporadically employed mothers were more likely to be delinquent. Their early study had already shown that the mothers who worked sporadically tended to be women with unfortunate family histories, tendencies to delinquent behavior, and husbands who were emotionally disturbed and had poor work habits. In other words, the delinquency of the boys is associated with the character and habits of the mothers rather than with their work status.

Maccoby has reanalyzed the reanalysis of the Gluecks' data, bringing out the real moral of their tale—namely, that the chief variable differentiating between delinquency or nondelinquency in the child appears to be the quality of supervision given to him by his mother. "If the mother remains at home but does not keep track of where her child is and what he is doing, he is far more likely to become a delinquent (within this highly selected sample) than if he is closely watched. Furthermore, if a mother who works does arrange adequate care for the child in her absence, he is not more likely to be delinquent (indeed possibly less so!) than the adequately supervised child of a mother who does not work." [13]

She goes on to point out another important lesson to be learned from the reordered data; among the working mothers, a majority did not in fact arrange adequate supervision for their children in their absence. "Thus we are reminded of the problem of obtaining good substitute care for the children of working mothers in these days of isolated nuclear

[11] Nye, 1957; 1958.   [12] Glueck, 1950; 1957.   [13] Maccoby, 1958.

families containing few grandmothers, maiden aunts, or older daughters who will assume a responsible role in child care."

Nye also found that the association between maternal employment and juvenile delinquency largely evaporated when key variables were held constant. However, although in his study the differences between children of working and nonworking mothers became statistically non-significant, a difference did remain, showing more delinquent behavior in families of employed mothers. Since the differences were all in the same direction, Nye concluded that there was in fact some connection between maternal employment and delinquency, but that it was slight and far less important than other factors. He too ascribed the difference to "less effective direct controls" by the working mother over her children.

Two studies, on the other hand, report less delinquency among the children of working than of nonworking mothers. Bandura and Walters found, in a group of middle-class boys, more working mothers among the nondelinquent than among the delinquent ones—although the numbers were too small for statistical significance.[14] And a Detroit study found, among school-age children who had case records with the police department, only one out of four whose mother worked, although among all children of this age one out of three had a working mother.[15]

Myrdal and Klein report that a study carried out in Britain has shown the rate of delinquency among children whose mothers go out to work is no higher than among those whose mothers stay at home, other conditions being equal.[16]

These and other studies seem to indicate that, when relevant variables are controlled, there is no significant association between juvenile delinquency and maternal employment per se. Despite its limitations, there is striking consistency in the evidence concerning the direct effects on children of their mothers' employment outside the home. None of the studies reviewed has shown that, when relevant factors such as socio-economic status are controlled, maladjustment and developmental or behavior problems are increased by the mother's working. The evidence is, of course, limited to the measures used by the various studies. Moreover, to demonstrate absence of perceptible ill effects is not to demonstrate the presence of beneficent effects. Current theories of child development point to the advantage—other things being equal—of having the mother in the home at least during the child's preschool years, for his sake and also for the mother's. The factfinding report of the Midcentury White House Conference on Children and Youth comments: "It may well be questioned whether most mothers can, without undue

[14] Cited by Maccoby, 1958; p. 154.   [15] Cited in Pope, 1955.
[16] Myrdal and Klein, 1956; p. 134.

strain, carry a full-time job and still give responsive and attentive care to the physical and emotional needs of small children." [17]

But other things are often not equal. And our evidence is highly relevant in situations where it is expedient, advisable, or necessary for the mother to work. The situation is, of course, defined not only by external circumstances and the mother's individual makeup but also by the child's individual needs and susceptibilities. Our studies deal with prevailing norms in groups of children and not with the individual children who may have special need to be close to or removed from their mothers.

The other sweeping generalization consistent with the studies reviewed concerns the great importance of the arrangements made for children while their mothers work. This emerged specifically in relation to two studies dealing with juvenile delinquency and is also supported by the large body of research relating to child development regardless of whether the mother works.

Effects on Family Life

Some of the evidence concerning the effects of the mother's outside employment on the family also bears directly on the child's development and adjustment, while some is more indirect in its bearing.

That so many mothers attempt the dual job of homemaking and wage earning is due to changes which have occurred during relatively recent years: the development of means for making housekeeping easier and less time consuming, earlier marriage, and longer life expectancy. Numerous youth surveys show that most girls today expect to work before marriage and perhaps until the first child is born. And statistics show an increasing tendency for women to return to the labor force either when the children enter school or when the last one leaves home.

The increased life expectancy, along with technological changes that reduce the time required for housekeeping, has resulted in a typical life cycle that contrasts dramatically with that of the average woman of years gone by. In the 1890's, according to the figures of the National Manpower Council,[18] a woman could expect to marry at about 22, bear her last child at about 32, have the last child leave home when the mother was about 55, and die at about 68. Today, the average girl marries at about 20, has her last baby before she is 30, and sees him enter school before she is 35.[19] He is likely to leave home before she is 50. After this she can look forward to an increased span of active life, since the average life expectancy of women has lengthened by about 10 years.

[17] White House Conference, 1950.
[18] National Manpower Council, 1957.   [19] SSA, 1959.

As for the dual job itself, it merits far more comment than can be given here. Our life today seems to require more of many adults than a human being should be expected to accomplish. Yet, despite the incidence of heart attacks and ulcers—more frequent among men than among women—a surprising number seem to manage. One road to feasibility for the two-job woman has been the greater sharing of homemaking responsibilities between husband and wife. A man is no longer considered a sissy if he helps with such domestic tasks as taking clothes to be machine washed, shopping, dishwashing, baby tending, etc. The change appears to be much more marked in the middle than in the lower class—perhaps because this is the typical course of change, perhaps because the working mother is more of an innovation on the higher income level than on the lower. Nevertheless, the sharing of household duties has increased also in middle-class families where the mother does not work.

Some misgivings have been expressed lest the change in husband-wife roles prove harmful for the sex identification of the children. More often, however, students of family life dwell on the positive aspects of the shift: the view of marriage as a partnership in which both members share responsibility for homemaking, child rearing and income earning. Part of this plus, under favorable circumstances, goes to the children in the form of a more responsible and functional role in the household, a more appealing view of marriage as a dynamic partnership and—for the girls—a stimulating vista of "the many lives of modern woman." [20]

A great deal needs to be learned, however, about the sex-role image imparted to children in this day of more and more working mothers. Two studies already mentioned have suggested that the impact of the mother's outside employment may be different for girls and for boys. A number of studies considered the implications of decreasing sex-role differentiation, and at this point the evidence supports only the statement that we need to know more. One suspects, however, that here again the crucial factors will be found to lie in the family climate, the quality of the marriage, and the personal makeup of the parents, rather than in the precise content of the evolving parental roles. Moreover, although there has been some convergence in specific activities, the father (when he is present) is still typically viewed as the primary breadwinner and the mother as the primary homemaker. As we have seen, the father *is* present in the majority of homes where the mother works.

There has been a good deal of concern also about the effect of maternal employment on the marital relations of the parents, which in turn affects the child's growth and development. Here again the evidence suggests that the woman's employment in itself is not a determining

[20] Gruenberg and Krech, 1952.

factor. One of our best known specialists in research on the family is quoted as saying, "Consensus of the research to date is that gainful employment of the wife is not a significant factor either in marriage success or marriage failure. It is a peg on which conflict can be hung, a socially approved area in which to disagree." [21]

On the other hand, a Detroit study found that 25 per cent of the respondents of both sexes felt that the wife's participation in the labor force "disrupts interpersonal relations" in the family and 40 per cent said that it "disrupts family life." [22]

It seems obvious that the amount of disruption would be conditioned by attitudes of the family and the working mother toward her employment. A study not yet released shows that husbands of working women are more likely to accept or actively to favor their employment than husbands of nonworking wives. A panel conducted by the YWCA showed analogous attitudes. The daughters of working mothers tended to approve the mother's outside employment, and to feel that they themselves gained by their increased responsibility in the home. The daughters of nonworking mothers held the opposite view—and were accused by the other girls of wanting their mothers to stay at home for purely selfish reasons.[23] Both studies suggest the ability of people to adjust to existing conditions—although undoubtedly the preference of husband and children affects the decision of many women to work or not to work.

Several investigators have tried to discover the kind of shifts that occur in the family power structure when the wife works, testing the hypothesis that the wife who earns money will carry more weight in decision making than the homebody wife. One of them, studying a sample of Irish Roman-Catholic families, concluded that his findings did show this to be the case.[24] Two others, using broader samples, came to the opposite conclusion: that the wife's influence in family decisions was not significantly affected by her earning power, but rested on other and more basic factors. One of them found, however, that the sharing of decisions and tasks was greater in families where the wife worked.[25] This is merely a confirmation of familiar observations and assumptions, but since so many assumptions are not confirmed it is worth mentioning one that is. The difference in findings may relate to the rather specialized sample of the dissenting study, in which the authoritarian male-dominated household is traditional.

A primary reason for accepting the mother's employment, both by husbands and by children, is the simple fact that it augments the family income. Questions have been raised about how much a working mother can contribute after the costs of her employment have been deducted

[21] Applebaum, 1952; p. 13.   [22] University of Michigan, 1957.
[23] Working mothers, 1958.   [24] Heer, 1958.
[25] Blood and Hamblin, 1958; Hoffman, 1960.

from her earnings. The questions are valid, especially for mothers who work at ill-paid employment, and most especially if the costs of adequate child care are high. There is no doubt, however, that in many two-parent homes the family income is substantially raised when the wife works. Census figures, as well as other studies and reports, bear out Feldman's statement that the wife's earnings "have materially accelerated both the steady rise in average family income and the steady rise in the number of families in the middle income group." [26]

The mother's attitude toward her own working both reflects and conditions the attitudes of her husband and children. It has often been remarked that women today are likely to feel guilty if they do work and to feel guilty (as well as faintly inferior) if they do not. Hoffman has attempted to explore the extent of the working mother's guilt feelings and their apparent effect on her child-rearing practices. She found that mothers who liked their jobs were more apt to feel guilty than those who did not; and that those who felt guilty were less likely to assign household responsibilities to their children than those who did not, and more likely to be affectionate and indulgent. However, whether the mother liked her job or not was strongly related to the kind of job it was; and the kind of job it was reflected her socioeconomic status. Pending publication of the complete report, a question remains to what extent the mother's demands on her child reflected her socioeconomic status rather than her degree of guilt.[27]

The guilt-free mothers in this study were the mothers with low status jobs. Another investigation, however, reports that lower class mothers were more anxious than upper class mothers about the effects of their working on their children.[28] The apparent conflict in evidence cannot be talked away. One is tempted to speculate, however, whether the greater anxiety of the lower class mothers had to do with their greater difficulty in arranging for adequate child care during their absence.

It is unfortunate that we have so little systematic evidence about the mothers' own view of their employment and its consequences. We do, of course, have a great deal of unsystematic evidence which suggests— as observed before—that a great many mothers feel guilty, whether they work or not. And we have the disquieting assurance from psychiatrists and family counselors that if a mother feels guilty, anxious, or uncertain about what she is doing, there are likely to be unfortunate repercussions on the child. Perhaps the greatest boon that could be given to working mothers and their children in this phase of our evolution would be freedom from anxiety and guilt. Apparently nonworking mothers need it just as much, but they are not the present topic of discussion.

We have been talking mainly about two-parent families, because these

[26] Feldman, 1958; p. 107; Blaisdell, 1958; Holmes, 1958.
[27] Hoffman, 1959.   [28] Heer, 1958.

are in the majority and are the ones most frequently involved in family research concerning maternal employment. The problems of adjusting to the mother's absence from the home are likely to be increased if there is no spouse to share responsibilities; and the responsibility carried by school-age children is more likely to become too great, unless the mother has adequate income or adequate ingenuity and stamina to prevent this.

There is sometimes an unfortunate impulse to exclude one-parent families from discussions of healthy family life. It would be unfortunate and unnecessary, however, to write off more than 2 million mothers and their children as being shut out from a healthy family life. Actually, some broken families do a good deal better than some unbroken ones in achieving healthy family life and producing well-adjusted children. Two studies, for example, have shown the emotional adjustment of children from well-functioning one-parent homes to be superior to that of children from unbroken and unhappy homes—a finding in keeping with many reports of psychiatrists and counselors.[29]

Certainly one would wish for every child a happy home with two parents in it. Since the wish is obviously vain, it is comforting to be assured by systematic investigation and professional opinion, as well as by our own observations, that there can be family health in one-parent homes.

Any thinking we do about maternal employment must take account of the rate at which change is occurring, and this is especially true in connection with effects on the family. The "quiet revolution" in women's work habits, like any revolution, involves many changes—some welcome and some unwelcome—and itself occurs in a context of change. Some changes which ultimately appear desirable may seem undesirable while we are adjusting to them. Quite aside from the effects of maternal employment, the family appears to be undergoing major changes today. Some of them relate to the shift of functions from the immediate family to the peer group, the school, and other organizations outside the home In considering such changes we can take comfort both in the infinite varieties of family function that have proved adequate for other societies and in the basic flexibility of the family in our own.

In a book based on the materials produced for the Midcentury White House Conference, the authors remark, "All the evidence points to the infinite capacity of the family to change—to change its composition, to redefine the way it shares the care of children with other social institutions—and yet to retain its over-all responsibility for them."[30] Still on the subject of change, Myrdal and Klein point out: "To combine a career with a family may be difficult at present; but it is already less so than it was 30 years ago, and it is likely to become easier as time goes on

---

[29] Landis, 1955; Nye, 1957.   [30] Witmer and Kotinsky, 1952; p. 209.

and technical efficiency increases, in particular if we set our minds to solving the problem." [31]

The review of evidence concerning the family yields less consistent results than the evidence concerning the direct effects on children of their mothers' outside employment. Yet with two exceptions, both based on slight samples, the findings reported seem to say that the quality of the family life influences the effects of a mother's outside employment more than her employment influences the quality of the family life. There are indications that the activities and responsibilities of mother and father overlap more in families where the wife works, but not that this in itself is unfavorable to family life. On the contrary, a number of signs suggests the opposite.

General Comment

All in all, the research evidence available so far suggests that the mother's working is only one of many factors impinging on children, and—despite individual variations—that on the whole it is a secondary rather than a primary factor, so far as child development and adjustment are concerned. The primary factors, it would seem, have to do with family climate and functioning, the personality and temperament of the parents, the kind of care and training the child receives—whether the mother works or not. These may, of course, be affected by her working. But the impact of her employment seems to be affected by these primary factors more than they are by the fact of her working. This conclusion has surprised a number of investigators who reached it independently, and the last word has not yet been said (it never is). Yet if one thinks of problems in homes where mothers do *not* work, the surprise may dwindle. Words like Momism, overprotection, inadequate supervision, rejection, neglect, are not specific to families of working mothers.

A corollary generalization is that the primary factors strongly affect the kind of arrangements made for child care and for maintaining the well-being of family and homes if the mother does work; and that these arrangements in turn can be crucial. The evidence also hints that middle-income mothers are more likely than low-income mothers to achieve adequate supervision of children while the mother works—whether because they possess the means to do so, because they have been made more aware that it is important, or for both reasons.

References

APPLEBAUM, STELLA B.: Working Wives and Mothers. Public Affairs Pamphlet No. 188. New York: Public Affairs Pamphlets, 1952. 33 pp.

[31] Myrdal and Klein, 1956; p. 123.

546   Children and Parents

BLAISDELL, RICHARD S.: More Women Are Working. Journal of Home Economics, 1958, 50, 261–265.

BLOOD, ROBERT O., JR., AND HAMBLIN, ROBERT L.: The Effect of the Wife's Employment on the Family Power Structure. Social Forces, 1958, 36, 347–359.

BOWLBY, JOHN: Maternal Care and Mental Health. New York: Columbia University Press, 1952: 194 pp.

BOWLBY, JOHN, AINSWORTH, MARY, BOSTON, MARY, AND ROSENBLUTH, DINA: The Effects of Mother-Child Separation: A Follow-Up Study. British Journal of Medical Psychology XXIX, Parts 3 and 4, pp. 211–244. 1956.

BRONFENBRENNER, URIE: Socialization and Social Class Through Time and Space. [In] Maccoby, E. E.; Newcomb, T. M.; and Hartley, E. L.: Readings in Social Psychology. New York: Henry Holt, 1958. 674 pp. (p. 400–425)

ESSIG, MARY, AND MORGAN, D. C.: Adjustment of Adolescent Daughters of Employed Women. Journal of Educational Psychology, 1946, 37, 219–233.

FELDMAN, FRANCES L.: Supplementary Incomes Earned by Married Women. [In] National Manpower Council: Work in the Lives of Married Women. New York: Columbia University Press, 1958. 220 pp. (p. 93–155)

GLASS, NETTA: Eating, Sleeping, and Elimination Habits in Children Attending Day Nurseries and Children Cared for at Home by Mothers. American Journal of Orthopsychiatry, 1949, 19, 697–711.

GLUECK, SHELDON, AND GLUECK, ELEANOR: Unravelling Juvenile Delinquency. New York: Commonwealth Fund, 1950. 399 pp.

GLUECK, SHELDON, AND GLUECK, ELEANOR: Working Mothers and Delinquency. Mental Hygiene, 1957, 41, 327–353.

GRUENBERG, SIDONIE M., AND KRECH, HILDA SIDNEY: The Many Lives of Modern Women: A Guide to Happiness in Her Complex Role. Garden City, N. Y.: Doubleday, 1952, 255 pp.

HAND, HORACE B.: Working Mothers and Maladjusted Children. Journal of Educational Sociology, 1957, 30, 245–246.

HARTLEY, RUTH E.: Children's Concepts of Male and Female Roles. Merrill-Palmer Quarterly of Behavior and Development, 1959–60, 6, 83–91.

HEER, DAVID M.: Dominance and the Working Wife. Social Forces, 1958, 36, 341–347.

HEINICKE, CHRISTOPH M.: Some Effects of Separating Two-Year-Old Children From Their Parents: A Comparative Study. Human Relations, 1956, 9, 103–234.

HOLMES, EMMA G.: Job-Related Expenditures of Working Wives. U. S. Department of Agriculture, Agricultural Research Service, Institute of Home Economics. (Presented at the 36th Annual National Agricultural Outlook Conference, Nov. 19, 1958, Washington 25, D.C.) 6 pp. (mimeographed).

KOHN, MELVIN L.: Social Class and Parental Authority. American Sociological Review, 1959, 24, 352–366.

LANDIS, JUDSON T.: A Comparison of Children of Divorced Parents and Children of Happy or Unhappy Non-divorced Parents on Parent-Child Relationships, Dating Maturation, and Sex and Marriage Attitudes. Paper read before the National Council on Family Relations, Minneapolis, Minnesota, 1955.

LEWIS, HILDA: Deprived Children: The Mersham Experiment, London: Oxford University Press, 1954, 163 pp.

MACCOBY, ELEANOR E.: Effects Upon Children of Their Mothers' Outside Employment. [*In*] National Manpower Council: Work in the Lives of Married Women. New York: Columbia University Press, 1958. 220 pp. (pp. 150–172).

MEAD, MARGARET: Some Theoretical Considerations on the Problem of Mother-Child Separation. American Journal of Orthopsychiatry, 1954, 24, 471–483.

MYRDAL, ALVA, AND KLEIN, VIOLA: Women's Two Roles: Home and Work. Routledge and Kegan Paul, 1956. 208 pp.

NATIONAL MANPOWER COUNCIL: Womanpower. New York: Columbia University Press, 1957. 371 pp.

NATIONAL MANPOWER COUNCIL: Work in the Lives of Married Women. Proceedings of a Conference on Womanpower held October 20–25, 1957, at Arden House. New York: Columbia University Press, 1957. 220 pp.

NYE, F. IVAN: Child Adjustment in Broken and in Unhappy Unbroken Homes. Marriage and Family Living, 1957, 19, 356–361.

NYE, F. IVAN: Two-Job Mothers. National Parent-Teacher, 1957, 52, 16–18.

POPE, ELIZABETH: Is a Working Mother a Threat to the Home? McCall's, 1955, 82, 29; 70; 72–73.

RABIN, A. I.: Kibbutz Children—Research Findings to Date. Children, 1958, 5, 179–184.

RHEINGOLD, HARRIET L., AND BAYLEY, NANCY: The Later Effects of an Experimental Modification of Mothering. Child Development, 1959, 30, 363–372.

SEARS, ROBERT R., MACCOBY, ELEANOR E., AND LEVIN, HARRY: Patterns of Child Rearing. White Plains, New York: Row, Peterson, 1957. 549 pp.

SIEGEL, ALBERTA ENGVALL, STOLZ, LOIS MEEK, HITCHCOCK, ETHEL ALICE, AND ADAMSON, JEAN: Dependence and Independence in the Children of Working Mothers. Child Development, 1959, 30, 533–546.

SIMONSON, K. M.: Examination of Children From Children's Homes and Day Nurseries. Copenhagen. 1947. [*In*] Bowlby, John: Maternal Care and Mental Health. New York: Columbia University Press, 1952. 194 pp.

SOCIAL SECURITY ADMINISTRATION: Facts About Families, 1959 (March). 17 pp. (mimeographed).

UNIVERSITY OF MICHIGAN: A Social Profile of Detroit: A Report of the Detroit Area Study. Survey Research Center of the Institute of Social Research, 1957. 83 pp.

WHITE HOUSE CONFERENCE ON CHILDREN AND YOUTH, MIDCENTURY: Fact Finding Report—A Digest. Midcentury White House Conference on Children and Youth, Inc., 1950. 170 pp.

WITMER, HELEN LELAND, AND KOTINSKY, RUTH: Personality in the Making: The Fact-Finding Report of the Midcentury White House Conference on Children and Youth. New York: Harper & Bros., 1952. 454 pp.

WORKING MOTHERS [What It Means to a Teen-Age Girl to Have Her Mother Go to Work] (December 1957, YWCA Magazine) Children, 1958, 5, 39.

59. CHILDREN AND PARENTS IN THE KIBBUTZ AND AMERICA

Howard Halpern

§ Is the family necessary for the best personality development of parents and children? In some cultures children are placed for substantial periods of time in special child-care institutions, such as private schools in the United States and England, residential schools in Russia, and communal schools in the kibbutzim of Israel. These children have parents, but certain cultural values of the society take precedence over close parent-child relationships. The increasing proportion of employed mothers of young children in the United States has aroused deep interest in non-family methods of child-rearing. The article that follows compares child-rearing in the kibbutz and America.

The fight for survival plus the desire to actualize a cherished social ideal have combined in Israel to create the collective settlements known as the "Kibbutzim." Each Kibbutz is a largely autonomous unit, in which every member is an owner of the Kibbutz and, in a sense, the Kibbutz owns every member. The work, the profits and the property of these settlements are communally shared. Policy is collectively determined. And, to a very large extent, the children are collectively reared. The purpose of this paper is to discuss the effects of this collective child rearing, not on the child—for much has been said about this—but on the parents and their marriage, and to compare some aspects of child rearing in the Kibbutz with current trends in American child rearing.

While there are variations in the way children are cared for among the many Kibbutzim, depending somewhat on the ideology, piety and national origin of the members, there is a relatively common pattern that is clearly identifiable.

From birth, the infant is in charge of a trained nurse or *metapelet,*

SOURCE: "Alienation from Parenthood in the Kibbutz and America," *Marriage and Family Living,* 24 (February, 1962), 42–45. Reprinted by permission of the publisher and the author.

The article was presented at the annual meeting of the American Association of Marriage Counselors, May 20, 1961, New York City. It derived from observations made by the author in 1960 when he conducted a workshop in child psychotherapy at Bar Ilan University, Israel, and from various publications.

The author received his doctorate in clinical psychology from Columbia University. He is co-director of the Student Consultation Center in New York City. Other of his articles have been published in various professional journals.

who is usually responsible for about six infants. These infants do not live in their parents' apartment but in a special nursery or infants' house. Despite this, the infant's mother has the primary relationship with her child, at least during the first six months. The mother feeds her child (usually by breast feeding), keeps him clean and comfortable and gives him the needed fondling, cooing and warmth of contact. During this first half-year the *metapelet* serves as the mother's teacher and guide, as well as the housekeeper of the nursery.

Gradually, however, the *metapelet* begins to take over the rearing of the child, so that usually by the end of the first year she is almost totally responsible for it. In the second year, the child is transferred from the infants' house to the toddlers' house where a new *metapelet* is in charge. She takes on all the tasks and responsibilities that in our culture are traditionally the function of the mother. She teaches the child how to feed himself, she toilet trains him, she comforts and soothes him, she leads him to increased independence, she teaches him the social do's and don'ts and helps him to master the difficulties of group living.

From his second year on, the child is with his parents daily in the two or three hours between the parents' return from work and the child's bedtime; on the Sabbath or on holidays he is with his parents almost the entire day. This time is devoted by both parents exclusively and warmly to the children. The writer was impressed by the spontaneous, joyous greeting exchanged by parent and child at these times, and can still see the dazzling smile of one ten year old boy as he burst into his parents' apartment at the end of the day, shouting "*Shalom.*" Others have also been impressed by these evening encounters. General Sir Arthur Wauchope has written

> I have often been witness to these meetings. The children's cries of joy and the unrestrained signs of affection show at once that the daily separation during hours of labor causes no lessening of devotion on one side or the other. On the contrary, I believe the relationship between parents and children is peculiarly happy in these communal communities.[1]

Despite these genuinely happy vignettes, or maybe because of them, the writer left Israel with the feeling that there were profound differences in the emotional underpinnings of the parent-child relationship when compared to the home and family structure of our society. In fact, it seemed that the Kibbutz parents' concept of the parental role differed drastically from that of American parents. One story particularly raised many troubling questions for the author.

Late at night, in one of the older and well-established Kibbutzim, one of the men of the Kibbutz stole into the building where the younger

---

[1] General Sir Arthur Wauchope, "Communal Settlements in Palestine," *Jewish Frontier*, (October, 1941), p. 12.

children were housed and went to the bed of a six year old girl, molesting her quite comprehensively. The next morning she told her story, and it was easily verified. One group of parents had long felt that the hourly rounds by the teacher or nurse on duty offered insufficient protection and emotional security for their children. They knew of the studies indicating a higher rate of nightmares and bedwetting among Kibbutz children. Therefore, they used this incident to propose that the parents in the Kibbutz take turns sleeping in the children's building. Each couple would thus be required to sleep at the children's house once every three weeks. This proposal aroused loud and overwhelming opposition at the weekly Kibbutz meeting. Such coddling, some parents felt, would undermine the children's development of independence and self-confidence. Others flatly stated that they did not want to undergo the inconvenience of having to sleep in the children's house once every third week.

It seems to me that this scene, this decision, would not easily take place in our society, at least at the present. It is difficult for me to picture a group of American parents in which the majority would openly oppose this relatively untaxing way to provide their children more protection and comfort.

If there is this alienation from the parental role as we know it, what accounts for the zestful, enthusiastic relationship of Kibbutz parents with their children? I believe that the notable exuberance in the parent-child interaction is related to this alienation. The parents share all the joys of growing up with their children but little of the pains. When a child is wounded, physically or emotionally, it is the *metapelet* who responds to the tears and who offers consolation and comfort. It is the *metapelet* who engages in the struggle of toilet-training and other struggles in the exasperating process of teaching the growing child to replace the pleasure principle with the reality principle. Should the child become ill, he is sent to stay in the infirmary where the medically trained nurses, not his parents, tend to his needs. In short, the parents and children have between them a bond of countless hours of warmth, of laughter and of fun, but they do not share a bond based on going through the hell and misery of growing up together. This is the root of the alienation. The relationship between parents and children in the Kibbutz is like that often found between grandparents and grandchildren in our familial framework. Grandparents traditionally have the maximum amount of enjoyment with the minimum of responsibility and turmoil. This often makes for a very happy and affectionate relationship between grandparents and grandchildren, and this is the atmosphere that seems to exist between the Kibbutz parents and their children.

One may wonder whether Kibbutz parents, who are alienated in this way from the traditional parental self-concept, suffer from the alienation.

Are there benefits inherent in the experience of personally rearing children that leave the Kibbutz parents somewhat impoverished for not having had this experience? What are these benefits of personally rearing children—as in our culture—for the husband and wife as individuals and for their relationship to each other?

Bearing and rearing children does serve many positive functions in the growth toward maturity on the part of the parents. For the mother, at least, it may gratify a profound biologically rooted need. For both parents, child rearing may satisfy desires to create, to guide and to shape a new individual. Parents ready for the developmental task of parenthood can gain from it an expanded capacity for giving, sacrificing, protecting and loving. In short, it is a powerful force against the immaturity, the self-involvement, the narcissism of the parents. It pushes them to grow up. In their concern for the lives and well-being of their offspring, parents attach themselves to the inexorable, biological process of the preservation of the species, thus also attaining a sense of immortality.

The Kibbutz parents would seem to be deprived of these growth forces found in active parenthood. But even though the Kibbutz parents assume a role similar to that of the grandparents of our culture, they do have ways of compensating for the opportunities for maturing found in personal child rearing. For while they may act as grandparents to their own children, they do have a child to raise—and that child is the Kibbutz itself.

The growth, the progress, the success of the Kibbutz is the ever-present, burning concern of each Kibbutz member. The desires to create, to shape and to guide are gratified in the maternal or parental relationship a member may have to the Kibbutz. This involvement in the Kibbutz's welfare brings him from narcissistic self-concern to a point where he can give and sacrifice for something outside himself. And in his energetic concern for the Kibbutz and the ideals it represents, he tries to contact immortality.

Thus, many of the maturing forces present in the task of rearing children find a substitute in the parents' relationship to the Kibbutz. But is there something lacking? Is there not something of tenderness, of a deeply protective feeling toward a cherished and somewhat helpless baby that cannot be substituted for by a parental feeling toward a collective settlement? Can a parent learn the soft strength of love in relation to the surrogate child represented by the Kibbutz? It seems unlikely, so that many Kibbutz parents may be cheated out of this dimension of the child-rearing experience and be the poorer and harder as a result.

The alienation from the old parental self-concept that we see occurring in the Kibbutz is happening in many parts of the world today, including our American society. Twenty or thirty years ago, nursery schools were rare, and the number of children attending them were few.

Many felt that parents who sent their children to nursery school wanted to be rid of them, and this was a terrible accusation. Now in many segments of American society, nursery schools are commonplace, and it is the good mother, the concerned mother who enrolls her child in these schools. Or note the increase in camps and campers. Countless children leave their parents each summer to live in a woodland communal settlement with occasional Sunday visits from their parents. Day camps and after-school programs also take over many of the old parental tasks of protection, discipline and socialization. Cub Scouts, Boy Scouts, Girl Scouts, Little Leagues and community centers of all kinds are booming. This trend may indicate a tendency on the part of many parents to put an intermediary between themselves and their children. It seems there must be a difference in the parental self-concept of a mother informally observing or guiding the spontaneous group play of her children as compared to that of a Den Mother instructing her pack in making a leather bookmark at the weekly den meeting. And there must be a difference in the self-concept of a father who plays ball with his children and their friends in a casual choose-up game, as compared to the father involved in the details of organizing, scheduling, uniforming and coaching a Little League team.

The trend is toward greater parental freedom from the directly personal, deeply intimate, minute-by-minute total involvement in the child's development that has long characterized the role of the parent in the western family setting. In the service of this drive for parental freedom, there has been the explosive growth of these parent-surrogate institutions, which serve many of the functions of the Israeli Kibbutz, in that they offer the children guidance, instructions, impulse control, socialization, warmth and a sense of belonging, and they afford for the parents a sense of dutiful involvement with their children from a comfortable and liberating distance.

There seems to be much that is healthy in this surge toward parental liberation. Healthy for the child, in that he has a greater chance of escaping the entanglements of his parents' neuroses, and healthy for the parents who must now face themselves and each other as two individuals. It is almost impossible for Kibbutz parents and it is becoming increasingly difficult for American parents to use their children as the mortar holding together a destructive marriage or as a pawn in their marital conflicts. It is becoming increasingly disappointing in the Kibbutz and in America to expect children to fulfill the ungratified longing for love and companionship found in a barren marriage. Nor can parents easily hope to live their own lives through their children, or to expect the children to rescue them from their own emptiness or their own boredom. As parents achieve greater freedom from personal child-rearing, they are compelled to confront their separateness and the stark reality of their marriage relationship. It is to be hoped that much growth can be fostered by such honest self-confrontation.

One danger of this trend toward parental liberation and alienation in American society is similar to that already noted in Kibbutzim—that less opportunity is afforded the parent for the flowering of his softer self, his capacity for love and for unconditional involvement. This danger is smaller here than in the Kibbutz because the traditional family framework is still basically intact and has not been fully surrendered to collective child rearing. But there is another problem in the alienation from the traditional parental role that is of much greater seriousness in our society than in the Kibbutz. I refer to the fact that while the Kibbutz gives its members a sense of total commitment to something they cherish, the American parent-surrogate institutions, from Cub Scouts to summer camps, do not involve a great emotional investment on the part of American parents.

So parents in America, increasingly alienating themselves from traditional parental roles, are in peril of having no other strong forces pulling them toward maturity as part of the natural pattern of living. Neither their child nor the surrogate institutions they place between themselves and the child carry enough magnetism to draw the parents out of their narcissistic self-concern, to expand their self-concept to include many people and richer values, or to deepen their capacity to love and sacrifice.

Perhaps this is a partial explanation of the increase in narcissistic display and consumption, the packaging of personalities, the diluted and superficial involvement in ideas and ideals and the decreasing pride in craft and accomplishment. Parents have gained great freedom from responsibility, but are at a loss for substitutes for these growth-provoking responsibilities. So they join PTAs, religious institutions and fund-raising drives for countless charities, not just as something to do but in the hope of stretching themselves. Much of this activity is presently frantic and based on a longing to be deeply committed, rather than on real commitment.

But in a world with hydrogen bombs perched on launching pads, with a population explosion potentially more dangerous than an H-bomb explosion, with so much tyranny to be toppled by freedom, so much hatred to be tempered by love, so much ugliness to be transformed by beauty, it is difficult to agree with the hero of *Look Back in Anger* that there are no great causes left any more. The Kibbutz member in Israel shows each day his willingness to invest himself without stint in the growth of his Kibbutz. He is willing to work long hours under very trying conditions and then stay up half the night planning and arguing about Kibbutz policy. He is ready to sacrifice his life on the many Kibbutzim guarding hostile borders. His whole life takes on richer meaning as part of the fabric of this ideal, this offspring which he adores. The boundaries of his self-concept enlarge to encompass the Kibbutz and this gives him a sense of strength and maturity.

And it is possible that if Americans are to rise above the small self-involvement fostered by their increased alienation from personal child-rearing, they must find, as a magnet toward maturity, their own personal great cause, their own counterpart of the Israeli Kibbutz.

Chapter 19: Children with Serious Family Problems

60. WHO GETS THE CHILDREN?

Morris Ploscowe

§ Divorce brings a marriage to an end but does not destroy the fact of parenthood. The divorced wife is still a mother, the divorced husband a father. Since the mother and father no longer live in the same household and in fact may place a thousand or more miles between them, serious questions arise as to which parent the child will live with and how he can retain some kind of personal relationship with the other parent. It falls to the judge who hears the divorce case to arrange for the custody of the child and his opportunities for being with the absent parent. Judge Ploscowe has both a legal and a humane interest in this important problem of "Who gets the children?"

. . . While courts and judges differ in their judgments and in their evaluations of specific situations, there are certain principles that are generally followed in awarding custody. These principles are deemed to be for the best interests of the child. However, they are only guides to the court, which may depart from them in any given situation.

1. *Mothers are generally preferred in custody disputes, particularly where very young children are involved.* This preference of the law for mothers as against fathers finds statutory expression in the California Civil Code (Sec. 138). "As between parents adversely claiming the custody" of a minor child, states the California Statute, neither is entitled to custody as a matter of right, "but other things being equal, if the *child is of tender years, it should be given to the mother.*"

A recent California case demonstrates how this principle is applied.

SOURCE: Morris Ploscowe, *The Truth about Divorce* (New York: Hawthorn Books, 1955), pp. 228–43. Copyright © 1955 by Hawthorn Books, Inc. Reprinted by permission of the publisher.

The author, with long experience as a judge in the Magistrates' Courts of New York City, has published extensively in both popular and professional journals. Besides the book from which this selection is taken, he has also written *Sex and the Law.*

The evidence reveals that both parents have great affection for the child and he for them, and that at the time of the hearing both parents were able to offer the child a good home, a yard to play in, their own personal care, love, and attention during the day as well as night, and the love and affection of those strangers with whom the child would come in daily contact, namely, the stepfather if the child were permitted to remain in the custody of his mother, or defendant's uncle and aunt in the event custody was awarded to the father. We think it clear that *the advantages which the child would receive in the home of his mother were equal to those of the father,* and *in view of the child's tender years—three—his custody should be with his mother* unless it has been shown that she is no longer a fit and proper person to have such custody. We are unable to find any substantial evidence supporting the court's finding of unfitness. No one [states another California court] will give such complete and selfless devotion and so unhesitatingly and unstintingly make the sacrifices which the welfare of the child demands as the child's own mother.[1]

Before one charges California legislators and courts with having succumbed to the persuasive influence of the "Mammy" songs of Hollywood musicals, one should ponder the following facts of divorce litigation. In the first place, a large percentage of the children of divorce are very young. The father, who has a living to earn, cannot be handicapped by having to care for young children. As a result, when families break up, when husbands and wives go their separate ways, children are generally left in the custody of the mother. Moreover, women bring most of the divorce actions. Where they are successful in obtaining the divorce (and they are successful in most cases since there is no contest) the custody of the children is awarded to them in the vast majority of cases. The New Jersey Study noted that for every decision awarding custody to the father, there are ten giving custody to the mother.

Courts deprive the mother of the custody of young children after divorce only on a clear showing that the mother is morally unfit to bring up a child or that having had the child she has been neglectful of her responsibilities. Where a mother is an alcoholic, or a habitué of barrooms, beer parlors and night clubs; where her mental or physical condition is such that she cannot properly care for her children; or where she has been indiscreet in her adulteries; it is likely that the court will forget the usual preference for the mother and award custody to the father or to some other relative.

2. *An award of custody is usually made to the successful party in the divorce action.* "In awarding the custody of a child in a divorce proceeding, unless otherwise manifestly improper," states an Oregon court, "a preference should be given to the party *not* in fault."[2] However, the award of custody to the successful party in the divorce action is not a

[1] Robertson v. Robertson 1945, 72 Cal. App. 2d. 129, 135, 164. P. 2d. 52, 56.
[2] Sachs v. Sachs 1933, 25 P. 2d. 159, (Ore.).

matter of right. A child is not awarded like a prize in a raffle to the winner in the divorce contest. The successful party must also show that he is the better parent for the child and that it will be more advantageous for the child to be brought up by him rather than by the losing spouse.

The previous derelictions of the husband and wife are considered by the court on the question of the fitness to have the child. A plaintiff who has won a divorce and who technically is an injured and innocent party and not guilty of derelictions, starts out, therefore, with an advantage in this connection. But it is only an advantage. It is not decisive of the issue. As the court put it in one New York case:

> The children of a broken marriage are not responsible for the breach yet suffer through it. The Court must then provide for the care, custody and control of the children in the conditions which exist, as wisely as it can. Apportionment *between the parents of the blame for the broken marriage may not be the decisive factor in the determination.* . . . Nonetheless the past conduct of the parents, the unwillingness of one or both to carry out their marital obligations are factors which may not be disregarded in determining which parent will provide the better home.[3]

We have seen in the *Bunim* case (*supra*) that the trial court awarded the custody of the children to a mother who was divorced because of her adultery, in the belief that she was the better parent for the children. This attitude is not unusual when the trial court looks at the derelictions of the parent from the point of view of the child rather than that of the opposing spouse. When all things are considered, if the losing party in the divorce action is in fact the better parent for the child and can provide a better home, custody will be awarded to him, no matter what his past moral lapses or derelictions may have been. This is illustrated by an old Massachusetts case in which the husband, a Congregational minister, sought a divorce on the ground that his wife had committed adultery and bigamy. He was granted the divorce, but could not obtain the custody of his two sons. He had contended that where a wife was found guilty of adultery and bigamy, the court had no discretion and must as a matter of law turn over the custody of the children to the husband. The trial court, however, decided that it did have discretion and for reasons which are not clear from the opinion, preferred a bigamous wife to a Congregational minister. This action was sustained on appeal. "We know of no absolute rule of law," stated the appellate court, "that the father is entitled to the custody of children when he obtains a divorce . . . on the ground of bigamy and adultery."[4]

Similarly, in a Michigan case, although the wife was a proverbial hell on wheels toward her husband, having beaten him on a number of occa-

---

[3] Harrington v. Harrington 1943, 290 N.Y. 126, 130, 48 N.E. 2d. 290.
[4] Haskell v. Haskell 1890, 152 Mass. 16, 24 N.E. 859.

sions and threatened him with a revolver, she was apparently a good mother for the couple's three-year-old child. The husband had no difficulty in obtaining the divorce for his wife's cruelty, but he was unable to obtain the custody of the child. A Wisconsin husband was also able to obtain a divorce because his wife deserted him. But the fact that she ran away from her husband and would not put up with his idiosyncrasies, did not bar her right to have their two children. The Wisconsin court found that the desertion was in part due to the "radical differences that had grown up between the husband and the wife." Since there was no showing that the mother was not morally fit to have the children, custody of the two daughters was awarded to her, despite the fact that her husband obtained the divorce.[5]

It is apparent, therefore, that lack of success in the divorce action will not prevent an award of custody to the loser, especially if the loser is the mother of the child and is not unfit to bring up the child.

3. *The preference of a child for a particular parent is not conclusive in a custody award.* When children are no longer infants, they may have a decided preference as to which parent they would like to live with. This preference of the child for one parent or the other, however, is not decisive of the issue of who will be awarded custody of the child after divorce. However, the preference of a child for a particular parent will be given considerable weight in the custody decision.

There are statutes in states such as Ohio and Utah which provide that children of four years and ten years respectively, may in any custody dispute, select the parent with whom they want to live. These statutes, however, do not compel a court to award custody to the parent selected, unless such parent is a fit person for the child. Generally, even without such statutes, a court will give effect to the preference of a child for a particular parent. In one New York case for example, the separation agreement provided that the four children of a couple contemplating a divorce could select the parent with whom they wanted to live. The two older children chose the father and the two younger children the mother. The court noted that it was not bound by these preferences and had the power, if it so desired, to award custody to someone else. However, in view of the fact that both the father and the mother appeared to be fit persons to bring up the children, the court saw "no sound reason" for not permitting each child to remain with the parent of his choice.

The child's wishes may not be permitted to control the award of custody if the behavior of the parent selected does not meet with the approval of the court. We have seen in the *Bunim* case that the majority of the court of appeals placed a great deal more emphasis in the custody decision on the mother's adulteries than the daughters' preferences. Similarly in another outstanding New York case (*Glendening v. Glen-*

[5] Twohig v. Twohig 1922, 186 N.W. 592, (Wisc.).

dening) the appellate court was more influenced by a father's devotion and care rather than a child's preference.

The custody battles of the Glendenings had kept many lawyers busy. The mother left the father and the child when the child was an infant. However, she had frequently tried to get the child back. Her latest attempt to gain control of the child occurred when the boy was sixteen years of age. Despite the fact that the boy had lived with the father for many years, his preference was for the mother. A lower court sought to give effect to his preference. But the appellate court upset the custody award to the mother and permitted the father to retain custody and control of the boy. Examining the comparative records of the father and the mother, and the care which the boy had received while in the father's custody, the majority of the appellate court found it "very difficult to see" how any court could find that the boy should be taken from the father. Nevertheless, the dissenting judge pointed out that the father had had a far greater opportunity than the mother to win the boy's love and affection. Yet he had failed to do so. He saw no reason why the boy's desire to be with the mother should not be granted.

It should be noted, however, that if a child has a deep-seated aversion to one parent and love and affection for the other, the child itself may frustrate any custody award by the simple process of running away from the hated parent. This was the situation involved in the case of the battling Brussels. Custody of two daughters, thirteen and eleven, was awarded to the father because the mother was deemed by the court to be unfit. The girls, however, refused to stay with the father and kept continually running away to the mother and to other relatives. Despite many contempt proceedings which the father brought in an effort to enforce the custody decree in his favor, a court was finally compelled to modify the custody award and leave the girls temporarily with an aunt and uncle. The court suggested psychiatric guidance to remove the strong reluctance of the children to stay with the father. The lesson of the entire proceeding, however, was that two determined little girls literally thumbed their noses at the ponderous procedures of the law and won a partial victory for themselves, namely, temporary freedom from the control of their father, whom they disliked.

4. *Parents have a superior right to children over grandparents or other relatives.* Some of the most heartbreaking custody cases arise where parents after the breakup of the marriage leave a child in the care of grandparents, or with uncles or aunts. The child becomes attached to his new surroundings and to the grandparents, aunts or uncles. The latter also become very much attached to the child. Despite this attachment, these relatives may eventually be faced by a demand for the child from one of the parents. The fundamental legal rule in such cases is quite clear. The parent is preferred in the matter of custody over any other relative of

the child. This is illustrated by a California case in which a husband divorced his wife, and their two small daughters were turned over to the custody of the paternal grandparents. Two years later, the mother who had remarried, wanted the children in her own home. The probation officer who made an investigation concluded that it would not be for the best interests of the children to take them from the home of the grandparents. Custody was accordingly left with them. But the appellate court took a different view.

> While these grandparents may be able to give to these infants greater material advantages (stated the court), the right of a parent to the care and custody of a child cannot be taken away merely because the court may believe that some third person can give the child better care and greater protection. One of the natural rights incident to parenthood, . . . is the right to the care and custody of a minor child, and this right can only be forfeited by a parent upon proof that the parent is unfit to have such care and custody. . . . As between a mother and the grandparents of a child, the rights of the mother are paramount; and the grandparents should not be permitted to retain custody where there is no showing that a mother, seeking the custody of her two small girls, is not presently a fit and proper person to have their custody.[6]

Despite the fact that the law favors parents, as against other relatives, many courts refuse to give effect to this preference and to take children away from a home and an environment in which they are both happy and contented. They refuse to take a chance in transferring a child from a home that they know is beneficial to one whose influence is unknown or may at best be dubious. In one New York case, for example, the mother had left two children with her parents. The children had lived with these grandparents for a number of years and the latter became quite attached to them. The mother died. Thereupon the father demanded custody of the children. But he had no real substitute to offer for the excellent care which the grandparents were giving to the children. He wanted them either to live with his sister, who had eight children of her own, or to place them in boarding schools. This did not appeal to the court, which found that a transfer of custody was not in the best interests of the children and left them with the grandparents. Similarly, courts will deny a parent the right to custody if they find that the parent has neglected the child in the past, or appears to be an unfit person for the child. This was the situation in the famous *Gloria Vanderbilt* custody dispute. The contest in that case was between the mother who had been awarded custody after divorce and an aunt with whom the child had been left. The mother obviously had a superior legal right to the child, yet the court awarded custody of Gloria to Mrs. Whitney,

[6] Wilkinson v. Wilkinson 1951, 233 P. 2d. 639, (Cal.).

her aunt. The court found that when the mother had the child she was indifferent to her and would leave her in the care of nurses and relatives for long periods, and that the life the child led with the mother was "unsuitable, unfit, improper and calculated to destroy the child's health," and was "neglectful of her spiritual, mental and moral education." On the other hand, life with Aunt Whitney was characterized by the court as "fit, suitable and appropriate, tending to promote the child's welfare and happiness." Under these circumstances, the custody of the child was awarded to the aunt, for it was obviously in the best interests of the child to do so.[7]

It is apparent that legal rules in custody proceedings are flexible. Courts do not hesitate to depart from them where they feel that the best interests of the child require it. It is this uncertainty, as to what courts will do in particular custody situations, which fosters much litigation.

5. *Courts do not like divided custody arrangements.* Where there is considerable bitterness between parents and considerable competition for the child's loyalty and affection, there is temptation to apply the rule, equality is equity. Divide up the custody periods—give each parent an equal right to the companionship and custody of the child. Let the child spend six months of the year or two weeks of the month with one parent and the other six months of the year or two weeks of the month with the other parent. This may resolve the immediate dispute, but such custody arrangements are fraught with disaster for the child.

The child, under such arrangements, shuttles back and forth between two different households. The child may have to adjust himself to a new stepfather in one home and a new stepmother in the other. He may also have to compete for affection and attention with a different set of half-brothers and half-sisters in each home. Such a child will find it unusually difficult to develop the sense of belonging and the sense of security which is so necessary to the normal psychological development of children. One case properly called a child subject to these conditions, "a wanderer from home to home." Appellate courts are aware of these facts and on occasion upset arrangements which require a child to spend a stated number of weeks or months with each parent. In one such case, where custody of the child was divided between both parents for six-month periods, the court said,

> Were the little boy to be regarded as a plaything existing alone for the pleasure and entertainment of the parents, there might be some justification in changing his place of residence twice a year; but as his welfare is of paramount importance, he should be accorded if possible, such a home as will conduce to his physical and moral well being and enable him to acquire a suitable education. . . . No argument is required to support the

[7] In re Vanderbilt 1935, 245 A.D. 211, 281 N.Y.S. 171.

proposition *that a permanent abode is for the child's best interest and rarely indeed will a divided custody by parents who have separated, prove beneficial.*[8]

Nevertheless, despite such judicial attitudes, courts frequently approve custody arrangements where a child must spend the school year with one parent and the vacation period with the other. Sometimes also, courts modify custody arrangements so as to give an older boy a chance for greater association with his father, even though this may involve a split custody with the mother.

It should also be noted that courts are not partial to the separation of brothers and sisters. They would like, wherever possible, to keep them together in one household, so that they can grow up in some close approximation to a normal family life. However, here again circumstances may require a splitting up of the family. This is what happened in the case noted above, where the parents split up four children between themselves, in accordance with the children's preferences.

6. *Courts are reluctant to permit children to be taken out of the state.* In a recent New York case a wife, after a battle with her husband, left him and their two children and ran off to Florida to get a divorce. She liked the calm and sunshine of Florida so much that she decided to settle there permanently. But she missed the children. She came back to New York, after the divorce, and sought their custody. She was able to persuade a referee that the best interests of the children would be served by having them live with her in Florida. But she struck an unsympathetic judge who could find "no exceptional reasons" why the court should permit the wife "to remove the children over one thousand miles from their father." The court stressed the need of the children for love, affection and attention from *both* parents. This is obviously difficult to obtain where parents are separated from children by great distances. Since the wife had created the situation by moving to Florida, it was the court's opinion that she could correct it "by moving back to the metropolitan area." In any event, she received no assistance from the court in her plan to deprive the father of custody and take the children with her to the sunnier clime of Florida.[9]

There are, however, no absolute rules with respect to the removal of children from the jurisdiction of a particular court, or a particular state. This will be permitted despite a natural reluctance to do so where a court feels that it is warranted by all the circumstances. In a recent Oregon case, for example, the husband objected strenuously to his divorced wife taking their child to Australia to live. The mother had spent most of her life in the Orient and had married her husband in India. Her mother, a wealthy widow, who wanted to furnish a home for her

[8] Caldwell v. Caldwell 1909, 141 Iowa 192, 119 N.W. 599.
[9] Whittemore v. Whittemore 1951, 109 N.Y.S. 2d. 216.

daughter and grandson, lived in Australia. The Oregon Supreme Court permitted the mother to take the child to Australia, stating in the course of its opinion

> If we deny plaintiff the right to establish a new home for her son beyond the borders of the United States, we are convinced that her . . . devotion will never permit her to abandon her son and go thence alone. She will reluctantly and unwillingly remain in this country . . . in an unhappy environment. . . . We would in effect penalize her by a species of exile. . . . If the mother is so coerced to live in the United States with her boy, she will have to support herself and during her working hours be compelled to entrust the care of her child to the supervision of strangers. . . . We believe the consequent unhappiness of a mother so required to live and labor in a strange world to which she is linked against her will by judicial decree would undoubtedly tincture and perhaps eventually warp unfavorably the life of the child entrusted to her custody. The resultant atmosphere, . . . might be far less conducive to the welfare of the child than the promise of a more idyllic pattern of life and living offered by a new home in Australia.[10]

In view of the above facts, the best interests of the child seemed to require migration to Australia.

Thus, though courts are generally opposed to having children taken out of the state the hard facts of any given situation may require such a solution.

7. *A court may deem a parent unfit to bring up a child and deny a parent the right to custody because of his unpopular political belief or unconventional religious views.* Ordinarily courts do not interfere in parental conflicts over the religious or political training of children. When Mrs. Sisson, who was bedridden, found that her husband was subjecting her child to the influence of a fanatical religious sect, the Meggido, she sought the aid of the courts to prevent this. The lower courts were able to assist her through a modification of custody arrangements. But the court of appeals refused to interfere in this dispute over the training of a child pointing out that

> The court cannot regulate by its processes the internal affairs of the home. Dispute between parents when it does not involve anything immoral or harmful to the welfare of the child is beyond the reach of the law. The vast majority of matters concerning the upbringing of children, must be left to the conscience, patience and self-restraint of father and mother. No end of difficulties would arise should judges try to tell parents how to bring up their children.[11]

However, courts do indirectly affect the unbringing of children when they deny the custody of children to parents who have expressed un-

[10] Edwards v. Edwards 1951, 227 P. 2d. 975, (Ore.).
[11] Sisson v. Sisson 1936, 271 N.Y. 285, 287, 2 N.E., 2d. 660.

popular or unconventional political or religious views. This, the poet Shelley discovered as far back as 1811. After the death of his wife, he tried to obtain the custody of his children from the grandparents with whom they had been left. The fact that Shelley had been living in adultery would not have disqualified him from having the children under the English law as it then existed. English gentlemen were apparently expected to have mistresses. But Shelley had committed a much worse offense. He has expressed heretical, political and atheistic religious views in his writings which the judge considered "highly immoral." He was therefore not considered to be a "fit" parent for the children and custody was left with the grandparents.

A New Jersey court in 1936 reached a similar result, when, after a divorce, it denied the custody of two young children to Mrs. Eaton, who was an atheist and who had attended lectures on "Communism and IWW ism." This court held that she had no right to teach her un-American beliefs to her children and awarded custody to the father.

Nevertheless, despite precedents such as these, the New York Court of Appeals recently refused to sanction the grant of custody to a grandmother as against the mother of a child, despite the fact that the mother was accused of being a Communist, and having no regard for the religious upbringing of her child. In the eyes of the grandparents, the mother had also committed the additional offense of marrying a Negro.

Despite the authority of New York's Court of Appeals, many judges will sympathize with the New Jersey court in the Eaton case, especially in view of the great tensions over Communism. Accordingly, a person who would normally be granted custody of a child may find that he has been stigmatized as an "unfit parent" and denied custody because of his alleged subversive political and religious activities and opinions.

8. *The courts usually insist upon a right of visitation for the parent deprived of custody.* Courts feel that no matter what may have caused the differences between the parents which resulted in divorce, children belong to both parents and are entitled to the affection, attention and interest of both the mother and the father. Accordingly, when custody is awarded to one parent by a court, there is usually provision for the other parent to visit the child at stated times and during specific periods, so that the child can have the benefit of his companionship and guidance. It is highly desirable for the parents themselves to work out the details of visitation rights after divorce. They know when and where it will be convenient to exercise the right of visitation and what arrangements may be best for the child. Provisions concerning visitation, agreed on by the parents, if reasonable, are usually incorporated into the decree awarding custody. But if the parents do not agree, then the court will be required to use its discretion and to prescribe the limitations and extent of the right of visitation. Where and when such visitation will take

place will depend upon such factors as the age of the child, the distance between the father's and mother's residences, the free time of the father and the mother, the degree of hostility between the parents, the availability of some neutral ground where visits to the child can take place, etc.

Where there is a deep-seated hostility between the parents, the exercise of the right of visitation is usually fraught with difficulties and unpleasantness. The parent having the custody surrenders the child to the visiting parent only with greatest reluctance. He will try to restrict the right of visitation as much as he can and make it as inconvenient as possible for the other parent to visit the child. He may seek to deprive the other parent of the right of visitation altogether. Where the breach of the court's decree is a flagrant one, the court may be appealed to by a parent to secure his rights. Jail for contempt is one weapon that a court can use to enforce its decree. Another is a change in the custody arrangements. Courts may also penalize a mother who deprives a father of rights of visitation by depriving her of alimony or even of maintenance or support money for the child.

It should be noted that in this guerilla warfare between parents over the exercise of the right of visitation, the child is the principal victim. No court can repair the emotional damage done to a child by the continuous conflict of his parents.

The right of visitation, like other rights in the child, may be denied if it is not conducive to the child's welfare. If a father's idea of visiting with a child is to take him on a tour of barrooms; if he uses the period of visitation to instill hatred and disrespect for the mother; or if the child is violently averse to visits from the parent who does not have custody, visitation rights may be eliminated from the custody decree. Similarly, if past experience shows that a parent's contact with the child has a deleterious effect upon himself emotionally or physically, then visitation rights may be denied.

61. SOME RELATIONSHIPS OF STEP-CHILDREN TO THEIR PARENTS

Charles E. Bowerman and Donald P. Irish

§ After a thorough review of the literature on stepparents, the authors report the results of a careful study of the affection of children for their own parents and stepparents. In their conclusion the authors note that "In all the aspects thus far examined, homes involving step-relationships proved more likely to have stress, ambivalence, and low cohesiveness than did normal homes. . . . The presence of stepparents in the home affected also the adjustment of the children to their natural parents, usually somewhat diminishing the level of adjustment."

A Review of the Literature

The "wicked stepmother" of folklore has long existed in our legends. The concept of the "neglected stepchild" occurs commonly in our linguistic usage. The multifarious and presumably negative results of broken homes have received abundant popular comment. But no comprehensive analyses of the problems involved in step-relationships have yet been made. A thorough examination of the research literature for the past forty years reveals that there have been relatively few systematic inquiries concerned with the stepchild. Excluding discussions of individual cases, the scholarly literature yields fewer than forty published articles or books which analyze empirical data.

German scholars appear to have demonstrated the earliest interest and to have published the first studies almost five years before any Americans did so. Among them, Rühler contended that the child is unable to cope adequately with the alteration of the home situation brought about by the entrance of a new parent.[1] Wittels, in a publication of the same year, utilized a theoretical framework stemming from Freud and Levy-Bruhl and stressed the disruption of libidinous relations to the parent as a causal factor in changes in the personalities of stepchildren

SOURCE: *Marriage and Family Living*, 24 (1962), 113–21. Reprinted by permission of the publisher and the authors.

Charles E. Bowerman is on the staff at the University of North Carolina, and Donald P. Irish is at Hamline University, St. Paul, Minn. Dr. Bowerman has published other significant material on the family. The present article represents a portion of a project supported by PHS research grant M-2045, from the National Institute of Mental Health, and directed by Dr. Bowerman.

[1] Alice Rühler, "Das Stiefkind," in *Schwerezichbare Kinder*, Dresden, 1927.

he observed.[2] Stern was a third contributor, discussing four cases.[3] Hoenig examined ten different types of step-relationships and concluded that injury was done to the life of the child in a broken home before the establishment of the new full family was obtained.[4]

Kühn was apparently the first investigator to procure data from a substantial number of subjects, obtaining pertinent essays from 500 children.[5] She stated that the entrance of a stepmother into the family brought various stimuli to conflict and asserted that the widespread and deep-seated prejudice in general provoked tension. Mudroch, utilizing observations from almost a thousand subjects, over a third of whom came from families with a "disturbed structure," discussed the difficult role of the stepmother.[6] Neumann analyzed the responses of nearly 500 German eighth graders who wrote compositions on "What do you know about . . . stepmothers, especially about the relations to your own?"[7] VonLincke examined the stepmother motif in German folklore.[8]

In English, an early treatment, that of Fortes, was concerned with the connection between delinquency and abnormal family conditions, including step-relationships.[9] (The Gluecks, Lumpkin, Monahan, and others in America have more recently examined these correlations, although in studies that did not focus primarily on stepchildren.) Meriam has dealt principally with the social work and legal aspects of the stepfather role.[10] Several scholarly expositions advanced formulations in stimulating treatments but provided no additional empirical data beyond case illustrations.[11] Heilpern[12] and Deutsch[13] each considered

[2] Fritz Wittels, "Stepchildren," in *Set the Children*, London: Allen and Unwin, 1932, Chapter XI, pages 198–224; and New York: W. W. Norton and Company, 1933. Translated from *Die Befreiung des Kindes* by E. and C. Paul, and published by Hippokrates Verlag, 4th edition, 1927.
[3] Erich Stern, "Beitrag zur Psychologie des Stiefkindes," *Zeitschrift für Kinderforschung*, 24 (1928), pp. 144–57.
[4] C. Hoenig, "Die Stiefelternfamilie des Stiefkindes," *Zeitschrift für Kinderforschung*, 24 (1928), pp. 188–331.
[5] Hannah Kühn, "Psychologische Untersuchungen über das Stiefmutterproblem: Die Konfliktmöglichkeiten in der Stiefmutterfamilie und ihre Bedeutung für die Verwahrlosung des Stiefkindes," *Zeitschrift für angewandte Psychologie*, 45 (1929–1930), pages 1–185.
[6] R. Mudroch, "Das Stiefkind," *Versammlung für Kinderforschung*, 4 (Bratislava, 1932), pages 216–28.
[7] G. Neumann, "Untersuchungen über das Verhaltnis Zwischen Stiefmutter und Stiefkind," *Zeitschrift für Pädagogische Psychologie*, 34 (1933), pp. 348–67.
[8] Werner VonLincke, "Das Stiefmuttermotiv in Märchen der germanischen Völker," *Germanische Studien*, 142 (1933).
[9] M. Fortes, "Step-parenthood and Juvenile Delinquency," *Sociological Review*, 25 (1933), pp. 153–58.
[10] Adele Stuart Meriam, *The Stepfather in the Family*, Chicago: University of Chicago Press, 1940; and "Stepfather in the Family," *Social Service Review*, 14 (December, 1940), pp. 655–77.
[11] James H. S. Bossard, *Parent and Child: Studies in Family Behavior*, Philadelphia: University of Pennsylvania Press, 1953, Chapter VII, "The Child with a Sequence

step-relationships within the framework of psychoanalytic theory. The former focused upon the psychological problems of stepchildren; while the latter, in her oft-cited work, concentrated her interest on stepmothers in varied settings, with diverse motivations.

Social work students have examined step-relationships within the families of clients of metropolitan social agencies. White undertook to discover the factors that brought over forty stepchildren to a child guidance clinic during the course of a year and to discern if these were attributable to the step-relationships.[14] Pfleger reviewed the background of the "stepmother stereotype" in the legends and fiction of diverse preliterate as well as national cultures and then endeavored to analyze case records to see if the mythology provided initial psychological barriers for stepmothers to surmount.[15] She examined (a) feelings expressed about being a stepmother, (b) feelings toward the stepchildren, associated with the relationship, and (c) the children's attitudes manifested toward their stepmothers.

William C. Smith has published a comprehensive review of the literature, summarizing the data and insights with regard to step-relationships. His major volume,[16] supplemented by additional articles,[17] presents exploratory views and advances some thoughtful hypotheses, most of which remain yet to be tested.

More recently, in an extensive study of 2009 remarriages, many of which involved stepchildren, Jessie Bernard considered the attitudes of stepparents toward their spouse's children, the patterns of adjustment which newly married pairs developed with regard to the children, and the validity and relevance of the folk myths about step-relationships.[18] Although the data she used were the responses of *friends* of the couples

---

of Parents," pp. 125–54; and Edward Podolsky, "The Emotional Problems of the Stepchild," *Mental Hygiene*, 39 (1955), pp. 49–53.

[12] Else P. Heilpern, "Psychological Problems of Stepchildren," *The Psychoanalytic Review*, 30 (1943), pp. 163–76.

[13] Helene Deutsch, *The Psychology of Women*, New York: Grune and Stratton, 1944–1945, Two Volumes. Volume II, Chapter XII: "Stepmothers," pp. 434–55.

[14] Annie M. White, "Factors Making for Difficulty in the Step-parent Relationship with Children," *Smith College Studies in Social Work*, 14 (1943), p. 242, Abstract.

[15] Janet Pfleger, "The 'Wicked Stepmother' in a Child Guidance Clinic," *Smith College Studies in Social Work*, 17 (1946–1947), pp. 125–26, Abstract.

[16] William C. Smith, *The Stepchild*, Chicago: The University of Chicago Press, 1953.

[17] William C. Smith, "The Stepchild," *American Sociological Review*, 10 (1945), pp. 237–42; "Re-marriage and the Stepchild," in Morris Fishbein and Ernest W. Burgess (eds.), *Successful Marriage*, New York: Doubleday and Company, 1947, pp. 339–55; "Adjustment Problems of the Stepchild," *Proceedings* of the Northwest Annual Conference on Family Relations (1948), pp. 87–98; and "The Stepmother," *Sociology and Social Research*, 33 (May-June, 1949), pp. 342–47.

[18] Jessie Bernard, *Remarriage: A Study of Marriage*, New York: Dryden Press, 1956. Chapter 8: "Establishing Dynamic Equilibrium: Remarriages with Children," pp. 210–26 and Chapter 12: "The Success of Remarriage: Children of the First Marriage," pp. 301–29.

involved and not of the principals themselves, the investigation was useful in suggesting many hypotheses for direct inquiry. Bernard's study also serves to provide data from the parent generation to complement inquiries, like the present ones, in which the data were secured from the children involved.

William J. Goode has made a significant contribution to the understanding of step-relationships. He reached 425 divorced respondents, all mothers of children, through a thorough and quite effective procedure to secure a representative sample within a county.[19] Many of these women had remarried since their divorce. The data he provides illumine the processes and phases of adjustment through which divorced mothers of varied situations may go and the manner in which stepfathers are introduced into the family group.

A number of scholars have examined the differences in adjustment of children in broken and unbroken homes. Few, however, have attempted to discern "whether children are better adjusted in homes psychologically broken but legally and physically intact, compared with legally broken homes." Ivan Nye, in a study similar in method and problem to the present research, found within a sample of almost 800 high school youth that, as a group, "adolescents in broken homes show . . . better adjustment to parents than do children in unhappy unbroken homes." He pointed out that "reconstructed" families, those into which a stepparent had been incorporated, often brought about enhancement of the child-parent adjustments as a result of remarriage.[20]

The Research Populations

The findings reported in this paper stem from two separate, though related, studies. Data for the first were collected in the State of Washington in the spring of 1953, while the data for the second and larger study were secured in North Carolina and Ohio in the spring of 1960. In both inquiries, questionnaires were administered by classroom teachers to junior and senior high school students. The analyses being presented here are derived from those portions of the data provided by the 2145 stepchildren found among the almost 29,000 teen-agers who were involved in these two endeavors. The total number of subjects comprised about 90 per cent of all the white pupils enrolled in the 7th through 12th grades within the selected cities and counties.[21]

---

[19] William J. Goode, *After Divorce*, Glencoe: The Free Press, 1956. Chapter XXI, "The Children of Divorce," pp. 307–30.
[20] F. Ivan Nye, "Child Adjustment in Broken and in Unhappy Unbroken Homes," *Marriage and Family Living*, 19 (November, 1957), 356–61.
[21] Greensboro and Lexington cities and Chatham, Harnett, and Lee counties of North Carolina; the cities of Hamilton and Urbana and Delaware and Morrow counties in Ohio; and Kitsap County, Washington. The parochial schools also

In the Puget Sound area, the 572 such stepchildren constituted 12.2 per cent of the sample secured there (N = 4685), and the mother-stepfather homes were encountered 3.2 times as often as were father-stepmother families. Similarly, the 772 Ohio stepchildren comprised 7.5 per cent of the 10,388 participants, and the parental pattern distribution had a stepfather-stepmother ratio of 3.8. In North Carolina, 710 stepchildren accounted for but 5.4 per cent of the 13,164 students, with a parallel stepparent pattern ratio of 4.8. In all three states, very high proportions of respondents were "Protestant" in religious preference, although the proportion of Catholics ranged from 2.5 per cent in the Southern state to 13 per cent in the Mid-West and Far-Western areas.[22]

Child-Parent Adjustment Scales

Scales were utilized to measure the adjustment and orientations of the respondents to each of their parents. The analyses have been made contrasting the adjustments of children living under three different parent patterns: living with both natural parents, having a mother and stepfather, and residing with a father and stepmother. Scale scores have been grouped for presentation, placing all of the children into high, medium, or low adjustment categories.

For the Washington sample the scale consisted of five items.[23] The questions were asked with reference to mother and father separately, and four or five response choices were provided for each. Categories were combined to develop the closest approximation to a perfect Guttman-type scale, resulting in seven score groups, ranging from 3 to 9. The items were simple-scored and formed a quasi-scale.

The scale developed for measuring affectional orientation toward mother and father in the North Carolina–Ohio study was longer but quite comparable in content to that used in the Washington inquiry. Each scale was comprised of nine items with four or five alternative replies.[24] After categories were combined and simple-scored, these items formed a quasi-scale with fifteen score groups ranging from 0 to 14.

---

participated in Ohio. Only white, public schools were included in North Carolina. Herein, the Negro respondents in Ohio and Washington are excluded from the data analyzed, and only white subjects are involved in all three areas.

[22] Additional contrasts in the distribution of parent patterns may be found in the authors' "Frequencies and Characteristics of Broken Homes among Adolescents," an unpublished manuscript, 17 pages.

[23] "Do you talk over your personal matters with your mother (father)?" "Do you ever feel that your mother (father) neglects you and your wishes?" "In general, how well do you get along with your mother (father)?" "Does your mother (father) understand you and your problems?" "Has your mother (father) given you the love and attention you think you should have?"

[24] "Does your mother (father) seem to understand you and your problems?" "Do you confide your inner thoughts and feelings with your mother (father)?" "Do you feel that you can depend on your mother (father) for support and encouragement

Responses for mother and father were given identical weights, so these scores may be compared. However, since the scales in the two investigations were based on somewhat different items, the frequency distributions of scale scores for the two samples cannot be compared. Yet the analysis which follows reveals that the patterns of relationships are essentially the same in each of the samples.

Analysis of the Data

Affectional Orientation to Parents

If one examines the data in Table 1 for those subjects who resided with both real parents, it is evident that the average level of affection in every combination is higher toward mothers than toward fathers. The extent of this difference, however, varies considerably according to the age and sex of the respondents. The younger children (7th through 9th grades) were considerably closer to each parent, according to our indices, than were the older subjects (10th through 12th grades). Within each of the two age groups, males were more intimately related to fathers than were females, and the latter were closer to mothers than were the males. Among the possible dyadic combinations, the closest in degree was that between younger females and their mothers; while the most "distant" occurred between older females and their fathers.[25]

When the scores toward stepparents are contrasted with those toward real parents of the same sex, it is quite apparent that for the majority of our subjects stepparents had not been able to attain the same level of affection and degree of closeness as had real parents. However, in this regard, it is evident that the differences in magnitude between males and females or between the younger or older adolescents in our populations are neither large nor consistent. "The general consensus among remarried parents," Bernard asserts, "seems to be that very young or quite grown-up children tend to assimilate a new parent more easily than do adolescents."[26] An analysis of the data in terms of the age at which the

---

when you really need it?" "Are there times when you like your mother (father) less than at other times?" "How close is your relationship with your mother (father)?" "Do you feel that you can talk over your personal problems with your mother (father)?" "Do you ever have feelings of dislike for your mother (father)?" "Do you ever try to avoid your mother (father) because of your feelings toward her (him) at that time?" "Do you ever get annoyed with your mother (father) because of the way she (he) treats you?"

[25] If one extended this finding to speculate about the relationship between family composition and family unity, the most "emotionally homogeneous" families would be those with all male children whose affection for mother and father were approximately equal; while the least "homogeneous" affectional ties would be expected in those families with all female children whose relationships with their mother and father were most widely divergent in intensity.

[26] Bernard, *op. cit.*, page 216.

TABLE 1 *Affection for Parents, by Grade in School, Sex, and Parent Pattern: Washington and North Carolina–Ohio Samples*

Parent Pattern	WASHINGTON SAMPLE					NORTH CAROLINA–OHIO SAMPLE				
	Total	MALES		FEMALES		Total	MALES		FEMALES	
		7–9	10–12	7–9	10–12		7–9	10–12	7–9	10–12
Both Parents										
Mother: %high*	30.3	26.4	20.7	40.7	32.2	46.7	48.7	34.8	55.7	42.5
%low*	15.1	13.7	14.4	14.7	17.6	16.9	12.7	21.6	13.4	23.0
N	3510	984	773	890	841	17,738	4982	3596	5411	3749
Father: %high	8.4	12.9	8.2	6.1	5.6	34.4	47.5	31.6	32.2	22.6
%low	31.4	23.2	27.8	34.0	41.5	29.2	18.3	30.9	29.3	41.7
N	3488	984	769	880	833	17,738	4982	3596	5411	3749
Mother-Stepfather										
Mother: %high	28.4	26.7	17.6	38.2	28.4	42.8	43.9	30.8	50.8	39.4
%low	20.8	18.1	20.9	23.6	20.6	23.9	20.0	31.8	19.0	29.7
N	423	116	91	110	102	1112	310	195	358	249
StepFa: %high	5.5	10.5	4.4	5.6	1.0	17.8	30.2	12.2	16.4	9.2
%low	49.0	37.7	46.2	47.7	65.7	55.8	41.6	56.3	56.4	72.0
N	416	114	91	107	102	1115	308	197	360	250
Father-Stepmother										
StepMo: %high	10.1	10.4	5.1	10.0	20.0	19.8	22.5	15.9	22.0	18.9
%low	49.6	56.3	56.4	50.0	32.0	55.6	45.1	59.4	54.2	66.0
N	129	48	39	20	25	252	71	69	59	53
Father: %high	14.2	14.6	15.4	14.3	12.0	39.4	58.3	29.4	41.7	24.1
%low	35.1	27.1	30.8	57.1	40.0	29.5	18.1	29.4	31.7	42.6
N	134	48	39	21	25	254	72	68	60	54

* Washington sample: scores 8 and 9 were classed as "high"; 3–5 as "low." North Carolina–Ohio sample: 10–14 were "high"; 0–4, "low."

subjects *became* stepchildren is contemplated, and such a breakdown should more directly test her contention. Also to be noted in both sample totals are the very similar score distributions for stepmothers and step-fathers in contrast to the more divergent score proportions for real fathers and mothers.

Since they have more distant relationships to stepparents, one might expect that stepchildren would compensate by developing exceptionally close ties to their real parents. Although children in homes with a mother and stepfather have slightly lower scores, on the average, toward their mothers than do those youngsters who live in homes that have remained unbroken, the level of affection toward stepfathers is usually markedly lower than toward real fathers. Thus, the *difference* in attitudes toward parents is greater in this type of step-home than in homes containing both real parents. Perhaps any tendency to compensate for the attenu-ated relationship toward stepfathers by establishing even closer than customary bonds with the mother is partially offset by the effect on the relationship of a greater amount of discord in the home. Other evidence from these studies makes this assumption tenable.[27]

TABLE 2   *Affectional Orientation to Stepparents, by Sex of Respondent and Reason for Loss of Parent—North Carolina–Ohio Sample*

Orientation scores	TO STEPFATHER				TO STEPMOTHER			
	MALE		FEMALE		MALE		FEMALE	
	Death	Di-vorce	Death	Di-vorce	Death	Di-vorce	Death	Di-vorce
10–14	20.4%	25.6	12.6	14.7	13.1	22.6	13.8	27.9
5– 9	28.3	29.1	19.3	25.9	32.8	24.2	29.0	26.3
0– 4	51.3	45.3	68.1	59.4	54.1	53.2	67.2	55.8
Total %	100.0	100.0	100.0	100.0	100.0	100.0	100.0	100.0
Total N	152	289	182	367	61	62	58	43

For the father-stepmother families the situation was somewhat differ-ent. Generally, the relationships with fathers in such homes were close slightly more often than toward fathers in unbroken homes. Since the affectional level toward stepmothers was quite low, adolescents in these homes tended to have closer bonds with the real father than with the stepmother. However, the average levels of the relationships toward the two parents tended to be lower than occurred in either of the other parent patterns.

[27] Using data from this project, Earle found the level of marital discord to be higher in stepparent homes than in first marriages. See John R. Earle, *Parental Conflict in First Marriages and Remarriages as Reported by a Sample of Adolescents,* Chapel Hill: The University of North Carolina, unpublished master's thesis, 1961.

The recurring implication in Smith's discussions of the stepchild is that the adjustment of the stepchild to his parents, singly and jointly, is more difficult and at a less harmonious level than is that of the child in a normal home. Our data substantiate his contention. Over-all, the adjustment toward stepparents is usually poorer than toward the real parent of the same sex, for both boys and girls and with regard to both stepmothers and stepfathers. Further, in most of the parent-child and age-sex combinations the stepfather appears to fare better in comparison with the real fathers than do stepmothers in contrast with mothers in normal homes. Nonetheless, the identity of sex roles does tend to place the girls closer to their mothers and the boys closer to their fathers, whether they be real or stepparents.[28]

Adjustment and Nature of Previous Break

The late James Bossard believed that significant studies of family settings would need to "distinguish between cases where the children's parents have been divorced, and where death terminated the procreative family. . . ."[29] Bernard also expressed interest in this factor. In one context she asserted that "the remarriages of the widowed seemed to be more successful than those of the divorced."[30] Further on, however, she also stated that "the entrance of a new parent tends to have an adverse effect if it takes place after death and a benign effect if it takes place after divorce."[31] If such differentials do exist, they clearly should appear in a comparison of the adjustment scale scores of the children who have acquired stepparents by these two divergent sets of circumstances.

Since the Washington data involved too few cases for the breakdown required to test these relationships, our results on this issue are limited to the North Carolina–Ohio sample. Table 2 shows the comparison of orientation scores toward stepparents, for the latter sample, between children whose homes had been broken by divorce and those broken by death. Although differences in scores toward stepfather are small, all comparisons show higher average adjustment toward the stepparent when the previous marriage had been broken by divorce. Both comparisons are significant at the .10 level, by the Chi-square test, for combined male and female frequencies.

Average orientation scores toward the real parent were approximately the same for the two types of broken home. The dispersion, however, was greater with regard to the real parent who had divorced, a greater per cent being in both high and low score groups than was the case for

[28] For a more extended, though earlier, consideration of the affectional relations toward stepparents for the Washington sample see: Charles E. Bowerman, "Family Background and Parental Adjustment of Stepchildren," *Research Studies of the State College of Washington,* 24 (June, 1956), pp. 181–82. Abstract.
[29] Bossard, *op. cit.,* page 151.   [30] Bernard, *op. cit.,* page 111.
[31] *Ibid.,* page 321.

parents who had been widowed. The moderate size of these differences, in spite of the consistent direction for stepparents, lends support to Goode's contention that emphasis should be placed on the nature of the relationships rather than upon mere form. He states that the differential effects of divorce and remarriage on children "are more properly measured by *differences in the steadiness of warmth and love, in understanding, rather than by the simple structural differences to be found between broken and unbroken homes.*"[32]

Presumably numerous influences interact to bring about the seemingly complicated result that children of the divorced may tend more often to adjust to their stepparents *both better and worse* than those who have experienced bereavement before a remarriage. Among those factors which may be involved, several can be suggested: the younger age and smaller number of children, on the average, who acquire a stepparent after a divorce, contrasted with a death experience; differentials in the timing before remarriages and, thus, in the intensity and content of the children's memories; factors which operate in a divorce situation to select the parent that will retain custody of given children; differences in personal attributes and the probability of remarriage; the comparative facility of the stepfather role in contrast to the difficulty of the stepmother role, and the probability of each following divorce or death of parents; disruptive influences of former spouses in the aftermath of divorce; and even class differentials in death and divorce frequencies and consequences. Precise and representative data related to children involved in remarriages in this country are lacking. Furthermore, little is known of the consequents of remarriage following divorce or death of one's spouse. Consequently, our discussion of these factors must be recognized as merely suggestive.

Why might a larger proportion of children of divorce adjust *better* to stepparents than is the case with children of bereavement? First, on the average, children who acquire a stepparent following divorce probably do so more promptly after the event, at an earlier age, and in fewer numbers (per family) than do those who have experienced the death of a mother or father. Not only do the differentials in mortality and re-marriageability by age contribute to this result, but also often the ready availability of a prospective partner (if a "triangle" were involved), and the proprieties surrounding bereavement, are factors which introduce a stepparent into families earlier when divorce rather than death has broken the home. Presumably younger children, particularly if very young, and more youthful parents, too, establish step-relationships more readily than will older ones. In addition, a remarriage in some respects may be less disruptive for those that have had a shorter experience in a post-marriage one-parent milieu than for those who have

[32] Goode, *op. cit.*, page 317.

undergone a lengthier period with but one parent as an influence and confidant.

Furthermore, assuming that the average initial number of children involved in a post-divorce remarriage is slightly smaller and that the sibling and child-parent patternings are in some ways then more often simpler than in a postbereavement remarriage (for example, more frequent parent-child combinations of the same sex), these influences, too, would accentuate the proportion of those making "good" adjustments.

Those who have experienced pre-divorce tensions may tend to reject the parent now out of the home and to anticipate and experience a stepparent as an improvement; whereas the tendency to idealize a deceased parent, and the presence of accumulated and, presumably, positive residues on the part of both the children and the surviving parent may impede the acceptance of a surrogate. The contrasting content in the memories of children in these two circumstances, coupled with the different degrees of flexibility linked to the time-lapse factor, could also increase the number who achieved satisfying relationships with their stepparents, when a divorce rather than a parental death figured in the family background.

A cluster of factors also operates to affect the selection of a new marriage partner, to whom the child is to adjust: which partner, when there are children, is more apt to select or be selected, and what attributes may be more likely to "survive" to interact in a second marriage. Some persons who have been divorced benefit by the experience, gain in "maturity," develop a determination to succeed in marriage and parenthood, and consequently engender improved relationships. Bereavement, which strikes persons generally without regard to their marital or parental fitness, perhaps serves less well to spur new approaches to family living and may actually hinder the acceptance of new patterns in the subsequent marriage.

Moreover, although customary custody arrangements following divorce leave the children with the mother, or sometimes with the parent of the same sex, the traditional patterns are sometimes altered to provide that the "more competent" parent retains the children, thereby leaving the decision concerning a remarriage and the selection of a stepparent to the more adequate partner, increasing to some degree the probability of success.

On the other hand, why might a greater proportion of children from divorced homes also be found to adjust *less well* to stepparents than do those who lost a parent by death? Divorce often is symptomatic of those personalities who have failed to achieve an adequate adjustment to their spouses, and perhaps also occurs more often among those parents who were less competent as parents. The inadequacies of those persons then influence the decision to bring a stepparent of certain qualities into the family circle, and their marital attributes continue to operate within the new setting as well. Furthermore, the influence of previous tensions and deep conflicts may carry over directly or covertly into the personality, marital, and parental patterns brought to a new marriage. Oftentimes, an implication of failure and inadequacy may be directed toward a divorced parent, even a preferred one, and may militate against adequate child-parent adjustment; whereas such a qualification or imputation is not a factor in the child's assessment of a bereaved parent.

In addition, the difficulties engendered by the custody of children being split between the two parents or the intrusions otherwise of a former spouse produce disruptive effects upon some children of divorce not experienced by those with a parent deceased.

It is recognized that the social significance and psychological meaning of the behaviors and expectations implied or specified in the scale items probably are not the same for families of diverse socio-economic statuses. However, while divorce now accounts for more stepparent-stepchild relationships than death, both death and divorce proportionately more often break homes in the lower economic segments of our population. Differentials in modal behavior patterns; re-marriageability rates by sex, age, previous marital status; value systems and levels of expectation; educational achievement; and economic security may serve to alter the consequences and thereby tend to polarize the results of divorce by class.

Parental Preferences

Somewhat similar to the parent comparisons which can be made with the affectional orientation scales were the specific "parent preference" items included in the questionnaires of each of the inquiries.[33] Extended discussions of the parental preferences of stepchildren, in contrast to those residing in normal homes, can be found elsewhere.[34] The data from both samples consistently reveal the same patterns.

Briefly, stepchildren are more likely to express a preference for one parent or the other than are those who live with both real parents. Girls and the older adolescents are more apt to express a preference than are

---

[33] Washington State: "Which parent do you like best as a parent?" North Carolina-Ohio: "How would you compare the feelings of liking, closeness, or affection you have for your father with those you have toward your mother?" Each query provided five response choices, ranging from much stronger or a little stronger toward one parent through an equivalent "about equal" category on to a little or much stronger feeling toward the other parent.

[34] Donald P. Irish, *The Parental Preferences of Kitsap County Youth*, Seattle: The University of Washington, unpublished doctoral dissertation, 1957, Chapter VIII, "The Step-child and Parental Preference," pages 253–308 (for the Washington sample) and "The Adolescent Project: Parental Preference Patterns of Adolescents from Broken Homes," *Research Previews*, 8, #4 (June, 1961), pages 1–10 (Institute for Research in Social Science, University of North Carolina, for the North Carolina-Ohio sample).

the boys and our younger respondents. Stepchildren more often prefer the real parent over the stepparent.

The data show also that the frequency of preference is greatest when the adult is of the same sex as the child. Since these relationships occur whether the adult is a real or stepparent, for both the younger and older respondents, the tendency to identify with the parent of one's own sex is apparent. The sharing together of attitudes, interests, and activities of a sub-culture, by each sex, is presumably a prominent factor in producing these patterns.

However, while these influences usually prove insufficient to swing the affectional preference of the majority of the children to the *step*parent of the same sex, there is usually enough leverage involved to increase the proportion who indicate that they feel "the same" toward both parents. This "balanced" emotional position may represent a "way station" or intermediate position for these children, who can remain loyal and close to their natural parent of the opposite sex while yet signifying an affinity for the stepparent of the same sex and showing that the latter has been able to win at least an equal place in their affections. As the usual pattern is one of divergence in emotional attachment to the parents separately, equivalent affection for parents on the part of a child is an indication of achievement for a father in competition with a mother or for a stepparent in relation to a real parent, assuming that such equivalence is a status to be valued.

Other Factors Associated with Affectional Orientations

Bearing on the topics already discussed are a number of other aspects of child-parent interactions related to adjustment and parent-preferences: namely, parental discriminations felt by stepchildren who have siblings; feelings of rejection or acceptance; and the presence, absence, and directionality of desires to emulate parents or to identify with them. Quite comparable data have been secured for these factors in both investigations. Although the analyses and interpretations will be extended in later reports, a résumé of the relationships is included.

Felt Discrimination

The Cinderella story and others in our folklore provide traditional illustrations of discriminatory practices and attitudes that stepparents may manifest. Folk beliefs portray stepparents as particularly prone to discriminate unfairly among children. The responses reported herein represent the *perceptions of the children* concerning the presence or absence of parental discrimination. These feelings are an important factor psychologically whether or not an objective appraisal would show that the parents charged with discrimination actually practiced it.

The items most pertinent to this concern were not the same in the two samples.[35] Since the Washington State question elicited the feelings more directly and avoided qualifications due to age, differences in sibling patterns, and so on, the following conclusions are from that sample. For each of the parent-child age-sex combinations, stepparents were believed to discriminate more often than were natural parents; and children in step-homes were more often "not sure" than were those living with both real parents. Stepparents of the opposite sex were more often suspected of discrimination than were those of the child's own sex. Stepchildren of both sexes believed that the stepmother discriminated more than did stepfathers. These differences were all significant at the .01 level.

Thus, these findings further substantiate that the relationships of stepchildren to their stepparents, particularly, but toward their natural parents as well, are marked by greater levels of uncertainty of feelings, insecurity of position, and strain than are those to be found in normal homes. Further analyses will control for varied types of sibling patterns, using the larger sample.

Feelings of Rejection

Closely parallel to feelings about discrimination are children's feelings that they may be or are rejected by one or both of their parents. The items utilized in the samples were quite comparable.[36] The results again were very similar; and the relationships proved to be significant at the .01 level.

Children residing with both natural parents least often felt rejected by either or both parents. Both boys and girls felt somewhat more often rejected by the natural parent in a stepparent home and felt much more often rejected by the stepparent than they did with natural parents, of their own sex, in a normal home. Boys generally expressed such feelings of rejection less often than the girls, within each parent pattern. Again, among the Washington respondents, those who were "unsure" regarding being wanted were found with greater frequency in the homes with step-relationships, for each parent-child sex combination. Very parallel findings resulted from questions closely similar in content: "Do your parents ever compare you unfavorably with other young people?" and "Do your parents seem to go out of their way to hurt your feelings?"

---

[35] Washington State sample: "Have your parents favored other children over you?" ("yes," "not sure," "no" response categories toward each parent). North Carolina-Ohio sample: "How does the amount of discipline you get compare with what your brothers and sisters get?" ("I get much more," "I get a little more," "Some get more, some get less," "I get less," "have no brothers and sisters").
[36] Washington State sample: "Have you ever felt that your parents wished you were not in the family?" ("yes," "not sure," and "no" for each parent). North Carolina-Ohio sample: "Do your parents ever make you feel like you are not wanted?" ("Both parents do," "mother does," "father does," "neither does").

An inverse question was asked of the Washington teen-agers, and their responses provide corroborative evidence: "Do you ever wish you were living in a different family?" Children of both sexes least often rejected their own family when they resided with both natural parents, rejected it somewhat more frequently in a mother-stepfather home, and rejected it most often in father-stepmother families. The data once again highlight the greater difficulties faced by stepparents, particularly stepmothers.

Desire to Emulate Parents

Also related to affections toward, and preferences for, parents are the wishes of children to emulate their parents.[37] Consonant with the assumptions underlying the foregoing analysis, it was expected that a greater proportion of stepchildren would wish to emulate their biological parent in more or most ways than would desire to imitate their stepparent in comparable fashion. The highest proportion of respondents wishing to emulate either or both parents was found among those living with both natural parents. In the homes involving step-relationships, as anticipated, children of both sexes wished more often to emulate their natural parent, rather than the stepparent. However, each parent, regardless of relationship, had greater influence with the children of his own sex.

Summary

In all the aspects thus far examined, homes involving step-relationships proved more likely to have stress, ambivalence, and low cohesiveness than did normal homes. The reactions of adolescent children indicate that stepmothers have more difficult roles than do stepfathers, with the consequent implications for interactions within the family. Stepdaughters generally manifested more extreme reactions toward their parents than did stepsons. The presence of stepparents in the home affected also the adjustment of the children to their natural parents, usually somewhat diminishing the level of adjustment.

[37] The same question was used in the two samples, though with slightly different response categories: "Would you like to be the kind of person your mother (father) is?" Since the replies to this item by the North Carolina-Ohio subjects have not yet been machine-processed, the generalizations are based on the data from the Washington sample only.

Chapter 20: Forestalling and Solving Problems

62. MARITAL CONFLICT: ITS COURSE AND TREATMENT AS SEEN BY CASEWORKERS

Dorothy Fahs Beck

§ This preliminary report on an extensive research project has as one central concept marital balance, or the dovetailing of the partners' needs and the reciprocal methods of meeting them to the extent than a mutually satisfactory equilibrium is reached. The breakdown of marital balance tends to result in conflict. A discussion of casework treatment brings out not only the stages in the process of conflict and the possible dissolution of the marriage but also the processes of resolving the conflict and restoring balance.

Because of the high prevalence and serious consequences of marital problems among family agency clients, casework on marital problems was chosen as having precedence for practice-focused research under the leadership of the Family Service Association of America. As the initial project* in this area, the association undertook, with the help of funds from the National Institute of Mental Health, to "explore and attempt to formulate in conceptual terms the underlying processes involved in the resolution or alleviation of marital problems through casework." The project has been based on the assumption that "skilled and perceptive caseworkers understand a good deal more about what they are doing in the treatment of marital problems than they usually

SOURCE: *Social Casework*, 47 (1966), 211–21. Reprinted by permission of the author and Family Service Association of America.

The author's background is given in the footnote for article 10.

* This first project is known in the field as the FSAA Research Project on the Treatment of Marital Problems. It is being financed in part by Public Health Service Grant MH-602 from the National Institute of Mental Health, under the title "Casework on Marital Problems: A Conceptual Exploration."

communicate." The core purpose throughout has been to tap some of this unformulated knowledge and integrate it in ways that would contribute to theory building and to the development of subsequent research in this area. This paper represents a brief interim attempt at such a formulation.*

The reflections of practice wisdom used as sources for the project have been gathered through two major channels: (1) the collection of responses from more than 400 caseworkers in 104 member agencies throughout the country to a series of more than 60 difficult, unstructured questions and (2) the stimulation of local study groups to prepare reports in depth on special topics. This gathering of practice wisdom has resulted in the accumulation of some 9,000 pages of comment and 28 study group reports. These resources have been further supplemented by occasional tape-recorded interviews with caseworkers and by a review of relevant research and related studies developed in previous local agency projects and elsewhere. These materials are being subjected to an intensive content analysis by a team of research analysts and assistants.† The results will be reported in detail in a series of monographs.

At this point the central contribution that has emerged from this analysis is best reflected in a longitudinal view of the marital relationship over time and, more particularly, in a conceptualization of the process of escalation of marital conflict and its reduction through casework. This is the focus of this paper. In the selection of conflict as the central theme, no implication is intended that all marital problems involve conflict. Nor can the research context of the study be taken to mean that the formulations ventured have been validated through formal research. The details, gleaned mainly from the workers' comments, reflect instead their informal observations, based primarily on experience with troubled marriages. In selecting, organizing, and interpreting these observations, the writer has been guided by the natural time sequence of the marital career, the logic of the processes involved, the focus on conflict, and the implications of the workers' core concept of balance. In most instances the resulting formulations are suggested, rather than clearly identified, in the responses received and do not in any case rest on consensus

* This formulation will be expanded and refined in a summary monograph on the project.

† The research analysts who have worked at one time or another on the project are Mrs. Elsbeth Couch, Sheila Day, Mrs. Hazel Froscher, Wingate Froscher, Mrs. Elinor Haberman, Mrs. Artie Helgason, Mrs. Julia Matlaw, Robert Roberts, Mrs. Ruth Ronall, Mrs. Mary Schreiber, and Mrs. Hedda Spielman. Mrs. Mina Holtzberg was associate director of the project for the first year and a half of its existence. The contributions of each will be specifically identified in the final monographs. Project assistants who have worked on the content analysis are Phyllis Cohen, Mrs. Carol Glassheim, Miriam Kagan, and Mrs. Isabel Kottak. The FSAA Research Committee has served throughout in an advisory capacity. The contributions of all are gratefully acknowledged.

among respondents. To encompass in a brief paper a total longitudinal view, they are being presented here in bold outline form with minimum elaboration and qualification and with full awareness that many refinements are needed.

The Concept of Marital Balance

At the outset, one central concept—that of *marital balance*—must be defined. By this term workers mean a dovetailing of the partner's needs and patterns of reciprocity in meeting them such as will maintain over the long run an equilibrium in gratifications that is acceptable to both. This balance in satisfactions and rewards is apparently essential for the long-term stability of the family as a system. The concept does not imply that all the needs of each partner must be met, but simply that the core needs specific to a given marital relationship must be satisfied. The level of giving and receiving need not be equal, provided the ratio of gratification to frustration is acceptable to both. Mutuality in emotional support and affection are central components but not the only ones, and even here perfect balance is not necessary. It matters little whether the dovetailing of need-gratification patterns is accomplished by sameness or difference, provided each partner likes to initiate the kind of behavior the other likes to receive. The needs met may also be either "neurotic" or "healthy." The relationship visualized is not seen as static; on the contrary, it is seen as one that fluctuates with changing needs, growth of family members, changes in family composition, and stress and crises. These fluctuations, from the courtship period to the restoration of marital balance that is a central goal of treatment, constitute one theme of this paper.

Courtship and Early Years of Marriage

The caseworkers' comments about choice of mate are consistent with this concept of balance. Essentially, each partner is seen as attempting to find among the eligible alternatives a mate who will meet as nearly as possible his emotional and reality needs as he feels them at the time. Ideally, the courtship process itself tests and retests the viability and the rewards of the relationship—the degree of meshing of the two personalities, of the partners' expectations, and of their values. Some discover before it is too late that the relationship is unrewarding and turn back. Others proceed along a course of increasing warmth and intimacy, mutual regard, and progressive commitment, to the final step of marriage with high hopes.

Once the marriage rites have been celebrated, however, and the glow of the morning fades, the realities of the task ahead become clear in the bright light of noon. Somehow the two must integrate into a satisfying partnership and a conjoint career, plan two designs for family living, two sets of expectations for the relationship, and two dreams for the future.

Breakdown of Marital Balance

While this is a difficult and universal task, failure to accomplish it is not seen as the major cause of loss of balance. Of more serious consequence are such factors as a gross error in the choice of mate, extreme immaturity, insatiable neurotic needs, unrealistic fantasies, and a lack of the skills needed to adjust to change or resolve conflicts.

To some extent the descriptions of marital breakdown read like a Greek tragedy. The factors leading to happiness or unhappiness are seen, to an important degree, as "present at the moment of choice." Perhaps the needs of only one partner were considered in the decision or the partners' needs dovetail in only one dimension. Perhaps, as in some seemingly perfect matings, the characteristics originally felt as the most desirable become in time the most hated. Other threats stem not from the original choice but from the impact of change over time—from differential growth rates, differential access to opportunities, or the emergence of the reverse side of an ambivalence. Added sources of imbalance cited are the inevitable crises and changes that are the common lot of man. The responses, as well as data from the FSAA census,[1] suggest that the birth of the first child and the demands of the nursery years are particularly stressful for the marital relationship.

Fortunately, failures in balance are often reversible. Most partners have the capacity to grow and change and can be helped to do so by their mates, the total family group, life experience, and treatment. Particularly important to the maintenance or restoration of balance are flexibility in coping with change, facility in communication, and skill in the control and resolution of conflict and in problem solving. As one caseworker wrote: "Breakdowns occur not because of differences, but because of the inability to handle these differences together." If this task proves insurmountable, a conflict spiral may begin and escalate tragically.

The Conflict Spiral

What, then, are the stages and course of conflict itself? From the question responses and from the study group reports—particularly the report from the Family Service of Delaware County[2]—and from the literature,[3] a composite picture of the escalation of conflict emerges that may be tentatively formulated as follows.

Latent Stage

Marital conflict is seen as beginning with a latent stage of variable length, which may last indefinitely or be so short as to go completely unnoticed. This stage in marital conflict does not readily lend itself to problem solving by the partners. Differences, whether small or large, are not overtly recognized, discussed, or dealt with realistically. The incipient conflict that results may be disguised by a façade of mutuality, may be held at arm's length by a process of mutual withdrawal, or may be obscured by reliance on alternate gratifications. Hence, irritations and resentments slowly accumulate and smolder and lead to progressive disenchantment. Although this latent stage may persist indefinitely, it frequently evolves into a series of further stages.

The Trigger

Sooner or later, if a new development intrudes to upset the balance, one or both of the spouses may be overwhelmed. Something felt as threatening suddenly reactivates earlier dissatisfactions or noticeably undercuts the gratifications received. Normal defenses cannot be maintained, and one spouse can no longer serve as need satisfier to the other. The balance is therefore upset. This added stress triggers some dramatic new action—some direct, though perhaps ill-advised, problem-solving effort.

The Clash

This unexpected, usually sudden, action precipitates an open clash or blowup. Under its impact, the submerged conflict can no longer be kept under control, and long-suppressed emotions burst forth. The sense of threat becomes mutual. To the more unaware partner, this crisis may seem incomprehensible—"a bolt out of the blue." To the other, it represents an attempt at solution of a smoldering problem.

At this point the road appears to fork. Some go one way, some another. The clash itself may set in motion readjustments long overdue or the conflict may stabilize at some intermediate level that seems to meet the particular needs of a couple. Other couples attempt to return to their prior state of avoidance and denial, but the truce is an uneasy one. Some abandon investment in the marriage and seek gratification elsewhere. Some vacillate between open conflict and reconciliation. Some commit their full energies to winning the conflict itself.

Spread of Conflict

If both partners choose open confrontation and retaliation, the tempo accelerates. Each round of attack and counterattack, each increase in demands, each session of increasingly frank and hostile criticism leaves a residue of smoldering anger and a bitter aftertaste. Increasingly, blame is not shared but mutually projected. The goal becomes victory, not accommodation. Each seeks to restore his own sense of adequacy at the expense of the other. Flexibility is reduced and negative behavior reinforced; thus exploration for new solutions is blocked. While some try to retard the spiraling conflict by making repeated attempts to reach out to the spouse, reconciliation is usually temporary. After an interlude, the quarrels begin again. What may have begun as a struggle confined to one area may in time spread to all areas of family living.

Search for Allies

Eventually, if the couple cannot solve the conflict alone, they reach out for allies. If there are children, they are likely to be drawn in— perhaps as substitute spouses, confidants, or accomplices or, perhaps, as judges, mediators, or bearers of messages. Regardless of the role they adopt, the children are burdened with thankless and hopeless tasks that exact a heavy toll. If the conflict persists long enough, the secrecy norms that protect the privacy of the family are eventually violated. Family boundaries are pierced and the fiction of solidarity is broken. The purpose of the move may be constructive—to seek counsel, essential resources, or solace and reassurance from friends. On the other hand, it may be to recruit allies, to enhance power resources, or to confirm the rightness of a cause. The paramour, as an ally to one spouse and threat to the other, presents possibly the most serious and direct threat to the existing marriage, for the new love relationship may well supplant the old, at least for a time.

With each expansion in the circle of allies, the positions of the opposing camps become more polarized and less subject to compromise. Eventually, the pile-up of hostility and the erosion of rewards is so great that the marital balance is completely destroyed and the continuation of the marriage made untenable—except, perhaps, for those who draw major satisfactions from the conflict itself.

Search for Alternate Sources of Gratification

Instead of open conflict, some partners look for vicarious fulfillment through their children or for alternate gratifications in work, social activities, or another love affair. But the more one partner builds an independent life, the more he reduces his emotional investment in the marriage. Eventually, he comes to see his spouse as an encumbrance, if not an active threat.

Dissolution of the Marriage

The final scene in this tragic drama comes when at least one of the partners is sufficiently motivated to take public responsibility for the decision to separate, to pay its price, and to impose it on the partner. At this point, one or both engage a lawyer as a further ally in the conflict. Usually the beginning of formal legal action represents a point of no return. Even before the decree itself is final, it is nearly impossible to reverse the spiral. A mutually satisfying marital balance cannot be rebuilt when nothing remains of the bright promise of courtship except the burning embers of hatred.

When Do Couples Apply for Help?

This all too brief picture of the stages of conflict presumes that there has been no intervention through casework or psychotherapy and that the marital partners have achieved no resolution through their own efforts. When in this typical sequence of conflict are couples likely to come to a family agency?

Most couples seek help from the agency only after the problem has become overt and stressful—that is, after the point of trigger or clash. The only significant exception involves couples who come because of problems with their children and who later learn that these stem from difficulties in their own marital relationships.

While help may be sought at almost any point thereafter, the motivation for the application tends to shift as the conflict escalates. In the early stages, spouses often come in together out of a mutual concern to save the marriage. In later stages, one partner is more likely to seek to enlist the worker as an ally in making the spouse behave, come home, stop his physical abusiveness, or interrupt his extramarital affair. About a fourth of all applicants with marital problems come after separation is an accomplished fact.[4]

Couples Who Can Be Helped

The chances of helping clients with marital problems vary greatly in accordance with the stage of the conflict when they seek out the agency and with the assets they bring with them. Optimum timing seems to require a preceding period of substantial anxiety. The first threat of divorce, the first revelation of infidelity, or the first temporary separation can increase accessibility to casework. The optimum time for application would thus seem to be shortly after the first major clash.

Certainly, the first application should not be delayed much beyond this point. Once infidelity or desertion has become chronic or a major source of satisfaction to either partner, or hostility has escalated to the point where all gratifications in the relationship have been lost, the situation is difficult to reverse. For a good chance of success, both partners must still see the marriage as worth saving and have real hope that it can be saved. They must seek help before the destructive patterns have become strongly entrenched and reinforced by secondary gains and before anger and hurt have spread to all areas of the marriage. Once the search for allies has involved the children as direct partisans or the conflict has extended to relatives and others outside the family, treatment becomes difficult.*

In the FSAA census,[6] those with marital problems who delayed application until after they had separated averaged less than half as many interviews as similar applicants who were still living with their spouses at the time of application. These and other figures suggest that too little and too late can be just as disastrous in marriage as elsewhere.

Among the clues to a favorable outcome most often mentioned were the presence of some remaining positives in the relationship (especially the willingness of the couple to seek help as a pair), the willingness of the original applicant to accept some responsibility for the problem, acceptance of casework as the method for resolving the conflict, and ability to relate to the worker in a predominantly positive manner.

Various inappropriate approaches to the worker cited as clues to a poor prognosis seem, on the other hand, to reflect later phases of the conflict, particularly efforts to draft the worker as an ally, to appoint him as judge, or to press him to punish or discipline the spouse. So also does a fixed, unyielding projection onto the partner.

Taken as a group, the workers' references to direct or indirect indicators of stage of conflict total about half of the more than 1,400 prognostic-clue comments and constitute an even higher proportion of those on points of accessibility to treatment.

In evaluating the assets of the two partners for the very difficult task of reversing the conflict spiral, workers look primarily to current functioning rather than past history. Among the positive clues noted were some ego strength, some ability to communicate, an absence of extreme behavioral deviance, and a margin of energy sufficient for the process of change.

Within the ego-strength category, nonrigid defenses and capacity for object relations ranked highest in frequency of mention as favorable predictors. Next came capacity for self-awareness, appropriate range and level of affective responses, capacity to control motility, and capacity to tolerate frustration, anxiety, and criticism. Unfortunately, the caseworkers' comments leave unclear what degree and combination of assets are needed for success and the extent to which these assets must be possessed by both partners.

---

* It is of special interest in this connection that the Harrisburg Study Group[5] found that where nonprofessional outsiders had become involved before the time of application the case was usually moving toward divorce at the time treatment was terminated.

Of key importance also is the worker himself—the totality of his personality, capacity for relationship, knowledge, orientation, and skill. More than two thirds of the respondents commenting on what makes the various casework techniques effective gave central importance to worker characteristics. Certainly, it is the total interplay of the worker and the two partners that in the end makes success possible.

Treatment of Marital Conflict

How then is conflict interrupted or moderated once the couple applies for service? How is marital balance improved, restored, or newly established? Often workers are unable to reverse the spiral. But when they do succeed, what is the process, step by step, by which they accomplish this result?

Establishing a Relationship with Both Partners

The first of several central tasks is that the worker establish a relationship of warmth, confidence, and trust with both partners, not only as individuals but as a marital pair. Both partners must be helped to tolerate the admission of an outsider into the most intimate aspects of their marital relationship and into a conflict that divides them but is crucial to both. A closely related requirement is that both partners come to understand and accept the potential role of the agency and the worker and their own future role in the casework process. Regardless of the natural pressures on the worker to become an active partisan, judge, or prosecutor, he must not permit himself to enter into the conflict as an ally of either side. Instead, he must be free to act as enabler and catalyst. When the two partners see each other as enemies and the battle has been joined, these are difficult requirements; they are nevertheless essential. A frequent pitfall reported for the early diagnostic period is over-identification with one spouse.

From these requirements, a related structural one also follows: If at all possible, both partners should be seen and involved in the treatment process. Four out of five respondents commenting on this point thought this was essential. Yet the more the conflict has escalated, the more difficult it becomes to involve the reluctant spouse. Workers have spelled out a number of diagnostic indications for working with one partner only and agree that progress can often be made by this more limited approach.[7] They differ, however, on whether they believe that treatment limited to one partner should be termed *marital counseling*.

Maximizing Motivation

The need to mobilize the motivation of both partners was especially stressed. For this caseworkers utilize what Lilian Ripple has called "the push of discomfort and the pull of hope." Discomfort is maximized by helping the spouses to face the extent of their own hostility, their current lack of fulfillment, the destructive effects of the conflict on themselves and their children, and its possible future consequences in terms of divorce or separation. They must also come to see that their current approaches are self-defeating and their secondary gains not worth the price.

At the same time, the couple must be helped to look to the future with renewed hope. Workers encourage the partners to identify what they want and expect from the marriage, what they want changed, and whether, in fact, they wish to continue the marriage at all. When goals are unrealistic, the partners are encouraged to modify them to more modest and realistic ones.

But goals alone are not enough to maximize the pull of hope. The partners must also have confidence that progress toward these goals is truly possible. Here the worker's own optimism, confidence, and knowledge of the experience of others are all crucial. If these can be conveyed to the couple, a start can be made. Facilitating an immediate solution to some small problem or relieving environmental stress can also rekindle hope. Once small positive gains are achieved, discouragement fades and the essential work can proceed with renewed vigor.

Identifying the Dynamics of the Conflict

Hope will have been kindled in vain, however, unless it is soundly based on realities and a plan of action designed for the specific problems of each specific marriage. The question on what workers need to know to diagnose a marital case brought forth the largest volume and greatest range of responses of any question in the study. Obviously, in any particular case, a worker can explore only for the most relevant clues.

Some of the most central diagnostic questions posed by caseworkers are these: What upset the balance? When did this happen and why? How extensive and how entrenched has the conflict become? Under what circumstances does it intensify or recede? What assets, vulnerabilities, and needs does each partner bring to the relationship? What in each is now threatening the other? What functions does the fight itself serve for the participants? What are its costs? When, how, and with whom should treatment begin? Should both partners be involved and how? Or should one or both be referred for psychiatric care? Is the marriage itself basically a viable one? How much change in the balance is feasible? Desirable? What pacing of change can be tolerated? What defenses need to be protected in the process? Sound answers to these central questions provide much-needed guidelines, while extensive misjudgments may lead to tragedy.

Helping the Couple Understand the Circular Interaction

As the worker selectively feeds back some of his more immediate observations, the spouses begin to sort out fact from fear and fancy, to distinguish inner feelings from outer realities, to focus on basic rather than superficial problems, and to identify distortions and recurrent elements in the conflict. To clarify the processes at work, the worker makes therapeutic use of both the here-and-now interactions between the partners and the interactions of both with the worker. Once the participants come to recognize some of their own individual contributions to the circular process of conflict, they may begin to control its escalation. They also develop a greater commitment to treatment.

Focusing the Conflict

The next essential is to bring the marital conflict into direct focus and to reverse the process of spread. Wherever the conflict has been denied or disguised, the mask is removed. Where it has been internalized, it is brought back into the arena of interaction. Where it has become diffused over many areas, it is refocused. Where parents and in-laws have intruded or been drawn in as allies, issues related to emancipation from the families of origin are worked through. Where children have been used as tools in the conflict or as substitute targets for parental hostility, they are freed insofar as possible. Where outsiders have been drafted as allies, they are progressively disengaged. Where a partner's energies and loyalties have been dissipated in seeking outside gratification, he is encouraged to rechannel his energies back into the marriage. The central purpose throughout is to return the conflict to its point of origin— to the husband-wife relationship. Once it has been directly confronted, it can be more readily interrupted or gradually tempered, and positive gratifications can be slowly restored.

Directly Confronting the Conflict

When the issues between the partners are finally out in the open, the hostile interaction may assume frightening proportions. At such crisis points, workers apparently do not hesitate to use their professional authority to introduce direct external controls. They seem to feel that, regardless of method, safe conditions for the direct expression of the long pent-up anger must be assured.

In particular, they insist that hostile feelings and anxieties be expressed verbally—not in physical abuse or other acting out—and preferably within the treatment situation. If the prohibition against physical attack does not succeed, some workers make a referral for legal protection. At other times, a spouse may be urged to interrupt temporarily an outside liaison; such an interruption may even be made a condition for the continuation of treatment. Or a wife may be asked to delay separation for a trial period while the couple and the worker try together to resolve the most urgent problems. If one spouse becomes overly anxious, or immobilized, or ill from a psychosomatic response, he may be referred to a medical resource.

More usual and less openly directive approaches include taking the focus off blame, keeping the partners from becoming defensive, and fostering mutual responsibility. As discussions proceed, the worker's support is shifted flexibly from one partner to the other as first one, then the other, must be protected from a barrage of criticism. Once one partner becomes more flexible and less defensive, the other feels less need to gain a point.

In this difficult process the worker acts as catalyst and educator. Whenever feasible, he arranges joint interviews and begins to foster and teach the direct communication and feedback so essential to identifying the mutual adjustments needed to restore equilibrium. He offers and teaches a new kind of listening. When feelings run high, he helps both participants become more objective. At the same time he keeps the discussions as fluid and flexible as possible, pushing for exploration by raising questions. Occasionally, he directly confronts one partner or both with obvious inconsistencies. The focus throughout is typically on the present interaction. The net effect is the gradual loosening of rigid patterns as a preliminary to new, creative solutions.

For this type of process, most workers see great value in a discriminating use of joint interviews. They differ, however, about when they should be used and the extent to which they are appropriate when major weaknesses in communication or gross hostilities are present. Some include additional sessions with the entire family, particularly in situations where the conflict involves other family members, such as the children, or where there is need for enhanced awareness of the total family interaction and the network of alliances.

Reducing the Intensity of the Conflict

Once the conflict has been confronted, how is its intensity reduced? Actually, reduction begins even in the first exploratory discussions. The mere verbalizing of the problems and the ventilation of feelings to a safe and understanding outsider lightens the burden on each partner and thus reduces pressures. Feelings can be further diluted if the caseworker deals with the partners' guilt about revealing family secrets to an outsider and gives assurance that their problems are not unique.

A second important step toward reducing the intensity of the conflict is the strengthening of each partner's self-esteem. When the spouse who has felt rejected or depreciated is given acceptance, his fear of the dominance of the stronger partner lessens and the power differential is reduced. Being more accepting of himself, he is more able to express himself in ways that will stimulate understanding and acceptance by the partner. If, at the same time, the self-esteem of the more dominant partner is also fostered, he may, in turn, be able to risk a softening of his demands and attacks.

A third approach mentioned involves identifying and sensitizing each to the components of his own and the partner's behavior that trigger hostile interaction. Once this has been accomplished, modification of the vicious cycle is easier. In the process, the unmet needs of each become clearer and the partners are stimulated to think of ways of meeting them. A reverse approach involves reducing the sensitivity of the spouses to the trigger. Once the special sensitivities of each are mutually understood, the tendency to challenge them is lessened.

Along with analyzing the circular interaction and stressing to each his own positives, caseworkers try to identify what it is that each partner likes about the other. Each is helped to relate to the other as a truly separate person. Differences then may be seen in a new light—perhaps as assets instead of liabilities. In addition, each is helped to seek more effectively the response he needs from the other. In time, each may learn to support in the other a positive and secure self-image that will not require the downgrading of the partner.

Fostering the Development of New Solutions

Ultimately, however, the resolution of the conflict requires not only a reduction in intensity but also new, creative solutions. At some point the old behavior of one must be met by a new and quite different response from the other. This in turn must be answered in a new way by the first if the circular process of conflict is really to be interrupted.

For most clients, the first step toward a new response has already been taken, for coming to the agency represents in itself a new approach to problem solving and creates a mind-set conducive to change. The explorations inherent in treatment also open up new perspectives and encourage the examination of alternatives. Sometimes the worker fosters new attitudes: for example, the modification of constricted attitudes toward sex. Some workers report planting "seed ideas" or making direct suggestions. These may concern a possible new form of interaction, a new way of handling the self, or a return to a discarded form of interaction. Others consider such direct advice-giving inappropriate.

Sometimes readiness for the new requires intensive nurturing. Old patterns may have to be broken, energies redirected, or new interests cultivated. Often one spouse must be prepared for anticipated novel behavior of the other or for temporary disturbances in balance during a transition period. On the other hand, new "codes of behavior" or revised definitions of role expectations may be needed.

While the specific approaches differ with each couple, there are some common denominators. Many caseworkers report, for example, that after a period of mutual exploration, identifiable tasks are laid out by agreement in "bite-sized bits." If the partners see a new approach as promising, a commitment may be obtained that it will be tried for some definite time-limited period. The worker then lends his ego and courage and uses his creative skill to devise and support a real test of the new solution.

His first task may well be to enable one partner to overcome a strong reluctance to make the first move. Once that partner has risked trying to meet in some new way the needs of the other, the worker may encourage appreciation and reciprocity. When this is forthcoming, he identifies this response to the initiator of the exchange, who may then reciprocate. The fostering of this positive type of spiral is continued through the numerous setbacks, crises, and regressions inevitable in the integration of any new approach.

Finally, in successful cases, the new positive pattern of interaction is firmly established and integrated. At this point the new patterns of reciprocity provide their own built-in reinforcements that help to perpetuate the gains. If, in the process, flexible techniques of problem solving and communication feedback have also been learned, the couple may be able themselves to restore balance in other areas.

An inevitable by-product of the successful resolution of the more immediate conflict is, however, the subsiding of the anxiety that up to this point has motivated treatment. Unless other concerns emerge that really challenge the couple, they move naturally toward termination. At this point, the worker too must be willing to let go as the partners again turn to each other for their major satisfactions and draw once again behind them the curtains of privacy.

Outcomes of Treatment of Marital Conflict

Finally, when treatment is terminated successfully and the marriage is maintained and strengthened, what are the specific types of outcomes achieved?

Viewed globally, the primary effects are seen as interactional rather than intrapsychic. They affect a whole relationship network that begins with the husband-wife relationship but extends well beyond it to relationships with the children, the family as a whole, relatives, and many others.

Among the more specific comments on improved relationships between the partners, improvements in the couple's ways of resolving problems were noted with particular frequency. Outcomes stressed in this area included the reduction of conflict-provoking behavior, less actual conflict, more appropriate modes of conflict resolution, and a re-channeling of conflict energies into more positive relationships with the partner. Improvements in patterns of communication were also empha-sized. In successful cases communication was reported to become freer, more direct, and less hostile as the partners became more able to listen, to share feelings of all kinds, and to express the negative ones in a less destructive way. Noted also were clarification of role perceptions and role allocations, increased acceptance by each of his respective role, increased ability to plan together, and more agreement on joint and family goals.

Changes in atmosphere were also described. The image of the partner becomes more realistic and more positive than it was prior to treatment. Interpretations of the behavior of the mate are more objective and valid and reflect increasing understanding. Partners show, on the one hand, greater tolerance and acceptance of each other's limitations and idiosyn-crasies and, on the other, an increased respect for, and recognition of, each other's assets.

Corresponding changes were also noted in partners' perceptions of their own specific marriage and of marriage in general. The spouses increasingly recognize marriage as a partnership and succeed in resolv-ing their ambivalence about continuing life with their own particular mates. Distortions and disabling attitudes carried over from earlier life situations are lessened, and there is an increased understanding of the conflict and a greater capacity to keep it limited. Both have a greater sense of security in the relationship and more hope for the future.

Casework treatment is not seen as resulting in a totally new pattern of interaction between the spouses. Rather, there is some moderation of extremes in the behavior of each, fostering a more flexible, satisfying interdependence, or, in more general terms, improving the current bal-ance, restoring an old balance, or establishing a new one. There is, for example, more mutual consideration and concern; increased demonstra-tion of affection, warmth, and empathy; better satisfaction of sexual needs; increased freedom and spontaneity in the interaction; and more sharing.

As would be expected, these changes in relationships between the partners affect, in turn, their performance as parents. They no longer need to use their children as scapegoats or as instruments for the expres-sion of their hostility toward each other. They are less likely to see their children as rivals, competitors, or need satisfiers and more likely to see them as individuals with needs of their own. They are also more able to resist manipulation by their children. The result in successful cases is more consistent discipline of the children when this is called for or more affection, understanding, and approval where this is appropriate. These changes are reflected, in turn, in improved functioning of the children themselves.

The re-establishment of the husband-wife relationship as the primary axis also affects relationships with parents and relatives. As each is helped to emancipate from his family of origin and to turn to his partner for his major satisfactions, both are more able to recognize and discourage undue interference from their families. The result is less antagonism and conflict with parents and in-laws and also less dependence on them. Those relationships that remain are more positive and mutually satisfying.

As the partners turn again to each other as a major source of gratification, their relationship with other outsiders also changes. Since they no longer need them as allies or confidants, they use them more appropriately and are more ready to set limits on their interference in the marriage.

Changes are also observed in the partners as individuals. There is less use of denial and projection, more acceptance of a share of the responsibility for existing problems, an increased willingness to examine their own roles in the conflict, and more flexible defenses. The treatment of marital problems through casework is not seen as resulting in fundamental personality changes or in the resolution of deep intrapsychic conflicts, but rather as a growth-promoting process in which the task of resolving the conflict provides the primary growth stimulus.

Taken as a whole, the picture given is an optimistic one. One must not, however, overlook the darker side—the failures in treatment. The FSAA census statistics[8] indicate, for example, that nearly half of the marital cases terminate prematurely at client initiative. In others, relationships deteriorate or continue in deadlock in spite of treatment. Some clients bring conflicts too deep or irreversible for casework help, with the result that one partner or both must be referred for psychiatric treatment. Still others come too late and proceed inexorably toward divorce without fully weighing the consequences.

It is important, here, to point out that workers' general concept of success is based on modest, not dramatic, gains. Where the partners bring only very limited strengths or are very poorly mated, the containment of the conflict or the arresting of the destructive process may be deemed success. Moreover, success also does not depend on maintaining the marriage. Helping one partner resolve his ambivalence and move out of a destructive marriage with minimum damage is also considered a success.

Research Implications

At this point many questions remain unanswered. Workers were not asked, for example, what they found to be the ratio of success to failure, or how often specific types of positive outcomes occurred. These are subjects more appropriately left for more formal research assessment. The focus in this project was rather on the identification of the wide range of variables and relationships involved and on the understanding of the development and resolution of conflict.

It is also important to remind the reader once more that the sketch given of the course and treatment of marital conflict does not rest on validated research. It represents simply one possible organization of the varied perceptions of caseworkers at one point in time. It is to be hoped that the many formulations given here will be tested, refined, and amplified, first by discussion and systematic case analysis, and then by formal research.

This team approach to the building of practice theory must be pressed further. What, more specifically, is marital balance, and how can it be studied? How, in detail, do its fluctuations relate to the equilibrium of the total family? Under what conditions does conflict escalate, stabilize, or recede? How do clients differ in these respects from couples who do not come to agencies? Which couples can be helped to resolve their conflicts? Which should be referred elsewhere or helped to separate? What complex combination of processes is most effective for each? How can the processes and results be tested? When this project is finished, most of these questions will remain unanswered.

It is important that casework practice and research continue as partners to develop and test theory and new methods of service. Only thus can the family service field learn how to help most effectively the hundreds of thousands of troubled families who each year turn to agencies for help. Perhaps in the process the field can also contribute increasingly to the basic understanding of one of man's core problems—that of how to resolve conflicts, whether between marital partners, between groups at the community level, or between nations.

References

1. Dorothy Fahs Beck, *Patterns in Use of Family Agency Service*, Family Service Association of America, New York, 1962. (Census figures cited in this paper are for the most part based on supplementary analyses of data collected in connection with this study that are not included in the published report.)

2. Family Service of Delaware County, Media, Pennsylvania: *Processes Involved in Marital Conflict and Its Resolution.* Mimeographed study group report. *Study group participants:* Helen LaMar (Leader), Mrs. Louise Bernstein, Mrs. Lucille Conover, Mildred Darlington, Mrs. Ruth Hammershaimb, Eleanor Hesch, Winifred Miller, Mrs. Mary D. Noonan, Elizabeth M. Robinson, Mrs. Maria E. Shelmire, Mrs. Ellen Wiesen. (This study group identified and named the first three stages of conflict described in this paper.)

3. Willard Waller and Reuben Hill, *The Family: A Dynamic Interpretation,* rev. ed., Dryden Press, New York, 1951; Willard Waller, *The Old Love and the New: Divorce and Readjustment,* Liveright, New York, 1930; Norman W. Bell, "Extended Family Relations of Disturbed and Well Families," *Family Process,* Vol. I, September 1962, pp. 175–93.

4. Beck, *op. cit.*

5. Family and Children's Service, Harrisburg, Pennsylvania: *The Effect of the Involvement of Other Persons with Marriage Partners in a Situation of Marital Conflict.* Mimeographed study group report. *Study group participants:* Mrs. Elsie S. Stonesifer (Leader), Mrs. Muriel Gunderman, Mrs. Adeline Miller, Mrs. Mary Phillips. *Consultants:* Dr. Miles D. Garber, Mrs. Lenore Stone Meffley, Glen Winter.

6. Beck, *op. cit.*

7. Family and Children's Service of Greater St. Louis, St. Louis, Missouri: *Choice and Implementation of Casework Treatment of Disturbances in Marriage Resulting from Severe Individual Pathology.* Mimeographed study group report. *Study group participants:* Sue Vesper (Leader), Mrs. Mary E. Greene, Mrs. Frankie W. Spearman. *Consultant:* Ruth Downing.

8. Beck, *op. cit.*

63. FAMILY TREATMENT CONCEPTS

Frances H. Scherz

§ An earlier approach to social work centered on the troubled individual. Gradually a shift toward family treatment occurred as the family was recognized as the most important influence on human development. The author introduces the concept of family equilibrium and the more basic concept of marital equilibrium. The family, not the individual, is the focus of treatment.

SOURCE: *Social Casework,* 47 (1966), 234–40. Reprinted by permission of the author and Family Service Association of America.

Frances H. Scherz is Director of Casework, Jewish Family and Community Service, Chicago, Illinois. Her paper was presented at the Biennial Meeting of the Family Service Association of America held in Detroit, Michigan, November 10–13, 1965.

Family treatment is in a stage of development similar to that of the young child who is struggling to establish his identity by asking: Who am I? Who am I in relation to my parents? How am I different from them? In this developmental stage, which is a normal part of his growth, the child is in a state of productive and exciting confusion. Family treatment is also in a state of exciting confusion. It is good that this is so because it serves to prevent a premature crystallization of concepts and theories of family treatment that are now emerging. Even so our practice must continue while theoretical speculations continue to be put forward, formulated, altered, and reformulated.

At this point there are almost as many definitions of family treatment as there are practitioners in the field and writers on the subject. The one used in this article is the working definition developed by the Committee on Family Diagnosis and Treatment of the Midwestern Regional Committee of the Family Service Association of America: "Family treatment is the process of planned intervention in an area of family dysfunctioning. Family treatment is centered upon the dynamic functioning of the family as a unit, and some form of multiple interviewing is the primary treatment technique. Shifts to other treatment techniques (individual, joint, and total-family interviews) are related to the emergence of new diagnostic data or treatment developments, and are undertaken in the context of the total-family treatment goal. Since the goal of treatment requires focus on the family, some form of multiple interviewing remains the major treatment technique."[1]

According to this definition family treatment is a new therapeutic model. It focuses on the system of interpersonal relationships of the total family; each family system is made up of a unique blend of biological, social, psychological, and cultural components that are expressed through the patterns of relationships among family members. Theories of personality are, of course, relevant to all forms of treatment. But when the family system is the unit of attention, the worker must also apply knowledge derived from theories of group interaction and group communication. The conceptual framework for family diagnosis must incorporate these theories. Moreover, in practice, in the course of exploration and treatment, the family must be viewed as a network of forces and of roles discharged through interactional and transactional processes.

In this article I shall discuss some of the assumptions and concepts that underlie the working definition given above. The essential assumption is that the family is the most important shaper and influencer of human destiny, the matrix in which human development takes place. How the individual matures, how he learns to manage himself in the family and the outside world, how he conducts himself in relation to

[1] *Casebook on Family Diagnosis and Treatment,* Family Service Association of America, New York, 1965, p. viii.

stress—in other words, his identity as an individual—is largely determined by intrafamilial patterns of conflict and integration.

These patterns are the family's accustomed ways of behaving and the rhythms it develops in the course of the continuous process of resolving differences as it faces new developmental tasks in each successive phase of family life. Eric Berne describes these patterns as "games" a family fashions and plays according to complex rules it develops both consciously and unconsciously.[2] The rules are designed to help the family perform its life tasks: ensure the security and physical survival of its members; provide a context for emotional and social functioning, sexual differentiation, and the training of children; and support the growth of individual family members. Each newly formed family develops a unique set of rules that are based on the meshing of the individual members' needs and responsive to the family's changing tasks. The rules shape the family network. The games, or the forms of conflict and integration, are played out through explicit roles—parent, husband, wife, son, daughter, breadwinner, and so forth—and through implicit emotional roles.

The Concept of Family Equilibrium

Recognition of the dynamic interplay between these complex sets of rules and patterns of conflict and integration has led to the concept of family equilibrium, viewed as the family's design to provide avenues of stability and change in the interest of performing life tasks and fulfilling growth needs as economically as possible. Economy of operation is achieved by agreements, compacts, alliances, and collusions that are shaped by the rules and, in turn, shape the patterns of conflict and integration. At any given time, or even throughout the course of a family's life, the equilibrium may be either predominantly adaptive or predominantly maladaptive. Often it is adaptive in some respects and maladaptive in others. In any event it is always designed to meet the family's operational needs.

The significance of family equilibrium and marital equilibrium is readily apparent in the phenomena of scapegoating and projective identification. Additional evidence is to be seen in the familiar treatment situation in which one family member becomes sicker as another becomes healthier. A ten-year-old boy (the less competent of two brothers) put this very well in a family interview when he said: "If my grades go up, Steve's grades will go down." What caseworkers have observed in their practice points to the fact that the more fixed the maladaptive family equilibrium is and, therefore, the less adequate for coping with

---

[2] Eric Berne, *Transactional Analysis in Psychotherapy*, Grove Press, New York, 1961, pp. 98–115.

new tasks, the more the family needs to cling to established ways as if it would be totally destroyed if the equilibrium were shifted.

Inherent in the concept of family equilibrium is the idea that each family member has a stake in stability and in change; when an individual is in trouble, the family is in trouble, and vice versa. Each family member is a beneficiary of family well-being and a victim of family maladaptation; he is also a producer of, and participant and collaborator in, the family system network for good and ill. He has his own problems, wishes, and goals that must be understood, but they can be understood only in the context of his family. Also inherent in the concept of family equilibrium is the idea that the nature of a family's equilibrium is closely related to its stage of development and the tasks characteristic of that stage. For example, family maturational tasks requiring a shift in family equilibrium may precipitate crises at certain transitional stages in the family's life—from the early years of marriage to the child-rearing years, from those years to the middle years, and so on.

Marital equilibrium is basic to family equilibrium. Therefore, the concept of marital complementarity—that marital interaction is based on intermeshing needs, hopes, and wishes—is an integral component of the theory of family treatment. An important current idea is that most persons choose as a marital partner a person whose personality structure is basically identical with their own and that the conflicts and defensive patterns of the partners dovetail. The nature and depth of psychopathology in each partner in a disturbed marriage are identical; basic conflicts, points of fixation and regression, and general ego integration are the same, despite differences in behavioral expression. The new family unit created by marriage develops its own rules and operational dynamics and has its own unique modes of adaptation and maladaptation.

One of the caseworker's major therapeutic endeavors in family treatment is to understand the nature of the family's equilibrium through learning to know the sets of rules and the patterns of conflict and integration that govern that equilibrium. Such knowledge is gained through direct observation of the processes of family interaction. The worker must also know at what stage the family is in its development and the specific forces or incidents that have upset its equilibrium, causing family dysfunctioning that requires treatment intervention. Having this knowledge, the worker can assess the nature and degree of change in equilibrium that is necessary, desirable, and possible. To use Berne's theory, one might say that a major goal of family treatment is to interrupt the destructive games, change or modify the overt and covert rules, and set in motion more constructive games with new or modified rules. Family treatment, then, attempts to influence the family system network for the purpose of reducing or altering dysfunctional stress on all members of the family. When treatment is effective, individual and family symptoms and problems disappear or are reduced.

In emphasizing the concept of family equilibrium, I wish to convey the idea that neither individual pathology nor particular presenting problems are, in and of themselves, overriding determinants in choosing the treatment method. Individual neuroses, character disorders, or psychoses may need to be explored, but they do not necessarily require individual treatment. Similarly, such presenting problem constellations as marital conflict, parent-child conflict, and problems of aging may suggest the use of different kinds of interviews during the exploratory period, but they do not necessarily determine the treatment method to be employed. More significant than individual pathology or presenting problems in determining treatment methodology are such factors as the degree of alienation and of intimacy in the family; the identity needs of each individual; the ability of each family member to perceive and respond to the feelings, actions, beliefs, values, and aspirations of other family members; and problems of self-esteem. Assessment of these factors should help the worker decide when various forms of family treatment are appropriate. The intent of the family approach is to discover in what ways the individual symptoms or presenting problem constellations represent family dysfunction. If there is an indication that the family's current problem—no matter how it is described—should concern the total family, family interviews should be used to shift the focus from the individual so that the entire family can be involved in working on the problem.

Communication

Communication is the index of family operations, and so the family system network is influenced through working with family interaction as it is expressed in communication. Communication is the means whereby the family transacts the business of life. It is carried on at all levels—conscious, preconscious, and unconscious. It takes many forms—verbal, nonverbal, attitudinal, and behavioral. It is revealed through the explicit and implicit use of roles and the expression of emotion, which may be bland or highly charged. The family's characteristic modes of communication reveal the cultural forces impinging on it; the social and personal values it embraces; its view of itself in relation to the outside world; its fears, permissions, taboos, and secrets; its defenses and adaptations; and the affective needs and responses of its members: in short, they reveal the family's life style. The messages family members communicate to each other may be congruent or incongruent. They may reflect the double-bind communication found in neurotic and psychotic family dysfunctioning. They may be clear, direct, and constructive in some areas of family communication, but clouded, confused, and confusing in others. It is through understanding the family's communication at all levels and its content, form, and affect that the worker gains knowledge of the family's life style, its adaptive and maladaptive equilibrium, and the immediate area of crucial dysfunction. Communication, then, is the channel for diagnosis.

Communication is also both the medium for treatment and a treatment goal. In the broadest sense, in family treatment the worker moves from observing the patterns of family communication to identifying the patterns that are crucial in family dysfunctioning, and then to working on better ways of communicating. A variety of techniques may be used: teaching family members how to communicate verbally; developing understandable connections between behavior, feeling, and verbalization; reducing or correcting misperceptions; clarifying the nature of double-bind messages; and trying to understand the roots of the difficulty in communicating. In using these techniques, the worker provides an example of clear, direct communication. A major treatment goal is to enable the family to open lines of communication by focusing on the development of a constructive fusion of verbalization, meaning, feeling, and behavior.

Communication between the family and the worker is the basic ingredient in the therapeutic relationship. The worker's activity is conditioned by such factors as whether he is functioning, for example, as a model parental ego and superego figure with the psychologically chaotic family, or as a moderator or catalyst with the relatively healthy family, or as an auxiliary ego with the family that is caught in neurotic double-bind communication. Families seem to establish modes of communication with the worker that are characteristic of them in such matters as trust, incorporation, identification, and the like and to express these modes through family defenses of projection, denial, displacement, and so on. In other words, there appear to be identifiable features in a family's communication with the worker that reflect its adaptive and maladaptive operations.

On the whole there appear to be fewer interfering transference phenomena in family treatment than in individual treatment because the emphasis is on family interpersonal communication rather than on individual intrapsychic problems. Intensity of feeling is more likely to be expressed to other family members than to the worker. Moreover, the family members are often engaged in seeking satisfaction of their affectional needs from each other rather than from the worker. Complicating transference reactions seem more likely to develop when exploration begins with individuals—which points to the value of holding family interviews very early in the contact in a new case. Experience shows that it is more difficult to shift from individual to family treatment than from family to individual treatment because of the likelihood that strong transference phenomena will appear during individual treatment.

Despite the fact that individual transference is limited in family treatment, it is not easy to develop appropriate treatment communication. The worker may encounter massive family defenses or resistance displayed through the beclouding of issues by excessive verbalizing, fighting, withdrawing, and the like. When this happens, the form that resistance takes, whether behavioral or verbal, should be explored as a family phenomenon because of the possibility that the resistance expressed by the one member is also felt by the others. It is not uncommon for one family member to use himself and be used by the others to express resistance for all of them. In one family interview a child refused to take off her coat. When the worker questioned this, the parents reinforced her behavior, saying that the office was cold. In this way the family was questioning the purpose of coming for treatment. Resistance may, however, be expressed in different ways by each family member, which may tempt the worker to shift to individual treatment. The worker should pay attention to the form resistance takes rather than the specific verbal content. One family engaged in bitter fighting during a number of interviews, each member turning to the worker at points to enlist him as the judge of who was right or wrong. The worker struggled to keep himself removed but could not always succeed and found himself lost in the minutiae of the content. When it became clear to him that the family not only obtained great gratification from the battles but also used fighting as a way of excluding him and denying the need for treatment, he told them this repeatedly until the fighting abated and the family became involved.

Whether dealing with family resistance or family defenses—and whether one or another family member takes the center of the stage in a particular interview or withdraws—the worker should keep in mind that the behavior is serving a purpose for all family members and that his communications must be addressed to all of them.

Other difficulties in communication—such as explosive hostility, excessive passivity or withdrawal, or nonverbalization—may also be encountered, and they may propel the worker away from family treatment. The purpose and meaning of these kinds of behavior should be understood, however, before the worker makes a shift in treatment. It is not uncommon, for example, for a family member to sit passively for many interviews, seemingly unobservant and nonparticipating, only to become suddenly active in interviews or to reveal that productive changes in his behavior have been taking place in the home, at school, or on the job. Perhaps the most difficult aspect of communication in family treatment is the worker's having to enter actively into the family system, in the sense that he is often forced to expose and express his personal and professional values. Although workers have always influenced people through their own values, the family interactional process creates a climate in which the worker must often intervene directly, with the result that he is uncomfortable and, at times, confused and self-doubting.

Family Constellations

I should like now to present a few ideas about family constellations that may offer broad guidelines to the use of family treatment. I shall describe briefly four typical constellations in relation to the nature of family equilibrium, the family tasks, the areas of dysfunction, the broad treatment methodology to be employed, and the treatment goals. I should like to emphasize, however, that these are not to be interpreted as distinct classifications or typologies of families. No family unit will exactly fit any one of the broad descriptions outlined.

1. One family constellation presents a socially and psychologically unstable equilibrium. This type of family can be described as chaotic. There is a lack of individuation among family members, and they fuse their identities and rely indiscriminately on one another. They function as a family of siblings; there is little explicit or implicit role differentiation between the spouses or between them and their children. This family often comes to the agency because the members' action orientation to life has created problems for them in the social environment, because they have failed in role performance in marriage and child rearing, because their primitive behavior makes it difficult for them to know how to manage themselves in the outside world, or because active or latent psychosis creates special problems of communication in the family. Frequently the members of this family behave in rigid, stereotyped ways and have ineffective patterns of control. They have little capacity for abstract thought. Life is lived in the present for immediate gratification and release of tension. The pervasive life style of the family is characterized by a lack of structure or stability and frequently by low self-esteem, fear of close relations, and overpowering affectional needs.

When such a constellation emerges, family treatment is frequently the treatment of choice; the action orientation of the members of such families and their lack of individuation may make one-to-one treatment intolerable or incomprehensible, and sibling competitiveness may not permit focus on one person. They are more likely to perceive the nature and implications of dysfunctional behavior and communication when they are worked with transactionally. Sometimes rivalry over having narcissistic affectional needs met is so intense that concurrent, supplementary nurturing of an individual or the marital pair is indicated. In some cases, initiated at a particular point of stress the narcissistic affectional needs and hurt self-esteem of a family member are so great that individual treatment may need to be the forerunner of some form of family treatment.

Appropriate treatment techniques for such a family include demonstration of the nature of the dysfunctional behavior to increase perception of its consequences, education in the use of language and communication, demonstration and teaching of role performance, and exposition of connections between behavior and affect. For some time emphasis may have to be placed on the content and form of the behavior rather than on its meaning and sources.

The immediate goal is to establish some structure and stability in explicit role performance through suggesting a series of tasks that the family can perform successfully. With some families, the long-range goal may be the achievement of an equilibrium of adequate role performances that will permit some individual identity. If the latter is possible, treatment may move, for example, to conjoint treatment of parents for the purpose of reinforcing parental development and concurrent individual treatment of a child to reinforce individual identity.

2. The second family constellation presents a flexible, adaptive equilibrium that has been equal to most of the maturational tasks but is temporarily dysfunctional or regressive because of an acute crisis brought about by disabling illness, death, employment changes, or the like. Family-unit treatment is often effective in quickly mobilizing and solidifying the family so that a new equilibrium can be established, perhaps through calling upon existing strengths or through bringing to the fore latent strengths and supports. Experience shows that this kind of family can often find a new equilibrium more quickly when family members work on a problem together. For example, when the family unit works with common feelings of loss, grief, and rage over the death of a family member—giving each other permission to mourn—the children may be helped to give up their anxiety-provoking fantasies about their responsibility for the death. Similarly when residual conflicts between aged parents and adult children are aroused by the need for a new living plan for the aged member, family-unit interviews may aid in reducing the conflicts enough for effective plans to be worked out.

The main technique is the furtherance of open communication among family members. The worker functions as a catalyst in helping the family identify feelings, clarify misperceptions, and develop new perceptions about each other and the family's life situation.

3. Between the two kinds of family constellation already described, there is a grouping that includes a variety of family constellations in which the equilibrium can be broadly described as neurotic. The overall equilibrium presents, side by side, adaptation, maladaptation, and

ambivalence in explicit and implicit role performance. Internalized conflicts and high ambivalence in family relationships are characteristic. The over-all treatment plan depends on whether the crucial area of dysfunction is fixed, regressive, or representative of minor maturational delay. Also significant is the level and stage of personal and family development and the degree of flexibility in ego adaptation. The broad treatment goals may involve loosening fixed alliances, shifting the family members to new alignments, or changing the nature of family equilibrium. All combinations of family treatment techniques may be employed.

One family constellation within this broad category presents a disturbed equilibrium because of an inability to master certain maturational tasks, in spite of a history of marital complementarity and reasonable child-rearing practices. The equilibrium can be described as temporarily regressive in the area of dysfunction. The problem may occur because the specific maturational task comes at a time when there are other crucial tasks for the family—for example, employment difficulties on the part of the father at the same time his adolescent son is moving into competition with him. Or the disequilibrium may be caused by structural changes in the family, such as the birth of a child, the departure of a child for college or marriage, retirement from work, and so forth. In other words, when maturational tasks prompt a resurgence of partially resolved conflicts in such areas as identity formation, separation, and the like, or when the task is accompanied by special social stresses, some form of family treatment may be effective. Treatment techniques are used that enable the family to analyze misperception in communication; that enable them to work on such problems as identity, separateness, and interdependence; and that show links between past experiences and present tasks.

Another family constellation in this grouping presents a neurotic equilibrium in which characteristic adaptive modes are based on highly ambivalent, regressive, or fixated interaction that prevent the accomplishment of maturational tasks. One of the main diagnostic clues for the identification of this constellation is the family's use of double-bind or ambivalent communication in a specific or encapsulated area. With such a family it frequently appears that the marital equilibrium is stable, though a child manifests specific problems; closer scrutiny reveals the ambivalent marital equilibrium, which is held steady by the parents' using the child as a tool. Family-unit treatment may be the preferred initial technique for the purpose of clarifying and later reducing or resolving double-bind communication. The child's presence seems to further exposure of the neurotic binds.

Some of these families show neurotic dysfunction that is in a fluid, uncrystallized state, with evidence of a high degree of available, appropriate affect and a quality of flexible, perceptive communication that makes some form of continuing family treatment a good choice. They can use the worker as an auxiliary ego to work on the meaning and sources of double-bind, incongruent communications. When the dysfunction indicates a mild maturational delay with regressive features—which is often the case with the young married partners who have not yet mastered the developmental tasks of adolescence—the most effective treatment technique is the joint interview.

4. The family constellation that has a psychotic equilibrium is often characterized by pervasive double-bind communication. The literature is replete with evidence that families described as schizophrenic use pervasive double-bind communication in the total family unit or express it through one member. Our experience supports the evidence that family-unit treatment is the treatment of choice in such cases and that such a family can be worked with in a noninstitutional setting.

Conclusion

In an over-all sense, some form of family treatment appears to be effective when the family's therapeutic assets include the following: freedom to interact, some verbal communication, recognition of a family problem, shifting equilibrium as expressed in flexible family alliances, ability to use group diagnostic sessions, and acceptance of the principle of family treatment.

It may well be that experience will show that some form of family treatment is suitable for all families. Moreover, it may eventuate that the main therapeutic problems will be technical in nature, that is, problems of knowing when and how to alter family equilibrium, when and how to work with the family unit or with various combinations of family members, how shifts in diagnosis and treatment objectives affect the use of specific techniques, and how to use a growing body of knowledge about specific relationship and communication techniques. The goal of family treatment is to influence the family system by loosening, shifting, or changing maladaptive family equilibrium and by strengthening adaptive equilibrium so that family energy can be released to meet its tasks and the individual freed to grow.

64. THE INTERGENERATIONAL APPROACH IN CASEWORK WITH THE AGING

Jean M. Leach

§ Helping older people work out their problems is one of the newer fields of social work. In this article, the older person, even though he does not live with a son or daughter, is viewed as a family member. Casework is seen as involving an intergenerational process.

The voluntary family agency is receiving a steadily increasing number of requests for help in meeting the needs of older persons. By strengthening its program of services to the aging, the family agency has reaffirmed social work's concern with the welfare of all family members, regardless of age. Like other family agencies, Family Service of the Cincinnati Area has been re-examining its own services and those offered elsewhere in the community to ensure that all the services needed will be made available to the aging person.

This article is based on the experiences of ten caseworkers in the agency who have been meeting in a biweekly workshop throughout the period of the agency's participation in the Project on Aging of the Family Service Association of America. Certain insights that are reported here emerged as the caseworkers attempted to deepen their understanding of the emotional forces that affect the lives of aging clients.

An analysis of the requests made to the agency for services to older persons revealed that most come from younger family members—children, grandchildren, nieces, and nephews. Almost always the request is precipitated by a crisis in the older person's life: an illness that makes a different living arrangement necessary for him; the death of a spouse, relative, or friend with whom he has lived; a reduction in income; or a change in housing. In all these instances the older person is experiencing the loss of a relationship or an arrangement that has strongly influenced his self-image. He reacts to this loss in accordance with his established pattern of defense, which must be understood by the caseworker who undertakes to help him.

SOURCE: *Social Casework*, 45 (1964), 144–49. Reprinted by permission of the author and Family Service Association of America.

Jean M. Leach is Casework Director, Family Service of the Cincinnati Area, Cincinnati. This paper was presented at the Biennial Meeting of the Family Service Association of America, held in San Francisco, at a session on November 15, 1963.

Most of the older persons referred to the agency live apart from their younger relatives, though they may be in close touch with them. Few families are seen in which the pattern has been for three generations to live together, but often the possibility of it is being considered—sometimes with dread—when the request for service is made.

The caseworkers in the workshop felt the need to develop criteria for evaluating the capacity of the older client and his younger relatives to live together harmoniously. They were concerned about the extent to which our society seems to encourage independent, or even isolated, living for the aged, as if this were the most desirable arrangement from an emotional standpoint. Dr. Stanley Cath[1] has pointed out that there seems to be little awareness that continuing object relationships help to protect an older person against regression and deterioration, while "isolated living without the stimulating input of meaningful and repeated human contact accelerates regressive and degenerative changes. . . ." Cath urges study of the problems associated with isolated living, because "human interaction is a barrier against their [older persons'] regression." He believes that guideposts for intelligent planning can be obtained from studying the interaction between members of different generations and the particular functions those of one generation serve for those of another. One should not expect that three generations of one family will always be able to live together happily. But it is important that caseworkers and members of other helping professions be able to predict when this arrangement will probably be a satisfactory solution and when it will not.

Past Functioning and Relationships

As an antidote to the depression that usually follows a loss, the caseworker tries to involve the older person in planning the changes necessitated by his altered circumstances and thus to slow down or reverse the depression and promote healthy ego functioning. Understanding how the client has solved problems in the past is of primary importance, and often younger relatives can give the worker helpful information. Usually, however, the most significant data are provided by the older person himself after the caseworker has established a satisfactory relationship with him.

During the diagnostic phase the caseworker pays particular attention to the quality of the relationship between the older client and the younger relative who makes the request for help. This relationship is crucial; unless the caseworker understands it, he may find himself blocked from being helpful. The son who feels frustrated because he

[1] Stanley H. Cath, "Psychodynamics of the Three-Generation Home," *Tufts Folia Medica*, Vol. VIII, April–June 1962, pp. 43–53.

has failed to provide for his parent may need to defeat or complicate the efforts of the caseworker, whose success would be too threatening. A daughter's request for help may be an indirect way of embarrassing siblings who have remained detached from the problem.

The extent to which the older person and his younger relative have discussed the decision to seek help is revealed when the caseworker explains his desire to include the older person in any planning that affects him. At this point some applicants insist that, to be successful, the worker's approach to the older person must be circuitous. They may, for example, suggest that the caseworker pay the older person a social visit in order to observe him. Such suggestions reveal that the younger person cannot bring himself to admit to the aging person his inability to meet certain needs and his resort to professional intervention. The guilt, anger, and ambivalence that accompany this situation must be taken into account by the caseworker trying to provide service to the family.

The caseworker needs to be acquainted with the older client and with the younger relatives or friends with whom he is most involved emotionally. They should be interviewed together and perhaps separately. The insight derived from using a family-centered approach enables the worker to know what kind of living arrangements would be best for the older client if a change must be made. Often adult foster home care for him is threatening and thus unacceptable to a son or daughter with guilt feelings; these feelings need to be recognized and sufficiently resolved before such a plan can be successful. Homemaker service, no matter how skillful the homemaker, may fail for similar reasons. Sometimes the older client sabotages the best-laid plan in order to continue his neurotic struggle with his younger relative.

Often the solicitude expressed by the younger relative is only a fragile defense against the hostility that characterizes his relationship with the older person. His negative feelings emerge quickly as the caseworker explores possible plans with both of them.

Mrs. A asked help in planning for her adoptive mother. The mother, who lived alone in her own home, was ill and refused to accept any personal or household help. She had literally barricaded herself in her house, admitting only her physician, to whom she complained about her ungrateful daughter. Mrs. A could not pay for expensive nursing care. She was willing to do her mother's cooking and cleaning, but her offer had been refused. As the caseworker sought to understand the past relationship between Mrs. A and her mother, it became apparent that the mother had been telling Mrs. A all her life that she should be grateful for having been given a home. To ensure attention from her, the mother provoked her guilt. Paying the cost of an agency homemaker who could provide the services recommended by the physician would permit Mrs. A to contribute to her mother's care.

As the workshop participants have attempted to understand the older client, they have become increasingly aware of how much a person's capacity to adapt to new situations depends on his past experiences. If the caseworker can learn how these have shaped the client's self-image and sense of identity, he will be able to identify the client's previous defense patterns and thus to predict more accurately his response to his changing situation.

The Effect of the Parent-Child Relationship

The parent-child relationship is perhaps the most significant determinant of the course of the aging process and of the way in which the person meets the problems associated with aging; it appears to be as crucial to his preparation for aging and to continued congenial relationships with his adult children as it is to the development of the young child. To determine whether or not an older person can expect to establish a satisfactory living arrangement with his children, the caseworker carefully examines the early relationship between them and its course over the years.

The quality of a person's childhood relationship with his parents strongly influences his feelings toward them throughout his life. If it promoted his independence while meeting his normal dependency needs, he is better able to resolve his conflict between dependence and independence and to move away from his parents without guilt and crippling anxiety. At the same time he has no need to renounce the relationship; it remains warm and friendly even if he lives at some distance from them. A child so reared expects and wants to share his and his children's life with his parents and to plan with and for the parents whenever they need his help. In essence, they have given him permission to enjoy life's experiences, just as they have done. These older persons welcome grandchildren and do not need to compete with their own child for the grandchildren's affection. They are willing to share their material goods with their child and even to deprive themselves of personal pleasures for the child's sake. If the child achieves greater success than they did, they are proud and pleased rather than resentful and jealous. It is a source of satisfaction for them to contribute in a variety of small but important ways to the child's success as a parent, without making him feel inadequate or dependent.

Planning Living Arrangements

Caseworkers are often confronted with the remnants of unresolved parent-child conflicts and tensions that complicate current relationships in a client's family. Frequently, in these instances, the child left home as soon as he could support himself. Then there followed a period during which the parents and the child drifted farther apart and he avoided seeing them. He usually claims that the pressing demands of work, children, or marriage have made it impossible for him to maintain a close relationship with his aging father or mother. As long as the parent remained relatively healthy, the child did not feel guilty enough to try for a closer relationship. He is forced to make the effort, however, when the parent becomes less able to manage his own life. The unresolved neurotic conflict from the past now returns in full force and interferes with the child's ability to help the parent and the parent's ability to accept help from the child. The problem is complicated further by the guilt they both feel about past failures. The caseworker must understand this neurotic struggle in order to know what kind of help is most needed and what kind of services and resources are appropriate.

Mr. J, an eighty-one-year-old widower, was referred to the agency by a caseworker at a clinic. He suffered from diabetes, and his right foot had been amputated a year earlier. He had an income of ninety-nine dollars a month from Social Security. During the five years since his wife's death he had lived in furnished rooms—currently a small, dismal second-floor room for which he paid six dollars a week. He ate all his meals in restaurants and claimed he could not afford the diet prescribed for him. Mr. J's four children were married and lived in the same city as he, but they did not maintain close ties with him. When the caseworker attempted to involve them in planning with and for their father, she learned that they still resented his lack of responsibility toward them when they were young. Their mother had worked to help support them while he had spent his income as he pleased, without regard to their needs.

After his foot was amputated, one of his daughters had taken him into her home during his convalescence. Her children had given up their bedroom to him. While he lived there Mr. J had criticized the way his grandchildren were disciplined. He asked neighbors to take him to and from the clinic, though his son-in-law had offered to do it, and he further embarrassed his daughter by asking the neighbors to buy beer for him. At the earliest possible moment, his daughter had sent him back to a furnished room. Although this arrangement does not meet Mr. J's physical needs or afford the companionship he so obviously requires, it seems unlikely that casework help will make it possible for him and any of his children to live together comfortably under one roof.

In such a situation—and there are many similar ones—the caseworker must continue working with the older client and his younger relatives, even though they are unable to spend much time together without re-experiencing their past anger and disappointments. When parents cannot be completely independent financially or physically, their children must become involved in whatever planning has to be done. Since feelings of obligation become an additional burden for both generations in this instance, the caseworker can help both the parent and the children ventilate these feelings so that they can tolerate each other better. Since the focus here is on the strained interaction between two or three generations, and service to one generation is dependent on the responses of the others, this is properly called an intergenerational approach to casework with the aging. Interviews that include family members of various ages are held from time to time, and their attitudes and reactions are taken into account in making plans for the older person.

When study of the early parent-child relationship reveals unresolved neurotic conflicts that have always produced tension and conflict, the caseworker can anticipate that the family will not be able to live together comfortably. In these situations he should suggest a plan that ensures sufficient independence for both the older client and his children. Because of guilt feelings in the children, which sometimes lead them into greater intimacy with their aging parents than either can tolerate emotionally, such a plan may be difficult to carry out. Under these circumstances the caseworker attempts to help the family accept separate living arrangements without an overwhelming sense of failure.

> Mr. R, a college professor, telephoned from his home five hundred miles away to ask the agency to investigate his widowed mother's circumstances. She had written that she was not feeling well enough to continue living alone. He said he had never felt close to her. Throughout his childhood she had nagged him and his father, who had been miserable in the marriage. Mr. R had been relieved when he could move far away from her.
>
> Since his father's death he had provided the major part of his mother's income, and he was willing to continue doing so. Now she wanted to live with him and his family. In view of their previous experience together, he doubted whether they could combine their households happily. His children scarcely knew her, and he did not regret this.
>
> As the caseworker came to know Mr. R's mother, he too doubted the wisdom of combining the households. The mother was self-centered and uninterested in almost everything except her food and personal comfort. She had become extremely obese and refused to eat less, although her physician had urged her to do so. It was apparent that periodically she used provocative demands for attention to reassure herself that she was alive. It was also clear that her needs were insatiable—beyond the ability of her son and the caseworker to meet, whether they worked alone or together. In this instance the best plan seemed to be to help her move to a home for the aged, where her needs might be met through the joint efforts of many persons.

Successful Aging

When family living is available to the older person (often, of course, it is not), it is usually the happiest and most satisfactory solution—if he has the emotional health to enjoy it. Certain personality characteristics that appear to be associated with emotional health during the adult years have been identified. Resiliency and flexibility are considerable assets, and a sense of humor can convert an intolerable situation into a bearable one. Perhaps nothing contributes more to success in aging than genuine self-confidence. Self-trust and trust of others enable a person to be somewhat adventurous and to use his time in satisfying pursuits, and a capacity to form and maintain relationships with people from various walks of life helps him to enlarge his understanding of himself and others. If he has successfully resolved the dependence-independence struggle he can make decisions consistent with the responsibilities of maturity and can form close relationships without feeling threatened or regressing to a childlike state. A mature conscience enhances a person's ability to make unconflicted decisions about difficult problems. Abandoning fantasies of omnipotence leads to self-awareness and to a sense of humility that enables a person to accept his life as part of a continuum rather than as the be-all and end-all of human existence.

Mrs. S appeared to be an emotionally healthy person. When she was sixty-eight she volunteered her services to the agency, explaining that her husband had died the previous year and that she now had time to devote to others. She was invited to come to the agency to discuss her interests and its needs. In the interview, Mrs. S spoke with pride and pleasure of her son and her grandchildren, with whom she and her husband had always shared their holidays and special family events. She said that good parents do not intrude in their children's lives and talked of the virtues of independence. The interviewer thought Mrs. S could be helpful as a friendly visitor to homebound older persons, and this volunteer duty was assigned to her.

Several years later, the caseworker who supervised the volunteers noticed Mrs. S's concern over her failing eyesight, which was beginning to interfere with her driving. Mrs. S spoke sadly of the inevitability of a change in her living arrangements now that she was becoming less able to take care of her own needs. When the worker broached the subject of a joint conference with her son. Mr. S told of his concern about her and his repeated efforts to persuade her to move into his home. She had avoided this move because she did not want to be an "interfering relative."

Mrs. S finally agreed to a family conference, during which it became obvious that this family group could live together happily and that its members were fond of one another. The daughter-in-law was not threatened by the prospect of Mrs. S's increased dependency due to her failing eyesight; the grandchildren looked forward with pleasure to reading to their grandmother, just as she had so happily read to them when they were younger. Over the years the family members had established and maintained sound patterns of communication that reflected respect and affection for one another. Under these circumstances it was possible for Mrs. S to live out her declining years with her son and his family.

Resolving Family Conflicts

Sometimes past conflicts must be resolved before a joint living arrangement is possible. Working these through inevitably requires considerable time; often independent living arrangements must be continued until the family members are ready to live together.

Mrs. P telephoned the agency for information about her mother's eligibility for Old-Age Assistance. Her father had recently died after a prolonged illness that had exhausted all the family savings. She revealed her concern about her mother, who felt that though she could not support herself she should not impose on any of her children. Mrs. P had offered her mother a home, but this had created problems in her marriage because the P's themselves had only a marginal income. She felt ashamed that she and her siblings were not providing for their mother, and she knew her father would grieve if he realized that his wife had to seek public assistance. The intake worker suggested that the children and their mother might need help in deciding on the best course of action.

Mrs. P began to retreat, implying that her mother was aware that the other children were not equally concerned. Mrs. P's unmarried younger sister was teaching in the East. Her life was "different," and the others all resented her success and independence; she was the only child in the family with a college education. They did not think she should abandon her career to provide a home for their mother; in fact, they thought that the mother might not be happy living with her, because the two had little in common. But they did feel she was more obligated than they to contribute to the mother's support, both because she had no other family responsibilities and because she had received the most advantages from their parents. Mrs. P's brother had five children, one of whom was retarded. He had a large house in a rural area, but his income was too small for him to be able to help.

Mrs. P's own involvement with her mother was apparent, and she finally revealed her guilt about the pain she had caused her mother by having an out-of-wedlock pregnancy while she was in high school. Over the years their relationship had been a hostile-dependent one, and it was now blocking Mrs. P from planning with her mother. After the caseworker, in a series of interviews, had helped Mrs. P resolve her guilt, a family conference was planned for Mrs. P, her brother, and her mother. In preparation for this meeting the caseworker offered to communicate with Mrs. P's sister through a family agency in the East.

At the family conference, Mrs. P invited her mother to live with her—an arrangement made possible by a monthly sum to be sent by the sister in the East, which would supplement the mother's Social Security benefits. Although the mother accepted this plan, everyone understood that it posed many problems, because of the continued operation of unresolved conflicts that created strains in the relationships between mother and daughter and between grandmother and granddaughter. The family accepted the need for continued casework service while the mother and daughter re-established their home together.

Conclusion

Studying the quality of relationships between family members by using the intergenerational approach has helped caseworkers identify families in which living arrangements that include members of three generations can be successful and happy. Their observations reaffirm the importance of early professional intervention in disturbed family life. The older client may need a corrective parental experience, provided by the caseworker, before he can form a healthier relationship with his children.

The family caseworker can help younger persons prepare themselves emotionally to share their lives and their homes with older relatives if this course of action should be decided upon. When the grandparents live in the same household, the grandchildren have an opportunity to be reared in the presence of persons who have learned about life from long years of experience. Although the realities encountered by the grand-child struggling to grow up may be different, the feelings associated with growing and achieving are not new to the grandparent. He can understand and appreciate the child's feelings, and he has learned in addition to integrate them and evaluate them from the perspective that comes with age. The child reared in a three-generation family may benefit from the experience and wisdom of his grandparents.

Correlations Table

Correlation of This Book with Marriage and Family
Texts Published or Revised since 1960

*The reader should use the index to locate
short discussions of any specific subject.*

Text chs.	BELL *Marriage and Family Interaction*, rev. ed. Dorsey, 1967	BLOOD *Marriage* Free Press, 1962	BOWMAN *Marriage for Moderns*, 5th ed. McGraw-Hill, 1965	BURGESS, LOCKE, AND THOMAS *The Family, from Institution to Companionship*, 3d ed. American Book, 1963
	Related Articles in *Marriage and the Family in the Modern World: A Book of Readings*			
1	1, 2	(Intro., 1–4) 13, 14, 18, 20, 21	1	1, 2
2	3, 4	8–12, 22, 33, 34, 38, 39	2–4, 13	8–12
3	5–7	15–17, 19	15, 24–26	
4	8–12, 18–20, 23	24–26	18, 20, 21	
5	24–26	27–32, 56, 57	22	
6	21, 22		33, 34, 38	
7	27–29	23	27–30, 56, 57	
8	30–32		23	5–7
9	33, 34	35, 44–46	35, 36, 39	24, 25, 27, 28, 52–55
10	35	47, 48	19, 37, 40, 41	16, 56–59
11	13–17, 36, 38–42, 44	49–51, 60, 61		17–21, 23, 26–30
12	37, 45	62–64		22, 38, 39
13		36, 37, 58		33–35
14	52–55, 58–61			
15	56, 57	40, 41	52–55	
16	47–49		62–64	3, 4, 36, 37, 40, 41
17	43, 46, 50, 51, 62–64			
18				47, 48
19				31, 32, 44, 45
20		5–7, 52–55		46, 49, 50, 51, 60, 61
21		59		
22				13–15, 42, 43, 64
23		42, 43		62, 63

Text chs.	CAVAN American Family Crowell, 1969	CLEMENS Design for Successful Marriage, 2d ed. Prentice-Hall, 1964	DUVALL Family Development, 3d ed. Lippincott, 1967	FARBER Family: Organization and Interaction Chandler, 1964
		Related Articles in *Marriage and the Family in the Modern World: A Book of Readings*		
1	1, 2	1, 2	13, 14	1
2	3	8–12		2, 5–12
3		33, 34	1–4	
4		24–26	5–7	13, 14
5		13, 14, 36, 37	8–12	18–26, 33, 34, 38, 39, 49, 51
6		15–17, 18, 20, 21, 27–32	15–17, 24–26, 33–35, 40, 41	40, 41, 59
7	7	19, 22, 38, 39	52, 53	4
8	5, 6	23	54, 55	36, 37
9	45	5–7, 35	36, 37, 59	15–17, 27–32, 35, 42, 43, 47–51
10	19	3, 4, 40–43	27, 44–51, 58, 60, 61	44–46
11	13, 14, 40, 41	19	28–32, 56, 57	3, 52–58
12	27, 28, 56, 57		18–23, 38, 39	62–64
13	18, 20, 21		42	
14	8–12, 22, 23, 38	52–55	43	
15	29, 30	56–59	62–64	
16	17, 24–26			
17	16, 17, 35–37, 39, 44			
18	33, 34, 47–49, 51	44–51, 60–64		
19	31, 32, 50, 52–55, 58–61			
20	15, 42, 43, 46			
21	4, 62–64			

Text chs.	KENKEL *The Family in Perspective*, 2d ed. Appleton-Century-Crofts, 1966	KEPHART *The Family, Society, and the Individual,* 2d ed. Houghton Mifflin, 1966	KIRKPATRICK *The Family as Process and Institution,* 2d ed. Ronald Press, 1963	LANDIS AND LANDIS *Building a Successful Marriage,* 5th ed. Prentice-Hall, 1968
		Related Articles in *Marriage and the Family in the Modern World: A Book of Readings*		
1		1, 2, 13, 14	1, 2	1–4
2				15–17
3		8–12	5–12	18, 20, 21
4				
5		3, 4	3, 4	
6				
7	8–12, 59	5–7		22
8	3, 4		13, 14, 16	
9	1, 2, 5–7, 33, 34	18–23		24–26
10	52–55		40, 41	39
11	24–26	17, 24–26	56–59	27–32
12	27–32	27–32	17–21, 24–26	19
13	49–51		22	23
14		33, 34	27–32	33, 34
15	24–26		23	35–38, 44–49, 51
16	18–23, 38, 39		33, 34	
17	13, 14, 35–37	15, 16, 35–41	36, 37	40, 41
18	15–17, 40, 41, 44–49, 51		16, 35, 38, 39	
19	50, 56–61	50, 52–59, 61	52–55	
20	42, 43, 51, 62–64	47, 49, 51, 60	15, 42–48	
21			49, 51	
22		44–46, 48	50, 60, 61	
23		62–64	62–64	
24				54, 55
25				52, 53
26				50, 56–61
27				62–64

	LANDIS *Making the Most of Marriage*, 3d ed. Appleton-Century-Crofts, 1965	LANTZ AND SNYDER *Marriage* Wiley, 1962	LEE AND LEE *Marriage and the Family*, 2d ed. Barnes and Noble, 1961	LESLIE *Family in Social Context* Oxford, 1967
Text chs.	Related Articles in *Marriage and the Family in the Modern World: A Book of Readings*			
1	1–4	5–7	1, 2	1, 2
2		1–4	3, 4, 8–12	
3		13, 14	5–7, 19	
4	15–17		36, 37	8–12
5	27	24	62, 63	
6	36, 37	17, 25, 26		3, 4
7		18, 20, 21	13, 14, 27, 28	
8		28–32		
9	24	8–12, 22, 33, 34, 38	56, 57	13, 14
10	25, 26	19	17, 24–26	5–7
11	13, 14, 18, 20, 21	23	18–22, 27–30	40, 41
12	28–30		23	17, 18, 20, 21, 24–26
13		15, 16, 35–37, 39, 44–46	35, 38, 39	27–32
14	8–12, 22	40–43	33, 34	19, 22, 23, 33, 34
15	19		52, 53	35, 47, 48
16	38	47, 48		52–55
17	33, 34, 39	27, 52–59	54, 55	15, 16
18		49–51, 60, 61	31, 32, 50, 51, 60, 61	47–50, 60–64
19	23	62–64	40–43, 64	51
20	31, 32		44–45	42, 43
21	35, 40, 41, 44–46		15, 46, 47–49	
22	5–7, 47, 48			
23			16	
24–27				
28				
29	52–55			
30	56–59			
31				
32				
33	42, 43			
34	49–51, 60, 61			
35	62–64			

Text chs.	PETERSON Education for Marriage, 2d ed. Scribner, 1964	SAXTON Individual, Marriage and the Family Wadsworth, 1968	SIMPSON People in Families World, 1966	STROUP Marriage and Family Appleton-Century-Crofts, 1966
	Related Articles in *Marriage and the Family in the Modern World: A Book of Readings*			
1	1–4	1–4	1–4	1, 2
2		24–26		3, 5–12
3	17, 24–26		8–12, 40, 41	4
4	13, 14	27–32	13, 14, 18, 20, 21	13, 14
5		13, 14, 18, 20, 21	22–26	18, 20, 21
6	27–32	8–12, 22, 23, 38, 39	27–30	
7	18, 20, 21	15–17, 33–37	19, 33, 34, 38, 39	17, 24–26
8	22	44–49, 62, 63	15–17	19, 22, 38, 39
9	19, 38, 39	19, 51	5–7	27–32
10	5–12, 36, 37	5–7, 40, 41		23
11	23		35–37, 47, 48	33, 34
12	16, 33, 34	50, 52–61		16, 35
13	35, 40, 41, 44–46		52, 53, 59	40, 41
14	52–61			
15			27–30, 56–58	36, 37
16				
17				
18			49	52–55
19			50, 60, 61	
20	47–51, 62–64		51	
21			44–46	58–61
22			54–55	
23			42, 43	56, 57
24			31, 32	42, 43, 64
25				15, 44–48
26			62–64	49–51
27				62, 63

Text chs.	UDRY *Social Context of Marriage* Lippincott, 1966	WILLIAMSON *Marriage and Family Relations* Wiley, 1966	WINCH *Modern Family*, rev. ed. Holt, Rinehart, and Winston, 1963
	Related Articles in *Marriage and the Family in the Modern World: A Book of Readings*		
1		1, 2	1–4
2	1–12	3	8–12
3	15, 16	4	59
4	27–28, 56, 57	5–7, 36, 37	5–7
5	18, 20, 21	13, 14, 56, 57	
6	29–32	15–17	
7	17, 24–26	8–12, 18, 20, 21	
8	8–12, 19, 33, 34, 38, 39	27–30	31, 32, 45, 54, 55
9	22	24–26	
10	23	19, 22, 38, 39	19, 22, 33, 34, 38, 39
11	35	33, 34	13, 14
12		23	16, 36, 37
13	13, 14	35, 40	52, 53
14	36, 37, 40, 41		
15			50, 58, 60, 61
16		52–55	27, 28, 56, 57
17	42, 43, 52–55, 58, 59		40–43, 64
18	47–51, 60, 61	31, 32, 58–61	22
19	62–64	42–45, 47, 48	17, 24–30
20		41, 46, 49, 50, 51	18, 20, 21, 23
21		62–64	35, 44
22			15, 46–49
23			51
24			62, 63

Index

Index